THE CATHOLIC DOCTRINE

OF

THE CHURCH OF ENGLAND.

The Parker Society.

Instituted A.D. M.DCCC.XL.

For the Publication of the Works of the Fathers and Early Writers of the Reformed English Church.

THE CATHOLIC DOCTRINE

OF

THE CHURCH OF ENGLAND,

AN EXPOSITION

OF THE

THIRTY-NINE ARTICLES,

BY

THOMAS ROGERS, A.M.,

CHAPLAIN TO ARCHBISHOP BANCROFT.

EDITED FOR

The Parker Society,

BY THE

REV. J. J. S. PEROWNE, M.A.,

FELLOW OF CORPUS CHRISTI COLLEGE, CAMBRIDGE.

Wipf and Stock Publishers
199 W 8th Ave, Suite 3
Eugene, OR 97401

The Catholic Doctrine of the Church of England
By Rogers, Thomas
ISBN: 1-59752-204-X
Publication date 5/18/2005
Previously published by Cambridge, 1854

INTRODUCTORY NOTICE.

Of the life of Thomas Rogers, the author of the following Treatise on the Articles, but very scanty notices have been preserved. Wood says, (Athen. Oxon. Vol. II. col. 162-6. Lond. 1815):

"Thomas Rogers, a most admirable theologist, an excellent preacher, and well deserving every way of the sacred function, was born, as I conceive, in Cheshire, and came full ripe to the university before 1568. About which time being made one of the students of Ch. Ch. took holy orders very early, and afterwards the degree of master of arts, scil. an. 1576, before which time he was a sedulous and constant preacher of God's word. What his preferments were successively afterwards, I know not, only that he was chaplain to doctor Bancroft, bishop of London, and at length rector of Horninger near to S. Edmonds-Bury in Suffolk, where and in the neighbourhood he was always held in great esteem for his learning and holiness of life and conversation. His works are these:

A Philosophical Discourse, entit. The Anatomy of the Mind. Lond. 1576, oct. [Bodl. 8vo. H. 18. Art. BS.] Before which is a copy of verses in praise of it, written by his contemporary Will. Cambden of Ch. Ch.

Of the End of the World, and second Coming of Christ, &c. Lond. 1577, qu. [Bodl. 4to. E. 5. Th. BS. again 8vo. 1582 and 1583.][1]

[[1] In this work is a translation* of some old 'Germanical rhythmes by John Stoffler,' which Rogers says he heard recited by Melancthon:

* This is a mistake. The work itself is only a translation. See below, p. vii. The verses are ascribed to Cyprian, who "by his Latin verses doth shew that old and common prophecy turned into Germanical rythme by John Stoffler." These English verses are not the translation of the "Germanical rythme" but of the Latin lines. Moreover it was not Rogers that heard Melancthon but Schelto à Geveren whom Rogers translates.—Ed.

The English Creed; wherein is contained in Tables an Exposition on the Articles which every Man is to subscribe unto. Where the Articles are expounded by Scripture, and the Confessions of all the reformed Churches; and Heresies are displayed. Lond. 1579, and 85, fol.

General Session, containing an Apology of the comfortable Doctrine concerning the End of the World and second Coming of Christ. Lond. 1581, qu.

The English Creed; consisting with the true, ancient Catholic and Apostolic Church in all the Points and Articles of Religion, which every Christian is to know, and believe that would be saved, &c.—In two parts. The first printed at London in 1585, the second there 1587, and both in fol. [Bodl. N. 2. 7. Jur.]

An Exposition on the 39 Articles of the Church of England. Lond. 1586, &c. qu.[1] Which book, at the first appearance, met not with that welcome entertainment, which seemed due to the author's endeavours. For besides the two extremes, Papists and Schismatics, who were highly enraged, many Protestants of a middle temper were much offended thereat. Some conceived it presumption for a private minister to make himself the mouth of the church, to render her sense

When after Christes birth there be expirde
  Of hundreds fifteen, yeeres, eightie and eight,
Then comes the tyme of daungers to be ferde
  And all mankind with dolors it shall fraight.
For if the world in that yeere doo not fall,
  If sea and land then perish ne decaie,
Yet empires all and kingdomes alter shall,
  And man to ease himselfe shall have no way.
fol. 16.

These have not been noticed by Ritson, who, probably, had not seen *The Anatomy of the Mind,* which adds two other names to his *Bibliographia Poetica.*

1. *Abraham Fowler,* who prefixed an alliterative poem, (imperfect in the Bodleian copy) entitled *Needeles Hædera.*

2. *Josua Hutten,* who also contributed a *Dialogue between himself and the Book.*]

[[1] My edition is, London, printed by John Legatt, 1621, 4to. the dedication to Dr Bancroft, archb. of Cant. is dated at Horniger, near St Edm. Bury in Suff. 11 of March, an. 1607. 'Your grace's poor chaplaine always at command, Thomas Rogers.' KENNET.]

in matters of so high concernment. Others were[2] offended, that his interpretation confined the charitable latitude, formerly allowed in those articles. Howsoever it was, sure it is, the work in some years wrought itself in good esteem, as dedicated to, and countenanced by, Dr Bancroft beforementioned[3].

A Golden Chain taken out of the rich Treasure-House of the Psalms of David. Lond. [1579] 1587, in tw.

The Pearls of K. Solomon, gathered into common Places.—Taken from the Proverbs of the said King. Printed with the former book.

Historical Dialogue touching Antichrist and Popery; drawn and published for the Comfort of our Church, &c. Lond. 1589, oct. [Bodl. 8vo. B. 169. Th.]

Serm. on Rom. 12. *ver.* 6, 7, 8. Lond. 1590, qu.[4]

Miles Christianus, or, a Defence of all necessary Writings and Writers, written against an Epistle prefixed to a Catechism made by Miles Moses. Lond. 1590, qu. This Miles Moses was Bach. of Div. and published besides the former things, *The Arrangement of Usury in six Sermons.* Lond. 1595, qu.

Table of the lawful Use of an Oath, and the cursed State of vain Swearers. Lond.

Two Dialogues, [*or Conferences concerning kneeling in the very Act of receiving the Sacramental Bread and Wine in the Supper of the Lord.*] Lond. 1608. [Bodl. 4to. M. 17. Art.] He also translated into English, (1) *A Discourse of the End of the World and Second Coming of Christ*[5]. Lond.

[[2] See Tho. Fuller's *Ch. Hist.* lib. 9. an. 1584.]

[[3] There are two copies of this book in the Bodleian. One printed London 1633, 4to. R. 29. Th. The other at Cambridge in 1691. 4to. Rawl. 132. The latter is interleaved, and contains a MS. comparison between Rogers's view of the subject and bishop Burnet's, drawn up by Nicholas Adams of Corpus Christi Coll. Oxon. in 1704.]

[[4] A copy in the library of the archb. of Canterbury at Lambeth.]

[5] Already noticed above. See p. v. note.—ED.

1577, 78, oct. written by Schelto à Geveren of Emden in Friesland. (2) *General Discourse of the damnable Sect of Usurers,* &c. Lond. 1578, qu. written by Philip Cæsar. To which is added, *A Treatise of the lawful Use of Riches:* written by Nich. Heming. (3) *The Profession of the true Church, and Popery compared.* Lond. 1578, oct. (4) *Exposition on the 84th Psalm.* Lond. 1581, oct. written by Nic. Heming for the instruction of the ignorant in the grounds of religion; and confutation of the Jews, Turks, &c. (5) *S. Augustine's heavenly Meditations, called, A private Talk with God.* Lond. 1581, in tw. purified by our translator T. Rogers, and adorned with annotations of scripture. (6) *Of the Foolishness of Men and Women in putting off the Amendment of their Lives from Day to Day.* Lond. 1583, and 86, oct. written by Joh. Rivius. (7) *Of the Imitation of Christ.* Lond. 1584, 89. [1592 and 1596] in tw. [and 4to.] written in three books by Tho. de Kempis; and for the worthiness thereof oft since translated into sundry languages. Now newly translated by Tho. Rogers, corrected, and with most ample texts and sentences of holy scripture illustrated. (8) *A Method to Mortification, called heretofore The Contempt of the World,* &c. Lond. 1586, in tw. written by Didac. Stella. (9) *S. Augustin's Prayers.* Lond. 1591, in tw. &c. Purged by our translator (T. Rogers) from divers superstitious points, and adorned with manifold places of scripture. (10) *S. Augustine's Manual, containing special and picked Meditations and godly Prayers.* Lond. [1581] 1591, in tw. with corrections by the translator. (11) *Enemy of Security; or a daily Exercise of Godly Meditations.* Lond. 1580[1], and 91, in tw. written by Joh. Avenar, public professor of the Hebrew tongue in the university of Wittenberge. (12) *Enemy to Atheism: or Christian Godly Prayers for all Degrees.* Lond. 1591, in tw. written in the German language

[[1] I have this book printed in 1579, small 8vo. or 12mo. newlie corrected, with a dedication to Sir Francis Walsingham. COLE.]

by Jo. Avenar, translated out of Lat. by our author, T. Rogers. (13) *Soliloquium Animæ: The fourth Book of the Imitation of Christ.* Lond. 1592, in tw. written by Tho. de Kempis before-mentioned. What other things our author hath written and translated I know not; nor anything else of him, only that he was a zealous opposer of the doctrine of the Sabbath, and the first that publicly stood up against Dr Nich. Bownd's opinion of it in his preface to the *Exposition of the 39 Articles,* &c. which made the other party (the Puritan) angry, and so far to be enraged as maliciously to asperse and blemish him. Whereupon he wrote a vindication of himself in MS. now in the hands of a near relation of his. At length after a great deal of pains taken for the benefit of the church he gave up the ghost at Horninger before-mentioned, otherwise called Horningshearth: whereupon his body was buried in the chancel of the church there, under a rough, unpolished and broken grave-stone, without name or epitaph, 22 Feb. in sixteen hundred and fifteen, as the register of that church tells us; which, I presume, follows the English accompt and not the common, as many country registers do. I find one Tho. Rogers, a Cheshire man born, to have been admitted student of Ch. Ch. 1547, aged 24, or more, being then Bac. of Arts, and soon after made Master. What relation he had to the former Tho. Rogers I know not. Another Tho. Rogers I find, who was born in Glocestershire, in or near to Tewksbury, lived mostly in his latter days in the parish of S. Giles in the Fields near London, and published a poem entitled, *The Tears or Lamentations of a sorrowful Soul.* Lond. 1612, qu. written by Sir Will. Leighton, knight, one of his majesty's band of pensioners. To which, the said Tho. Rogers added, of his own composition, a poem called *Glocester's-Mite*[2]. But

[[2] Wood is certainly wrong in this statement, that Thomas Rogers was the publisher of Sir Will. Leighton's poem. He was misled by the Bodleian copy of these two poems, which are bound together, and so misplaced by the binder as to render it difficult to distinguish the one from the other. They are however very

this Tho. Rogers is quite different from the divine beforementioned.

[Tho. Rogers, A.M. institutus ad rectoriam de Horningherth, dioc. Norw. 11 Dec. 1581. *Reg. Vac.* BAKER.]"

The work now reprinted first made its appearance, though in a different form and under a different title, in two parts, the first of which was published, according to Wood, in 1579, and the second in 1585. A copy of this edition the present Editor has been unable to discover. The second edition noticed by Wood was also in two parts, published at some interval of time; and a copy of it is in the University Library at Cambridge. The first part bears the title of "The English Creede, consenting with the True Auncient Catholique and Apostolique Church in al the points and articles of Religion which everie Christian is to knowe and beleeve that would be saved. The Firste Parte in most loyal maner to the Glorie of God, credit of our Churche and displaieng of al hærisies and errors, both olde and newe, contrarie to the faith, subscribed unto by Thomas Rogers.

different works. *Gloucester's Myte* is a funeral tribute to the memory of Prince Henry, and was printed in 1612. *The Teares*, &c. are various religious poems, and sonnets which were set to music by Leighton, who, in his preface, declares his intention to print the notes by which his hymns, &c. are to be sung or played. This work was printed one year after Rogers's production, with which it has not the smallest connexion.

A very sufficient specimen of Leighton's *Teares* will be found in the *British Bibliographer*, i. 378; but that our readers may have no occasion to regret the scarcity of the book, four lines shall be offered to their religious contemplation.

Our fathers, Lord, were comforted,
  Strength'ned, relieved, and blest
Onely by grace, and iustified
  As righteous men, in Jesus Christ.—

It is now only just to Rogers that he should not be omitted entirely, and the concluding stanza of his *Myte* shall end this note.

Our soules are siluer plates thy fame to hold;
Our zeall rich diamonds to make th' impression;
The characters we print, refined gold
To keep thy name all ages in succession.
  Then sleepe, sweet Henry, prince of endless fame,
  Whilst we record thy euerlasting name.]

Allowed by Auctoritie. At London. Imprinted by John Windet for Andrew Maunsel, at the Brasen Serpent in Paul's Churchyard, 1585." This part contains an analysis of the first nineteen Articles, and is dedicated to Edmund [Scambler] Bishop of Norwich. The second part, completing the work, bears a similar title, but is dedicated to Sir Christopher Hatton, the Lord Chancellor. It was published in 1587. The whole work is printed in a thin folio. The Articles are broken up into Propositions, and each Proposition is presented in the form of an analytical conspectus. Of the manner in which this was done the following instance, taken at random, may suffice to convey an idea:

7. Article.

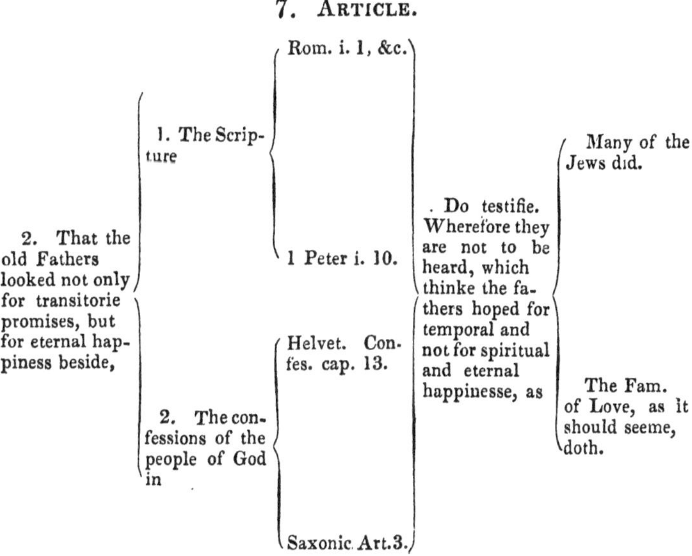

In 1607 the book was published in quarto; and the analytical form in which it had hitherto appeared was abandoned. This edition, which was the last published during the author's life-time, has been in almost every instance followed in the present reprint. Where the corrections of later editions have been adopted, the reading of the edition of 1607 has been carefully noticed.

But the quarto varied considerably from the folio in other respects as well as in form. In the folio the only references are to Scripture and the Confessions of the Protestant churches. Errors and heresies are noticed, but no authorities are given in support of the statements made respecting them. Nor are the notices of heresies themselves by any means so numerous as in the later edition.

Again, several distinct Propositions were added in the quarto. In it the Fifth and Eighteenth Articles, which in the folio are treated as single Propositions, are divided into three and two respectively. Similarly, the third Proposition of the Seventh Article, the last of the edition of 1585, in that of 1607 is expanded into three.

Other variations are as follows:

In the folio, there is appended to the Third Proposition of the Tenth Article, a caution against the doctrine of human perfectibility, which was subsequently omitted.

In the Seventeenth Article the Propositions 5—9 are differently worded: 5. Why some are elected and not others. 6. Who are they which shall be saved. 7. What are the effects of predestination. 8. The use of the doctrine of predestination both to the godly and wicked. 9. What may keep men both from desperation and also from security.

In the Nineteenth Article there is an Eighth Proposition, which was afterwards omitted. It is this: "There is no salvation without the church; and therefore every man is firmlie to joyne thereunto, and never to depart therefrom by schisme and contention."

But the chief difference between the two editions lies in the altered exposition of the Third Article, an alteration to which there attaches some historical interest. In the folio of 1585, the author adopts Calvin's view of the descent into hell. He there writes: "That our Saviour Christ descended into Hell, together with our Church, (1) the ancient creeds,

Apostolical [and] Athanasian; the Confession of the Church of Helvet. ii. cap. 11; Basil, Art. 4; Ausburgh, Art. 3; Suevia. Art. 2, do testify. Which word Hell in this Article, as we take it, signifieth: not the place of everlasting torments where Dives was and is, Luke xvi. 23; all the reprobate together shall be, Matt. xxv. 41. In which place Christ as man was not, forasmuch as (1) His body lay in the grave, Matt. xii. 40; xvi. 4; Luke xi. 29; (2) His soul was commended into the hands of God the Father, Ps. xxxi. 5; Luke xxiii. 46, [and was] in Paradise, (so is it set down as a thing well to be observed): and not in Hell, Luke xxiii. 43. [But] The terrors and torments of the body and soul which Christ suffered; as appeareth Isa. liii. 6, 10; Ps. cxvi. 3; Matt. xxvi. 38; xxvii. 46; Luke xxii. 42." Controversy, however, as to the true interpretation of the Article was already rife. Calvin's view had indeed been very generally received, more perhaps from deference to his authority, than from any careful investigation of the subject. But in the year 1579, Hugh Broughton, a learned Hebraist, maintained that the hell of the Creeds and the Article was the Greek *Hades*, or place of disembodied spirits, and not the place of eternal punishment. This interpretation, which at first met with very considerable opposition, gradually gained ground, and Archbishop Whitgift, who among others had formerly controverted it, at length came round to it himself[1]. There can be little doubt indeed that a great revolution of opinion on this point had been effected before Thomas Rogers's work on the Articles appeared in its present form in 1607. Hence we find that in this edition he speaks far less confidently than before[2], and whilst mentioning different views that had been entertained of the doctrine, does not strongly advocate any.

The Editor is unable to add anything to Wood's account

[1] See Strype's Whitgift, Book IV. chap. 13 and 19. pp. 431, 483. Lond. 1718. Heylin, Hist. Presb. 350. Soames's Elizabethan Church Hist. p. 476.

[2] Thus p. 61, he says, "But till we know the native and undoubted sense of this article and mystery of religion," &c.

of Rogers. Fuller, in the place referred to by Wood, speaks at some length of the work on the Articles. And Rogers himself notices his share in the Sabbatarian controversy, Preface, § 23. He also defends himself in some observations on the Thirty-Fourth Article, from a misrepresentation of his view respecting the use of the cross in Baptism. By the authors of the misrepresentation in question, he is mentioned along with others well-known for their theological attainments, as a divine of learning and repute.

Two severe and protracted attacks of illness have prevented the Editor from bringing his labours to a conclusion so soon as he could have wished and had intended. Further delay has been occasioned not only by the great rarity of some of the books referred to, but by the extreme looseness and inaccuracy of the author's quotations. Some of these the Editor has been able to correct. Many he has unhappily been compelled to give up. None but those who have actually made the experiment can conceive of the time and labour necessary to verify the numerous references made by many of the writers of the Elizabethan period.

The Editor has to express his sincere thanks to those friends who have assisted him in his researches. His acknowledgements are due especially to the Rev. Professor Corrie, Master of Jesus College, who, besides other aid, kindly permitted reference to his rare and almost unique collection of the books of the Family of Love; to the Rev. J. J. Blunt, Margaret Professor of Divinity; and to the Rev. F. Proctor, late Fellow of St Catharine's Hall.

Corpus Christi College,
January 2, 1854.

CONTENTS.

ADDENDA ET CORRIGENDA.

Page 9, line 24. The edition of 1607 has *mercate-town.*

... 61, note 6. The references to Hume's Rejoinder and Gifford's Catechism were afterwards found. They are as follows:

For we say that Christ descended personallie into Hell, both bodie and soule and suffered actuallie all the torments thereof, for our redemption. Otherwise, were he but a potentiall Saviour, and all wee actually condemned.—Alex. Hume, A Reioynder to Doctor Hil concerning the Descense of Christ into Hell, p. 38.

...it is as sure (as what is most sure) that upon the tree, that is upon the crosse, hee descended into the lowermost Hell; that is into the heaviest torments that Hell could yeeld, &c.—Ibid. p. 138.

For wee holde and will die for it, that Christ in his owne person bodie and soule, did descend into all the torments, that hel could yeelde.—Ibid. p. 152.

What is it to be made the curse, but to have the bitter anguish of God's wrath in his soule and body: which is the fire that shall never be quenched.—A Catechisme, conteining the summe of Christian Religion, &c.—Newly set foorth by G. G. London, 1583. fol. B. 5.

... 246, line 4. *for* from Christians, *read* for Christians.

... 285, ... 1. *for* venial and mortal, *read* venial and not mortal.

THE CATHOLIC DOCTRINE

OF THE

CHURCH OF ENGLAND.

THE

FAITH, DOCTRINE
and religion, professed, & protected
in the Realm of England, and dominions of the same:

Expressed in 39 Articles, concordably agreed upon by the Reverend Bishops, and Clergy of this Kingdom, at two several meetings, or Convocations of theirs, in the years of our Lord, 1562, and 1604:

THE SAID ARTICLES ANALYSED INTO Propositions, and the Propositions proved to be agreeable both to the written word of God, and to the extant Confessions of all the neighbour Churches, Christianly reformed.

THE ADVERSARIES ALSO OF NOTE, AND name, which from the Apostles' days, and primitive Church hitherto, have crossed, or contradicted the said Articles *in general, or any particle, or proposition arising from any of them in particular, hereby are discovered, laid open, and so confuted.*

Perused, and by the lawful authority of the Church of England, allowed to be public.

Rom. xvi. 17.
I beseech you, Brethren, Mark them diligently, which cause divisions, and offences, contrary to the doctrine which ye have received, and avoid them.

PRINTED BY IOHN LEGATT, PRINTER
to the University of Cambridge. 1607.

TO THE MOST REVEREND FATHER IN GOD, AND HIS RIGHT HONOURABLE GOOD LORD RICHARD[1], BY THE DIVINE PROVIDENCE, ARCHBISHOP OF CANTERBURY, AND PRIMATE OF ENGLAND, AND COUNSELLOR TO THE MOST HIGH AND MIGHTY PRINCE, JAMES, KING OF GREAT BRITAIN, FRANCE, AND IRELAND.

MOST reverend father in God, there is no one thing in this world, that of men truly zealous and christian in these latter days of the world with greater earnestness hath been desired, than that by a joint and common consent of all the churches rightly, and according to the canons of the sacred scriptures, reformed, there might be a draught made and divulged, containing and expressing the sum and substance of that religion, which they do all both concordably teach and uniformly maintain.

Archbishop Cranmer.

That holy man (of happy remembrance) D. Cranmer, who sometime enjoyed that room in our church which your grace now worthily possesseth, in the days of that most godly young prince, king Edward the Sixth, employed a great part of his time and study for the effecting of that work; and imparted his thoughts with the most principal persons, and of rarest note in those days for their wisdom, piety, and credit, among the people of God throughout Christendom. M. Calvin, understanding of his intent, addressed his letters unto the said archbishop, and offered his service, saying, "That, might his labours stand the church instead, *Ne decem quidem maria*, it would not grieve him to sail over ten seas to such a purpose[2]."

Unity of doctrine in all churches reformed.

2. But, this proving a work of much difficulty, if not altogether unpossible in men's[3] eyes, especially in those days, to be brought about; the next course and resolution was, that every kingdom and free state, or principality, which had

[1 Bancroft. He succeeded Whitgift as Primate. See Soames's Elizabethan Rel. Hist. p. 604. n.]

[2 Quantum ad me attinet, si quis mei usus fore videbitur, ne decem quidem maria, si opus sit, ob eam rem trajicere pigeat.—Calv. Epist. p. 100. Genev. 1576.]

[3 man's, 1607.]

abandoned the superstitious and antichristian religion of the church of Rome, and embraced the gospel of Christ, should divulge a brief of that religion, which among themselves was taught and believed, and whereby, through the mercy of God in Christ, they did hope to be saved: which to God his great glory and the singular benefit and comfort of all churches, both present and to come (as the extant Harmony[1] of all their confessions doth most sweetly record), with no great labour was notably performed.

This work of theirs told the churches in those days, and doth us, and will inform our posterity, that not only in every particular state and kingdom, but also throughout Christendom where the gospel was entertained, the primitive and apostolical days of the church were again restored. For the multitudes of them that did believe (I speak both jointly of all, and severally of each reformed people, not of every particular person, fantastic, false apostles, and perverse teachers or professors in any church, who were not wanting even in the apostles' days) touching the main and fundamental points of true religion were then of one heart and of one soul, and did think and speak one thing, and live in peace[a].

[a] *Ab initio Reformationis ardebant amore veritatis omnes ordines: politici, ecclesiastici, plebei.* Jezler. *de diutur. belli Euch.* p. 49.

Unity of doctrine in the church of Eng. in K. Ed. 6. his days.

3. The said archbishop (for unto whom better, after God and the king, can we ascribe the glory of this worthy act?) he wrought this unity and uniformity of doctrine in this kingdom in the halcyon days of our English Josias, K. Edward the Sixth of that name: and the same doctrine, so by his means established in the time of peace (a notable work of peace), like a manly, heroical, and heavenly captain, under our general Jesus Christ, he resolutely, even with his heart-blood and in the fiery torments, afterwards confirmed in the days of persecution.

An. 1552. A certain learned man, speaking of the religion here then professed, and writing unto the lords of our late queen's council, doth say, "He" (meaning the papist his adversary, who charged our church with discord and disagreements

[[1] This work was published at Geneva in the year 1581, and was entitled "Harmonia Confessionum Fidei Orthodoxarum et Reformatarum Ecclesiarum, quæ in præcipius quibusque Europæ Regnis, Nationibus et Provinciis, sacram Evangelii doctrinam pure profitentur, &c." For an account of it, see Niemeyer. Collect. Conf. Præf. Lips. 1840. An English Translation appeared in 1586.]

about matters of religion) "he ought" (saith he), "if he had been able, to have brought out the public confession and articles of faith, agreed in K. Edward's time; and have shewed any in England, that, professing the gospel, dissenteth from the same." So esteemed he (and with him many thousands of learned and judicious men) of the doctrine then ratified by authority, and professed in this kingdom.

K. Edward 6.

But those days of our church's peace continued not long (through our unthankfulness and sins); neither on the other side was our persecution permanent (through the goodness of God,) though for the time exceeding vehement and violent. For, *nubecula fuit, et cito transiit,* it vanished away quickly, as do many raging storms, even upon the sudden; yet not through the power of gunpowder and treasons, but through the force of ardent prayers unto the Almighty. For, *Arma ecclesiæ preces.*

Q. Mary.

4. We find that M. Latimer (that sacred and reverend father) addicted himself very seriously in those days unto the exercise of prayer: and his principal and most usual prayers were, first, for himself; next, for the afflicted church of England; and lastly, for lady Elizabeth, the deceased K. Edward's and queen Mary's sister.

The prayers of the persecuted saints for the reducing of true religion into the realm.

For himself he prayed that, as God had made him a minister and preacher of his truth, so he might constantly bear witness unto the same, and have the grace and power to maintain it in the face of the world, even till the hour of his death. For the church of England he prayed, that God would be pleased once again to restore the free preaching of the gospel to this realm; and this with all possible fervency of spirit he craved at the hands of God. And for lady Elizabeth, that he would preserve and make her a comfort to his then comfortless people in England. And the Almighty and our heavenly Father both heard and granted all and every of his petitions.

F. Latimer.

M. Gualter (that learned, painful, and excellent divine at Tigure), dedicating his holy and christian Comments upon the Lesser Prophets unto D. Parkhurst, bishop of Norwich (who in the days of the forementioned queen Mary voluntarily had exiled himself so far as Switzerland, for his preservation, if it might be, unto better times), saith of the said Parkhurst that, when he lived in Tigure, lady Elizabeth was ever in his

Bp. Parkhurst.

mouth: her faith, her wisdom, her magnanimous spirit, her virgineous and chaste behaviour, he would ever celebrate with high words and commendations; and that God would guard and safeguard her person for the good of his people, was his daily prayer: yea (saith the same Gualter), *orabant idem tecum pii omnes*[1], "it was not your prayer only, but all God's people so prayed besides." And their prayers were not made in vain. For both queen Mary lived not long; and L. Elizabeth was placed in the royal throne; superstition was expulsed, and true religion again, to the singular comfort and multiplication of God's people in this kingdom, very solemnly restored.

Q. Elizab.

True doctrine restored an. 1558, and an uniformity of the same established, and published, an. 1562.

5. Notwithstanding an uniformity of doctrine to be taught, embraced, and professed, by authority of the prince and state, was not published till certain years after the queen's attaining the kingly diadem; but then Articles of Religion, to the number of thirty-nine, drawn yet three years afore, were commended to the consideration and perusal of the whole clergy of both provinces in an orderly and lawful assembly or convocation of theirs at London; and by a sweet and unanimous readiness thereupon by them allowed. This was effected in the year of our Lord 1562, the same year that the merciless massacre at Vassey in France was committed by the duke of Guise, and the same very time also that all the protestants in that country of France, for holding and professing the same doctrine, were sentenced unto death and destruction by the parliament at Paris; after which their condemnation ensued those horrible and more than savage murders and slaughters of the religious, and only for their religion[2], at Carrascone, at Tholouse, Amiens, Tours, Sens, Agen, Aurane, and many other cities, towns, and villages throughout France.

An. 1562.

Arch. Parker.

A principal contriver of this uniformity in religion, and thereby unity among us, was another predecessor of your grace's, even D. Parker, the first archbishop of Canterbury in the said queen's days.

[1 Hæc (sc. Elizabetha) tibi semper in ore erat; illius fidem, prudentiam, fortitudinem, pudicitiam semper prædicare, utque hanc nobis Dominus incolumem servaret, assidue precari solebas. Orabant idem tecum, &c.—Rod. Gualter. Hom. in Proph. Min. Epist. nuncup. in Hos. Proph. ad fin. Tigur. 1572.]

[2 This religion, 1607.]

Hereupon wrote Beza[3] from Geneva, *Doctrinæ puritas viget in Anglia pure et sincere*[4]; "Religion flourisheth in England:" Zanchius, from Strasborough, *Per hanc reginam factam*; "By her" (meaning queen Elizabeth's) "coming to the crown, God again hath restored his doctrine and true worship:" and Danæus, "The whole compass of the world hath never seen anything more blessed, nor more to be wished, than is her government."

So now again flourished those apostolical times (as I may say) of unity and uniformity of doctrine in our church. For then were there no contentions, nor dissensions, nor thorny and pricking disputations among us, about questions of religion; *tantum res nobis fuit cum satellitibus quibusdam pontificiis*[5] (as bishop Jewel said), "we then skirmished only with the papists." As it was with the building of Solomon's temple, so was it with us then: we set upon the building of God's house (which is his church) without deane[6], without noise and stirs. The adversaries without heard us, and heard of our doings abroad by the pens of the learned Jewel, Nowel, Calfhill, and such other architects of ours: to ourselves we were comely as Jerusalem, to our enemies "terrible as an army of banners."

6. Also what afore, *viz.* an. 62[7], they had agreed upon, the same at another assembly at London, *an.* 71, and the 13 of Q. Elizabeth, according to an act of parliament then made[8], the said clergy of England (the archbishops and bishops first beginning, and giving the example), by their several subscriptions with their own hands, most readily did prove.

Subscription required unto the book of Art. an. 1571.

Howbeit in the year next ensuing, *scil. an.* 72, (a year many ways memorable, especially for the great and general massacre of above an hundred thousand protestants in France,

An. 1572.

[[3] Hereupon Beza, &c. 1607.]

[[4] .... in eo regno .... ubi puritas doctrinæ vigeat.—Bez. Epist. XII. p. 101. Genev. 1575. The editor has been unable to verify the references to Zanchius and Danæus.]

[[5] See Zurich Letters. First Series. Park. Soc. Ed. Epist. LVI.]

[[6] Din, later editions.] [[7] In the year 1562, later editions.]

[[8] *The Act for Ministers of the Church to be of sound Religion* enjoins subscription to the Articles, "comprised in a book imprinted, intituled *Articles whereupon, &c.*"—Lamb's Hist. Account, 26. See also Fuller's Ch. Hist. Bk. IX. § 55. p. 72. Lond. 1655.]

chiefly in Paris and the country thereabout adjoining, begun on St Bartholomew's eve[1]; for pope Gregory's excommunicating of Q. Elizabeth, for defending this doctrine and religion which here we speak of; and thirdly, for the erecting of private presbyteries now first in England), divers of the inferior ministers in and about London, and elsewhere in this kingdom, not a little disturbed the quiet of our state and peace, some of them by untimely and inconsiderate admonitions, pamphlets, and libels; other by obstinate refusing to subscribe, as both law did enjoin, and their fathers in Christ and superiors afore them had done. But these men speedily both by learning were answered and by authority censured, suspended, or deprived[2].

Bartholomæus flet; quia Gallicus occubat Atlas.

Unity of doctrine still continued.

7. And yet not one of the recusants, and so not one of England's clergy, either now or afore, did ever oppugn the received public and catholic doctrine of our church; but most willingly approved and applauded the same, as the truth of God.

For even the admonitioners themselves (which said that they did strive for true religion, and wished the parliament even with perfect hatred to detest the church of England, whereof notwithstanding they were members), even they do say how they (meaning the bishops and their partakers) hold[3] the substance of religion with us, and we with them[4]. And again: "We (all of us) confess one Christ." And their champion doth acknowledge that her majesty hath delivered us from the spiritual Egypt of popery.

So that for doctrine (I mean still for the main points of doctrine) there was now a sweet and blessed concord among

[1 "This same year happened a cruel massacre in Paris, the French Protestants being bidden thither under the pretence of a nuptial solemnity, but never were such black favours given at a wedding. Admiral Coligny (the pillar of the reformed Church) being slain in his bed on Bartholomew eve, whose day then and for some years after was there remarkable for wet weather.

Bartholomeus flet, quia Gallicus occubat Atlas.
Bartholomew bemoans with rain
The Gallic Atlas thereon slain."

Fuller, Ch. Hist. Bk. IX. Sect. iii. § 10.]

[2 See Strype's Whitgift, Book I. Chaps. vi. and vii.]

[3 They hold, 1607.]

[4 See Admonition to the Parliament, Art. 3.]

us: which unity continued all that holy and reverend father's, I mean archbishop Parker's, time, which was till the 17. year of Q. Elizabeth[5].

8. After him succeeded in the said archiepiscopal chair B. Grindal, a right famous and worthy prelate, and for religion so sound, as in K. Edward's days (had the prince lived a while longer) he had been promoted unto the bishoprick of London, upon the translation of B. Ridley unto Durham; for these things had the state then in purpose. But God otherwise had decreed for their advancements, as that the one of them should pass through the fire unto the kingdom of heaven, and the other escape the dangers of many storms and waters, before he came unto any preferment at all. And so accordingly Ridley was burned and Grindal banished, and both of them deprived either of life or living, or both; and that for one and the same cause and doctrine, which they had preached, and we profess.

Archbishop Grindal.

But, the tempest being over-blown, and Q. Elizabeth herself having likewise escaped the bloody hands of her cruel enemies, yea, and gunpowder trains, and treasons too, in most barbarous manner laid to have blown up her saint-like and sanctified body and soul into the heavens (and all for her constant favouring and embracing this very doctrine), her majesty, not forgetful what he had endured for the cause of Christ and his church, advanced the zealous confessor and tried soldier unto the see, first of London (afore designed him), next of York, and lastly of Canterbury.

The care of this archbishop was great to further the glory of God; but, through the envy and malice of his ill-willers, his power was but small; his place high, but himself made low, through some disgraces[6], by his potent adversaries; which he meekly and patiently endured till his dying day.

9. During the time of this man's troubles, among other, two things especially deserve observation. One is, the flocking of Jesuits into the kingdom[7], who afore then never came

The factious increase, and grow confident.

[5 Seventeenth year, and queen Elizabeth, later editions.]

[6 He was confined and sequestered for refusing to forbid the 'Exercises' or 'Prophesyings' as they were termed. See Strype's Grindal, Bk. II. chap. ix.]

[7 See Strype's Grindal, Bk. II. ch. xi. p. 256. Lond. 1710. Fuller, Ch. Hist. Bk. IX. Sect. iii. § 41. And Sect. iv. § 6.]

among us; the other is, the insolency and boldness of our home-faction.

The Jesuits indicted councils, summoned synods, enacted and reversed orders, and exercised papal jurisdiction among us; we not witting, nor so much as dreaming of any such matter.

The brethren (for so did they now style themselves) in their churches and charges would neither pray, nor say service, nor baptize, nor celebrate the Lord's supper, nor marry, nor bury, nor do any other ecclesiastical duty according to the law; but after their own devisings. And abroad[1] (as if they had been acquainted with the jesuitical proceedings, or the Jesuits with their practices) they had their meetings, both classical and synodical; they set down decrees, reversed orders, elected ministers, exacted subscriptions, and executed the censures of suspension and excommunication, where they thought good.

The Jesuits had for their provincial, first, Robert Parsons, *alias* Cowbuck, then Weston, and lastly Garnet; which Garnet continued in that office till the year 1605, when he was apprehended, and for most horrible and hellish treasons, as an arrant traitor, put to death in Paul's church-yard the same year. And the brethren had their (I know not what) chief men; all of these residing in and about London, and in special favour both with the gentry[2] and vulgar people of their several factions, and so continued multiplying their number and growing strong, even headstrong in boldness and schism, till the dying day of this most grave and reverend archbishop, which was in the month of July, 1583.

Unity of doctrine still holdeth among us.

10. Some four months afore whose death the said brethren, at a certain assembly of their own appointing, among other things (as I find) decreed that, if subscription unto the book of Articles of Religion (afore-mentioned and still meant) should again be urged, the said brethren might subscribe thereunto according to the statute: which declareth, that what diversity and disagreement soever was about other matters, yet abode there still a blessed unity among us touching the foundation of the christian religion. And this was in 25. year of Q. Elizabeth.

Archbishop Whitgift.

11. Next unto him D. Whitgift, then bishop of Wor-

[[1] Fuller, Ch. Hist. Bk. IX. Sect. i. § 56.] [[2] Gentiles, 1607.]

cester (a man deservedly unto that dignity promoted, and for his manifold pains in writing, teaching, and defending the truth, his wisdom in governing, and his well-demeaning of himself every way, worthy the double honour which he did enjoy, or the state could advance him unto), from thence was translated unto the see of Canterbury.

No sooner was he confirmed in his office, but, observing both the open and intolerable contempt, in many places, of all church-orders by authority prescribed, and hearing both of many secret conventicles and unlawful assemblies in his province, and of the tumults and garboils abroad, and even at his very admission unto his charge raised in Scotland, and that for the self-same cause which by the brethren here in England was maintained; and foreseeing the dangers and troubles likely to ensue, for which he should give an account, if in time he sought not means to prevent them; he thought it his bounden duty (for the preservation of unity and purity in religion, the preventing of further schism, and the discovery of men's inclinations either unto peace or faction), that all and every minister ecclesiastical having cure of souls within the province of Canterbury, under his own hand and by subscription, should testify his consent both unto the points of religion in the convocation *an.* 62 approved, and likewise unto other articles necessary for concord's sake of all and every man, minister especially, to be acknowledged; and accordingly by due course of law called then thereunto: which was done the very first year of his removal, and of her majesty the 26[3].

Subscription the second time called for.

This of the brethren was termed the woeful year of subscription; but that they should so do there was no cause, unless they are grieved that factious spirits and malcontented ministers and preachers were discovered, and their erroneous and schismatical opinions brought into light. And surely never was there subscription hitherto by authority urged in this land, but divers new fancies (held yet for truths not to be doubted of among the brethren) were thereby detected, for God's people to avoid as monsters: neither hath our church lost by imposing, nor the adversaries gained, at the long run, by refusing subscription.

An. 1584.

12. In the years 71 and 72, when subscription first was

[3 Fuller, Bk. IX. Sect. V. § 9, and VI. § 14.]

How basely the brethren conceive of the doctrine, by the bishops agreed upon, and established by the prince.

required, the whole land will witness, that many and sundry books (as well in Latin as English) then and afterward flew abroad. In which we read how then and in those days the truth of God did in a manner but peep out (as it were) at the screen; that Cranmer, Parker, Grindal, and all the other martyrs, preachers, and learned men (which first in our age "brought the light of the gospel into this realm) did see a little and had a glimpse of the truth, but oversaw many things which in these days of the sunshine of the gospel men of meaner gifts do see, and yet may not utter them without great danger of the laws (through the iniquity of the times), though the said things now seen be comprised in the book of God, and also be a part of the gospel, yea, the very gospel itself; so true are they and of such importance as, if every hair of our heads were a life (say the brethren), we ought to afford them in defence of these matters; the Articles of Religion, penned and agreed upon by the bishops and clergy, and ratified by the prince and parliament, in comparison of these things now revealed and newly come to light, are but childish and toys[1]."

Thus write they (as your grace best knoweth, and I would have quoted the places where they may be read, had I either not written unto yourself, or did write unto a man unacquainted with their books). And, had they here stayed, their words had been able (without the more grace of God) to have moved the parliament and all the people of this land (as they have prevailed but too much already with their too credulous favourites), to think our church, for all the reformation wrought and uniformity in doctrine established, to be much awry, and far from the truth it should profess. But setting down (as they have done) and publishing both what the truth is which now breaketh out and offereth itself, by their ministry, to the view of the whole world (which afore did but peep out at the screen), and what the things be which they of mean gifts do see, and our fathers, the martyrs, bishops, and preachers, both in king Edward's days and afterwards (known and acknowledged to be men of excellent parts), either did not see at all, or oversee, and what likewise the points of doctrine newly now revealed, their *æternum evangelium* (which without great danger may not be preached

[[1] See Soames, Eliz. Rel. Hist. pp. 184, 193.]

in England, no more than the doctrine and articles of the church of England may be preached at Rome; and for defence whereof they ought to afford even their very lives, were they so many as the hairs of every of their heads) is, and be, they demonstrate themselves to be most childishly vain and idle in their imaginations, which they take yet to be illuminations of the Spirit.

13. For all their doings and discourses (to say the best of them) are but to erect a new (which they term a true) ministry, and their discipline among us. The uncouth doctrine of the factious brethren.

Themselves do say, "The controversy betwixt them and us is not as (the bishops and their well-willers) they would bear the world in hand, for a cap, a tippet, or a surplice; but for greater matters concerning a true ministry, and regiment of the church, according to the word[2]: the one whereof, that is, a true ministry, they shall never have, till archbishops and bishops be put down, and all ministers made equal; the other also will never be brought to pass, till kings and queens do subject themselves unto the church, and submit their sceptres, and throw down their crowns before the church, and lick up the dust of the feet of the church, and willingly abide the censures of the church, that is, of the presbytery. For as the church is subject unto the civil magistrate, in respect of his civil authority, so must the magistrate, the king and queen, subject themselves and be obedient to the just and lawful authority of the church. The civil magistrate is none officer at all of the church. For church-officers be *non magnates aut tetrarchæ*, not gracious or honourable lords, but ministers of the church. The presbytery is the church, and every congregation or church should and must in it have a presbytery."

This is the light which indeed the martyrs never saw; the religion which our brethren strive for; the truth which they may not preach; not childish doctrine, like the bishops' articles, but the wise gospel, the main and material points of religion, now in these last days last of all (yea, after the eighth thorough breaking of H. N.[3] his *Evangelium Regni*)

[[2] See the Admonition to the Parliament. Art. 2. ad fin.]

[[3] Henry Nicholas, a Dutchman, founder of a sect of Anabaptists, calling themselves the Family of Love. For an account of their opinions see Fuller, Ch. Hist. Bk. IX. Sect. xiv. § 37, and especially Henry More's Theological Works.]

revealed, and for furtherance whereof they are to lend and spend even all their lives, if occasion be ministered.

14. Strange and strong delusions: first, to take these and other such assertions for truths and heavenly mysteries, which are but the fancies of troubled brains, not grounded nor truly gathered from God's word.

Next, to teach one another and all their favourers, how they should be as ready and prepared even for these matters to give other their livings, and to give their lives (were they as many as the hairs of all their heads), as Cranmer, Ridley, Latimer did; and Parker, Grindal, and all other preachers would, and every christian man and woman should (if they be called thereunto), for the apostolical and catholic doctrine of our church; which all God's people do know, and the brethren themselves (as afore hath been noted) do confess, is originally from God and his written word.

These and many more (too many here to be recapitulate) such fantasies of theirs, or frenzies rather, this first subscription brought first to light; and yet happy had it been for God's church and people, they had never been broached.

Of the second subscription urged an. 1584.

15. Semblably, the next subscription called for by the last archbishop, your lordship's predecessor, *an.* 84, discovered even the very thoughts and desires of those (brethren before, but now styled) faithful brethren, which have and do seek for the discipline and reformation of the church.

Many treatises afore, but now and divers years ensuing, they flew about and abroad like atoms[1]; and by them the same things which afore, but in a differing sort, and in other words, they publish.

For touching church-officers, they name who and how many sorts they be of them, viz. doctors, pastors, governors, deacons, and widows[2]; no more, no fewer.

They say every church must be furnished with a teacher and a pastor, as with two eyes; with elders, as with feet; with deacons, as with hands[3]. Every congregation must have eyes, hands, and feet; and yet neither all, nor at all any congregation, is to have an head, answerable to those feet, hands, and eyes.

[1 Atomies, 1607.]

[2 See Bancroft, Survey of Pretended Holy Discipline, chap. i. p. 3. Lond. 1593.]

[3 Ibid. chap. vii. p. 97.]

The doctor, by their doctrine, must be a distinct minister from the pastor, and only teach true doctrine, and neither exhort, nor apply his doctrine according to the times, and his auditory, nor minister the sacraments. For these things the pastor is to perform: which pastor also, whensoever he administereth the sacraments, must necessarily make a sermon, or else he committeth sacrilege.

And concerning discipline, by their doctrine, every congregation must have absolute authority to admonish, to censure, to excommunicate, and to anathematize all offending persons, yea even kings and princes, if they be of the congregation. And no prince but must be of some parish, and under one presbytery or other, always. Where this power is not, in their judgments, one of the tokens of a true church is wanting. For this discipline with them is a mark of the church, and numbered among the articles of their faith.

16. This (say they) is the great cause, the holy cause, which they will never leave suing for, though there should be a thousand parliaments in their days, until either they obtain it, or bring the Lord in vengeance and blood against the state and the whole land for repelling the same. The discipline is God's holy yoke, God's sceptre, the kingdom, and throne of Christ[4].

The brethren's divine conceits of their discipline.

Our controversy (say they) is, whether Jesus Christ shall be king, or no. Again, the end of all our travail is, to build up the walls of Jerusalem, and to set up the throne of Jesus Christ, our heavenly king, in the midst thereof; the advancing whereof is a testimony unto us that we shall have part in that glory which shall be revealed hereafter.

So learn we now from their said books, learned and demonstrative discourses (which the fathers and our forefathers never saw, nor had learned), both that their discipline established and exercised is a visible mark of a true church; and to desire the advancement of the same, an invisible token of an elect child of God: so as neither is that a church, at least no true church, where their discipline is not; neither they but titular Christians, no true Christians indeed, which either sigh or seek not to have it established, and presbyteries in every parish to be advanced.

[[4] See Bancroft, Dangerous Positions, &c. Bk. II. chap ii. p. 45. Lond. 1593.]

The brethren renew and continue their base conceits of the public articles of our religion, in comparison of their new gospel.

17. The Articles of our Religion (concluded upon by the reverend clergy of our church), with these learned and all-seeing brethren, are but the bishops' decrees, the articles of the convocation-house, and reveal some little truth: but these wise brethren (so faithful have they been between God and his church) they have not failed to shew us the whole counsel of God.

And yet these faithful brethren, either through forgetfulness or frailty, or (which I rather think) forced thereunto by the power of truth, do plainly confess, that those very decrees of our bishops, and articles of the convocation-house, even that little, little part of the gospel, which the said bishops and martyrs brought to light, and hath enlightened the whole realm, containeth the very fundamental points of Christianity.

Whereof I still gather, that had their newly-revealed, termed learned discourses, and doctrines, touching discipline and their presbyteries (howsoever with goodly and glorious titles, to ravish poor hearts with the desire thereof, brandished and set out) never been divulged or preached, we may be saved; but, without knowing and believing the articles or doctrine of our church (which yet is not ours, but God's) there is no salvation ordinarily to be looked for of any man: so true, and of such necessity, is this; so impertinent and unneedful, the other.

18. *Octogesimus octavus mirabilis annus*[1]*:* it was prophesied to be a wonderful year, long afore it came, and will never be forgotten now it is past.

An. 1588. Queen Elizabeth opposeth her authority against the brethren, their books and writings.

Among the things for which the year eighty-eight is famous, one, and not of least regard, is that, afore it expired, these books of the brethren, by a proclamation from queen Elizabeth, were denounced schismatical and seditious; and the doctrine in them contained erroneous, tending to persuade and bring in a monstrous and apparent dangerous innovation within her dominions and countries; and to make a change, even a dangerous change, of the form of doctrine then in use. And therefore the said books were commanded to be brought in, and delivered into the hands of authority;

[1 Now began that fatal year generally foretold that it would be wonderful, as it proved no less, &c. Fuller, Bk. IX. Sect. vii. § 14.]

and special charge given, that no more of that nature should come abroad, or be printed.

Whereby (so much as in that blessed queen, whose name with eternal honour shall be recorded) these new fancies of the brethren were hissed and exploded out of this christian kingdom; and the articles, or public doctrine of our church, confirmed, countenanced, and by the royal prerogative of that peerless prince more strongly ratified and commended to her awful and good subjects than afore.

19. The zeal of learned and godly men hereupon was inflamed, and their courage so increased, as whereas afore this time but one or two, or a very few (the first whereof was your lordship's immediate predecessor, whose memory be always honourable among the saints), did encounter the brethren, and oppugned their fancies: now an army of most valorous and resolute champions and challengers rose up, which then and divers years ensuing (among whom as your grace was the first in time which gave the onset, so are you to be reckoned with the first and best for zeal, wisdom, and learning) did conflict with these brethren, defended the prelacy, stood for the prince and state, put the new doctors to the foil, profligated the elders, set upon the presbytery and so battered the new discipline as hitherto they could never, nor hereafter shall ever fortify and repair the decays thereof.

Most learned and worthy men set themselves against the brethren and the presbyterian discipline.

20. Notwithstanding, what the brethren wanted in strength and learning, they had in wiliness; and, though they lost much one way in the general and main point of their discipline, yet recovered they not a little advantage another way, by an odd and a new device of theirs, in a special article of their classical instructions.

A stratagem of the brethren.

For while these worthies of our church were employing their engines and forces, partly in defending the present government ecclesiastical, partly in assaulting the presbytery and new discipline, even at that very instant the brethren (knowing themselves too weak either to overthrow our holds, An. 1595.
and that which we hold, or to maintain their own) they abandoned quite the bulwarks which they had raised, and gave out were impregnable; suffering us to beat them down, without any, or very small resistance: and yet, not careless of their affairs, left not the wars for all that, but from an odd corner,

and after a new fashion, which we little thought of, (such was their cunning,) set upon us afresh again by dispersing in printed books (which for ten years' space before they had been in hammering among themselves to make them complete) their sabbath speculations, and presbyterian (that is, more than either kingly or popely) directions for the observation of the Lord's day.

This stratagem of theirs was not observed then, neither, I fear me, is regarded as it should be yet; and yet did, and since hath, and doubtless in time to come, if it be not timely seen unto, with unsound opinions and paradoxes will so poison many, as the whole church and commonweal will find the danger and inconvenience of them: so plausible are they to men either popularly religious, or preposterously and injudiciously zealous.

Certain fruits and effects of the sabbatarian doctrine published by consent of the brethren.

21. In this their sally, as I said before, they set not upon the bishops and their calling, their chancellors, &c., as popish and antichristian; they let them alone, seeing and knowing they are too well backed for them to subvert: but (which are of great all, and almost of the same antiquity with bishops divers of them, and I had almost said as necessary) they ruinate, and at one blow beat down all times and days, by just authority destined to religious and holy uses, besides the Lord's day, saying plainly and in peremptory words, that the church hath none authority, ordinarily, or from year to year perpetually to sanctify any other day to those uses, but only the Lord's day.

They build not presbyteries expressedly (though under hand, if it be well marked, they do erect them in their exercises of the sabbath:) but they set up a new idol, their Saint Sabbath (erst in the days of popish blindness St Sunday) in the midst and minds of God's people.

By the former they have opened not a gap, but a wide gate, unto all licentiousness, liberty, and profaneness on the holydays, which is readily and greedily apprehended of all sorts of people everywhere, especially of their favourites, to the high dishonour of God, decay of devotion, hinderance of christian knowledge and wisdom in all sorts, especially in the vulgar multitude and poor servants, advantage of the common enemies, and gross contempt of the necessary and laudable orders of our church. By the latter they have introduced a new, and more than either Jewish or popish superstition into the land, to no small blemish of our christian profession, and scandal of the true servants of God, and therewith doctrine most erroneous, dangerous, and antichristian.

22. Their doctrine summarily may be reduced unto these two heads, whereof the one is, that the Lord's-day, even as the old sabbath was of the Jews, must necessarily be kept, and solemnized of all and every Christian, under the pain of eternal condemnation both of body and soul.

The sum of the sabbatarian doctrine broached by the brethren.

The other, that under the same penalty it must be kept from the highest to the lowest, both of king and people, in sort and manner as these brethren among themselves have devised, decreed, and prescribed.

The former of these is like that of the false apostles, which came from Judea unto Antioch, and taught the brethren, that unless they were circumcised after the manner of Moses, they could not be saved: whom the apostles, Paul and Barnabas first, and afterwards Peter, James, and the rest at Jerusalem both zealously did resist, and in their synod, or convocation, powerfully suppress.

The latter, as bad as that, hath been the mother of many heretical assertions and horrible conclusions.

I have read (and many there be alive which will justify it) how it was preached in a market-town in Oxfordshire, that to do any servile work or business on the Lord's-day is as great a sin as to kill a man, or to commit adultery. It was preached in Somersetshire, that to throw a bowl on the Sabbath-day is as great a sin as to kill a man. It was preached in Norfolk, that to make a feast or wedding-dinner on the Lord's-day is as great a sin as for a father to take a knife and cut his child's throat. It was preached in Suffolk (I can name the man, and I was present when he was convented before his ordinary for preaching the same), that to ring more bells than one upon the Lord's-day to call the people unto the church is as great a sin as to commit murder.

When these things I read and heard, mine heart was stricken with an horror, and so is it still, when I do but think of them; and calling into mind the Sabbath Doctrine[1], at London printed for J. Porter and T. Man, anno 1595,

[[1] This work was written by a Dr Bound, and was republished with some additions in 1606.]

which I had read afore (wherein very many things are to this effect), I presently smelt both whose disciples all those preachers are, and that the said doctrine had taken deep impression in men's hearts, and was dispersed (while our watchmen were otherwise busied, if not asleep) over the whole kingdom.

The brethren's doctrine of the Sabbath called in by authority, and forbidden any more to be printed.

23. It is a comfort unto my soul, and will be till my dying hour, that I have been the man and the means[1], that these sabbatarian errors and impieties are brought into light and knowledge of the state; whereby whatsoever else, sure I am, this good hath ensued, namely, that the said books of the sabbath (comprehending the abovementioned, and many more such fearful and heretical assertions) have been both called in, and forbidden any more to be printed and made common. Your grace's predecessor, archbishop Whitgift, by his letters, and officers at synods and visitations, anno 1599, did the one; and sir John Popham, lord chief justice of England, at Bury St Edmunds, in Suffolk, anno 1600, did the other.

Anno 1599, 1600.

And both these most reverend, sage, and honourable personages by their censures have declared (if men will take admonition), that this sabbath doctrine of the brethren agreeth neither with the doctrine of our church, nor with the laws and orders of this kingdom; disturbeth the peace both of the commonweal and church; and tendeth unto schism in the one, and sedition in the other: and therefore neither to be backed, nor bolstered by any good subject, whether he be church or commonweal man.

Purity of doctrine all queen Elizabeth's reign maintained in England.

24. Thus have errors and noisome doctrines, like boils and botches, ever and anon risen up, to the overthrow of our church's health and safety, if it might be; but yet such hath been the physic of our discipline, as what by lancing, purging, and other good means used, the body still hath been upholden and preserved from time to time.

And well may errors (like gross humours and tumours) continue among us, (as never church was, or will be quite without them, while it is militant here upon earth:) yet are they not of the substance at all of our religion, or any part of our church's doctrine (no more than ill humours which be in, are of the body; or dregs in a vessel of wine be any part either of the vessel or wine) which remaineth, as at the first,

[[1] Fuller, Book IX. Sect. viii. § 22.]

most sound, and uncorrupted; and so continued even until the dying day of that most illustrious and religious princess, queen Elizabeth.

The very brethren themselves do write, that,

In regard of the common grounds of religion, and of the ministry, we are all one. We are all of one faith, one baptism, one body, one spirit, have all one Father, one Lord; and be all of one heart against all wickedness, superstition, idolatry, heresy; and we seek with one christian desire the advancement of the pure religion, worship, and honour of God. We are ministers of the word by one order; we administer prayers and sacraments by one form; we preach one faith and substance of doctrine. And we praise God heartily, that the true faith, by which we may be saved, and the true doctrine of the sacraments, and the pure worship of God, is truly taught, and that by public authority, and retained in the book of articles. Anno 1602.

Hitherto the said brethren. And this was their verdict of our church's doctrine in the last year save one of queen Elizabeth's reign; than which nothing was ever more truly said or written: and this unity and purity of doctrine she left with us, when she departed this world.

25. Now, after Elizabeth reigned noble James, who found this our church, as all the world knoweth, in respect of the grounds of true religion, at unity; and that unity in verity, and that verity confirmed by public and regal approbation. King James. Anno 1603.

These ecclesiastical ministers therefore (though a thousand for number) who at his majesty's first coming into this kingdom either complained unto his highness of (I know not what) errors and imperfections in our church, even in points of doctrine (as if she erred in matters of faith), or desired that an uniformity of doctrine might be prescribed (as if the same had not already been done to his hands,) or (as weary belike of the old, by queen Elizabeth countenanced and continued) desired his majesty to take them out a new lesson (as did the seventy-one brethren of Suffolk), are not to be liked. King James abused and troubled with false informations, and petitions of the brethren.

Neither can we extol the goodness of our God sufficiently toward our king, and us all, for inspiring his royal heart with holy wisdom to discern these unstayed and troublesome spirits; and enabling his highness with power, and graces from above, to decree orders and directions for the general benefit and peace of the whole church; neither suffered he his eyes to sleep, nor his eye-lids to slumber, nor the temples of his head to take any rest, till he had set them down afore all other, though never so important and weighty affairs of the crown and kingdom.

King James patroniseth the doctrine and religion countenanced by queen Elizabeth.

26. Myself have read, and thousand thousands, with an hundred thousand of his subjects besides, have either read or heard of proclamations after proclamations (to the number of six, or seven at the least), of books and open speeches of his majesty, uttered in the parliament-house, and all of them made vulgar within a year, and little more, after his happy ingress into this kingdom and taking the administration of this most famous and flourishing empire upon himself; whereby the doctrine in this land allowed, and publicly graced and embraced of all sorts at his entrance into the realm, hath been not only acknowledged to be agreeable to God's word, sincere, and the very same which both his highness, and the whole church and kingdom of Scotland, yea, and the primitive church professed; but also by his authority regal and paramount (as one of the main pillars, supporting his estate) ratified to continue; and all hope either of allowing or tolerating in this kingdom of any other doctrine, religion, or faction whatsoever, opposite or any way thwarting the faith and confession of the church of England, in most plain, pithy, and peremptory words and speeches cut off.

Domini incarnati. Anno 1604.

The year 1562 was not more famous for the uniformity of doctrine in religion then concluded, than the year 1604 is memorable, and will be for seconding the same: neither got the clergy in those days more credit in composing the articles of our unity in faith, than did the last convocation (whereat your grace, then bishop of London, was present, and president) in ratifying the acts and articles of their antecessors; neither was queen Elizabeth more honoured in establishing them at the first, than is our king James renowned, and more and more will be, for approving under the great seal of England the late and last constitutions and canons ecclesiastical.

Subscription the third time urged.

27. Whereby no person shall hereafter be received into the ministry, nor neither by institution or collation admitted to any ecclesiastical living, nor suffered to preach, to catechise,

or to be lecturer or reader of divinity in either university, or in any cathedral, or collegiate church, city or market-town, parish-church, chapel, or in any other place in this realm, except, &c., and except he shall first subscribe to these three articles, &c.; whereof the third is, that he alloweth the book of Articles of Religion, &c.; nor any licensed to preach, read, lecture, or catechise, coming to reside in any diocese, shall be permitted there to preach, read, lecture, catechise, or minister the sacraments, or to execute any other ecclesiastical function (by what authority soever he be thereunto admitted), unless he first consent and subscribe to the three articles[1].

Neither shall any man teach either in public school, or in private house, except he shall first subscribe to the first and third articles simply, &c.[2]

Neither shall any man be admitted a chancellor, commissary, or official, to exercise any ecclesiastical jurisdiction, except, &c. and shall subscribe to the Articles of Religion, agreed upon in the convocation in the year 1562, &c.

And likewise all chancellors, commissaries, registers, and all other, that do now possess or execute any places of ecclesiastical jurisdiction or service, shall before Christmas next in the presence of the archbishop or bishop, or in open court, under whom, or where they execute their offices, take the same oaths, and subscribe, as before is said; or upon refusal so to do, shall be suspended from the execution of their offices, until they shall take the said oaths, and subscribe, as aforesaid[3].

Of the subscription called for.

28. In which constitutions the wisdom of his highness sheweth itself to be excellent, who indeed (as exceeding necessary, both for the retaining[4] of peace in the church, and preventing of new doctrine, curious speculations, and offences, which otherwise daily would spring up and intolerably increase) calleth for subscription, in testimony of men's cordial consent unto the received doctrine of our church, but exacteth not their oaths, as some do; much less oaths, vows, and subscription too (but only in a particular respect, and that of a very few in public office), as our neighbours have done.

[1 Constitutions and Canons Ecclesiastical, &c. xxxvi, vii.]
[2 Ibid. lxxvii.] [3 Ibid. cxxvii.]
[4 Retain, 1607.]

Again, he requireth subscription, but not of civil magistrates; not of the commons (as elsewhere some do), not of every man, yea, of women as well as of men (as did the persecuted church at Franckford in queen Mary's days), not of noble, gentlemen, and courtiers (as in Scotland was exacted in our king's minority); but only of ecclesiastical ministers, teachers, and spiritual officers, or of those which would be such: and so do the reformed churches in France and Germany at this very day.

Last of all, his majesty calleth for subscription unto articles of religion; but they are not either articles of his own lately devised, or the old newly turkened[1], but the very articles agreed upon by the archbishops and bishops of both provinces, and the whole clergy in the convocation holden at London, and that in the year of our Lord God 1562, and unto none other; even the same articles, for number thirty-nine, no more, no fewer; and for words, syllables, and letters, the very same, unaugmented, undiminished, unaltered.

Can. 2, 127.

Ibid.

The church of England settled and constant in her religion.

29. And being the same, the whole world is to know, that the church of England is not in religion changed, or variable like the moon, nor affecteth novelty or new lessons; but holdeth stedfastly and conscionably that truth, which by the martyrs and other ministers in this last age of the world hath been restored unto this kingdom, and is grounded upon God's written word, the only foundation of our faith.

And being the same, all men again may see, that we are still at unity both among ourselves at home, and with the neighbour churches abroad in all matters of chiefest importance and fundamental points of religion, though our adversaries the papists would fain beat the contrary into the common people's heads.

And being the same, there is now (as also from the first restoration of the gospel among us there hath been) an uniformity likewise of doctrine by authority established, which at the king his first arrival among us was so much desired by the brethren.

And finally, being the same, let us not doubt but persuade

[[1] Furbished, later Editions. Bancroft, in his Survey of the Pretended Holy Discipline, uses the word, *turkised:* "And yet he taketh the same sentence out of *Esay* (somewhat turkised) for his poesie as well as the rest." Chap. i. p. 6. Lond. 1593.]

ourselves, that we shall find the anti-christian church of Rome too the same, which for the same doctrine, and for none other cause, persecuteth all christian churches, but ours of England especially, with sword, fire, and powder in most hostile, yea, and hellish manner: the effect of whose hatred against us as we have often seen, so especially had we felt the same the next year after our king's ratification of these articles, had not our ever merciful God most miraculously detected both the treason and traitors. For which his favours his holy name be glorified of us and our posterity, throughout all generations.

Anno 1605.

The brethren no changelings.

30. So our church is the same. But be the brethren, the faithful, and godly brethren too, the same now which they have also been? If they be, then will they not deny (which anno 1572 they writ), that we hold the substance of religion with them; nor (which anno 1602 they published, and is afore remembered) that the true faith, by which we may be saved, and the true doctrine of the sacraments, and the pure worship of God be truly taught, and that by public authority, and retained in the book of articles. And in this confession I pray God they may constantly persevere.

Howbeit even these men (which in a generality do allow the doctrine of our church) being called by authority to acknowledge their assent unto every article thereof in particular, they do not a little debase the estimation of this doctrine of ours, and shew themselves but too apparent and professed dissenters from the same. And though all of them do and will approve some, yet not one of them will subscribe unto all and every of the articles.

For unto the articles of religion, and the king's supremacy, they are willing to subscribe. And they may subscribe (as afore hath been noted) unto such of them, as contain the sum of christian faith and the doctrine of the sacraments. But unto the same articles, for number 39, agreed upon in this convocation at London, anno 1562, they neither will, nor dare, nor may subscribe. For neither the rest of the articles in that book, nor the Book of Common Prayer, may be allowed, no, though a man should be deprived from his ministery for it, say the said brethren in a certain classical decree of theirs. The late politician is not afraid to move the high and most honourable court of parliament, that impropriations may be let to farm unto incumbent ministers, viz. which faithfully preach in the churches the true doctrine of the gospel, according to the articles of religion, concerning faith and sacraments; meaning that such ministers as preach the same doctrine, if they proceed to the rest of the articles, concerning either conformity in external and ceremonial matters, or uniformity in other points of doctrine contained in that book, should not be partakers of that benefit, or of benefices impropriate.

Why the brethren will subscribe unto some, but not unto all the Articles.

31. If it be demanded, what the causes may be, why they will subscribe unto some, but will not unto all; or why they will unto those Articles which concern faith and the sacraments, but will not unto the rest subscribe; the reasons hereof be two: whereof

The one is for that, in their opinion, there is no law to compel them to subscribe unto all. For (say the brethren resiant I know not where) we have always been ready to subscribe to the Articles of Religion concerning the doctrine of faith and of the sacraments, which is all that is required by law. Also the brethren in Devonshire and Cornwall, We are ready (say they) to subscribe to the third (which concerneth the book of Articles of Religion) so far as we are bound by statute concerning the same, *viz.* as they concern the doctrine of the sacraments and the confession of the true faith. And the two-and-twenty London brethren tell king James to his head, how the subscription which he calleth for is more than the law requireth.

Their other reason is, because (as the Lincolnshire do say) sundry, (as the London brethren affirm) many things in that book be not agreeable, but contrary to God's word.

32. If these things be true which they do allege, surely then are those men to be chronicled for the faithful, the godly and innocent brethren indeed, whom neither present benefices can allure, nor the angry countenance and displeasure of a king, even of the puissant and powerful king of Great Britain, can force to do anything at his beck and pleasure, either against law or for which there is no law; and who had rather to forego all their earthly commodities and livings, yea, and to go from their charges and ministery, and to expose themselves, their wives, and children, to the miseries of this world (grievous for flesh and blood to endure), than to

approve anything for true and sound by their hands, which is opposite or not agreeable to the revealed will and scriptures of God.

But if these allegations of theirs be but weak and sinful surmises, or rather, apparently most false, scandalous, and slanderous imputations to their prince, their mother-church, and this state; then doubtless, as even the[1] Christians now living cannot but take them, so the ages to come will everlastingly note and censure them, both for disloyal subjects, that so traduce a truly and most christianly religious king; ill-deserving children, that so abuse their honourable and reverend fathers and superiors of state and authority; turbulent spirits, not peaceable men, which raise such broils, troubles, and divisions in the church and kingdom (the issues whereof no tongue can foretel and are fearful being thought of) without cause; and, finally, neither faithful nor godly preachers, but ungodly broachers of untruths and slanders, and the very authors and fautors of horrible confusion and faction in God's church, whose peace they should seek and promote even with their dearest blood.

33. Since the statute for uniformity in rites and doctrine was first enacted, more than thirty-five years have passed, in all which space neither the brethren now being, nor the brethren afore them living, have hitherto shewn of the thirty-nine Articles, for names and titles, which—for number, how many—the articles be, which ecclesiastical ministers necessarily must, how many which they may not, or need not unless they list, subscribe unto; which I am sure they, or some of them, at one time or other would have expressed, had the law favoured their recusancy, and they been able to have justified their maxim, which is, that they are not compellable by subscription to approve them all. Again, since the first establishment of that statute-law, the most reverend fathers and truly reformed ministers of this church (sound for judgment, profound for learning, zealous for affection, sincere for religion; faithful in their churches, painful in their charges; more profitable many ways, of as tender consciences every way as any of these brethren combined, according both to their bounden duties and as they are persuaded) to the very purport and true intent of the

[1 As they even, 1607.]

said statute, have always both with their mouths acknowledged and with their pens approved the thirty-nine articles of our religion for truths not to be doubted of, and godly.

Yea, and the brethren too themselves (which now so scrupulously, when they are orderly called thereunto, do hold back their hands, and will subscribe but choicely unto some of them) even they with their mouths (which is equivalent and all one) have, and that according to the statute (or else their livings be void), upon the first entrance into all and singular their ecclesiastical benefices, openly both read and testified their consent unto the said articles, for number even nine-and-thirty, acknowledging them, I say, all of them to be agreeable to God's word; whereof the people in their several charges be ready witnesses, to testify so much before God and the world.

34. Again, of these brethren, that will subscribe but unto which they please of these articles, there be some who fain would beat into men's heads (if they could tell how to make it credible), that the doctrine of our church is altered from that it was in the reign of queen Elizabeth.

A late device of the brethren to shun subscription.

But this assertion being too gross, egregiously untrue, and no way justifiable, they secondly give out and report (so industrious be they to invent new shifts to cloak their inveterate and rooted pertinacy) how the purpose, if not doctrine, of our church is of late altered from that it was. And therefore though they can be well content to allow of the old doctrine and ancient intention; yet unto the old doctrine and new intention of our church they cannot subscribe, might they either gain much or lose whatsoever they have thereby. Besides, this new intendment, contrary to the old purpose, if not doctrine of our church, is become now the main and principal obstacle, why they cannot subscribe unto the Book of Common Prayer and Book of Ordination, as erst they (some of them) four times have done, when as well the intention as doctrine of our church was pure and holy.

Lastly, they seem not obscurely to intimate unto the state, that were they sure, or might be assured, that the purpose of our church were the same which it was, neither varied from the doctrine, they would be prest and as ready, even four, if not forty times more, to subscribe unto the fore-mentioned books of common prayer and of ordination, as aforetimes they did, when they were out of doubt the intention of our church was correspondent to her doctrine, that it was sound and good. I have four times subscribed (saith a brother) to the Book of Common Prayer with limitation, and reference of all things therein contained (not unto the purpose only, or doctrine only, but) unto the purpose and doctrine of the church of England. Yet cannot the same man with a good conscience so much as once more subscribe, which formerly, and that with a good conscience, had subscribed four times. His reason is, because the purpose, if not doctrine, of our church (to which he referred his subscription) appeareth to him, by the late canons, book of conference, and some speeches of men in great place, and others, to be varied somewhat from that, which he before (not without reason) took it to be.

The purpose and doctrine of our church, continue the same.

35. The purpose of our church is best known by the doctrine which she doth profess; the doctrine by the thirty-nine Articles, established by act of parliament; the articles by the words whereby they are expressed; and other purpose than the public doctrine doth minister, and other doctrine than in the said articles is contained, our church neither hath nor holdeth; and other sense they cannot yield than their words do import. The words be the same, and none other than erst and first they were; and therefore the sense the same; the articles the same; the doctrine the same, and the purpose and intention of our church still one and the same.

If then her purpose be known by her doctrine and articles, and their true sense by their very words, needs must the purpose of our church be the same, because her doctrine and articles for number, words, syllables, and letters, and every way be the very same.

And so our church's intention in her public doctrine and articles revealed, being good at the first, it is so still. For her purpose, continuing one and the same, cannot be ill at the last, which was good (and so believed and acknowledged, even by the brothers' subscription) at the first; or good in good queen Elizabeth's, and ill in illustrious king James his days.

Neither the doctrine nor purpose of our church altered.

36. If the premisses sufficiently explain not the constancy of our church's purpose in professing religion sincerely, then cast we our eyes upon the propositions, which she publicly maintaineth; and, if we find them the same, which ever

they have been, then need we not doubt (the brethren themselves being judges) but the articles again, their sense, the doctrine, purpose, and intention of the church of England (the proposition interpreting, as it were, the said articles) is the very same it ever was.

Now that propositions (pregnantly and rightly gathered, and arising from the articles) be the same, and for substance unaltered (though upon good considerations some few be added to the former); and all of them approved for true, and christian, by the lawful and public allowance of our church, the book here ensuing plainly will declare, and so demonstrate withal, not the doctrine only, but intention also, of our church to be the same and not changed; and being unchanged, the books then of common prayer, and of ordination too, considered in the purpose and intention of the church of England, and reduced to the propositions (as the brethren would have them), be well allowed and authentically approved; and the said brethren with as good conscience now again and afresh may subscribe unto all the articles, even concerning the Book of Common Prayer, and of Ordination, as well as of the king's supremacy, and of religion, as afore often and always they did.

37. For myself, most reverend father in God, what my thoughts be of the religion in this realm at this instant professed, and of all these articles, if the premisses do not, that which here followeth will sufficiently demonstrate. Twenty, yea, twenty-two years ago, voluntarily, of mine own accord, and altogether unconstrained, I published my subscription unto them: my faith is not either shaken or altered, but what it then was it still is; years have made those hairs of mine grey which were not; and time, much reading, and experience in theological conflicts and combats have bettered a great deal, but not altered one whit, my judgement, I thank God.

Nothing have I denied, nothing gainsaid, which afore I delivered.

The propositions are (and yet not many) more; the method altered; quotations added, both for the satisfaction of some learned and judicious friends of mine, requesting it at mine hands, and for the benefit both of the common and unlearned, and of the studious and learned reader.

The whole work expresseth as well my detestation and renunciation of all adversaries and errors, opposite, crossing, or contradicting the doctrine professed by us, and protected by our king, or any article or particle of truth of our religion; as my approbation of that truth which in our church by wholesome statutes and ordinances is confirmed.

There is not an heretic, or schismatic (to speak of) of any special mark, that from the apostles' times hitherto hath discovered himself and his opinions vulgarly in writing, or in print against our doctrine, but his heresy, fancy, or phrensy may be here seen against one proposition or other. The sects and sect-masters, adversaries unto us, either in the matter or main points of our doctrine or discipline, to one of our articles or other, wholly, or in part, which here be discovered to be taken heed of and avoided, are many hundreds.

38. This, and whatever else here done, either to the confirmation of the truth or detestation of heresies and errors, I do very meekly present unto your grace, as after God and our king best meriting the patronage thereof.

Myself am much, the whole church of England much more, bound unto your lordship; yea, not we only now living, but our successors also and posterity, shall have cause in all ages, while the world shall continue, to magnify Almighty God for the inestimable benefits which we have, and shall receive from yourself, and your late predecessors (Dr Whitgift, Grindal, Parker, Cranmer, of famous and honourable remembrance, bishops of our church, archbishops of the see of Canterbury) for this uniform doctrine by some of your lordships drawn and penned, by all of you allowed, defended, and (as agreeable to the faith of the very apostles of Christ, and of the ancient fathers, correspondent to the confessions of all reformed churches in Christendom, and contrariant in no point unto God's holy and written word) commended unto us, both by your authority and subscriptions.

Now the all-merciful God and heavenly Father, which so inspired them and your lordship with wisdom from above, and enabled you all to discern truth from falsehood, and sound religion from atheism, idolatry, and errors, vouchsafe of his infinite goodness to increase his graces more and more upon your grace, to his own glory, the church's benefit, and your own everlasting comfort.

And the same God which both mercifully hath brought, and miraculously against all hellish and devilish practices of his and our enemies continued the light of his truth among us, give us all grace with one heart and consent, not only to embrace the same, but also to walk and carry ourselves as it beseemeth the children of light, in all peaceableness and holiness of life, for his Son, our Lord and Saviour Christ, his sake.

At Horninger, near St Ed. Bury in Suff. the eleventh of March, anno 1607.

Your grace's poor Chaplain,

always at command,

THOMAS ROGERS.

CONSTITUTIONS AND CANONS ECCLESIASTICAL,

Anno 1604.

Whosoever shall hereafter affirm, that the church of England, by law established, under the king's majesty, is not a true and an apostolical church, teaching and maintaining the doctrine of the apostles; let him be excommunicated *ipso facto*, and not restored, but only by the archbishop, after his repentance and public revocation of this his wicked error. Can. 3.

Whosoever shall hereafter affirm, that any of the 39 articles agreed upon by the archbishops and bishops of both provinces and the whole clergy, in the convocation holden at London, in the year of our Lord God 1562, for the avoiding of diversities of opinions, and for the establishing of consent touching true religion, are in any part superstitious or erroneous, or such as he may not with a good conscience subscribe unto; let him be excommunicated *ipso facto*, and not restored, but only by the archbishop, after his repentance and public revocation of such his wicked errors. Can. 5.

Whosoever shall hereafter separate themselves from the communion of saints, as it is approved by the apostles' rules in the church of England, and combine themselves in a new brotherhood, accounting the Christians who are conformable to the doctrine, government, rites, and ceremonies of the church of England, to be profane and unmeet for them to join with in christian profession; let them be excommunicated *ipso facto*, and not restored, but by the archbishop, after their repentance and public revocation of such their wicked errors. Can. 9.

THE TITLES

OF THE

THIRTY-NINE ARTICLES.

ART.

I. OF Faith in the Holy Trinity.
II. Of the Word of God, which was made very Man.
III. Of the Going down of Christ into Hell.
IV. Of the Resurrection of Christ.
V. Of the Holy Ghost.
VI. Of the Sufficiency of the Scripture for Salvation.
VII. Of the Old Testament.
VIII. Of the three Creeds.
IX. Of Original, or Birth-sin.
X. Of Free-will
XI. Of the Justification of Man.
XII. Of good Works.
XIII. Of Works before Justification.
XIV. Of Works of Supererogation.
XV. Of Christ alone without sin.
XVI. Of Sin after Baptism.
XVII. Of Predestination and Election.
XVIII. Of Obtaining eternal salvation only by the Name of Christ.
XIX. Of the Church.
XX. Of the Authority of the Church.
XXI. Of the Authority of General Councils.
XXII. Of Purgatory.
XXIII. Of Ministering in the Congregation.
XXIV. Of the Speaking in the Congregation in such a tongue, as the people understand not.
XXV. Of the Sacraments.
XXVI. Of the Unworthiness of the Ministers, which hinder not the effects of the Sacraments.
XXVII. Of Baptism.
XXVIII. Of the Lord's Supper.
XXIX. Of the Wicked which do not eat the Body and Blood of Christ in the use of the Lord's Supper.
XXX. Of both Kinds.
XXXI. Of the Oblation of Christ finished upon the Cross.
XXXII. Of the Marriage of Priests.
XXXIII. Of Excommunicate Persons, how they are to be avoided.
XXXIV. Of the Traditions of the Church.
XXXV. Of Homilies.
XXXVI. Of Consecration of Bishops and Ministers.
XXXVII. Of the Civil Magistrate.
XXXVIII. Of Christian men's goods, which are not common.
XXXIX. Of a Christian man's Oath.

THE CATHOLIC DOCTRINE

BELIEVED AND PROFESSED IN

THE CHURCH OF ENGLAND.

Article I.

Of faith in the Holy Trinity.

There is but (1) *one living, and true God, everlasting, without body, parts, or passions; of infinite power, wisdom, and goodness:* (2) *the maker and preserver of all things, both visible and invisible.* (3) *And in unity of this Godhead there be three persons, of one substance, power, and eternity, the Father, the Son, and the Holy Ghost.*

The Propositions.

1. There is but one God, who is living, true, everlasting, &c.
2. God is the maker and preserver of all things.
3. In the Unity of the Godhead there is a Trinity of persons.

Proposition I.

There is but one God, who is living, true, everlasting, without body, parts, or passions: of infinite power, wisdom, and goodness.

The proof from the word of God.

That there is but one God, who is, &c., is a truth which may be gathered from the all-holy and sacred scripture: and is agreeable to the doctrine of the reformed churches. For both God's word giveth us to know that God is one, and no more[a], the living[b] and true God[c], everlasting[d], without body,

[a] Thou shalt have none other gods before me, Exod. xx. 3. The Lord our God is Lord only, Deut. vi. 4. Who is God beside the Lord? Psal. xviii. 31. Hath not one God made us? Mal. ii. 10. There is none other God but one, 1 Cor. viii. 4.

[b] Mine heart and my flesh rejoice in the living God, Psal. lxxxiv. 2. Ye are the temple of the living God, 2 Cor. vi. 16.

[c] For a long season Israel hath been without the true God, 2

parts, or passions[e]; of infinite power[f], wisdom[g], and goodness[h]: and God's people in their public Confessions[1] from Ausburgh, Helvetia, Bohemia, France, Flanders and Wittemberg testify the same.

[Conf. Aug.] Art. I. [Helv.] 2. Art. III. [Boh.] Cap. 3. [Gall.] Art. I. [Belg.] Art. II. [Wittemb.] Cap. 1.

Chron. xv. 3. The Lord is the God of truth; he is the living God, and an everlasting king, Jer. x. 10. This is life eternal, that they know thee to be the only very God, &c. John xvii. 3. Ye turned to God from idols to serve the living and true God, 1 Thess. i. 9.

[d] O my God, &c. thy years endure from generation to generation, &c. thy years shall not fail, Psal. cii. 24, 26, 27. He is the living God, and remaineth for ever, Dan. vi. 26.

[e] O Lord my God, thou art exceeding great, thou art clothed with glory, and honour; which covereth himself with light as with a garment, &c., Psal. civ. 1, &c. God is a spirit, John iv. 24. The Lord is the Spirit, 2 Cor. iii. 17. He is not a man that he should repent, 1 Sam. xv. 29. I will not execute the fierceness of my wrath, I will not return to destroy Israel: for I am God, and not man, Hos. xi. 9.

[f] The sound of the cherubims' wings was heard into the utter court, as the voice of the Almighty God, when he speaketh, Ezek. x. 5. I will be a father unto you, &c. saith the Lord Almighty, 2 Cor. vi. 18. We give thee thanks, Lord God Almighty, Rev. xi. 17.

[g] Great is our Lord, and great is his power: his wisdom is infinite, Ps. cxlvii. 5. To God only wise be honour, and glory for ever and ever, 1 Tim. i. 17. To God, I say, only wise, be praise through Jesus Christ for ever, Amen. Rom. xvi. 27.

[h] Praise ye the Lord, because he is good, for his mercy endureth for ever. Psal. cvi. 1; cvii. 1; cviii. 1, &c.

[[1] Ecclesiæ magno consensu apud nos docent....quod sit una essentia divina, quæ appellatur et est Deus, æternus, incorporeus, impartibilis, immensa potentia, sapientia, bonitate, creator et conservator omnium rerum, visibilium et invisibilium.—Harm. Conf. Genev. 1581. Sect. II. p. 40. Ex August. Conf. Art. I. Deum credimus et docemus unum esse essentia sive natura, per se subsistentem, sibi ad omnia sufficientem, invisibilem, incorporeum, immensum, æternum.....summum, bonum, vivum,......omnipotentem, et summe sapientem, clementem sive misericordem, justum atque veracem.—Ibid. p. 23. Ex Helvet. Conf. Post. cap. 3.......Nostri docent.....secundum essentiam ...... unum tantum, verum, solum, æternum, omnipotentem, incomprehensibilem Deum, unius æqualis individuæ divinæ essentiæ.—Ibid. p. 29. Ex Bohem. Conf. cap. 3. Credimus et agnoscimus unicum Deum, qui sit unica et simplex essentia spiritualis, æterna, invisibilis, immutabilis, infinita, incomprehensibilis, inenarrabilis, omnipotens, summe sapiens, bona, justa et misericors.—Ibid. p. 33. Ex Gall. Conf. Art. I. Corde credimus et ore confitemur, unicam esse et simplicem essentiam spiritualem, quam Deum vocamus, æternum, incomprehensibilem, inconspicuum, immutabilem, infinitum, qui totus est sapiens, fonsque omnium bonorum uberrimus.—Ibid. p. 36. Ex Belg. Conf. Art. I. Credimus et confitemur, unum solum, verum, æternum, immensum esse Deum, omnipotentem creatorem, &c.—Ibid. p. 47. Ex Virtemb. Conf. c. 1.

Errors and adversaries unto this truth.

Then, impious and execrable are the opinions of Diagoras and Theodorus, who flatly denied there was any God[i].

Of Protagoras[k], and the Machivilian atheists, which are doubtful whether there be a God.

Of such as feigned unto themselves divers and sundry gods, as did the Manichees[2], the Basilidians[3], the [l]Valentinians, the Messalian[4] heretics, the gentiles and heathen people; whereof some in place of God worshipped beasts unreasonable, as the Egyptians did a calf, an ox[5], cats, vultures, and crocodiles: the Syrians a fish[m], and pigeons[6]; the Persians a dragon; some as gods have adored men, under the names of Jupiter, Mars, Mercury, and such like[n]; and some even at this day for God do worship kine, the sun, and what they think good; so the inhabitants of Baly[7] in the East Indies.

August. contr. Manich. Lib. ii. c. 1, 2. Clemen. Alex. Strom. Lib. v. 11. Epiphan. Exod. xxxii. Gand. Merula de Mirabil. Lib. III. c. 56. Merula de Mirab. Lib. III. c. 48. Hist. of Bel. Voyage of the Holland Ships.

[i] Deos esse dubitabat Protagoras: nullos esse omnino Diagoras [Melius] et Theodorus Cyrenaicus putaverunt.—M. T. Cic. de Nat. Deor. Lib. I. [c. 1.]

[k] Protagoras Deos in dubium vocavit; Diagoras exclusit.—Lactan. [Opp. Par. 1748. Tom. I. Lib. I.] de Fals. Rel. cap. 2. [p. 7.]

[l] Valentinus, XXX. Deorum prædicator, saith Cyril, [Opp. Par. 1720.] Catech. VI. [17, p. 97.]

[m] Piscem Syri venerantur.—Cic. [de Nat. Deor. III. 15, 39.]

[n] Gods are come down to us in the likeness of men: and they called Barnabas Jupiter, and Paul Mercurius, &c. Then Jupiter's priest, &c. Acts xiv. 11, &c. Who knoweth not that the city of the Ephesians is a worshipper of the great goddess Diana? Acts xix. 35.

[[2] Duos enim deos, unum bonum, alterum malum esse perhibetis.—Aug. Opp. Paris. 1836-8. Tom. I. col. 1123. De Mor. Eccl. et Manich. Lib. I. cap. 10.]

[[3] Πάλιν ὁ Μωϋσῆς οὐκ ἐπιτρέπων βωμοὺς καὶ τεμένη πολλαχοῦ κατασκευάζεσθαι, ἕνα δ' οὖν νέων ἱδρυσάμενος τοῦ Θεοῦ, μονογενῆ τε κόσμον, ὥς φησιν ὁ Βασιλείδης, καὶ τὸν ἕνα, ὡς οὐκ ἔτι τῷ Βασιλείδῃ δοκεῖ, κατήγγελε Θεόν.—Clem. Alex. Opp. Oxon. 1715. Tom. II. Strom. Lib. v. c. 11. p. 690.]

[[4] Ἀλλ' ἐκεῖνοι μὲν (sc. Μασσαλίανοι) ἐξ Ἑλλήνων ὡρμῶντο....καὶ θεοὺς μὲν λέγοντες, μηδενὶ μηδὲν προσκυνοῦντες κ.τ.λ.—Epiphan. Opp. Paris. 1622. Tom. I. p. 1067. Adv. Hær. Lib. III. Tom. II. Hær. 80.]

[[5] Bovem, quem ipsi Apim nominabant alias Ægyptii, sacrificiis exquisitis adorabant; præter hunc etiam ex animalibus venerabantur feles, crocodilos, vultures, ibes, et ichneumones.—Gand. Merula de Memorab. Lib. III. c. 56, p. 232. Lugd. 1556.]

[[6] Syrii columbas olim adorabant.—Ibid. c. 48, p. 226.]

[[7] Churchill's Voyages. Lond. 1747. Vol. VIII. p. 417.]

Theodoret. [Hæret. Fab.] Lib. IV. c. 10.

Of the Anthropomorphites[1], which ascribed the form and lineaments of man unto God, thinking God to be like unto man.

Panormit. C. Quanto Abbas. Extravag. Joan. xxii. Extravag. de Transl. Episc. Quanto. Alcor. Francisc. Lib. I. Horæ B. Virginis Mar. secundum usum Sarum. p. 51. Russe Commonwealth, c. 19.

Of such as put their trust and confidence, to be reposed in God alone, either in men living, as do both the Persians in their soldan[o], and the papists in their pope, who with them is God[2], their Lord and God[3], of infinite power[4]; or in saints departed this life, as do the same papists both in their St Francis[5], whom they term The Glory of God, prefigured by Esay when he said, Holy, holy, holy, &c.; and in their Thomas Becket, whom they say God hath set over the works of his hands[6]; or in beasts unreasonable, as doth the Mord-wite Tartar[7]; or finally in riches and other senseless creatures, as do the atheists, and irreligious worldlings.

[o] Tu es nostra fides, et in te credimus; will the Persian say unto the Soldan.—P. Bizarus, Rer. Pers. l. xi. [p. 304. Franc. 1601.]

[[1] *Αὐδαῖος δέ τις....ἀνθρωπόμορφον ἔφησε τὸν Θεὸν, καὶ τὰ τοῦ σώματος αὐτῷ περιτέθεικε μόρια.*—Theodoret. Opp. Lut. Par. 1642-84. Tom. IV. p. 241. Hæret. Fab. Lib. IV. c. 10.]

[[2] Quinto not. quod factum a papa ut a vicario Jesu Christi attribuitur factum a Deo, cujus locum papa tenet in terris.—Panormit. Lugdun. 1534. Secundo super Prim. Decretal. de Translat. Prelat. cap. 3. Quanto Episcopus Fo. 19. Cf. de Translat. Episcop. Quod factum a papa ut a vicario, &c. censetur factum a Deo. —Secunda super Prim. Decret. Fo. 6.]

[[3] Dominus Deus noster papa.—Extravag. Joann. XXII. ad calc. Sext. Decretal. Par. 1585. Tit. xiv. Gloss. in cap. 4. col. 153.]

[[4] ...excepto peccato, potest papa quasi omnia facere quæ potest Deus.—Panorm. Prim. super Prim. Decr. Tit. vi. de Elect. cap. 6. Fo. 123. 2. Conf. ibid. cap. 34. Fo. 156.]

[[5] Franciscum figuravit Esaias capite sexto, qui audivit duos Seraphin, dicentes, Sanctus, sanctus, sanctus.—Alcoranus Franciscanorum. Francoph. 1542. Fol. non.]

[[6] Gloria et honore coronasti eum, Domine. *R.* Et constituisti eum super opera manuum tuarum.—Horæ Beatiss. Virg. Marie ad legit. Sarisbur. Eccles. ritum. Paris. 1535. Fol. xix.]

[[7] For his religion, though he acknowledge one God, yet his manner is to worship for God that living thing that he first meeteth in the morning, and to swear by it all that whole day, whether it be horse, dog, cat, or whatsoever else it be.—Russe Commonwealth. Lond. 1591. p. 74. c. 19.]

Proposition II.

God is the maker and preserver of all things.

The proof from God's word.

That the world, and all things both visible and invisible therein, both were made and are preserved by the almighty and only power of God, are truths grounded upon the holy scripture, and agreeable to the Confessions of God's people.

For touching the creation of the world, we read that in the beginning God created the heaven and the earth, &c. He made heaven and earth; by him were all things created which are in heaven, and which are in earth, things visible and invisible, whether thrones, or dominions, or principalities, or powers, all things were created by him, and for him; by his Son he made the worlds; and all these acknowledged by the churches, primitive and reformed, at this day[8].

Gen. i. 1, &c. Psal. cxxiv. 8; cxxxiv. 3. Col. i. 16. Hebr. i. 2. Creed, Apost. and Nicene. Confess. Helv. II. c. 6, 7. Basil. Art. I. of France, Art. VII. Fland. Art. XII.

And touching the preservation of all things by him created: "My soul, praise thou the Lord," &c., (saith the Psalmist) "which covereth himself with light as with a garment, spreadeth the heavens like a curtain; which layeth the beams of his chambers in the waters, and maketh the clouds his chariot, and walketh upon the wings of the wind; which maketh the spirits his messengers, and flaming fire his ministers," &c.

Psal. civ. 1, &c.

"Are not two sparrows sold for a farthing, and one of them shall not fall on the ground without your Father?" yea, "and all the hairs of your head are numbered," saith our Saviour

Matt. x. 29, 30.

[[8] Dei hujus sapientis æterni et omnipotentis providentia, credimus cuncta in cœlo, et in terra, et in creaturis omnibus conservari et gubernari. Deus hic bonus et omnipotens creavit omnia cum visibilia, tum invisibilia, per verbum suum coæternum, eadem quoque conservat per Spiritum suum coæternum, &c.—Harm. Conf. Sect. III. pp. 59, 60. Genev. 1581. Conf. Helv. Post. cap. 6, 7. Credimus etiam Deum omnia creasse per verbum suum æternum; id est per suum unigenitum Filium: et omnia sustentare ac vegetare per Spiritum suum, id est, virtute propria, ideoque Deum, omnia, sicuti creavit, providere et gubernare.—Ibid. p. 61. Conf. Basil. Art. I. Disp. 2. Credimus Deum cooperantibus tribus personis, sua virtute, sapientia ac bonitate incomprehensibili, condidisse universa, id est, non tantum cœlum et terram, omniaque iis contenta, sed etiam invisibiles spiritus, &c.—Ibid. p. 362. Conf. Gall. Art. VII. Credimus Patrem per Verbum suum, hoc est, per Filium, cœlum, terram, et reliquas naturas omnes ex nihilo creasse, quum illi visum est opportunum, singulisque suum esse, formam, et varia officia tribuisse, ut Creatori suo inservirent: eumque nunc illas omnes etiam fovere, sustentare et regere, pro æterna sua providentia, et immensa virtute.—Ibid. p. 63. Conf. Belg. Art. XII.]

Acts xvii. 24, 25, 26. Christ. "God that made the world and all things that are therein, he is Lord of heaven and earth, he giveth life and breath and all things; and hath made of one blood all mankind to dwell on all the face of the earth, and hath assigned the times, which were ordained before, and the bounds of their habitation," saith St Paul.

Heb. i. 3. "The Son is the brightness of the glory, and the engraved form of his person, and beareth up all things by his mighty word."

Conf. Helv. II. c. 7. Conf. Basil. Art. I. II. Conf. Gal. Art. VIII. Conf. Belg. Art. XII. XIII. The churches of God in Helvetia, Basil, France, and Flanders[1] testify the very same.

The errors and adversaries unto these truths.

Hereby are condemned all heretics and errors impugning either the creation of the world by God, or his providence in the continuing and preservation of the same.

Of the former sort was,

1. First, Aristotle[2] and his followers, which said, the world was eternal and without beginning.

Tertul. Lib. I. contr. Marc. 2. Next, the Marcionites[3], that held how God made not the world, as being too base a thing for him to create.

Iren. Epiph. Philaster. 3. Simon Magus, Saturninus, Menander, Carpocrates, Cerinthus[4], who ascribed the world's creation unto angels.

[[1] See the preceding note, and add the following: Credimus Deum omnia non tantum creasse, sed etiam regere et gubernare, ut qui pro sua voluntate disponat et ordinet quicquid in mundo evenit.—Harm. Conf. III. p. 62. Conf. Gall. Art. VIII. Credimus Deum hunc Opt. Max. postquam res omnes creasset, minime eas sortis aut fortunæ arbitrio regendas commisisse, sed ipsummet illas ex præscripto sacrosanctæ suæ voluntatis ita assidue regere et gubernare, ut nihil in hoc mundo absque illius decreto atque ordinatione contingat.—Ibid. p. 64. Conf. Belg. Art. XIII.]

[[2] ....τὸ δὲ σύμπαν ἀνώλεθρόν τε καὶ ἀγέννητον.—Aristot. Opp. Basil. 1550. p. 279. De Mundo, c. iv. ad fin.]

[[3] Cum Deum hoc gradu expellimus, cui nulla conditio tam propria et deo digna, quam creatoris, testimonium præsignarit, narem contrahentes impudentissimi Marcionitæ convertuntur ad destructionem operum creatoris. Nimirum inquiunt grande opus, et dignum Deo, mundus.—Tertull. Opp. Lutet. 1634. p. 438. D. Adv. Marc. Lib. I. c. 8.]

[[4] Simone Mago primo dicente semetipsum esse super omnia Deum et mundum ab angelis ejus factum.—Iren. Opp. Oxon. 1702. p. 129. Contr. Hær. Lib. II. c. 9. cf. Lib. I. c. 20. Saturninus quidem similiter ut Menander, unum Patrem incognitum omnibus ostendit, qui fecit angelos, archangelos, virtutes, potestates. A septem autem quibusdam angelis mundum factum, et omnia quæ in eo.—Ibid. p. 196. Lib. I. c. 22. Carpocrates autem et qui ab eo, mundum quidem, et ea quæ in eo sunt, ab angelis multo inferioribus ingenito Patre factum esse dicunt.—

4. The Manichees[5], who gave the creation of all things unto two Gods, or beginnings; the one good, whereof came good things; the other evil, whence proceeded evil things. Epiph. Aug. contr. Manich. c. 49.

5. The same Manichees[6], and Priscillianists[7], which did affirm man to have been the workmanship not of God, but of the devil. D. Aug. de fide contr. Manich. c 40. Con. Brac. cap. 11.

6. The Family of Love[8], who deliver that God by them made heaven and earth. Display of the Family of Love. H. 8. b.

7. The Papists, who give out how sacrificing priests are the creators of Christ[p].

Of the latter sort were

The Stoic philosophers and the Manichee[9], who are the great patrons of destiny, fate, and fortune. Socrat. Hist. Lib. I. cap. 22.

[p] Qui creavit me sine me, (jam) creatur mediante me, Stella Cleric. [Daventr. 1490.]

Ibid. p. 99. Lib. I. c. 24. Εἰ τοίνυν ποιητὴς οὐράνου καὶ γῆς ὑπάρχει ὁ Θεὸς ὁ Πατὴρ τοῦ Κυρίου ἡμῶν Ἰησοῦ Χριστοῦ, μάτην τὰ πάντα τῷ συκοφάντῃ Σίμωνι εἴρηται, τὸ ὑπ' Ἀγγέλων τὸν κόσμον ἐν ἐλαττώματι γεγεννῆσθαι.—Epiph. Opp. Paris. 1622. Tom. I. p. 60. Adv. Hær. Lib. I. Tom. II. ὁμοίως δὲ ἔλεγε καὶ αὐτὸς (Μένανδρος) τὸν κόσμον γεγονέναι ὑπ' Ἀγγέλων.—Ibid. p. 61. σχέδον δὲ οὐδὲν ἕτερον παρὰ τὸν προειρημένον Καρποκρᾶν ἀλλὰ τὰ αὐτὰ τῷ κόσμῳ κακοποιὰ φάρμακα ἐκβλυστάνει (Κήρινθος). τὰ ἴσα γὰρ τῷ προειρημένῳ εἰς τὸν Χριστὸν συκοφαντήσας ἐξηγεῖται....καὶ τὸν κόσμον ὁμοίως ὑπὸ Ἀγγέλων γεγεννῆσθαι.—Ibid. p. 110. Qui [Simon Magus] et audebat dicere mundum ab angelis factum.—Philastrius in Bibliothec. Patr. Paris. 1624. Tom. IV. col. 8. Lib. de Hær. Similiter de Saturnino et Carpocrate.—Ibid. col. 9. 10.]

[5 Οὗτος (sc. Μανὴς) δύο σέβει Θεοὺς ἀγεννήτους, αὐτοφυεῖς, ἀϊδίους, ἕνα τῷ ἕνι ἀντικείμενον, καὶ τὸν μὲν ἀγαθὸν, τὸν δὲ πονηρὸν εἰσηγεῖται, κ.τ.λ.—Epiph. Opp. Paris. 1622. Tom. I. p. 642. Adv. Hær. Lib. II. Tom. II. Manichæus enim duas dicit esse naturas, unam bonam et alteram malam; bonam quæ fecit mundum, malam de qua factus est mundus.—August. Opp. Paris. 1836-8. Tom. VIII. col. 1602. A. De Fide contr. Manich. cap. 49. This treatise was probably not written by St Augustine.]

[6 Paulus apostolus clamat, Seminatur in corruptione, resurget in incorruptione. ....Et vos contra reclamatis, carnem hominis non posse resurgere, et eam tenebrarum principem habere auctorem.—Ibid. col. 1598. c. cap. 40.]

[7 Si quis plasmationem humani corporis, diaboli dicit figmentum esse, et conceptiones in uteris matrum, operibus dicit dæmonum figurari, propter quod resurrectionem carnis non credit, sicut Manichæus et Priscillianus dixerunt, anathema sit.—Concil. Binnii. Colon. Agrip. 1606. Tom. II. fol. 641. Concil. Bracar. cap. 12.]

[8 They hold that as God made heaven and earth by Jesus Christ, viz. the word: so did he it by them.—Displaying of the Family of Love by J. R. (John Rogers) Lond. 1579. H. 8. b.]

[9 Καὶ εἱμαρμένην εἰσάγει (ὁ Μανιχαῖος) καὶ τὸ ἐφ' ἡμῖν ἀναιρεῖ....'Εμπεδοκλέους καὶ Πυθαγόρου καὶ Αἰγυπτίων ταῖς δόξαις ἀκολουθήσας.—Socrat. Hist. Eccl. Cant. 1720. p. 55. Lib. I. c. 22.]

Disp. of the Fam. H. 5. b. The Family of Love[1], which may not say, God save any thing; for they affirm that all things be ruled by nature, and not ordered by God.

The old philosophers, who thought that inferior things were too base for God to be careful of[q].

And lastly, the Epicures, who think God is idle, and governeth not the same. Of which mind was Cyprian[2], who held, that God, having created the world, did commit the government thereof unto certain celestial powers. (In exposit. Symb.)

Proposition III.

In the Unity of the Godhead there is a Trinity of persons.

The proof from God's word.

The scripture saith:

In the beginning God the Father[r], the Son[s], and the Holy Ghost[t], created the heaven and the earth.

By (1) the Word of (2) the Lord were the heavens made,
Psal. xxxiii. 6. and all the host of them by the (3) breath of his mouth.

Lo, the heavens were opened unto (1) him; and (John)
Matt. iii. 16, 17. saw (2) the Spirit of God descending like a dove, and lighting upon him; and lo, a voice from heaven, saying, This is (3) my beloved Son, in whom I am well pleased.

Gal. iv. 6. Because ye are sons, (1) God hath sent forth (2) the

[q] Dii magna curant, parva negligunt.—Cic. de Nat. Deor. Lib. II. [c. 66.]

[r] The Father by the Son made the worlds, Heb. i. 2.

[s] In the beginning was the Word, and the Word was with God, and that Word was God. The same was in the beginning with God, Joh. i. 1, 2.

[t] In the beginning God created the heaven and the earth, &c.; and the Spirit of God moved upon the waters, Gen. i. 1, 2.

[[1] They may not say, *God save any thing*. For they affirm that all things are ruled by nature, and not directed by God.—Displaying of the Family of Love. H. 5. b.]

[[2] Etenim ut breviter aliqua etiam de secretioribus perstringamus, ab initio Deus cum fecisset mundum, præfecit ei et præposuit quasdam virtutum cœlestium potestates, quibus regeretur et dispensaretur mortalium genus. Quod ita factum Moyses indicat in Deuteronomii cantico, ubi dicit: Cum divideret Excelsus gentes, statuit terminos gentium secundum numerum angelorum Dei, &c. Ruffinus was the author of this Exposition of the Creed.—Cypr. Opp. Oxon. 1682. Exposit. in Symb. p. 21.]

Spirit of his (3) Son into your hearts, which crieth Abba, Father, saith the apostle: and again, The grace of (1) our Lord Jesus Christ, and the love (2) of God, and the communion of the (3) Holy Ghost be with you all. 2 Cor. xiii. 14.

And St John; there are three which bear record in heaven, (1) the Father, (2) the Word, and (3) the Holy Ghost, and these three are one. 1 John v. 7.

This truth hath always been, and seriously is, confessed in the church of Christ[3]. Creed Apost. Nice. Athan. Conf. Helv. I. Art. VI. and II. c. 3. Aug. Art. I. Gal. Art. VI. Belg. Art. VI. Bohem. c. 3. Wittemb. c. 1. Suev. Art. I.

Errors and adversaries unto this truth.

Then cursed are all opinions of men contrary hereunto: whereof

Some denied the Trinity, affirming there is one God, but not three persons in the Godhead; so did the Montanists[4], and Marcellians[5], and so do the Jews[6] and Turks[7]. Socrat. Eccl. Hist. Lib. I. c. 23. Theod. Hær. Fab. Lib. II. Lud. Carrettus, Lib. Divinor. Visor. ad Judæ. Pol. of the Turk. Emp. c. 5.

[3 De Deo sic sentimus, Unum substantia, Trinum personis, &c.—Harm. Conf. II. p. 27. Conf. Helvet. Prior. Art. VI. Eundem nihilominus Deum, immensum unum et indivisum credimus et docemus personis inseparabiliter et inconfuse esse distinctum in Patrem, Filium, et Spiritum Sanctum.....ita ut sint tres non quidem Dii, sed tres personæ consubstantiales, coæternæ et coæquales, &c.—Ibid. p. 23. Conf. Helvet. Post. cap. III. Ecclesiæ.....docent....quod sit una essentia divina.... et tamen tres sint personæ ejusdem essentiæ et potentiæ, et coæternæ, Pater, Filius, et Spiritus Sanctus.—Ibid. p. 40. Conf. Aug. 1531. Art. I. Sancta scriptura nos docet in illa singulari et simplici essentia Divina, subsistere tres personas, Patrem, Filium, et Spiritum Sanctum.—Ibid. p. 33. Conf. Gall. Art. VI. ....In unicum solum Deum credimus (qui est unica essentia, incommunicabilibus proprietatibus in tres personas re vera ab æterno distincta) nempe in Patrem, Filium, et Spiritum Sanctum.—Ibid. p. 36. Conf. Belg. Art. VIII. ....Nostri docent, per fidem agnoscere et ore profiteri sanctam Trinitatem, Deum videlicet Patrem, Filium, et S. Spiritum, tres esse distinctas personas sive hypostases, &c.—Ibid. p. 29. Conf. Bohem. cap. III. Credimus....unum solum....esse Deum....et in hac una ac æterna divinitate tres esse per se subsistentes proprietates seu personas, Patrem, Filium, et Spiritum Sanctum.—Ibid. p. 47. Conf. Wittemb. cap. I. ....Articuli, quos huc usque Christiana Ecclesia de sacrosancta Trinitate firmiter credidit: Videlicet, Deum Patrem et Filium et Spiritum Sanctum unam esse essentiam et personas tres, &c.—Ibid. p. 50. Conf. Suev. Art. I.]

[4 *Οἱ μὲν γὰρ τοῦ ὁμοουσίου τὴν λέξιν ἐκκλίνοντες, τὴν Σαβελλίου καὶ Μοντάνου δόξαν εἰσηγεῖσθαι αὐτὴν τοὺς προσδεχομένους ἐνόμιζον· καὶ διὰ τοῦτο βλασφήμους ἐκάλουν ὡς ἀναιροῦντας τὴν ὕπαρξιν τοῦ υἱοῦ τοῦ Θεοῦ.*—Socrat. Hist. Eccl. Cant. 1720. Lib. I. c. 23, p. 57.]

[5 *Μάρκελλος δὲ ὁ Γαλάτης....ἠρνήθη τῶν ὑποστάσεων τὴν τριάδα.*—Theod. Opp. Lut. Par. 1642-84. Tom. IV. p. 224. Hæret. Fab. Lib. II. c. 10.]

[6 כי הנצרים יתפללו אל אל משלל ומיוחד והיהודים לא כן. Christiani Deum trinum et unum adorant. Quod Judæi haudquaquam faciunt.—Epist. Ludov. Carreti ad Judæos qui inscribitur Lib. Divin. Vis. b. iii. Paris. 1552.]

[7 Touching the Godhead, they acknowledge with the Jews and Christians

Clem. Alex. Strom. Lib. v. Epiphan. Clem. Alex. Strom. Lib. IV.

Some, as the Gnostics[1], Marcionites[2], and Valentinians[3], affirm there be more Gods than one, and yet not three persons, nor of one and the same nature, but of a diverse and contrary disposition[4].

Philastr. Zanc. de 3. El. par. 1. Lib. VII. c. 1.

Some think there be three Gods, or Spirits, not distinguished only, but divided also, as did the Eunomians[5], and Tritheites[6].

Calv. Epist.

Some fear not to say, that in worshipping the Trinity, Christians do adore three devils, worse than all the idols of the papists; such blasphemers were the heretics[7] Blandrat, and Alciat.

Athanas. ad Epictet.

Some will have a quaternity of persons, not a Trinity, to be worshipped: so did Anastasius the emperor command; and the Apollinarians[8] did hold.

that there is one only God:...... Neither do they acknowledge any distinction of persons in the Godhead, either of Trinity in Unity, or of Unity in Trinity as do the Christians.—The Policy of the Turkish Empire, Lond. 1597. c. 5. init.]

[1 See above, p. 37, note 3. and cf. Clem. Alex. Strom. Lib. III. c. 10, p. 542. *μετὰ μὲν τῶν πλειόνων τὸν Δημιουργὸν, κ.τ.λ.*]

[2 *Ἔλαβε δὲ τὴν πρόφασιν [ὁ Μαρκίων] ἐκ τοῦ προειρημένου Κέρδωνος.... προσθεὶς δὲ πάλιν ἐκείνῳ....ἕτερόν τι παρ' ἐκείνου δείκνυσι, λέγων τρεῖς εἶναι ἀρχάς· μίαν μὲν τὴν ἄνω ἀκατονόμαστον καὶ ἀόρατον, ἣν καὶ ἀγαθὸν Θεὸν βούλεται λέγειν, μηδὲν δὲ τῶν ἐν τῷ κόσμῳ κτίσασθαι. ἄλλον δὲ εἶναι ὁρατὸν Θεὸν, καὶ κτίστην, καὶ δημιουργόν. Διάβολον δὲ τρίτον, ὡς εἰπεῖν, καὶ μέσον τῶν δύο τούτων, κ.τ.λ.*—Epiph. Opp. Paris. 1622. Tom. I. p. 303. Adv. Hær. Lib. I. Tom. III. Hær. xlii. c. 3.]

[3 This reference the editor has been unable to verify. It is probably an inference rather than a direct quotation.]

[4 Dispositions, 1607.]

[5 Eunomiani....aiunt tres esse diversas qualitatis substantias, ut auri, argenti, et æris: et patrem quidem fecisse filium, et iterum filium, qui sit creatura, fecisse spiritum, &c.—Philastr. Lib. de Hær. in Biblioth. Patr. Paris. 1624. Tom. IV. col. 17.]

[6 Non defuerunt, nec desunt, qui dicant Spiritum Sanctum, veram quidem esse personam, eamque Deum; sed a persona Patris et Filii, non solum distinctam, verum etiam disjunctam; eoque ita verum esse Deum, ut alius sit a Patre et a Filio Deus: sic Tritheitæ.—Zanchius de Trib. Elohim. Neustad. Palatin. 1597. Par. I. Lib. VII. cap. 1. p. 380.]

[7 Etsi autem non protulit ipse (Blandrata) horribilem blasphemiam, quæ mox sequetur, totam tamen ejus culpam sustinet. Dixit enim intimus ejus sodalis Joannes Paulus Alciatus, quem adhuc pro anima sua habet, tres Diabolos a nobis adorari pejores omnibus idolis Papatus: quia statueremus tres personas.—Calvin. Opp. Amstelod. 1667-71. Tom. VIII. Part. 2. p. 162. a.]

[8 The author is mistaken here. Athanasius is stating the argument of those heretics who denied the passibility of our Lord's body, objecting that if he had a human body, born of the Virgin, it could not be consubstantial with the divine Word; and that a quaternity, instead of a Trinity of Persons, must necessarily follow.—Athanas. Opp. Paris. 1627. Tom. I. p. 588. Ad Epictet. contr. Hær. Epist. See also the Magdeburg Eccl. Hist. Cent. IV. c. 5. fol. 384.]

Some do grant and acknowledge the names of three in the Godhead, but deny their persons; such were the Noëtians, Praxeneans, and Hermogeneans[9]. These did say how the same God was called by divers names in the holy scripture; and therefore that the Father became flesh, and suffered, because one and the same God is called the Father, the Son, and the Holy Ghost. For which cause they were termed Patripassians. In this number was Servetus[10].

Again, some do grant the names and persons of three, and yet deprive not only the Son and Holy Ghost of their divinity, but the whole Trinity also of their properties. For they say, there be three in heaven, *viz.* the Father, the Word, and Holy Ghost; howbeit (say they) the Father only is very God; the Word is the breath of the Father; and the Holy Ghost is the Spirit created by God of nothing, through the Word: spoiling so both the Son, and Holy Ghost of their Deity, and the whole Trinity of their properties. Such were the Arian and Macedonian heretics, hence by-named Pneumatomachons[11], because they waged battle with the Holy Ghost.

And some do bring in other names of Deity, besides of the Father, Son, and Holy Ghost, as did the Priscillianists[12]. Concil. Bracar. cap. 2.

[9 Οὗτος δὲ (sc. Νοητὸς) ... *τὸν αὐτὸν Πατέρα καὶ Υἱὸν καὶ ἅγιον Πνεύμα, ἐν σαρκὶ πεπονθότα καὶ γεννηθέντα ἡγησάμενος.*—Epiph. Opp. Par. 1622. Tom. I. p. 481. Adv. Hær. Lib. II. Tom. I. Hær. lvii. c. 2. ...Unicum Deum non alias putat credendum, quam si ipsum eundemque et Patrem et Filium et Spiritum sanctum dicat.—Tertull. Opp. Lut. 1634. p. 635. B. Adv. Prax. c. 2. ...ne ut vestra perversitas infert, pater ipse credatur natus et passus.—Ibid. p. 644. C. Hermogenes seems to have held the eternity of matter. Christum Dominum non alium videtur aliter cognoscere, alium tamen facit quem aliter cognoscit immo totum quod est Deus aufert, nolens illum ex nihilo universa fuisse.—Ibid. p. 265. D. Adv. Herm. c. 1. "We hear of no sect called Hermogeneans."—Neander, Ch. Hist. Vol. II. p. 276. Eng. Trans. Bohn.]

[10 The Patripassians held that God the Father united himself to the man Christ, his Son, so as in and with him to be born and suffer.—See Mosheim's Eccles. History (Soames's Edit.), Vol. I. pp. 205, 270. The doctrine of Servetus was different from this. He seems to have regarded the Word and the Spirit as economies, or dispensations, produced in, and formed by, the supreme Being, and that the Word was joined to the man Christ. See Mosheim, Vol. III. p. 559.]

[11 See Socrates, Eccles. Hist. Cantab. 1720. Lib. IV. c. 4.]

[12 Si quis extra S. Trinitatem, alia (nescio quæ) divinitatis nomina introducit, dicens quod ipsa divinitas sit Trinitas, sicut Gnostici et Priscillianus dixerunt. anathema sit.—Concil. Binnii. Colon. Agr. 1606. Tom. II. p. 641. Conc. Bracar. cap. 2.]

Article II.

Of the Word of God which was made very man.

The Son, which is (1) the Word of the Father, begotten from everlasting of the Father, the very and eternal God, of one substance with the Father, (2) took man's nature in the womb of the blessed virgin, of her substance: so that (3) two whole and perfect natures, that is to say, the Godhead and manhood were joined in one person, never to be divided, whereof is one Christ, very God, and very man; (4) who suffered, was crucified, dead, and buried, to reconcile his Father to us, and to be a sacrifice, not only for original guilt, but also for all actual sins of men.

The propositions.

1. Christ is very God.
2. Christ is very man.
3. Christ is God and man, and that in one person.
4. Christ is the Saviour of mankind.

Proposition I.

Christ is very God.

The proof from God's word.

John i. 1. In the beginning was the Word, and the Word was with God, and that Word was God. This is written of Christ. Therefore Christ is God.

Psal. ii. 7. Acts xiii. 33. Heb. i. 5. Christ was begotten of the Father from everlasting. Therefore very God.

John xvii. 3. This is life eternal, that they know thee to be very God, and whom thou hast sent, Jesus Christ.

Matt. i. 23. They shall call his name Emmanuel, which is by interpretation, God with us.

Heb. i. 3. Christ, he is the brightness of the glory, and the engraved image of (the Father) his person, and beareth up all things by his mighty hand, therefore very God.

And this both hath been of the ancient Christians[u], and is the faith[1] of the reformed churches.

Conf. Helv. I. Art. 11, [and] II. c. 11. Boh. c. 4. 6. Aug. Art. 3. Gal. Art. 13, 14. Belg. Art. 10. Wittemb. c. 2. Suevica, Art. 2.

The errors and adversaries unto this truth.

Miserably therefore do they err, which either deny or impugn the Deity of our Saviour, as did certain old heretics, viz.

The Arians, whereof some were called Douleians[2], be-

Theod. Hær. Fab. Lib. IV.

[u] I believe in God the Father, &c., and in Jesus Christ his only Son our Lord. (Symb. Apost.) The Godhead of the Father, of the Son, and of the Holy Ghost is all one; the Glory equal, the Majesty co-eternal. Such as the Father is, such is the Son. The Father uncreate, the Son uncreate. The Father incomprehensible, the Son incomprehensible. The Father eternal, the Son eternal. The Father is Almighty, the Son Almighty. The Father is God, and the Son is God. The Father is Lord, and the Son is Lord.—Symb. Athanas. I believe in God the Father Almighty, &c., and in one Lord Jesus Christ, the only-begotten Son of God, begotten of his Father, before all worlds, God of God, Light of Light, very God of very God: begotten, not made; being of one substance with the Father.—Symb. Nicen.

[[1] Hic Christus verus Dei filius verusque Deus, &c.—Harm. Conf. VI. p. 99. Conf. Helv. Prior. Art. XI. Credimus præterea et docemus filium Dei dominum nostrum Jesum Christum.....esse genitum, non tantum cum ex virgine Maria carnem assumsit, nec tantum ante jacta fundamenta mundi, sed ante omnem æternitatem, et quidem a patre ineffabiliter.....Proinde Filius est patri juxta divinitatem coequalis et consubstantialis, Deus verus non nuncupatione, aut adoptione, aut ulla dignatione, sed substantia atque natura, &c.—Ibid. p. 99. Conf. Helv. Post. XI. Primum autem docentur de Christo credi hæc, Quod sit verus, æternus et de natura Patris cœlestis, unigenitus, et ab æterno genitus filius atque ita simul cum Patre et Sancto Spiritu unus verus et individuus Deus, &c.—Ibid. p. 106. Conf. Bohem. cap. VI. Item docent quod Verbum, hoc est Filius Dei, assumpserit humanam naturam in utero beatæ Virginis Mariæ ut sint duæ naturæ, Divina et Humana in unitate personæ inseparabiliter conjunctæ; unus Christus, vere Deus, et vere homo.—Ibid. p. 116. Conf. Aug. 1531. Art. III. Credimus quicquid ad salutem nostram requiritur, nobis in uno demum illo Jesu Christo offerri et communicari.... Credimus Jesum Christum Sapientiam, et Filium æternum Patris naturam nostram assumpsisse, ita ut una sit persona Deus et homo.—Ibid. p. 109. Conf. Gall. Art. XIII. XIV. Credimus Jesum Christum respectu naturæ ipsius divinæ esse unicum Dei filium ab æterno genitum, non factum aut creatum....seu ejusdem cum Patre essentiæ, illique coæternum, &c.—Ibid. II. p. 38. Conf. Belg. Art. X. Credimus et confitemur, Filium Dei Dominum nostrum Jesum Christum ab æterno Patre suo genitum, verum et æternum Deum, Patri suo consubstantialem.—Ibid. p. 118. Conf. Wittemb. cap. II. Servatorem quoque nostrum Jesum Christum, eundem verum Deum, &c.—Ibid. Conf. Suevic. Art. II. § 2.]

[[2] Χρόνῳ δὲ ὕστερον καὶ ἕτερος συνέστη σύλλογος, ἐκ τῶν Ἀρειάνων χωρισθείς· τὴν δὲ προσηγορίαν ἐκ τῆς ἀσεβείας ἐσχήκασι· Δουλειανοὶ γὰρ ὠνομάσθησαν, τὸν μονογενῆ τοῦ θεοῦ υἱὸν δοῦλον τοῦ πατρὸς τολμήσαντες

cause in scorn they termed the only-begotten of God the Father's servant.

Irenæus.

The Cerinthians[1].

Euseb. Eccl. Hist. Lib. III. c. 27.

The Ebionites[2], among whom some said that Christ Jesus was a mere man; others acknowledged him to be God, but not from everlasting.

Basil. Lib. II. contra Eunom.

The Eunomians[3].

Concil. Bracar. cap. 3.

The Samosatenians[4], who thought that Christ was not the Son of God before his incarnation.

Liberatus.

The Nestorians[5], whose opinion was, that Christ became God by merit, but was not God by nature.

Theod. Lib. IV. Hæret. Fab.

The Macedonians[6], which utterly denied the Son to be of one substance with the Father.

Gregor. Ep. 23, Lib. VIII.

The Agnoites[7], who held that the divine nature of Christ was ignorant of some things.

Again, some late heretics even to the death never would

καλέσαι.—Theodoret. Opp. Lut. Par. 1642-84. Tom. IV. p. 238. Hæret. Fab. Lib. IV. c. 4.]

[1 Jesum autem subjecit (Cerinthus) non ex virgine natum; ... fuisse autem eum Joseph et Mariæ filium, similiter ut reliqui omnes homines.—Iren. Adv. Hær. Oxon. 1702. p. 102. Lib. I. c. 25.]

[2 *Λιτὸν μὲν γὰρ αὐτὸν καὶ κοινὸν ἡγοῦντο, κατὰ προκοπὴν ἤθους αὐτὸ μόνον ἄνθρωπον δεδικαιωμένον.....ἄλλοι δὲ παρὰ τούτους τῆς αὐτῆς ὄντες προσηγορίας, τὴν μὲν τῶν εἰρημένων ἔκτοπον διεδίδρασκον ἀτοπίαν, ἐκ παρθένου καὶ τοῦ ἁγίου πνεύματος μὴ ἀρνούμενοι γεγονέναι τὸν Κύριον· οὐ μὴν ἔθ' ὁμοίως καὶ οὗτοι προϋπάρχειν αὐτὸν, θεὸν λόγον ὄντα καὶ σοφίαν ὁμολογοῦντες, τῇ τῶν προτέρων περιετρέποντο δυσσεβείᾳ.* — Euseb. Eccl. Hist. Cant. 1720. Lib. III. c. 27. p. 121.]

[3 Καὶ εἷς υἱός. *μονογενὴς γὰρ, περὶ οὗ ἐνῆν μὲν τὰς τῶν ἁγίων φωνὰς παραθέμενον, δι' ὧν υἱὸν καὶ γέννημα καὶ ποίημα καταγγέλλουσι ταῖς τῶν ὀνομάτων διαφοραῖς καὶ τὴν τῆς οὐσίας παραλλαγὴν ἐμφανίσαντας, ἀπηλλάχθαι φροντίδων καὶ πραγμάτων.*—The words of Eunomius quoted by Basil. Opp. Par. 1721-30. Tom. I. p. 238. Adv. Eunom. Lib. II. c. 1.]

[4 Si quis dicit filium Dei Dominum nostrum, antequam ex virgine nasceretur, non fuisse, sicut Paulus Samosatenus, &c. dixerunt, anathema sit.—Concil. Binnii. Colon. Agripp. 1606. Vol. II. p. 641. Concil. Bracar. c. 3.]

[5 ...Nestorius *confitens* existentiam divinitatis filii Dei, Christum purum hominem *credidit* conceptum atque formatum, et postea in Deum provectum, hoc est hominem deificatum et non verbum carnem factum.—Liberat. Breviarium. Par.1675. c. 2. p. 5.]

[6 *Οὗτος ὁ Μακεδόνιος, τὸ μὲν ὁμοούσιον εἶναι τὸν υἱὸν τῷ πατρὶ πολυτελῶς ἀπεκήρυξεν.*—Theodoret. Opp. Tom. IV. p. 238. Hæret. Fab. Lib. IV. c. 5.]

[7 Itaque scientiam quam ex humanitatis natura non habuit, ex qua cum angelis creatura fuit, hanc se cum angelis, qui creaturæ sunt, habere denegavit. Diem ergo et horam judicii scit Deus et homo: sed ideo quia Deus est homo. Res autem valde manifesta est, quia quisquis Nestorianus non est, Agnoita esse nullatenus potest. Nam qui ipsam Dei sapientiam fatetur incarnatam, qua mente valet dicere, esse aliquid, quod Dei sapientia ignoret?—S. Greg. Mag. Opp. Paris. 1705. Tom. II. 1070. D. Epist. Lib. X. 39.]

acknowledge Christ Jesus to be the true and very God, as namely:

Certain Catabaptists[8]. Zuing. Lib. contra Catab.

Blandrat[9]. Beza, Ep. 19.

Matthew Hamant[10] (burnt at Norwich, anno 1579), one of whose heresies was, that Christ was a mere and sinful man. Holin. Chro. 1299.

Francis Ket[11] (burnt also at Norwich, anno 1588), who most obstinately maintained that Christ was not God till after his resurrection.

David George[12], sometime of Basil, who affirmed himself to be greater for power than ever Christ was. Hist. Davidis Georg.

In oppugning the Deity of our Saviour, with these heretics join the Jews[13] and Turks[14], which say, that Christ was a good man; such as Moses and Mahomet were; but not God. Hence Amurath the great Turk, in his letters unto the emperor Rodolph the Second, anno 1593, termed our Saviour in derision, The crucified God. Unto whom may be added the Family of Love[15]. Lud. Caret. Lib. Divinor Visor. ad Judæos. Policy of the Turkish Empire, cap. 5. pag. 16. Display of the Family of Love, H. 7. a.

[[8] Vos negatis Christum esse natura Dei Filium.—Zuingl. Opp. Tiguri. 1545. Tom. II. Elench. contr. Catabapt. p. 39.]

[[9] Itaque jam manifeste Blandrata transiens ad Samosateni castra non aliam quam humanam in Christo naturam agnoscit.—Beza, Epist. Genev. 1575. Ep. XIX. p. 119.]

[[10] ....It was objected that he had published these heresies following....that Christ is not God nor the Saviour of the world, but a mere man, a sinful man, and an abominable idol.—Holinshed's Chron. Lond. 1587. Vol. III. fol. 1299.]

[[11] Strype, Ann. of the Reform. Vol. III. p. 557. Bk. II. c. 17. Lond. 1728.]

[[12] Et quemadmodum Moses nulla injuria vel contumelia affectus est, quod dictus sit obscuratus et superatus a Christo Jesu secundum carnem, ita et Christum secundum carnem nulla injuria vel contumelia notari, si dicatur jam a Christo secundum spiritum (sc. Christo Davide) superatus et obscuratus antiquatusque, &c. —Hist. Dav. Georgii. à Nicol. Blesdikio. Daventriæ, 1642, p. 43.]

[[13] בהתגשמות דבר יהוה הוא אלהות המשח אשר יאמינו הנצרים כי יאמרו היהודים כבר כתוב אני יהוה לא שניתי ..... super incarnatione verbi divini, quæ est divinitas Christi, quam credunt Christiani, Judæi vero aiunt, jam scriptum est, Ego dominus non mutor.—Lud. Carret. Epist. ad Jud. b. III. Paris. 1553.]

[[14] Likewise touching Christ, ...with the Jews they deny him to be the Son of God and the Messiah and Saviour of the world.—Pol. of Turk. Emp. c. 5. p. 16. Again, p. 18. b. It is a common opinion and tradition amongst the Turks that, Moyses, Christ and Mahomet....were each of them sent from God and were most excellent, holy, and good men, all of them highly favoured and beloved of God.]

[[15] They deny that Christ is equal with God the Father in his Godhead, upon this place of Scripture, My Father is greater than I.—Displaying of the Family of Love by J. R. (John Rogers). Lond. 1579. H. 7. a.]

Proposition II.

Christ is very man.

The proof from God's word.

Holding the humanity of Christ, we join with the blessed prophets and evangelists, who either prophesied of his future incarnation[a] and conception in the womb of a virgin[b], or plainly avouched, and writ, both that the Virgin Mary was his mother, and that, as very man, he grew and increased in strength, endured hunger[c] and thirst[d], wept, and slept, and suffered death.

Matt. i. 18, 23 Luke i. 27, 31, 34. Luke ii. 40. Luke xix. 41. John iv. 7. Mark iv. 38. Matt. xxvii. 50. Mark xv. 37. Luke xxiii. 46. John xix. 30, 33. Symb. Apost.

Hence the ancient fathers and Christians:

I believe in God, the Father Almighty, &c. and in Jesus Christ, &c. which was conceived by the Holy Ghost, born of the Virgin Mary, suffered under Pontius Pilate, was crucified, dead, and buried.

Symb. Athan.

The right faith is, that we believe and confess, that our Lord Jesus Christ, the Son of God, is God and man; God, of the substance of the Father, begotten before the world; and man, of the substance of his mother, born in the world; perfect God and perfect man, of a reasonable soul and human flesh subsisting; equal to the Father as touching his Godhead, and inferior to the Father as touching his manhood.

Symb. Nicen.

I believe in one God, the Father Almighty, &c. and in one Lord Jesus Christ, &c., who for us men, and for our salvation came down from heaven, and was incarnate by the Holy Ghost of the Virgin Mary, and was made man, &c.

Conf. Helv. I. Art. XI. & II. c. 11. Confess. Basil. Art. IV. Confess. Bohem. cap. 6. Confess. Belg. Art. XVIII. Confess. Gall. Art. XIV. Conf. August. Art. III. Confess. Wittemb. c. 2. Confess. Suevica, Art. II. Harmon. Confess. Præf.

The very same testify God's people in Helvetia, Basil, Bohemia, the Low Countries, France, Ausburgh, Wittemburgh, Suevia[1], with many more besides.

[a] The seed of the woman shall break thine head, Gen. iii. 15. The sceptre shall not depart, &c. until Shiloh come, Gen. xlix. 10.

[b] Behold, a Virgin shall conceive, and bear a Son, Isai. vii. 14.

[c] When he had fasted forty days and forty nights, he was afterward hungry, Matt. iv. 2.

[d] He said, I thirst, John xix. 28.

[[1] Hic Christus,...homo verus, quum juxta præfinitum tempus hominem totum, id est, anima et corpore constantem assumpsisset in una individuaque persona duas, sed impermixtas naturas, &c.—Harm. Conf. VI. p. 104. Conf. Helv. Prior. Art. XI. Eundem quoque æterni Dei æternum filium credimus et docemus hominis factum esse filium, ex semine Abrahæ atque Davidis.... conceptam purissime ex Spiritu sancto, et natum ex Maria semper virgine, &c.—Ibid. p. 100.

The errors and adversaries unto this truth.

Therefore most wicked were the opinions of those men which held, viz. that,

1. Christ really and indeed had neither body nor soul, but was man in appearance only, as the Manichees[2], the Eutychians[3], the Marcionites[4], and the Saturnians[5].

2. Christ had a body without a soul: as thought the

Aug. Lib. XIV. contra Faust. Niceph. Lib. XVIII. cap. 52. Philast. Beza, Ep. 81. Iren. Lib. I. c. 22.

Conf. Helv. Post. cap. XI. Credimus æternum Dei Verbum Carnem factum esse: id est, hunc Filium Dei, humanæ naturæ in una persona unitum, &c.—Ibid. p. 105. Conf. Basil. Prior. Art. IV. Disp. 7. Item [docentur de Christo] quod sit etiam verus et naturalis homo, noster verus frater, qui animam et corpus, id est, veram integramque naturam humanam habeat, quam efficacitate Sancti Spiritus, ex pura virgine Maria, absque omni peccato assumpsit, &c.—Ibid. p. 107. Conf. Bohem. cap. VI. Confitemur itaque Deum promissionem implevisse, quum Filium illum suum unicum et æternum in hunc mundum misit: *qui formam servi assumpsit, similis hominibus factus*, et veram naturam humanam cum omnibus ipsius infirmitatibus (excepto peccato) vere assumpsit, dum conceptus est in utero beatæ Virginis Mariæ, virtute Spiritus Sancti, absque ulla maris opera.—Ibid. p. 112, 13. Conf. Belg. Art. XVIII. Credimus Jesum Christum,...naturam nostram assumpsisse, ita ut una sit persona Deus et Homo; homo, inquam, et corpore et anima passibilis, nobisque per omnia, excepto peccato, similis, utpote cujus caro sit vere semen Abrahæ et Davidis, quanvis arcana et incomprehensibili Spiritus Sancti virtute fuerit suo tempore in utero beatæ illius Virginis concepta.—Ibid. p. 109. Conf. Gall. Art. XIV. Christus, vere homo, &c.—Ibid. p. 116. Conf. August. 1531. Art. III. See p. 47, note 1. Credimus et confitemur Filium Dei.... Jesum Christum....in plenitudine temporis factum hominem....ut Jesus Christus verus Deus et verus homo sit, una tantum persona non duæ.—Ibid. p. 118. Conf. Wittemb. cap. II. Servatorem quoque nostrum Jesum Christum, eundem verum Deum, etiam verum hominem factum naturis quidem impermixtis, at ita in eadem persona unitis, ut in omnia secula nunquam rursus solvantur.—Ibid. Conf. Suevic. Art. II. § 2. The passage intended in the Preface to the Harm. Conf. is probably this: Ecce posterioribus temporibus, infelix ille fœtus ubiquitatis prodiit qui veram doctrinam de persona Christi, et ejus naturis, siquidem recipiatur, penitus evertit.]

[2 Qui enim nisi dæmones, quibus est amica fallacia, istis persuaderent, quod Christus fallaciter passus, fallaciter mortuus sit, fallaciter cicatrices ostenderit; id est, non vere passus, nec vere mortuus sit, nec illæ veræ fuerint ex veris vulneribus cicatrices?—August. Opp. Paris. 1836-8. Tom. VIII. p. 434. c. contra Faust. Lib. XIV. 10.]

[3 Ὁ Εὐτυχὴς δύο μὲν καὶ αὐτὸς πρὸ τῆς ἑνωσέως ἔλεγε φύσεις τὰς ὕστερον ἑνωθείσας· μετὰ δὲ τὴν ἕνωσιν εἰς μίαν κραθῆναι ταύτας φύσιν, καὶ συγχυθῆναι, καὶ φυρμὸν παθεῖν ἐδογμάτιζεν. ὥστε καὶ τὴν θεότητα τὰ τῆς ἀνθρωπότητος πάσχειν, καὶ τὸ ἀνάπαλιν.—Niceph. Eccl. Hist. Lut. Par. 1630. Tom. II. p. 881. Lib. XVIII. c. 52.]

[4 Christum autem putative apparuisse, id est quasi per umbram, et passum eum fuisse umbratiliter, non tamen in vera carne credebat.—Philastr. Lib. de Hær. in Biblioth. Patr. Paris 1629. Tom. IV. col. 12. Aiebat enim Marcion Filium δοκήσει, id est opinione tantum non autem reipsa carnem induisse.—Beza, Epist. Genev. 1575. Ep. lxxxi. p. 329.]

[5 Salvatorem autem innatum demonstravit (Saturninus), et incorporalem, et sine figura, putative autem visum hominem.—Iren. Adv. Hær. Oxon. 1702. Lib. I. c. 22. p. 97.]

Basil. contr. Eunom. Theodoret. Hæret. Fab. Lib. IV. Ruffin. Lib. II. cap. 20. Niceph. Lib. XVIII. cap. 53. Iren. Lib. I. cap. 1. Conf. Belg. Art. XVIII. H. N. prophecy of the Spirit, cap. 19, sent. 9. Epiphan. Euseb. Eccl. Hist. Lib. III. cap. 27. Iren. Lib. I. cap. 24. Tertul. Lib. de car. Christ. Athanas. Lib. de Incar. Christi.

Eunomians[1], the Arians[2], the Apollinarians[3], with the Theopaschites[4].

3. Christ took not flesh of the Virgin Mary; so did the Valentinians[5] think, and so think the Anabaptists[6], and the Family of Love[7], who make an allegory of the incarnation of Christ.

4. Christ took flesh only of the Virgin, but no soul; as the Arians[8].

5. Christ took flesh not of the Virgin only, but by the seed of man too; so said Ebion[9], and Carpocrates[10].

6. The flesh of Christ was spiritual, and his soul carnal; so dreamed the Valentinians[11].

7. The carnal body of Christ was consubstantial with the Father, as published the Apollinarians[12].

[1 The editor has been unable to verify this reference.]

[2 Σῶμα γὰρ αὐτὸν (sc. τὸν Λόγον) ἄψυχον ἔφη (Ἄρειος) εἰληφέναι, ἐνηργηκέναι δὲ τὰ τῆς ψυχῆς τὴν θεότητα.—Theod. Opp. Par. 1642-84. Tom. IV. p. 232. Hæret. Fab. Lib. IV. c. 1.]

[3 Apollinaris.... hæresim.... generavit, asserens solum corpus non etiam animam a Domino in dispensatione susceptum.—Autores Histor. Eccles. Basil. 1535. Lib. XI. p. 253. Ruffin. Lib. II. c. 20.]

[4 Ἀρείῳ συμφύρονται.... τρεπτὴν ἔχειν φύσιν τὸν Θεὸν λόγον, καὶ σάρκα ἀνειληφέναι ἄψυχον....Ἀπολλιναρίῳ.... ἄνουν σῶμα. — Niceph. Eccl. Hist. Tom. II. p. 882. Lib. XVIII. cap. 53.]

[5 Εἰσὶ δὲ οἱ λέγοντες προβαλέσθαι αὐτὸν (sc. τὸν Δημιουργὸν) καὶ Χριστὸν, υἱὸν ἴδιον, ἀλλὰ ψυχικόν ... εἶναι δὲ τοῦτον, τὸν διὰ Μαρίας διοδεύσαντα καθάπερ ὕδωρ διὰ σωλῆνος ὁδεύει.—Iren. Adv. Hær. Lib. I. c. 1. § 13. p. 32.]

[6 Idcirco contra Anabaptistarum hæresin qui negant Christum carnem humanam sumpsisse, confitemur, &c.—Collect. Conf. Lips. 1840. p. 371. Conf. Belg. Art. XVIII.]

[7 There appears to be a mistake in the reference. But see Evang. Reg. cap. XIII. For this same Messias, or Anointed, is the Sabbath-day, &c. See also cap. XXI. XXII. and Henry More's Theolog. Works, Lond. 1708. Book VI. c. 16. p. 181.]

[8 Ἀλλα καὶ ἀρνοῦνται ψυχὴν αὐτὸν (Χριστὸν) ἀνθρωπείαν εἰληφέναι αὐτὸ τοῦτο προκατασκευάζοντες. σάρκα γὰρ ὁμολογοῦσιν ἀληθινὴν ἀπὸ Μαρείας αὐτὸν ἐσχηκότα, καὶ πάντα ὅσα ἐστὶν ἐν τῷ ἀνθρώπῳ, χωρὶς ψυχῆς.—Epiph. Opp. Par. 1622. Tom. I. p. 743. Adv. Hær. Lib. II. Tom. II. c. 19.]

[9 Λιτὸν μὲν γὰρ αὐτὸν καὶ κοινὸν ἡγοῦντο....ἐξ ἀνδρός τε κοινωνίας καὶ τῆς Μαρίας γεγενημένον.—Euseb. Eccl. Hist. Cant. 1720. Lib. III. c. 27. p. 121.]

[10 Jesum autem e Joseph natum, &c. (Carpocrates dicit).—Iren. Adv. Hær. Lib. I. c. 24. p. 99.]

[11 Convertor ad alios æque sibi prudentes, qui carnem Christi animalem affirmant, quod anima caro sit facta, ergo et caro anima. Et sicut caro animalis, ita et anima carnalis, &c. Licuit et Valentino ex privilegio hæretico carnem Christi spiritalem comminisci.—Tertull. Opp. Lutet. 1634. p. 367. B. 370. D. De Carne Christi, c. 10, 15.]

[12 Οὗτοι δὲ ἢ ἀλλοίωσιν τοῦ λόγου φαντάζονται, ἢ δόκησιν τὴν οἰκονομίαν τοῦ πάθους ὑπολαμβάνουσι, πότε μὲν ἄκτιστον καὶ ἐπουράνιον λέγοντες τὴν τοῦ Χριστοῦ σάρκα, πότε δὲ ὁμοούσιον τῆς θεότητος.... Ταῦτα γὰρ ὑμῖν ἐπινε-

8. The human nature of Christ before his passion was Niceph. Lib.
devoid of human affections; so thought the Severites[13]. XVII. cap. 29.

Proposition III.

Christ is God and man, and that in one Person.

The proof from God's word.

That the divine and human natures of Christ are united
in one person, it accordeth with the holy scripture. For, John i. 14.
the word was made flesh, and dwelt among us: (and we
saw the glory thereof, as the glory of the only-begotten of
the Father,) full of grace and truth, saith the evangelist John.
And Matthew: Jesus when he was baptized, &c. Lo, a voice Matt. iii. 17.
(came) from heaven, saying, This is my beloved Son, in whom
I am well pleased.

He that descended is even the same that ascended far Eph. iv. 10.
above all heavens, that he might fill all things, saith S. Paul.

Again, Christ Jesus, being in the form of God, thought Phil. ii. 6, 7, 9, 11.
it no robbery to be equal with God, but made himself of no
reputation, and took on him the form of a servant, and was
made like unto men, and was found in shape as a man, &c.;
wherefore God hath also highly exalted him, &c., that every
tongue should confess that Jesus Christ is the Lord, unto the
glory of God the Father.

And the same apostle, There is one God, and one Me- 1 Tim. ii. 5, 6.
diator between God and man, even the man Christ Jesus, who
gave himself a ransom for all men.

Upon these, and the like grounds,

I believe in God, the Father Almighty, &c. and in Jesus Symb. Apost.
Christ his only Son our Lord, which was conceived by the
Holy Ghost, born of the Virgin Mary.

The right faith is, That we believe, and confess, that our Symb. Athan.
Lord Jesus Christ, the Son of God, is God and man, &c., who
although he be God and man, yet he is not two, but one

νόηται λέγειν, ἵνα ....τὴν θεότητα βλασφημήσητε, λέγοντες, φησὶν, ἡμεῖς τὸν ἐκ Μαρίας λέγομεν ὁμοούσιον τοῦ πατρός.—Athanas. Opp. Colon. 1686. Tom. I. De Incarnat. Christi, pp. 615. B. 621. D.]

[13 .....ἡ ἐκ παρθενοῦ τῷ Σωτῆρι Χριστῷ προσληφθεῖσα σὰρξ πρὸ τοῦ πάθους ἄφθαρτος ἦν· ἡμεῖς γὰρ, ἔλεγον, ἀνάγκῃ φύσεως τὰ ταύτης περιφέρομεν πάθη, πεῖναν, φημὶ, καὶ δίψαν καὶ τὰ ἑξῆς. ὁ δὲ Χριστὸς ἅτε δὴ πάσχων ἕκων οὐκ ἐπίσης ἡμῖν τοῖς τῆς φύσεως νόμοις δουλεύων ἦν.—Niceph. Eccl. Hist. Par. 1630. Tom. II. p. 781. Lib. XVII. cap. 29.]

Christ. One, not by conversion of the Godhead into flesh, but by taking of the manhood unto God. One altogether, not by confusion of substance, but by unity of person.

Symb. Nicen.

I believe in one Lord Jesus Christ, the only-begotten Son of God, begotten of the Father before all worlds, God of God, Light of Light, very God of very God, begotten, not made, being of one substance with the Father, by whom all things were made: who for us men, &c. came down from heaven, and was incarnate, &c. He suffered, and was buried, &c. and he shall come again, &c. say the ancient and first Christians.

Conf. Helv. I. cap. 11. & II. Art. XI. Basil. Art. IV. Bohem. Art. VI. Gal. Art. XV. Belg. Art. XIX. Aug. Art. III. Wittemb. cap. 2. Suevica, Art. II. Harmon. Confess. Præf.

The very same is the belief and confession of all the reformed churches at this present, and always hath been[1].

Errors and adversaries unto this truth.

Detestable therefore is the error,

Hartman. Schedel.

Of the Acephalians[2], who denied the properties of the two natures in Christ.

Niceph. Lib. XVI. cap. 33.

Of the Severites, of Eutyches, and Dioscorus[3], who affirmed the divinity and humanity of Christ to be of one and the same nature.

Volater. Lib. XVII.

Of the Monothelites[4], who denied that two wills, viz. a divine and human, were in Christ.

[1 See the last Proposition, p. 50. note 1, and add the following: Agnoscimus ergo in uno atque eodem Domino nostro Jesu Christo, duas naturas, Divinam et Humanam; et has ita dicimus conjunctas vel unitas esse, ut absorptæ aut confusæ aut immixtæ non sint, &c.—Harm. Conff. VI. p. 100. Conf. Helv. Post. cap. 11. Atque ita in his duabus naturis, neque mutatis, neque confusis proprietatibus harum, et admirabili tamen earundem communicatione, seu unione, una sit et individua persona, unus Christus Emanuel, &c.—Ibid. p. 107. Conf. Bohem. cap. 6. Credimus in una eademque persona quæ est Jesus Christus, vere et inseparabiliter duas illas naturas sic esse conjunctas, ut etiam sint unitæ; manente tamen unaquaque illarum naturarum in sua distincta proprietate, &c.—Ibid. p. 110. Conf. Gall. Art. XV. Credimus etiam per hanc conceptionem, personam Filii conjunctam atque unitam fuisse inseparabiliter cum humana natura, ita ut non sint duo Filii Dei, nec duæ personæ, sed duæ naturæ in unica persona conjunctæ, &c.—Ibid. p. 113. Conf. Belg. Art. XIX.]

[2 Acephalorum pessima hæresis Calcedonense concilium impugnavit.... Hi quippe duarum substantiarum proprietatem in Christo negabant, unam tantum in ejusdem persona naturam prædicantes.—Hartman. Schedel. Lib. Cronic. Nuremberg. 1493. fol. cxli. b.]

[3 Ἀλλ' οὐδ' ἐπίσης Εὐτυχεῖ καὶ Διοσκόρῳ, πρὸς δὲ καὶ Σευήρῳ (ἡ ἐν Χαλκηδόνι σύνοδος) εἰς μίαν φύσιν συγχέει τὴν θεότητα καὶ ἀνθρωπότητα τοῦ ἑνὸς Χριστοῦ.—Niceph. Eccl. Hist. Lut. Par. 1630. Tom. II. p. 705. c. Lib. XVI. c. 33.]

[4 Monothelitæ ex argumento nomen sumsere. Duas in Christo voluntates negabant; divinam videlicet et humanam, quum contra sit.—Volaterran. Comment. Urban. 1603. Lib. XVII. col. 630. D.]

Of Theodorus Mesechius[5], who said that the Word was one thing, and Christ another.

Magdeburg. Eccles. Hist. Cent. 6, cap. 5, fol. 319.

Of Nestorius[6], who denied the two natures of Christ to be otherwise[7] united, than one friend is joined to another, which only is in good will and affection.

Niceph. Lib. XVIII. cap. 48.

Of Servetus[8], who said of Christ that he was the pattern of all things, and but a figure of the Son of God; and that the body of Christ was compact of three uncreated elements; and so confounded and overthrew both natures.

Beza, Ep. 81. Confess. Gal. Art. XIV.

Proposition IV.

Christ is the Saviour of mankind.

The proof from God's word.

Christ to be the Saviour of mankind, we find it perspicuously in the holy scripture, which teacheth us that Christ was crucified, dead, and buried; and that to reconcile his Father unto us[a], and to be a sacrifice for all sins of men[b].

Matt. xxvii. 26, &c.

[a] We were reconciled to God by the death of his Son, Rom. v. 10. God hath reconciled us unto himself by Jesus Christ, 2 Cor. v. 18; by his cross, Ephes. ii. 16. It pleased the Father, &c. by him to reconcile all things unto himself, Col. i. 19, 20.

[b] He hath borne our infirmities, and carried our sorrows, Isai. liii. 4. He is the Lamb of God, which taketh away the sin of the world, Joh. i. 29. Christ hath redeemed us from the curse of the law when he was made a curse for us, Gal. iii. 13. God hath made him, sin for us, which knew no sin, that we should be the righteousness of

---

[5 Peculiaris erroris autor extitit Theodorus Mesethenus:—Aliud esse Verbum, aliud esse Christum.—Magdeburg. Eccl. Hist. Basil. 1560, &c. Cent. VI. c. 5. fol. 319.]

[6 Φησὶ γὰρ ἐνωθῆναι τὸν Θεὸν λόγον τῷ ἐκ Μαρίας ἀνθρώπῳ, ὥσπερ εἴ τις φίλος φίλῳ ἕνωσιν διὰ σχέσεως ποιοῖτο.—Niceph. Eccl. Hist. Tom. II. p. 875. c. Lib. XVIII. c. 48.]

[7 To be any otherwise, 1633, and all the later editions.]

[8 Docebat Servetus Filium ex Deo fuisse non reipsa sed figurative; .... sentiebat Servetus τὸν λόγον tum cœpisse existere, quum mundus creatus est, ac etiam ideam quandam fuisse ex tribus increatis elementis compositam.—Beza, Epist. Genev. 1575. Ep. lxxxi. p. 328. Ac proinde omnes illas hæreses...detestamur, ac nominatim quidem diabolicas *Serveti* imaginationes, Domino nostro Jesu Christo *imaginariam deitatem* tribuentis; ut quem videlicet dicat ideam et exemplar fuisse rerum omnium, et *Filium Dei personatum* sive *figurativum* appellat; denique corpus ei fabricantis ex tribus increatis elementis compactum, ac proinde utranque naturam miscentis ac destruentis.—Coll. Conf. Lips. 1840. p. 333. Conf. Gall. Art. XIV.]

Symb. Apost. Hence I believe the forgiveness of sin.

Symb. Ath. He suffered for our salvation.

Symb. Nicen. For us men and for our salvation he came down from heaven, say our forefathers in their confessions; as do also our brethren[1] throughout Christendom.

Conf. Helv. I. cap. 11. & II. Art. XI. Basil. Art. IV. Bohem. Art. VI. Gal. Art. XIII. XVI. XVII. Belg. Art. XX. XXI. August. Art. III. Saxon. Art. III. Wittemb. cap. 2. Suevica, Art. II. Harmon. Conf. Præf.

The errors and adversaries unto this truth.

Wicked then are all opinions and assertions contrarying and crossing this truth: as

God in him, 2 Cor. v. 21. He is the reconciliation for our sin, and not for ours only, but also for the whole world, 1 John ii. 2.

[[1] Is sacrosanctam, Divinitatis unione, carnem....in mortem tradidit, ad universi peccati expiationem....Qui ut solus est Mediator, intercessor, hostia, &c.—Harm. Conf. Sect. VI. p. 104. Conf. Helv. Prior. Art. XI. Docemus....Jesum Christum....generis humani, adeoque totius mundi esse servatorem, &c.—Ibid. p. 102. Conf. Helv. Post. cap. XI. Hunc Jesum Christum credimus....crucifixum et mortuum pro peccatis nostris. Atque ita unica sui ipsius oblatione Deo Patri nostro cœlesti pro nostris, et omnium fidelium peccatis satisfecisse, ac nos cum eo reconciliasse.—Ibid. p. 105. Conf. Basil. Art. IV. Hoc enim omnino constat, quod post lapsum Adæ nemo....ad veram cum Deo reconciliationem pervenire possit, nisi tantum per unicum mediatorem inter Deum et hominem Jesum Christum in fide viva, qui solus morte et sanguine suo imaginem peccati et mortis a nobis tollit, &c.—Ibid. p. 106. Conf. Bohem. cap. VI. Credimus quicquid ad salutem nostram requiritur, nobis in uno demum illo Jesu Christo offerri et communicari, &c..... Credimus Deum immensam suam in nos caritatem ac bonitatem in eo demonstrasse, quod filium miserit qui moreretur et resurgeret, et justitiam omnem impleret, ut nobis cœlestem vitam acquireret. Credimus eo unico sacrificio quod Jesus Christus in cruce obtulit, nos esse Deo reconciliatos.... testamur Jesum Christum esse integram et perfectam nostram ablutionem, in cujus morte plenam satisfactionem nanciscimur, qua liberemur ab omnibus peccatis quorum rei sumus, &c.—Ibid. pp. 109, 10. Conf. Gall. Artt. XIII. XVI. XVII. Credimus Deum.... Filium suum misisse, ut naturam illam assumeret quæ per inobedientiam peccarat, ut in ea ipsa natura et satisfaceret, et de peccato, per acerbam ipsius mortem et passionem, justas pœnas sumeret.... Credimus Jesum Christum summum illum Sacerdotem esse....qui sese nostro nomine coram Patre ad placandam ipsius iram cum plena satisfactione obtulit, sistens seipsum super altare crucis, et sanguinem suum ad purgationem peccatorum nostrorum profudit.—Ibid. p. 114. Conf. Belg. Artt. XX. XXI. Christus....vere passus, crucifixus, mortuus et sepultus, ut reconciliaret nobis Patrem, et hostia esset, non tantum pro culpa originis, sed etiam pro omnibus actualibus peccatis hominum.—Ibid. p. 116. Conf. Aug. Art. III. Dominus noster Jesus Christus....constitutus est Mediator, Propitiator, Redemptor, Justificator, et Salvator. Hujus unius obedientia et merito placatur ira Dei.—Ibid. p. 117. Conf. Saxon. Art. III. Credimus....Jesum Christum....in plenitudine temporis factum hominem, ad expianda peccata et procurandam æternam salutem humani generis, &c.—Ibid. p. 118. Conf. Wittemb. cap. II. Nec in iis quicquam variarunt quæ Ecclesia ex sacrosanctis Evangeliis docta credit de Servatore nostro Jesu Christo....in cruce mortuo ac sepulto.—Ibid. Conf. Suevic. Art. II.]

That the Father in his Deity, not the Son in his humanity, did suffer: which error the Patripassians[2] did hold. D. August. de Trin. Lib. v.

That Christ, as well in his divinity as in his humanity, suffered for mankind: an error of Apollinaris[3] of old, and of Islebius[4] and Andreas Musculus of late years. Magdeburg. Eccles. Hist. Cent. 4, cap. 5. Beza, Ep. 60.

That the whole and Holy Trinity was crucified, as said Petrus Antiochenus[5].

That Christ really and indeed hung not on the cross; for his Passion was in shew only, said the Cerdonites[6], the Eutychians[7], and the Manicheans[8]: and another man, said the Theopaschites[9], and Basilides[10]; yea, the very devils and not Christ, said the Manichees[11], suffered and hung on the cross. Iren. Lib. I. cap. 23. Nic. Lib. XVIII. cap. 52. August. con. Fa. Lib. XV. cap. 10. Antonin. Tit. xiii. cap. 5. sect. 3 Theod. Ter. August. Lib. de Fide, cap. 32, 33.

[2 The passage referred to is probably this: Excidit nobis, quosdam male intelligentes vocari Patripassianos, qui dicunt ipsum Patrem natum ex femina, ipsum Patrem passum, ipsum esse Patrem qui est Filius, duo esse nomine, non res duas?—August. Opp. Paris. 1836-8. Tom. v. col. 435. c. Sermo 52.]

[3 Ipsum unigenitum Deum, judicem omnium, autorem vitæ, mortis destructorem mortalem esse fecit, ac propria ejus divinitate passionem suscepisse, &c.—Magdeburg. Eccl. Hist. Basil. 1560, &c. Cent. IV. c. 5. fol. 383.]

[4 Quanquam non potest satis bene disputari.... de sententia Islebii et Musculi Andreæ, contendentium Christum in utraque natura passum esse, &c.—Beza, Epist. Genev. 1575. Ep. lx. ad init. p. 261.]

[5 Peter, surnamed the Fuller, Bishop of Antioch. See Felicis Papæ III. Epist. xi. in Concil. Coll. Harduin. Tom. II. col. 817—824. *Μετὰ γὰρ τὸ εἰπεῖν ἅγιος ἀθάνατος, ὅπερ ἐστι τὸ πνεῦμα τὸ ἅγιον, τότε ἐπάγεις ὁ σταυρωθεὶς δι' ἡμᾶς, ἐλέησον ἡμᾶς.*]

[6 Irenæus does not speak of this as one of the notions of Cerdon. And as the reference is to cap. 23. the allusion should doubtless be to the heresy of Basilides. Quapropter neque passum eum (sc. Christum), sed Simonem quendam Cyrenæum .... transfiguratum ab eo, uti putaretur ipse esse Jesus.—Iren. Adv. Hær. Oxon. 702. p. 98. Lib. I. c. 23.]

[7 Εὐτυχὴς Θεὸν μὲν ὡμολογεῖ τεχθῆναι ἀπὸ τῆς ἀχράντου παρθένου καὶ Θεοτόκου......πεπλασμένην δὲ τὴν σάρκα ἐδόξαζε.....διὸ καὶ πάντα τὰ σωματικὰ τοῦ Θεοῦ φαντασιώδη ἔλεγεν εἶναι. καὶ αὐτὸ δὲ τὸ σταυρῷ παγῆναι φύσιν ἐκείνην τὴν θείαν καὶ ἀπερίγραπτον φαντασιώδως γενέσθαι ὡρίζετο.—Niceph. Eccl. Hist. Par. 1630. Tom. II. p. 876. A. Lib. XVIII. c. 48.]

[8 Qui (sc. Manichæus) Christum laudans asseverat falsas cicatrices ostendisse in membris suis.—August. Opp. Tom. VIII. col. 453. Contra Faust. Lib. XV. 10. See also Lib. XIV. c. 10.]

[9 There seems to be some error in the reference to Antoninus.]

[10 Παθεῖν δὲ τοῦτον (sc. Χριστὸν) οὐδαμῶς λέγει, ἀλλὰ Σίμωνα τὸν Κυρηναῖον ὑπομεῖναι τὸ πάθος νομισθέντα εἶναι Χριστόν.—Theod. Opp. Par. 1642-84. Tom. IV. p. 195. Hæret. Fab. Lib. I. c. 4. Christum autem [dicit Basilides]...... sine substantia carnis fuisse: hunc passum a Judæis non esse, sed vice ipsius Simonem crucifixum esse.—Tertull. Opp. Paris. 1634. p. 250. B. De Præscript. Hæret. 46.]

[11 Omnis sana fides Christum pro nobis passum confitetur: et Manichæus iniquus dæmones illas passiones asserit pertulisse.—August. Opp. Tom. VIII. Ap-

H. N. Instr. Art. IV. sent. 17, 29. Witness Th. Aquin. on 1 Pet. iii.

That the whole Passion of Christ is to be understood allegorically, and not according to the letter; as the Family of Love[1] do think.

That Christ[2] on the cross hath suffered (1) for the redemption of mankind, and shall suffer again for the salvation of the devils; such heretics there have been; (2) as Jesus, but shall again suffer as Jesus Christ (which was one of Francis Ket his heresies, for which he was burned); (3) for men, but one mother Jane is the saviour of women: a most execrable assertion of Postellus[3], the Jesuit.

Jesuit's Cat. Book I. cap. 10. Niceph. Lib. XVIII. cap. 52. Lonic. Tur. Hist. Tom. I. Lib. I. See Art. XXII. XXXI. Test. Rhem. in Rom. viii. 17. Ibid. in Col. i. 24.

The fantasies of the Jacobites[4] and Turks[5].

The popish doctrine touching the mass, prayers unto saints, pardons, and purgatory, which make the Passion of Christ either of none effect, or to put away but original sin only.

That albeit our Saviour hath suffered[6] for all men in general, yet both each man must suffer for himself in particular, and the works of one man may satisfy the justice of God for another[7]: which are popish errors.

pend. col. 1594. c. De Fide contr. Manich. cap. 32. Et ideo dum timet dicere Manichæus, quia ista facta non sunt; et iterum timet dicere, quia in divina substantia facta sunt; .... coactus est dicere quia non Christus sed princeps tenebrarum cum suis sociis illa omnia passus est.—Ibid. c. 33.]

[1 The editor has been unable to meet with the work of Henry Nicholas here referred to.—See H. More, Theolog. Works, Lond. 1708. pp. 181, 2.]

[2 Et nota quod dicit, semel mortuus est, quasi non iterum moriturus: ad destruendam hæresim quæ dicit eum semel passum ad redemptionem hominum, et iterum passurum in aëre ad redemptionem dæmonum.—Thom. Aquin. in Petr. Epist. I. 3. Paris. 1543. p. 94.]

[3 The Jesuits deny that Postell was one of their society. At Venice he became acquainted "with a superstitious old beldame called mother Jane, whom he made his mother .... he printed a book, entitled, The Victory of Women. In which he maintained that our Saviour Jesus Christ redeemed the superior world only, that is man; and that his mother Jane was sent from God to save the inferior world, that is, women, &c."—The Jesuits' Catechism, transl. from French into English, 1602. Book I. c. 10. p. 28.]

[4 Ἀρείῳ συμφύρονται, κ.τ.λ. (vid. p. 52. note 4.)......*καὶ πῆ μὲν ἄφθαρτον καὶ ἄκτιστον καὶ οὐράνιον, καὶ ἀπαθὲς καὶ λεπτὸν σῶμα ἀναλαβεῖν τὸν Θεὸν λόγον, καὶ μὴ ἡμῖν ὁμοούσιον δογματίζουσι. καὶ τὰ τῆς σαρκὸς κατὰ φαντασίαν ἡμῖν ἐνεργεῖν. πῆ δὲ ὡς ἡ σὰρξ αὐτοῦ εἰς φύσιν μετεβλήθη θεότητος, καὶ ὁμοούσιος αὐτῇ γέγονεν.*—Niceph. Eccl. Hist. Tom. II. p. 882. Lib. XVIII. cap. 53.]

[5 Lonic. Chron. Turc. Francof. 1584. Tom. I. Lib. II. Pars II. cap. 21. p. 120, &c.]

[6 Christ's pains or passions have not so satisfied for all that Christian men be discharged of their particular suffering or satisfying for each man's own part, &c.—Test. Rhem. Rhemes, 1582. Annot. in Rom. viii. 17. p. 402.]

[7 Therefore these also (*i.e.* the passions of good men) through the communion

That Christ died not for the sins of all men; and that some sins are so filthy and enormous, as Christ his blood upon true repentance of the delinquent's part cannot wash them away: which was Cain's, Fr. Spira's[8], and other desperate persons' error. Gen. iv. Hist. F. Spira.

That whatsoever is written touching Christ his sufferings, must in us, and with us, be fulfilled; the false doctrine of H. N.[9] Prophecy of the Spir. cap. 19, sent. 3.

Article III.

Of the going down of Christ into Hell.

As Christ died for us, and was buried: so also it is to be believed, that he went down into hell.

The proposition.

Christ went down into hell.

The proof from God's word.

Sundry be the texts of scripture for Christ his descension into hell.

Mine heart was glad (saith David, a figure of Christ), and my glory rejoiced; my flesh also shall rest in hope. For why? Thou shalt not leave my soul in hell. Ps. xvi. 9, 10. Acts ii. 26, 27.

of saints and the society that is not only between the head and the body, but also between one member and another, are not only satisfactory and many ways profitable for the sufferers themselves, but also for other fellow-members in Christ, &c.—Ibid. p. 538.]

[8 At ego postquam ejuravi Christi sacramenta, cœpi esse odio Deo, ac video indignationis oceanum omnes æstus suos in meum caput versare, prærupto veluti quodam aggere, qui antea vim inundationis sævæ prohibebat: id est, sublata Christi intercessione, quo jam mediatore uti non possum. Quocirca jaceo in abysso peccatorum meorum Stygiæ aquæ cæca voragine obrutus. Hinc est horror quem cernitis, hinc desperatio, hinc certissima mortis æternæ imago oculis meis obversatur.... Scio mihi non esse ullam spem reliquam de salute, &c.—Franc. Spieræ Hist. pp. 118, 119, Basil. 1550. For his own account of himself, see pp. 98, sqq. See also, Bacon's Relation of the fearful estate of Francis Spira in the year 1548.]

[9 Behold, hereto, as to a kingdom of God full of all lovely being, hath God chosen us; .... which we now inherit in this same Day of his Love, to the end that now, in the very last, the Scripture, and all what God hath spoken through his holy Prophets, and what is written of Christ, should also in us, and with us, become fulfilled (Luke xxiv. c.) to the honour or glory of God and to our joy.—Prophesy of the Spirit of Love. 1574. p. 38. cap. 19. 3.]

Psal. xxx. 2, 3. O Lord my God, I cried unto thee, and thou hast healed me. Thou, Lord, hast brought my soul out of hell.

Ps lxxxvi. 12, 23. I will thank thee, O Lord my God, with all my heart; and will praise thy name for evermore. For great is thy mercy towards me; and thou hast delivered my soul from the nethermost hell.

Eph. iv. 9, 10. In that he ascended, what is it but that he had also descended first into the lowest parts of the earth? He that descended is even the same that ascended far above all heavens, that he might fill all things.

1 Cor. xv. 55. O death, where is thy sting? O hell, where is thy victory?

Confess. Helv. II. cap. 11. Basil. Art. II. August. Art. III. Suevica, Art. II. Also that Christ went down into hell all sound Christians, both in former days[a] and now[1] living, do acknowledge; howbeit in the interpretation of the article there is not that consent as were to be wished: some holding that Christ descended into hell:

1. As God only, and not man; as they do which say how Christ descended powerfully and effectually, but not personally into hell; and that the Deity exhibited itself, as it were present in the infernal parts, to the terror of the devil and other damned spirits.

2. As man; and that, as some think, in body only, as when death as it were prevailed over him lying in the grave: as others deem, in soul only, when he went unto the place of the reprobate, to the increasing of their torments.

3. As God and man in one person; as they do, which affirm that Christ in body and soul went, some think, as it were into hell, when upon the cross and elsewhere he suffered the terrors and torments prophesied of Esa. liii. 6, 10; Psal. cxvi. 3; and mentioned Matt. xxvi. 38, or xxvii. 46; Luke xxii. 42; some say even into hell (the very place destined for

[a] He descended into hell.—Symb. Apost., Athan.

[[1] Hunc Jesum Christum credimus .... secundum carnem sepultum, descendisse ad inferos.—Harm. Conf. Sect. VI. p. 105. Conf. Basil. Prior. Art. IV. Disp. 8 et 9. Idem (sc. Christus) descendit ad inferos.—Ibid. p. 116. Conf. Aug. Art. III. Quique (sc. Christus) ad inferna descendit.—Ibid. p. 113. Conf. Suev. Art. II. With regard to the Helvetic Confession to which the author refers, there is no direct mention in it of the descent into hell, but only a general recognition of everything contained in the Nicene, Athanasian, and other similar creeds.]

the reprobate), which he entered into the very moment of his resurrection, at which time he shewed and declared himself a most glorious conqueror both of death and hell, the most powerful enemies.

Errors and adversaries unto this truth.

But till we know the native and undoubted sense of this article, and mystery of religion, persist we adversaries unto them which say:

That Christ descended not into hell at all, calling this article an error and a fable, as Carlile[2] doth. Carli. against D. Smith, pag. 28, 77.

That Christ, being dead, descended into the place of everlasting torments, where in soul he endured for a time the very pains which the damned spirits without intermission do abide: Bannister's[3] error. Treatise of Bannister's Errors.

That Christ alive upon the cross humbled himself *usque ad inferni tremenda tormenta*[3], even unto the dreadful torments of hell: endured for a time those torments, *quales reprobi in æternum sensuri sunt*[4], which the reprobates shall everlastingly suffer in hell: even despaired of God's mercy, finding God at this time, *non patrem, sed tyrannum*[5], "not a father, but a tyrant," and overcame despair by despair, death by death, hell by hell, and Satan by Satan: suffered[6] actually all the torments of hell for our redemption, and descended into the heaviest torments that hell could yield: suffered[7] the Paget's Catech. Latin. Pisc. in Luc. xii. 50. Ferus in Matth. xxvii. Hume's Rejoind. p. 38, 138, 152. Household Catech.

[[2] Neither Matthew, neither Mark, neither Luke, neither John, neither Peter, nor Paul, who wrote exactly of Christ's death, resurrection and ascension, made any mention of Christ's descending into hell, and therefore we cannot believe that sentence without error, neither affirm it without a lie, nor approve it in our belief without offence, and danger of drawing others to credit fables. Of this fable they (the apostles) make no mention. "A Discourse, concerning two divine Positions," &c. by Christopher Carlile. Lond. 1582. fol. 28, 77.]

[[3] The editor has been unable to meet with these works.]

[[4] Piscator. Comment. in Nov. Test. Herborn. Nasso. 1621. p. 505. Observat. 17. in Luc. XII. where, reprobi in gehenna in, &c.]

[[5] Exuit enim Christus hac hora Deum, non abjiciendo, sed non sentiendo.... sic et Deus pater nunc non patrem sed tyrannum agit....Ut non solum supplicium a nobis meritum, verum etiam desperationem nostram in se transtulerit.....ut famem fame, timorem timore, horrorem horrore, desperationem desperatione, mortem morte, infernum inferno: breviter Satanam Satana vinceret.—Ferus, Comment. in Matth. Mogunt. 1559. Lib. IV. pp. 516, 17. in cap. xxvii.]

[[6] The editor has been unable to meet with the work here referred to, as also with Gifford's Catechism referred to below.]

[[7] "A short Catechism for Householders." 1614. B. III. Where, second death, sorrows of death, and abjection, &c.]

Gifford's Catech. torments of hell, the second death, abjection from God: and was made a curse, that is, had the bitter anguish of God's wrath in his soul and body, which is the fire that shall never be quenched.

Canis. Catech. That Christ personally in soul went down into Lake Limbo, to fetch from thence[1], as Canisius, to loose from Vaux Catech. thence[2], as Vaux[3] saith, the souls of our forefathers, which afore his death (as the papists dream) were shut up in the Test. Rhem. an. Luc. xvi. 22. close prison of hell[4].

Coster. Instit. Lib. v. That Christ by his descension hath quite turned hell into Paradise, Costerus[5] the Jesuit's error.

Article IV.

Of the Resurrection of Christ.

Christ did truly (1) *arise again from death, and took again his body, with flesh, bones, and all things appertaining to the perfection of man's nature,* (2) *wherewith he ascended into heaven, and there sitteth* (3) *until he return to judge all men at the last day.*

[[1] Quid credendum profert quintus articulus, descendit ad inferos, et resurrexit? Christum docet postquam mortuus esset in cruce, secundum animam quidem ad inferos usque penetrasse tum ut mortis ac Satanæ devictorem, tum ut Patrum in limbo sedentium liberatorem sese declararet, &c.—Canis. Opus. Catechist. Colon. 1606. Cap. I. Quæst. XIII. p. 22.]

[[2] And out of that place called *Lymbus Patrum* he loosed the souls of the blessed Fathers from captivitie, and caried them away with him.—A Catechism or a Christian Doctrine, &c. by Laurence Vaux, p. 6. Antverp. 1574.]

[[3] As Vaux he saith, 1607.]

[[4] The bosom of Abraham is the resting-place of all them that died in perfect state of grace before Christ's time, heaven before being shut from men. It is called in Zachary (ix. 11) *a lake without water,* and sometimes *a prison* (Isai. xlii. 7), but most commonly of the divines, *Limbus patrum,* for that it is thought to have been the higher part or brim of hell, the places of punishment being far lower than the same which therefore be called *Infernum inferius, the lower hell.* (Aug. in Psalm. LXXXV.) Where this mansion of the fathers stood, or whether it be any part of hell, St Augustine doubteth: but that there was such a place, he nor no catholic man ever doubted: as all the fathers make it most certain, that our Saviour descending to hell went thither specially, and delivered the said fathers out of that mansion.—Test. Rhem. Rhemes, 1582. p. 187. Annot. Luc. xiv. 22.]

[[5] Descendit.—Propria virtute, non delatus, non dejectus, non detrusus; sed gloria magna, potentia, claritate, qua sic inferni loca illustravit, ut tenebrosum carcerem in Paradisum verteret.—Coster. Libellus Sodalitatis, Antverp. 1588. p. 413. Instit. Lib. v.]

The propositions.

1. Christ is risen from the dead.
2. Christ is ascended into heaven.
3. Christ shall come again at the last day, to judge all men, even the quick and the dead.

Proposition I.

Christ is risen from the dead.

The proof from God's word.

The resurrection of Christ may easily be proved from the holy scriptures, in which it is evident, first, that Christ should[a]; and next, that he did rise from death unto life, both by his appearing to Mary Magdalen, to divers women, to two, to ten, to all the disciples, to more than five hundred brethren at once, to sundry persons by the space of forty days together, and by the testimony also of the apostles, Peter and Paul.

John xx. 14. Matt. xxviii. 9. Luke xxiv. 13, 15, 30, 31. John xx. 19. John xx. 26. 1 Cor. xv. 6. Acts i. 3. Acts i. 22, & ii. 32. 1 Pet. i. 3.

A truth both believed and acknowledged by God's people[6] from age to age.

Acts xvii. 2, 3. Rom. x. 9. 1 Cor. xv. 4, 5, &c. Symb. Apost. Athan. Nicen. Conf. Helv. I. Art. XI. and II. c. 11. Basil. Art. IV. Bohem. c. 6. Gal. Art. XV. XVI. Belg. Art. XX. August. Art. III. Suevica, Art. II. Harmon. Conf. Præf.

[a] Thou wilt not suffer thine holy One to see corruption, Psal. xvi. 10. After he is killed, he shall rise again the third day, Mark ix. 31, and x. 34. Luke ix. 22.

[[6] Idem (Christus), ut esset plena nobis perfectaque immortalitatis nostræ spes et fiducia, suam ipse carnem, de morte suscitatam, in cœlum ad omnipotentis patris dexteram collocavit.—Harm. Conf. sect. VI. p. 104. Conf. Helvet. Prior. Art. XI. Credimus... Dominum nostrum Jesum Christum vera sua carne, in qua crucifixus et mortuus fuerat, a mortuis resurrexisse.—Ibid. p. 101. Conf. Helvet. Post. c. XI. Hunc Jesum Christum credimus...... tertia die resurrexisse a mortuis.—Ibid. p. 105. Conf. Basil. Prior. Art. IV. Disp. 8 et 9. ...quæ (opera et affectiones Christi)...... immota fide et credendæ sunt et profitendæ, quales sunt,...... mors, sepultura, resurrectio, ascensio in cœlos, sessio ad dexteram Dei, et reversio inde ad judicium vivorum et mortuorum.—Ibid. p. 107. Conf. Bohem. cap. vi. Credimus Deum immensam suam in nos caritatem ac bonitatem in eo demonstrasse, quod filium miserit, qui moreretur et resurgeret, &c.—Ibid. p. 110. Conf. Gall. Art. XVI. The resurrection of our Lord is also alluded to as an acknowledged fact in Art. XV. Deus...... Filium suum.........propter justificationem nostram e mortuis excitavit &c.—Ibid. p. 114. Conf. Belg. Art. XX. Idem (sc. Christus)...... vere resurrexit tertia die, &c.—Ibid. p. 116. Conf. August. Art. III. Quique (sc. Christus)......a mortuis tertio die in immortalem vitam revocatus, cumque hanc destinatis ad hoc testibus, variis argumentis comprobasset, &c.—Ibid. p. 118. Conf. Suevic. cap. II.]

Errors and adversaries unto this truth.

Utterly false then and unchristian is the opinion of those men,

Which utterly deny the resurrection of any flesh, as did the Sadducees[a], the false apostles[b], Simon Magus[1], and the Manichees[2].

Epiph. August. contra Faust. Lib. IV. c. 16. Matt. xxviii. 13, 15. Lud. Caret. l. divinor. visor. Holinsh. 1299. Hist Davidis George.

Which would acknowledge no resurrection of Christ, as would not, nor will the Jews[3], nor heretic Hamant[4], nor David George[5], one of whose errors was, that the flesh of Christ was dissolved into ashes, and so rose no more.

Philaster.

Which affirm (as did Cerinthus[6]) that Christ shall rise again, but yet is not risen.

Which say, how our Saviour, after his resurrection, was so deified, as he retained no more the parts and properties of his body and soul, nor the union of both natures, but is merely God. So thought the Schwenkfeldians.

Display in Allen's Conf.

Which take the resurrection of Christ to be but an allegory, and no true and certain history, as do the Family of Love[7].

[a] The Sadducees say there is no resurrection, Matt. xxii. 23. They deny there is any resurrection, Luke xx. 27. They say there is no resurrection, neither angel, nor spirit, Acts xxiii. 8.

[b] How say some among you, that there is no resurrection of the dead? 1 Cor. xv. 12.

[[1] *Φθορὰν δὲ ὑφηγεῖται σαρκὸς καὶ ἀπώλειαν μόνον, ψυχῶν δὲ κάθαρσιν κ.τ.λ.*—Epiph. Opp. Paris. 1622. Tom. I. p. 58. c. Adv. Hær. Lib. I. Tom. II.]

[[2] ...dicitis, nunc esse resurrectionem tantummodo animarum per prædicationem veritatis; corporum autem, quam prædicaverunt Apostoli, futuram negatis.—August. Opp. Paris. 1836-8. Tom. VIII. col. 330. Contra Faust. Lib. IV. 2.]

[[3] Not stated in the "Liber Divin. Vis."; may be considered as implied perhaps in the general denial of the divinity of Christ.]

[[4] ...that Christ did not rise again from death to life by the power of his godhead.—Holinshed, Chron. Lond. 1587. Vol. III. fol. 1299.]

[[5] Dei verbum incarnatum, et servili redemtionis officio per mortem, resurrectionem, et ascensionem perfunctum, mox rediisse unde venerat, humanæ naturæ statu deposito. Qui ut ante illam progressionem, ita nec postea carnis substantiam habuerit......Hist. Dav. Georg. p. 48. Daventr. 1642.]

[[6] Christum nondum resurrexisse a mortuis, sed resurrecturum annuntiat.—Philastr. Lib. de Hær. in Biblioth. Patr. Tom. IV. col. 10. Paris. 1624.]

[[7] See Henry More's Enthusiasm Triumph. Lond. 1662. Sect. XXXIV. p. 24.]

Proposition II.

Christ is ascended into heaven.

The proof from God's word.

In saying how Christ with his body is ascended into heaven, and there sitteth and abideth, we do agree with the prophets, evangelists, and apostles, with the ancient fathers, and God's people our brethren[8], throughout all Christendom.

Psal. xlvii. 5; lxviii. 18; cx. 1. Matt. xxii. 44; xxvi. 64. Acts i. 9. Luke xxiv. 51. Rom. viii. 34. Eph. iv. 8. Symb. Apost. Athan. Nicen. Conf. Helv. I. Art. XI. & II. c. 11, Basil. Art. IV. Bohem. c. 6. Gal. Art. XV. Belg. Art. XX. August. Art. III. Saxon. Art. III. Suevic. Art. II.

The errors and adversaries unto this truth.

But we altogether dissent from Hamant[9], the English heretic, which denied the ascension of Christ.

Holinsh. Chr. fol. 1299.

Also from Ket the heretic and apostata, which likewise denied our Saviour's ascension, affirming that his human nature is not in heaven but in Judea, gathering a church and people.

Also from the German ubiquitaries and papists, they saying that Christ, as man, is not only in heaven, but in earth too at this instant, wheresoever the Deity is[c]; these affirming the human nature of Christ is wheresoever the sacrament of the altar is administered[d].

Also from the Montanists[10], Cataphrygians, and Carpocra- Philast. Theodor.

[c] Ja. Smidelinus ubiquitatis apostolus, Beza, [Epist. Genev. 1575.] Ep. lxi. [p. 274, with a slight verbal alteration.]

[d] *Ergo* it is not in heaven, unless heaven be upon earth.

[[8] See last Proposition, p. 63. n. 6, and add: In eadem illa carne sua credimus ascendisse Dominum nostrum Jesum Christum supra omnes cœlos aspectabiles, in ipsum cœlum supremum, sedem videlicet Dei et beatorum, ad dexteram Dei Patris.—Harm. Conf. VI. p. 101. Conf. Helv. Post. cap. XI. (Credimus) ipsum corpore et anima in cœlum ascendisse, ibique sedere in dextera, id est, gloria Dei Patris cœlestis.—Ibid. p. 105. Conf. Basil. Art. IV....sic etiam natura humana manserit mansuraque sit in æternum, finita, suam illam naturalem formam, dimensionem atque adeo proprietatem habens, cui nimirum veritatem humanæ naturæ non ademerit resurrectio, et glorificatio, sive assumptio ad dexteram patris.—Ib. p. 110. Conf. Gall. Art. XV. Deinde [Christus] adscendit ad cœlos, ut sedeat ad dexteram Patris &c.—Ib. p. 116. Conf. August. Art. III. Ipse autem, unicam pro peccatis offerens hostiam, in perpetuum sedet ad dexteram Dei &c.—Ib. p. 117. Conf. Sax. III. In cœlos ad dexteram patris evectus est.—Ib. p. 119. Conf. Suev. II.]

[[9] Holinsh. Chron. Lond. 1587. Vol. III. fol. 1299.]

[[10] Cujus [Christi] animam in cœlum susceptam prædicat [Carpocras]: carnem vero in terra dimissam æstimat.—Philastr. Lib. de Hær. in Biblioth. Patr. Paris. 1624. Tom. IV. col. 10. Theodoret does not ascribe any such opinion to these heretics.]

tians, who held how Christ not in body but in soul ascended into heaven.

Catec. Trid. in Symb verba, Descendit ad inferos, et ascendit ad cœlos.--Vaux Cat. c. 1. Test. Rhem. an. marg. pag. 633.

From the papists[1], who say that Christ ascending into heaven carried with him the souls which he loosed from captivity and bondage of the devil, even the souls of the righteous, afore that time not in heaven but in limbo.

And lastly, from those German divines[2], which think that our Saviour carried with him into heaven the faithful people, in soul and body, raised at his resurrection.

D. Ma. hom. in Evang. in festo Ascen. Dom. et in Epist. Dom. Ascen. D.

Proposition III.

Christ shall come again at the last day, to judge all men, even the quick and the dead.

The proof from God's word.

Acts x. 38, 40, 42. "God anointed Jesus of Nazareth with the Holy Ghost, and with power, &c." "Him God raised up the third day, &c. And he commanded us to preach unto the people, and to testify that it is he that is ordained of God a judge of quick and dead," saith St Peter.

Rom. ii. 16. "God shall judge the world by Jesus Christ."

2 Tim. iv. 1, 8. "Jesus Christ shall judge the quick and dead, at his appearing, and in his kingdom, &c. Henceforth is laid up for me the crown of righteousness, which the Lord the righteous Judge shall give me at that day, and not to me only, but unto all them also that love his appearing," saith St Paul.

Jam. v. 9 "The Judge standeth before the door," saith St James.

Symb. Apost. Nicen. Athan. Conf. Helv. II. c. 11, et 1, Art. I. Basil. Art. IX. Bohem. cap. 6, Belg. Art. XXXVII. August. Art. III. Suevic. Art. II.

And this God's church and people do firmly believe, and faithfully confess[3].

[[1] Docendum erit, propterea Christum dominum ad inferos descendisse, ut, ereptis dæmonum spoliis, sanctos illos patres ceterosque pios e carcere liberatos secum adduceret in cœlum.—Catechism. Conc. Trident. Rom. 1566. In Symb. verba, Descendit, &c. p. 39. Piorum animas, quas ab inferis eripuerat, secum in æternæ beatitudinis domicilium introduxit.—Ibid. p. 47. Vaux, Catechism. p. 6. See above p. 62. n. 6. The marginal Annotation (on Heb. xi. 40) is, The Patriarkes and other just not in heaven before Christ.—Test. Rhem. Rhemes, 1582. p. 633.]

[[2] Ascendit triumphans, multos homines sanctos excitatos e pulveribus terræ secum in hoc triumpho in cœlos ducens, &c.—Geo. Major. Opp. Witeberg. 1570. Tom. III. p. 348. Hom. Sec. in Fest. Ascen. Dom.]

[[3] Ex cœlis autem idem ille redibit in judicium .... Redibit autem Christus, adserturus suos, et aboliturus adventu suo Antichristum, judicaturusque vivos et mortuos.—Harm. Conf. Sect. vi. p. 101. Conf. Helv. Post. XI. Hunc adventurum ad sæculorum omnium finem, verum rectumque judicem, ac sententiam in omnem

Errors and adversaries unto this truth.

On the other side, both they abroad and we at home abhor them for their opinions, which said that

There shall be no general judgment at all, as did the Manichees[4], and do the atheists. Philaster.

That the devils and the most ungodly, some of them, and namely so many as in hell do call upon God for mercy, and forgiveness, say the Turks[5], yea all of them, say the Origenists[6] and Catabaptists[7], shall be saved. Pol. of the Turk. Emp. cap. 23. Aug. Conf. Art. XVII. Bulling. cont. Cat. Lib. I. Tract. I.

That the wicked shall not be judged at all, but shall die as the brute beasts, and neither rise again in body nor come unto judgement: an error of the Family of Love[8]. Displ. of the Fam. H. 6. b.

That Christ shall not be the future judge; so thought both David George, Coppinger, and Arthington: for that George[9] rumoured himself to be the judge of the whole world, Hist. D. Geor.

carnem, ad id judicium prius suscitatam, laturum, ac pios supra æthera evecturum impios corpore et anima ad æternum exitium damnaturum, expectamus.—Ibid. p. 104. Conf. Helv. Prior. Art. XI. Credimus ultimum Judicium fore: in quo caro nostra resurget, et quilibet, prout in hac vita egit, a Christo Judice recipiet, &c.—Ibid. p. 105. Conf. Basil. Art. X. Disp. 25. Conf. Bohem. cap. VI. See above, p. 63, note 6. Postremo credimus ex Dei verbo, Dominum nostrum Jesum Christum ...e cœlo rursus venturum,...ut judex vivorum et mortuorum appareat, &c.—Ibid. p. 115. Conf. Belg. Art. XXXVII. Idem Christus palam est rediturus, ut judicet vivos et mortuos etc.—Ibid. p. 116. Conf. August. III. In cœlos ad dexteram patris evectus est, unde eum expectamus judicem vivorum et mortuorum.—Ibid. p. 119. Conf. Suevic. cap. II.]

[4 Manichæi ... resurrectionem negantes, judicium non sperantes, &c.—Philastr. Lib. de Hær. in Biblioth. Patr. Paris. 1624. Tom. IV. col. 15.]

[5 They affirm, That all those souls which in the midst and extremity of their torments do call upon the name of God, and crave aid and help from his Majesty, afterwards they shall be released, and received up into paradise. And that none shall rest or remain for ever in hell without hope of redemption: but only such as do utterly despair of salvation, &c.—Pol. of Turk. Emp. Lond. 1597. p. 70.]

[6 Damnamus et Origenistas, qui finxerunt diabolis et damnatis finem pœnarum futurum esse.—Syll. Conf. Oxon. 1827. p. 176. Conf. August. 1540. Art. XVII.]

[7 Ex abominandorum Anabaptistarum numero adhuc alii supersunt, qui arbitrantur Deum postremo post judicium omnium miserturum. Nam ipsum non posse in æternum irasci. Præterea sæculi aut æternitatis nomen non semper perpetuitatem sed quandoque diuturnitatem significare. Itaque tandem aliquando omnes impios una cum diabolis salvandos esse.—Bullinger. Adv. Anabapt. (Simler. Vers. Lat.) Tiguri. 1560. p. 72. b. Lib. II. c. 15.]

[8 Whosoever is not of their sect they accompt him as a beast, that hath no soul, and shall yield no account for his doing: but as a beast shall die, and not rise again in body or soul. And to prove it, they allege a place out of Esdras, that, whoso is not of God, shall be as a drop of water that falleth from the house, and cometh to nothing.—Displaying of the Fam. of Love. Lond. 1579. H. 6. b.]

[9 Per hunc Christum Davidem.... judicium postremum futurum.—Hist. Dav. Georg. Daventr. 1642. p. 50.]

Conspir. for pretend. Refor. pag. 47, 55. Arthing. seduc.

and Coppinger[1] and Arthington published how one William Hacket was come to judge the world, and themselves to be his angels for the separating the sheep from the goats.

Extravag. de sent. Excom. C. a nobis, et 24. q. 2.

That besides Christ the pope is judge of the quick and dead: an error of the papists[2].

Conf. Aug. Art. XVII.

That afore the judgement there shall be a golden world; the godly, and none besides, enjoying the same peaceably and gloriously, as the Jews[3] imagine.

H. N. in his Instruct. præf. sent. 5.

That the belief, touching the general judgement of Christ over the living and dead, is a doctrine mystical, or a mystery (no history), as H. N.[4] teacheth.

H. N. Ibid. sent. 1, Art. VIII. § 35, and in his Evang. c. 1. § 1. Allen's Confess. in the Display.

That the righteous are already in godly glory, and shall from henceforth live everlastingly with Christ, and reign upon earth, as the Family of Love[4] holdeth.

[[1] Coppinger told him . . . . that they the said Coppinger and Arthington were ordained to separate the lambs from the goats, before the Lord Jesus at the last day . ... They opened not at any time Hacket's chief pretended office unto Arthington: videlicet, to represent and to participate with Jesus Christ's office (of severing with his fan the good from the bad) until the very time, &c. Then Coppinger asked him (Hacket) what his pleasure was to be done. Go your way both (said he as Arthington reports) and tell them in the city that Christ Jesus is come with his fan in his hand to judge the earth.—Conspiracy for Pretended Reformation, London, 1592. pp. 47, 8. 55. It is not unknown throughout all England there were two false prophets set on work in London, to proclaim that Christ Jesus was come to judge the world with his fan in his hands, Hacket that cursed condemned wretch was that supposed Christ Jesus the Judge, &c.—Arthington's Seduction, &c. London. p. 2.]

[[2] Nec obstat, quod Ecclesiæ legitur attributa potestas ligandi atque solvendi homines super terram, tanquam non possit solvere et ligare sub terra sepultos, &c. —Corpus Jur. Canon. Antv. 1648. Decret Greg. Lib. v. Tit. xxxix. De Sent. Excom. cap. 28. p. 287. Sunt...quædam crimina de quibus etiam post mortem accusari potest quilibet, vel damnari, velut hæresis.—Ibid. Decret. Grat. Pars II. Caus. XXIV. Quæst. ii. cap. 5. p. 340.]

[[3] Damnamus Anabaptistas qui nunc Judaicas opiniones spargunt, fingunt ante resurrectionem pios regna mundi occupaturos esse, ubique deletis aut oppressis impiis.—Syll. Conf. Oxon. 1827. pp. 175, 6. Conf. August. 1540. Art. XVII.]

[[4] . . . . to bring unto the believers a great light of the true being of Jesus Christ, and the glorious day of his godly clearness: as also to express . . . that Jesus Christ hath not left us as orphans: but as our faithful Father; for to beget us anew, out of the safe-making water or doctrine of his service, and out of his holy spirit of love, also to judge us with his righteousness, and to bring us into his rest; is come again unto us, according to his promises, to the end that they all, which love God and his righteousness, and Christ and his upright being; might presently enter into the true rest, which God hath prepared from the beginning, for his elect; and inherit the everlasting life.—H. N. Evangelium Regni, Lond. 1652. cap. I. § 1. p. 2. We the elders of the holy understanding shall reign upon the earth in righteousness, and under the obedience of love, judge the world with equity.—Displaying of the Fam. by J. R. Lond. 1579. D. 2. See also, Hen. More's Theolog. Works, Lond. 1708. Bk. VI. c. 16. pp. 183, 4.]

Article V.

Of the Holy Ghost.

The Holy Ghost (3) *proceeding from the Father and the Son,* (2) *is of one substance, majesty, and glory with the Father and the Son,* (1) *very and eternal God.*

The propositions.

1. The Holy Ghost is very and eternal God.
2. The Holy Ghost is of one substance, majesty and glory with the Father and the Son.
3. The Holy Ghost proceedeth from the Father and the Son.

Proposition I.

The Holy Ghost is very and eternal God.

The proof from God's word.

The Holy Ghost to be very and eternal God, the scriptures teach us. For he is the Creator of all things. In the beginning God created the heaven and the earth, &c.; the Spirit of God moved upon the waters. O Lord, how manifold are thy works, &c. If thou hide thy face, they are troubled; if thou take away their breath, they die, and return to their dust: if thou send forth thy Spirit, they are created: *ergo,* the Holy Ghost is God. (Gen. i. 1, 2. Psal. civ. 24, 29, 30.)

Christians are to be baptized in the name of the Holy Ghost, as well as of the Father and the Son. Therefore is he very God. (Matt. xxviii. 19.)

Ananias lied unto God, and Sapphira tempted God, when both he lied unto the Holy Ghost, and she tempted the Spirit of the Lord. (Acts v. 3, 4, 9.)

As God, he chooseth, assigneth, and sendeth forth men for the ministry of the gospel; as God, he decreeth orders for his church and people; and as God he is to be invocate and prayed unto, as well as the Father and the Son. (Acts xiii. 2, 4. Acts xv. 28. 2 Cor. xiii. 14.)

Upon this and the like words, I believe in the Holy Ghost; I believe in the Holy Ghost, the Lord and giver of life. The catholic faith is this, that we worship one God in Trinity, and Trinity in Unity, &c. The Father is God, the Son is God, and the Holy Ghost is God; and yet they are not three Gods, but one God, &c., say the ancient fathers; (Symb. Apost. Symb. Nicen. Symb. Athan.)

Conf. Helv. II. Art. VI. et II. c. 3. Basil. Art. I. Bohem. c. 3. Belg. Art. VIII. Aug. Art. I. Wittemb. c. I. Suevica, Art. I. Gal. Art. VI. Harmon. Confess. Præfat.

which also is the faith and confession of all God's people at this day[1].

The errors and adversaries unto this truth.

This maketh to the condemnation of the Pneumatomachies, whereof

Epiphan. Vinc. Lyr. l. advers. hær. Beza, Epist. 1. Zanc. de 3. El. Lib. IV. c. 1. Holinsh. Chr. fol. 1299. Theod. Lib. V. cap. 3. Philast. Soz. Lib. IV. c. 27. Athan. Zanc. de 3. El. par. Lib. II. c. 5.

Some impugn the Deity of the Holy Ghost, as did in old time Samosatenus[2], and Photinus[3]: of late years, Servetus[4], Ochinus[5], abroad, and Francis Ket[e], Hamant[6], and certain Brownists[7][f] among us at home. Some affirm the Holy Ghost to be but a mere creature, as did Arius[8], the Semi-Arians[9], the Macedonian heretics[10], the Tropicks[11], Ochinus[12]. Some

[e] Burnt at Norwich 14 Jan. 1588.

[f] "Who whisper in corners that we must not believe in the Holy Ghost," saith Bredwell, writing against Glover, p. 122.

[[1] Credimus ... in Deum Spiritum Sanctum.—Harm. Conf. II. p. 28. Conf. Basil. Art. I. Disp. 1. For the references to the other Confessions see above, p. 43, n. 3.]

[[2] Οὗτος δὲ οὐ λέγει μόνον Θεόν, διὰ τὸ πηγὴν εἶναι τὸν Πατέρα, ἀλλὰ μόνον Θεόν, ἀναιρῶν ὅσον τὸ κατ' αὐτὸν τὴν τοῦ Υἱοῦ θεότητα καὶ ὑπόστασιν, καὶ τοῦ ἁγίου Πνεύματος.—Epiphan. Opp. Paris, 1622. Tom. I. p. 609. A. Adv. Hær. Lib. II. Tom. II.]

[[3] Photini ergo secta hæc est: Dicit Deum singulum esse ... neque ullam Dei Verbi, aut ullam Spiritus Sancti putat esse personam.—Vincent. Lir. Adv. Hær. Paris, 1619. Comm. I. c. XVII. p. 25.]

[[4] Quis te fascinavit, mi frater? Servetumne quæso, ... qui Sancti Spiritus hypostasin ac divinitatem est inficiatus, &c.—Bez. Epist. Genev. 1575. Ep. i. p. 10.]

[[5] Zanchius de Trib. Elohim. Neustad. Palat. 1597. Par. II. Lib. IV. cap. 1. p. 636. sqq.]

[[6] Holins. Chron. Lond. 1587. Vol. III. fol. 1299.]

[[7] I hear besides, that there is one among you, who whispereth already in corners, &c.—Bredwell's Detection, London, 1568. p. 122.]

[[8] Οὐ γὰρ οἶδεν αὐτὸ (sc. τὸ πνεῦμα) τῆς κτίσεως μόριον, οὐδὲ πρῶτον ποίημα ὀνομάζει, κατὰ τὴν Ἀρείου, καὶ Εὐνομίου, καὶ Μακεδονίου βλασφημίαν.—Theod. Opp. Par. 1642-84. Tom. IV. p. 258. Hær. Fab. Lib. V. c. 3.]

[[9] Spiritum autem non de divina substantia, nec Deum verum, sed factum atque creatum spiritum prædicantes, ut eum conjungant et comparent creaturæ.—Philastr. Lib. de Hær. in Biblioth. Patr. Paris, 1624. Tom. IV. col. 16.]

[[10] Εἰσηγεῖτο δὲ (Μακεδόνιος) τὸν Υἱὸν Θεὸν εἶναι, κατὰ πάντα τε καὶ κατ' οὐσίαν ὅμοιον τῷ Πατρί. τὸ δὲ ἅγιον Πνεῦμα ἄμοιρον τῶν αὐτῶν πρεσβείων ἀπεφαίνετο, διάκονον καὶ ὑπηρέτην καλῶν, καὶ ὅσα περὶ τῶν θείων Ἀγγέλων λέγων τις οὐκ ἂν ἁμάρτοι.—Sozom. Eccl. Hist. Cant. 1720. Lib. IV. c. 27. p. 173.]

[[11] Οἱ δὲ Τροπικοί, τὸ Πνεῦμα καὶ αὐτοὶ τοῖς κτίσμασι συναριθμοῦσιν.—Athanas. Opp. Colon. 1686. Tom. I. p. 192. A. Epist. ad Serapionem.]

[[12] Christus, inquit (Ochinus), Spiritus Sancti nomine, innuit Spiritum suum, id est animam, quæ creatura est, &c.—Zanch. De Trib. Eloh. Par. II. Lib. ii. c. 5. p. 515.]

have assumed the style and title of the Holy Ghost unto themselves, as did Simon Magus[13], Montanus[14], and Manes[15]. D. Iren. Euseb. Lib. v. c. 18. Chrys. Lib. de S. S.

Some have given the title of the Holy Ghost unto men, and women.

So Hierax[16] said, Melchisedech was the Holy Ghost. Epiphan.

Simon Magus[17] termed his Helene the Holy Ghost. Epiphan.

The Helchesaites[18] said, the Holy Ghost was a woman, and the natural sister of Christ. Epiphan.

Many Papists, and namely the Franciscans, blush not to say that St Francis is the Holy Ghost. Alcor. Fr. Lib. I.

Proposition II.

The Holy Ghost is of one substance, majesty, and glory, with the Father and the Son.

The proof from the word of God.

The Holy Ghost effected the incarnation of Christ, teacheth all things, leadeth into all truth, giveth utterance to his servants, and gifts unto his people, placeth rulers in the church, and overseers to feed the flock of God, sealeth the elect unto the day of redemption, as well as the Father and the Son: and these three, *viz.* the Father, the Word, and the Holy Ghost, are one. Therefore is the Holy Ghost of one substance, majesty, and glory with the Father and the Son. Matt. i. 18, 20. Luke i. 35. John xiv. 26. John xvi. 13. Acts ii. 4. 1 Cor. xii. 8. Acts xx. 28. Eph. iv. 30. 1 John v. 7.

And this was the belief of the ancient fathers.

I believe (say they) in the Holy Ghost, the Lord, and giver of life, &c., who with the Father and the Son together is worshipped and glorified, who spake by the prophets. Symb. Nicen.

[13 Hic igitur a multis quasi Deus glorificatus est, et docuit semetipsum esse qui inter Judæos quidem quasi Filius apparuerit, in Samaria autem quasi Pater descenderit, in reliquis vero gentibus quasi Spiritus Sanctus adventaverit.—Iren. Adv. Hær. Oxon. 1702. p. 94. Lib. I. c. 20.]

[14 Eusebius does not state this. See Bp. Kaye's Tertull. p. 21. 3d Edition.]

[15 Ἦλθε Μάνης ὁ ἀληθῶς μανεὶς, ὁ φερωνύμως τῇ πλάνῃ τὸ ὄνομα ἔχων, καὶ λέγει· ἐγώ εἰμι ὁ Παράκλητος, ὃν ἐπηγγείλατο ὁ Σωτὴρ τοῖς ἀποστόλοις.—Chrys. Opp. Paris. 1834-9. Tom. III. p. 980. D. De Spiritu Sancto, § 10. This treatise is generally regarded as spurious.]

[16 Φάσκει δὲ οὗτος (sc. Ἱέρακας) ὡς ἄνω μοι ἐν τῇ τῶν Μελχισεδεκιανῶν αἱρέσει δεδήλωται, περὶ τοῦ ἁγίου Πνεύματος, ὅτι αὐτός ἐστιν ὁ Μελχισεδέκ, κ.τ.λ.—Epiphan. Opp. Tom. I. p. 711. Adv. Hær. Lib. II. Tom. III. Hær. 67.]

[17 Ἑαυτὸν εἶναι δύναμιν Θεοῦ τὴν μεγάλην, τὴν δὲ σύζυγον πορνάδα πνεῦμα ἅγιον εἶναι τετόλμηκε λέγειν.—Ibid. p. 56. Adv. Hær. Lib. I. Tom. III. Hær. 20.]

[18 Χριστὸν δὲ ὀνόματι ὁμολογοῦσι [Ἐλκέσαιοι]......... καὶ εἶναι τὸ ἅγιον Πνεῦμα ἀδελφὴν αὐτοῦ, θηλυκῷ σχήματι ὑπάρχουσαν.—Ibid. p. 462. Adv. Hær. Lib. II. Tom. I. Hær. 54.]

Symb. Athan.

The Godhead of the Father, of the Son, and of the Holy Ghost, is all one, the glory equal, the majesty coeternal. Such as the Father is, such is the Son, and such is the Holy Ghost, &c. And in this Trinity none is afore or after other, none is greater or less than another; but the whole three Persons be coeternal together, and coequal.

Conf. Helv. I. Art. VI. & II. c. 3. Basil. Art. I. Boh. c. 3. Gal. Art. I. Belg. Art. VIII. Aug. Art. I. Wittemb. c. 1, 2. Suevica, Art. I. Zanc. de 3 El. par. 2. Lib. V. c. 1. Aug. contr. Max. Arian. Ruffin. Lib. I. cap. 25. Niceph. Lib. IX. cap. 47. Conf.

The very same do all reformed churches[1] believe and confess.

The errors and adversaries unto this truth.

The premisses do make against the Tritheites[2], which affirm the Holy Ghost to be inferior unto the Father.

Against the Arians[3], who said the Holy Ghost was inferior to the Son.

Against the Macedonian heretics[4], who held the Holy Ghost to be but a minister, and a servant of the Father and the Son; yet of more excellent majesty and dignity than the angels[5].

August. Art. VIII.

Against many erroneous spirits[6], which deliver the Holy Ghost to be nothing else but the motion of God in his creatures; as did the Samosatenians.

Pol. of the Turk. Emp. c. 5. Hutchinson in his Image of God, c. 24. pag. 112. a.

A bare power and efficacy of God, working by a secret inspiration; as the Turks[7], and certain English Sadducees[8] do imagine.

[1 Credimus Spiritum Sanctum...esse ejusdem cum Patre et Filio essentiæ majestatis et gloriæ, verum ac æternum Deum.—Harm. Conf. II. p. 48. Conf. Wittemb. cap. III. For the other references see above, p. 43, n. 3.]

[2 Ita tamen (sentiunt) ut...prædicent Filium...et Spiritum Sanctum esse Deos inferiores.—Zanch. de Trib. Eloh. Neustad. Palat. 1597. Pars II. Lib. V. cap. 1. § 1. p. 657.]

[3 Objicis mihi, quod dicam Spiritum Sanctum æqualem esse Filio. Dico plane. "Da," inquis, "testimonia ubi adoratur Spiritus Sanctus." Ut video, hinc eum vis ostendi æqualem Christo, si adoratur ut Christus.—August. Opp. Paris, 1836-8, Tom. VIII. col. 1066. Contra Maxim. Lib. II. 3.]

[4 (Macedoniani) quidicunt...Sanctum...Spiritum cum Patre et Filio nihil habere commune.—Autor. Hist. Eccl. Basil. 1535. Lib. XI. p. 235. Ruffin. Lib. II. c. 25.]

[5 (Μακεδόνιος) ἓν τῆς τριάδος λέγειν τὸ Πνεῦμα τὸ ἅγιον ἀπηρνεῖτο...διάκονον γὰρ αὐτὸ εἶναι καὶ ὑπουργὸν εἰσηγεῖτο, καὶ βραχύ τι τῶν ἀγγελικῶν διάφερον ταγμάτων.—Niceph. Eccl. Hist. Lutet. 1630. Tom. I. p. 800. Lib. IX. cap. 47.]

[6 Damnant et Samosatenos...qui...de Spiritu Sancto astute et impie rhetoricantur, quod...significet...Spiritus motum in rebus creatum.—Syll. Conf. Oxon. 1827. p. 166. Conf. August. 1540. Art. I.]

[7 Albeit they do acknowledge that there is a Holy Ghost...yet do they not acknowledge it to be a distinct person in the Godhead: but they do by a gross conceit imagine it to be only a bare power and virtue in God working by a secret kind of inspiration.—Policy of the Turk. Emp. Lond. 1597. cap. V. p. 16.]

The inheritance allotted to the faithful[9], and the being or virtuous estate of Christ[10]; as dreameth H. N. H. N. in his Instruct. præf. sent. 7. Idem in his Spir. Land. præf. § 14.

The affection of charity, or love, within us; an error of Petrus Lombardus[11]. Sent. Lib. I. dist. § 5. 2.

God's love, favour and virtue, whereby he worketh in his children; so thought Ochinus[12] and Servetus[13]. Zanch. de 3. El. par. 2. Lib. IV. cap. 1. Zanch. ibid. Lib. I. c. 2.

Proposition III.

The Holy Ghost proceedeth from the Father and the Son.

The proof from God's word.

The proceeding of the Holy Ghost from the Father and the Son, we gather from the holy Scripture, which teacheth how the Father sendeth the Comforter, which is the Holy Ghost, in the name of the Son, and the Son sendeth the Comforter, the Spirit of truth, from the Father; he proceedeth of the Father, and is sent of the Son. John xiv. 26. John xv. 26. Ibid. John xvi. 7.

So with us say the ancient fathers and Christians.

He proceedeth from the Father and the Son. Symb Nicen.

The Holy Ghost is of the Father, and of the Son, neither made, nor created, but proceeding. So there is one Father, not three Fathers; one Son, not three Sons; one Holy Ghost, not three Holy Ghosts: which is the faith of the modern Christians[14]. Symb. Athan. Conf. Helv. II. c. 3. Gal. c. 6. Belg. Art. VIII. 11. Wittemb. c. 3. [Bohem. cap. 3.]

[[8] If he (the Holy Spirit) be God, then is he a substance; not an inspiration coming from God, as our English Sadducees and outlandish libertines do teach.—Hutchinson, Image of God, ch. xxiv. p. 135. Park. Soc. Ed.]

[[9] The editor has been unable to meet with the work referred to.]

[[10] Yea, the Holy Spirit of love: which is a comforter of the heart; whom the Father sendeth in the name of the truth; the being of Christ; he teacheth and declareth, &c.—A True Testification of the Spiritual Land of Peace. Set forth by H. N. Præf. 14. p. 4. b.]

[[11] ... addendum est, quod ipse idem Spiritus Sanctus est amor sive charitas, qua nos diligimus Deum et proximum.—Petr. Lombard. Sentent. Col. Agr. 1576. Lib. I. Distinct. xvii. p. 44. B.]

[[12] Spiritus ille Ochinianus tres adfert significationes Spiritus...Altera; significari hac voce Dei favorem et virtutem per quam operatur, præsertim in electis—Zanch. de Trib. Eloh. Par. II. Lib. IV. cap. 1. § 2. p. 637.]

[[13] Fingit (Servetus)...Spiritum Dei virtutem et ἐνέργειαν—Ibid. Lib. I. cap. 2. § 2. p. 480.]

[[14] Eundem nihilominus Deum...docemus personis inseparabiliter et inconfuse esse distinctum, Patrem, Filium, et Spiritum Sanctum, ita ut Pater ab æterno Filium generaverit, Filius generatione ineffabili genitus sit, Spiritus Sanctus vero procedat ab utroque &c.—Harm. Conf. Sect. II. p. 23. Conf. Helv. Post. cap. III.

Errors and adversaries unto this truth.

Basil. Serm. de Spir. Sanct.

This discovereth all them to be impious, and to err from the way of truth, which hold and affirm that the Holy Ghost proceedeth neither from the Father, nor the Son, but is one and the same person that Christ is; as the Arians do[1].

Russ. Commonweal, c. 23. Guagnin. de Relig. Moscov. Faber de Relig. Moscov.

That the Holy Ghost proceedeth from the Father, but not from the Son; as at this day the Grecians[2], the Russians[3], the Moscovites[4], maintain.

L. Sent. Lib. I. distinct. 14.

That there is a double proceeding of the Holy Ghost, one temporal, the other eternal; an error of Peter Lombard[5], uncontrolled hitherto, and therefore well liked of the Papists.

ARTICLE VI.

Of the sufficiency of the holy Scripture for salvation.

Holy Scripture (1)*containeth all things necessary for salvation: so that whatsoever is not read therein, nor may*

Spiritum Sanctum ab æterno ex Patre et Filio procedentem.—Ib. p. 34. Conf. Gall. Art. VI. Spiritus Sanctus vero potentia est et virtus quæ a Patre et Filio emanat.—Ib. p. 360. Credimus etiam et confitemur Spiritum Sanctum a Patre et Filio ab æterno procedere.—Ib. p. 38. Conf. Belg. Artt. VIII. XI. Credimus...Spiritum Sanctum, ab æterno procedere a Deo Patre et Filio—Ib. p. 48. Conf. Vittemb. cap. III. Spiritus Sanctus autem procedit a Patre et Filio.—Ibid. p. 29. Conf. Bohem. cap. III.]

[[1] Μηδὲ (τις) Υἱοῦ προσηγορίαν ἐπὶ Πνεύματος τιθέναι βιαζέσθω—Basil. Opp. Par. 1721-30. Tom. II. p. 585. Hom. de Spir. S. in App. The homily, however, says nothing about the Arians. The passage meant perhaps is in the Hom. c. Sabell. Arium &c.: Οὐδὲ πάλιν Υἱοῦ καὶ πνεύματος ἓν πρόσωπόν ἐστιν ἐπειδὴ εἴρηται· εἰ δέ τις πνεῦμα Χριστοῦ οὐκ ἔχει, οὗτος οὐκ ἔστιν αὐτοῦ· ὁ δὲ Χριστὸς ἐν ὑμῖν. ἐντεῦθεν γὰρ ἠπατήθησαν τινὲς, Πνεῦμα καὶ Χριστὸν τὸν αὐτὸν εἶναι.—Ibid. p. 193.]

[[2] Concerning the divine nature and the three persons, in the one substance of God, that the Holy Ghost proceedeth from the Father only, and not from the Son.—Russe Commonwealth. Lond. 1591. p. 97. c. 23.]

[[3] Spiritum quoque sanctum a Patre tantum et non a Filio procedere confitentur.—Guagnin. de Relig. Moscov. in Collect. Script. de Russ. &c. Relig. Spiræ Nemet. 1582. p. 233.]

[[4] Spiritum Sanctum a solo Patre nec a Filio procedere perinde atque Græci tuentur [Moscovitæ].—Faber. Relig. Moscov. Ibid. p. 182.]

[[5] Præterea diligenter adnotandum est, quod gemina est processio Spiritus Sancti: æterna videlicet, quæ ineffabilis est, qua à Patre et Filio æternaliter, et sine tempore processit: et temporalis, qua a Patre et Filio ad sanctificandam creaturam procedit.—Petr. Lombard. Sentent. Col. Agr. 1576. Lib. I. Distinct. XIV. p. 37.]

be proved thereby, is not to be required of any man, that it should be believed as an article of the faith, or be thought requisite, [and] necessary to salvation. (2) *In the name of the Holy Scripture we do understand those canonical books of the Old and New Testament, of whose authority was never any doubt in the church.*

Of the names and number of the Canonical Books.

Genesis.	*The* 1. *Book of Chronicles.*
Exodus.	*The* 2. *Book of Chronicles.*
Leviticus.	*The* 1. *Book of Esdras.*
Numbers.	*The* 2. *Book of Esdras.*
Deuteronomium.	*The Book of Esther.*
Josue.	*The Book of Job.*
Judges.	*The Psalms.*
Ruth.	*The Proverbs.*
The 1. *Book of Samuel.*	*Ecclesiastes, or The Preacher.*
The 2. *Book of Samuel.*	*Canticles, or Song of Solomon.*
The 1. *Book of Kings.*	4. *Prophets the greater.*
The 2. *Book of Kings.*	12. *Prophets the less.*

(3) *And the other books (as Hierome saith) the church doth read for example of life, and instruction of manners; but yet doth it not apply them to stablish any doctrine; such are these following:*

The 3. *Book of Esdras.*	*Baruch the Prophet.*
The 4. *Book of Esdras.*	*Song of the* 3 *Children.*
The Book of Tobias.	*The Story of Susanna.*
The Book of Judith.	*Of Bel and the Dragon,*
The rest of the Book of Hester.	*The Prayer of Manasses.*
The Book of Wisdom.	*The* 1. *Book of Maccabees.*
Jesus the Son of Sirach.	*The* 2. *Book of Maccabees.*

(4) *All the books of the New Testament, as they are commonly received, we do receive, and account them for canonical.*

The Propositions.

1. The sacred Scripture containeth all things necessary (to be known and believed) for the salvation of man.

2. All the books in the volume of the Bible are not canonical, but some, and namely those here specified, are.

3. The 3. and 4. books of Esdras, the book of Tobias, &c. are apocryphal.

4. Of the New Testament all the books are canonical.

Proposition I.

The sacred Scripture containeth all things necessary (to be known and believed) for the salvation of man.

The proof from God's word.

The holy scriptures to be sufficient to instruct us in all things necessary to be known and believed for man's salvation, the Word of God teacheth.

Deut. iv. 2. "Ye shall put nothing unto the word which I command you (saith the Lord), neither shall ye take ought therefrom."

Ibid. xii. 32. "Whatsoever I command you, take heed you do it: thou
Josh. i. 7. shalt put nothing thereto, nor take ought therefrom. Thou shalt not turn away from it to the right hand, nor to the left, that thou mayest prosper whithersoever thou goest."

Prov. xxx. 5, 6. "Every word of God is pure, &c. Put nothing unto his words, lest he reprove thee, and thou be found a liar."

John xx. 31. "These things are written, that ye might believe, &c., and that in believing ye might have life through his name."

2 Tim. iii. 16, 17. "The whole scripture is given by inspiration of God, and is profitable to teach, to improve, to correct, and to instruct in righteousness, that the man of God may be absolute, being made perfect unto all good works."

Rev. xxii. 18, 19. "If any man shall add unto these things, God shall add unto him the plagues that are written in this book: and if any man shall diminish of the words of this book, God shall take away his part out of the book of life, and out of the holy city, and from those things which are written in this book."

Conf. Helv. I. Art. I. 4. & II. c. 1. Basil. Art. X. Bohem. c. 1. Gal. Art. II. IV. V. Belg. Art. VII. Saxon. Art. I. Wittemb. c. 30, Suevica, Art. I.

Hereunto God's people both always have, and at this present do subscribe[1].

[[1] Scriptura canonica, verbum Dei, Spiritu S. tradita, et per prophetas apostolosque mundo proposita, omnium perfectissima et antiquissima philosophia, pietatem omnem, omnem vitæ rationem sola perfecte continet.—Harm. Conf. Sect. I. p. 9. Conf. Helv. Prior. Art. I. Ceterum de traditionibus hominum quantumvis speciosis et receptis, quæcumque nos abducunt vel impediunt, ut de inutilibus et noxiis, sic illud domini respondemus, Frustra me colunt docentes doctrinas hominum.—Ibid. Art. IV. Credimus et confitemur scripturas canonicas sanctorum prophetarum et apostolorum utriusque Testamenti, ipsum verum esse verbum Dei...Et in hac scriptura sancta habet universalis Christi ecclesia plenissime exposita, quæcunque pertinent cum ad salvificam fidem, tum ad vitam Deo placentem, recte informandam. Quo nomine distincte a Deo præceptum est, ne ei aliquid vel addatur vel detrahatur.—Ibid. p. 3. Conf. Helv. Post. cap. I. Confitemur quod quemadmodum nemo mandare potest, ea quæ Christus non mandavit: ita etiam nemo prohibere possit, quæ ipse non prohibuit.—Ibid. p. 7. Conf. Basil. Art. X.

The errors and adversaries unto this truth.

Therefore adversaries be we to all adversaries to this truth: especially to such as scorn, and contemptuously reject the book of God; as both did the Circumcellians[2], which defaced Aug. contra Petil. Lib. I. c. 27.

[Art. XI. Disp. 26]. Initio docent ministri ecclesiarum nostrarum uno consensu de sacra scriptura veteris et novi Testamenti...quod vera certa et fide digna sit, cui nulla alia humana scripta, quæcunque aut qualiacunque sint, æquiparari possint, ...verum et certum testimonium est...propitiæ voluntatis Dei, quam de se patefecit, sine qua scripturæ patefactione, nulla cognitio salutaris, neque fides, neque accessio est ad Deum.—Ibid. p. 8. Conf. Bohem. cap. I. Hic unicus Deus talem se patefecit hominibus, primum, &c....deinde multo clarius in verbo suo, quod quidem initio certis quibusdam visis et oraculis patribus patefecit: deinde vero iis libris perscribi voluit, quos sacram scripturam vocamus.—Ibid. p. 10. Conf. Gall. Art. II. Hos libros (sc. supra dictos) agnoscimus esse *canonicos*, id est, ut fidei nostræ normam et regulam habemus, idque non tantum ex communi ecclesiæ consensu, sed etiam multo magis ex testimonio et intrinseca Spiritus Sancti persuasione, &c.—Ibid. Art. IV. Credimus verbum his libris comprehensum ab uno Deo esse profectum, quo etiam uno, non autem hominibus, nitatur ipsius auctoritas. Cumque hæc sit omnis veritatis summa, complectens quicquid ad cultum Dei et salutem nostram requiritur, neque hominibus, neque ipsis etiam angelis fas esse dicimus, quicquam ei verbo adjicere vel detrahere, vel quicquam prorsus in eo immutare.—Ibid. Art. V. Credimus autem sacram hanc scripturam perfectissime omnem Dei voluntatem complecti, et in illa abunde ea omnia doceri, quæcunque ab hominibus credi necesse est, ut salutem consequantur. Itaque cum illic exactissime fuse descripta sit omnis divini cultus ratio, quam Deus a fidelibus exigit: nulli hominum (quamvis apostolica dignitate prædito, ac ne ulli quidem angelo e cœlo demisso, ut divus Paulus loquitur) fas est aliter docere, quam jam pridem in sacris scripturis edocti sumus. Quum enim vetitum sit, ne quis Dei verbo quidquam aut addat aut detrahat, satis eo ipso declaratur sacram hanc doctrinam omnibus suis numeris et partibus perfectam ac absolutam esse—Ibid. p. 13. Conf. Belg. Art. VII. Cum certissimum sit, Deum sibi in genere humano, propter filium, et per eum, colligere ad vitam æternam ecclesiam voce doctrinæ, quæ scripta est in libris prophetarum et apostolorum: adfirmamus clare coram Deo et universa ecclesia in cœlo et in terra, nos vera fide amplecti omnia scripta prophetarum et apostolorum &c.—Ibid. p. 14. Conf. Sax. Art. I. Sacram scripturam vocamus eos canonicos libros veteris et novi Testamenti, de quorum autoritate in ecclesia nunquam dubitatum est. Hanc scripturam credimus et confitemur esse oraculum Spiritus Sancti, cœlestibus testimoniis ita confirmatum ut si angelus de cœlo aliud prædicaverit anathema sit....Sed, quod nonnulli sentiunt in hac scriptura non contineri omnem doctrinam, nobis ad veram et perpetuam salutem cognitu necessariam :...videtur facilius posse dici quam probari.—Ibid. p. 15. Conf. Wirtemb. cap. XXX....Mandavimus concionatoribus nostris ne quid deinceps populo pro concione proponant, quod non aut in divinis scripturis sit traditum, aut ex iis certum habeat fundamentum...Et certe...nihil christianæ veritatis sanæque doctrinæ illi deesse poterit, qui totis viribus scripturam illam divinam consectari, et amplecti studuerit.—Ibid. p. 19. Conf. Suev. Art. I. § 1.]

[2 Traditionem objiciunt, persecutionem objiciunt, falsum baptisma objiciunt: de solis Maximianistis ad omnia respondete. Quod enim majores eorum tradiderunt sanctos codices flammis, occultum esse arbitrantur: sed cum sacrilegio schismatis inquinatos in suis honoribus receperunt, hoc certe occultare non possunt.—August. Opp. Paris. 1836-8. Tom. IX. col. 357. Contra Litt. Petil. Lib. I. 27.]

Apol. Steph. fol. 358. and burnt the holy scriptures; and Pope Leo the X.[1], who termed the holy gospel a fable of Christ; and do the profane Atheists[2].

Nash in Christ his tears, p. 59. a.

Also to such as debase the credit and estimation of the holy scriptures; as David George[3] did; and both do the Papists[4], who have an opinion, that the Scriptures of God are not sufficient to instruct mankind unto salvation; and the Anabaptists[5], which deem not the holy Bible to be the word of God, with the Family of Love, in whose books nothing is more frequent than the terming of God's reverend ministers and preachers Scripture-learned.

Hist. David. Georg. Lindan. Lib. I. cap. 1. Bullin. contra Catabap. Lib. I.

Also to them, which with God's word do equal their own doctrines, injunctions, precepts, and traditions; as do the Papists. For of their doctrine say the Rhemists, "Whatsoever the lawful apostles, pastors or priests of God's church preach in the unity of the same church (meaning the new church of Rome), is to be taken for God's own word." To the same purpose, but more blasphemously, Stapleton[6]: "As the Jews were to believe Christ, so are we simply, and in every thing to believe the church (of Rome), whether it teacheth truth or errors."

Test. Rhem. An. 1 Thess. ii. 12. Stap. antid. Evang. in Luc. x. 16, p. 528.

Whatsoever by the authority of the church is commanded, ought of all men to be esteemed as the very gospel, saith

Tract. de propriet. Monach. c. 4.

[1 See Bale's Pageant of Popes (Eng. Transl.), Lond. 1574. Bk. VII. fol. 179. b.]

[2 Because some late writers of our side have sought to discredit the story of Judith, of Susanna, and Daniel, and of Bel and the Dragon, they think they may thrust all the rest of the Bible (in like manner) into the Jewish Talmud, and tax it for a fabulous legend.—Christ's Teares over Jerusalem, by Tho. Nashe. Lond. 1593.]

[3 ... et hanc præsentem revelationem, quam perfectionis spiritum vocat, multimodis superare superiorum ætatum revelationes, et esse omnium rerum divinarum quæ revelandæ erant veluti complementum.—Hist. Dav. Georg. Daventr. 1642. p. 38.]

[4 Docent catholicæ Christi ecclesiæ adversarii, verbum Dei solis sacræ scripturæ limitibus esse comprehensum, finibusque inclusum: nec quicquam præterea pro verbo Dei christianis agnoscendum, quod non sacris in literis contineatur. Quod initio a veritate longe esse alienissimum demonstrabimus, veramque fidei Christianæ regulam et credendi normam necessario aliud esse constituendam, sicuti et hactenus a Patribus priscis, theologisque omnino omnibus, quam solam scripturam sacram.—Lindanus, Panopl. Evangel. Col. Agrip. 1560. Lib. I. c. 1. p. 1.]

[5 Thomas Muncerus....docebat....scripturam externumque verbum non esse verum Dei verbum, sed solum testimonium veri verbi, &c.—Bulling. Adv. Anabapt. (Simler. Vers. Lat.) Tiguri. 1560. p. 1. b. Lib. I. c. 1.]

[6 Sicut Christo Judæi, sic nos ecclesiæ simpliciter credere debemus; non quidem sive vera doceat sive non, sed sive id nobis constet sive non.—Stapleton. Opp. Lut. Par. 1620. Tom. III. p. 163. Antid. Evang. in Luc. x. 16.]

abbot Trithemius[7] of popish precepts: and our English Rhemists: "He, that despiseth the church's or her lawful pastors' precepts, offendeth no less than if he contemned God's express commandments." And of their traditions; "He, that refuseth ecclesiastical traditions, deserveth to be thrown out of the church among the heathen, as well as he which refuseth the gospel," saith Didacus Stella[8], and the council of Trent. With like affection of godliness, and reverence, embrace we, and worship the books of the Old and New Testament, and ecclesiastical traditions, saith the council[9]. The like opinion have the Moscovites[10] of traditions.

Test. Rhem. An. 1 Thess. iv. 8.

Stella in Luc. x. fol. 20.

Concil. Trid. Sess. 4.

Russ. Com. cap. 23.

To them, finally, are we adversaries, which above the Scriptures do prefer their own (1) inventions; as did the philosophers; whereof one said of Moses, that good man maketh a trim discourse, but proveth nothing; and the Grecians, to whom the gospel is foolishness: and (2) imaginations; as did the Manichees[11], David George[12], and do the Turks, and Family of Love[13]: (3) or traditions; as do the Papists, who more cruelly do punish the violaters of their own traditions and ordinances, than they do the breakers of God's commandments: (4) or

1 Cor. i. 23. Epiphan. Hist. D. Geor. Policy of the Turkish Emp. cap. 3. Display, a. 6.

[[7] Quicquid ergo auctoritate ecclesiæ præcipitur; tanquam evangelium ab omnibus habeatur.—Trithem. Opp. Mogunt. 1605. p. 728. De Propr. Monach. cap. 4.]

[[8] Non minus meretur inter ethnicos ejici qui ecclesiasticas traditiones recusat, quam qui evangelium recusat.—Stella in Luc. Lugd. 1583. Tom. II. in. cap. x. fol. 20.]

[[9] Sacrosancta œcumenica et generalis Tridentina synodus...omnes libros tam veteris quam novi Testamenti, cum utriusque unus Deus sit auctor, nec non traditiones ipsas, tum ad fidem, tum ad mores pertinentes, tanquam vel ore tenus à Christo, vel a Spiritu Sancto dictatas, et continua successione in ecclesia catholica conservatas, pari affectu ac reverentia suscipit ac veneratur.—Concil. Harduin. Paris, 1714. Tom. x. col. 22. Conc. Trid. Sess. IV.]

[[10] They hold with the Papists, that their church *traditions* are of equal authority with the written word of God.—Russe Commonwealth, Lond. 1591. c. 23.]

[[11] *Καὶ ἀφ' ἑαυτοῦ διανοηθεὶς, (ὁ Σκυθιανὸς) ἐπλάσατο ῥήματα τοιαῦτα, οὐκ ἀπὸ τῆς θείας γραφῆς εὑράμενος, καὶ Πνεύματος ἁγίου φθογγῆς, ἀλλὰ ἀπὸ λογισμῶν ἀνθρωπείας φύσεως τῶν δειλαίων φάσκων.*—Epiphan. Opp. Paris. 1622. Tom. I. p. 619. Adv. Hær. Lib. II. Tom. II. Hær. 66. Epiphanius speaks of Scythianus as the first originator of the Manichæan heresy, which was afterwards more fully developed by Manes.]

[[12] See above, p. 78, note 4.]

[[13] Articles gathered out of the books of H. N. and which are taught by the Family of Love. 1. Inprimis, that H. N. can no more err or miss the right, than Moyses, the prophets, or Christ and his apostles....8. Item, that his books are of equal authority with the holy scripture, and are written with the same spirit.—Displaying of the Fam. Lond. 1579. A. 6.]

statutes, edicts, judgments, proclamations, &c., proceeding from the brain of man; as Machiavel doth, and his scholars.

Proposition II.

All the books in the volume of the Bible are not canonical, but some are.

That some books, and namely those above mentioned, are canonical, it hath been granted by the best learned and most godly of long time. And as all Reformed Churches in the world are of the same judgment with us, so in their public confessions[1] some have so accounted and judged of them as we do.

Confess. Gal. Art. III. Belg. Art. IV.

Adversaries to this truth.

Therefore (to speak first of the canonical books of the Old Testament) much have they offended which either rejected all, or allowed but some of the books of the Old Testament: of the former sort were the Severians[2], Basilides[3], Carpocrates[3], and the Manichees[4]; are the Catabaptists[5]: of the latter were sundry, whereof

Trithem. de Eccles. scrip. Epiphan. Epiphan. Aug. de bono perf. Lib. II. c. 11, Zuingl. Lib. cont. Catabap. D. Whit. de S. Scrip. contr. Bellar. q. I. c. 3.

Some received no more but only the five books of Moses; as the Sadducees[6].

Some, of all the books in the Old Testament, reject the

[[1] See Coll. Conf. Lips. 1840. p. 329. Conf. Gall. Art. III. and Ibid p. 361. Conf. Belg. Art. IV. The two lists of canonical books agree entirely with that in the Article.]

[[2] Vetus testamentum non suscipiunt. Trithem. de Script. Eccl. p. 8. § 8. In Fabric. Biblioth. Eccl. Hamb. 1718.]

[[3] The editor has been unable to verify these references.]

[[4] ... Quod et Manichæi non accipiunt, qui non solum omnes veteris instrumenti scripturas in ulla auctoritate non habent; verum etiam eas quæ ad novum pertinent Testamentum sic accipiunt, ut suo quodam privilegio, imo sacrilegio, quod volunt sumant, quod nolunt rejiciant. — August. Opp. Paris. 1836-8. Tom. X. col. 1411. De Dono Persev. 26.]

[[5] In hoc aliquando fuistis, ut totum vetus instrumentum negaretis, &c.... Verba eorum quæ hic tractamus, paulo diligentius expende. Paulus, inquiunt, docet anathema esse quicquid non in evangelio atque sermonibus apostolorum contineatur. Vides ut aperte vetus instrumentum fastidiunt?—Zuing. Opp. Tigur. 1545. Tom. II. Lib. contr. Catabapt. pp. 10, 11.]

[[6] Primi omnium Sadducæi nullas scripturas recipiebant, nisi quinque libros Mosis.—Whitak. Opp. Theolog. Genev. 1610. Tom. I. col. 261. De S. Script. Controv. I. Quæst. I. c. 3. Park. Soc. Ed. p. 30.]

works of Moses, and namely his four last books; as the Moscovites[7]. Russ. Com. c. 23.

Some embraced the law only, and the prophets; as the Samarites[8]. Cyril. Cat. 18.

Some esteemed neither the law, nor the prophets; as the Appelleans[9]. Tertul. de præs. Hæret.

Some had in contempt the book of the Canticles; as Sebastian Castellio[10]. Beza in vita Calv.

And some the Book of Job; as the Anabaptists[11]. Whitak. de S. Scrip. contra Bellar. q. I. c. 3.

Proposition III.

The third and fourth Books of Esdras, the Book of Tobias, &c. be Apocrypha.

That divers, and namely these books mentioned, are Apocrypha, we are neither the first that said, nor they alone, which affirm the same. For so judge of them did the ancient council at Laodicea[12], and do the churches reformed, and namely in France[13], and Belgia[14]. Can. 59. Conf. Gal. Art. 3. Conf. Belg. Art. IV.

[7 They will not read publicly certain books of the canonical scripture, as the books of Moses: specially the four last, Exodus, Leviticus, Numeri, and Deuteronomy, which they say are all made disauthentic, and put out of use by the coming of Christ.—Russe Commonwealth, c. 23.]

[8 Μετάβηθί μοι λοιπὸν ἐπὶ Σαμαρείτας οἳ, νόμον δεχόμενοι μόνον, προφήτας οὐκέτι καταδέχονται· οἷς ἀργὸν ἔοικε τὸ παρὸν ἀνάγνωσμα τοῦ Ἰεζεκιήλ. προφήτας γὰρ, ὡς ἔφην, οὐ δέχονται.—Cyril. Hierosol. Opp. Paris. 1720. Catech. 18.]

[9 Legem et prophetas repudiat (Apelles).—Tertull. Opp. Lutet. 1634. p. 254. A. de Præscrip. Hæret. 51.]

[10 Domi vero Sebast. ille Castellio...indignatus quod suas ineptias in Gallica novi Testamenti versione Calvinus non probasset, eousque efferbuit, ut exotica quædam docere non contentus, palam etiam Canticum Salomonis, tanquam impuram et obscœnam cantionem ex canone expungi juberet.—Beza, in Vit. Calvin. prefixed to Calvin. Opp. Tom. I. Amstelod. 1671.]

[11 Jobi librum Anabaptistæ hodie rejicere atque irridere dicuntur &c.—Whitak. Opp. Theol. Tom. I. col. 261. De S. Script. Quæst. I. c. 3. Park. Soc. Ed. p. 33.]

[12 Ὅτι οὐ δεῖ ἰδιωτικοὺς ψαλμοὺς λέγεσθαι ἐν τῇ ἐκκλησίᾳ, οὐδὲ ἀκανόνιστα βιβλία, ἀλλὰ μόνα τὰ κανονικὰ τῆς καινῆς καὶ παλαίας διαθήκης.—Concil. Harduin. Paris. 1715. Tom. I. col. 791. Concil. Laodicen. Can. 59. The 60th Canon contains a list of the canonical books, in which those of the Apocrypha are omitted.]

[13 See above, p. 80, note 5.]

[14 Differentiam porro constituimus inter libros istos sacros, et eos quos Apocryphos vocant: utpote quod Apocryphi legi quidem in ecclesia possint, et fas sit ex illis eatenus etiam sumere documenta, quatenus cum libris canonicis consonant.

The adversaries unto this truth.

So that they are to be held, and taken heed of, as seducers, which upon the church would thrust either other men's works and devices, not comprised in the Bible, as would

Euseb. Eccl. Hist. Lib. IV. c. 8.

Some, the new prophets, Barcobas and Barcolf, of Basilides[1] the heretic.

Tertul. de Hæret. Magdeburgh. Eccles. Hist. Cent. 3. cap. 11. Epiphan.

Some, the manifestations of Marcion[2] the heretic.

Some, the mysteries of Manes[3] the heretic.

Others, Esaias' Ascensorium of Hierax[4] the heretic.

Others, the Gospel after the Egyptians, after St Andrew, St James the lesser, St Peter, St Bartholomew, the twelve Apostles, Barnabas, Nicodemus, Thaddeus.

The Canons of the Apostles, others.

Others, the acts of St Abdie, St Andreas, St Paul, Peter, Philip, Thomas.

Others, the Revelation of St Paul, Peter, Stephen, Thomas[5].

Others, the books of the Anabaptists, of H. N., with popish legends, and the like.

Concil. Trid. Sess. 4, decr. de Can. Script.

Or, the books Apocrypha, within the volume of the Bible;

at nequaquam ea est ipsorum autoritas et firmitudo, ut ex illorum testimonio aliquod dogma de fide et religione christiana certo constitui possit.—Coll. Conf. p. 362. Conf. Belg. Art. VI.]

[1 *Ὧν εἰς ἡμᾶς κατῆλθεν......Ἀγρίππα Κάστορος ἱκανώτατος κατὰ Βασιλείδου ἔλεγχος......ἐκφαίνων δ' οὖν αὐτοῦ τὰ ἀπόῤῥητα φησὶν αὐτὸν εἰς μὲν τὸ εὐαγγέλιον τέσσαρα πρὸς τοῖς εἴκοσι συντάξαι βιβλία· προφήτας δὲ ἑαυτῷ ὀνομάσαι Βαρκαββᾶν καὶ Βαρκώφ, κ.τ.λ.*—Euseb. Eccl. Hist. Cant. 1720. Lib. IV. c. 7. p. 145.]

[2 This should rather be "the manifestations of Apelles the heretic," for the allusion is to him, in the passage of Tertullian which is doubtless intended. Habet præterea privatas, sed extraordinarias lectiones suas, quas appellat phaneroseis Philumenes cujusdam puellæ, quam quasi prophetissam sequitur.—Tertull. Opp. Lutet. 1634. p. 254. B. De Præscrip. Hæret. 51.]

[3 Manichie, 1607. Statim autem inter discipulos de novo quodam et inaudito dogmate disputare cœpit.—Magdeburg. Eccl. Hist. Basil. 1559, &c. Cent. III. cap. XI. col. 295.]

[4 *Βούλεται δὲ τὴν τελείαν αὐτοῦ σύστασιν ποιεῖσθαι ἀπὸ τοῦ Ἀναβατίκου Ἠσαΐου κ.τ.λ.*—Epiphan. Opp. Paris. 1662. Tom. I. p. 711. D. Adv. Hær. Lib. II. Tom. II.]

[5 Most of these spurious writings are mentioned by Eusebius (Eccl. Hist. Lib. III. c. 25. p. 118): *ὧν οὐδὲν*, he observes, *οὐδαμῶς ἐν συγγράμματι τῶν κατὰ διαδοχὰς ἐκκλησιαστικῶν τις ἀνὴρ εἰς μνήμην ἀγαγεῖν ἠξίωσεν.*—See also Epiphan. Opp. Tom. I. p. 506.]

as the Papists[6], who therefore anathematize and curse so many as take them not for canonical.

Proposition IV.

Of the New Testament all the books are canonical.

Although some of the ancient fathers and doctors accepted not all the books contained within the volume of the New Testament for canonical; yet in the end they were wholly taken and received by the common consent of the church of Christ in this world, for the very word of God, as they are at this day almost in all places where the gospel is preached and professed.

Howbeit, we judge them canonical, not so much because learned and godly men in the church so have, and do receive and allow of them, as for that the Holy Spirit in our hearts doth testify that they are from God. They carry a sacred, and divine authority with them, and they do also agree in all points with the other books of God in the Old Testament.

Errors and adversaries unto this truth.

Therefore in admitting all and every of these books, and acknowledging them to be canonical, we demonstrate ourselves to be against

Such as rejected all the New Testament, as did the Jews, and our Matthew Hamant[7]. Holin. Chron. fol. 1299.

Such, as allowed part, but not the whole New Testament; and these were of divers sorts: whereof

Some allowed of the evangelists, only Matthew, as the Cerdonites[8], and Ebionites[9]; others only Luke, as the Eus. Lib. III. c. 27. Iren. Lib. I. c. 26.

[6 After including the apocryphal books in the list of the canonical scriptures, the council proceeds: Si quis autem libros ipsos integros cum omnibus suis partibus, prout in ecclesia catholica legi consueverunt, et in veteri vulgata Latina editione habentur, pro sacris et canonicis non susceperit, et traditiones prædictas sciens et prudens contempserit, anathema sit.—Concil. Harduin. Paris. 1714. Tom. x. col. 23. Concil. Trident. Sess. IV. Decret. de Canon. Script.]

[7 Holinsh. Chron. Lond. 1587. Vol. III. fol. 1299.]

[8 This is not stated by Eusebius. In the place referred to he is speaking of the Ebionites, who he says only acknowledged the gospel according to the Hebrews.—Eccles. Hist. Cant. 1720. p. 121. Lib. III. c. 27.]

[9 Solo autem eo, quod est secundum Matthæum, evangelio utuntur (Ebionæi).—Iren. Adv. Hær. Oxon. 1702. p. 102. Lib. I. c. 26.]

Iren. ibid. Ibid. Lib. III. c. 11. August. Lib. de util. cred. Euseb.

Marcionites[1]; others only John, as the Valentinians[2].

Some accepted only the Acts of the Apostles, as the Tatians; others, of all other books rejected the said Acts, as the Manichees[3], and the Severites[4].

Iren. Lib. III. c. 12.

Some, of St Paul's epistles, took the Epistles unto Timothy and Titus only to be canonical, as Marcion[5] the heretic.

Theodor. arg. in Epist. Pauli ad Titum. Althemer. in c. e. Epist. Ja. Wigand. Syntag. Lib. V. See Whitak. against W. Rainolds, c. 7.

Some, as apocryphal, refused the Epistle unto Philemon[6]: others the Epistle unto the Hebrews, the Epistle of St James, as Althemerus[7]; others, the first, and second Epistles of John, with the Epistle of Jude, as Wigandus[8]; others, the Epistle unto the Hebrews, of James, the two last of John, and of Jude, as cardinal Cajetane[9].

Lib. de 600. error. Pontif.

Some rejected the book of St John's Revelations, or the Apocalypse, as Heshusius[10]: we are also against them which

[1 See below, note 5.]

[2 Hi autem, qui a Valentino sunt, eo quod est secundum Johannem plenissime utentes &c.—Ibid. p. 190. Lib. III. c. 11.]

[3 Nihil mihi videtur ab eis impudentius dici....quam scripturas divinas esse corruptas...Si enim dicerent eas sibi penitus accipiendas non putasse...esset utcunque tergiversatio eorum rectior, vel error humanior. Hoc enim de illo libro fecerunt qui Actus Apostolorum inscribitur.—August. Opp. Paris. 1836-8. Tom. VIII. col. 103. De Util. Cred. 7.]

[4 *Χρῶνται μὲν οὖν οὗτοι νόμῳ καὶ προφήταις, καὶ εὐαγγελίοις, ἰδίως ἑρμηνεύοντες τῶν ἱερῶν τὰ νοήματα γραφῶν· βλασφημοῦντες δὲ Παῦλον τὸν Ἀπόστολον, ἀθετοῦσιν αὐτοῦ τὰς ἐπιστολὰς, μὴ δὲ τὰς πράξεις τῶν Ἀποστόλων καταδεχόμενοι.*—Euseb. Eccl. Hist. Lib. IV. c. 29. p. 193.]

[5 Marcion, et qui ab eo sunt, ad intercidendas conversi sunt scripturas, quasdam quidem in totum non cognoscentes, secundum Lucam autem evangelium, et epistolas Pauli decurtantes, hæc sola legitima esse dicunt, quæ ipsi minoraverunt.—Iren. Adv. Hær. Lib. III. c. 12. p. 198. 2.]

[6 The editor has been unable to verify this reference.]

[7 This work has not been met with.]

[8 Judæ epistolam etiam hæc arguunt non esse genuinam, quod non apostolum sed servum &c.—Wigand. Syntagma, Basil. 1585. Pars II. p. 393.]

[9 Was not Cajetane a pillar of your church?...Doth not this famous cardinal of Rome set down in plain words that "the author of the epistle to the Hebrews doth gather insufficient arguments to prove Christ to be the Son of God: that the second and third of John are not canonical scripture: that the epistle of Jude is apocryphal... and namely of S. James' epi. that the salutation is profane, having nothing of God nor of Jesus Christ?—Whitaker's Answer to M. Rainolds' Refutation. Lond. 1585. cap. I. p. 7.]

[10 Manifestus et non tolerandus error est, quod pontificii suo arbitrio sacræ scripturæ canonem dilatant...et quos libros orthodoxi Patres libero judicio a canonica scriptura Spiritus Sancti separarunt, apostolicis literis adæquant, videlicet Tobiam &c....Apocalypsin Johannis.—Heshusius, Sexcenti Errores, &c. Francof. ad Mœn. 1585. I. Loc. de Sacr. Scrip. p. 5. It does not seem however that Heshusius himself questioned the canonicity of the book, as he twice refers to it in his preface.]

allowed neither the whole New Testament, nor those books wholly, which they embraced, as the Marcionites[11], who defaced all those places in the gospel after Luke, and in the epistles, which concerned either the divinity or humanity of our Saviour Christ.

Iren. Lib. II. cap. 29.

And lastly are we against them which receive the whole New Testament, but deface and put out such texts as mislike them; as the Turks[12], who scrape out whatsoever they find touching the passion of Christ, alleging how it was added purposely by the Jews in derision of Christians.

Aul. Tur. Lib. II. pag. 50.

Article VII.

Of the Old Testament.

(1) *The Old Testament is not contrary to the New. For both in the Old and New Testament everlasting life is offered to mankind by Christ, who is the only Mediator between God and man, being both God and man.* (2) *Wherefore they are not to be heard, which feign that the old fathers did look only for transitory promises. Although the law given from God by Moses, as touching* (3) *ceremonies and rites, do not bind Christian men,* (4) *nor the civil precepts thereof ought of necessity to be received in any commonwealth; yet, notwithstanding,* (5) *no Christian man whatsoever is free from the obedience of the commandments which are called moral.*

[11 Et super hæc, id quod est secundum Lucam Evangelium circumcidens, et omnia quæ sunt de generatione Domini conscripta auferens, et de doctrina sermonum Domini multa auferens, in quibus manifestissime conditorem hujus universitatis suum Patrem confitens Dominus conscriptus est; semetipsum esse veraciorem, quam sunt hi, qui evangelium tradiderunt, apostoli, suasit discipulis suis; non evangelium, sed particulam evangelii tradens eis. Similiter autem et apostoli Pauli epistolas abscidit, auferens quæcunque manifeste dicta sunt ab apostolo de eo Deo, qui mundum fecit, quoniam hic Pater Domini nostri Jesu Christi, et quæcunque ex propheticis memorans apostolus docuit, prænuntiantibus adventum Domini.—Iren. Adv. Hær. p. 104. Lib. I. c. 29.]

[12 Inter sacras literas habent nostra evangelia, quæ vocant *Ingil*, sed ex iis decerpunt et adimunt passionem Christi, dicentes, eam in irrisionem Christianorum a Judæis adjunctam esse.—Aulæ Turcicæ &c. Descriptio, Basil. 1577. Lib. II. p. 50.]

The propositions.

1. The Old Testament is not contrary to the New.
2. The old fathers looked for eternal happiness through Christ, as well as for temporal blessings.
3. Christians are not bound at all to the observation of the Judaical ceremonies.
4. The judicial laws of the Jews are not necessarily to be received or established in any commonwealth.
5. No Christian man whatsoever is freed from the obedience of the law moral.

Proposition I.

The Old Testament is not contrary to the New.

The proof from God's word.

That the Old Testament is not contrary to the New, it may be proved by many invincible arguments; yet it is most apparent, in that our Saviour Christ, very God, and very man, (as above, Art. II., hath been declared) is offered unto mankind for his eternal salvation by them both. For

Acts iii. 25. Gal. iii. 8, 16. Gen. xxii. 18. We learn that there is one, and no Christs more, in the New; and we learn the same in the Old.

Matt. xvi. 16. Acts xiii. 33. Psal. ii. 7. That Christ is the Son of God in the New; we learn the same in the Old.

Heb. ii. 14, 15, 16. Esa. xi. 1, & liii. 3. That Christ is very Man in the New; we learn that he should be so from the Old.

Matt. ii. 1. Mic. v. 2. That Christ was born at Bethlehem in the New; we learn that he should be so from the Old.

Matt. i. 23. Esa. vii. 14. That Christ was born of a virgin in the New; we learn that he should be so from the Old.

Matt. ii. 11. Esa. lx. 6. That Christ was honoured of wise men in the New; we learn that he should be so from the Old.

Matt. xxi. 1. Zech. ix. 9. That he rode upon an ass unto Jerusalem, from the New; we learn that he should so do from the Old.

Luke xxii. 47. Zech. xi. 12. That he was betrayed in the New; we learn that he should be so from the Old.

Acts viii. 33. 1 Cor. xv. 3. 1 Pet. ii. 24. Esa. liii. 5. That he suffered not for his own, but for our transgressions, in the New; we learn that he should so do from the Old.

Acts ii. 24, 31. 1 Cor. xv. 4. In the New that he rose again from the grave; from the Old, that he should so do.

And in the New, that he ascended into heaven; and in the Old, that he should so do. Matt. xii. 40 Psal. xvi. 10. Jonas i. 17. & ii. 10. Ephes. iv. 8. Psal. lxviii. 18.

The adversaries unto this truth.

We are then adversaries to all them which reject, as of no reckoning, the Old Testament; as did both old heretics, as Basilides, Carpocrates, and the Manichees[1]; and the new Libertines[2], who say the Old Testament is abrogated. See afore Art. VI. Prop. 2. Bulling. cont. Anab. Lib. III. c. 14.

Proposition II.

The old fathers looked for eternal happiness through Christ, as well as for temporal blessings.

The proof from God's word.

The old fathers to have looked not only for transitory promises, but also for eternal happiness through Christ, the holy scripture doth manifest.

St Paul saith,

Brethren, I would not have you ignorant that all our 1 Cor. x. 1.
fathers were under the cloud, and all passed through the Red
Sea; and did eat the same spiritual meat; and did all drink 3, 4.
the same spiritual drink: (for they drank of the spiritual rock
that followed them; and the rock was Christ).

By faith Noe was made heir of the righteousness which Heb. xi. 7.
is by faith.

By faith Moses, when he was come to age, refused to be Ibid. 24, 25, 26.
called the son of Pharaoh's daughter, and chose rather to
suffer adversity with the people of God, than to enjoy the pleasures of sin for a season; esteeming the rebukes of Christ greater riches than the treasures of Egypt: for he had respect unto the recompense of the reward, &c.

All these through faith obtained good report, and received Ibid. 39, 40.
not the promise; God providing a better thing for us, that they without us should not be made perfect.

[[1] See page 80, note 8.]

[[2] Sexto et ultimo loco inter abominandos Anabaptistas eos statuimus, qui vetus Testamentum rejiciunt, qui testimonia quæ ex illo adducuntur ad declaranda et confirmanda dogmata christianæ fidei, aut ad errores et falsa dogmata refutanda non recipiunt, et aiunt, Testamentum vetus abrogatum esse, quod Paulus doceat, Hebr. viii. Mosem item habere tectam et velatam faciem.—Bulling. Adv. Anabapt. Tiguri. 1560. Lib. II. cap. xv. p. 74.]

John viii. 56. Rom. iv. 18. Abraham rejoiced to see my day. Abraham above hope believed under hope, that he should be the father of many nations.

1 Pet. i. 10. Of which salvation the prophets have inquired and searched.

This truth was never doubted of in the church of God, and publicly acknowledged by some confessions[1]. Helv. II. c. 13. Saxon. Art. III.

The adversaries unto this truth.

They are not then to be heard, which think the fathers, and faithful people before Christ his time, hoped only for temporal, and not for spiritual; and if for spiritual, yet not for eternal happiness; as did many of the Jewish atheists, and Sadducees, and do the Family of Love, which make the promises of happiness by temporal blessings to be accomplished in this transitory life. Psal. liii. 1. Acts xxiii. 28.

Hence H. N.[2] very strangely allegorizeth of the land of promise, when he calleth it, The good land of the upright, and concordable life; and saith that The lovely being or nature of the love is the life, peace, and joy, mentioned Rom. xiv. 6; and the land of promise, wherein honey and milk floweth, spoken of Exod. iii. a. xiii. a. Deut. viii. b. This and more a great deal to this effect hath H. N. In his book entit. 'The spir. Land of peace,' c. 18. § 10, & c. 25. § 4.

Proposition III.

Christians are not bound at all to the observation of the Judaical ceremonies.

The proof from the word of God.

That neither the whole law ceremonial of the Jews, nor any part thereof, is necessarily to be observed of us Christians,

[[1] ... certissimum est, eos qui ante legem et sub lege fuerunt, non omnino destitutos fuisse evangelio. Habuerunt enim promissiones evangelicas insignes, &c.... Habuerunt autem veteres non tantum externas vel terrenas, sed spirituales etiam cœlestesque promissiones in Christo.—Harmon. Conf. Genev. 1581. pp. 124, 5. Conf. Helv. Post. c. xiii. Ut autem beneficia hujus Mediatoris nota essent generi humano, et nobis applicarentur, edita est promissio statim initio post lapsum primorum parentum, &c.—Ibid. p. 129. Conf. Saxon. Art. III.]

[[2] But as long as they dwell in the horrible confused land, they understand not that they are decayed and corrupted, nor yet that they have missed the true entrance to the good land of the upright and concordable life, &c.—H. N. Spiritual Land of Peace, cap. xviii. 10. p. 32. For the same lovely being of the love, is the life, peace (Rom. xiv. b.), and joy, and the land of promise (Exod. iii. a. xiii. a.; Deut. viii. b.), wherein honey and milk floweth.—Ibid. cap. xxv. 4. p. 40. b.]

the holy scripture teacheth us by Peter's vision, the apostles' decree, and by the doctrine of St Paul.

Acts x. 13. Acts xv. 24, 29. Gal. ii. 3, 4. and iv. 10, 11. Eph. ii. 14, 15. Col. ii. 16, 17.

As all believe, so some churches[3] publicly acknowledge the same.

Conf. Gal. Art. XXIII. Belg. Art. XXV.

Errors and adversaries to this truth.

In a wrong opinion, therefore, be they who are of mind, either that the law ceremonial wholly is to continue, and be in use, or that part thereof is yet in force, and must be.

The former of these was the opinion of the false prophets, the Cerinthians[4], the Ebionites[5], and is of the Jews, Armenians, and Family of Love[6]: the latter is an error of our home Sabbatarians. For, say they,

Acts xv. 1, 2. Euseb. Iren. Lib. I. c. 26. H. N. Evang. c. 13. sect. 4, 9.

The sabbath was none of the ceremonies which were justly abrogated at the coming of Christ.

D. B. Sab. doctrine, I. Book, p. 11.

When all Jewish things have been abrogated, only (be their very words) the sabbath hath continued still in the church in his [own] proper force, that it might appear that it was of a nature far differing from them.

Ibid. p. 20.

Whereas all other things were so changed, that they were clean taken away, as the priesthood, the sacrifices, and sacraments, *this day* (meaning the sabbath-day) *was so changed,*

Ibid. p. 41.

[[3] Credimus omnes legis figuras adventu Jesu Christi sublatas esse, quamvis earum veritas et substantia nobis in eo constet, in quo sunt omnes impletæ.—Harmon. Confess. p. 129. Conf. Gall. Art. XXIII. Credimus omnes ceremonias et figuras legis, omnes denique umbras cessasse, Christi adventu: adeo ut earum quoque usus inter Christianos jam tolli abolerique debeat.—Ibid. Conf. Belg. Art. XXV.]

[[4] This opinion is not attributed to Cerinthus by Eusebius. But see Hieron. Epist. in Opp. August. Par. 1836-8. Tom. II. col. 260. Si hoc verum est, in Cerinthi et Ebionis hæresim delabimur, qui credentes in Christum propter hoc solum a patribus anathematizati sunt, quod legis ceremonias Christi evangelio miscuerunt.]

[[5] Apostolum Paulum recusant (Ebionæi) apostatam eum legis dicentes...et circumciduntur, ac perseverant in his consuetudinibus, quæ sunt secundum legem, uti et Hierosolymam adorent, quasi domus sit Dei.—Iren. Adv. Hær. Oxon. 1702. p. 102. Lib. I. c. 26.]

[[6] For this same Messias or anointed, is the sabbath-day (Exod. xx. b.; Deut. v. b.), which the Lord hath commanded to be always had in remembrance that we (when the same cometh) might rest therein and hallow or sanctify the same: wherein the law, the service of the priesthood of Aaron, out of Levi, and the elders' testament, doth cease (Heb. vii. 8. b.), and hath accomplished his service. For the same anointed which cometh at that time (Act. i. b.; Phil. iii. c.) out of heaven, with his anointing of the holy Ghost; in the spirit, and is the very-like-being (Col. i. b.; Heb. i. a.) of the godhead itself, he is a priest (Ps. cx. a.; Heb. v. vi. vii. b. ix. b. x. b.) of the most highest, higher and greater of dignity than Aaron, &c.—H. N. Evang. Regni. Lond. 1652. p. 69. cap. xiii. § 4, 5. See also Ibid. § 8, 9.]

that it yet remaineth: which sheweth, that though all the other were ceremonial, and therefore had an end, this (sabbath) [only] was moral, and therefore abideth still.

Ibid. p. 7. The commandment (of sanctifying every seventh day, as in the *Mosaical* Decalogue) is natural, moral, and perpetual (is their doctrine[1].)

Proposition IV.

The judicial laws of the Jews are not necessarily to be received, or established in any commonwealth.

The proof from God's word.

Acts xv. 20, 28, 29. The truth hereof appeareth by the apostles' decree; which sheweth whereunto only the primitive church necessarily was tied.

Rom. xiii. 1. 1 Pet. ii. 13, 14. By the apostles' doctrine, which enjoineth Christians to yield obedience unto the ordinances of their lawful governors and commanders whosoever.

Acts xvi. 37. Acts xxii. 25, &c. Acts xxv. 11, 12. By the apostles' example, and namely of the blessed St Paul, who took benefit, and made good use of the Roman and imperial laws.

Adversaries unto this truth.

This truth neither is, nor ever was, oppugned by any church. Only among ourselves some think us necessarily tied unto all the judicials of Moses; as the Brownists[2]. For they say, The laws judicial of Moses belong as well unto Christians as they did unto the Jews. (Barrow's discov. pag. 127.)

1 Reply, sect. 1, 2. Anatom. of abuses, 2 Part. D. b. Others, that we are bound, though not unto all, yet unto some of the judicials; as holdeth T. C.[3], and Philip Stubs[4].

[[1] Nic. Bownde's Doctrine of the Sabbath, Lond. 1595. Book I. pp. 11, 20, 41, 7.]

[[2] But the statutes and judgements of God which are delivered and expounded unto us by his holy prophets, endure for ever; the pure wisdom, the upright justice, the true exposition and faithful execution of his moral law: which laws were not made for the Jews' state only (as Mr Calvin hath taught) but for all mankind, especially for all the Israel of God, from which laws it is not lawful in judgement to vary or decline either to the one hand or to the other.—Barrow's Discovery of the False Church, 1590. p. 96.]

[[3] There are also civil punishments, and punishments of the body likewise, appointed by the word of God, in divers places in Exodus. He that sacrificeth to other gods, and not to the Lord alone shall die the death....The execution of this

Proposition V.

No Christian man whosoever is freed from the obedience of the law moral.

The proof from God's word.

Think not that I am come to destroy the law or the pro- Matt. v. 17,
phets: I am not come to destroy them, but to fulfil them. 18, 19.
For truly I say unto you (saith our Saviour Christ) till heaven and earth perish, one jot or one tittle of the law shall not scape, till all things be fulfilled: whosoever therefore shall break one of these least commandments, and teach men so, shall be called the least in the kingdom of heaven, &c.

If thou wilt enter into life, keep the commandments, &c. Matt. xix.
Thou shalt not kill; Thou shalt not commit adultery; Thou 17, 18, 19.
shalt not steal; Thou shalt not bear false witness; Honour thy father and thy mother.

Do we make the law of none effect through faith? God Rom. iii. 31.
forbid: yea, we establish the law. Circumcision is nothing, 1 Cor. vii. 19.
and uncircumcision is nothing, but the keeping of the commandments of God. The public confessions of the churches Art. xxiii.
of God in France[5] and Belgia agree with this doctrine. Art. xxv.

law appeareth in the Chro. by king Asa, who made a law, that all those that did not seek the Lord should be killed. And thus you see the civil punishment of contemners of the word and prayers.—Cartwright, First Reply, p. 28. ...Although the judicial laws are permitted to the discretion of the prince and magistrate, yet not so generally as you seem to affirm, and as I have oftentimes said, that not only it must not be done against the word, but according to the word and by it.—Ibid. p. 36. See also Second Reply, 1575. p. 95.]

[4 S. What kind of punishment would you have appointed for these notorious bloody swearers? P. I would wish (if it pleased God) that it were made death: For we read in the law of God, that whosoever blasphemed the Lord, was presently stoned to death, without all remorce. Which law *judicial* standeth in force to the world's end.—Stubs' Anatomie of Abuses, Lond. 1585. p. 82.]

[5 Legis tamen doctrina et prophetis nobis utendum est, tum ad vitam nostram formandam, tum ut eo magis in promissionibus evangelicis confirmemur.—Harm. Conf. p. 129. Ex Gall. Conf. Art. xxiii. Interim tamen manet nobis illarum [sc. ceremoniarum legis] veritas et substantia in Christo, in quo omnes impletæ fuerunt. Ideoque legis et prophetarum testimoniis adhuc utimur, ut nos ipsos in evangelii doctrina confirmemus: et omnem vitam nostram honeste ad Dei gloriam juxta ipsius voluntatem, componamus.—Ibid. Ex Belg. Conf. Art. xxv.]

The errors and adversaries unto this truth.

Whereby are condemned, as most wicked and unsound, the opinions

Aug. contra Faust. Epist. xi. and lxxiv. Of the Manichees[1], who found fault with the whole law of God as wicked, and proceeding not from the true God, but from the prince of darkness.

Bredwell detect. p. 119. Of Brownist Glover[2], whose opinion was, That love now is come in the place of the ten commandments.

Sim. Pauli meth. par. 2. de lege Dei, pag. 54. Of Johannes Islebius, and his followers, the Antinomies[3], who will not have God's law to be preached, nor the consciences of sinners to be terrified and troubled with the judgments of God.

Bannister's error. Of Bannister[4] (among ourselves) who held, how it is utterly evil for the elect so much as to think, much less to speak or hear of the fear of God (which the law preacheth).

ARTICLE VIII.

Of the three Creeds.

(1) *The three Creeds, Nicene Creed, Athanasius' Creed, and that which is commonly called the Apostles' Creed, ought thoroughly to be received and believed. For* (2) *they may be proved by most certain warrants of holy Scripture.*

The propositions.

1. The Nicene, Athanasian, and Apostolical Creeds ought to be received and believed.

[1 Unde autem tibi videtur legem Moysi nihil a Paganismo distare?—August. Opp. Par. 1836-8. Tom. VIII. col. 461. Cont. Faust. Lib. XVI. c. 10. Cf. etiam Libb. XVII-XIX. Non quod Legem juxta Manichæum...destruamus.—Ibid. Tom. II. col. 262. Epist. 75. al. 11. Legem per famulum Dei Moysem datam, non a vero Deo dicunt (Manichæi), sed a principe tenebrarum.—Ibid. col. 1289. Epist. 236. al. 74.]

[2 Bredwell's Detection, London, 1568. p. 119.]

[3 Clamores et furores Antinomorum de tollenda legis doctrina ex ecclesia, &c.—Sim. Paul. Method. Sec. Pars, Magdeb. 1573. De Lege Dei, p. 54. b. Cf. p. 2. b. disputatio...ab Islebio mota, &c.]

[4 This work the editor has been unable to meet with.]

2. The three Creeds, *viz.* the Ni., Athan., and of the Apostles, may be proved by the holy scripture.

Proposition I.

The Nicene, Athanasian, and Apostolical Creeds, ought to be received and believed.

This proposition the churches of God, both anciently and in these days[5], do acknowledge for true. Conf. Helv. II. c. 11. Gal. Art. v. Belg. Art. IX. Saxon. Art. I.

The adversaries unto this truth.

Therefore much out of the way of godliness are they, which term the Apostles' creed, a forged patchery; as Barrow doth[6]: and Athanasius', Sathanasius' creed; so did Gregorius Paulus[7] in Polonia, and the new Arians[8] and Nestorians in Lithuania. Bar. dis. p. 76. Genebr. Lib. IV. p. 1158. Surius, Chr. pag. 329.

Myself, some twenty-eight years ago, heard a great learned man, whose name upon another occasion afore is expressed (to whose acquaintance I was artificially brought), which in private conference between him and myself termed worthy Zanchius a fool, and an ass, for his book *De Tribus Elohim*, which refuteth the new Arians; against whose founders the creeds of Athanasius and Nicene were devised. Him attentively I heard, but could never since abide for those words; and indeed I never saw him since.

[[5] Quæcunque de incarnationis Domini nostri Jesu Christi mysterio, definita sunt ex scripturis sanctis, et comprehensa symbolis ac sententiis quatuor primarum et præstantissimarum synodorum, celebratarum Niceæ, Constantinopoli, Ephesi et Chalcedone, una cum beati Athanasii Symbolo,...credimus corde syncero, &c.—Harm. Conf. VI. p. 103. Conf. Helv. Post. c. xi. Quamobrem etiam tria illa symbola, nempe Apostolicum, Nicænum et Athanasianum, idcirco approbamus, quod sint illi verbo Dei scripto consentanea.—Ibid. I. p. 11. Conf. Gall. Art. v. Itaque libenter tria illa *symbola* hic recipimus, nempe Apostolorum, Nicenum et Athanasii.—Ibid. II. p. 38. Conf. Belg. Art. IX. Et hæc ipsa symbola (sc. Apost. Nic. et Athan.), et eorum nativam sententiam sine corruptelis semper constanter amplexi sumus, et Deo juvante, perpetuo amplectemur.—Ibid. I. p. 14. Conf. Saxon. I.]

[[6] Barrow's Discovery of the False Church. 1590. p. 76.]

[[7] In Polonia...Gregorius Paulus...tres esse Deos, symbolum Athanasii esse Sathanasii, &c.—Genebrard. Chronograph. Lugd. 1609. Lib. IV. p. 746.]

[[8] In Lituania sunt multi Arriani et Nestoriani...qui vocant...symbolum non Athanasianum, sed Sathanasianum, &c.—Surius, Comment. Brev. Rer. Gest. &c. Colon 1574. p. 251.]

Proposition II.

The three Creeds, viz., the Nicene, Athanasian, and of the Apostles, may be proved by the Holy Scripture.

The proof from God's word.

Than this assertion nothing is more true: for the creeds, I mean these three creeds, speak first,

Of one and the same God, who[1] we are to believe is for essence but one, in persons three, *viz.* the Father, the Creator; the Son, the Redeemer; the Holy Ghost, the Sanctifier. Next of the people of God, which we must think and believe is,

Deut. vi. 4. Mal. ii. 10. 1 Cor. viii. 4. Eph. iv. 5, 6. Matt. iii. 17. Gal. iv. 6. 1 John v. 7. Ps. cxxxiv. 3. Esa. liii. 4. Rom. v. 18. Gal. iii. 13. Eph. ii. 16. 1 John ii. 2. 2 Cor. i. 21, 22. 1 Pet. i. 2. Eph. i. 3, 4, & ii. 21. Col. i. 22. Esa. liv. 2. Ps. lxxxvii. 4. Esa. lxiv. 22. Rev. xxi. 4.

The holy and catholic Church.

The communion of saints,

Pardoned of all their sins,

And appointed to arise from death, and to enjoy eternal life, both in body and soul.

Acts i. 8, &c. Eph. ii. 14. Rev. v. 9. Eph. iv. 15. 1 Cor. x. 16. Heb. x. 25. 1 Joh. i. 7. Matt. xviii. 23, &c. Col. ii. 13. Joh. v. 28. 1 Cor. xv. Phil. iii. 21. Joh. vi. 39. 1 Pet. i. 4.

Adversaries unto this truth.

Therefore we are enemies to all adversaries of this doctrine, or any whit of the same in them comprised, whether they be Atheists, Jews, Sadducees, Ebionites, Tritheites, Anti-Trinitarians, Apollinarians, Arians, Manichees, Nestorians, Origenians, Turks, Papists, Familists, Anabaptists, or whosoever.

ARTICLE IX.

Of Original, or Birth-sin.

(1) *Original sin standeth not in the following of Adam, (as the Pelagians do vainly talk;) but* (2) *it is the fault and corruption of the nature of every man, that naturally is ingendered of the offspring of Adam, whereby man is very far gone from original righteousness, and is*[2] *inclined to*

[[1] whom, 1607.]

[[2] So 1607 and 1633. And is of his own nature inclined &c., 1675.]

evil, so that the flesh lusteth[3] *against the spirit; and therefore in every person born into the world, it deserveth God's wrath and damnation.* (3) *And this infection of nature doth remain, yea in them that are regenerated, whereby the lust of the flesh, called in Greek φρόνημα σαρκὸς, which some do expound the wisdom, some the sensuality, some the affection, some the desire, of the flesh, is not subject to the law of God. And although there is no condemnation for them that believe and are baptized, yet the apostle doth confess that* (4) *concupiscence and lust hath of itself the nature of sin.*

The propositions.

1. There is original sin.
2. Original sin is the fault, and corruption of the nature of every man, &c.
3. Original sin remaineth in God his dear children.
4. Concupiscence, even in the regenerate, is sin.

Proposition I.

There is original sin.

The proof from God's word.

In the holy Scripture we find of original sin, the cause, the subject, and the effects: the cause thereof is Adam's fall, partly by the subtle suggestions of the devil, partly through his own freewill; and the propagation of Adam his corrupted nature unto his seed and posterity. Rom. v. 15. 1 Cor. xv. 21. Gen. iii. 4. 2 Cor. xi. 3.

Except a man be born again, he cannot see the kingdom of God, saith our Saviour Christ. Joh. iii. 3. As by one man sin entered into the world, and death by sin, and so death went over all men: forasmuch as all men have sinned, saith St Paul. Rom. v. 12. As new-born babes, desire the sincere milk of the word, that ye may grow thereby, saith St Peter. 1 Pet. ii. 2. And St James, Of his own will begat he us with the word of truth, that we should be as the first-fruits of his creatures. James i. 18. And the forementioned Apostle Paul again, You that were dead in trespasses and sins, &c., and were by nature the children of wrath, as well as others. But God, which is rich in mercy, through his great love wherewith he loved us, even when we were dead by sins, hath quickened us together in Christ, &c. Eph. ii. 1, 3, 4.

[[3] Lusteth always against &c., 1675.]

The subject thereof is the old man, with all his powers, mind, will, and heart. For in the mind there is darkness, and ignorance of God, and his will: and in the will, and heart of man there is concupiscence, and rebellious affections against the law of God.

And the effects of this birth, or original sin, are first actual sins; and they both inward, as ungodly affections; and outward, as wicked looks, profane speech, and devilish actions; next, an evil conscience, which bringeth the wrath of God, death, and eternal damnation.

All churches of God believe this, and some in their public confessions[1] testify so much.

Matt. xii. 34. Rom viii. 7. 1 Cor. ii. 14. 1 John iii. 1, & v. 19, 20. Matt. v. 19. Acts vii. 39, & xv. 9. Rom. i. 21. James i. 13, 14. Matt. xv. 19. 1 John iii. 21. Rom. i. 18. Col. iii. 5, 6. John viii. 24. Rom. v. 12. James i. 15. Rom. v. 18. Conf. Helv. I. Art. VIII. & II. c. 8. Basil. Art. II. Bohem. c. 4. Gal. Art. IX.. XI. Belg. Art. XV. August. Art. I. Saxon. Art. II.

[[1] Atque hæc lues, quam originalem vocant, genus totum sic pervasit, ut nulla ope iræ filius inimicusque Dei nisi divina per Christum curari potuerit.—Harm. Conf. Sect. IV. p. 72. Conf. Helv. Prior. Art. VIII. Fuit homo ab initio a Deo conditus ad imaginem Dei, &c.... sed instinctu serpentis et sua culpa a bonitate et rectitudine deficiens, peccato morti variisque calamitatibus factus est obnoxius. Et qualis factus est lapsu, tales sunt omnes qui ex ipso prognati sunt: peccato, inquam, morti, varisque obnoxii calamitatibus.—Ibid. p. 67. Conf. Helv. Post. cap. VIII. Confitemur hominem ab initio secundum Dei imaginem... integre factum. Est autem sua sponte lapsus in peccatum: per quem lapsum totum humanum genus corruptum et damnationi obnoxium factum est.—Ibid. p. 72. Conf. Basil. Art. II. Homo... mandatum Dei transgressus est in eo, quod diabolo et mendacibus verbis hujus obtemperavit &c.... atque ita tam se quam genus suum in peccatum et mortem, omnisque generis in hoc vita miserias, et pœnas insuper æternas præcipitavit.—Ibid. p. 74. Conf. Bohem. cap. IV. Credimus hominem, creatum purum et integrum et imagini Dei conformem, sua ipsius culpa excidisse a gratia quam acceperat... adeo ut ipsius natura sit prorsus corrupta, et... omnem illam integritatem, sine ulla prorsus exceptione, amiserit.—Ibid. p. 77. Conf. Gal. Art. IX. Credimus hoc vitium esse vere peccatum, quod omnes et singulos homines, ne parvulis quidem exceptis adhuc in utero matrum delitescentibus, æternæ mortis reos coram Deo peragat.—Ibid. Art. XI. Credimus Adami inobedientia peccatum quod vocant originis, in totum genus humanum sparsum, et effusum fuisse. Est autem peccatum originis corruptio totius naturæ et vitium hereditarium, quo et ipsi infantes in matris utero polluti sunt, &c.—Ibid. p. 79. Conf. Belg. Art. XV. Item docent quod post lapsum Adæ, omnes homines naturali modo propagati nascentes habeant peccatum originis Intelligimus autem peccatum originis... reatum, quo nascentes propter Adæ lapsum rei sunt iræ Dei et mortis æternæ: et ipsam corruptionem humanæ naturæ propagatam ab Adam.—Ibid. p. 80. Conf. Aug. 1540. Art. II. Item docent, quod post lapsum Adæ omnes homines secundum naturam propagati nascantur cum peccato, hoc est sine metu Dei, sine fiducia erga Deum, et cum concupiscentia.—Ibid. Conf. 1531. Dicimus omnes homines post lapsum primorum parentum, qui nascuntur ex commissione maris et feminæ, nascentes secum afferre peccatum originis, &c.... Hos defectus et hanc totam depravationem dicimus esse peccatum, non tantum pœnam peccati, &c.—Ibid. p. 85. Conf. Sax. Art. II.]

The errors and adversaries unto this truth.

Thus armed with authority, and forces from the word of God, and assisted with the neighbour churches, we offer battle,

1. To the Jews[2], Carpocratians[2], and Family of Love[3], who flatly deny there is any original sin.

Frier Laur. a Villavincentia de form. S. concion. Lib. I. c. 13. Clem. Alex. Strom. Lib. III. Display in Allen's Conf.

2. To the Papists, which say, that

Original sin is of all the least sin, and less than any venial sin.

Original sin is only the debt of punishment for the sin of Adam, and not his fault.

Original sin is not properly sin. All this hath Ruardus Tapperus[4].

Tapp. Tract. de Pec. Orig.

Such as are infected only with original sin are free from all sensible punishment[5].

Th. Aquin. Lib. IV. dist. 16, q. 1. Art. II.

3. To Florinus, and Blastus[6], who make God the author of sin.

Conf. Helv. II. c. 8, ex Iren.

4. To the Sabbatarians among us, who teach, that the life of God in Adam before his fall could not continue without a sabbath[7].

Sab. Doct. I. Book, p. 15.

The sabbath was ordained before the fall of Adam[8], and that not only to preserve him from falling, but also that

Ibid.

[[2] These references the editor has been unable to verify.]

[[3] The passage meant is perhaps this: They hold that they ought not to say David's Psalms as prayers; for they are righteous and without sin.—Displaying of the Fam. &c. Lond. 1579. H. 8. b.]

[[4] Ideo docet idem beatus Thomas... Quod peccatum originale quamvis maximum sit malum, quia totius naturæ corruptio, minimum tamen est peccatum, et minus minimo peccato veniali.—Tapp. Opp. Colon. 1582. Tom. I. Art. II. p. 40. b. Quidam putant originale peccatum esse reatum pœnæ pro peccato primi hominis, id est, debitum vel obnoxietatem qua addicti sumus pœnæ temporali et æternæ pro primi hominis actuali peccato, &c.—Ibid. p. 37. b. Nec proprie peccatum erat in primo parente gratiæ et justitiæ originalis privatio, &c.—Ibid. p. 42. a.]

[[5] Peccatum originale non contrahitur per aliquam delectationem ejus qui ipsam contrahit. Ergo videtur quod non sit ejus curatio per aliquam pœnam, &c.—Thom. Aquin. in Quat. Libr. Sentent. Venet. 1586. In Lib. IV. Dist. XVI. Quæst. 1. Art. II. p. 98.]

[[6] Damnamus præterea Florinum et Blastum... et omnes qui Deum faciunt authorem peccati.—Coll. Conf. Lips. 1840. p. 478. Conf. Helv. Post. VIII.]

[[7] The life of God, which was in him (Adam), could not continue without those holy and spiritual means appointed for that purpose, and therefore he was commanded to keep holy the seventh day.—Nich. Bownde's Doct. of the Sabbath. Lond. 1595. Bk. I. p. 15.]

[[8] Now if Adam because he might fall, did stand in need of this day, to preserve him from falling, how much more we, &c. ... if it was needful for Adam (I say) being now most perfect, to have a day allotted out unto him, by true sanctifying of which he might still abide in his perfection, &c.—Ibid.]

Ibid. II. Book, p. 182. being holy and righteous still, he might have been preserved in the favour of God[1]; which D. B. delivereth in his sabbath-doctrine.

5. We are also adversaries to the like curiously affected who enquire[2],

Whether it was God's will that Adam should fall?
Whether God enforced our first parents to fall?
Why God stayed not Adam from falling? &c.

Proposition II.

Original sin is the fault and corruption of the nature of every man, &c.

The proof from God's word.

Original sin is not the imitation of Adam his disobedience: for the scripture speaketh of no such thing; neither doth God's people so think; and some churches, by their extant confessions, with us deny the same; as the church in France, and the Low Countries[3]: but it is partly the imputation of Adam his disobedience unto us, and partly the fault and corruption of man's nature, as the churches[4] also acknowledge.

Conf. Gal. Art. x. Conf. Belg. Art. xv. Rom. v. 12, 16. Conf. Aug. Art. II. Saxon. Art. II. Wittemb. c. 4. Rom. iii. 23. & vii. 18. Eph. ii. 3. Conf. Helv. II. c. 8. Gal. Art. x. Bohem. cap. 4. August. Art. II. Saxon. Art. II. Wittemb. c. 4.

[1 Nay, what a blockish presumption were it for a man to think that Adam was bound to sanctify the Sabbath, according to the Commandment; that being holy and righteous still, he might have been preserved in the favour of God for ever, and that we ourselves...might make less account of these means, &c.—Ibid. Bk. II. p. 182.]

[2 Reliquas quæstiones, an Deus voluerit labi Adamum, aut impulerit ad lapsum? aut quare lapsum non impediverit? et similes quæstiones deputamus inter curiosas, &c.—Coll. Conf. p. 478. Conf. Helv. Post. VIII.]

[3 Credimus totam Adami sobolem hac contagione infectam esse, quam peccatum originale vocamus, vitium videlicet ex propagatione manans, non autem ex imitatione duntaxat, sicut Pelagiani senserunt.—Harm. Conf. Sect. IV. p. 77. Conf. Gall. Art. x. Pelagianorum errorem damnamus, qui hoc peccatum originis nihil aliud esse asserunt, quam imitationem.—Ib. p. 80. Conf. Belg. Art. xv.]

[4 Peccatum autem intelligimus esse nativam illam hominis corruptionem, ex primis illis nostris parentibus, in nos omnes derivatam vel propagatam, qua concupiscentiis pravis immersi, ... nihil boni ex nobis ipsis facere, imo ne cogitare quidem possumus.—Ib. p. 67. Conf. Helv. Post. VIII. Peccatum originale ... vitium videlicet ex propagatione manans.—Ib. p. 77. Conf. Gall. Art. x. ... Innatum et hæreditarium peccatum originis in quo omnes concipimur et in hunc mundum nascimur.—Ib. p. 74. Conf. Bohem. cap. IV. Ib. p. 80. Conf. Aug. 1540. Art. II. Vid. supra, p. 96. n. 1. Est itaque peccatum originis, et propter lapsum primorum parentum et propter hanc depravationem quæ lapsum secuta est, nascentes reos esse iræ Dei et dignos æterna damnatione, &c.—Ibid. p. 85. Conf. Saxon. Art. II. Credimus et confitemur hominem initio justum ... postea autem propter inobedientiam Spiritu sancto privatum, ... Idque malum non in uno tantum Adamo constitisse, sed propagari in omnem posteritatem ejus.—Ibid. p. 88. Conf. Virtemb. cap. IV.]

The adversaries unto this truth.

Adversaries unto this truth are,

The Pelagians[5], and Family of Love[6], who say that original sin cometh not by propagation, but by imitation. (August. de Pec. Meritis, c. 1, 2, 3. Display in Allen's Conf.)

Such as ascribe original sin in no sort unto man, but either unto God, as did the Hermogenians[7], or unto the devil, as did the Valentinians[8]. (Tertul. August.)

The Manichees[9], who preached that this sin is another and a contrary substance within us, and proceedeth[10] not from our corrupted nature. (August. de Hæres.)

The Apollinarians[11], who held original sin to be from nature. (Athan. de Incarn. Christi.)

The Papists[12], who affirm, that some persons, and namely the Virgin Mary, is free from this original sin. (Concil. Trid. Sess. 5. decr. de Pec. Orig. Alb. Mag. c. 74, super Evang. Missus est, &c. Paulus de Palatio, in Matt. c. 11, p. 463.)

Proposition III.

Original sin remaineth in God his dear children.

The proof from God's word.

"I allow not that which I do; for what I would, that do I not; but what I hate, that do I; saith St Paul." (Rom. vii. 15.)

[5 Sentiunt ... ipsum peccatum non propagatione in alios homines ex primo homine, sed imitatione transisse.—August. Opp. Paris. 1836-38. Tom. x. col. 196. De Peccat. Mer. Lib. I. 9.]

[6 This reference the editor has been unable to verify.]

[7 ... Nescio qua possit evadere sententia Hermogenis, qui Deum, quoquomodo de materia malum condidit, sive voluntate, sive necessitate, sive ratione, non putet mali auctorem.—Tertull. Opp. Lut. 1634. p. 273. D. Adv. Herm. c. 16.]

[8 The editor has been unable to verify this reference.]

[9 Carnalem concupiscentiam, qua caro concupiscit adversus spiritum, non ex vitiata in primo homine natura nobis inesse infirmitatem; sed substantiam volunt esse contrariam; sic nobis adhærentem, ut quando liberamur atque purgamur separetur a nobis, et in sua natura etiam ipsa immortaliter vivat.—August. Opp. Tom. VIII. col. 52. De Hæres. xlvi.]

[10 Proceeded, 1607.]

[11 *Τί γὰρ περὶ τῆς ἁμαρτίας ὁριζόμενοι ταῦτα λαλεῖτε, φυσικὴν εἶναι τὴν ἁμαρτίαν λέγοντες, κατὰ τὸν ἀσεβέστατον Μανιχαῖον; ταῦτα οὕτως φρονεῖτε, κατήγοροι γινόμενοι τοῦ δημιουργοῦ τῆς φύσεως.*—Athanas. Opp. Colon. 1686. Tom. I. p. 627. c. De Incarn. Christi.]

[12 Declarat tamen hæc ipsa sancta synodus, non esse suæ intentionis comprehendere in hoc decreto, ubi de peccato originali agitur, beatam et immaculatam virginem Mariam, Dei genetricem.—Concil. Harduin. Paris. 1714. Tom. x. col. 29. Conc. Trid. Sess. v. Decret. de Pecc. Orig. 5. ... originale peccatum, a quo fuit beatissima virgo in utero sanctificata.—Albert. Mag. Opp. Lugd. 1651. Tom. xx. p. 38. Super Missus. Quæst. 36. § 2. The editor has been unable to meet with the work of Paulus de Palatio here referred to.]

Gal. v. 17. "The flesh lusteth against the spirit, and the spirit against the flesh: so that ye cannot do the same things that ye would."

James i. 14. "Every man is tempted, when he is drawn away by his own concupiscence, and is enticed."

1 Pet. ii. 11. "Dearly beloved, I beseech you as strangers abstain from fleshly lusts, which fight against the soul."

Conf. Helv. I. Art. VIII. & II. c. 8. Basil. Art. II. Gal. Art. XI. Saxon. Art. XI. Nothing is more true in the judgement of God's people[1].

The errors and adversaries unto this truth.

We stand therefore in this point,

Concil. Basil. Sess. 36. Test. Rhem. annot. Rom. v. 14. Against the Papists[2], who say, that original sin was not at all, much less remained in the Virgin Mary.

Giselb. Lib. altercat. Synag. & Eccles. c. 8. Against Giselbertus[3], whose doctrine is, that baptism once received, there is in the baptized no sin at all, either original or actual.

[1 Nam si quid frugis hic bonæ superstes est, vitiis nostris assidue debilitatum, in pejus vergit. Superat enim mali vis, et nec rationem persequi, nec mentis divinitatem excolere sinit.—Harm. Conf. IV. p. 72. Conf. Helvet. Prior. Art. VIII. Docemus ...in regeneratis remanere infirmitatem. Cum enim inhabitet in nobis peccatum, et caro in renatis obluctetur Spiritui, in finem usque vitæ nostræ, non expedite omnino perficiunt regenerati quod instituerant.—Ibid. p. 71. Conf. Helv. Post. IX. Not stated in the Confession of Basle. Vid. Ibid. p. 72. Conf. Basil. Art. II. Affirmamus quoque hoc vitium, etiam post baptismum, esse vere peccatum quod ad culpam attinet quamvis qui filii Dei sunt minime idcirco condemnentur ... præterea hanc perversitatem semper edere fructus aliquos malitiæ et rebellionis; adeo ut etiam qui sanctitate excellunt, quamvis ei resistant, multis tamen infirmitatibus et delictis sint contaminati, quamdiu in hoc mundo versantur.—Ibid. p. 77. Conf. Gall. Art. XI. Alia sunt peccata in renatis retinentibus fidem et bonam conscientiam, quæ non sunt corruptelæ fundamenti, nec sunt delicta contra conscientiam, sed sunt reliquiæ peccati originis, caligo, dubitationes, carnalis securitas, &c.—Ibid. p. 87. Conf. Saxon. Art. XI.]

[2 Nos vero ... doctrinam illam disserentem gloriosam virginem Dei genetricem Mariam, præveniente et operante divini numinis gratia singulari, nunquam actualiter subjacuisse originali peccato; sed immunem semper fuisse ab omni originali et actuali culpa, sanctamque et immaculatam; tanquam piam et consonam cultui ecclesiastico, fidei catholicæ rectæ rationi et sacræ scripturæ, ab omnibus catholicis approbandam fore tenendam et amplectendam diffinimus et declaramus, &c.—Concil. Harduin. Paris. 1715. Tom. VIII. col. 1266. Concil. Basil. Sess. XXXVI. Sin did reign, and thereupon death and damnation even till Moses *inclusivè*, that is to say, even till the end of his law. And that not in them only which actually sinned as Adam did, but in infants which never did actually offend, but only were born and conceived in sin ... Christ only excepted, being conceived without man's seed, and his mother for his honour and by his special protection (as many godly devout men judge) preserved from the same.—Test. Rhem. Rhemes, 1582. Annot. Rom. v. 14.]

[3 There is apparently an error in the reference.]

Against the Family of Love[4], who affirm that the elect and regenerate sin not. H. N. Document. sent. c. 2. § I. c. 13. § 5.

Against the Carpocratians[5], whereof some boasted themselves to be every way as innocent as our Saviour Christ. Iren. Lib. I. c. 24.

Against the Adamites, both old[6] and new[7], who said they were in so good a state as Adam was before his fall, therefore without original sin. Epiphan. Æneas Sylv. Hist. Bohem. c. 41.

Against the Begadores in Almaine[8], affirming they were impeccable, and had attained unto the very top and pitch of perfection in virtue and godliness. Carranza, Summa Conc.

Proposition IV.

Concupiscence, even in the regenerate, is sin.

[The proof from God's word[9].]

Concupiscence in whomsoever lusteth against the Spirit, Gal. v. 17.

[[4] There is demanded, How the children of Love or of God do behave themselves, &c. ... As touching this matter, there is much found witnessed in the holy scripture, (Levit. xix.; Deut. vi.; Mark xii.; Luke x.; Rom. xiii.), and it is also clearly testified in the serviceable Word (4 Spc. 23.) of the Holy Spirit of Love, that the true children of God have a good disposition and nature: and that they keep themselves always therein, uprightly, graciously, and peaceably, both before God and man ... for they are even from the youth up of their new birth, exercised in all well-doing and love. For that cause also, they cannot bring forth anything else but all good and love.—H. N. (Henry Nicholas) Documental Sentences, cap. II. § 1. For at that time when we have turned our love so wholly to the Word and his requiring; there can no assaulting indamage or hinder us: yea, although there came an hundred thousand. For we are so fast-knit and established with the love of our heart, on the Word and his requiring, that they all are not able to pluck us from the Word, nor to make us consent to any evil or vanity. For the Lord the strong God is then our helper, and releaser from all evil. (Matth. vi. b.; Luke xi. a.)—Ibid. cap. XIII. § 5.]

[[5] Quapropter et ad tantum elationis provecti sunt, ut quidam quidem similes se esse dicant Jesu ... Si quis autem plus quam ille contempserit ea, quæ sunt hic, posse meliorem quam illum esse.—Iren. Adv. Hær. Oxon. 1702. p. 100. Lib. I. c. 24.]

[[6] Εἰ δὲ δόξειε τινὰ, ὡς καὶ τοῦτο λέγουσιν, ἐν παραπτώματι γενέσθαι, οὔκετι τοῦτον συνάγουσι. φάσκουσι γὰρ αὐτὸν τὸν Ἀδὰμ τὸν βεβρωκότα ἀπὸ τοῦ ξύλου, καὶ κρίνουσι ἐξεώσθαι ὡς ἀπὸ τοῦ Παραδείσου, τουτέστι τῆς αὐτῶν ἐκκλησίας.—Epiphan. Opp. Paris. 1622. Tom. I. p. 459. Adv. Hær. Lib. II. Tom. I.]

[[7] Inter hæc et alia apud Bohemos nefanda et inaudita prius emersit hæresis. Picardus quidem ex Gallia Belgica ... Filium Dei se dixit, et Adam vocari ... Aiebat ceteros homines servos esse, se vero, et qui ex eis nascerentur, liberos.—Æn. Sylv. Hist. Bohem. Helmsted. 1699. cap. xli. p. 62.]

[[8] In eodem (sc. Concil. Vienn. General. sub Clem. V. celebrato) damnati sunt errores Begardorum et Beguinarum mulierum Alemaniæ. Primus, quod homo in vita præsenti tantum et talem perfectionis gradum potest acquirere, quod reddetur penitus impeccabilis, et amplius in gratia proficere non valebit.—Carranza, Summa Omn. Concil. Lovan. 1681. p. 381.]

[[9] Omitted in 1607.]

1 Pet. ii. 11. Rom. vii. 23. Rom. viii. 1. Gal. v. 17, 21. James i. 14, 15. Col. iii. 5.

fighteth against both the soul and the law of the mind, and therefore (but that there is no condemnation to them which are in Christ Jesus) it bringeth death and damnation.

"Mortify therefore your members which are upon earth," (saith St Paul unto the Colossians) "fornication, uncleanness, the inordinate affection, evil concupiscence, &c.; for the which things' sake the wrath of God cometh on the children of disobedience."

1 Pet. ii. 11.

And unto all Christians St Peter, "I beseech you, as strangers, abstain from fleshly lusts."

Confess. Helv. II. c. 9. Sax. Art. II. x.

To the same purpose is both the doctrine, and confessions[1] of God's people.

Errors and adversaries unto this truth.

Therefore we mislike their opinions, as unsound, which say that concupiscence either is no sin at all, or but a venial sin: the former was an assertion of the Pelagians[2], and is of the Papists; that latter was one of Glover's[3] errors.

Conf. Aug. Art. II.

Francis, the monk of Colen, counted concupiscence no sin, but said it was as natural, and so no more offensive before God for man to lust, than for the sun to keep his course.

Lomb. Lib. II. Dist. 32.

Petrus Lombardus[4] saith, that concupiscence afore baptism is both a punishment and a sin; but after baptism is no sin, but only a punishment.

Catech. Trid. præcept. 9.

The church of Rome both teacheth[5], that the power of lusting is not, but the use of wicked concupiscence is evil, and

[[1] Harm. Conf. IV. p. 71. Conf. Helv. Post. cap. ix. See above, p. 100, n. 1. ...Expresse nominamus hæc mala depravationem quæ sæpe nominatur ab antiquis scriptoribus mala concupiscentia... Hanc malam concupiscentiam dicimus esse peccatum.—Ibid. p. 86. Conf. Saxon. Art. II. Reprehendendus est etiam error adversariorum ... qui dicunt malum concupiscentiæ nobiscum nascens non esse peccatum nec malum pugnans cum lege seu voluntate Dei ... confiteatur vero dolore, adhuc in renato multa peccata et magnas sordes esse dignas ira Dei.—Ibid. Art. IX.]

[[2] Damnant Pelagianos qui negant peccatum originis et sentiunt defectus illos seu concupiscentiam esse res indifferentes seu pœnas tantum, &c.—Coll. Conf. p. 80. Conf. Aug. 1540. Art. II.]

[[3] See below, p. 103, note 7.]

[[4] Nec post baptismum remanet (concupiscentia) ad reatum, quia non imputatur in peccatum, sed tantum pœna peccati est: ante baptismum vero, pœna est et culpa.—Pet. Lombard. Sent. Col. Agr. 1576. Lib. II. Dist. XXXII. p. 212.]

[[5] Itaque hoc interdicto (sc. Non concupisces, &c.) non ipsa concupiscendi vis, qua tum ad bonum, tum ad malum uti licet, sed usus pravæ cupiditatis, quæ carnis concupiscentia, et peccati fomes vocatur, ac, si animi assensionem adjunctam habeat, semper in vitiis numeranda est, omnino prohibetur.—Catech. Conc. Trid. Rom. 1566. p. 288.]

numbered amongst most grievous sins; and decreeth[6] how concupiscence is not sin, but proceedeth from sin, and inclineth unto sin. Concil. Trid. Sess. 5. decreto de Pec. Orig.

Glover[7], the Brownist, said, that the intemperate affections of the mind, issuing from concupiscence, are but venial sins. Bredwell, Detect. 69, 119.

ARTICLE X.

Of Free-Will.

(1) *The condition of man after the fall of Adam is such, that he cannot turn and prepare himself, by his own natural strength and good works,* (2) *to faith and calling upon God: Wherefore we have no power to do good works pleasant and acceptable to God,* (3) *without the grace of God*[8] *preventing us, that we may have a good will, and working with us, when we have that good will.*

The propositions.

1. Man of his own strength may do outward and evil works before he is regenerate.

2. Man cannot do any work that good is and godly, being not yet regenerate.

3. Man may perform and do good works, when he is prevented by the grace of Christ, and renewed by the Holy Ghost.

[6 Hanc concupiscentiam quam aliquando Apostolus peccatum appellat, sancta synodus declarat ecclesiam catholicam nunquam intellexisse peccatum appellari, quod vere et proprie in renatis peccatum sit; sed quia ex peccato est, et ad peccatum inclinat.—Concil. Harduin. Paris. 1714. Tom. x. col. 29. Concil. Trid. Sess. v. Decr. de Pecc. Orig. 5.]

[7 Then, because he saw likewise, that the way was not so smooth and fair, but you should prick your feet often with the thorns of concupiscence, and ray your clothes with the clay of intemperate affections, he telleth you those be but venial sins against which you have not grace given you of God.—Bredwell's Detection. Lond. 1568. p. 69. In p. 119 the following are given as some of Glover's opinions: 1. That the first motions are no sin. 2. That there are sins of their own nature venial.]

[8 Grace of God by Christ preventing us, 1675.]

Proposition I.

Man of his own strength may do outward and evil works before he is regenerate.

The proof from God's word.

We deny not, that man, not regenerate, hath free-will to do the works of nature, for the preservation of the body, and bodily estate; which thing had and have the brute beast, and profane gentiles, as it is also well observed in our neighbour churches[1]. Besides, man hath free-will to perform the works of Satan, both in thinking, willing, and doing that which is evil. For the imaginations of the thoughts of man's heart only are evil continually, evil even from his youth. A truth confessed by our brethren[2].

Confess. Helv. II. c. 9. August. Art XVIII. Saxon. Art. III. IV. VII.

Gen. vi. 5. Ibid. viii. 21. Conf. Helv. II. c. 9. & I. Art. IX. Bohem. c. 4.

Errors and adversaries unto this truth.

A false persuasion is it therefore, that man hath no power to move either his body so much as unto outward things, as Laur. Valla[3] dreamed; or his mind unto sin, as the Mani-

Simon Pauli Meth. par. 2. de Lib. Ar.

[[1] Ceterum nemo negat in externis et regenitos, et non regenitos habere liberum arbitrium. Habet enim homo hanc constitutionem cum animantibus aliis (quibus non est inferior) communem, ut alia velit, alia nolit.—Harm. Conf. Sect. IV. p. 70. Ex. Helv. Conf. Post. c. IX. De libero arbitrio docent, quod humana voluntas habeat aliquam libertatem ad efficiendam civilem justitiam et deligendas res rationi subjectas.—Ibid. p. 81. Conf. Aug. Art. XVIII. Expresse discernimus disciplinam seu justitiam quam potest efficere homo non renatus, a justitia fidei, et novitate de qua concionatur evangelium.—Conf. Saxon. Art. III. Semper in ecclesia homines recte eruditi ... docuerunt in homine libertatem voluntatis talem esse ad regendos externos motus membrorum, qua etiam non renati utcunque disciplinam, quæ est externa obedientia juxta legem, præstare possint.—Ibid. Art. IV. ... Externam disciplinam homines naturalibus viribus utcunque præstare possunt.—Ibid. Art. VIII. Syll. Conf. pp. 249, 259, 262.]

[[2] Quoad malum sive peccatum, homo non coactus vel a Deo vel a diabolo, sed sua sponte, malum facit; et hac parte liberrimi est judicii.—Harm. Conf. Sect. IV. p. 69. Conf. Helv. Post. cap. IX. Sic homini liberum arbitrium tribuimus, ut qui scientes et volentes agere nos bona et mala experimur quod mala quidem agere sponte nostra queamus.—Ibid. p. 72. Conf. Helv. Prior. Art. IX. ... Hominis libera voluntas, quæ tamen ad malum conversa, per libidinem et cupiditates malas, perverseque concupiscendo, malum deligit. ... duæ legis tabulæ, prima et secunda, Mosi a Deo datæ sunt ut in primis se noscerent homines, quod in peccatis concepti et nati, et statim ab ortu et natura sua peccatores sint, plenique cupiditatum et inclinationum seu proclivitatum malarum.—Ibid. p. 74. Conf. Bohem. cap. IV.]

[[3] Error Vallæ ... nullam omnino esse humanæ voluntatis libertatem, etiam quod ad locomotivam attinet, sed omnia etiam impiorum hominum scelera fieri fatali necessitate.—Sim. Paul. Meth. Pars Sec. Magdeb. 1572. De Lib. Arb. p. 93. b.]

chees[4] maintained, affirming how man is not voluntarily brought, but necessarily driven unto sin. Aug. Ep. 28.

Proposition II.

Man cannot do any work that good is and godly, being not as yet regenerate.

The proof from God's word.

"The wisdom of the flesh is enmity against God: for it is not subject to the law of God, neither indeed can be. They that are in the flesh cannot please God." Rom. viii. 7, 8.

"The natural man perceiveth not the things of the Spirit of God; for they are foolishness unto him: neither can he know them, because they are spiritually discerned." 1 Cor. ii. 14.

"No man can say that Jesus is the Lord, but by the Holy Ghost." 1 Cor. xii. 3.

"We are not sufficient of ourselves to think anything as of ourselves, but our sufficiency is from God." 2 Cor. iii. 5.

"Without me ye can do nothing," saith our Saviour Christ. John xv. 5.

Which is the confession[5] of the godly reformed. Conf. Helv. I. Art. IX. & II. c. 9. Basil. Art. II. Bohem. c. 4. August. Art. XVIII. Belg. Art. XIV.

The adversaries unto this truth.

Adversaries unto this truth are all such as hold that naturally there is free-will in us, and that unto the best things. So thought the Pharisees, the Sadducees, the Pelagians[6], and August. de Pec. Mer. Lib. III.

[4 The passage intended is probably this: ... Manichæus ... dicit ... naturam boni cogi male facere ab ea natura mali, quæ bonum non potest velle.—Aug. Opp. Paris. 1836-8. Tom. x. col. 1551. c. contr. Julianum, Lib. I. c. 97.]

[5 ... Bona vero amplecti et persequi nisi gratia Christi illustrati, excitati et impulsi non queamus.—Harm. Conf. IV. p. 72. Conf. Helvet. Post. cap. IX. Proinde nullum est ad bonum homini arbitrium liberum nondum renato, vires nullæ ad perficiendum bonum.—Ibid. p. 70. Conf. Helv. Post. cap. IX. ... Natura nostra vitiata est, ac in tantam propensionem ad peccandum devenit, ut nisi eadem per Spiritum sanctum redintegretur, homo per se nihil boni faciat aut velit.—Ibid. p. 72. Conf. Basil. Art. II. Voluntas enim hominis quæ antea libera erat, nunc ita corrupta, perturbata et debilitata est ut nunc deinceps a se sineque gratia divina, nullum plenum delectum seu arbitrium optionemve, et neque studium aut propensionem, nedum facultatem habeat, bonum quod Deo placeat deligendi.—Ibid. p. 75. Conf. Bohem. cap. IV. Sed non habet (humana voluntas) vim sine Spiritu sancto efficiendæ justitiæ spiritualis, &c.—Ibid. p. 81. Conf. Aug. 1540. Art. XVIII. Nulla enim mens, nulla voluntas Dei voluntati acquiescit, in qua Christus ipse non sit prius operatus, quod et ipse nos docet, dicens, sine me nihil potestis facere.—Ibid. p. 79. Conf. Belg. Art. XIV.]

[6 Sunt enim quidam tantum præsumentes de libero humanæ voluntatis arbitrio, ut ad non peccandum nec adjurandos nos divinitus opinentur, semel ipsi

Idem contra Petil. cap. 19. Zuing. contra Catabapt.

the Donatists[1]: and the same affirm the Anabaptists[2] and Papists. For say the Papists,

Gab. Biel. 3, Sent. dist. 37.

Man by the force and power of nature may love God above all things[3].

Conc. Trid. Sess. 6, c. 1.

Man hath free-will to perform even spiritual and heavenly things[4].

Test. Rhem. an. Matt. xx. 16. Ibid. annot. marg. p. 408.

"Men believe not but of their own free-will." "It is in a man's free-will to believe, or not to believe, to obey, or disobey, the gospel or truth preached[5]."

Hills' quart. 13. reas.

The Catholic (Popish) religion teacheth free-will[6].

Proposition III.

Man may perform and do good works, when he is prevented by the grace of Christ, and renewed by the Holy Ghost.

The proof from God's word.

In a man prevented by the grace of Christ, and regenerate by the Holy Spirit, both the understanding is enlightened,

naturæ nostræ concesso liberæ voluntatis arbitrio.—August. Opp. Paris. 1836-8. Tom. x. col. 243. De Pecc. Mer. Lib. II.]

[1 Petil. dixit: Dicit enim Dominus Christus, *Nemo venit ad me, nisi quem Pater attraxerit.* Cur autem vos non liberum arbitrium unicuique sequi permittitis, cum ipse Dominus Deus liberum arbitrium dederit hominibus, viam tamen justitiæ ostendens, ne quis forsitan nescius deperiret?—Ibid. Tom. IX. col. 433. Contr. Litt. Petil. Lib. II. § 185.]

[2 Jam liberum arbitrium et proxime istud operum justitiam erigunt: si enim nostræ est vel electionis vel potestatis ambulare in resurrectione Christi, aut cum eo in mortem sepeliri, jam liberum est cuique et Christianum esse et optimum.—Zuingl. Opp. Tigur. 1545. Tom. II. p. 18. b. Elench. Contr. Catabapt.]

[3 Si quis voluerit ingredi ad vitam æternam, necesse est ut servet mandata ex charitate: quia necesse est, ut servet mandata meritorie, et par consequens ex charitate.—Gab. Biel. Comment. in Sent. Brixiæ. 1574. in Lib. III. Dist. 37. p. 356.]

[4 Primum declarat sancta synodus ad justificationis doctrinam probe et sincere intelligendam, oportere ut unusquisque agnoscat et fateatur, quod cum omnes homines in prævaricatione Adæ innocentiam perdidissent, facti immundi, et ut Apostolus inquit; natura filii iræ... usque adeo servi erant peccati, et sub potestate diaboli ac mortis, ut non modo gentes per vim naturæ; sed ne Judæi quidem per ipsam etiam literam legis Moysi inde liberari aut surgere possent: tametsi in eis liberum arbitrium minime extinctum esset, viribus licet attenuatum et inclinatum.—Concil. Harduin. Paris. 1714. Tom. x. col. 33. Concil. Trident. Sess. VI. Decr. de Justif. cap. I.]

[5 Test. Rhem. Rhemes, 1582. p. 58. Annot. on Matt. xx. 16, and p. 408. Marg. Annot. on Rom. x. 16.]

[6 The Catholic (doctrine) affirmeth that we have free-will.—Hills' Quartron of Reasons of Catholic Religion, Antwerp. 1600. Reason XIII. p. 66.]

so that he knoweth the secrets and will of God, and the mind is altogether changed, and the body enabled to do good works.

To this purpose the scriptures are plentiful.

"I will put my law in their inward parts, and write it in their hearts." Jer. xxxi. 33.

"No man knoweth the Father but the Son, and he to whom the Son will reveal him." Matt. xi. 27. Luke x. 22.

"Blessed art thou, Simon, the son of Jonas; for flesh and blood hath not revealed it unto thee, but my Father which is in heaven." Matt. xvi. 17.

"No man can say that Jesus is the Lord, but by the Holy Ghost." 1 Cor. xii. 3.

"To one is given by the Spirit the word of wisdom; and to another the word of knowledge by the same Spirit; and to another faith by the same Spirit; and to another the gifts of healing by the same Spirit; and to another the operations of great works; and to another prophecy; and to another the discerning of spirits; and to another diversities of tongues; and to another the interpretation of tongues; &c." 1 Cor. xii. 8.

God, he "purifieth man's heart;" "worketh in us both the will and the deed;" "the Spirit helpeth our infirmities; for we know not what to pray as we ought, &c." "Such were some of you, but ye are washed, but ye are sanctified, but ye are justified, in the name of the Lord Jesus, and by the Spirit of our God." Acts xv. 9. Phil. ii. 13. Rom. viii. 26. 1 Cor. vi. 11.

"Unto you it is given for Christ, that not only ye should believe in him, but also suffer for his sake." Phil. i. 29.

And this do the churches[7] of God believe and confess. Confess. Helv. II. c. 9. August. Art. XVIII. Bohem. c. 4. Saxon. Art. IV.

[[7] In regeneratione, intellectus illuminatur per Spiritum sanctum ut et mysteria et voluntatem Dei intelligat. Et voluntas ipsa non tantum mutatur per Spiritum sed etiam instruitur facultatibus, ut sponte velit et possit bonum.—Harm. Conf. Sect. IV. p. 70. Conf. Helv. Post. cap. IX. Efficitur autem spiritualis justitia in nobis, quum adjuvamur a Spiritu sancto.—Ibid. p. 81. Conf. August. 1540. Art. XVIII. Etsi enim ipsa (humana voluntas) sua sponte volensque prolapsa concidit, a se tamen viribusque propriis non potuit a lapsu resurgere, neque hodie etiam absque Dei propitia ope quicquam potest.—Ibid. p. 75. Conf. Bohem. cap. IV. Homo nequaquam potest se liberare a peccato et morte æterna, viribus naturalibus: sed hæc liberatio et conversio hominis ad Deum et novitas spiritualis fit per Filium Dei vivificantem nos Spiritu suo sancto, ut dictum est: si quis Spiritum Christi non habet, hic non est ejus. Et voluntas accepto Spiritu sancto, jam non est otiosa.—Ibid. p. 86. Conf. Saxon. Art. IV. al. Art. V.]

ARTICLE XI.

Of the Justification of Man.

We are accounted righteous before God, only for (1) *the merit of our Lord and Saviour Jesus Christ* (2) *by faith, and* (3) *not for our own works or deservings.*

Wherefore that we are justified by faith only is a most wholesome doctrine, and very full of comfort, &c.

The propositions.

1. Only for the merit of our Lord and Saviour Christ, 2. Only by faith, 3. Not for our own works or deservings,	are we accounted righteous before God.

Proposition I.

Only for the merit of our Lord and Saviour Christ we are accounted righteous before God.

The proof from the word of God.

By Christ his blood only we are cleansed.

John i. 29. He is "the Lamb of God, which taketh away the sin of the world."

Rom. iii. 24. "We are justified freely by his grace, through the redemption that is in Christ Jesus."

1 Cor. vi. 20. 1 Pet. i. 19. 1 John i. 7. We are bought with a price, even with the precious blood of Christ, the Lamb undefiled and without spot, which cleanseth us from all sin.

By his only righteousness we are justified.

Rom. v. 19. "By the obedience of one many be made righteous."

Ibid. x. 4. 1 Cor. i. 30. 2 Cor. v. 21. Phil. iii. 20. "Christ is the end of the law for righteousness unto every one that believeth." "He of God is made unto us wisdom, and righteousness, and sanctification, and redemption:" and "we are made the righteousness of God in him." And therefore "from heaven we look for the Saviour, even the Lord Jesus Christ."

Conf. Helv. II. c. 15. Bohem. c. 6. Gal. Art. XVIII. Belg. Art. XXII. August. Art. IV. Wittemb. Art. V. Suevica, c. 3. And this is the faith and confession[1] of all churches reformed.

[[1] Certissimum est autem omnes nos esse natura peccatores et mortuos ... justificari autem id est absolvi a peccatis et morte, a Judice Deo, solius Christi gratia

Errors and adversaries to this truth.

This truth is neither believed nor acknowledged,

Of the Atheists, who are neither persuaded of the life to come, nor understand the mysteries of man's salvation through the merits of Christ.

Nor of the Pharisees and their followers, who think that by civil and external righteousness we are justified before God. Matt. v. 20.

Nor of Matthew Hamant[2], who held that man is justified by God's mere mercy without respect unto the merits of Christ. Holin. Chro. fol. 1299.

Nor of Galeotus Martius[3], which was of opinion that all nations and persons whosoever, living according to the rules of nature, should be saved and inherit everlasting happiness. P. Jovius, Elog. doct. vir. p. 97.

Nor of the Turks[4], who think that so many as either go Lonic. Turc. Hist. Com. I. Lib. II. par. 2. c. 14, 15, 18.

et nullo nostro merito aut respectu.—Harm. Conf. Sect. IX. p. 168. Conf. Helv. Post. cap. XV. Et hæc justitia, seu justificatio est remissio peccatorum, sublatio pœnæ æternæ, quam Dei severa justitia deposcit, et Christi justitia seu imputatione hujus convestiri, &c.... Viva autem et nunquam exarescens scaturigo hujus justificationis est ipse Dominus noster Jesus Christus solus, operibus illis suis salvificis, &c.—Ibid. pp. 176-7. Conf. Bohem. cap. VI. Credimus totam nostram justitiam positam esse in peccatorum nostrorum remissione ... omnique virtutum et meritorum opinione abjecta, in sola Jesu Christi obedientia prorsus acquiescimus, quæ quidem nobis imputatur, tum ut tegantur omnia nostra peccata, tum etiam ut gratiam coram Deo nanciscamur.—Ibid. p. 183. Conf. Gall. Art. XVIII. Quæ fides Jesum Christum cum omnibus suis meritis amplectitur, illumque sibi, ceu proprium effectum vindicat, nihilque deinceps extra illum quærit... Christus igitur ipse est nostra justitia, qui omnia sua nobis merita imputat, &c.—Ibid. p. 184. Conf. Belg. Art. XXII. ... quod gratis nobis propter Christum donentur remissio peccatorum et justificatio per fidem, qua credere et confiteri debemus, hæc nobis dari propter Christum, qui pro nobis factus est hostia, et placavit patrem.—Ibid. p. 187. Conf. Aug. 1540. Art. IV. The confession of 1531 has, Item docent, quod homines non possint justificari coram Deo propriis viribus, meritis aut operibus, sed gratis justificentur propter Christum, per fidem; quum credunt se in gratiam recipi et peccata remitti propter Christum qui sua morte pro nostris peccatis satisfecit. Hanc fidem imputat Deus pro justitia coram ipso. —Ibid. p. 188. Homo enim fit Deo acceptus, et reputatur coram eo justus propter solum Filium Dei, Dominum nostrum Jesum Christum, per fidem.—Ibid. p. 218. Conf. Virtemb. Art. v. Primum igitur, quum jam aliquot annis, ad justificationem hominis requiri propria ejus opera traditum sit, nostri hanc totam divinæ benevolentiæ Christique merito acceptam referendam, solaque fide percipi docuerunt.—Ibid. p. 221. Conf. Suev. cap. III.]

[2 Holinsh. Chron. Lond. 1587. Vol. III. fol. 1299.]

[3 Scripsit etiam (Galeottus) et malo quidem infortunio, quædam in sacra moralique philosophia: nam ex ea lectione, quum omnibus gentibus integre et puriter veluti ex justa naturæ lege viventibus æternos cœlestis auræ fructus paratos diceret, a cucullatis sacerdotibus accusatus damnatusque est.—Paul. Jov. Elog. Vir. Doct. p. 90. Basil. 1577.]

[4 Docetur in libris Turcarum atque Æthiopum, eum, qui peregrinatione sus-

on pilgrimage unto Mecca, or do kiss the sepulchre of Mahomet, are justified before God, and thereby do obtain remission of their sins.

Display in Allen's Conf.

Nor of the Family of Love[1], who teach by the shedding of Christ his blood is meant the spreading of the Spirit in our hearts.

Nor of the Papists, whose doctrine is, that

Test. Rhem. an. Rom. viii. 17.

1. Though Christ hath suffered for all men in general, yet not only each man must suffer for his own part in particular, but also that the works of one man may satisfy for another[2].

Ibid. annot. Col. i. 24.

Vaux, Catech. cap. 4. Test. Rhem. an. Joh. xiii. 10.

2. They teach next, that sins venial are done away and "purged by prayer, alms-deeds, by the worthy receiving of the blessed sacrament of the altar, by taking of holy water, knocking upon the breast with holy meditation, the bishop's blessing and such like[3]," by holy water and such ceremonies, sacred ceremonies[4], as

Test. Rhem. an. marg. pag. 258.

Confiteor, tundo, conspergor, conteror, oro,
Signor, edo, dono, per hæc venialia pono:

that is,

I am confest unto the priest;
I knock mine heart and breast with fist;
With holy water I am besprent,
And with contrition all yrent;

cepta, Mecham semel adierit, æternæ beatitudinis certum esse, nec unquam vel purgatorio igni, vel aliis pœnis infernalibus afficiendum.—Lonicer. Turc. Hist. Francf. 1584. Tom. I. p. 112. Lib. II. Part. 2. c. 14. In templo cum per tres horas continuas precationi indulserunt, inde quanto possint impetu cursim in proximi montis fastigium tendunt, ea festinatione, ut per totum corpus sudor diffundatur. Nam una cum sudore omnes peccati labes defluere persuasum habent.—Ibid. p. 114. c. 15. Hoc sepulcrum (sc. Mahometis) illud est, quod Turcæ et Æthiopes magna religione et frequentia petunt, remissionem peccatorum sibi pollicentes, si illud exosculati fuerint.—Ibid. p. 117. c. 18.]

[[1] The reference appears to be to "A Confession made by two of the Family of Love, &c." in the "Displaying of the Family," by J. R. (John Rogers), Lond. 1579. If so there is an error in the reference. See Hen. More's Theolog. Works, Lond. 1708. Bk. VI. c. 16. pp. 182-3.]

[[2] See above, p. 58, notes 6, 7.]

[[3] Vaux, Catech. Antv. 1574, c. 4. p. 70.]

[[4] And because this (the washing of the disciples' feet) was only a ceremony, and yet had such force, both now and afterward used of the apostles, that it purged smaller offences and filthiness of the soul, as St Ambrose and St Bernard gather, it may not seem strange that holy water and such ceremonies may remit venial sins.—Test. Rhem. Rhemes, 1582. Annot. Joh. xiii. 10. "Venial sins taken away by sacred ceremonies," is the marginal annotation on the above passage, p. 258.]

I pray to God and heav'nly host;
I cross my forehead at every post;
I eat my Saviour in the bread;
I deal my dole when I am dead:
And doing so, I know I may
My venial sins soon put away.

And sins mortal, not by the merits of Christ only, but many ways besides are cleansed, think the said Papists; as by the merits of dead saints, namely of St Mary the Virgin:

Threnosa compassio dulcissimæ Dei Matris
Perducat nos ad gaudia summi Dei Patris[5].

The pitiful compassion of God's best pleasing Mother
Bring us to the joys of God the Sovereign Father.

And of Thomas Becket:

Horæ B. Virg. S. Mar. secundum usum Sarum.

Tu per Thomæ sanguinem, quem pro te impendit,
Fac nos, Christe, scandere, quo Thomas ascendit[6].

By the blood of Thomas, which he for thee expended,
Make us, Christ, to climb up where Thomas ascended.

By Agnus Deis[7], whereof they say,

Peccatum frangit, ut Christi sanguis, et angit[8]. Cerem. Lib. I. tit. 7.

It breaketh sin, and doeth good,
As well as Christ his precious blood.

By reading certain parcels of scripture, according to their vulgars;

Per Evangelica dicta,
Deleantur nostra delicta[9]. Breviar. secundum Sarum.

Through the sayings and words evangelical,
Our sins blot out, and vices all.

Proposition II.

Only by faith are we accounted righteous before God.

The proof from God's word.

"Only believe;" "all that believe in Christ shall receive Mar. v. 36. Acts x. 43.

[5 Horæ Beatiss. V. Mariæ ad Usum Sarisb. Eccl. Par. 1535. fo. xxii. where "summi cœli patris."]

[6 Ibid. fo. xix.]

[7 Agnos Deis, 1607 and 1633.]

[8 Ceremon. Lib. Rom. 1560. Lib. I. Tit. 7. p. 38.]

[9 Per hæc sancta evangelica dicta deleantur peccata atque universa mala delicta nostra. Amen.—Horæ Beatiss. Virg. Mar. &c. fo. ii.]

Acts xiii. 39. remission of sins;" "from all things, from which ye could not be justified by the law of Moses, by Christ every one that believeth is justified."

Rom. i. 16. "The gospel is the power of God unto salvation to every one that believeth."

Rom. iv. 5. "To him that worketh not, but believeth in him that justifieth the ungodly, his faith is counted for righteousness."

Rom. x. 4. "Christ is the end of the law for righteousness to every one that believeth."

Gal. ii. 16. "Know that a man is not justified by the works of the law, but by the faith of Jesus Christ, &c."

Gal. iii. 8, 9. "God would justify the gentiles through faith, &c. They which be of faith, are blessed with faithful Abraham."

Ephes. ii. 8. "By grace are ye saved, through faith, and that not of yourselves."

Phil. iii. 8, 9. "Yea, doubtless, I think all things but loss for the excellent knowledge sake of Christ Jesus my Lord, for whom I have counted all things loss, and do judge them to be dung, that I might win Christ, and might be found in him, not having mine own righteousness, which is of the law, but that which is through the faith of Christ, even the righteousness which is of God through faith."

Confess. Helv. II. c. 16. Basil. Art. VIII. Bohem. c. 6, 7. Gal. Art. XX. Belg. Art. XXII. August. Art. IV. Saxon. Art. III. VIII. Wittemb. Art. IV. Suevica, cap. 3.

The churches of Christ by their public confessions[1] give testimony unto this truth.

[[1] Ergo quia fides Christum justitiam nostram recipit, et gratiæ Dei in Christo omnia tribuit, ideo fidei tribuitur justificatio, &c.—Harm. Conf. Sect. IX. p. 169. Conf. Helv. Post. cap. XV. Confitemur remissionem peccatorum per fidem in Jesum Christum crucifixum.—Ibid. p. 174. Conf. Basil. Art. VIII. (al. Art. IX. Disp. 22.) Hæc sola fides et hæc intimi cordis in Jesum Christum Dominum nostrum fiducia justificat, seu justum facit hominem coram Deo, absque ullis operibus, &c. ... Eos qui, per solam fidem in Christum Jesum, gratia divina gratis absque ullis meritis justi facti sunt et Deo accepti, &c.—Ibid. pp. 176-8. Conf. Bohem. capp. vi. vii. Credimus nos sola fide fieri hujus justitiæ participes, &c.—Ibid. p. 183. Conf. Gall. Art. XX. Merito igitur jureque dicimus cum D. Paulo, nos sola fide justificari seu fide absque operibus legis.—Ibid. p. 185. Conf. Belg. Art. XXII. Hic honos Christi non debet transferri in nostra opera. Ideo Paulus dicit, gratis salvati estis. Item, ideo ex fide gratis, ut sit firma promissio, &c. —Ibid. pp. 187-8. Conf. Aug. 1540. Art. IV. See also Proposit. I. note 1. p. 109. In ecclesiis nostris dicitur, fide sola justificamur, quod sic intelligimus et declaramus: Gratis propter solum Mediatorem, non propter nostram contritionem seu alia nostra merita donamur remissione peccatorum et reconciliatione.—Ibid. p. 206. Conf. Saxon. Art. III. Primum statuat renatus se reconciliatum esse Deo, sola fide, id est, fiducia Mediatoris, et personam certo reputari justam propter Filium Dei Mediatorem, gratis propter ipsius meritum.—Ibid. p. 214. Conf. Saxon. Art. VIII. [IX.] Sentimus, veteres ac majores nostros recte dixisse. Nos coram Deo sola fide justificari.—Ibid. p. 218. Conf. Virtemb. Art. V. Conf. Suev. cap. III. See above, Proposit. I. note 1. p. 109.]

The errors and adversaries unto this truth.

Partakers of the profit and sweetness of this doctrine are not they which be altogether ignorant of this mystery.

Nor they who know the same, but apply it not to their own souls and consciences, but altogether despise the same; as did Pilate, in condemning Christ; Herod, in killing James; Agrippa, in not defending Paul; the Jews, in persecuting the apostles; and do the devils, and many ungodly persons, tyrants, false Christians, and apostates. Matt. xxvii. 24. Acts xii. 1. Acts xxvi. 26. James ii. 19.

Nor they which teach not a sure confidence in Jesus Christ, but an historical knowledge of him; as do the Papists[2]. Canis. Cat. c. 1. Vaux, Cat. c. 1. Test. Rhem. ann. Rom. iv. 24.

Nor they which hold that all and every man is to remain doubtful whether he shall be saved or no; as do the same Papists[3]. 1 Tim. iii. 15. Concil. Trid. sess. 6. c. 9. Test. Rhem. annot. Rom. v. 1.

[[2] The notion mentioned in the text is nowhere expressly laid down in the Catechism. Its language is as follows: *Quid fidei nomine intelligitur?* Dei donum et lumen quo illustratus homo, firmiter assentitur atque adhæret iis, quæ ut credantur, sunt divinitus revelata, et ab ecclesia nobis proposita. Cujusmodi sunt, Deum esse trinum et unum, e nihilo creatum mundum, Deum factum esse hominem, &c.—Canis. Opus Catechist. Colon. 1606. cap. I. Quæst. iv. p. 3.

Faith is the gift of God, and light whereby we be lightened within, and assuredly be induced to believe all things that be revealed in Christ's church to us, either by word written, or unwritten.—Vaux. Catech. Antv. 1574. c. I. p. 3. *For us to whom it shall be reputed.* By this it is most plain against our adversaries, that the faith which was reputed for justice to Abraham, was his belief of an article revealed to him by God, that is to say, his assent and credit given to God's speeches: as in us his posterity according to the Spirit, it is here plainly said that justice shall be reputed to us by believing the articles of Christ's death and resurrection, and not by any fond special faith, *fiducia*, or confidence of each man's own salvation, to establish the which fiction, they make no account of the faith catholic, that is, wherewith we believe the articles of the faith, which only justifieth, but call it by contempt an historical faith: so as they may term Abraham's faith, and our lady's faith, of which it was said, Beata quæ credidisti. Blessed art thou that hast believed. And so in truth they deny as well the justification by faith as by works.—Test. Rhem. Rhemes, 1582. Ann. Rom. iv. 24. p. 393. In the Annot. on 1 Tim. iii. 15, it is said that the church as free from all error is to be believed. "We must believe, hear, and obey the same, as the touch-stone, pillar, and firmament of truth. For all this is comprised in that principle, *I believe the catholic church.* And therefore the council of Nice said, I believe in the church, that is, I believe and trust the same in all things."—Ibid. p. 572.]

[[3] Sed neque illud asserendum est, oportere eos, qui vere justificati sunt, absque ulla omnino dubitatione apud semetipsos statuere, se esse justificatos; neminemque a peccatis absolvi ac justificari, nisi eum qui certo credat se absolutum et justificatum esse; &c.—Concil. Harduin. Paris. 1714. Tom. x. col. 36. Conc. Trid. Sess. VI. cap. 9.

Let us have. Whether we read, *Let us have peace,* as divers also of the Greek doctors (Chrysost. Orig. Theodor. Œcum. Theophyl.) do, or, *We have peace,* it

Nor they which teach that man is justified,

2 Tim. i. Bale, Myst. of Iniquit. p. 53.

Either by works without faith, as did the false apostles in Asia, and do the Turks and Anabaptists[1]:

Acts xv. 1. Eus. Lib. III. c. 24. Test. Rhem. an. Luke vii. marg.

Or by faith and works, as both the pseud-apostles at Hierusalem, the Ebionites[2], and the Papists[3], with the Russians[4];

Luke x. 28. John iii. 18. James ii. 25. Russ. Commweal, c. 23.

Or neither by faith, nor works, as they which contemn both faith in Christ Jesus, and good works too, hoping yet to be saved, as the carnally secure worldlings.

Catech. c. 3. De formand. S. concion. Lib. I. c. 11. Test. Rhem. an. Act. viii. 18.

Neither shall they be partakers of the sweetness of this truth, which say, that for Christians to trust only by Christ his passion, or by faith only to be saved, is a breach of the first commandment, as Vaux[5]; is the doctrine of devils, as Friar Laurence à Villavincentia[6]; and the doctrine of Simon Magus, as do the Rhemists[7].

maketh nothing for the vain security and infallible certainty which our adversaries say every man ought to have upon his presumed justification by faith, that himself is in God's favour and sure to be saved: *peace towards God*, being here nothing else but the sincere rest, tranquillity and comfort of mind and conscience, upon the hope he hath that he is reconciled to God. Sure it is that the catholic faith, by which and none other men be justified, neither teacheth nor breedeth any such security of salvation. And therefore they have made to themselves another faith which they call *Fiduciam*, quite without the compass of the creed and scriptures.—Test. Rhem. Rhemes, 1582. Ann. Rom. v. 1. p. 394.]

[1 Rather should the Anabaptists seem to be of your sort (sc. the Papists) than of theirs. For they have in a manner the same opinion of free will, and of justification by works, that you have.—Bale, Mystery of Iniquity. Genev. 1545. p. 53.]

[2 *Δεῖν δὲ πάντως αὐτοῖς τῆς νομικῆς θρησκείας, ὡς μὴ ἂν διὰ μόνης τῆς εἰς τὸν Χριστὸν πίστεως, καὶ τοῦ κατ' αὐτὴν βίου σωθησομένοις.*—Euseb. Eccl. Hist. Cant. 1720. Lib. III. c. 27. p. 121.]

[3 Not only faith (as you may perceive), but love or charity, obtaineth remission of sins.—Test. Rhem. Marg. Annot. (Luke vii. 47) p. 157. *This do and thou shalt live.* Not by faith only, but by keeping God's commandments we obtain life everlasting: not only by believing but by doing.—Annot. Luke x. 28. He that believeth in Christ with faith which worketh by charity (as the apostle speaketh) shall not be condemned at the latter day nor at the hour of his death, &c.—Annot. John iii. 18. p. 224. This apostle allegeth the good works of Rahab, by which she was justified, and S. Paul (Heb. xi.) saith she was justified by faith. Which are not contrary one to the other, for both is true, that she was saved by faith, as one saith: and that she was saved by her works, as the other saith.—Annot. James ii. 25. p. 647.]

[4 For the means of justification they agree with the papists, that it is not by faith only apprehending Christ, but by their works also.—Russe Commonwealth, Lond. 1591. c. 23. p. 98.]

[5 Vaux, Catech. Antwerp. 1574. c. iii. p. 28. In answer to the question, Who breaketh the first commandment by presumption of God's mercy?]

[6 This reference the editor has been unable to verify.]

[7 This wicked sorcerer Simon is noted by S. Irenæus, Lib. I. c. 20 and others, to have been the first heretic and father of all heretics to come in the church of

Nor they, finally, which maintain how the truly righteous apprehend not Christ by faith, but have him and his righteousness essentially and inherent within them: which is an error of the Catharists[8], Papists[9], Osiandrians[10], and Family of Love[11].

Isidor. etym. Lib. VIII. c. de hæres. Concil. Trid. Sess. 6, cap. 16, 7. Calvin. contra Osiand. epist. fol. 303. Theod. Beza, Epist. I. Display in Allen's Confess.

Proposition III.

We are accounted righteous before God, not for own works or deservings.

The proof from God's word.

Besides what hath been said, that works have no place nor portion in the matter of our justification, it is evident in the holy scripture, where we find, that

All men be sinners, and destitute of the glory of God; and therefore that no man can be justified by his own works.

Eternal life cometh unto us, not by desert, but partly of promise, partly of gift.

The just shall live by faith; and the law is not of faith.

Moreover, as the godly in old time were, so Christians in these days are, and shall be justified: but the godly were justified, not for any good works or worthiness of their own: so justified was Abraham, the Jews, the Samaritans, Paul, the Eunuch, the Jailor, and the Ephesians.

All churches reformed[12], with a sweet consent, applaud, and confess this doctrine.

Ps. xiv. 2, 3. Ps. liii. 2, & li. 4. Rom. iii. 12. Acts ii. 39. Acts iii. 25. Acts xiii. 32. 2 Tim. i. 1. John xvii. 2. Rom. vi. 23. 1 John v. 11. Rev. ii. 10. Gal. iii. 11, 12. Rom. iv. 1, 2. Gal. iii. 6. Heb. xi. 17. Acts ii. 44, &c. Acts viii. 12. Acts xxii. 16, &c. 1 Tim. i. 14, 16. Phil. iii. 6, 9. Acts viii. 36. Acts xvi. 31, &c. Eph. ii. 4, 5. Conf. Helv. II. c. 16. Basil. Art. VIII. Bohem. c. 7. Gal. Art. XXII. Belg. Art. XXIV. August. Art. VI. 20.

God. He taught only faith in him, without good life and works, to be enough to salvation.—Test. Rhem. Annot. Acts viii. 18.]

[[8] This assertion, as regards the Catharists, is merely inferential. Isidore only says: *Cathari* propter munditiam ita se nominaverunt. Gloriantes enim de suis meritis, negant pœnitentibus veniam peccatorum.—Isidor. Opp. Col. Agrip. 1617. Etymol. Lib. VIII. c. 5. fol. 65, G.]

[[9] Quæ enim justitia nostra dicitur, quia per eam nobis inhærentem justificamur, illa eadem Dei est, quia a Deo nobis infunditur per Christi meritum.—Concil. Harduin. Paris. 1714. Tom. x. col. 39. Conc. Trid. Sess. VI. cap. 16.]

[[10] Admittit quidem (Osiander)...remissionem peccatorum intercedere in homine justificando: sed in primo et summo gradu locans spectrum essentialis justitiæ quod ipse finxit, nihil aliud relinquit gratuitæ Dei acceptationi, quam ut sit inferior quædam appendix.—Calv. Opp. Amstel. 1667-72. Tom. IX. Epist. contr. Osiand. p. 190. a. Osiandri fanaticum delirium de essentiali justitia non multo magis, opinor, te vel sanæ quenquam mentis hominem exercuerit.—Bez. Epist. Genev. 1575. Ep. I. p. 12.]

[[11] Touching Christ's perfection....we utterly deny this to be wrought as you affirm in us: for neither doth he work this perfection in us, nor by us, but merely without us.—Ans. to Lett. of the Fam. in the Displ. Lond. 1579. fol. N. 8.]

[[12] Interim...non sentimus per opera bona nos salvari...Gratia enim soliusque Christi beneficio servamur. Opera necessario ex fide progignuntur; at improprie his salus attribuitur, quæ propriissime ascribitur gratiæ.—Harm. Conf. Sect. IX.

The errors and adversaries unto this truth.

Adversaries hereunto are,

Matt. v. 21, &c. Matt. xv. 2. The Pharisees, who thought men were justified by external righteousness, moral and ceremonial.

2 Tim. i. Acts xv. 2. The false apostles in Asia and at Jerusalem.

Gab. Biel. Lib. II. Dist. 27. q. 1. The pharisaical Papists[1], who against the justification by faith alone, do hold a justification by merits, and that of congruity, dignity, and condignity.

Concil. Trid. Sess. 6, Can. 32. The said Papists teach, besides[2], that life eternal is due unto us of debt; because we deserve it by our good works.

Petrus à Soto, Asser. cath. de bonis oper. They teach, finally[3], that by good works our sins are purged.

p. 172. Conf. Helv. Post. c. XVI. Justitiam et satisfactionem pro peccatis nostris non tribuimus operibus quæ fidei fructus sunt.—Ibid. p. 174. Conf. Basil. Art. VIII. [IX]. Deinceps docetur quare et quo consilio seu fine pietatis Christianæ opera bona præstari debeant, nimirum non hac de causa ut homines justificationem aut salutem per hæc et remissionem peccatorum consequantur.—Ibid. p. 180. Conf. Bohem. c. VII. ...Profitemur bona opera quæ duce ipsius Spiritu edimus, non respici a Deo, ut per ea justificemur, aut filii Dei censeri mereamur, &c.—Ibid. p. 184. Conf. Gall. Art. XXII. Hæc vero opera...ad nos...justificandos, nullius sunt prorsus momenti. Fide enim in Christum justificamur et quidem priusquam bona ulla opera ediderimus.—Ibid. p. 186. Conf. Belg. Art. XXIV. Sentiendum est nos consequi remissionem peccatorum, et personam pronuntiari justam gratis, &c. —Ibid. p. 190. Conf. Aug. 1540. Art. VI. Item docent...quod oporteat bona opera ...facere...non ut confidamus per ea opera justificationem coram Deo mereri.—Id. Edit. 1531. ...Diserte docet Paulus gratis nobis donari remissionem peccatorum, et justificationem, non propter nostrorum operum dignitatem, &c.—Ibid. p. 193. Conf. Aug. 1540. Art. XX. Principio quod opera nostra non possint reconciliare Deum, aut mereri remissionem peccatorum et gratiam et justificationem.—Ibid. p. 199. Edit. 1531.]

[1 Actus meritorius est actus a voluntate libere elicitus ad retribuendum aliquod præmium acceptatus....Meritum condigni sive de condigno est actus a voluntate elicitus ad præmium alicui secundum debitum justitiæ retribuendum. Consistit autem justitia illa in quadam proportione meriti ad præmium et æqualitatem...Meritum de congruo est actus libere elicitus, acceptatus ad aliquid retribuendum; non ex debito justitiæ, sed ex sola acceptantis liberalitate. Et hoc meritum non coexigit æqualitatem dignitatis cum retributo, neque in operante nec in opere, nec in retribuente.—Gab. Biel. Comment. in Sentent. Brixiæ, 1574. In Lib. II. Dist. XXVII. Quæst. I. p. 138.]

[2 Si quis dixerit, hominis justificati bona opera ita esse dona Dei, ut non sint etiam bona ipsius justificati merita: aut ipsum, justificatum bonis operibus, quæ ab eo per Dei gratiam, et Jesu Christi meritum, cujus membrum est, fiunt, non vere mereri augmentum gratiæ, vitam æternam, et ipsius vitæ æternæ, si tamen in gratia discesserit, consecutionem atque etiam gloriæ augmentum; anathema sit.—Concil. Harduin. Tom. X. col. 43. Conc. Trid. Sess. VI. De Justific. Can. 32.]

[3 Sentiendum itaque,...bonis operibus, quæ ex divina gratia fiunt, ita esse fidendum, ut et ad expianda peccata, iram Dei placandam, et vitam æternam consequendam necessaria sint, et utilia.—Petr. à Soto, Assert. Cathol. Fid. Antwerp. 1557. De Bon. Oper. p. 20.]

ARTICLE XII.

Of Good Works.

Albeit that good works, which are the fruits of faith, and follow after justification, cannot put away our sins, and endure the severity of God's judgement; (1) *yet are they pleasing and acceptable to God in Christ,* (2) *and do spring out necessarily of a true and lively faith, insomuch that by them a lively faith* (3) *may be as evidently known as a tree discerned by the fruit.*

The propositions.

1. Good works do please God.
2. No work is good except it spring from faith.
3. Good works are the outward signs of the inward belief.

Proposition I.

Good works do please God.

The proof from God's word.

Though God accepteth not man for his works, but for his dear Son's sake; yet, that good works, after man his justification, do please God, it is a clear truth everywhere to be read in the holy scripture. For,

God hath commanded them to be done, and requireth righteousness, not only outward of the body, but also inward of the mind, and hath appointed for the virtuous and godly rewards both in this life, and in the world to come, and to the wicked punishments spiritual, corporal, and of body and soul eternal in the pit of hell.

And this is believed and acknowledged by the churches[4].

Matt. v. 16. John xv. 12. Phil. ii. 14, &c. 1 Thess. iv. 3, &c. 2 Tim. ii. 19. James ii. Matt. v. 22, 28. Acts xxiv. 16. Matt. v. 5. Mark x. 29, 30. 1 Tim. iv. 8. Matt. vii. 21, & x. 32. Luke xiv. 13, 14. Rom. ii. 10. Isai. lix. 1, 2. John ix. 31. 1 John iii. 21. Deut. xxviii. 15, &c. Jer. v. 25. Rom. xiii. 2. Matt. x. 33. Matt. xxi. 41, &c. 1 Cor. vi. 9, 10. Heb. xii. 14, &c. 25. Rev. xxi. 8. Conf. Helv. II. c. 16. Basil. Art. VIII. Bohem. c. 7. Gal. Art. XXII. Belg. Art. XXIV. August. Art. VI. & XX. Saxon. Art. III. V. VI. Wittemb. c. 7. Suevica, c. 4.

[[4] Placent vero approbanturque a Deo opera, quæ a nobis fiunt per fidem, &c.—Harm. Conf. Sect. x. p. 172. Conf. Helv. Post. cap. xvi. Fiunt itaque opera fidelium non ut satisfaciant pro peccatis suis sed solummodo ut his Deo Domino nostro pro maximis beneficiis nobis in Christo exhibitis, se aliquo modo gratos esse declarent.—Ibid. p. 174. Conf. Basil. Art. VIII. [IX.] Ex his manifestum fit et planum, ea opera quæ ex fide fiunt Deo placere, et luculenta gratia affici, &c.—Ibid. p. 182. Conf. Bohem. cap. VI. Tantum abest...ut bene et sancte vivendi studium fides extinguat, ut etiam illud augeat, et inflammet in nobis unde bona opera necessario consequuntur.—Ibid. p. 183. Conf. Gall. Art. XXII. Hæc vero opera a sincera fidei hujus radice emanantia, ideo demum bona et Deo grata sunt, quia per illius gratiam sanctificantur.—Ibid. p. 186. Conf. Belg. Art. XXIV. Item docent quod quum fide reconciliamur, necessario sequi debeat justitia bonorum operum

The errors and adversaries unto this truth.

This truth is oppugned by adversaries of divers kinds. For Some hold, that seeing man is justified by faith, he may live as he listeth; as the Libertines[1].

Some think that to attend upon virtue, and to practise good works, is a yoke too heavy, and intolerable; as the Simonians[2].

Iren. Theod.

Some utterly cast off all grace, virtue, and godliness, as did the Basilidians[3], the Aetians[4], the Circumcellians[5], and do the Machivilians and Atheists. Some permit, though not all manner, yet some sins: so allowed was both whoredom and

Iren. Lib. I. c. 23. Epiph. Lib. III. Aug. contra Pet. Lib. I. c. 24.

quæ Deus nobis mandavit....Placet igitur hæc obedientia, &c.—Ibid. p. 189. Conf. Aug. 1540. Art. VI. Quanquam...hæc nova obedientia procul abest a perfectione legis, tamen est justitia et meretur præmia, &c.—Ibid. p. 196. Art. XX. Item docent ...quod oporteat bona opera mandata a Deo facere propter voluntatem Dei, &c.—Ibid. p. 190. Conf. 1531. Art. VI. Præterea docent quod necesse sit bona opera facere...propter voluntatem Dei.—Ibid. p. 201. Art. XX. ...Tenenda est norma de bonis operibus,...et hæc opera interiora et exteriora fiunt cultus Dei, quum fiunt in fide et referuntur ad hunc finem ut Deus hac obedientia celebretur.—Ibid. p. 211. Conf. Saxon. Art. VI. [VII.] Et tamen sciat oportere inchoari obedientiam et justitiam bonæ conscientiæ, et hanc...in reconciliatis Deo placere, propter mediatorem, &c.—Ibid. p. 215. Art. VIII. [IX.] Ceterum etsi vita æterna datur propter Filium Dei renatis tamen simul etiam est merces bonorum operum, &c.—Ibid. p. 217. Art. IX. [X.] Docemus bona opera divinitus præcepta, necessario facienda esse et mereri, gratuita Dei clementia, sua quædam sive corporalia sive spiritualia præmia.—Ibid. p. 219. Conf. Virtemb. cap. VII. Nam quicquid lex tradit, huc spectat, hoc unum requirit, ut tandem ad Dei imaginem solidam reformemur, &c.—Ibid. p. 223. Conf. Suev. cap. IV.]

[[1] Unumquemque oportere naturalem inclinationem sequi, atque sic agere et vivere ut libebit, &c.—Calv. Opp. Amstel. 1667-72. Tom. VIII. p. 391. b. Instr. adv. Libert. cap. XX.]

[[2] Secundum enim ipsius gratiam (dicit Simon) salvari homines, sed non secundum operas justas. Nec enim esse naturaliter operationes justas, sed ex accidenti; quemadmodum posuerunt, qui mundum fecerunt angeli, per hujusmodi præcepta in servitutem deducentes homines.—Iren. Adv. Hær. Oxon. 1702. Lib. I. cap. 20. p. 95. οὐ γὰρ διὰ πράξεων ἀγαθῶν, ἀλλὰ διὰ χάριτος τεύξεσθαι τῆς σωτηρίας· οὗ δὴ χάριν οἱ τῆς τούτου (sc. Σίμωνος) συμμορίας πᾶσαν ἐτόλμων ἀσέλγειαν.—Theod. Opp. Lut. Par. 1642-84. Tom. IV. p. 193. Hær. Fab. Lib. I. c. 1.]

[[3] Contemnere autem et idolothyta, et nihil arbitrari, sed sine aliqua trepidatione uti eis: habere autem et reliquarum operationum usum indifferentem et universæ libidinis.—Iren. Adv. Hær. Lib. I. cap. 23. p. 98.]

[[4] Καὶ γὰρ οὐκ ἄγεται αὐτοῖς περὶ βίου σεμνότητος, οὐ περὶ νηστείων, οὐ περὶ ἐνταλμάτων Θεοῦ, οὐ περί τινος ἑτέρου τῶν εἰς ζωὴν ἀνθρώποις ἐκ Θεοῦ προστεταγμένων.—Epiphan. Opp. Paris. 1622. Tom. I. p. 916. Adv. Hær. Lib. III. Tom. I.]

[[5] Vestros autem fructus si consideremus; omitto tyrannicas in civitatibus et maxime in fundis alienis dominationes, omitto furorem Circumcellionum, et præcipitatorum ultro cadaverum cultus sacrilegos et profanos, bacchationes ebrietatum, et sub uno Optato Gildoniano decennalem totius Africæ gemitum: &c.—August. Opp. Paris. 1836-8. Tom. IX. col. 355. Contr. Litt. Petil. Lib. I. cap. 24.]

unclean pollutions, by the Carpocratians[6] and Valentinians[7], and is of the Jesuits[8] and Papists[9]: and perjury in the time of persecution by the Basilidians[10], Helchesaites[11], Priscillianists[12], Henricians[13], and Family of Love[14]; and violating of promise, yea and oaths made unto heretics, as they call them, by the Papists[15].

Cl. Alex. Str. Lib. III. Epiph. Theodoret. Spar. discov. pag. 13. Constit. Othonis, de concub. Cler removendis. Philast. Iren Euseb. Lib. VI. c. 38. August. D. Bernard. sup. Cant. ser. 65. Display H. 5. b. Conc. Const. Sess. 19, & Cochlæus Hist. Hussit. Lib. II. p. 75.

[6 *Οἱ δὲ ἀπὸ* Καρποκράτους *καὶ* Ἐπιφάνους *ἀναγόμενοι, κοινὰς εἶναι τὰς γυναῖκας ἀξιοῦσιν.* After mentioning the abominable impurities practised and encouraged by these heretics, he observes, *τοιαῦτα δὲ οἶμαι τῶν κυνῶν καὶ συῶν καὶ τράγων λαγνείαις νομοθετεῖν τὸν* Καρποκράτην *ἔδει.*—Clem. Alex. Opp. Oxon. 1715. p. 511. Strom. Lib. III. c. 2. Εἰσὶ *δὲ ἐν ἀσωτίᾳ διατελοῦντες οὗτοι, καὶ πᾶν ὁτιοῦν ἐργαζόμενοι πρὸς εὐπάθειαν σωμάτων, κ.τ.λ.*—Epiphan. Opp. Tom. I. p. 104. Adv. Hær. Lib. I. Tom. II. Hær. 27.]

[7 Καὶ *γὰρ τὰς* Ἑλληνικὰς *ἑορτὰς ἐπετέλουν, καὶ εἰδωλοθύτων μετελάμβανον καὶ φιληδονίαις δουλεύουσι, καὶ πᾶν ὁτιοῦν πονηρὸν ἀδιακρίτως τολμῶσιν.*—Theod. Opp. Tom. IV. pp. 200, 1. Hæret. Fab. Lib. I. c. 7.]

[8 The stews are in Rome *cum approbatione*. The stews are in Rome as lawful as any citizen: as lawful as any magistrate: as lawful as any order of religion. The stews are at Rome *cum approbatione* as lawful as the pope is himself.—A Sparing Discoverie of our English Jesuits, 1601. p. 13.]

[9 ... Præcipimus, ut ubi clerici et maxime in sacris ordinibus constituti, qui in domibus suis vel alienis detinent publice concubinas, eas prorsus a se removeant infra mensem, &c. In the annotation on this constitution, various interpretations are given of the word 'publice'; after which the annotator proceeds: Tu dic publice, quando multitudini se patere non expavet...secus ergo si secrete intra domum propriam vel alienam detineat hanc concubinam: nam tunc pœnam hujus constitutionis non incurret: cum domus rem secretam, non autem publicam denotat.—Constitut. Othon. Parrhis. 1506. De Concub. Cler. Remov. Fol. xxii.]

[10 Prohibet etiam pati martyrium homines pro nomine Christi, dicens ita ignoras quid desideras, &c.—Philastr. Lib. de Hær. in Biblioth. Patr. Paris. 1624. Tom. IV. col. 9. Quapropter et parati sunt ad negationem qui sunt tales, imo et magis ne pati quidem propter nomen possunt, cum sint omnibus similes.—Iren. Adv. Hær. Lib. I. cap. 23. p. 99.]

[11 *Φησὶ δὲ ὅτι τὸ ἀρνήσασθαι ἀδιάφορόν ἐστι· καὶ ὁ μὲν νοήσας, τῷ στόματι ἐν ἀνάγκαις ἀρνήσεται· τῇ δὲ καρδίᾳ οὐχί.*—Euseb. Eccl. Hist. Cant. 1720. Lib. VI. c. 38, pp. 300, 1.]

[12 Nec in eo malo debemus Priscillianistarum esse participes...Ipsi enim soli, vel certe maxime ipsi reperiuntur, ad occultandam suam quam putant veritatem, dogmatizare mendacium: atque hoc tam magnum malum ideo justum existimare, quia dicunt in corde retinendum esse quod verum est; ore autem ad alienos proferre falsum, nullum esse peccatum.—August. Opp. Tom. VI. col. 756. Ad Consent. Lib. cap. 2.]

[13 Denique indixere (ut dicitur) latebras sibi, firmaverunt sibi sermonem nequam. Jura, perjura: secretum prodere noli...Patet vos...flagitiose præsumere de perjurio.—Bernard. Opp. Par. 1719. Vol. I. col. 1494. In Cant. Ser. lxv. § 2.]

[14 They may answer to every demandant (not being one of their sect) in such sort as they think best shall please him. For they say they are bound to deal truly with no man in word or deed that is not of their congregation: alleging that he is no neighbour, and that therefore they may abuse him at their pleasure.—Display of the Fam. Lond. 1579. fol. H. 5. b. See also Ibid. fol. H. 4. b. and Sents. 10 and 47. of the Admonition to Christ. Vittel.]

[15 Præsens sancta synodus ex quovis salvoconductu per imperatorem, reges,

Policy of the Turkish Emp. cap. 24. Some (as the Turkish priests[1] called Seiti and Chagi) take it to be no sin, but a work meritorious, by lies, swearing, yea forswearing, to damnify Christians what they can. Much like unto these are the equivocating Jesuits, in deluding and deceiving Protestant princes, and their officers, by their doubtful speeches, even when they are sworn to answer plainly and truly by their lawful magistrates.

Matt. vii. & xxiii. Some suppose that God is pleased with lip-service only, and outward righteousness, as the hypocritical Pharisees, or pharisaical hypocrites.

Proposition II.

No work is good, except it spring from faith.

The proof from God's word.

All which man doth is not pleasing unto God, but that only which proceedeth from a true faith in Jesus Christ: so saith God in his word.

Rom. viii. 8. "They that are in the flesh cannot please God."

Gal. v. 6. "In Jesus Christ neither circumcision availeth any thing, neither uncircumcision; but faith, which worketh by love."

Tit. i. 15. "Unto the pure are all things pure; but unto them that are defiled and unbelieving is nothing pure."

Heb. xi. 6. "Without faith it is impossible to please God."

et alios sæculi principes, hæreticis vel de hæresi diffamatis, putantes eosdem sic a suis erroribus revocare, quocumque vinculo se adstrinxerint, concesso, nullum fidei catholicæ, vel jurisdictioni ecclesiasticæ præjudicium generari, vel impedimentum præstari posse seu debere declarat, quo minus, dicto salvoconductu non obstante, liceat judici competenti et ecclesiastico de hujusmodi personarum erroribus inquirere, et alias contra eos debite procedere eosdemque punire, quantum justitia suadebit, si suos errores revocare pertinaciter recusaverint, etiam si de salvoconductu confisi, ad locum venerint judicii, alias non venturi: nec sic promittentem, cum fecerit quod in ipso est, ex hoc in aliquo remansisse obligatum.—Concil. Harduin. Paris. 1715. Tom. VIII. col. 462. Concil. Constant. Sess. XIX. ...petebat (Hieronymus) audiri, sub salvo tamen conductu: qui ei sic datus est, ut justitia semper salva maneret, et quantum fides orthodoxa exigeret. Qualis et Joanni Hus datus fuisse creditur. Quod si rex Sigismundus in suo conductu, ea cautela usus non fuit, concilium tamen declaravit, aliter hæreticis conductum dari non debere.—Cochlæ. Hist. Hussit. apud S. Vict. prope Mogunt. 1549. Lib. II. p. 72.]

[[1] Both of these sorts of priests, the *Seiti* and the *Chagi* are, for the most part, a most wicked and detestable kind of men. For being much and often called, or rather hired, to testify as witnesses in matters before the magistrate, they will for a ducat take a thousand false oaths, especially if it be against a Christian; against whom to use perjury or false witness they hold it no impiety, but rather a good and meritorious deed.—Policy of the Turk. Emp. Lond. 1597. p. 74.]

And although the works of the believing do please God, yet are they not so perfect that they can satisfy the law of God. Therefore even of the regenerate and justified saith our Saviour Christ: "Pray, Forgive us our debts;" "Say, We are unprofitable servants." And St Paul, Matt. vi. 12. Luke xvii. 10. Rom. vii. 14.

"We know that the law is spiritual, but I am carnal, &c."

"We, which have the firstfruits of the Spirit, even we do sigh in ourselves, &c., and have infirmities." Rom. viii. 23.

"Ye cannot do the same thing that ye would." Gal. v. 17.

Which is the faith and confession of the churches[2]. Conf. Helv. II. cap. 16. Basil. Art. VIII. Bohem. cap. 7. Gal. Art. XXII. Belg. Art. XXIV. August. Art. XX. Saxon. Art. III. V. VI. Wittemb. c. 7. Suevica, c. 4.

Errors and adversaries unto this truth.

Therefore we mislike and condemn the opinions of the Valentinians and Papists.

The Valentinians[3] say, that please God do spiritual Iren. Lib. I. c. 1.

[2 Docemus enim vere bona opera enasci ex viva fide per Spiritum Sanctum, et a fidelibus fieri secundum voluntatem vel regulam verbi Dei.—Harm. Conf. Sect. IX. p. 171. Conf. Helv. Post. cap. XVI. ...Hæc (sc. fides) per opera charitatis se sine intermissione exercet &c.—Ibid. p. 174. Conf. Basil. Art. VIII. [IX. Disp. 22.] ...Hæc duo fides et charitas scaturigo sunt et norma omnium virtutum et bonorum operum, &c.—Ibid. p. 180. Conf. Bohem. cap. VII. Recipimus autem per fidem hanc sancte vivendi gratiam.—Ibid. p. 183. Conf. Gall. Art. XXII. Tantum abest igitur ut fides hæc justificans homines a recta sanctaque vivendi ratione avocet...ut contra absque illa nemo unquam quicquam boni propter Deum...agere atque operari possit.—Ibid. p. 186. Conf. Belg. Art. XXIV. Inter bona opera præcipuum est...fides ipsa et parit multas alias virtutes quæ existere non possunt, nisi prius corda fidem conceperint.—Ibid. p. 195. Conf. Aug. 1540. Art. XX. Et quia per fidem accipitur Spiritus Sanctus jam corda renovantur et induunt novos affectus, ut parere bona opera possint....Nam sine fide nullo modo potest humana natura, primi aut secundi præcepti opera facere—Ibid. p. 201. Conf. 1531. Art. XX. ...hæc externa disciplina, etiam sicubi est honestissima, nequaquam est impletio legis, nec meretur remissionem peccatorum, nec est justitia illa, qua coram Deo accepti sumus, &c.—Ibid. p. 204. Conf. Saxon. Art. III. Totum beneficium Filii Dei considerandum est: ita enim vult peccatum et mortem tollere, et nos ex regno diaboli eripere ut prorsus abolito peccato et deleta morte restituat in nobis æternam vitam.—Ibid. p. 210. Art. V. [VI.]. ...Hi veri cultus non possunt præstari sine luce Evangelii et sine fide.—Ibid. p. 212. Art. VI. [VII.] Non est autem sentiendum quod iis bonis operibus quæ nos facimus in judicio Dei...confidendum sit. Omnia enim bona opera, quæ nos facimus sunt imperfecta nec possunt severitatem divini judicii ferre.—Ibid. p. 219. Conf. Virtemb. cap. VII. Hanc fidem vocat D. August....evangelicam, efficacem, videlicet per dilectionem. Hac demum regeneramur, et restituitur in nobis imago Dei. Hac quum perversi nati simus, nostris cogitationibus a puero ad malum tantum pronis, evadimus boni rectique.—Ibid. p. 222. Conf. Suev. cap. IV.]

[3 Ἡμᾶς μὲν γὰρ ἐν χρήσει τὴν χάριν λαμβάνειν λέγουσι· διὸ καὶ ἀφαιρεθήσεσθαι αὐτῆς. αὐτοὺς δὲ ἰδιόκτητον ἄνωθεν ἀπὸ τῆς ἀῤῥήτου καὶ ἀνονομάστου συζυγίας συγκατεληλυθυῖαν ἔχειν τὴν χάριν· καὶ διὰ τοῦτο προστεθήσεσθαι αὐτοῖς. διὸ καὶ ἐκ παντὸς τρόπου δεῖν αὐτοὺς ἀεὶ τὸ τῆς συζυγίας μελετᾶν μυστήριον...διὰ τοῦτο οὖν ἡμᾶς καλοὺς ψυχικοὺς ὀνομάζουσι, καὶ ἐκ κόσμου

men[1], (which are themselves only,) not by faith, but only by their knowledge of divine mysteries; and natural men do please him by their bodily labour and upright dealing.

Epiphan. The said Valentinians[2] feigned three sorts or degrees of men: the first spiritual, who through bare knowledge; the next natural, who by labour and true dealing shall be saved; the third they call material, men utterly incapable of divine knowledge, and religious speculations, who must perish both in soul and body.

The Papists teach, that

Tapp. p. 188. They not only are[3] good works which God commandeth, but they also which be either voluntarily done of ourselves, or enjoined us by priests[4].

Andrad. de fide, Lib. III. They are good works, and acceptable before God, which are done without faith[5].

Tapp. p. 189. Works of themselves, without respect unto Christ, please God[6].

εἶναι λέγουσι, καὶ ἀναγκαίαν ἡμῖν τὴν ἐγκράτειαν, καὶ ἀγαθὴν πρᾶξιν, ἵνα δι' αὐτῆς ἔλθωμεν εἰς τὸν τῆς μεσότητος τόπον· αὐτοῖς δὲ πνευματικοῖς τε καὶ τελείοις καλουμένοις μηδαμῶς.—Iren. Adv. Hær. Oxon. 1702. pp. 31, 32. Lib. I. c. 1. § 12.]

[1 Spiritual men do please God, 1633, and the later editions.]

[2 Ἀνθρώπων δὲ τρία γένη ὑφίστανται, πνευματικὸν, χοϊκὸν, ψυχικὸν, καθὼς ἐγένοντο Καΐν, Ἀβὲλ, Σήθ. καὶ ἐκ τούτων τὰς τρεῖς φύσεις, οὐκέτι καθ' ἓν, ἀλλὰ κατὰ γένος, καὶ τὸ μὲν χοϊκὸν εἰς φθορὰν χωρεῖν, καὶ τὸ ψυχικὸν ἐὰν τὰ βελτίονα ἕληται, ἐν τῷ τῆς μεσότητος τόπῳ ἀναπαύεσθαι· ἐὰν δὲ τὰ χείρω, χωρήσειν καὶ αὐτὸ πρὸς τὰ ὅμοια. τὰ δὲ πνευματικὰ, ἃ ἂν κατασπείρῃ ἡ Ἀχαμὼθ, ἔκτοτε ἕως τοῦ νῦν δικαίαις ψυχαῖς παιδευθέντα ἐνθάδε, καὶ ἐκτραφέντα διὰ τὸ νήπια ἐκπεπέμφθαι, ὕστερον τελειότητος ἀξιωθέντα, νύμφας ἀποδοθήσεσθαι τοῖς τοῦ Σωτῆρος Ἀγγέλοις δογματίζουσι κ.τ.λ.—Epiphan. Opp. Paris. 1622. Tom. I. p. 192. Adv. Hær. Lib. I. Tom. II. Hær. 31.]

[3 They only are not, 1607.]

[4 Philippus Melancthon contra docet...hæc ipsa [bona] opera ideo facienda quia a Deo præcepta sunt, non ut illis quicquam mereamur. Quæ vero et nostra electione, nostroque arbitrio, aut superiorum præscripto vel consilio assumpserimus, apud Deum nullius haberi momenti...Quem ejus errorem...improbat Alb. Pighius, &c....Non igitur ea sola opera Deo placent et bona sunt quæ Deus præcepit, nec solum ea quæ fiunt in proximi utilitatem; sed quæcunque conformia sunt, secundum omnes circumstantias suæ regulæ, &c.—Tapp. Opp. Col. Agrip. 1582. Art. xi. Tom. II. pp. 115, 6.]

[5 ...satis abunde explicavimus, D. Paulum ea appellare opera legis, quæ cum non ex fide proficiscantur, externum tamen quoddam virtutis specimen habent....Ne tamen omni prorsus præmio destituta esse videantur, Mosis illa verba adjungit, Qui fecerit ea homo, vivet in eis: hoc est, supplicia legis violatoribus constituta effugiet.—Andrad. Orthodox. Explic. Colon. 1564. Lib. VI. De Justific. pp. 527, 8. Cf. Lib. III. De Peccat. pp. 274, 5.]

[6 See above, note 3.]

Men perfectly may keep the laws of God[7]. In which error also be the Anabaptists[8] and Family of Love[9]. Tapp. ibid. Bullin. contra Anabapt Lib. IV. c. 3. Display L. 6. a.

Proposition III.

Good works are the outward signs of the inward belief.

The proof from God's word.

Many are the reasons why good works are to be done, in part cited afore, p. 107, yet not the least cause is, that men may be known what they are. For the scripture saith, and sheweth, that thereby are known the good trees from the bad, the wheat from the chaff, the true disciples from the false, the sons of God from the children of Satan, the regenerate from the unbelievers. Matt. vii. 16. Matt. iii. 12. John xiii. 35. Luke vi. 36. Ephes. v. 1. 1 John iii. 10. James ii. 18. 1 Pet. i. 17. Eph. iv. 17.

Hereunto the saints and churches[10] do subscribe. Conf. Helv. II. c. 16. Basil. Art. VIII. Bohem. c. 7. Gal. Art. XXII. Belg. Art. XXIV. Saxon. Art. III. Wittemb. c. 7. Suevic. c. iv.

[7 This is apparently not expressed in the place referred to.]

[8 Quemadmodum in præcipuo dogmate justificationis et salutis per fidem Anabaptistæ graviter impingunt, ita in doctrina de fine seu usu et observatione legis multum aberrant: de quibus tamen nos accusant, quod falsa doceamus, et aiunt docere nos legem ab homine servari non posse, cum tamen omnes scripturæ legem servare jubeant.—Bulling. Adv. Anabapt. (Simler Vers. Lat.) Tiguri, 1560. p. 123. b. Lib. IV. c. 3.]

[9 Happily ye may object (as some have done that I have communed with), and say, it is impossible to do and keep the commandments.—*Answer.* What the scriptures last before recited [Eccles. xii. Fear God, and keep his commandments] doth require you have heard, and many more there might be alleged to the same effect, &c.—Letter of the Fam. in the Displaying. Lond. 1579. fol. L. 6. a.]

[10 Non...vilipendimus aut condemnamus opera bona: quum sciamus hominem nec conditum nec regenitum esse per fidem, ut ocietur; sed potius ut indesinenter quæ bona et utilia sunt, faciat.—Harm. Conf. Sect. IX. p. 172. Conf. Helv. Post. cap. XVI. Quæ (sc. opera) fidei fructus sunt.—Ibid. p. 174. Conf. Basil. Art. VIII. [IX.] Disp. 22. Christiani in bonis operibus exercere se debent...ut hoc modo probent et demonstrent fidem suam, et ex his quod sint veri Christiani, hoc est viva membra et sectatores Christi esse agnoscantur.—Ibid. p. 180. Conf. Bohem. cap. VII. Unde (sc. e fide) bona opera necessario consequuntur.—Ibid. p. 183. Conf. Gall. Art. XXII. Credimus veram hanc fidem...nos regenerare, atque veluti novos homines efficere, ut quos ad novam vitam vivendam excitet, et a peccati servitute liberos efficiat.—Ibid. p. 186. Conf. Belg. Art. XXIV. Quum autem in hac ipsa consolatione, fiducia qua acquiescimus in Filio Dei, vere sit motus accensus a Spiritu sancto, quo vivificatur cor, et liberatur ab externa morte, dicitur hæc conversio, regeneratio ...Et fit homo jam vere domicilium Dei, qui est in eo efficax, &c.—Ibid p. 209. Conf. Saxon. Art. III. Docemus bona opera divinitus præcepta, necessario facienda esse.—Ibid. p. 219. Conf. Virtemb. cap. VII. Nolumus autem hoc sic intelligi, quasi salutem ac justitiam in ignavis animi cogitationibus fideve charitate destituta (quam informem vocant) ponamus: quandoquidem certi sumus neminem justum aut salvum fieri posse nisi amet summe Deum et imitetur studiosissime.—Ibid. p. 222. Conf. Suev. cap. IV.]

Errors and adversaries unto this truth.

The faithful shew their works, yet neither to have them seen of men, as did the hypocritical Pharisees; nor thereby to merit heaven, as do the pharisaical Papists, whose doctrine is, that

Matt. vi. & vii.

Good works are meritorious[1].

Test. Rhem. an. Rom. ii. 6. 1 Cor. iii. 8. 2 Cor. v. 10. Heb. vi. 10. James ii. 22. Concil. Trid. Sess. 14, c. 3.

Good works (as contrition, confession, and satisfaction done in penance) not only do merit, but are besides a sacrament for to attain reconciliation with God, and forgiveness of sins[2].

Conc. Trid. Sess. 6, Can. 32.

Life eternal is due unto good works by the justice of God[3].

[[1] Though the holy apostle's special purpose be in this epistle to commend unto the Gentiles that trusted so much in their moral works, the faith in Christ: yet lest any man should think or gather untruly of his words, that Christian men's works were not meritorious or the cause of salvation, he expressly writeth, that God giveth as well everlasting life and glory to men, for and according to their good works, as he giveth damnation for the contrary works.—Test. Rhem. Rhemes, 1582. p. 387. Annot. Rom. ii. 6. *Every man shall receive according.* A most plain text for proof that men by their labours, and by the diversities thereof, shall be diversely rewarded in heaven: and therefore that by their works proceeding of grace, they do deserve or merit heaven, and the more or less joy in the same.—Ibid. p. 430. Ann. 1 Cor. iii. 8. *Either good or evil.* Heaven is as well the reward of good works, as hell is the stipend of ill works. Neither is faith alone sufficient to procure salvation, nor lack of faith the only cause of damnation: by good deeds men merit the one, and by ill deeds they deserve the other.—Ibid. p. 480. Ann. 2 Cor. v. 10. *God is not unjust.* It is a world to see what wringing and writhing the Protestants make to shift themselves from the evidence of these words, which make it most clear to all not blinded in pride and contention, that good works be meritorious, and the very cause of salvation, so far that God should be unjust, if he rendered not heaven for the same.—Ibid. p. 613. Ann. Hebr. vi. 10. *Faith did work with.* Some heretics hold, that good works are pernicious to salvation and justification: other that though they be not hurtful, but required, yet they be no causes or workers of salvation, much less meritorious, but are as effects and fruits issuing necessarily out of faith. Both which fictions, falsehoods, and flights from the plain truth of God's word, are refuted by these words, when the apostles saith, That faith worketh together with good works: making faith to be a coadjutor, or co-operator with works, and so both jointly concurring as causes and workers of justification: yea afterward he maketh works the more principal cause when he resembleth faith to the body, and works to the spirit, or life of man.—Ibid. p. 646. Ann. James ii. 22.]

[[2] Sunt autem quasi materia hujus sacramenti [sc. Pœnitentiæ], ipsius pœnitentis actus, nempe contritio, confessio et satisfactio: qui quatenus in pœnitente ad integritatem sacramenti, ad plenamque et perfectam peccatorum remissionem ex Dei institutione requiruntur, hac ratione partes pœnitentiæ dicuntur. Sane vero res et effectus hujus sacramenti, quantum ad ejus vim et efficaciam pertinet, reconciliatio est cum Deo.—Concil. Harduin. Paris. 1714. Tom. x. col. 91. Conc. Trid. Sess. xiv. cap. 3.]

[[3] See above, p. 116, note 2.]

Article XIII.

Of Works before Justification.

Works done before the grace of Christ, and the inspiration of his Spirit, (1) are not pleasant to God, forasmuch as they spring not of faith in Jesus Christ, (2) neither do they make men meet to receive grace, or (as the school-authors say) deserve grace of congruity: yea rather, (3) for that they are not done as God hath willed and commanded them to be done, we doubt not but they have the nature of sin.

The propositions.

1. Works done before justification please not God.
2. Works done before justification deserve not grace of congruity.
3. Works done before justification have the nature of sin.

Proposition I.

Works done before justification please not God.

The proof from God's word.

Before men do please God, nothing that they do can please him. But men please not God, being not renewed, and justified by the Spirit. For, before men be regenerate, they are not grapes, but thorns; not[4] figs, but thistles; not good, but evil trees; not lively, but dead boughs; not engraffed, but wild olives; not friends, but enemies; not the sons of God, but the children of wrath; which bring forth no good fruit. As the churches[5] also acknowledge. Matt. vii. 16. Matt. xii. 33. Luke vi. 43. John xv. 4. Rom. xi. 17, 23. Rom. v. 10. Ephes. ii. 3. Confess. Helv. II. c. 15. August. Art. XX.

Errors [and] adversaries unto this truth.

Hereby the vanity of them is perceived which think, before man's justification his deeds do please God; such are the Papists, and were the Basilidians.

The Papists teach, that

[4 Nor, 1607.]

[5 Sed et non possent Deo placere dilectio et opera nostra si fierent ab injustis: proinde oportet nos prius justos esse quam diligamus aut faciamus opera justa.—Harm. Conf. Sect. IX. p. 169. Conf. Helv. Post. cap. XV. Humanæ vires sine Spiritu sancto, plenæ sunt impiis affectibus et sunt imbecilliores quam ut bona opera possint efficere coram Deo.—Adhæc, sunt in potestate diaboli, &c.—Ibid. p. 201. Conf. Aug. 1531. Art. XX.]

Andrad. de Fide, Lib. III. Tapp. p. 189.

Works done without faith do please God.

Good works, not in respect of Christ only, but in themselves considered, please God[1].

Clem. Alex. Strom. Lib. II.

The Basilidians[2] placed the doers of civil and philosophical righteousness, performed without faith in Christ, in the very heavens.

Proposition II.

Works done before justification deserve not grace of congruity.

[The proof from God's word[3].]

Eph. iv. 22. Rom. viii. 7. Eph. ii. 3. Rom. v. 8. Tit. i. 15.

The unregenerate, not yet justified, have nothing in them to move God to be gracious unto them; and being as they are, old, not new creatures; enemies, not favourers of godliness; the children of wrath, not of God; sinners, not virtuously bent; infidels, and not believers; of congruity deserve no grace at God's hands, which is the faith too and confession[4] of other churches.

Conf. Helv. II. c. 16. Bohem. c. 7. Belg. Art. XXIII. August. Art. IV. XX. Saxon. Art. III. & VIII. Wittemb. Art. V.

[1 See above, p. 122, note 3.]

[2 The passage meant may possibly be the following: *Ἦν μὲν οὖν πρὸ τῆς τοῦ Κυρίου παρουσίας εἰς δικαιοσύνην Ἕλλησιν ἀναγκαία φιλοσοφία· νυνὶ δὲ χρησίμη πρὸς θεοσέβειαν γίνεται, προπαίδειά τις οὖσα τοῖς τὴν πίστιν δι' ἀποδείξεως καρπουμένοις.*—Clem. Alex. Opp. Oxon. 1715. Tom. I. p. 331. Strom. Lib. I. cap. 5. This however is the sentiment of Clemens himself, not of the Basilidians.—Cf. Ibid. cap. 20. p. 377. *καίτοι καὶ καθ' ἑαυτὴν ἐδικαίου πότε καὶ ἡ φιλοσοφία τοὺς Ἕλληνας κ.τ.λ.*]

[3 Omitted in 1607.]

[4 Referimus tamen mercedem hanc, quam Dominus dat, non ad meritum hominis accipientis: sed ad bonitatem...Dei promittentis atque dantis.—Harm. Conf. Sect. IX. p. 173. Conf. Helv. Post. cap. XVI. Deinceps docetur, quare et quo consilio...opera bona præstari debeant: nimirum non hac de causa ut homines justificationem aut salutem per hæc et remissionem peccatorum consequantur.—Ibid. p. 188. Conf. Bohem. cap. VII. ...De nobis ullisve meritis nostris nihil quicquam præsumimus.—Ibid. p. 185. Conf. Belg. Art. XXIII. ...Ut remissio peccatorum certa sit, docet eam gratis donari: hoc est non pendere ex conditione dignitatis nostræ, nec dari propter ulla præcedentia opera, aut dignitatem sequentium.—Ibid. p. 187. Conf. Aug. 1540. Art. IV. ...sentiendum est, donari nobis remissionem peccatorum et fieri nos ex injustis justos...gratis propter Christum, non propter dignitatem contritionis, aut aliorum operum præcedentium aut sequentium.—Ibid. p. 192. Art. XX. In the edition of 1531: Principio quod opera nostra non possint reconciliare Deum aut mereri remissionem peccatorum et gratiam et justificationem.—Ibid. p. 199. Et contumelia est Filii Dei fingere ulla nostra opera merita esse...deliramenta clare damnamus quæ fingunt disciplinam illam...mereri remissionem seu de congruo seu de condigno, &c.—Ibid. p. 205. Conf. Saxon. Art. III. Inanis est imaginatio fingentium obedientiam Deo placere sua dignitate et esse meritum condigni, ut loquuntur, et justitiam coram Deo quæ sit meritum vitæ æternæ.—Ibid. p. 214. Art. VIII. [IX.] Credimus...quod...necessariæ sint hæ virtutes, fides, spes, et charitas, et quod homo has virtutes non ex se concipere possit, sed accipiat ex favore et gratia Dei.—Ibid. p. 218. Conf. Virtemb. Art. V.]

Errors and adversaries unto this truth.

This overthroweth the popish assertions concerning merits of congruity[5]; and that by good works man is justified before God, and made heir of eternal life[6]. Test. Rhem. an. Act. x. 2. Concil. Trid. Sess. 6. c. 16.

As evil works deserve hell-fire, so eternal happiness is deserved by good works[7]. Andrad. de Fide, Lib. VI.

Proposition III.

Works done before justification have the nature of sin.

The proof from the word of God.

Whatsoever men do, not yet justified before God, it is sin: for of such persons the best works which they do, even their fasting[a], praying[b], alms-deeds[c], sacrificing unto God[d], pro-

[a] Wherefore have we fasted, and thou seest it not? We have punished ourselves, and thou regardest it not, Isai. lviii. 3. Did you fast unto me? Zech. vii. 5. They have their reward, Matt. vi. 16.

[b] He that turneth away his ear from hearing the law, even his prayer shall be abominable, Prov. xxviii. 9. When thou prayest be not as the hypocrites, &c.; they have their reward, Matt. vi. 5.

[c] Take heed that ye give not your alms before men, &c.; they have their reward, Matt. vi. 1, 2.

[d] Will I eat the flesh of bulls, or drink the blood of goats? Psal. l. 13. Bring me no more oblations in vain: incense is an abomination unto me, &c. Isai. i. 13. He that killeth a bullock is as if he slew a man; he that sacrificeth a sheep, as if he cut off a dog's neck; he that offereth an oblation, as if he offered swine's blood; he that remembereth incense, as if he blessed an idol, Isai. lxvi. 3.

[[5] After quoting Bede and St Augustine, the annotator continues, Whereby it appeareth that such works as are done before justification, though they suffice not to salvation, yet be acceptable preparatives to the grace of justification, and such as move God to mercy, as it might appear also by God's like provident mercifulness to the eunuch, though all such works preparative come of grace also; otherwise they could never deserve at God's hand of congruity or any otherwise toward justification.—Test. Rhem. Rhemes, 1582. Ann. Acts x. 2. p. 320.]

[[6] Atque ideo bene operantibus usque in finem, et in Deo sperantibus proponenda est vita æterna, et tamquam gratia filiis Dei per Christum Jesum misericorditer promissa, et tanquam merces ex ipsius Dei promissione bonis ipsorum operibus et meritis fideliter reddenda.—Concil. Harduin. Paris. 1714. Tom. x. col. 39. Conc. Trid. Sess. VI. cap. 16.]

[[7] Quod quidem D. Paulus satis aperuit ad Thessalonicenses scribens, Nos ipsi (inquit) in vobis gloriamur in Ecclesiis...Si tamen justum est apud Deum retribuere retributionem iis qui vos tribulant, et vobis qui tribulamini requiem, &c...quæ quidem satis indicant, non minus sempiternam felicitatem justorum esse præclaris operibus debitam, quam æternos cruciatus eorum sceleribus qui non noverunt Deum, neque obediunt Evangelio, &c.—Andrad. Orthodox. Explic. Colon. 1564. Lib. VI. De Justific. p. 517.]

phesying, and working of miracles, even in the name of Christ[e], yea, all their actions whatsoever[f], are abominable before God.

Conf. Helv. II. c. 15, 16. Bohem. c. 7. Belg. Art. XXIII. August. Art. IV. XX. Saxon. Art. III. & VIII. Wittemb. Art. V. Concil. Trid. Sess. 6. Can. 7.

And this is agreeable to the confessions[1] of our brethren.

The adversaries unto this truth.

Erred therefore hath the council of Trent, in pronouncing them accursed which hold that all works of man[2] whatsoever done before his justification are sin[3].

ARTICLE XIV.

Of Works of Supererogation.

Voluntary works, (1) *besides, over and above, God's commandments, which they call works of supererogation, cannot be taught without arrogancy and impiety.* (2) *For by them men do declare, that they do not only render unto God as much as they are bound to do, but that they do more for his sake, than of bounden duty is required: whereas Christ saith plainly, When ye have done all that are commanded to you, say, We be unprofitable servants.*

The propositions.

1. Works of supererogation cannot be taught without arrogancy and impiety.
2. Works of supererogation are the subversion of godliness and true religion.

[e] Lord, Lord, have we not by thy name prophesied? and by thy name cast out devils? and by thy name done many great works? Then will I profess to them, I never knew you: depart from me, ye that work iniquity, Matt. vii. 22, 23.

[f] Whatsoever is not of faith is sin, Rom. xiv. 23. Unto them that are defiled and unbelieving is nothing pure; but even their minds and consciences are defiled, Tit. i. 15. Without faith it is impossible to please God, Heb. xi. 6.

[[1] See above, p. 121, note 3, and p. 125, n. 5.] [[2] Men, 1607.]

[[3] Si quis dixerit opera omnia, quæ ante justificationem fiunt, quacunque ratione facta sint, vere esse peccata, vel odium Dei mereri...anathema sit.—Concil. Harduin. Paris. 1714. Tom. x. col. 41. Conc. Trid. Sess. vi. De Justificatione, Can. 7.]

Proposition I.

Works of supererogation cannot be taught without arrogancy and impiety.

The proof from God's word.

Works of supererogation (which are voluntary works besides, over and above the commandments of God) are often condemned in the holy scripture, where we are commanded to walk, not after the laws of men, but according to the statutes of God, and to hear, not what man speaketh, but what Christ doth say: and he, teaching the duty of Christians, setteth before them, as their rule and direction, the law and word of God; and more than that he doth neither urge nor require. Josh. i. 7. Ezek. xx. 1. Mark ix. 7. Matt. v. 19.

And against man's injunctions:

"They worship me in vain (saith he) who for doctrine teach the commandments of men." Mark vii. 7.

"Teach them to observe all things whatsoever I have commanded you." Matt. xxviii. 20.

"My sheep hear my voice, and know not the voice of strangers." John x. [5] 27.

Which doctrine, ordinances, and works whatsoever (besides, over and above that which God hath revealed and imposed), is called of the apostle, sometimes ordinances of the world, voluntary religion, sometime the doctrine of devils, and cursed. And the same is condemned in all churches[4] reformed after the word of God. Col. ii. 20. Ibid. 23. 1 Tim. iv. 1. Gal. i. 8. Confess. Helv. II. c. 16. August. Art. XX. Basil. Art. X. Gal. Art. XXIV. Belg. Art. XXII. Sax. Art. III. XVII.

[4 Diximus autem antea legem Dei, quæ voluntas Dei est, formulam nobis præscribere bonorum operum...Etenim non probantur Deo opera, et nostro arbitrio delecti cultus, quos Paulus nuncupat ἐθελοθρησκείας.—Harm. Conf. Sect. ix. p. 171. Conf. Helv. Post. cap. xvi. Hanc doctrinam (justificationis) horribiliter obruerunt olim quædam absurdæ persuasiones, in quibus indocti, contra auctoritatem scripturæ et veteris Ecclesiæ finxerunt homines legi Dei satisfacere....Et monachos perfectos esse, et ampliora et præstantiora opera præstare, quam lex Dei flagitat.—Ibid. p. 197. Conf. Aug. 1540. Art. xx. Fiunt itaque opera fidelium, non ut satisfaciant pro peccatis suis.—Ibid. p. 174. Conf. Basil. Art. VIII. [al. IX.] Disp. 24. ...vota monastica, peregrinationes, interdicta matrimonii et usus ciborum...ceteræque res omnes ejusmodi, quibus opinantur quidam se gratiam et salutem mereri. Ea vero omnia non tantum rejicimus, propter falsam meriti opinionem ipsis adjunctam, sed etiam quoniam sunt humana commenta et jugum ex hominum auctoritate conscientiis impositum.—Ibid. Sect. xvi. p. 181. Conf. Gall. Art. XXIV. Horrenda est omnino in Deum blasphemia, asserere Christum minime sufficere, sed aliis quoque rebus opus esse.—Ibid. Sect. ix. p. 185. Conf. Belg. Art. XXII. Idem accidit post apostolos amissa luce Evangelii...quæsita est remissio per exercitia monastica, per cœlibatum, per varias observationes, per oblationem in missa, per intercessionem hominum mor-

The errors and adversaries unto this truth.

Therefore both arrogant and ungodly be the Papists, which teach and speak in the commendation of such works; and namely, Petrus à Soto[1], the Rhemists[2], yea, and the council of Trent[3].

In his Assert. Cathol. fidei. Annot. marg. Luke x. 35. 1 Cor. ix. 23. 2 Cor. viii. 14. Conc. Trid. Sess. 6. c. 10.

tuorum, et multæ monstrosæ superstitiones excogitatæ sunt.—Ibid. p. 203. Conf. Saxon. Art. III. (Monachi finxerunt)...oportere satisfactiones esse opera non debita lege Dei....Dicimus opera indebita, de quibus ipsi loquuntur, non esse cultus Dei aut compensationes, sed pertinere ad hoc dictum: Frustra colunt me mandatis hominum.—Ibid. Sect. viii. p. 156. Art. XVII.]

[[1] After speaking of the command to love God, of which he says, Sed illi nullus quicquam superaddere potest, he proceeds: At vero quod ad rerum externarum usum attinet, habet vera fides juxta propheticam et apostolicam doctrinam quædam juberi vel prohiberi præceptis, quibus non obedire peccatum est, quædam vero proponi sub consilio, cui non parere nullum peccatum est, sed minus bonum, obedientia vero illorum gratior, per quam videlicet supererogamus nonnihil his, ad quæ ex necessitate tenemur.—Petr. a Soto. Assert. Cathol. Fid. Antverp. 1557. De Lege. p. 16.]

[[2] St Augustin saith that the apostle (1 Cor. ix.) according to this place did supererogate, that is, did more than he was needed or was bound to do, when he might have required all duties for preaching the gospel, but would not. *Li. de op. Monach. c.* 5. Wherefore it cometh that the works which we do more than precept be called works of supererogation; and whereby it is also evident against the protestants that there be such works.—Test. Rhem. Rhemes, 1582. Marg. Annot. p. 168. The passage of St Luke's Gospel (x. 35) upon which the above is a comment, is rendered in the Rhemish version, "And whatsoever thou shalt supererogate, I at my return will repay thee:" and the marginal gloss is, *supererogaveris, προσδαπανήσῃς. And I do all things for the gospel that I may be made partaker thereof.* A singular place to convince the protestants that will not have men work well in respect of reward at God's hand: the apostle confessing expressly, that all this that he doeth either of duty, or of supererogation above duty...all is the rather to attain the reward of heaven.—Ibid. p. 444. Ann. 1 Cor. ix. 23. *Let in this present time your abundance supply their want.* This place proveth plainly that the fastings and satisfactory deeds of one man be available to others, yea and that holy saints or other virtuous persons may, in measure and proportion of other men's necessities and deservings, allot unto them, as well the supererogation of their spiritual works, as those that abound in worldly goods may give alms of their superfluities to them which are in necessity. Which interchange and proportion of things the apostle doth evidently set down.—Ibid. p. 485. Ann. 2 Cor. viii. 14.]

[[3] Sic ergo justificati...per observationem mandatorum Dei et ecclesiæ, in ipsa justitia, per Christi gratiam accepta, co-operante fide bonis operibus, crescunt atque magis justificantur—Concil. Harduin. Paris. 1714. Tom. x. col. 36. Conc. Trid. Sess. VI. c. 10.]

Proposition II.

Works of supererogation are the subversion of godliness and true religion.

The proof from God's word.

Where the works of supererogation are taught, and in regard, the law of God there is broken, against the will of Christ, and men's traditions may be observed. Matt. v. 19. Mark vii. 7.

The holy scripture must be contemned, as not sufficient enough to bring men unto the knowledge of salvation, which St Paul saith is able to instruct in righteousness, that the man of God may be absolute, being made perfect unto all good works. 2 Tim. iii. 16, 17.

God, who is only wise, is made unwise, in not prescribing so necessary works. 1 Tim. i. 17.

Faith and other spiritual and most special virtues are brought into oblivion.

Perfection is imputed not unto faith in Jesus Christ, but unto works: and, which is most detestable, unto the works too not commanded, but forbidden of God, ordained by men.

The law of God is thought to be throughly satisfied, and more duties performed than man needed to have done.

The same think our brethren[4] of these works. Conf. Helv. II. &c. as in the former Prop.

The adversaries unto this truth.

Contrariwise the Papists of supererogatory works: they do merit (say they) remission of sins, and that not for the doers of them only, but for others besides[5]. Test. Rhem. an. 2 Cor. viii. 14.

They are tokens of the forgiveness of sins, so well as baptism; yea deliver from the wrath of God, so well as Christ[6]. Conf. Aug. Art. xx.

Are greater, and more holy, than are the works commanded in the Decalogue, or law moral[7]. Petrus à Soto Asser. Cath. de Lege.

And so preferring their own works and inventions before God his law, sacraments, and the blood of Christ, both ought this doctrine of works supererogatory to be counted the doctrine of devils, and the maintainers thereof taken for the subverters of godliness and true religion.

[[1] See above, p. 129, note 4.] [[5] See above, p. 130, note 2.]

[[6] There is apparently an error in the reference. But see, Syll. Conf. Oxon. 1827. p. 222, 3. Conf. Aug. 1540. Art. de Abus. &c. De Vot. Monach. Constat autem monachos docuisse quod factitiæ religiones mereantur remissionem peccatorum, &c....Item opponunt iræ Dei, non propitiatorem Christum, sed propria opera &c.]

[[7] See above, p. 130, note 1.]

ARTICLE XV.

Of Christ alone without sin.

Christ in the truth of our nature was made like unto us in all things, sin only except, (1) *from which he was clearly void, both in his life*[1] *and spirit. He came to be the Lamb without spot, who, by sacrifice of himself once made, should take away the sins of the world: and sin, (as St John saith) was not in him. But* (2) *all we the rest, although baptized, and born again in Christ, yet offend in many things; and if we say we have no sin, we deceive ourselves, and the truth is not in us.*

The propositions.

1. Christ is truly and perfectly righteous.
2. All men besides Christ, though regenerate, be sinners.

Proposition I.

Christ is truly and perfectly righteous.

The proof from God's word.

That Christ was pure from sin, it is abundantly to be seen in the holy scriptures.

Matt. i. 20. Luke i. 35. He was both conceived and born without sin.

1 John iii. 8. He appeared to loose, but not to fulfil, the works of Satan.

Heb. iv. 15. 1 Pet. ii. 22. 2 Cor. v. 21. 1 John iii. 5. He lived, and was tempted, yet without sin, and did no sin, knew no sin, nor had any sin in him.

Rom. v. 6, &c. Acts iii. 14. Acts vii. 52. Matt. xxvii. 24. John xix. 4, 6. He died a guiltless and just man, even by the testimony of Paul, Peter, Stephen, yea of his adversary and judge, Pilate.

Conf. Helv. I. Art. xi. & II. c. 11. Bohem. c. 4, 7. Gal. Art. xiv. Belg. Art. xviii. As ours, such are[2] the confessions[3] of the purer churches.

[[1] Flesh, 1691.] [[2] Such is, &c. 1607.]

[[3] Is (Christus)...carnem nostræ (peccato solum excepto, quoniam illibatam esse hostiam oportebat) per omnia similem...in mortem tradidit.—Harm. Conf. Sect. vi. p. 104. Conf. Helv. Prior. Art. xi. (Christum) juxta humanam (naturam)... nobis hominibus...per omnia similem, excepto peccato.—Ibid. p. 100. Conf. Helv. Post. cap. xi....qui (sc. Christus) animam et corpus...absque omni peccato assumsit.—Ibid. p. 107. Conf. Bohem. cap. 6. Homo, inquam,...nobisque per omnia, excepto peccato, similis.—Ibid. p. 109. Conf. Gall. Art. xiv. Qui (Filius Dei)... veram naturam humanam cum omnibus ipsius infirmitatibus, excepto peccato, vere assumpsit.—Ibid. p. 113. Conf. Belg. Art. xviii.]

Errors and adversaries to this truth.

Cursed therefore before God are the Jews, which said that Christ was a violater of the sabbath. Matt. xii. 10. Luke xiii. 14. John v. 16.

That he taught, being not lawfully authorized thereunto. Matt. xxi. 23.

That he forbad tribute to be given unto Cæsar. Luke xxiii. 2.

That he was the destroyer of the law. Matt. v. 17.

That he overthrew all religion, and moved the commons unto rebellion. Luke xxiii. 5.

In this state with the Jews are

The Marcionites[4], which said that he dissolved the law, the prophets, and all the works of God. Iren. Lib. I. cap. 29.

The Saturnians[5], which blazed that his coming into the world was to overthrow the God of the angels. Theodoret.

Our new heretics, viz. Matthew Hamant[6] in England, which divulged that Christ was a sinful man and an abominable idol; and Leonardus Vairus[7] among the papists, which hath written, that Christ was *Veneficus*, or a common poisoner of men and women. Holin. Chro. fol. 1299. Leon Vairus, De Fasc. Lib. II c. 11. circa finem.

Proposition II.

All men besides Christ, though regenerate, be sinners.

The proof from God's word.

All men either be regenerate or unregenerate; the unregenerate be all sinners, unrighteous, and sin in whatsoever they do. Proved p. 125. Proved, p. 127.

[4 Jesum autem (dixit Marcion)...in hominis forma manifestatum his qui in Judæa erant, dissolventem Prophetas et Legem, et omnia opera ejus Dei qui mundum fecit, quem et Cosmocratorem dicit.—Iren. Adv. Hær. Oxon. 1702. Lib. I. cap. 29. p. 104.]

[5 ... τὸν πατέρα φησὶ τοῦ Χριστοῦ καταλῦσαι βουλόμενον μετὰ τῶν ἄλλων ἀγγέλων καὶ τὸν τῶν Ἰουδαίων Θεὸν, ἀποστεῖλαι τὸν Χριστὸν εἰς τὸν κόσμον ἐπὶ σωτηρίᾳ τῶν εἰς αὐτὸν πιστευόντων ἀνθρώπων.—Theodoret. Opp. Paris. 1642-84. Tom. IV. p. 194. Hær. Fab. Lib. I. cap. 3.]

[6 See above, p. 49, note 11.]

[7 The statement in the text is a misrepresentation. Vairus is commenting on the words, "Like the deaf adder which...refuseth to hear the voice of the charmer &c." (Ps. lviii. 4), and says, Per quam quidem similitudinem obduratam contra Christum Judæorum perfidiam propheta ostendere vult: quia ipsi ne ejus et apostolorum verba audirent, aspidis more suas obturabant aures....Quid ergo venenum nisi frigidam pœnitentiam notat? quæ carni et sanguini contraria est. Ergo Christus et Apostoli venefici erant qui tale venenum concionando conficiebant, pœnitentiæ asperitatem docendo. Utque de Venefico in bonam partem sumpto intelligeretur, inquit, Venefici incantantis sapienter.—Leon. Vairus, De Fascino, Paris. 1583. Lib. II. c. xi. p. 157.]

Proved, pp. 99, 100. Proved, p. 120. The regenerate also be not without their sins, both original and actual.

Eccles. vii. 20. Gal. v. 17. "Besides, there is no man just in the earth that doth good and sinneth not," saith the preacher. "Ye cannot do the same things that ye would."

1 Tim. i. 15. "Christ Jesus came into the world to save sinners, of whom I am chief," saith St Paul.

James iii. 2. 1 John i. 8. "In many things we sin all," is St James' saying; and St John, "If we say we have no sin, we deceive ourselves, and the truth is not in us."

Matt. vi. 12. "Pray therefore, Forgive us our debts."

Conf. August. Art. xx. Sax. Art. III. A truth believed and confessed by all churches, expressedly by some[1].

The errors and adversaries unto this truth.

Many adversaries hath this truth had, and hath; as the Papists, the Manichees, the Catharans, the Donatists, the Pelagians, Family of Love, Marcionites, Adamites, and Carpocratians. For

Concil. Trid. Sess. 5. decreto de Pec. Orig. Test. Rhem. an. Col. i. 24. Annot. Mar. iii. 33. Stapl. Antid. Evang. in Matt. xii. 50. p. 118. The Papists say that the blessed virgin was pure from all sin, both original[2] and actual. For (these are their own words) "Our Lady never sinned."

Our Lady "sinned not so much as venially in all her life[3]:" she exactly fulfilled the whole law, that is, was without sin[4].

Also of St Francis they write, that for virtue and godliness he was like unto Christ, and hath fulfilled every jot of the law[a].

[a] Sicut Adæ Deo non parenti, omnis creatura rebellis extitit: sic B. Francisco, omnia præcepta divina implenti, creatura omnis famulata est: omnia Deus subjecit sub pedibus ejus.—Alcor. Franc. [Franceph. 1542. fol. I. i.]

[[1] In hac tanta infirmitate et immunditie naturæ, sancti non satisfaciunt legi.—Harm. Conf. IX. p. 196. Conf. Aug. 1540. Art. xx. See also above, p. 126, n. 4.]

[[2] Declarat tamen hæc ipsa sancta synodus, non esse suæ intentionis, comprehendere in hoc decreto ubi de peccato originali agitur, beatam et immaculatam virginem Mariam, Dei genetricem, &c.—Concil. Harduin. Tom. x. col. 29. Conc. Trid. Sess. v. De Pecc. Orig. can. 5.]

[[3] Test. Rhem. Rhemes, 1582. Annot. Col. i. 24. p. 538, and Annot. Mar. iii. 33, p. 94.]

[[4] Verum quidem est ... forte de facto neminem quidem fuisse (Beatiss. semper virginem propter honorem Domini semper excipio) qui totam legem exacte impleverit, id est, sine peccato fuerit.—Stapleton. Opp. Par. 1620. p. 36. Antid. Evang. in Matt. xii. 50.]

The Manichees[5] and Catharans[6] thought they could not sin so much as in thought.

Hier. in prol. Dial. contra Pelag.
Cyp. Lib. IV. ep. 2.

The Donatists dreamed how they were so perfect as they could justify other men[7].

Aug. Lib. II. contra Petil. c. 14.

Some were of opinion, as the Pelagians[8] and Family of Love[9], how they were so free from sin as they needed not to say, "Forgive us our trespasses." Which Family also teacheth how there be men living as good and as holy as ever Christ was[10];—an error of Christopher Vitels[11], a chief elder in the said Family;—and that he, which is a Familist, is either as perfect as Christ, or else a very devil.

Conc. Melit. cap. 8.
Displ. H. 6. B.
Answ. to the Fam. Libert. Lib. III.
Displ. H. 6. B.

Some deemed themselves as pure as Paul, Peter, or any men, as the Marcionites[12]; yea, as Adam and Evah before their fall, as the Adamites[13]; yea, as Jesus Christ himself, as the Carpocratians[14].

Iren. Lib. I. cap. 9.
Epiphan.
Iren. Lib. I. c. 24.

[[5] Ut præteream Manichæum, Priscillianum, &c.... quorum omnium ista sententia est; posse ad perfectionem, et non dicam ad similitudinem sed æqualitatem Dei humanam virtutem et scientiam pervenire; ita ut asserant se ne cogitatione quidem et ignorantia, quum ad consummationis culmen ascenderint, posse peccare.—Hieron. Opp. Par. 1693-1706. Tom. IV. col. 484. Dial. adv. Pelag. Prolog. in Lib. I.]

[[6] Miror autem quosdam sic obstinatos esse ut dandam non putent lapsis pœnitentiam, aut pœnitentibus existiment veniam denegandam, cum scriptum sit: Memento unde cecideris, et age pœnitentiam et fac priora opera, &c.—Cypr. Opp. Oxon. 1682. Epist. 55. p. 110. In Edit. Erasm. Lib. IV. Ep. 2.]

[[7] Linguæ autem dolosæ sunt eorum, qui cum facta sua noverint, non solum se dicunt justos esse homines, sed etiam justificatores hominum.—August. Opp. Paris. 1836-8. Tom. IX. col. 371. Contr. Litt. Petil. Lib. II. cap. 35.]

[[8] Item placuit, ut quicunque verba ipsa dominicæ orationis, ubi dicimus, *Dimitte nobis debita nostra*, ita volunt a sanctis dici, ut humiliter non veraciter, hoc dicatur, anathema sit... Hucusque de fide contra Pelagianos.—Concil. Harduin. Paris. 1715. Tom. I. col. 1219. Concil. Milevit. can. VIII.]

[[9] The passage intended is probably this: They scorn all those that say, *Good Lord, have mercy upon us, miserable sinners:* saying, they that so say declare themselves never to amend, but still to be miserable sinners, whereas we do live perfectly, and sin not.—Displaying, &c. Lond. 1579. fol. H. 5.]

[[10] This reference has not been found.]

[[11] They hold, that he which is one of their congregation is either as perfect as Christ, or, &c.—Displaying of the Fam. Lond. 1579. fol. H. 6. b.]

[[12] These were not the Marcionites, but the followers of the heretic Marcus. Καὶ μαθηταὶ δὲ αὐτοῦ τινες... τελείους ἑαυτοὺς ἀναγορεύοντες· ὡς μηδενὸς δυναμένου ἐξισωθῆναι τῷ μεγέθει τῆς γνώσεως αὐτῶν, μηδ' ἂν Παῦλον, μηδ' ἂν Πέτρον εἴπῃς, μηδ' ἄλλον τινα τῶν Ἀποστόλων· ἀλλὰ πλείω πάντων ἐγνωκέναι, κ. τ. λ.—Iren. Adv. Hær. Oxon. 1702. Lib. I. c. 9. p. 60.]

[[13] Ἡγοῦνται γὰρ τὴν ἑαυτῶν ἐκκλησίαν εἶναι τὸν Παράδεισον, καὶ αὐτοὺς εἶναι τοὺς περὶ Ἀδὰμ καὶ Εὐάν.—Epiphan. Opp. Paris. 1622. Tom. I. p. 450. Adv. Hær. Lib. II. Tom. I. Hær. 52. See above, p. 101, note 6.]

[[14] See above, p. 101, note 5.]

ARTICLE XVI.

Of Sin after Baptism.

(1) *Not every deadly sin willingly committed after baptism is sin against the Holy Ghost, and unpardonable. Wherefore the grant of repentance is not to be denied to such as fall into sin after baptism.* (2) *After we have received the Holy Ghost, we may depart from grace given, and fall into sin, and by the grace of God (we may) rise again and amend our lives. And therefore they are to be condemned which say, they can no more sin as long as they live here,* (3) *or deny place of forgiveness to such as truly repent.*

The Propositions.

1. Every sin committed after baptism is not the sin against the Holy Ghost.
2. The very regenerate may depart from grace given, and fall into sin, and yet rise again unto newness of life.
3. No men utterly are to be cast off as reprobates which unfeignedly repent.

Proposition I.

Every sin committed after baptism is not the sin against the Holy Ghost.

The proof from God's word.

Though every sin, in itself considered, deserveth damnation; yet is there a sin which shall be punished with many, and a sin which shall be punished with few stripes; a sin unto death, and a sin not unto death; a sin against the Father, and the Son, which shall be forgiven; and a sin against the Holy Ghost, which never shall be forgiven.

Luke xii. 47, 48. 1 John i. 5, 16. Matt. xii. 31. Mark iii. 29. Luke xii. 10.

So in their extant Confessions witness the churches in Bohemia, Saxony, and Helvetia[1].

Confess. Bohem. c. 4. Conf. Saxon. Art. x. Conf. Helv. II. c. 8.

Errors and adversaries unto this truth.

Diversely has this doctrine been oppugned. For

[[1] ... peccata secundum hos gradus et hoc ordine considerari et æstimari possunt. Primum omnium et maximum atque gravissimum peccatum omnino fuit Adami peccatum. ... Alterum est innatum et hæreditarium, &c. ... Tertium genus peccatorum est eorum quæ actualia vocantur, &c.—Harm. Conf. Sect. IV. p. 74. Conf. Bohem.

Some have thought all sins to be like and equal, as the Stoics[2], Pelagians[3], and Jovinians[4]. Concil. Milevit. D. Hieron. advers. Jovin.

Some have taught, as Manes the heretic, how none of the godly fathers, and others from the beginning of the world, till the 15. year of Tiberius the emperor (though earnestly they did repent) were saved; but were all punished alike with utter confusion[5]. Epiphan.

Some give out that such persons be utterly out of God's favour and condemned, which depart out of this world, either afore they are baptized, as the Papists[6] do, or afore they come unto years of discretion, as [the] Hieracites[7] did. Spec. peregr. quæst. dec. I. cap. 3. q. 5. Position. ingoldstad. de Purg. Epiphan.

Proposition II.

The very regenerate may depart from grace given, and fall into sin, and yet rise again unto newness of life.

The proof from the word of God.

That the regenerate may fall into sin, and yet rise again, it is a doctrine grounded upon the scriptures. For in them we evidently may see, that fall they may, partly by the admonitions of our Saviour unto the man healed of the palsy, John v. 14.

cap. IV. Necesse est igitur discerni peccata, quæ in sanctis in hac mortali vita manent, nec excutiunt Spiritum Sanctum, ab aliis peccatis propter quæ homo rursus fit reus iræ Dei et æternarum pœnarum.—Ibid. p. 87. Conf. Saxon. Art. x.... omnia alia peccata... qualicunque nomine nuncupentur, sive mortalia sive venialia, sive illud quoque quod vocatur peccatum in Spiritum Sanctum, quod nunquam remittitur. Fatemur etiam peccata non esse æqualia, &c.—Ibid. p. 68. Conf. Helv. Post. cap. VIII.]

[2 Alia est philosophorum et Stoicorum ratio ... qui dicunt omnia peccata paria esse.—Cyp. Opp. Oxon. 1682. Ep. lv. p. 107.]

[3 There seems to be an error in the reference.]

[4 ... hæc vera est Antichristi prædicatio quæ inter Johannem et ultimum pœnitentem nullam facit esse distantiam ... Si non licet a virtutibus paululum declinare, et omnia peccata sunt paria, &c.—Hieron. Opp. Par. 1693-1706. Tom. IV. col. 213. Adv. Jov. Lib. II.]

[5 Εἶτα ἔφη, ὅτι τὰ παλαιὰ ἔτη οὐδεὶς ἐσώθη, ἀλλὰ ἀπὸ τοῦ πεντεκαιδεκάτου ἔτους Τιβερίου Καίσαρος ἄχρι τῶν αὐτοῦ χρόνων.—Epiphan. Opp. Paris. 1622. Tom. I. p. 698. Adv. Hær. Lib. II. Tom. II. Hær. 66.]

[6 Secunda quæstiuncula est: qua pœna puniuntur pueri in limbo: sine baptismate cum solo originali defuncti. Ad quam sic respondetur, quod pœna conveniens puerorum, qui cum solo peccato originali decesserunt in limbo, est subtractio gratiæ et per consequens carentia visionis divinæ ad quam homo per gratiam ordinatur.—Bart. Sibylle Spec. Peregrin. Quæst. Lugd. 1516. Prim. Dec. cap. III. Quæst. v. fol. 104.]

[7 Οὐ δέχεται δὲ τοὺς παῖδας τοὺς τελευτῶντας πρὸ γνώσεως, ἀλλ' ἀποβάλλει αὐτοὺς τῆς νομιζομένης ἐλπίδος. φάσκει γὰρ τούτους μὴ κληρονομεῖν βασιλείαν οὐρανῶν, ἐπειδή φησι οὐκ ἠγωνίσαντο.—Epiphan. Opp. Paris. 1622. Tom. I. p. 711. Adv. Hær. Lib. II. Tom. II. Hær. 67.]

John viii. 11. Eph. iv. 21, 22. Coloss. iii. 8. Heb. iii. 12. 1 Tim. i. 19. 2 Tim. iv. 3. 2 Tim. ii. 22. 1 Pet. ii. 10. & v. 8. 2 Pet. iii. 17. 2 Sam. xi. 4. 1 Kings xi. 3. Matt. xxvi. 70, 72, 74.

and unto the adulteress; of St Paul unto the Ephesians, Colossians, Hebrews, and Timothy; and of St Peter unto all the godly; and partly by the examples of David, Solomon, Peter, who egregiously and very offensively did fall: and that they do fall, it is most evident by the fifth petition of the Lord's prayer, were nothing else to prove the same; but see afore, Art. XI. Prop. 3. Art. XII. Prop. 2. Art. XV. Prop. 2.

Rev. ii. Luke xxii. 55. Acts ii. 23, &c. & iii. 13. & iv. 10, &c. Matt. xxvi. 56.

Next, that being fallen, they may rise again and be saved, it is apparent both by the exhortations of the angel unto the churches of Ephesus, Pergamus, and Thyatira; and by the examples of Peter, who denied, and yet afterward confessed his master Christ; and of all the disciples, who fled, and yet returned.

Conf. Helv. II. c. 17. Bohem. c. 5, 8. Sax. Art. X. XI. Wittem. Art. XXXII. Suevica, Art. XV.

This both granted is, and published for truth, by the churches[1].

The adversaries unto this truth.

Magdeburg. Eccles. Hist. cent. XII. c. 5. Eus. Lib. VI. c. 43. Magdeburg. Eccles. Hist. cent. IV. c. 5.

Unto this truth subscribe will not

Either the Catharans[2], Novatians[3], Jovinians[4], which

[1 ... non ita arcte includimus ecclesiam, ut omnes illos extra ecclesiam esse doceamus ... in quibus aliquando deficit fides, non tamen penitus extinguitur, aut prorsus desinit ... scimus quid evenerit S. Petro negatori, et quid quotidie evenire soleat electis Dei fidelibus errantibus et infirmis.—Harm. Conf. Sect. x. p. 7. Conf. Helv. Post. cap. XVII. For the reference to Conf. Bohem. c. 5. see next Prop. p. 140, note 2. In c. 8. the doctrine referred to is merely implied, where it is said, that those are to be the subjects of church discipline, qui in manifestis peccatis sine pœnitentia et obdurato corde versantur, &c.—Harm. Conf. x. pp. 12, 13. Postulat Deus, et quidem juramento conversionem. Quare non placent ei retinentes propositum peccandi.—Ibid. IV. p. 87. Conf. Saxon. Art. X. Et ad ministerium hæc pertinent... vocem absolutionis impertire petentibus, qui non perseverant in manifestis delictis.—Ibid. x. p. 24. Conf. Saxon. Art. XI. Quod in hac ecclesia sit vera peccatorum remissio.—Ibid. x. p. 27. Conf. Virtemb. Art. XXXII. There is an error in the reference to the Conf. Suev.]

[2 Solos se mundos et Christianos esse contendebant: reliquos vero omnes immundos et hæreticos.—Magdeburg. Eccl. Hist. Basil. 1559. &c. Cent. XII. c. 5. fol. 852.]

[3 Ἐπειδήπερ τῇ κατὰ τούτων (sc. τῶν ἐξησθενηκότων κατὰ τὸν τοῦ διωγμοῦ καιρὸν) ἀρθεὶς ὑπερηφανίᾳ Νούατος τῆς Ῥωμαίων ἐκκλησίας πρεσβύτερος, ὡς μηκέτ' οὔσης αὐτοῖς σωτηρίας ἐλπίδος, μηδ' εἰ πάντα τὰ εἰς ἐπιστροφὴν γνησίαν καὶ καθαρὰν ἐξομολόγησιν ἐπιτέλοιεν, ἰδίας αἱρέσεως τῶν κατὰ λογισμοῦ φυσίωσιν καθαροὺς ἑαυτοὺς ἀποφηνάντων ἀρχηγὸς καθίσταται.—Euseb. Eccl. Hist. Cant. 1720. Lib. VI. cap. 43. p. 309.]

[4 Non posse peccare hominem [dicebat Jovinianus] aut a diabolo subverti, lavacro regenerationis plena fide accepto. ... Suo præterea baptismo plus tribuit, quam eorum qui a se dissentiebant.—Magdeburg. Eccl. Hist. Cent. iv. c. 5. fol. 381.]

think God's people be regenerate into a pure and angelical state, so that neither they be, nor can be, defiled with any contagion of sin.

Either the Libertines, whose opinions were, that

Whosoever hath God's Spirit in him cannot sin.

David sinned not after he had received the Holy Ghost[5]. Wilkinson against the Fa. of Love, Art. XIV.

Regeneration[6] is the restoring of the estate wherein Adam was placed afore his fall. Calv. contra Liber. fol. 217.

Or the Papists, who are of mind, that

The works[7] of men justified are perfect in this life. Tapp. p. 189.

No man[8] which is fallen into sin can rise again, and be saved, without their sacrament of penance. Conc. Trid. Sess. 6. Can. 29.

St Francis attained unto the perfection of holiness, and could not sin at all[a].

Proposition III.

No men utterly are to be cast off as reprobate which unfeignedly repent.

[The proof from God's word.]

Such as do fall from grace, and yet return again unto the Lord by true repentance, are to be received as members of God's church: and this by the scripture is verified. For there we read that

"God would have all men saved." Matt. xi. 28. 1 Tim. ii. 4.

[a] Vis ad apicem venire perfectionis? Vitam cum moribus attende B. Francisci.

[[5] That whosoever hath God's Spirit cannot sin, and that the prophet David did not sin, after that time he had received the Holy Ghost.—Wilkinson's Confut. of Certain Articles, &c. London, 1579. Artic. XIV. p. 66. b.]

[[6] Hoc enim principium sumunt; nempe regenerationem esse restitutionem innocentiæ, in qua Adam, antequam peccasset, constitutus erat. Hunc autem innocentiæ statum sic accipiunt, nihil dignoscere, nec inter album quod aiunt et nigrum discernere; quia hoc Adæ peccatum fuit, comedere de fructu scientiæ boni et mali.—Calv. Opp. Amstelod. 1667-72. Tom. VIII. p. 389. Instruct. Adv. Libert. cap. XVIII.]

[[7] Non solum opera justorum severum Dei judicium sustinent, ut reprehendi non possint, etiam diligentissime examinata discussis circumstantiis ac diaboli accusatione audita. Nihil enim culpæ, nihil deformitatis habent... verum etiam mercedem secundum justitiam, et non mere ex gratia accipiunt.—Tapp. Opp. Colon. Agr. 1582. Tom. II. Art. VIII. p. 17. b.]

[[8] Si quis dixerit, eum, qui post baptismum lapsus est, non posse per Dei gratiam resurgere; aut posse quidem, sed sola fide amissam justitiam recuperare sine sacramento pœnitentiæ,... anathema sit.—Conc. Harduin. Paris. 1714. Tom. X. col. 43. Conc. Trid. Sess. VI. De Justificatione, Can. 29.]

God is always ready to receive the penitent into favour: for "there is joy in heaven for the sinner that converteth." Luke xv. 7.

Christ is grieved when sinners will not repent. Luke xix. 41, 42, &c.

"He shall save a soul from death, and hide a multitude of sins, which converteth a sinner from going astray out of his way." James v. 20.

"The Lord would have no man to perish, but all men to come to repentance." 2 Pet. iii. 9.

"If we acknowledge our sins, he is faithful and just to forgive us our sins, and to cleanse us from all unrighteousness." 1 John i. 9.

He exhorteth his erring people to repent, and do their first works: neither refuseth he the sinner that repenteth, as appeareth in the example of the prodigal son, and of the debtor. Rev. ii. 5, 16. Luke xv. 20. Matt xviii. 26, &c.

God then being so gracious and merciful, man after his ensample is both by all good means to provoke sinners unto repentance, and, they testifying the same, to receive them into favour.

So did St Paul will the Galatians. "Brethren (saith he), if a man be fallen by occasion into any fault, ye which are spiritual restore such an one with the spirit of meekness, considering thyself, lest thou also be tempted." Gal. vi. 1.

So did he enjoin the Corinthians, when he said,

"If any hath caused sorrow, the same hath not made me sorry, but partly (lest I should more charge him) you all. It is sufficient unto the same man, that he was rebuked of many. So that now, contrariwise, ye ought rather to forgive, and comfort (him), lest the same should be swallowed up with overmuch heaviness." 2 Cor. ii. 5, 6, 7.

When also he said, "Receive him," (meaning Onesimus). Philem. 12.

And so teach the churches[1]. Confess. Helv. II. c. 14. Bohem. c. 5. August. Art. XI. Saxon. Art. III. Wittemb. Art. XII.

[[1] Docemus ... et omnibus peccatoribus aditum patere ad Deum, et hunc omnia omnibus fidelibus condonare peccata, excepto uno illo peccato in Spiritum Sanctum.—Harm. Conf. Sect. VIII. p. 140. Conf. Helv. Post. cap. XIV. ... Deinceps docetur de sacra pœnitentia, quæ doctrina omnibus peccatoribus consolationem præstat ingentem, et in genere omnibus hominibus, tam incipientibus discere, quam proficientibus Christianis, etiam lapsis peccatoribus, iis tamen qui per gratiam Dei conversi resipiscunt, ad salutem admodum utilis est et necessaria.—Ibid. p. 141. Conf. Bohem. cap. v. De pœnitentia docent, quod lapsis post baptismum contingere possit remissio peccatorum, quocunque tempore, quum convertuntur. Et quod

Errors and adversaries unto this truth.

Adversaries unto this truth are they,

First, which leave nothing but the unappeasable wrath of God to such as do sin after baptism: as did both in old time the Montanists[2] and Novatians[3], and of late years Melchior Hoffman[4], the arch-heretic of his days, and the anabaptists in Germany[5], and the Barrowists[6] among ourselves in England.

D. Hieron. adv. Marc. Cypr. Epist. 4. ad Antonian. Bullin. contra Anab. Lib. II. c. 13. Calv. Instit. Giffor. Reply. Magd. Eccles. Hist. cent. 4. cap. 5. H. N. spirit. land, cap. 33, § 5, cap. 34. § 11, c. 37, § 8, & Prov. cap. 5, § 15, and crying voice, § 6.

Next, who say, that, being once regenerate, sin is cut away, as with a razor, so that the godly cannot sin, and therefore need no repentance; so did the Messalians[7], and do the Family of Love[8].

ecclesia talibus, redeuntibus ad pœnitentiam, impertire absolutionem debeat.—Ibid. p. 147. Conf. Aug. 1540. Art. IX. Certissimum est prædicationem pœnitentiæ ad omnes homines pertinere, et accusare omnes homines. Ita et promissio universalis est, et omnibus offert remissionem peccatorum, &c.—Ibid. p. 152. Conf. Saxon. Art. III. Quum semper nobis agnoscenda sint peccata nostra et credendum quod remittantur nobis peccata propter Christum, sentimus semper etiam in hac vita nobis agendam esse pœnitentiam.—Ibid. p. 158. Conf. Virtemb. Art. XII.]

[2 Illi ad omne pene delictum ecclesiæ obserant fores, nos quotidie legimus: malo pœnitentiam peccatoris, quam mortem, &c.—Hieron. Opp. Paris. 1693-1706. Tom. IV. Pars I. col. 65. Epist. 27. ad Marc.]

[3 See above, p. 135, note 6.]

[4 Quod si quis accepta gratia denuo voluntarie peccaret, hunc nunquam deinceps in gratiam recipi.—Bulling. Adv. Anabapt. Tiguri. 1560. p. 656. Lib. II. cap. 13.]

[5 ... Novatianis non multum dissimiles nostrum quoque seculum habet quosdam ex anabaptistis ... Fingunt enim regenerari Dei populum in baptismo in puram et Angelicam vitam ... Quod si post baptismum quis delinquat, nihil præter inexorabile Dei judicium illi relinquunt.—Calv. Opp. Amstelod. 1667-72. Tom. IX. Institut. Lib. IV. cap. 1. § 23. p. 276.]

[6 With Novatus the wicked heretic, ye take away all hope of salvation from those which offend of knowledge willingly, inasmuch as ye make every obstinate persisting in the least error to separate from the faith and communion of Christ.—Gyfford's Reply to Barrow and Greenwood, Lond. 1591. p. 96.]

[7 Baptismum auferre priora peccata instar novaculæ; nec prodesse cuiquam nisi oratione prorsus exscindantur, ut deinceps non sit necesse jejunio corpus reprimere, aut doctrina refrenare, possitque omni petulantia carere.—Magdeburg. Eccl. Hist. Basil. 1559, &c. Cent. IV. c. 5. fol. 387.]

[8 Whosoever also cometh into this good city of Peace, he becometh altogether born anew in the Spirit, (1 Pet. 1. 2), under the obedience of the Love, through the said Love and her service. For he is changed in every part, as in senses, thoughts, and mind. (Rom. 12. Eph. 4. c.)—H. N. Spiritual Land of Peace. cap. XXXIII. 5. p. 51. Also there the one doth see no unclean thing in the other. For it is there, all of God, spiritual, holy, and good (Eph. 1. 2. Apo. 21. a.); and pure are all their works and thoughts.—Ibid. cap. XXXIV. 11. p. 53. For all there, whatsoever is manly, the same is every one; lords, kings, and priests: and do

Gen. iv. Acts i. History of Francis Spira. Luther on Gal. iii. 1. Gifford's Rep. to Barrow and Green. pag. 17.

Lastly, the desperate, whose sins being either infinite, or abominable, they think how God he neither can, nor will forgive them: such in times past were Cain and Judas; in our fathers', Franciscus Spira[1] and one Doctor Kraus[2]; and in our days, Bolton[3], even he that first hatched that sect in England, which afterward was termed Brownism.

Article XVII.

Of Predestination and Election.

(1) *Predestination to life is the everlasting purpose of God, whereby,* (2) *before the foundations of the world were*[4] *laid, he hath* (3) *constantly decreed by his counsel secret to us, to deliver from curse and damnation* (4) *those whom he hath chosen* (5) *in Christ out of mankind, and to bring them by Christ to everlasting salvation, as vessels made to*

bear their dominion over sin, death, devil, and hell.—Ibid. cap. xxxvii. 8. p. 57. In the true Love, the kingdom of heaven bideth stedfast; upon the earth; everlastingly; in perfection: and there cometh with the same, in the true Love, the eternal life, to the elected holy ones of God upon the earth.—H. N. Proverbs. Cap. v. 15. For that cause come now all to this hill (Esa. 2. a.) or house of Love: and purge, amend, (Ezech. 16.) or hallow your being under the obedience of the Love of Jesus Christ in the out-flowing waters of the same: to the end that your sins may become washed away (Act. 3. c.): and ye even so led into the rest (Heb. 3. b. 4) of all the children of God and holy ones of Jesu Christ.—First Epistle, (A Crying Voice, &c.) chap. ii. § 6.]

[1 Dei misericordiam proponitis: at Deus me abjecit. Allegatis Christi gratiam atque interpellationem? Ego Christum abnegavi. Credere me jubetis? nequeo. Sum hostis judicatus, vestrum mandatum mihi est impossibile. ... Hinc est quod in salo jactor desperationis ... Vult Deus me sustinere hanc pœnam peccati, vult in me statuere exemplum iræ suæ vestra causa, &c.—Hist. Fr. Spier. Basil. 1550. p. 109. See above, p. 59, note 8.]

[2 Idem anno Domini 1527 accidit illi misero Doctori Hallensi Kraus, qui dicebat: Ego negavi Christum, ideo jam stat coram Patre, et accusat me. Illam cogitationem, præstigiis diaboli captus, tam fortiter conceperat ut nulla adhortatione aut consolatione, nullis divinis promissionibus pateretur eam sibi excuti, atque ita desperavit, et seipsum miserrime occidit.—Luther. Opp. Witeberg. 1554, &c. Tom. v. p. 325, 6. Comm. in Gal. cap. 3.]

[3 I said that the fearful end of one Bolton, about twenty years past, would not be forgotten ... for the truth is, he did for the same causes that you do, utterly condemn the whole church of England, and was with sundry others separated from it. And (as it is constantly affirmed) he was an elder in their secret church, and afterward falling into deep despair, he could not be recovered, but did hang himself.—Gyfford's Reply, Lond. 1591. p. 17.]

[4 Was, 1607.]

honour. Wherefore, they which be endued with so excellent a benefit of God (6) *be called according to God's purpose by his Spirit working in due season:* (7) *they through grace obey the calling: they be justified freely: they be made sons of God by adoption: they be made like the image of his only-begotten Son Jesus Christ: they walk religiously in good works: and at length, by God's mercy, they attain to everlasting felicity.* (8) *As the godly consideration of predestination, and our election in Christ, is full of sweet, pleasant, and unspeakable comfort to godly persons, and such as feel in themselves the working of the Spirit of Christ, mortifying the works of the flesh, and their earthly members, and drawing up their mind to high and heavenly things, as well because it doth greatly establish and confirm their faith of eternal salvation to be enjoyed through Christ, as because it doth fervently kindle their love towards God: so, for curious and carnal persons, lacking the Spirit of Christ, to have continually before their eyes the sentence of God's predestination, is a most dangerous downfall, whereby the devil doth thrust them either into desperation, or into wretchlessness of most unclean living, no less perilous than desperation. Furthermore,* (9) *we must receive God's promises in such wise as they be generally set forth unto us in holy scripture: and,* (10) *in our doings, that will of God is to be followed, which we have expressly declared unto us in the Word of God.*

The Propositions.

1. There is a predestination of men unto everlasting life.
2. Predestination hath been from everlasting.
3. They which are predestinate unto salvation cannot perish.
4. Not all men, but certain, are predestinate to be saved.
5. In Christ Jesus, of the mere will and purpose of God, some are elected, and not others, unto salvation.
6. They who are elected unto salvation, if they come unto years of discretion, are called both outwardly by the word, and inwardly by the Spirit of God.

7. The predestinate are both justified by faith, sanctified by the Holy Ghost, and shall be glorified in the life to come.

8. The consideration of predestination is to the godly wise most comfortable, but to curious and carnal persons very dangerous.

9. The general promises of God, set forth in the holy scriptures, are to be embraced of us.

10. In our actions, the word of God, which is his revealed will, must be our direction.

Proposition I.

There is a predestination of men unto everlasting life.

The proof from God's word.

That of men, some be predestinate unto life, it is a truth most apparent in the holy scripture by the testimony both of Christ himself, who saith,

Matt. xx. 23. "To sit at my right hand, and at my left hand, is not mine to give, but (it shall be given) to them for whom it is prepared of my Father."

Ibid. xxii. 14. "Many are called, but few chosen."

Ibid. xxiv. 22. "For the elects' sake those days shall be shortened."

Luke xii. 32. "Fear not, little flock; for it is your Father's pleasure to give you a kingdom."

Ibid. xvii. 34. "I tell you, in that night there shall be two in one bed; the one shall be received, and the other shall be left."

John vi. 37. "All that the Father giveth me shall come unto me."

Witnessed also is this by the evangelist Luke, and Paul;
Acts xiii. 48. the one saith, how of the Gentiles at Antioch "so many as
Rom. viii. 29. were ordained unto eternal life believed;" and the other, "those whom he knew before he did also predestinate."

2 Cor. ii. 15, 16. "We are unto God the sweet savour of Christ, in them that are saved, and in them which perish: to the one we are the savour of death unto death; and to the other, the savour of life unto life."

Eph. i. 3, 4, 5. "Blessed be God, even the Father of our Lord Jesus Christ, which, &c., hath chosen us in him, before the foundation of the world, &c., who hath predestinate us to be adopted
Matt. xxv. 34, 41. through Jesus Christ unto himself, &c."

Jude 6. Gen. iv. 4. Rom. ix. 7, &c. Mal. i. 2, 3. Rom. ix. 13. Gen. xl. 20. The examples also of the elected creatures, man and angels; of the two brethren, Abel and Cain; Isaac and Ismael; Jacob and Esau; of the two eunuchs of K. Pharaoh;

of the two kingdoms, Juda and Israel; the two peoples, Jews and Gentiles; the two apostles, Peter and Judas; the two thieves upon the cross, the two men in the field, the two women at the mill; make to the illustration of this truth. Luke xxiii. 39, 40, 43. Matt. xxiv. 40, 41.

All churches consent with this doctrine.

The errors and adversaries unto this truth.

Err therefore do they which stand in opinion that

Some are appointed to be saved, but none to be damned.

In souls, some persons; but in soul and body together, none shall be saved. Of this mind were the old heretics, *viz.* the false apostles, the Carpocratians[1], the Valentinians[2], the Cerdonites[3], the Manichees[4], and the Hieracites[5], and of their opinion be the Family of Love[6]. 1 Cor. xv. 12. Clem. Strom. Lib. IV. Irenæus. Irenæus. August. contra Faust. Lib. IV. cap. 16. Epiphan. H. N. Instr. Art. v. § 24. Prophecy of the Spir. cap. 16. § 7.

Proposition II.

Predestination hath been from everlasting.

The proof from God's word.

Predestination began before all times. "It will be said" (saith our Saviour Christ), "Come, ye blessed of my Father, inherit ye the kingdom prepared for you from the foundations of the world." Matt. xxv. 34.

"God hath chosen us in Jesus Christ before the foundation of the world." Ephes. i. 4.

"God hath saved us, &c., according to his own purpose and 2 Tim. i. 9.

[1 This reference the editor has been unable to verify.]

[2 Τρίων οὖν ὄντων, τὸ μὲν ὑλικὸν, ὅ καὶ ἀριστερὸν καλοῦσι, κατὰ ἀνάγκην ἀπόλλυσθαι λέγουσιν ἅτε μηδεμίαν ἐπιδείξασθαι πνοὴν ἀφθαρσίας δυνάμενον· τὸ δὲ ψυχικὸν, ὃ καὶ δεξιὸν προσαγορεύουσιν, ἅτε μέσον ὂν τοῦ τε πνευματικοῦ καὶ ὑλικοῦ, ἐκεῖσε χωρεῖν ὅπου ἂν καὶ τὴν πρόσκλισιν ποιήσηται· τὸ δὲ πνευματικὸν ἐκπεπέμφθαι ὅπως ἐνθάδε τῷ ψυχικῷ συζυγὲν μορφωθῇ....καὶ τὸν Σωτῆρα δὲ ἐπὶ τοῦτο παραγεγονέναι τὸ ψυχικὸν (λέγουσι)...ὅπως αὐτὸ σώσῃ. And again a little below, ὡς γὰρ τὸ χοϊκὸν ἀδύνατον σωτηρίας μετασχεῖν. κ.τ.λ. Iren. Adv. Hær. Oxon. 1702. Lib. I. cap. 1. § 11. pp. 29, 30.]

[3 Irenæus mentions this as one of the dogmas of Marcion (Lib. I. cap. 29, p. 104), but he does not attribute it to Cerdo.]

[4 Ex qua vena falsitatis vos manare cognoscite, qui dicitis nunc esse resurrectionem tantummodo animarum per prædicationem veritatis; corporum autem quam prædicaverunt apostoli, futuram negatis—August. Opp. Par. 1836-8. Tom. VIII. col. 329, 30. Con. Faust. Lib. IV. cap. 2.]

[5 Βούλεται γὰρ καὶ οὗτος (sc. Ἱέρακας) τὴν σάρκα μὴ ἀνίστασθαι τὸ παράπαν, ἀλλὰ τὴν ψυχὴν μονωτάτην.—Epiphan. Opp. Paris, 1622. Tom. I. p. 709. Adv. Hær. Lib. II. Tom. II. Hær. 67.]

[6 These references have not been found.]

grace, which was given to us through Christ Jesus before the world was."

Confess. [Helvet.] 2. c. 10, 11. [Basil.] Art. I. [Gall.] Art. XII. The public confessions of the churches, namely in Helvetia, Basil, and France[1], bear witness hereunto.

Adversaries unto this truth.

Those wrangling sophisters then are deceived, who, because God is not included within the compass of any time, but hath all things to come as present continually before his eyes, do say, that God he did not in the time long ago past only, but still in the time present, likewise doth predestinate.

Proposition III.

They which are predestinate unto salvation cannot perish.

The proof from God's word.

John vi. 37. "All that the Father giveth me shall come to me; and him that cometh to me I cast not away;" saith Christ.

John x. 28, 29. "I give unto them eternal life, and they shall never perish, neither shall any pluck them out of my hand, &c.... None is able

Matt. xvi. 18. to take them out of my Father's hand." "The gates of hell shall not overcome the church."

Rom. viii. 30. "Moreover, whom he predestinated[2], them he also glorified."

Rom. xi. 29. "For the gifts and calling of God are without repentance."

1 John ii. 19. "They went out from us, but they were not of us: for if they had been of us, they would have continued with us."

So the churches of God; as afore in this Article.

The errors and adversaries unto this truth.

Wander then do they from the truth which think

[1 Deus ab æterno prædestinavit, vel elegit libere et mera sua gratia, nullo hominum respectu, sanctos quos vult salvos facere in Christo, juxta illud apostoli, Deus elegit nos in ipso, antequam jacerentur fundamenta mundi.—Harm. Conf. Sect. v. p. 93. Conf. Helv. Post. Art. x. Credimus...Jesum Christum ab æterno prædestinatum vel præordinatum esse a Patre, salvatorem mundi.—Ibid. p. 99. Art. xi. Confitemur Deum, antequam mundum creasset, eos omnes elegisse, quos hæreditate æternæ beatitudinis donare vult.—Ibid. p. 95. Conf. Basil. Art. i. [Disp. 3.]. Credimus ex hac corruptione et damnatione universali, in qua omnes homines natura sunt submersi, Deum alios quidem eripere, quos videlicet æterno et immutabili suo consilio sola sua bonitate et misericordia, nulloque operum ipsorum respectu in Jesu Christo elegit.—Ibid. Conf. Gall. Art. xii.]

[2 Predestinate, 1607.]

That the very elect, totally and finally, may fall from grace, and be damned.

That the regenerate may fall from the grace of God; may destroy the temple of God, and be broken off from the vine, Christ Jesus: which was one of Glover's[3] errors. Bredwell's Detect. p. 85.

That the number of those which be predestinate may both increase and be diminished: so thought the Pelagians.

Proposition IV.

Not all men, but certain be predestinate to be saved.

The proof from God's word.

We deny that all, and affirm that a certain chosen and select[4] company of men be predestinate: and so doth God's word. "Rejoice that your names are written in heaven." Luke x. 20.

"I know mine, and am known of mine," is the saying of Christ Jesus. John x. 14.

"I suffer all things for the elect's sake," saith St Paul. 2 Tim. ii. 10.

The very same with us do the churches[5] affirm. Conf. Helv. II. cap. 10. Basil. Art. I. Gal. Art. XII. Belg. Art. XVI.

Adversaries unto this truth.

We are therefore against them which teach, how not certain, but all, even the most ungodly, and damnable, yea, the very devils, shall be saved: of which opinion were the Origenists[6], and are the Catabaptists[7]. Wolf. Musc. in epist. ad Philip. præf.

All men be elected unto life everlasting. Bullin. contr. Catabap. Lib. I.

There is no hell, nor future and eternal misery at all;

[[3] Now he [Glover] saith: It is manifest in the word of God, that if we be not stirred up to take heed, we may quench and so put clean out the Spirit of Christ, we may fall away from the grace of God, we may destroy the temple of God, we may be broken off from the vine Christ Jesus, &c.—Bredwell's Detect. Lond. 1568. p. 85.]

[[4] So the edition of 1691. All the previous editions have 'chosen and company,' which might perhaps have been an error for, 'and chosen company.']

[[5] See last Prop. p. 146, note 1, and add: Credimus Deum...seipsum...demonstrasse...et misericordem et justum: misericordem quidem, eos damnatione et interitu liberando et servando quos in æterno suo consilio pro gratuita sua bonitate per Jesum Christum Dominum nostrum elegit, absque ullo operum ipsorum respectu. Justum vero, alios in illo suo lapsu et perditione relinquendo, &c.—Harm. Conf. Sect. v. p. 96. Conf. Belg. Art. XVI.]

[[6] Origenes, qui...fingit Satanam conversum iri, damnatorum pœnas cessaturas et alia his etiam absurdiora.—Wolfg. Muscul. Comm. in Pauli Epist. Basil. 1578. In Ep. ad Philip. Præf. p. 4.]

[[7] See above, p. 67, note 7.]

Nash, in Chr. his Tears, p. 58. Ramsey's and Allen's Conf.

but only either in man's opinion, as hold the Atheists[1]; or in the heart and conscience of man in this life, as the Familists[2] maintain.

No certain company be foredestined unto eternal condemnation.

Calv. Epist. Ministr. Basil. fol. 105.

None, more than others, be predestinate unto salvation; which was an error of Henry Bolseck[3].

In like sort we condemn such as either curiously enquire who, and how many, shall be saved or damned; or give the sentence of reprobation upon any men[4] whosoever; as do the Papists upon Calvin, Beza, and Verone, when they call them reprobates.

Test. Rhem. ann. Rom. xi. 33.

Proposition V.

Of the mere will and purpose of God some men in Christ Jesus are elected, and not others, unto salvation.

The proof from God's word.

In the scripture we read of man's predestination, the cause efficient to be the everlasting purpose of God[a]; the cause formal, God his infinite mercy and goodness[b]; the cause material, the blood of Christ[c]; the cause final, or end, why both

[a] That the purpose of God might remain according to election, Rom. ix. 11. Who doth predestinate us, &c. according to the good pleasure of his will, Ephes. i. 5. Not according to our works, but according to his own purpose and grace, 2 Tim. i. 9.

[b] I will shew mercy to whom I will shew mercy, Exod. xxxiii. 19, Rom. ix. 15.

[c] He hath chosen us in Christ, &c., and hath predestinated us through Christ unto himself, Eph. i. 4, 5. Ye were not redeemed with corruptible things, &c., but with the precious blood of Christ, as of a Lamb undefiled and without spot, which was ordained before the foundation of the world, but was declared in the last times for your sakes, 1 Pet. i. 18, 19, 20.

[[1] They follow the Pironicks, whose position and opinion it is, that there is no hell or misery but opinion.—Nashe's Christ's Teares over Jerusalem. Lond. 1593. p. 58. b.]

[[2] This reference has not been found.]

[[3] Hanc vero gratiam generalem esse: item non esse hos potius quam illos ad salutem prædestinatos.—Calvin. Opp. Amstelod. 1671. Tom. IX. Pars 2. p. 64. Epist. Ministr. Basil.]

[[4] ... the proud pens of Calvin, Beza, Verone, and such reprobates, &c.—Test. Rhem. Rhemes, 1582. Ann. Rom. xi. 33. p. 412.]

God the Father hath loved, and Christ for his elect hath suffered, is the glory of God[d], and the salvation of man[e].

And this do all the churches[5] militant, and reformed, with a sweet consent, testify and acknowledge.

Errors and adversaries unto this truth.

Hereby is discovered the impiety of those men which think that,

1. Man doth make himself eligible for the kingdom of heaven by his own good works and merits; so teach the Papists.

"The kingdom of heaven" (say they) "is prepared for them that are worthy of it, and deserve it by their well-doing[6]." Test. Rhem. an. Matt. xx. 23.

Licet electis gloria ex æterna Dei prædestinatione dimanet, non tamen provenit, nisi ex eorum operibus, &c. Sine nobis non glorificamur[7]. 1. Although from God's eternal predestination glory floweth to the elect, yet for all that it springeth not but from their own works, &c. Without ourselves we are not glorified. Stella in Luc. c. 10. fol. 35.

2. God beheld in every man whether he would use his grace well, and believe the gospel or no; and as he saw a man affected, so he did predestinate, choose, or refuse him.

3. Besides his will, there was some cause in God why he chose one, and cast off another man; but this cause is hidden from us.

4. Men by nature be elected and saved; an error of the Basilidians and Valentinians[8]. Clem. Alex. Strom. Lib. II. 4.

[d] Who doth predestinate us, &c. to the praise of the glory of his grace, Eph. i. 6. The Lord hath made all things for his own sake: yea, even the wicked for the day of evil, Prov. xvi. 4.

[e] Those whom he knew before, he did also predestinate to be made like to the image of his Son, that he might be the firstborn among many brethren, Rom. viii. 29. Hath not the potter power of the clay to make of the same lump one vessel to honour, and another unto dishonour? Rom. ix. 21.

[[5] See above, p. 146, note 1, and p. 147, note, 5.]

[[6] Test. Rhem. Rhemes, 1582. Ann. Matt. xx. 23. p. 58.]

[[7] Stell. in Luc. Evang. Lugd. 1583. Tom. II. fol. 35. Enarr. in cap. x.]

[[8] 'Ενταῦθα φυσικὴν ἡγοῦνται τὴν πίστιν οἱ ἀμφὶ τὸν Βασιλείδην· καθὸ καὶ ἐπὶ τῆς ἐκλογῆς τάττουσιν αὐτὴν, τὰ μαθήματα ἀναποδείκτως εὑρίσκουσαν καταλήψει νοητικῇ. Οἱ δὲ ἀπὸ Οὐαλεντίνου τὴν μὲν πίστιν τοῖς ἁπλοῖς

Theoph. in Matth. 22. Calvin. epist. Minist. Helv. fol. 104.

5. It is in man's[1] power to be elected, the error of Theophylact[2] and of Bolseck[3].

6. God is partial and unjust for choosing some, and refusing others; calling many, and electing but few.

Proposition VI.

They who are elected unto salvation, if they come unto years of discretion, are called both outwardly by the word, and inwardly by the Spirit of God.

The proof from God's word.

Though true it be, the Lord knoweth all and every of his elect, yet hath he revealed unto us certain notes and tokens whereby we may see and certainly know whether we be of that number, or not. For such as be ordained unto everlasting life, if they live long in this world, they one time or other be called unto the knowledge of salvation, by the preaching of God's word; they obey that calling, through the operation of the Holy Ghost working within them; they feel in their souls the same Spirit bearing witness unto their spirits how they are the children of God; and finally, they walk religiously in all good works.

These things are most evident, and clear in the holy Scripture, where is set down both the calling of the predestinate[a],

[a] Whom he predestinate them also he called, Rom. viii. 30. God separated me from my mother's womb, and called me by his grace, Gal. i. 15. He hath called you to his kingdom and glory, 1 Thess. ii. 12. He hath saved us, and called us with an holy calling, 2 Tim. i. 9. They that are on his side, called, chosen, and faithful, Rev. xvii. 14.

ἀπονείμαντες ἡμῖν, αὐτοῖς δὲ τὴν γνῶσιν, τοῖς φύσει σωζομένοις, κ. τ. λ.—Clem. Alex. Opp. Oxon. 1715. Tom. I. Strom. Lib. II. c. 3. p. 433. ... *φύσει σωζομένου, ὡς Οὐαλεντῖνος βούλεται, τινὸς, καὶ φύσει πιστοῦ καὶ ἐκλεκτοῦ ὄντος, ὡς Βασιλείδης νομίζει.*—Ibid. Tom. II. Lib. V. c. 1. p. 645.]

[[1] Man his power, 1607.]

[[2] *Πολλοὶ δὲ εἰσὶ κλητοὶ, πολλοὺς γὰρ καλεῖ ὁ Θεὸς, μᾶλλον δὲ πάντας· ὀλίγοι δὲ ἐκλεκτοὶ, ὀλίγοι γὰρ οἱ σωζόμενοι καὶ ἄξιοι τοῦ ἐκλεγῆναι παρὰ Θεοῦ· ὥστε τοῦ μὲν Θεοῦ τὸ καλεῖν, τὸ δὲ ἐκλεκτοὺς γενέσθαι, ἢ μὴ, ἡμέτερόν ἐστι.*—Theophylact. Opp. Venet. 1754-63. Tom. I. p. 119. A. In Matt. xxii.]

[[3] ... non ideo salutem consequi homines, quia electi sint; sed ideo eligi quia credant.... Hic autem impostor cum electionem ex fide pendere fingit, tum fidem ipsam non minus ex proprio motu hominis quam ex cœlesti inspiratione oriri.—Calv. Opp. Amstelod. 1671. Tom. IX. Pars II. p. 64. Epist. Minist. Helv.]

and their obedience to the word being called[b], and their adoption by the Spirit to be the children of God[c]; and last of all, their holiness of life, and virtuous conversation[d].

All churches reformed consent hereunto.

Errors and adversaries unto this truth.

Sundry adversaries hath this truth, and

First, the Papists, who teach that none are to think or persuade themselves that they are of the number of the predestinate unto salvation, but to be ever doubtful thereof[4].

Concil. Trid. Sess. 6. c. 12. Can. 15, Test. Rhem. annot. Rom. viii. 38. an. 1 Cor. ii. 12. an Phil. ii. 12.

[b] Your obedience is come abroad among all, Rom. xvi. 19. In Christ also ye trusted, after ye heard the word of truth, Eph. i. 13. Jesus Christ is in you, except ye be reprobates, 2 Cor. xiii. 5.

[c] Ye received the Spirit of adoption, whereby we cry, Abba, Father: the same Spirit bearing witness with our spirit that we are the children of God, Rom. viii. 15, 16. After this manner pray ye, Our Father, &c. Matt. vi. 9. And because ye are sons, God hath sent forth the spirit of his Son into your hearts, which crieth, Abba, Father, Gal. iv. 6.

[d] He hath chosen us in him, &c. that we should be holy and without blame before him in love, Eph. i. 4. We are his workmanship, created in Christ Jesus unto good works, which God hath ordained, that we should walk in them, Eph. ii. 10. For the grace of God, &c. hath appeared, and teacheth us that we should deny ungodliness and worldly lusts, and that we should live soberly, and righteously, and godly, in this present world, Tit. ii. 11, 12.

[[4] Nemo quoque, quamdiu in hac mortalitate vivitur, de arcano divinæ prædestinationis mysterio usque adeo præsumere debet, ut certo statuat se omnino esse in numero prædestinatorum, &c.—Concil. Harduin. Paris, 1714. Tom. x. col. 37. Conc. Trid. Sess. VI. cap. 12. Si quis dixerit hominem renatum et justificatum teneri ex fide ad credendum se certo esse in numero prædestinatorum; anathema sit.—Ibid. De Justif. can. 15.

I am sure. This speech is common in St Paul, according to the Latin translation, when he had no other assured knowledge but by hope: as *Rom.* 15, 14; 2 *Tim.* 1, 5; *Heb.* 6, 9: where the Greek word signifieth only a probable persuasion. And therefore except he mean of himself by special revelation, or of the predestinate in general, (in which two cases it may stand for the certitude of faith or infallible knowledge) otherwise that every particular man should be assured infallibly that himself should be justified, and not that only, but sure also never to sin, or to have the gift of perseverance, and certain knowledge of his predestination: that is a most damnable false allusion and presumption, condemned by the fathers of the holy council of Trent. *Sess.* 6, *c.* 9, 12, 13.—Test. Rhem. Rhemes, 1582.—Ann. Rom. viii. 38. *That we may know the things that of God are given to us.* The protestants that challenge a particular spirit revealing to each one his own predestination, justification, and salvation, would draw this text to that purpose. Which importeth nothing else, (as is plain by the apostle's discourse) but that the Holy Ghost hath given to the apostles, and by them to other Christian men, to know God's ineffable gifts bestowed upon the believers in this

The said Papists deliver, that so many persons as are not marked with the sign of the cross upon their forehead are damned and reprobate[1]; also, that they which will be saved must be Franciscans[2], at leastwise become members of the church of Rome[3].

Test. Rhem. annot. Apoc. ix. 4. Conform. F. Lib. I. fol. 101. Answer to the exec. of Just. cap. 8. pag. 192. Simon. Pauli meth. par. 2. de lege Dei.

Secondly, the Anti-nomies[4], which think the outward calling by the word (though they have not the inward calling by the Spirit, and be destitute of good works) a sufficient argument of their election unto life.

Demon. of Dis. epist. ded.

Thirdly, the Puritans, who, among other assurances given them from the Lord of their salvation, make their advancing of the presbyterial kingdom (by the putting down of bishops, chancellors, &c.) a testimony that they shall have part in that glory which shall be revealed hereafter[5].

Fourthly, the Schwenfeldians, and all such as, depending upon immediate and divine revelations, condemn and contemn the ordinary calling of God by the ministry of his word.

time of grace: that is Christ's Incarnation, Passion, presence in the Sacrament, and the incomprehensible joys of heaven.—Ibid. Ann. 1 Cor. ii. 12. p. 428. *With fear and trembling.* Against the vain presumption of heretics that make men secure of their predestination and salvation, he willeth the Philippians to work their salvation with fear and trembling, according to that other scripture, *Blessed is the man that always is fearful,* Proverb. 28, v. 14.—Ibid. Ann. Phil. ii. 12. p. 530.]

[1 *Nor any green thing.* The heretics never hurt or seduce the green tree, that is, such as have a living faith working by charity; but commonly they corrupt him in faith who should otherwise have perished for ill life, and him that is reprobate, that hath neither the sign of the cross (which is God's mark) in the forehead of his body, nor the note of election in his soul.—Ibid. Ann. Apocal. ix. 4. p. 716.]

[2 The passage meant is perhaps the following: Hic enim ordo (sc. S. Francisci) quoad sua membra repletus est quasi flumen sapientia &c.... Quare non immerito in Domino ordo honoratur et honorabitur. In medio populi gloriabitur. Et in ecclesiis Altissimi aperiet os suum. In medio populi exaltabitur. Et in multitudine electorum habebit laudem, &c.—Lib. Aureus Conf. Franc. Bonon. 1590. Lib. I. Pars II. p. 101.]

[3 ... the Catholique and Romane church,...out of whose companie and obedience ther is neither salvation in the next, nor anie true peace and securitie in this world.—(Alan's) Defence of English Catholics, &c. Chap. VIII. p. 192.]

[4 ... Antinomica sexta extitit, quæ furenter contendit quovis scelere pollutissimos salvari, modo credant Evangelii promissionibus.—Sim. Pauli, Method. Sec. Pars. Magd. 1573. De Lege Dei, p. 42. b.]

[5 ... but when he (Christ) cometh to shew himself in his glorious majesty; it shall be said unto all these sorts of adversaries: *Those mine enemies,* &c., Luke xix. 27. The which fearful sentence that we may avoid, let every one of us (as may stand with our several callings) carefully endeavour to advance this kingdom here, which (among other assurances given us from the Lord) shall be a testimony unto us that we shall have part, &c.—Demonstration of Discipline, Pref. to the Reader, prop. fin.]

Lastly, the Russians[6], Catabaptists[7], and Family of Love[8], who believe that themselves only, and none besides, shall be saved.

Spartan. de Relig. Ruthen. c. 2. Zuing. contr. Catab. fol. 107. Display H. 6, b. D. 5.

Proposition VII.

The predestinate are both justified by faith, sanctified by the Spirit, and shall be glorified in the life to come.

The proof from God's word.

Divers be the effects of man's predestination; but chiefly it bringeth to the elect justification by faith in this life[a], and in the life to come glorification[b]; always a conformity to the image of the only-begotten Son of God, both in suffering troubles here, and in enjoying immortal glory hereafter[c]; as testify all the churches in their confessions.

[a] Know that a man is not justified by the works of the law, but by the faith of Jesus Christ, Gal. ii. 16. They which be of faith are blessed with faithful Abraham, Gal. iii. 9.

[b] Moreover, whom he predestinate, them also he called; and whom he called, them also he justified; and whom he justified, them he also glorified, Rom. viii. 30. Come, ye blessed of my Father, inherit ye the kingdom prepared for you, Matth. xxv. 34.

[c] If we be children, we are also heirs, even the heirs of God, and heirs annexed with Christ; if so be that we suffer with him, that we may also be glorified with him, Rom. viii. 17. And as we have borne the image of the earthly, so shall we bear the image of the heavenly, 1 Cor. xv. 49.

[[6] Se vero solos esse veros christianos asseverant, sectatores Christi et Apostolorum, et sic esse de numero salvandorum.—Sacran. Rel. Ruth. cap. 2, p. 188. in Coll. Script de Russ. &c. Rel. Spir. Nem. 1582.]

[[7] The passage meant is perhaps this: Rursus cum eosdem nisi baptizati sint salvos factos esse negas, insignem temeritatem magna cum impietate mixtam prodis: qua Dei judicium ita tibi vendicas, quasi nemo salvari possit, præter quem tu salute dignum pronunciaveris, &c.—Zuingl. Opp. Tigur. 1545. Tom. II. Ad Lib. Balth. Resp. p. 105. b.]

[[8] See above, p. 67, note 8. The second reference the editor has been unable to verify. But the assertion is frequently to be met with in the works of H. N. Thus, There is no true christianity but the communalty of the holy ones in the love of Christ Jesus.—Joh. 17. c. Ephe. 4. a. b. Without the Family there is no forgiveness of sins; for this is the true christianity the Family of Love, &c.—See Wilkinson's Confutation. Lond. 1579. e. 3, 4.]

The errors and adversaries unto this truth.

Trittenhem. de Eccl. Script. Wolf. Musculus in epist. ad. Phil. præf. Euseb. Eccl. Hist. Lib. VII. c. 23. Philastrius.

This is flatly against Papias[1], Justinus[2], and all Millenaries[3], who deny the eternity of man's happiness, and dream of I know not what bliss in this life, to endure a thousand years, but no longer.

Also against the Manichees[4], who said the soul only shall be saved.

Clem. Alex. Strom. Lib. IV. Aug. contra Faust. Lib. IV. c. 16. See afore Art. IV. proposit. 1. Epiphan. Positiones Ingoldstad. de Purgat.

Also against those heretics which deny the resurrection of the flesh, as did the Carpocratians[5], Manichees[6], and others.

Likewise against the Hieracites[7], who have a phantasy, that no children departing this life before they come unto years of discretion and knowledge shall be saved. So the Papists do teach, that no infants dying unbaptized do go to heaven, but to another place adjoining unto hell, called Limbus Puerorum[8].

Proposition VIII.

The consideration of predestination is to the godly wise most comfortable; but to curious and carnal persons very dangerous.

The proof from God's word.

This doctrine of predestination is to the godly full sweet, pleasant, and comfortable, because it greatly confirmeth their faith in Christ, and increaseth their love toward God.

[1 Hic novitatem mille annorum primus invenit, post quos Christum denuo in carne regnaturum cum electis super terram somniavit.—Fabric. Biblioth. Hamburg. 1718. Trithem. de Script. Eccl. p. 7. § 9.]

[2 ...mille annis, quibus pii post resurrectionem ante judicium extremum et rerum consummationem, corporale regnum in hoc mundo habituri sunt: quod et senserunt Papias, Justinus, et alii.—Wolf. Musc. In D. Pauli Epist. &c. Basil. 1578. Præf. Ep. Philip. p. 4.]

[3 ... Νέπως ἦν ἐπίσκοπος τῶν κατ' Αἴγυπτον· Ἰουδαϊκώτερον τὰς ἐπηγγελμένας τοῖς ἁγίοις ἐν ταῖς θείαις γραφαῖς ἐπαγγελίας ἀποδοθήσεσθαι διδάσκων, καί τινα χιλιάδα ἐτῶν τρυφῆς σωματικῆς ἐπὶ της ξηρᾶς ταύτης ἔσεσθαι ὑποτιθέμενος.—Euseb. Eccl. Hist. Cant. 1720. p. 349. Lib. VII. c. 24.]

[4 Hominis quidem animam de Deo esse proprie putantes, corpus autem a diabolo factum esse arbitrantur.—Philastr. Lib. de Hær. in Biblioth. Patr. Paris. 1624. Tom. IV. col. 15.]

[5 There seems to be an error in the reference. But see August. Opp. Par. 1836-8. Tom. VIII. col. 40. c. De Hær. cap. 7. Resurrectionem corporis simul cum lege abjiciebat (Carpocrates).]

[6 See above, p. 64, note 2.] [7 See above, p. 137, note 7.]

[8 The work referred to has not been found; but see Spec. Peregrin. Quæst. Lugd. 1516. Prim. Dec. cap. iii. Quæst. v. fol. 102. In centro terræ sunt quatuor loca subalternatim posita. Primus est sinus sive limbus patrum perfectorum.

"I account the afflictions of this present time are not worthy of the glory which shall be shewed unto us." Rom. viii. 18.

"If God be on our side, who can be against us? who spared not his own Son, but gave him for us all to death; how shall he not with him give us all things also? who shall lay anything to the charge of God's chosen? it is God that justifieth; who shall condemn? &c." Ibid. 31, 34.

"Ye were sealed with the holy Spirit of promise, which is the earnest of our inheritance, until the redemption of the possession purchased unto the praise of his glory." Eph. i. 13, 14.

"Grieve not the holy Spirit of God, by whom ye are sealed unto the day of redemption." Eph. iv. 30.

But to the wicked and reprobate the consideration hereof is very sour, unsavoury, and most uncomfortable; as that which they think (though very untruly and sinfully) causeth them either to despair of his mercy, being without faith; or not to fear his justice, being extremely wicked: whereas neither from the word of God, nor any confession of the church, can any man gather that he is a vessel of wrath prepared to damnation; but contrariwise, by many and great arguments may persuade himself that God would[9] not his destruction; as in the next Proposition immediately ensuing plainly may appear.

Errors and adversaries to this truth.

Therefore they are to be taken as much out of the way which say, that this doctrine leadeth either unto desperation, which is without all comfort; or unto looseness of life, and so unto atheism, and therefore to be published neither by mouth nor book; and so thought both the Pelagians[10] and the Prosper. in Epist. ad Aug. de reliquiis Pelag. hæresis.

Secundus, purgatorium sive locus purgandorum. Tertius, limbus puerorum. Postremus est infernus damnatorum. See also above, p. 137, note 6.]

[9 Will'd, 1675.]

[10 ... ea quæ de epistola Apostoli Pauli Romanis scribentis ad manifestationem divinæ gratiæ prævenientis electorum merita proferuntur, a nullo unquam ecclesiasticorum ita esse intellecta, ut nunc sentiuntur, affirmant. Cumque ut ipsi ea exponant secundum quorum velint sensa deposuimus; nihil se profitentur invenisse, quod placeat, et de his taceri exigunt, quorum altitudinem nullus attigerit. Eo postremo pervicacia tota descendit, ut fidem nostram ædificationi audientium contrariam esse definiant; ac sic, etiamsi vera sit, non promendam: quia et perniciose non recipienda tradantur, et nullo periculo quæ intelligi nequeant, conticeantur.—Prosper. Opp. Venet. 1782. Tom. I. Epist. ad August. de Reliq. Pelag. Hær. p. 6.]

Magd. Eccl. Hist. Cent. 5. c. 5. p. 620. Display in an Epist. of the Families, I. 7. b.

Predestinates[1] (a sort of heretics so called) in old time, and the Family of Love[2] in our days, who term the doctrine of predestination a licentious doctrine, and say it filleth all the prisons almost in England.

Proposition IX.

The general promises of God set forth in the holy scripture are to be embraced of us.

The proof from God's word.

That men the better may avoid both desperation and carnal security, they are to have always in mind, that,

1. The promises of grace and favour to mankind are universal: as,

Matt. xi. 28. "Come unto me, all ye that are weary and laden, and I will ease you."

John iii. 17. "God sent not his Son into the world, that he should condemn the world; but that the world through him might be saved."

1 Tim. ii. 4. "God will that all men shall be saved, and come unto the knowledge of the truth."

2. The doctrine of the gospel for the free remission of sins, is to be preached not unto a few, but universally and generally unto all men.

Matt. xxviii. 19. "Go therefore, and teach all nations, baptizing them, &c."

Mark xvi. 15, 16. "Go into all the world, and preach the gospel to every creature. He that shall believe and be baptized shall be saved; but he that will not believe shall be damned."

3. The seals of the covenant be appointed to be given to all men, and members of the visible church, or which are desirous to be incorporated thereinto. For,

Matt. xxviii. 19. Matt. xxvi. 26, 27. 1 Cor. xi. 24, 25. All are to be baptized, and all are to participate of the bread and cup at the Lord's Supper.

4. As the disobedience of Adam brought condemnation

[[1] Hoc tempore Prædestinatorum hæresis cœpit serpere: qui ideo Prædestinati vocantur, quia de prædestinatione et divina gratia disputantes adserebant, quod nec pie viventibus prosit bonorum operum labor, si a Deo ad mortem prædestinati fuerint, nec impiis obsit, quod impie vivant, si a Deo prædestinati fuerint ad vitam.—Magdeburg. Eccl. Hist. Basil. 1559, &c. Cent. v. c. 5. fol. 620.]

[[2] At this present your brethren in Christ (for their good faith's cause they have in your licentious doctrine of predestination and free election) fill all the prisons almost in England.—Letter of the Family in the Displaying, &c. fol. I. 7. b.]

upon all men, so the blood and obedience of Christ is able and all-sufficient to wash away all sins, and that of all men.

5. No man ever truly repented but he was received again into favour; so was David after his adultery, Manasses after his idolatry, Peter after his apostasy, the thief upon the cross, the Ninevites.

2 Sam. xii. 13. 2 Chron. xxxiii. 12, 13. John xxi. 15, &c. Luke xxiii. 42, 43. Jonas iii. 10.

The adversaries unto this truth.

They are not to be heard then which say, that

The number of the elect is but small; and seeing we are uncertain whether we be of that company or no, we will proceed in our course as we have begun.

God is an accepter of persons, and so unjust in choosing some and refusing others.

God hath predestinate all those persons to eternal death which are not in the state of true repentance: which was one of Glover's errors[3].

Bredwell's Detect. p. 96.

It is the part therefore of all and every man

Not to refuse the mercies of God both generally and graciously offered unto all men by his word and sacraments.

Not to despair in respect either of the greatness or multitude of his sins.

Nor yet to provoke the Lord to execute his vengeance upon them, through profaneness of life, or security.

Proposition X.

In our actions the word of God, which is his revealed will, must be our direction.

The proof from God's word.

In our doings, but chiefly in the matter of predestination, we are to follow not our own judgement, and what seemeth good in our own opinions, but the will of God, and that will too, not which is concealed from us, *viz.* of God his omnipo-

[[3] And thus he [Glover] babbleth: First, God hath from the beginning purposed, appointed, elected, and chosen in Christ, such only to be in the state of salvation, the children of God, and heirs of everlasting life, which are in the state of true repentance and amendment of life, holy and blameless before God in love and charity, and so made according to the likeness and image of Christ. Secondly, God hath from the beginning purposed, appointed, predestinate, elect and chosen all such to be condemned to eternal death which are not in that state of true repentance and amendment of life.—Bredwell's Detection. Lond. 1568. p. 96.]

tency, whereby he governeth at his pleasure the things by
Psal. cxv. 3. himself created; whereof mention is made both in the Psalms,
Isai. xlvi. 10. Rom. ix. 15. in the prophet Isaiah, and other places of his word: but of
his favour and good pleasure towards man, revealed in the
Matt. iii. 17. holy scriptures by Jesus Christ, whom we are to hear.

Subscribed hereunto have and do God's church everywhere.

The adversaries unto this truth.

Theodor. Lib. III. de Hæret. fab. Beza, Ep. 81. Sleidan, com. Lib. VI. H. N. Evang. c. 13. § 6.

This truth is gainsaid by the Phrygians, Montanists, and Messalians[1], also by the Enthusiasts[2], Anabaptists[3], and Family of Love[4], which leave the written word of God, and rely upon their own dreams, visions, and lying revelations. Hence proceedeth the contempt of God's written word, and of the preachers, and all religious exercises thereof. For saith the Family of Love, "No difference is there between a ceremonial either letter-doctor christian and an uncircumcised heathen[5]."

In a letter of theirs unto the B. of Roch. in Wilk. Confut.

Article XVIII.

Of obtaining eternal salvation only by the name of Christ.

(1) *They also are to be had accursed that presume to say, that every man shall be saved by the law or sect which*

[1 Αἱ δὲ τῆς Πρισκίλλης καὶ Μαξιμίλλης προφητεῖαι ὑπὲρ τὸ θεῖον εὐαγγέλιον τετίμηνται παρ' αὐτοῖς (sc. τοῖς Μοντανίσταις.)—Theod. Opp. Par. 1642-84. Tom. IV. p. 227. Hær. Fab. Lib. III. c. 2. εἶτα ὑπὸ τοῦ σφᾶς ἐκβακχεύσαντος δαίμονος ἐξαπατηθέντες, ἀποκαλύψεις ἑωρακέναι φασί, καὶ τὰ ἐσόμενα προλέγειν ἐπιχείρουσιν.—Ibid. p. 243. Lib. IV. c. 11.]

[2 Itaque, mi Philippe, quæcunque ab istis Enthusiastis de Deo divinisque rebus extra verbum illud scriptum dicuntur, si quis rimari studeat, perinde mihi facere videtur ac si velit cum ratione insanire. Sunt autem extra verbum, non modo quæ sunt aperte commentitia, sed etiam quæ allegoricis illis fictionibus nituntur, &c.—Bez. Epist. Genev. 1575. Ep. vii. p. 63. This is doubtless the passage referred to: there is a mere allusion to the Enthusiasts in the 81st Epistle.]

[3 In hoc tempore vigebat novum doctrina genus eorum qui dicuntur anabaptistæ....Jactant etiam visiones et somnia, &c.—Sleidan. Comment. Argent. 1555. Lib. VI. fol. 87.]

[4 Where now then the law and the services do in such wise change by the believers of the Anointed; to wit, out of the figures into the true being; and out of the letter, or serviceable word, into the revealing of the holy Spirit of Christ; there is also then (by those same) the priest's office changed, &c.—H. N. Evang. Reg. London. 1652. cap. XIII. § 6. p. 70.]

[5 Wilkinson's Confutation, Lond. 1579. fol. A. 4.]

he professeth, so that he be diligent to frame his life according to that law, and the light of nature. For Holy Scripture doth set out unto us (2) *only the Name of Jesus Christ whereby men must be saved.*

The propositions.

1. The profession of every religion cannot save a man, live he never so virtuously.

2. No man ever was, is, or shall be saved, but only by the name or faith of Jesus Christ.

Proposition I.

The profession of every religion cannot save a man, live he never so virtuously.

The proof from the word of God.

This we cannot but acknowledge to be a truth, if we believe the scriptures; for they testify that

Jews and Gentiles are all under sin, culpable before God, and deprived of the glory of God. Rom. iii. 9, 19, 23.

All men that would be saved must be born again of the Holy Ghost. John iii. 3.

No man is justified by the works of the law, either ceremonial or moral. Gal. iii. 10. Acts xv. 24, 28. Col. ii. 16, 20. Gal. v. 18. Rom. iii. 20, 28.

God hateth the doctrine of the Nicolaitans, and of Balaam. Rev. ii. 15. Ibid. 14.

The reprobate, whose names are not written in the book of the life of the Lamb, they do worship the beast. Rev. xiii. 8.

Punishments eternal and intolerable are threatened both to the beast and the false prophet, and likewise to all such as will not go out of Babylon, and to all idolaters. Rev. xx. 10. Rev. xviii. 4. Rev. xxi. 8.

The Confessions[6] of God's people are to this end and purpose. Conf. Helv. I. Art. XII. & II. c. 12. Bohem. c. 6. Gal. Art. XXII. XXIII. Belg. Art. XXII. XXIII. August. Art. IV. V. XXI. Wittemb. Art. V. VI. Suevica, c. 3.

[6 Itaque in omni doctrina Evangelica primum ac præcipuum hoc ingeri debet, sola nos Dei misericordia et gratia Christique merito servari: quo ut intelligant homines quam opus habeant, peccata eis per legem et Christi mortem luculentissime sunt indicanda.—Harm. Conf. Sect. VII. p. 126. Conf. Helv. Prior. Art. XII. Docemus legem hanc (Dei) non datam esse hominibus, ut ejus justificemur observatione: sed ut ex ejus indicio infirmitatem potius, peccatum atque condemnationem agnoscamus, et de viribus nostris desperantes, convertamur ad Christum in fide: Aperte enim Apostolus, Lex iram, ait, operatur.—Ibid. p. 123. Conf. Helv. Post. cap. XII. Hoc enim omnino constat, quod post lapsum Adæ nemo hominum e servitute peccati et regno mortis condemnationisque se in libertatem vindicare, aut ad veram cum Deo reconciliationem pervenire possit, nisi tantum per unicum mediatorem inter Deum et hominem Jesum Christum in fide viva, &c.—Ibid.

Errors and adversaries unto this truth.

Then to be held accursed are they which affirm that

Acts xv. 1. Iren. Lib. I. cap. 26. Philastrius.

The observation of the Judaical ceremonies is necessary unto salvation; as did the false apostles, the Ebionites[1], and the Cerinthians[2].

Clem. Alex. Lib. II. 4. Paul. Jovius Elog. doct. Vir. p. 97. Præf. sua in Tuscul. quæst. H. N. præf. to his 3 Reform. § 2, 6.

Such throughout the world as lead an upright life, and be morally righteous, whatsoever their religion is, shall be saved; as many of the philosophers were, in the opinion of the Valentinian[3] and Basilidian heretics, of Galeatus Martius[4], and Erasmus Roterodam[5].

That men externally may possess any religion, and notwithstanding be saved, if their affections and heart be with the Family of Love[6].

Pol. of the Turk. Emp. Lonicer. Turk. Hist. Tom. I. Lib. II. par. 2. cap. 12. Damascene.

That all those which live uprightly and do good deeds, shall be of equal happiness in the kingdom of heaven, be they Turks, Christians, Jews, or Moors. A Turkish error[7].

That men may embrace and follow the sect and religion which they have most mind unto; and so doing, please God, and shall be saved. The Lampatians' doctrine[8].

Sect. vi. p. 106. Conf. Bohem. cap. VI. The references generally do not contain any *direct* support of the statement in the proposition.—See Harm. Conf. Sect. IX. p. 183, and VII. p. 129. Conf. Gall. Artt. XXII. XXIII. Ibid. Sect. IX. pp. 184, 5. Conf. Belg. Artt. XXII. XXIII. Ibid. pp. 188, 9. Conf. Aug. Artt. IV. V. Ibid. p. 218. Conf. Virtemb. Art. v. and Sect. VII. p. 131. cap. VI. Ibid. Sect. IX. p. 221. Conf. Suev. cap. iii.]

[1 See above, p. 89, note 5.]

[2 Docet autem [Cherinthus] circumcidi et sabbatizari, &c.—Philastr. Lib. de Hær. in Bibl. Patr. Paris, 1624. Tom. IV. col. 10.]

[3 See above, p. 126, note 2.] [4 See above, p. 109, note 3.]

[5 Ubi nunc agat anima Ciceronis fortasse non est humani judicii pronunciare. Me certe non admodum aversum habituri sint in ferendis calculis qui sperant illam apud superos quietam vitam agere...Si Judæis ante proditum Evangelium sufficiebat ad salutem rudis quædam et confusa de rebus divinis credulitas: quid vetat quo minus ethnico, cui ne Mosi quidem lex erat cognita, rudior etiam cognitio profuerit ad salutem: præsertim quum vita fuerit integra, nec integra solum verum etiam sancta? &c. Erasm. Epist. Præf. ad Cic. Tusc. Quæst. Lond. 1577.]

[6 The editor has been unable to verify this reference.]

[7 And they affirm, that there shall be no difference between Turks and Christians, Jews and Moors; neither shall one be known from another, but all such as have lived well, and have done good deeds in the sight of God, shall be of equal beauty and blessedness.—Pol. of the Turk. Empire. Lond. 1597. c. 23, p. 68. Nec ullum (aiunt) inter Turcas et Christianos fore discrimen, nec inter Æthiopas et Judæos, sed eandem eorum, qui coram Deo bona præstitissent opera, fore et formam et felicitatem.—Lonicer. Chron. Turc. Francof. 1578. Tom. I. Lib. II. Pars 2, c. 22, p. 121.]

[8 Λαμπετίανοι. οἱ ἀπὸ Λαμπετίου τινος οὕτω προσαγορευόμενοι, οἵτινες τοῖς

That no sect ever erred, or were out of the way to heaven. A fancy of the Rhetorians[9].

D. Aug. ep. ad Quod-vult Deum.

Proposition II.

No man ever was, is, or shall be saved, but only by the Name or faith of Jesus Christ.

The proof from God's word.

This we cannot but acknowledge to be true, if also we believe the scriptures, which say, that

"Among men there is given none other name under heaven, whereby we must be saved." Acts iv. 12.

"Through (Jesus Christ) his name, all that believe in him shall receive remission of sins." Acts x. 43.

"In thee (*viz.* Christ Jesus) shall all the gentiles be blessed." Gal. iii. 8.

And this is the faith and confession of the reformed churches[10].

Conf. Helv. I. Art. x. xi. & II. cap. 11, 13. Basil. Art. IV. Bohem. cap. 4, 10. Gal. Art. XIII. XVI. XVII. Belg. Art. XVII. XX. XXI. XXII. August. Art. III. Saxon. Art. III. Wittemb. c. 8. Suevica, cap. 2.

The errors and adversaries unto this truth.

Many ways this truth very heretically is oppugned. For,

Some teach that we are saved, not by Christ, but (as the

βουλομένοις ἐπὶ τὸ αὐτὸ ζῆν, καὶ ἐν κοινοβίοις διάγειν ἐπιτρέπουσιν ἑκάστῳ οἵαν ἂν ἐθέλῃ καὶ δοκιμάζῃ πολιτείαν ταύτην μετίεναι, καὶ ὃ προαιρεῖται σχῆμα ἀμφιεννῦσθαι. οὐδὲν γάρ φησιν ἠναγκασμένως ποιεῖν τὸν Χριστιανόν· ὅτι γέγραπται, ἑκουσίως θύσω σοι· καὶ πάλιν, ἐκ θελήματός μου ὁμολογήσομαι αὐτῷ. —Damascen. Opp. Venet. 1748. Tom. I. p. 109. De Hæres. 98.]

[9 A Rhetorio quodam exortam hæresim dicit nimium mirabilis vanitatis, quæ omnes hæreticos recte ambulare et vera dicere affirmet: quod ita est absurdum, ut mihi incredibile videatur.—August. Opp. Par. 1836-8. Tom. VIII. col. 59. D. Lib. de Hær. ad Quodvult-deum, 72.]

[10 Hujus igitur hominis...damnationi addicti...nunquam tamen curam gerere Deus pater desiit: id quod ex primis promissionibus, legeque tota...et a Christo in hæc destinato præstitoque perspicuum est.—Harm. Conf. Sect. VI. pp. 103, 4. Conf. Helv. Prior. Art. x. Hic Christus...carnem...in mortem tradidit, ad universi peccati expiationem.—Ibid. Art. xi. ...credimus hunc Jesum Christum, Dominum nostrum, unicum et æternum generis humani adeoque totius mundi esse servatorem, in quo per fidem servati sint, quotquot ante legem, sub lege et sub Evangelio salvati sint, et quotquot adhuc in finem usque seculi salvabuntur.—Ibid. p. 102. Conf. Helv. Post. cap. XI. See also Sect. VII. pp. 124, 5. Conf. Helv. Post. cap. XIII. Nec quisquam quicquam uspiam habet rerum omnium, quibus se possit a peccatis suis et condemnatione eripere et liberare aut redimere extra Christum, &c.—Ibid. pp. 105, 6. Conf. Bohem. cap. IV. Sed pro certo habendum esse existimamus... quod nec veteris, nec novi Testamenti hominibus contingat æterna salus, propter merita operum legis, sed tantum propter meritum Domini nostri Jesu Christi, per fidem.—Ibid. Sect. VII. p. 133. Conf. Virtemb. cap. VIII. For the references to the other confessions, see above, p. 56, note 1.]

Iren. Lib. I. Iren. Holin. Chro. fol. 1299. Beza resp. ad repetit. Jo. And. Cal. p. 8.

Valentinians[1] said) by the labour of their hands, and by their own good works; (as Simon Magus[2] boasted) by his fair Helene; (as Matthew Hamant[3]) by other means, and that all persons which worshipped Christ, are abominable idolaters; as Neuserus and Silvanus[4] believed by Mahomet, and therefore they revolted from Christianity unto Turcism.

Epiphan. Eus. Lib. VII. c. 31. Geneb. Chro. Lib. III. p. 358, 709. Hist. D. Geor. Stow. Conspiracy for pretended reformation.

Others confess that we are saved by the name of Christ, but either not by the right and true Christ; for they said, themselves and every of themselves were Christ: as in old time did Saturninus[5], Manes[6], Desider. Burdegal[7] and Eudo de Stella; and of late years, at Basil, David George[8], and in England, first, one John Moore[9], and afterward William Hacket[10]: the former was whipt for the same at Bethlehem, in the second of Queen Elizabeth; the other hanged and quartered in Cheapside, anno 1591.

Philaster.

Or by the true Christ, but either distinguish between Jesus and Christ, saying, Jesus was one man, and Christ another; as did the Marcionites[11].

[1 Iren. Adv. Hær. Oxon. 1702. Lib. I. cap. 1. § 11. p. 29. See above, p. 121, note 3.]

[2 Rather by himself. Quapropter et ipsum venisse, uti eam assumeret primam et liberaret eam a vinculis, hominibus autem salutem præstaret per suam agnitionem.—Ibid. Lib. I. cap. 20. p. 95.]

[3 See above, p. 109, and p. 49, note 10.]

[4 Nec enim illi (sc. Neuserus et Silvanus) duntaxat erroris, aut etiam blasphemiæ alicujus arguebantur in quam induci quispiam possit ex falsa scripturæ interpretatione, sed quod aperte Christum negarent, apostolica scripta ludibrio haberent, quid amplius? quod Mahumetis de Deo sententiam aperte amplecterentur, &c.—Bez. ad Repetit. Jac. Andr. &c. Calumn. Respon. Genev. 1578. p. 8.]

[5 It does not appear that Saturninus professed to be the Christ himself...τὸν δὲ σωτῆρα [φάσκει] ἀπεστάλθαι ἀπὸ πατρὸς κατὰ γνώμην τῶν δυνάμεων, ἐπὶ καταλύσει τοῦ Θεοῦ τῶν Ἰουδαίων καὶ ἐπὶ σωτηρίᾳ τῶν πειθομένων.—Epiphan. Opp. Paris. 1622. Tom. I. p. 63. Adv. Hær. Lib. I. Tom. II. Hær. 23.]

[6 Χριστὸν αὑτὸν μορφάζεσθαι ἐπειρᾶτο.—Euseb. Eccl. Hist. Cantab. 1720. p. 365. Lib. VII. c. 31.]

[7 Desiderius quidam Burdegalensis cuculla et tunica ex pilis caprarum amictus. Christum se simulans arte magica miracula quædam edere conatur.—Genebrard. Chron. Lugd. 1609. Lib. III. p. 474. Nothing apparently said about Eudo de Stella.]

[8 Attamen ejus (sc. Christi) Spiritum et animam adhuc restare, imo jam rediisse et denuo atque adeo præstantiori modo incarnatam vel hypostatice cum alicujus hujus temporis hominis spiritu velut unitam atque resuscitatam se nunc prodere per cœlestem et novam hanc Christi Davidis doctrinam, &c.—Hist. Dav. Georg. Daventr. 1642, p. 48.]

[9 The tenth of April was one William Geffrie whipped, &c....for that he professed one John Moore to be Christ our Saviour...they had lain prisoners nigh a year and a half, the one for professing himself to be Christ, the other a disciple of the same Christ.—Stow, Chron. Lond. 1587. fol. 1194.]

[10 See above, p. 68, note 1.]

[11 This opinion is not attributed to the Marcionites by Philastrius.]

Or, say there be two Christs, one revealed already in the days of Tiberius the emperor, who came for the salvation of the Gentiles; another yet to come, for the redemption of the Jews: so thought the same Marcionites[12]. Nestorius[13] held also there were two Christs, whereof one was very God, the other very man born of a woman.

Tertul. Lib. IV. contra Marc.

Vincent. Lir. adv. hæreses.

Or, publish how none were saved by the true Christ, till the 15. year of the foresaid Tiberius; an heresy of Manes[14], and his company.

Epiphan.

Others besides (as the Family of Love) understand all things written of Christ allegorically, and not according to the letter of God's word. For they teach, that whatsoever is written of Christ must in us, and with us be fulfilled[15].

H. N. Proph. of the Spir. c. 19. § 3.

Others have thought, yea have spoken blasphemously of the constant and holy martyrs, who, for the name of Christ, gave their lives in England in the reign of Queen Mary; some saying, they were stark fools, as did Christopher Vitel[16], a chief elder in the Family of Love; others, (as Westphalus, and Marbachius)[17] that they were the devil's martyrs.

Answer to the Fam. Let. Lib. III. a. Sturmius, Antipap. 4. par. 3, p. 189.

[12 Constituit Marcion alium esse Christum, qui Tiberianis temporibus a Deo quondam ignoto revelatus sit in salutem omnium gentium; alium qui a Deo creatore in restitutionem Judaici status sit destinatus, quandoque venturus.—Tertull. Opp. Paris. 1634. p. 506. c. Adv. Marc. Lib. IV. 6.]

[13 Nestorius autem, contrario Apollinari morbo, dum sese duas in Christo substantias distinguere simulat, duas introducit repente personas; et inaudito scelere duos vult esse filios Dei, duos Christos: unum Deum, alterum hominem; unum qui ex patre, alterum qui sit generatus ex matre.—Vincent. Lir. Adv. Hær. Paris. 1619. Comm. I. cap. XVII. p. 26.]

[14 See above, p. 137, note 5.]

[15 See above, p. 59, note 9.]

[16 The editor has been unable to verify this reference.]

[17 Scribitis in libris vestris: clamatis pro concionibus, de quibus in Galliis et Belgis, et in Anglia et Scotia supplicium sumptum est, *Martyres esse Diaboli*...Non vos homines condemnatis?...quid in omnibus parochiis Jacobus Fabricula? quid per hosce menses Marbachius Heidelbergæ?—Sturmius, Quart. Antipapp. Neap. Palat. 1580. Pars III. p. 189.]

Article XIX.

Of the Church.

(1) *The visible church of Christ,* (2) *is a congregation* (3) *of faithful men: in the which* (4) *the pure word of God is preached, and the sacraments be duly ministered, according to Christ's ordinance, in all those things that of necessity are requisite to the same. As* (5) *the church of Jerusalem, Alexandria and Antioch hath erred; so also* (6) *the church of Rome hath erred, not only in their living and manner of ceremonies, but also in matters of faith.*

The propositions.

1. There is a church of Christ, not only invisible, but also visible.
2. There is but one church.
3. The visible church is a Catholic church.
4. The word of God was, and for time is before the church.
5. The marks and tokens of the visible church are the due and true administration of the word and sacraments.
6. The visible church may, and from time to time hath erred both in doctrine and conversation.
7. The church of Rome most shamefully hath erred in life, ceremonies, and matters of faith.

Proposition I.

There is a church of Christ both invisible and visible.

The proof from God's word.

A true saying is it, the Lord and he only knoweth who are his. For to man the church of Christ is partly invisible, and visible partly. The invisible are all the elect, who be or shall be either in heaven triumphing; or on earth fighting against the flesh, the world, and the devil. These as members of the church, are said to be invisible; not because the men be not seen, but for that their faith and conscience to Godward is not perfectly known unto us.

The members of the visible church are some of them for God, and some against God; all of them notwithstanding deemed parts of the church, and accounted faithful, so long as they make no manifest and open rebellion against the gospel of Christ.

All this we gather from the holy scripture, where mention is made of the church invisible, and triumphing, Rev. ii. 26, 28; and iii. 5, 12; and vii. 14, 15; invisible and militant, in the Epistles of St Paul, Peter, and book of St John's Revelations, also of the church visible, and mixed with good and bad, by the parable of the sower, of the marriage, and of the virgins; as also by the saying of our Saviour Christ[a], and of St Paul[b].

Gal. iv 29. Eph. vi. 10, &c. 2 Tim. iii. 12. 1 Pet. v. 9, 10. Rev. xii. 7, 11. 17 & xvii. 14. Matt. xiii. Matt. xxii. Matt. xxv.

The churches bear witness hereunto[1].

Conf. Helv. I. Art. XIV. & II. cap. 17. Bohem. c. 8. Gal. Art. XXVII. Belg. Art. XXVII. August. Art. VII. Saxon. Art. XI. Wittemb. Art. XXXII. Suevica, Art. XV.

[a] Have not I chosen you twelve, and one of you is a devil? John vi. 70.

[b] For he knew who should betray him: therefore said, Ye are not all clean, John xiii. 11. In a great house are not only vessels of gold, and of silver, but also of wood, and of earth, and some for honour, and some unto dishonour, 2 Tim. ii. 20.

[[1] Quæ (sc. ecclesia) quidem quum solius Dei sit oculis nota, externis tamen quibusdam ritibus ab ipso Christo institutis, et verbo Dei velut publica legitimaque disciplina non solum cernitur cognosciturque: sed ita constituitur, ut in hac sine his nemo, nisi singulari Dei privilegio censeatur.—Harm. Conf. Sect. x. p. 9. Conf. Helv. Prior. Art. XIV. ...Ecclesia invisibilis appellari potest, non quod homines sint invisibiles, ex quibus ecclesia colligitur, sed quod oculis nostris absconsa, Deo autem soli nota, &c....Rursus non omnes qui numerantur in ecclesia, sancti et viva atque vera sunt ecclesiæ membra, &c.—Ibid. pp. 7, 8. Conf. Helv. Post. cap. 17. ...docetur...sanctam catholicam uniuscujusque temporis præsentem ecclesiam, quæ in terris militat, esse communitatem universorum christianorum, quæ in toto orbe terrarum hinc inde diffusa est....Hæc vera ecclesia...utrumque adhuc, tam triticum purum quam paleas, pios Dei et impios mundi filios, &c....in se continet.—Ibid. p. 10. Conf. Bohem. cap. 8. ...affirmamus ex Dei verbo, ecclesiam esse fidelium cœtum, qui in verbo Dei sequendo et pura religione colenda consentiunt.... Minime tamen inficiamur, quia fidelibus hypocritæ et reprobi multi sint permixti, sed quorum malitia ecclesiæ nomen delere non possit.—Ibid. p. 15. Conf. Gall. Art. XXVII. Quæ (sc. ecclesia) est vera congregatio seu cœtus omnium fidelium Christianorum...hæc ecclesia sancta nullo est aut certo loco sita et circumscripta, aut ullis certis ac singularibus personis astricta aut alligata.—Ibid. p. 17. Conf. Belg. Art. XXVII. Est autem ecclesia Christi proprie congregatio membrorum Christi, hoc est sanctorum qui vere credunt et obediunt Christo: etsi in hac vita huic congregationi multi mali et hypocritæ sunt admixti.—Ibid. p. 19. Conf. Aug. 1540. Art. VII. Dicimus igitur ecclesiam visibilem in hac vita cœtum esse amplectentium evangelium Christi, et recte utentium sacramentis....In quo tamen cœtu multi sunt non sancti, sed de vera doctrina consentientes.—Ibid. p. 21. Conf. Saxon. Art. XI. Credimus et confitemur quod una sit sancta, catholica, et apostolica ecclesia....Quod huic ecclesiæ in hac terra multi mali et hypocritæ admixti sunt.—Ibid. pp. 26, 7. Conf. Virtemb. Art. XXXII. Ecclesia sive congregatio Christi...est societas et cœtus eorum qui se Christo addicunt...Inter quos tamen multi etiam ad finem usque mundi immiscentur, qui etsi fidem christianam profiteantur, eam tamen re vera non habent.—Ibid. p. 29. Conf. Suev. Art. XV.]

The errors and adversaries unto this truth.

This truth hath many adversaries, whereof

See Artic. II. prop. 4. Art. XVIII. prop. 2.

Some renounce our Christ the Saviour of mankind, and so think his people are not the church; as the Jews, Turks, and hereticks have done[1].

Leon. Ramsey's and J. Allen's Conf. also H. N. document. Sent. chap. 6, § 1, chap. 3, § 5. Spir. Land, chap. 44, § 12. Proverbs, chap. v. § 15. Proph. chap. xvi. § 8. Vaux Catech. cap. 1. Test. Rhem. Annot. Acts xi. 24.

Some acknowledge no triumphing state of the godly in heaven, but dream of an ever-glorious condition in this world; as the Family of Love[2].

Some think the church Catholic to be visible; as the Papists[3].

[1 See above, pp. 57, 8, and p. 162.]

[2 No man ascendeth unto heaven, but he which cometh (John 3. 6; Eph. 4. a.) or descendeth from heaven. The which figureth forth unto us in clearness, that the earthly flesh and blood cannot ascend to heaven, inasmuch as it is not of the heaven, but of the earth. But the holy Being of God, which God the Father out of his holy heaven hath grounded, or set from the beginning, in the Manhood; and is in us, for our sins' cause, become mortal, hath the sure promises to rise up again in immortal glory: and that the same shall reach from the man on the earth even unto God in the heaven; for to make known out of the heaven unto the man on the earth the heavenly goods, and to bring the same unto him out of the heaven, and thereto the eternal life.—H. N. Document. Sent. Transl. out of Base-Almayne, chap. VI. § 1. Among us the death is now swallowed up (Oze. 13. b.) in the death: the everlasting life is come unto us in the renewing of our life.—Terra Pacis. A testification of the Spiritual Land of Peace, &c. Translated, &c. cap. xliv. § 12. In the true love the kingdom of heaven bideth stedfast upon the earth everlastingly in perfection: and there cometh with the same in the true love the eternal life to the elected holy ones of God upon the earth.—Proverbs of H. N. Translated, &c. p. 14. cap. v. § 15. Rejoice now in this same day, all ye holy prophets, angels, and apostles (Apoc. 18. c.) For this is the day (Deut. 5. a. Nahum 1. a.) of the vengeance of our Lord and God, for to revenge the blood of his holy ones, (Math. 23. d. Apoc. 16. a.) that the sinners have spilt or shed upon the earth, and for to declare or reveal his holy ones again gloriously upon the earth, to the end that they might inhabit (2 Pet. 3. b.) the same peaceably in all love, and reign thereover, or judge (Apo. 5. b. 22.) the same with righteousness, from henceforth world without end.—Prophecy of the Spirit of Love. Translated &c. 1574. cap. XVI. § 8.]

[3 The church is a visible company of people first gathered together of Christ and his disciples, continued unto this day in a perpetual succession, in one Apostolic faith, living under Christ the head: and in earth under his vicar, pastor, and chief bishop.—Vaux, Catech. Antv. 1574. cap. i. p. 8.

And a great multitude was added to our Lord. As before (c. 10) a few, so now great numbers of Gentiles are adjoined also to the visible church, consisting before only of the Jews. Which church hath been ever since Christ's ascension, notoriously seen and known: their preaching open, their sacraments visible, their discipline visible, their heads and governors visible, the provision for their maintenance visible, the persecution visible, their dispersion visible: the heretics that went out from them, visible: the joining either of men or nations unto them, visible: their peace and rest after persecutions, visible: their governors in prison, visible: the church prayeth for them visibly, their councils visible, their gifts and graces visible, their name (Christians) known to all the world. Of the protestants' invisible church we hear not one word.—Test. Rhem Rhemes, 1582. Ann. Acts xi. 24. p. 323.]

Some imagine the church militant is not visible at all; as the Libertines.

Some give out, that the visible church is devoid of sin and sinners; as did the Donatists[4], and do the Anabaptists[5], Family of Love[6], Brownists[a], and [7]Barrowists[b].

Aug. contra Petil. cap. 19. Calv. contra Libert. H. N. 1 Exhort. chap. 13, sect. 10 & 1 Epist. Præf.

Proposition II.

There is but one Church.

The proof from God's word.

When we do say, that the church is visible, invisible, and that there is a Western, East, Greek, Latin, English, church; we mean not that there be divers churches of Christ, but that

[a] A confused gathering together of good and bad in public assemblies is no church. The Brownists' answer to Mr Cartwright, p. 39.

[b] The assemblies of good and bad together are no churches, but heaps of profane people, saith Barrow in his Discovery, p. 33.

[[4] The passage meant is perhaps this: ...nimis exsecrabili et impia cæcitate vos a frumentis Christi, quæ per totum agrum, id est totum mundum usque ad finem crescunt, paucis in Africa zizaniis offensi præcidistis.—August. Opp. Par. 1836-8. Tom. IX. col. 354. D. Cont. Litt. Petil. Lib. I. cap. 24.]

[[5] Quod ad innocentiam perfectam attinet, quam isti imaginantur, fingentes hominem regeneratum ab omni peccato purum et immunem esse: atque regenerationem instar angelici esse status, in quo homo delinquere aut labi non possit: si res ita se haberet, quo pertineret oratio, quo nos Christus precari jussit, ut remittat Deus nobis debita nostra? Id enim ad infideles non pertinet.—Calv. Opp. Amstelod. 1667-71. Tom. VIII. p. 389. Instr. adv. Libert. cap. 18.]

[[6] It behoveth, that all their mind, will, and meaning stand minded to demand after, nor yet lust to hear any other thing (for to know the same) but only this, namely, which are the upright ways of the Lord (Eccli. 2. a. 3. 5.), how they should enter into those same and walk in them, and even so in the good pleasure or delight of the Most Highest, have their forth-going therein, for to grow up (Eph. 1. a. Col. 1. b. 1 Pet. 2. a.) in the upright virtues of God, and in the lovely Being of the Love, to the end that they might even so (growing up in the oldness of the godly wisdom and holy understanding) become perfect men in the old age (Eph. 4. b.) of the man Christ, &c.—First Exhortation of H. N. Lond. 1649. p. 89. cap. XIII. § 10. But all ye that love the truth and upright righteousness with us....endeavour you first of all hereto, namely, to accomplish the beginning of the true christian life, and to observe....all upright and reasonable exercises to an incorporating to the sincere righteousness: and going forth humbly and obediently therein ye shall attain unto the true fulfilling or perfection of the christian life in the Spirit in the coming of the glorious appearing of the uncovered face of God and Christ.—H. N. First Epistle, Pref. § 5.]

[[7] He (Calvin) at the first dash made no scruple to receive all the whole state, even all the profane ignorant people, into the bosom of the church, &c.—Barrow's Discovery of the False Church. 1590. p. 33.]

one and the same church is diversly taken, and understood, and also hath many particular churches; as the sea many rivers, and arms, branching from it. For the visible church is not many congregations, but one company of the faithful.

Rom. xii. 5. "We, being many, are one body in Christ, and every one, one another's members."

1 Cor. x. 9. "We, that are many, are one bread and one body."

1 Cor. xii. 12, 13, 27. "For as the body is one, and hath many members, and all the members of the body which is one, though they be many, yet are but one body: even so is Christ. For by one spirit are we all baptized into one body," &c. "Now ye are the body of Christ, and members for your part."

Rom. xii. 4, 5. "For as we have many members in one body, and all members have not the same office: so we, being many, are one body in Christ, and every one, one another's members."

Gal. iii. 28. "There is neither Jew nor Grecian; there is neither bond nor free; there is neither male nor female: for ye are all one in Christ Jesus."

Conf. Helv. II. cap. 17. Bohem. cap. 8. Gal. Art. XXVI. Belg. Art. XXVII. August. Art. XXVII. Wittem. Art. XXXII. Suevic. Art. XV.

All God's people agree with us in this point[1].

The errors and adversaries unto this truth.

The adversaries unto the eighteenth article be also, for a great part, adversaries unto this truth.

Furthermore, although it be acknowledged by many, and they too baptized for Christians, that there is but one church; yet the same persons do err, which condemn so many (as no members of Christ's church) which join not with them in their singular and private opinions, arrogating the style and title unto themselves only, and denying all other men to be either the church, or members of the body of Christ. Such are

[[1] Et quum semper unus modo sit Deus, unus mediator Dei et hominum Jesus Messias, &c....unus denique spiritus, una salus, una fides, unum testamentum vel fœdus, necessario consequitur unam duntaxat esse ecclesiam.—Harm. Conf. Sect. x. p. 3. Conf. Helv. Post. cap. 17. ...Ecclesia, domus Dei...corpus Christi spirituale, et artus conjuncti, quos inter se aptat et connectit unum caput Christus, Spiritus unus regenerationis, unum verbum Dei, &c.—Ibid. p. 11. Conf. Bohem. cap. 8. Credimus igitur nemini licere sese cœtibus subducere, et in seipso acquiescere, sed potius omnibus simul tuendam et conservandam esse ecclesiæ unitatem.—Ibid. p. 14. Conf. Gall. Art. XXVI. Credimus et confitemur unicam ecclesiam catholicam seu universalem.—Ibid. p. 17. Conf. Belg. Art. XXVII. Item docent, quod una sancta ecclesia perpetuo mansura sit.—Ibid. p. 19. Conf. August. Art. VII. ...quod una sit sancta...ecclesia.—Ibid. p. 26. Conf. Virtemb. Art. XXXII. The unity of the church is not stated in the Conf. Suevic.]

The Russes, who boast how themselves with the Grecians, are the only church of God[2]; themselves only are the men who shall be saved[3], all Christians beside themselves, are no better than Turks[4].

The Papists also, which say, that

The present church of Rome is God's church[5], God's Catholic church[6], the mystical body of Christ[7], "Papists, Catholics, and true Christians, are all one."

Muncer, and the Anabaptists termed themselves (clean opposite to the church of Christ) the elect of God; and said that all other men were wicked, and worthy to be slain[8].

The Family of Love, who publish how themselves only are the church, and all other men are heathen and beasts[9], themselves only are the Catholic church of God, the saints[10] of God, and his acceptable people[11], and that such

Alex. Guag. de Relig. Mosc. p. 231. Sacramus de Relig. Ruthen. cap. 1, pag. 188. Russ. Com. cap. 25, p. 103. b. Test. Rhem. an. mar. p. 323. Answ. to the Execut. of Inst. c. 7. p. 151. Quodlibets, pag. 342. Test. Rhem. an. mar. p. 323. Sleidan. Hist. Lib. v. Allen's Conf. Displ. H. 6. b. Vitel's Letter. Display D. 5. H. N. Instru. Art. VIII. sect. 35, Art. I. sect. 35, Art. VII. sect. 36. Fidel. Decl. chap. 4. sect. 11. H. N. Evang. chap. 4. sect. 7.

[2 Gloriantur Rutheni se solos cum Græcis veros Christianos esse.—Guagn. de Relig. Mosc. in Collect. Script. de Relig. Russ. Spir. Nem. 1582. p. 231.]

[3 Sacram. de Relig. Ruthen. cap. 2. Ibid. p. 188. See above, p. 82, note 5.]

[4 Russe Commonwealth. Lond. 1591. cap. 25. p. 103. b.]

[5 Not to be with the pope is to be with Antichrist.—Test. Rhem. Rhemes, 1582. Ann. Marg. p. 323.]

[6 ...the late English general and most impudent revolt from the unity of God's catholic and apostolic church.—Card. Alan's Sincere and Modest Def. against the Exec. of Just. cap. VII. p. 154.]

[7 ...but if any quintescence of grace or other good gift be in me, it floweth from her (sc. our holy mother the catholic Roman church), and is not mine, but as a wretched poor miserable (yet a lively) member of that body mystical &c.—Decacordon of Quodlibetical Questions, 1602. p. 342.]

[8 ...(Muncerus) cœpit eorum nomina conscribere qui facta societate per jusjurandum promittebant auxilia, quo videlicet impiis interfectis novi substituerentur principes ac magistratus: nam a Deo sibi mandatum esse profitebatur ut sublatis illis constitueret novos.—Sleidan. Comment. Argentorat. 1555. Lib. v. fol. 55.]

[9 See above, p. 67, note 8.]

[10 ...for he (H. N.) manifesteth according to the truth, that none among all the children of men shall be found meet (in the sight of the Lord) to bear the names of Christians (boast they never so much of their Christianity, freedom, or justification by Christ in their unregenerated life as they will) which hath not submitted themselves in true repentance under the obedience of God's holy law, which is administered unto them in the Service of Love, &c.—Letter of the Fam. in Displ. of the Fam. Lond. 1579. fol. K.]

[11 If then these which notwithstanding seem to be wise and understanding, and can prate much of spiritual and heavenly things, be yet strangers unto the holy Spirit and unto the true Love, and yet utterly without the body of Christ or the true christianity, and held captive with a wicked nature, so consider then, how wide and far-estranged that the brutish world, and all they that are enemies or resisters of the Doctrine of Love, must yet needs be from the same christian being.—H. N. Evang. Reg. Transl. out of Base-Almayne, cap. IV. § 7. The other references the editor has been unable to verify.]

as are no Familists, they have no living God, and shall perish.

The Puritans finally they say,

Dial. concer. the strife, p. 10. "If God have any church or people in the land, no doubt the title Puritan is given them[1]." Notable words: either God hath no church in England, or Puritans are the church.

The Mar-Prelate is not afraid to utter this speech,

Protest. p. 16. "They, against whom I deal (namely, the ecclesiastical officers, as bishops and their favourers and partakers) have so provoked the anger of the Lord, and prayers of his church, as stand long they cannot[2]." Others, of the said bishops and

2 Admon. the like, write thus, "They bid battle to Christ and his church, and it must bid defiance to them till they yield[3]."

Proposition III.

The visible Church is a Catholic Church.

The proof from God's word.

The visible church, properly understood, is but a part of the Catholic; yet, forasmuch as it is a congregation of the faithful, who are, for calling, governors and subjects, noble and base, rich and poor, teachers and learners; for sex, men and women; for age, old and young; for nation, Jews and Gentiles, Grecians and barbarians; for time and continuance, in all ages, even from our first parents; it may rightly be called a Catholic church.

This is grounded upon God's word, where we find that excluded is no calling[a], no sex[b], none age[c], no nation[d], and

[a] Preach the gospel to every creature, Mark xxvi. 15. Teach all nations, Matt. xxviii. 19. Not many (yet some) wise men after the flesh; not many (yet some) mighty; not many (yet some) noble are called, 1 Cor. ii. 26.

[b] Whosoever shall call on the name of the Lord, shall be saved, Acts ii. 21. The gospel is the power of God to salvation to every one that believeth, Rom. i. 16. There is neither Jew nor Grecian; there

---

[[1] See A Dialogue concerning the Strife of our Church. Lond. 1584. p. 49.]

[[2] The Protestatyon of Martin Marprelat, p. 16. Where, *the anger of God and the prayers of his Church against them.*]

[[3] See Second Admonition, p. 35, where, *bid the defiance.*]

that the church, as it hath been from the world's beginning, so shall it continue to the end. Rev. xiii. 8. Matt. xxviii. 20.

And this is the confession of the churches[4]. Conf. Helv. II. cap. 17. Bohem. c. 8. Belg. Art. XXVII. Wittemb. Art. XXXII.

Errors and adversaries unto this truth.

Unsound be they in religion therefore, which have and do as it were tie the church to a certain country, as the Donatists[5] did to Africa; a people, as the Jews[6] to themselves; persons, place, calling or time, as do the Papists, Aug. Lib. 2. cont. Pet. c. 15. Clenard, Ep. Lib. II. p. 196.

To certain persons, when they say,

The church is founded upon Peter and his successors[7]. Confess. Petrocen. cap. 26.

is neither bond nor free; there is neither male nor female: for you are all one in Christ Jesus, Gal. iii. 28.

[c] He that shall believe and is baptized shall be saved, Mark xvi. 16. By him every one that believeth is justified, Acts xiii. 39. He is the end of the law[8] to every one that believeth, Rom. x. 4.

[d] They shall come from the east and from the west, and from the north and from the south, and shall sit at table in the kingdom of God, Luke xiii. 29. The promise is made unto you and to your children, and to all that are afar off, &c. Acts ii. 39. In every nation, he that feareth God, and worketh righteousness, is accepted with him, Acts x. 35.

[[4] ...Ecclesiam: quam propterea catholicam nuncupamus, quod sit universalis et diffundatur per omnes mundi partes, et ad omnia se tempora extendat, &c.—Harm. Conf. Sect. x. p. 3. Conf. Helv. Post. cap. XVII. ...quæ (ecclesia) in toto orbe terrarum hinc inde diffusa est, et per sanctum evangelium ex omnibus gentibus, &c....congregatur.—Ibid. p. 10. Conf. Bohem. cap. VIII. Denique hæc ecclesia sancta nullo est aut certo loco sita et circumscripta, aut ullis certis ac singularibus personis astricta aut alligata. Sed per omnem orbem terrarum sparsa atque diffusa, &c.—Ibid. p. 17. Conf. Gall. Art. XXVII. Arbitramur autem...vere catholicam et apostolicam ecclesiam non ad unum certum locum aut gentem, nec ad unum certum hominum genus alligatam esse.—Ibid. p. 27. Conf. Virtemb. Art. XXXII. See also above, p. 165, note 1.]

[[5] Si autem nihil est verius quam id quod dixit Christus, ecclesiam suam per omnes gentes incipientem ab Jerusalem; nihil est mendacius quam id quod dicitis, in parte Donati, &c.—August. Opp. Paris. 1836. Tom. IX. col. 371. D. Contra Litt. Petil. Lib. II. c. 15. Cf. Epist. cv. (Opp. Tom. II. col. 444. A.) Vos enim eis dicitis...remansisse ecclesiam Christi in sola Africa partis Donati.]

[[6] Vivo hic inter Judæos, qui longe magis mirantur esse Christianos, quam nos miramur esse aliquos adhuc Judæos.—Clenard. Epist. Antv. 1566. Lib. II. p. 196.]

[[7] Quamobrem si talem esse volumus ecclesiam, quæ videri et cognosci possit, necesse est ut visibilem esse petram statuamus, super quam illa sit visibilis ædificata, ut petræ nomine Petrum Petrique successorem confitentem Christum intelligi velit mus.—[Hosius] Conf. Cath. Fid. in Synod. Patricov. Vienn. 1560. cap. XXVI. p. 44.]

[[8] Head of the law, 1607.]

All that will be saved must of necessity be subject to the bishop of Rome[1].

Bonifac. 8. c. Unam. Extr. de major. et obed.

The true church is united to the obedience of the pope of Rome[2].

Bel. de Eccl. milit. cap. 2.

To a certain place, when they say,

The church of Rome is the Catholic church[3].

Test. Rhem. an. 1 Tim. iii. 15.

The church of Rome is the mother of the faith[4].

Jus Canonic. distinct. 22.

To a certain calling, by their *Petrus à Soto*, to bishops and prelates[5].

Petr. à Soto Assert. p. 133.

To a certain time, as when the said Papists affirm, how

Coster. Enchir. Controv.

The time was, when holiness was only in the Virgin Mary[6], when faith rested only in the Virgin Mary[7], when all the faith was lost save only in our lady[8].

Disput. Conc. Basil. Acts and Mon. in K. H. 6. fol. 796

Festival. feria Serm. IV. post Festum Palmarum.

[[1] Porro subesse Romano Pontifici, omni humanæ creaturæ declaramus, dicimus, definimus, et pronuntiamus omnino esse de necessitate salutis.—Corp. Jur. Canon. Antv. 1648. Extravag. Comm. Lib. I. De Major. et Obed. Tit. VIII. cap. i. Bonifac. VIII. p. 133.]

[[2] Nostra autem sententia est, ecclesiam...unam et veram esse cœtum hominum ejusdem christianæ fidei professione et eorundem sacramentorum communione colligatum, sub regimine legitimorum pastorum, ac præcipue unius Christi in terris Vicarii Romani Pontificis.—Bellarmin. Disput. Prag. 1721. Tom. II. De Controv. Lib. III. cap. 2. § 9. p. 65.]

[[3] *In the house of God.* All the world being God's, yet the church only is his house, the rector or ruler whereof at this day (saith S. Ambrose upon this place) is Damasus. Where let our loving brethren note well how clear a case it was then, that the pope of Rome was not the governor only of one particular see but of Christ's whole house, which is the universal church, whose rector this day is Gregory the thirteenth.—Test. Rhem. Rhemes, 1582. Ann. 1 Tim. iii. 15. p. 572.]

[[4] Fidem quippe violat qui adversus illam (sc. Rom. ecclesiam) agit, quæ mater est fidei.—Corp. Jur. Canon. Gratian. Decret. Pars I. Distinct. XXII. can. 1. p. 26.]

[[5] Ecclesia igitur, quia, ut diximus, humana est congregatio, habet prælatos et superiores suos, ii sunt ministri Christi et dispensatores ministeriorum (mysteriorum?) Dei, ut Paulus inquit, iis alligata est ecclesia, &c.—Petri à Soto, Assert. Cath. Fid. Antv. 1557. p. 114.]

[[6] Tametsi namque ejus [ecclesiæ] plurima membra sint emortua et impia, non amittit tamen sancti nomen, quamdiu vel unus pietatem ex animo colens, retinet sanctitatem, quæ tempore passionis Dominicæ in sola virgine sacratissima viguit.—Coster. Enchirid. Controv. Col. Agrip. 1608. cap. ii. De Eccles. p. 90.]

[[7] Neither do I consent or agree unto the opinion of divers, which affirm that the Virgin only persevered in faith at the Lord's passion. Whereupon divers have not been ashamed to say that the faith was so debilitate and weakened that it seemed to be returned to one only old woman.—Æn. Sylv. in Disput. Concil. Basil. Foxe, Acts and Mon. 1563. fol. 287. Townsend's Edit. Vol. III. p. 614.]

[[8] Thenne that candell is brought agayne and another lyght there, and that betokeneth our blessed Lady, for all the fayth was lost save onely our Lady, and of her al other were enformed and taught.—The Festival. Feria Quarta post Fest. Palmarum. Ed. Faques fol. XXX. a.]

It is a bold assertion also, and very presumptuous of apostata Hill[9], that in England all men were Papists, without exception, from the first christening thereof, until the age of king Henry the Eighth.

Hill's Quar. I. Reas. p. 5.

Proposition IV.

The word of God was, and for time is, before the church.

The proof from God's word.

Forasmuch as the visible church of Christ is a congregation of men (either in the eyes of God, or in the judgment of the godly) faithful, it followeth that the word of God must be afore the church for time, as likewise for authority.

For time; because God's word is the seed; the faithful, the corn and the children: God's word is the rock or foundation; the faithful, the house.

Luke viii. 11, 12. 1 Pet. i. 23. Matt. xvi. 18. Ephes. ii. 20. Ephes. ii. 21.

For authority also the word is before the church; because the voice of the church is the voice of man, who hath erred and may err from the truth; but the voice of the word is God's voice, who cannot deceive nor be deceived.

2 Tim. iii. 16. 2 Pet. i. 21.

Of this judgement be the churches reformed[10].

Conf. Helv. I. Art. XIV. 2. cap. 13, 17. Bohem. c. 1, 8. Gal. Art. VII. Belg. Art. III. 7. Sax. Art. I. 11. Suevica. Art. I.

Adversaries unto this truth.

This maketh to the strengthening of us against those popish assertions of Viguerius[11], and such like, *viz.* that the church was before the word for time, and is above the word for authority.

Viguer. Inst. ad Chr. Theol. c. 10. § 3. v. 10. fol. 83. a.

[9 Hill's Quartron of Reasons. Antwerp, 1600; First Reason, p. 5. where, *this age*.]

[10 Sita est illa (sc. veritas et unitas ecclesiæ) non in cærimoniis et ritibus externis, sed magis in veritate et unitate fidei catholicæ. Fides catholica non est nobis tradita legibus humanis, sed scriptura divina.—Harm. Conf. Sect. x. p. 8. Conf. Helv. Post. cap. XVII. Hæc vero de sacra scriptura persuasio et fides, quod nimirum a Deo suggesta sit et inspirata, initium est et fundamentum christianismi nostri, qui a verbo extrinsecus, sicut a re intermedia ad hoc divinitus ordinata incipit.—Ibid. Sect. I. p. 9. Conf. Bohem. cap. 1. The references to the other Confessions are merely of an inferential kind.]

[11 Et si loquamur de ordine temporis, constat manifeste ecclesiam esse priorem scriptura exteriori. Ecclesia enim fuit tempore Abel...et tamen eo tempore adhuc scriptura exterior non erat....Quod autem ecclesia sit prior dignitate et virtute obligandi, apparet primo ex approbatione scripturæ. Nam nulla scriptura est canonica, nisi sit ab ecclesia approbata.—Viguer. Inst. Theol. Col. Agrip. 1607. cap. x. De Virtute Fid. § 3. v. 10. p. 277.]

Proposition V.

The marks and tokens of the visible church are the due and true administration of the word and sacraments.

The proof from God's word.

There is the visible church of Christ, where the word of God sincerely is preached, and the sacraments instituted by our Saviour are duly administered.

Hence is it, that our Lord and Saviour calleth them his
Luke viii. 21. "mother and his brethren, which hear the word of God, and do
John viii. 47. it;" and saith, "He that is of God, heareth God's word;" also,
Joh. x. 27. Rom. x. 14. "My sheep hear my voice:" and, "How shall they hear without a preacher?" saith St Paul.

Likewise the apostle St John,

1 John iv. 6 "He that knoweth God, heareth us; he that is not of
Ibid. v. God, heareth us not." Again, "They are of the world, therefore speak they of the world, and the world heareth them."

And touching the sacraments; first of baptism.

Matth. xxviii. 19, 20. "Go therefore, and teach all nations, baptizing them in the name of the Father, and the Son, and the Holy Ghost; teaching them to observe all things whatsoever I have commanded you."

Rom. vi. 3. 1 Cor. vi. 11. "We have been baptized into Jesus Christ." "Ye are washed, ye are sanctified."

1 Cor. xii. 13. "By one Spirit are we all baptized into one body."

Next, of the Lord's supper.

"The Lord Jesus, in the night that he was betrayed, took bread, and when he had given thanks, he brake it, and said, Take, eat, this is my body, which is broken for you; this do in remembrance of me."

1 Cor. xi. 23, 24, 25. Luke xxii. 19. "After the same manner also he took the cup, when he had supped, saying, This is the new Testament in my blood; this do, as oft as ye drink it, in remembrance of me."

Conf. Helv. I. Art. XIV. and 2. cap. 17. Bohem. cap. 8. Gal. Art. XXVII. 28. Saxon. Art. XI. Wittem. Art. XXXII. Suevic. Art. XV. The Christians in all reformed churches acknowledge these things[1].

[1 Harm. Conf. Sect. X. p. 9. Conf. Helv. Prior. Art. XIV. [al. XV.]. See above, p. 165, note. 1...sed illam docemus vere esse ecclesiam, in qua signa vel notæ in-

Some (and they also many of them very godly men) add ecclesiastical discipline for a note of the visible church. But because the said discipline in part is included in the marks here mentioned; both we, and in effect, all other well-ordered churches, over pass it in this place, as no token simply of the visible church.

Neither tie we the church so strictly to the signs articulate, that we think all those to be without the church, and no Christians, which neither do hear the word ordinarily and publicly read and preached, nor participate in the sacraments, if so be they would; and yet can neither hear the one, nor receive the other: as it falleth out sometimes, especially in the times of blindness and persecution.

The errors and adversaries unto this truth.

We renounce therefore as altogether unsound and antichristian, the opinions

1. Of the Papists, who both[2] deny the pure preaching of God's word, and the administration of the sacraments among Protestants, to be the marks of Christ his visible church; and affirm the tokens hereof to be antiquity, unity, universality, Petrus a Soto Assert. de Eccles.

veniuntur ecclesiæ veræ. Imprimis vero verbi Dei legitima vel sincera prædicatio, &c....Simul et participant sacramentis a Christo institutis, et ab apostolis traditis.—Ibid. p. 6. Conf. Helv. Post. cap. XVII. ...ubi tamen sit (ecclesia) quam minime contaminata...etiam de infra scriptis signis cognosci potest, Nimirum ubicunque Christus in concionibus sacris docetur, sancti evangelii doctrina pure pleneque annuntiatur, sacramenta de Christi institutione et mandato, sententia et voluntate administrantur, &c.—Ibid. pp. 10, 11. Conf. Bohem. cap. VIII. ...simul etiam palam affirmamus ubi verbum Dei non recipitur, nec ulla est professio obedientiæ quæ illi debetur, nec ullus sacramentorum usus, ibi proprie loquendo, non posse nos judicare ullam esse ecclesiam.—Ibid. p. 15. Conf. Gall. Art. XXVIII. Dicimus igitur ecclesiam visibilem in hac vita cœtum esse amplectentium evangelium Christi et recte utentium sacramentis, &c.—Ibid. p. 21. Conf. Saxon. Art. XI. Arbitramur...ecclesiam...in eo esse loco aut gente ubi evangelion Christi sinceriter prædicatur, et sacramenta ejus recte, juxta institutionem Christi, administrantur.—Ibid. p. 27. Conf. Virtemb. Art. XXXII. ...ubicunque sacrosanctum evangelium et sacramenta exercentur, facile inde sciri poterit, ubi et qui sint christiana ecclesia.—Ibid. p. 30. Conf. Suev. Art. XV.]

[[2] Hoc itaque inquirentibus, quod sit signum ecclesiæ veræ: respondemus primo, fraudulenter et subdole dici signa certa, quibus ecclesia dignosci potest, esse sinceram evangelii prædicationem, et rectam atque secundum Christi institutionem administrationem sacramentorum...Novi enim evangelici dicunt, se verum evangelium docere, et recte administrare sacramenta.—Petri à Soto, Assert. Cathol. Fid. Antwerp. 1557. De Ecclesia, p. 119.]

In his fortress. In his motives. De signis visib. Eccles. In his Quartron. In his Motiv.

succession, &c., as doth Stapleton[1], Bristow[2], Bozius[3], Hill[4], and Alabaster[5].

2. Of the Brownists[6], who make discipline (and that too of their own devising) such an essential argument of the visible church, as they think, where that is not, "the magistrates there be tyrants; the ministers, false prophets; no church of God is; antichristianity doth reign."

R. H. in Psal. cxxii. Bar. discov. p. 86. Ans. to Mr Cartwr. Letter, p. 13.

3. Of the same Brownists and Barrowists[7], who nei-

[1 The church hath certain other marks which can never fall upon heretics in any colour or pretence, as the true preaching of God's word every heretic pretendeth, and therefore it is more clear than the true preaching of God's word. Two such marks I will note. First, the church is described to be universal, to be a communion of all nations. Another clear and most undoubted mark of the church, most evident in scriptures, and such a one as cannot possibly be found among heretics, is...the continuance thereof. We catholics do say that the faith, doctrine, and word of God, which we do believe, follow, and preach, hath continued ever since Christ came, &c.—Stapleton, Fortress of the Faith, &c. Antwerp, 1565. Part I. c. 5. pp. 25, 27, 28.]

[2 Whereas it is most strongly proved by all this which I have here said...that there maketh most plainly for us, and against the heretics, all that ever was or can be of any christian man required...Our unity, universality, antiquity, succession everlasting, &c.—Bristow, Motives to the Catholic Faith. Antwerp, 1599. p. 171. b.]

[3 Bozius, De Signis Eccles. Dei. Lugd. 1595. Tom. I. Lib. III. capp. 5, 9. pp. 183, 215. Tom. II. Lib. XVII. capp. 1, 5. pp. 372, 412.]

[4 The catholic Roman religion on being received by so many nations...ever kept unity and concord, &c.... They all have one faith, one belief, one service, one number of sacraments, &c.—Hill's Quartron of Reasons, Reason 3. pp. 11, 12. See also Reasons 4 and 5, on the Conversion of Countries and Largeness of Dominion.]

[5 The catholic part...allege the judgement of the church, the definition of councils, the consent of fathers, the harmony of churches, the practice of all ages, and the rule of apostolical tradition, left by succession as the light through the heavens.—Alabaster, First Motive. See A Booke of the Seven Planets or Seven wandring Motives of William Alabaster's wit, Retrograded or removed by John Racster. London, 1598. p. 5.]

[6 See A Little Treatise uppon the firste Verse of the 122. Psalm by R. H. fol. G. and H. 3. 1583.—I have shewed that the ministry and sacraments of Christ belong not unto this people or congregation, and how such sacraments and ministry are sacrilegious and ungodly, yea, pernicious and damnable to the whole congregation and all the communicants, unless they repent and redress these faults.... whereby appeareth that the church upon some occasions may be without sacraments, &c.—Barrowe's Brief Discov. of the False Church, 1590. p. 34. But see how fondly and blasphemously Master Cartwright distinguisheth...For he will join the church to Christ without the discipline and government of Christ. He putteth asunder the church and the discipline of Christ, &c.... So then, if the power of the word to bind and loose so be taken from Christ or the church of Christ, what remaineth but an idol or counterfeit Christ, an idol or counterfeit church?—Answ. to Cartwright's Lett. Lond. pp. 33, 4.]

[7 They condemn all coming to church, all preaching, all institution of sacraments,...they never have any sacrament among them.—A Plaine Confutation of a Treatise of Brownism, &c. London, 1590. p. 114.]

ther allow frequenting of sermons, and ministering of the sacraments, nor have any sacraments administered among themselves.

4. Of the Family of Love, which have in utter contempt and derision both the preachers and the sacraments, scornfully terming the preachers scripture-learned men[8], ceremonial[9], and letter-doctors; and the water at baptism[10], elementish water.

Allison, Confut. of Green. and Bar. p. 113, 116.
H. N. Evang. cap. 33. sect. 11.
Fam. Let. to the Bishop of Roch.
H. N. Evang. c. 19, § 5.

Neither do we approve them who for these visible and external put down invisible and spiritual tokens of the visible church, as faith in Christ Jesus, and love towards the saints: which thing J. K. doth[11].

In his Confut. of Pop. 1.4.b.

Proposition VI.

The visible church may, and from time to time hath, erred both in doctrine and conversation.

The proof from God's word.

Had not this been most true, it had never been avouched both by our Saviour Christ and St Paul.

Our Saviour saith unto his disciples concerning doctrine, "Take heed, &c." "Believe it not." Matth. xxiv. 4.

"Beware of the leaven of the Pharisees, and of the leaven of Herod;" even of the doctrine of the Pharisees and Sadducees. Ibid. v. 23, 26. Mark viii. 15. Matth. xvi. 12.

"Many shall be deceived, yea, the very elect, if it were possible." Matt. xxiv. 11. Ibid. v. 24.

"Shall he find faith on earth?" Luke xviii. 8.

And concerning conversation and manners, he prophesied that iniquity shall be increased, and the love of many shall be cold. Matt. xxiv. 12.

St Paul writeth touching doctrine, that

"We know in part." 1 Cor. xiii. 12.

[[8] Whereout each one may by himself well perceive and mark, that it is meer lies (Jer. 23. c. d.) or untrue, what such scripture-learned, through the knowledge which they get out of the scripture, bring-in, institute, preach, and teach.—H. N. Evang. Reg. cap. XXXIII. § 11.]

[[9] ...no difference to be had betwixt a ceremonial, either letter-doctor christian, and an uncircumcised heathen, &c.—Letter of the Fam. to the Bp. of Roch. in Wilkinson's Confutation. Lond. 1579. fol. A. 4. b.]

[[10] Not that men should run forth with an handful of water, and so persuade themselves when they have the elementish water, that it is therewith enough for to be a christian.—H. N. Evang. Reg. cap. XIX. § 5.]

[[11] The editor has been unable to verify this reference.]

2 Thess. ii. 4. Ib. v. 9, 10, 11. "Antichrist sitteth in the temple of God, &c., whose coming is by the working of Satan, with all power, and signs, and lying wonders, and in all deceivableness, among them that perish; because they received not the love of the truth, that they might be saved; and therefore God shall send them strong delusion, that they should believe lies."

Philip. iii. 2. "Beware of dogs, beware of evil workers, beware of concision."

And touching conversation.

Galat. vi. 1. "Restore, &c., lest thou also be tempted."

Rom. vii. 19, 20. "I do not the good thing which I would; but the evil which I would not, that do I: if I do that I would not, it is no more I that do it, but the sin that dwelleth in me."

Ibid. v. 23. There is a fight even in the best men, and members of Christ.

Besides that churches visible and glorious have erred, it appeareth evidently by the superstition, heresies, yea, and atheism now reigning at Jerusalem, Alexandria, and Antioch.

Conv. Helv. II. [c. 17.] Saxon. Art. XI. Wittem. Art. XXXII. Suevic. Art. XV. This with us the churches in their confessions do acknowledge[1].

Errors and adversaries unto this truth.

Test. Rhem. an. 2 Thess. ii. 3. Ibid. Annot. 1 Tim. iii. 15. Ibid. Annot. Ephes. v. 24. Ibid. Annot. marg. p. 264. Gab. Biel. Lib. IV. Dist. 6. quæst. 2. The premises will not be granted for true, neither by the papists, which maintain that in faith and doctrine the church, meaning thereby the visible church, whose rector is the pope of Rome, never erreth[2], never hath erred[3], and never can

[[1] Proinde damnamus illas ecclesias ut alienas a vera Christi ecclesia, quæ tales non sunt, quales esse debere audivimus, utcunque interim jactent successionem episcoporum, unitatem, et antiquitatem. Quinimo præcipiunt nobis apostoli ut fugiamus idololatriam, et Babylonem, &c.—Harm. Conf. Sect. x. p. 7. Conf. Helv. Post. cap. XVII. Non sunt igitur membra ecclesiæ Dei, etiamsi titulum et imperia tenent, Saducæi, Pharisæi et similes pontifices, et alii qui aliam doctrinam proponunt, dissentientem ab evangelio, et stabiliunt idola pertinaciter.—Ibid. p. 22. Conf. Saxon. Art. XI. Quod hæc ecclesia, Spiritu Sancto ita gubernetur, ut etsi sinit eam esse in his terris imbecillem, &c.—Ibid. p. 27. Conf. Virtemb. Art. XXXII. Ibid. p. 29. Conf. Suev. Art. XV. See above, p. 174, note 1.]

[[2] This apostasy or revolt, by the judgement in manner of all ancient writers, is the general forsaking and fall off of the Roman empire....All which fathers and the rest Calvin presumptuously condemneth of error and folly herein, for that their exposition agreeth not with his and his fellows' blasphemous fiction that the pope should be antichrist. To establish which false impiety they interpret this revolt or apostasy to be a general revolt of the visible church from God, &c....But concerning this error and falsehood of the church's defection or revolt, it is refuted sufficiently by St Augustine against the Donatists in many places. Where he proveth that the church shall not fail to the world's end, &c.—Test. Rhem. Rhemes, 1582. p. 555. Annot. 2 Thess. ii. 3. The Marg. Annot. is, There can be

err[4]; nor yet by these which say, the church cannot err for manners. Such were the Donatists, and are the Anabaptists, with the Family of Love.

Ibid. an. 1 Tim. iii. 15. Catech. Trid. in exposit. Symb. Apost. Coster. Enchirid. controvers. cap. 3. De Summo Pontif. p. 136. See of this Article, proposition 1.

Proposition VII.

The church of Rome most shamefully hath erred in life, ceremonies, and matters of faith.

The proof.

Justly is the church of Rome condemned of us and all churches reformed, because she hath erred, and still very badly every way doth offend.

1. In life. For,

"At Rome the harlot hath a better life,
Than she that is a Roman's wife[5]."

W. Thomas, Hist. of Italy.

"O Roma, a Roma quantum mutata vetusta es?
Nunc caput es scelerum, quæ caput orbis eras[6]."

If ye spell Roma backward (saith John Bale[7]) ye shall find it to be Amor: love in this prodigious kind. For

Acts of the Eng. Votaries. 2 Book, Præf.

no apostasy of the visible church from God.—Ibid. But the church which is the house of God, whose rector (saith St. Ambrose) in his time was Damasus, and now Gregory the thirteenth, and in the apostles' time St Peter, is the pillar of truth, the establishment of all verity: therefore it cannot err.—Ibid. p. 572. Ann. 1 Tim. iii. 18. Conf. Ibid. p. 522. Annot. Eph. v. 24.]

[[3] If he [the Spirit] shall teach all truth and that for ever (as before c. 14, 16): how is it possible that the church can err or hath erred at any time or in any point?—Test. Rhem. Marg. Annot. p. 264.

...siquidem ad hunc articulum, Credo sanctam ecclesiam catholicam, omnes veritates totius canonis reducuntur: nam credere ecclesiam sanctam, catholicam, est credere eam sancte vere et sine errore approbasse, quæcunque approbavit, &c.—Gab. Biel. Comm. in Sentent. Brixiæ, 1574. In Lib. III. Dist. xxv. Quæst. Unic. p. 252. This is probably the passage intended.]

[[4] For the reference to Rhem. Test. Annot. on 1 Tim. iii. 15, see above, note 2. Prima igitur proprietas (sc. ecclesiæ) in symbolo patrum describitur, ut una sit.... Unus est etiam ejus rector ac gubernator, invisibilis quidem Christus....Visibilis autem is qui Romanam cathedram Petri apostolorum principis legitimus successor tenet, &c. Sed quemadmodum hæc una ecclesia errare non potest in fidei ac morum disciplina tradenda, cum a Spiritu Sancto gubernetur, ita ceteras omnes quæ sibi ecclesiæ nomen arrogant, &c.—Catech. Conc. Trid. Rom. 1566. In verba Symb. Credo Sanct. Eccl. Cathol. pp. 61, 65. Hac enim donatus est gratia cum successoribus suis beatus apostolus Petrus, ut ad ecclesiæ totius commodum, in fide immobilis consistat; atque ad Romanæ sedis fidem et doctrinam universa per orbem ecclesia, fidem suam religionemque conformet.—Coster. Enchirid. Controvers. Colon. Agripp. 1608. cap. III. De Summo Pontif. p. 136.]

[[5] W. Thomas' History of Italy, Lond. 1549. p. 39. b.]

[[6] See Flac. Illyr. Varia Doct. Vir. Poem. Basil. p. 417. Where, *est* and *erat*.]

[[7] Bale, Acts of the English Votaries, London, Book II. Pref. where, Ye shall find it love in this prodigious kind......for it is preposterous amor, a love out of order, or a love against kind.]

it is a preposterous Amor, love out of kind. Hence the Pasquil poets:

[*Via.*] Roma quid est? [*Pas.*] Quod te docuit præposterus ordo.
[*Via.*] Quid docuit? [*Pas.*] Jungas versa elementa, scies.
[*Via.*] Roma, amor est. [*Pas.*] Amor est. [*Via.*] Qualis?
[*Pas.*] Præposterus. [*Via.*] Unde hoc?
[*Pas.*] Roma mares. [*Via.*] Noli dicere plura, scio.

Again,

Roma, vale; vidi, satis est vidisse. Revertar,
Cum leno, aut meretrix, scurra, cynædus ero[1].

Conf. August. Art. IV.

2. In ceremonies, which are in number infinite. Gerson[2] writeth how divers men have run into desperation, others have killed themselves, finding that they were not able to keep and perform the ceremonies of the Romish church.

Eckius, Enchirid. de Hum. Const. Axiom. 2. Test. Rhem. an. marg. 258.

For use also they are vain and impious; as their leading up and down of an ass on Palm-Sunday, their battering of hell, their burial of the cross, &c.; yea, and damnable, because Romish ceremonies are held both necessarily to be observed as well as the laws of God[3], and also to merit heaven. For sins venial (say the Rhemists) be taken away by sacred ceremonies[4].

3. In doctrine. For proof hereof see the popish errors in every Article almost, if not Proposition of this book.

Again, look we unto the head of the antichristian synagogue, and we shall find that of them

Cyp. Valeram in his Treatise of the Pope, &c. out of Card. Benon.

Some have been conjurers, sorcerers, and enchanters; as were Pope Martin the Second, Sylvester the Second, and Third, Benedict the Eighth, Sergius the Fourth, John the Nineteeth, Twentieth, and One-and-twentieth, Gregory the Sixth, and Seventh; and such were all the popes (even eighteen for number) from Sylvester the Second unto Gregory the Seventh[5].

[1 Pasquill. Tomi duo Eleutheropoli, (Basil.) 1544. Tom. I. p. 70. Cf. Flac. Illyr. Varia Doct. Vir. Poem. Basil. p. 417. Where, *aut* omitted.]

[2 Gerson scribit multos incidisse in desperationem, quosdam etiam sibi mortem conscivisse, quia senserant, se non posse satisfacere traditionibus, et interim consolationem nullam de justitia fidei et de gratia audierant.—Syll. Conf. Oxon. 1827. p. 143. Conf. August. 1531. Art. v. Cf. Gerson. Opp. Antv. 1706. Tom. III. col. 16 sq. De Vit. Spirit. Anim. Lect. 2. 4.]

[3 Ecclesiasticæ consuetudines, ritus et ceremoniæ æque sunt observandæ atque leges divinæ.—Eckii Enchirid. Lugd. 1572. p. 124. De Hum. Constit. Axiom. 2.]

[4 See above, p. 110, note 4.]

[5 Martin II. by deceit and wicked acts was made pope.—Cyp. Valera, Two Treatises transl. from the Span. Lond. 1600. Of the Lives of the Popes, p. 50.

Some, heretics. For Siricius, Calixtus, Leo the Ninth, and Paschalis, condemned the marriage of priests, Liberius was an Arian, Marcellinus an idolater, Honorius a Monothelite[6].

Cath. Apol. II. part. p. 31. Test. Rhem. an. Luke xxii. 31. Biblioth. Simleri. Gerson. Ser. I. Pasch.

John the Two-and-twentieth held many errors, whereof W. Occham wrote a book[7], one whereof was, that the souls of the wicked should not be punished till the day of judgement[8].

Pope John the Twenty-third denied the soul's immortality[9].

Bish. Jewel. Def. fol. 644.

And some, worldly, profane, and devilish atheists; for Sixtus the Fourth builded a male-stews[10].

Act. and Mon.

Paul the Third received a monthly pension for 45,000 whores at Rome[11].

D. Spark. against I. de Albine. p. 399.

Leo the Tenth made a fable of the gospel of Christ[12].

Smeton cont. Hamilt. p. 104.

Hence it proceeded that

Rome hath been called Babylon, both by St Augustine[13]

De Civitat. Dei, Lib. XVIII.

And it is to be noted (as also noteth Cardinal Benon.) that all the popes being eighteen successively from Sylvester II. until Gregory VII. (no less a villain than an enchanter) were enchanters.—Ibid. p. 58.]

[6 Liberius in persecution might yield, Marcellinus for fear might commit idolatry, Honorius might fall to heresy, &c.—Test. Rhem. Rhemes, 1582. Ann. Luke xxii. 31. p. 206. The reference to the Cath. Apol. the editor has been unable to verify.]

[7 Bibliothec. Simler. Tigur. 1574. p. 259.]

[8 Gerson, speaking of Christ's descent into hell, says: Et credendum est satis ipsum dedisse hanc pacem gloriosam omnibus his qui erant in purgatorio et eos liberavit, &c. He then notices the case of the penitent thief, who he observes enjoyed this peace and rest immediately, without enduring purgatorial pains, and continues: Propter quod insuper apparet falsitas doctrinæ Papæ Joannis Vicesimi, quæ damnata fuit cum sono buccinarum vel turbarum coram rege Philippo, &c.—Gerson, Opp. Antv. 1706. Tom. III. Pars III. col. 1205. In Fest. Pasch. Serm.]

[9 This should be Pope John XXII., the same who is called by Gerson John XX. See Jewel's Works, Park. Soc. Ed. Vol. IV. p. 930. Def. of the Apol. Part VI.]

[10 After this Paul came Sixtus IV., who builded up in Rome stews of both kinds, getting thereby no small revenues and rents unto the church of Rome.—Foxe, Acts and Monum. Lond. 1844. Vol. III. p. 738.]

[11 Sparke's Answer to J. de Albine's Discourse against Heresies, p. 399. Oxford, 1591.]

[12 Leonis decimi ad omnem libidinem et voluptatem nati impietatem satis ostendit, quod Petro Bembo ex Evangelio quiddam proponenti respondit: Quantum inquit, nobis ac nostro cœtui profuerit ea de Christo fabula, satis est sæculis omnibus notum.—Smeton. Respons. ad Hamilton. Edinburg. 1579. p. 104. See also above, p. 78.]

[13 ....Babylonia quasi prima Roma....Res autem quas propter comparationem civitatis utriusque terrenæ scilicet et cœlestis, huic operi oportet inserere, magis ex Græcis et Latinis, ubi et ipsa Roma quasi secunda Babylonia est, debemus assumere.—August. Opp. Par. 1836-8. Tom. VII. col. 775. De Civ. Dei, Lib. XVIII. cap. 2. § 2.]

Præf. Lib. de Spirit. Sancto. Ch. Franek. Præf. ad. Paradox. De Consid. ad Eugenium.

and Hierom[1], and by Pope Pius the Fifth[2] was said *magis Gentilizare, quam Christianizare:* rather to Gentilize, or to be a city of heathens, than of Christians.

St Bernard[3] saith, how the Romans, in his time, were hateful unto heaven and earth, yea, and hurtful unto both, wicked against God, rash against holy things, and seditious among themselves.

Chron. Lib. IV. page 817.

Genebrard[4] (himself an antichristian Romanist) writeth that fifty popes successively, and within the space of 150 years, departed from the virtue of their elders, and shewed themselves abjurers of Christianity, and apostates, rather than catholic bishops.

Arnolph. in Conc. Rhem. inter opera Bernardi.

The pope was proclaimed Antichrist at Rhemes by the council there under Hugh Capet[5].

Errors and adversaries to this truth.

What the Papists are then it appeareth, whose doctrine (as hath been shewn) is, that the church of Rome neither hath, nor can err.

Stella in Lucæ, ix. fol. 430.

Erraverunt aliæ ecclesiæ (saith D. Stella), other churches, as of Antioch, Alexandria, Constantinople, &c. have erred: *sed nunquam ecclesia Romana,* but the church of Rome never yet erred[6].

[[1] Cum in Babylone versarer, et purpuratæ meretricis essem colonus, et jure Quiritum viverem, volui garrire aliquid de Spiritu Sancto, et cœptum opusculum ejusdem urbis Pontifici dedicare.—Hieron. Opp. Par. 1693-1706. Tom. IV. Pars I. col. 493. Præf. in Lib. Didym. de Spir. Sancto. Cf. Ibid. Pars II. col. 104. VIII.]

[[2] Nam cum idolorum cultus adeo insitus et innatus sit Romanis ut vel nostro tempore Pius V. Pontifex Maximus, qui ab illis pro sancto colitur Romam adhuc magis gentilizare quam Christianizare (ut verbis ejus utar) dicere coactus sæpe fuerit. —Chr. Franeken. Colloquium Jesuit. Basil. 1581. p. 57.]

[[3] Quid de populo loquar? Populus Romanus est. Nec brevius potui, nec expressius tamen aperire de tuis parochianis quod sentio. Quid tam notum sæculis quam protervia et fastus Romanorum? Gens insueta paci, tumultui assueta; Gens immitis et intractabilis usque adhuc, subdi nescia, nisi cum non valet resistere.—Bernard. Opp. Paris. 1719. Vol. I. col. 441. De Consid. Lib. IV. cap. 2. Cf. Vol. II. p. 107. Epist. ccxliii.]

[[4] This reference the editor has been unable to verify.]

[[5] Quid hunc Reverendi patres, in sublimi solio residentem, veste purpurea et aurea radiantem, quid hunc (inquam) esse censetis? Nimirum si charitate destituitur solaque scientia inflatur et extollitur, Antichristus est, in templo Dei sedens, et se ostendens tanquam sit Deus.—Concil. Labb. et Cossart. Tom. XIX. col. 132. Orat. Arnulph. in Conciliab. Remen. cap. XXVIII.]

[[6] Stella in Luc. Lugd. 1583. Tom. I. Enar. in cap. IX. fol. 430.]

Id constanter negamus (saith Costerus the Jesuit[7]), we constantly deny that Christ his vicars, and Peter's successors, the bishops of Rome, have either taught heresies, or can propound errors. Enchirid. Controvers. c. 3. de Summo Pontif. p. 136.

God preserveth the truth of Christian religion in the apostolic see of Rome, and it is not possible, that the church (meaning the church of Rome) can err, or hath erred at any time, in any point, say the Rhemists[8]. Test. Rhem. an. Matt. xxiii. 2. Ibid. Annot. marg. page 264.

Article XX.

Of the Authority of the Church.

(1) *The church hath power to decree rites or ceremonies,* (2) *and authority in controversies of faith. And yet it is not lawful for the church* (3) *to ordain anything that is contrary to God's*[9] *word,* (4) *neither may it so expound one place of Scripture,* (5) *that it be repugnant to another. Wherefore although* (6) *the church be a witness, and a keeper of holy writ, yet, as it ought not to decree anything against the same, so* (7) *besides the same ought it not to enforce anything to be believed for necessity of salvation.*

The propositions.

1. The church hath power to decree rites or ceremonies.
2. The church may not ordain what rites or ceremonies she will.
3. The church hath authority to judge and determine in controversies of faith.
4. The church hath power to interpret and expound the word of God.
5. The analogy of faith must be respected in the exposition of the scripture.
6. The church is the witness and keeper of God's written word.

[7 Id constanter negamus, Vicarios Christi, Petrique successores, Romanos Pontifices, vel hæresim docere alios posse, vel errorem proponere.—Coster. Enchirid. Controvers. Col. Agrip. 1608. cap. 3. De Summo Pont. p. 133.]

[8 See above, pp. 178, 9, notes 2, 3.] [9 God's written word, 1675.]

7. The church may not enforce anything to be believed, as necessary unto salvation, that is either contrary or besides the word of God.

Proposition I.

The Church hath power to decree rites or ceremonies.

The proof from God's word.

The church's authority to decree rites or ceremonies is warranted in the word of God; first, by the example of the apostles, who did ordain rites and ceremonies: among other things, that

1 Cor. xi. 4, 7, 14, &c. In the church men should not be covered.

1 Cor. xiv. 34. 1 Cor. xi. 5. Women should keep silence, and be covered.

1 Cor. xiv. 2. 1 Cor. xi. 2, 3, 4. A known tongue, understood of the common auditory, should be used with other things.

Next, by the general and binding commandment of God himself, who at all times will have everything in the church to be done unto edifying, honesty, and by order, as being not the author of confusion, but of peace. (1 Cor. xiv. 26. Ibid. v. 40. Ibid. v. 33.)

All Protestant churches confess the same[1].

(Conf. Helv. I. Art. XIII. and II. c. 22, 23, 24. Basil. Art. X. Bohem. c. 15, 17. Gal. Art. XXXII. Belg. Art. XXXII. August. Art. IV. V. VII. XV. Saxon. Art. XX. Suevica, c. 8, 14. Wittemb. cap. 27, 31.)

[1 Cœtus autem sacros sic peragendos esse censemus, ut ante omnia verbum Dei in publicum, loco publico et sacris destinato plebi quotidie proponatur, &c.—Harm. Conf. Sect. xv. p. 159. Conf. Helv. Prior. Art. XXIII. [XXIV.] Instruantur autem omnia pro decoro, necessitate, et honestate pia, ne quid desit, quod requiritur ad ritus et usus Ecclesia necessarios, &c.... Neque oportet preces publicas quo ad formam et tempus in omnibus Ecclesiis esse pares. Libertate enim sua utantur Ecclesiæ quælibet.—Ibid. pp. 156, 7. Conf. Helv. Post. capp. XXII. XXIII. Cf. Ibid. Sect. XVI. p. 174. Conf. Helv. Post. cap. XXIV. De hoc genere accessorio traditionibus humanis, constitutionibus, consuetudineque bona introductis ritibus, docentur...concordi consensu retinenda esse, secundum sancti Apostoli doctrinam: Omnia in communitate (scilicet Ecclesiastica) vestra, decenter et ordine fiant.... Et quanquam nostri non omnes ritus æque servant cum aliis Ecclesiis, id quod et fieri non potest, et non est necesse fieri, &c.—Ibid. Sect. XVII. pp. 212, 14. Conf. Bohem. cap. XV. Cf. Ibid. Sect. XVI. p. 179. Conf. Bohem. cap. XVII. Credimus expedire, ut qui electi sunt Ecclesiæ alicujus præfecti, inter se dispiciant qua ratione totum corpus commode regi possit. Ita tamen ut ab eo quod Dominus noster Jesus Christus instituit nusquam deflectant. Hoc autem non impedit quominus quædam singulis locis peculiaria sint instituta, &c.—Ibid. p. 216. Conf. Gall. Art. XXXII. Interim credimus utile quidem esse, ut seniores qui Ecclesiis præsunt, aliquam inter se ordinem constituant, ad conservationem corporis Ecclesiæ: modo studiose caveant ne quo pacto ab iis deflectant declinentve, quæ Christus ipse, unicus Magister noster, semel constituit.—Ibid. p. 217. Conf. Belg. Art. XXXII. De ritibus ecclesiasticis, qui sunt humana auctoritate instituti, docent, ritus illos servandos esse, qui sine peccato servari possunt, et ad tranquillitatem, et bonum ordinem in ecclesia conducunt, ut certæ feriæ, certæ cantiones piæ et alii similes ritus.—Ibid. p. 217. Conf. Aug. Art. XV. The other references to this

Errors and adversaries unto this truth.

This power being given by the supreme authority unto the church, they do greatly offend which do condemn either generally all, or particularly some rites and ceremonies, orderly and lawfully established. Of the former sort are

1. The Family of Love, who say of themselves, how they are a free people[2], in bondage unto no creature, nor to any created thing[3]; they have no several dissenting, or variable religions, either ceremonies[4]. H. N. Spirit. land, c. 31. § 6. Ibid. cap. 40. § 1. Ibid, cap. 39. § 7.

2. The Brownists[5], who teach that every Christian is to join himself unto that people among whom the Lord's worship is free, and not bound, or withholden with any jurisdiction of this world. R. H. on Psal. cxxii.

3. The Puritans[a], whereof some would have all matters

[a] Such a one was that Scottish minister which said unto the head of K. James, how he would hold conformity with his Majesty's ordinances for matters of doctrine; but for matters of ceremony, they were to be left in Christian liberty unto every man. This Dr Barlow reporteth in the Sum of the Conference, page 71. [London, 1604.]

Confession should be, doubtless, to the Second Part, De Abusibus Sublatis; where rites and ceremonies are treated of in detail. See Franke, Libb. Symbol. Pars I. pp. 32, 3, 41—47. Natura rationalis ordinem intelligit, et intellectus ordinis, non obscurum testimonium est de Deo....Ac Paulus jubet omnia in ecclesia fieri decore et ordine.—Ibid. p. 192. Conf. Saxon. Art. xx. [al. XII.] Nam quæ (traditiones) cum scriptura consonant, et ad bonos mores utilitatemque hominum institutæ sunt, tametsi in scripturis ad verbum expressæ non sint, nihilominus, &c....Hujus ordinis erant illa Pauli, ne mulieres apertis capitibus, viri obvelatis orarent in ecclesia... Tales multas sane ecclesia hodie jure observat, et pro occasione quoque condit novas, &c.—Ibid. p. 230. Conf. Suev. cap. XIV. Fatemur et hoc, quod episcopis liceat cum ecclesiæ suæ consensu, ordinationes dierum, festorum, et lectionum seu concionum ad ædificationem, et eruditionem veræ fidei in Christum instituere.—Ibid. p. 229. Conf. Virtemb. Art. XXXV.]

[[2] And all the people of this city are free also: and do all live in freedom, &c.—H. N. Spiritual Land of Peace, p. 47. b. cap. XXXI. § 6.]

[[3] The people of this land do, in their good-service, serve the Most High God, who is God only. And they are subject to no other gods, nor laws or ceremonies.... Also they are not subject to the creatures, nor to any created thing as properly to belong thereunto.—Ibid. cap. XL. § 1, 2.]

[[4] In which plentiful land there are no sundry chosen-out God-services, nor several religions, or ceremonies used.—Ibid. cap. XXXIX. §. 7.]

[[5] Is it not the callinge of everie Christian to remove himselfe from their communion which worship God vaynlie, as by the directinge of the blinde and dumme ministerie, that execrable abomination in God's sight: and to joyne onlie where the Lordes worshippe is free, and not bound or withholden in the bands of any jurisdiction of this world?—A Little Treatise uppon the firste verse of the 122. Psalm, by R. H. (Harrison?) fol. D. 6. 1583.]

of ceremonies to be left in christian liberty unto every man.

Others would have both temples to be left without service, sermons and sacraments, and princes to be scared with the fear of uproars and sedition; and all because they would be freed from the obedience unto ceremonies, not impious of themselves, imposed by the church: the father of these men was Illyricus[1], of whom Melanchthon writeth.

Epist. ad Pium. Lect. pag. 455.

Of the latter kind be

1. The Family of Love again, who utterly dislike our churches or temples, also our liturgies, and forms of serving our God, and finally, our designed times of meeting together for the worship of God.

H. N. Spirit. Land. c. 5. § 5.

Our churches[2] they blasphemously term common houses; and so we term brothel-houses, or the stews.

Ibid. H. N. Exhort. c. 15. § 12, 13. Ibid. cap. 16. § 14. Ibid. § 3.

Our liturgies and manner of serving of God they call foolishness of taken-on services[3], false and seducing God's services[4], of no man to be ordained[5], nor to be obeyed, or used, when they are established[6]. With these join the Barrowists,

[[1] Sed fateor me suasisse et Francis et aliis ne desererent ecclesias propter servitutem, quæ sine impietate sustineri posset. Nam quod Illyricus vociferatur, potius vastitatem fuisse faciendam in templis, et metu seditionum terrendos principes, ego ne nunc quidem tam tristis sententiæ autor esse velim.—Melancth. Epist. Lond. 1642. Lib. I. Ep. 107. col. 137.]

[[2] They build there (i. e. in the city of ignorance, which according to the allegory, is the abode of all who are not Familists) likewise divers houses of common assembly, which they call God's houses.—H. N. Spirit. Land. p. 13. b. cap. v. § 5.]

[[3] And they use there many-manner of foolishnesses of taken-on services, which they call religions, or God-services, &c.—Ibid.]

[[4] Seeing now then that it all is nothing else but knowledge and a painted or coloured holiness: ...so is it likewise a false and deceitful light: yea, so false and deceitful, that all simple and unlighted people (Jer. 23. c. d. Ezech. 23. b.)... become therewith seduced or beguiled, &c. Nevertheless in all this same so hath hereto...every sundry sect or opiniated assembly in their understanding of the knowledge their respect bent to the false sight: and they minister forth the same likewise, as though that same were the Word of the Lord (3. Reg. 22. b. Jer. 8. 23. e. Ezec. 13. b.) and the illumination of the Holy Spirit.—H. N. First Exhortation. Lond. 1656. p. 113. cap. xv. § 12, 13.]

[[5] ...that any man should become so arrogant...that he...should dare to teach or set forth anything through the imagination of the knowledge...as a word (1 Reg. 15. a. b. Jer. 5. 6. 7. 8. 14.) or commandment of the Lord: or yet to institute any services (out of the letter of the Scripture) according to his good thinking, &c.—Ibid. pp. 129, 30. cap. XVI. § 14.]

[[6] For certain take in hand and use, out of the imagination of the knowledge, (whereon they set their hearts at peace) false God-services, which they notwithstanding institute, or bring in, for true God-services (Col. 2. b. c.) religions, laws, and commandments of God: and plant the same knowledge into the people as though they ought of right to be obedient thereunto.—Ibid. p. 124. cap. XVI. § 3.]

who do write[7], that to have liturgies and forms of common prayer, is to have another Gospel, and another Testament. Barrow's Refut. p. 244.

Our Sabbath they contemn, yea they condemn; for they say, There ought to be no Sabbath-day[8]. Our Sabbatarians go not so far, yet come they near unto these Familists, when they divulge that Displ. H. 8. b.

The church hath no authority ordinary and perpetually to sanctify any day but the seventh day, which the Lord himself hath[9] sanctified[10]. D. B. Doct. of the Sabb. I. book. p. 31.

The church cannot take away this liberty of working six days in the week[11]. These assertions are against all holy-days lawfully established. Barrow yet goeth further than do these men; for he saith, how the observing of times, as it is in our church, is an error fundamental[12]. T. C. I. Reply, p. 120. Barrow's Refut. p. 31.

They also be alike culpable, who, approving some rites and ceremonies, do yet tie the church, or people of God, to the observation of the ceremonies, either Mosaical, as many have done, and do[13]; or of the Romish Church, as do the Papists[14], and the half-Papists, the Family of Love[15]. See Art. VII. Prop. 3. Concil. Trid. Sess. 7. Can. 13. H. N. Evang. c. 31. Sect. I.

[[7] First the whole public worship and administration enjoined of their church was blamed unto him and refused as idolatrous, devised by man after the prescript of a rotten Popish Leitourgie, and proved such unto him by express scriptures.—Barrowe's Refut. of Giffard, 1591, p. 244.]

[[8] They hold there ought to be no Sabbath-day, but that all should be like: and for that they allege, The Son of Man is Lord over the Sabbath-day.—Displaying, &c. Lond. 1579. H. 8. b.]

[[9] Had sanctified, 1607.]

[[10] Yet I do not see...where the Lord hath given any authority to his Church ordinarily and perpetually to sanctify any day, except that which he hath sanctified himself.—Nich. Bownde. Doct. of the Sab. Lond. 1595. Book I. p. 31.]

[[11] But that it [the Church] hath power to make so many holy-days (as we have) wherein no man may work any part of the day, and wherein men are commanded to cease from their daily vocations of ploughing and exercising their handicrafts, &c., that I deny to be in the power of the Church.—Cartwright's First Reply. New Edition, p. 152.]

[[12] And evil provide they for their prince's honour that make her the author of such abominable idolatrous stuff as these Romish fasts, your Embers, Saints' eves, Lents, are, &c. ?...What can you there plead for your superstitious devotions towards our Lady, keeping a day, an eve, &c.... We poor Christians can see no other mystery in the matter, but that it is detestable idolatry, even that very pouring out your drink-offerings and burning incense to the queen of heaven.—Barrowe's Refut. of Giffard, pp. 31, 3.]

[[13] See above, pp. 88, 9.]

[[14] Si quis dixerit receptos et approbatos ecclesiæ catholicæ ritus in solemni sacramentorum administratione adhiberi consuetos, aut sine peccato a ministris pro libito omitti, aut in novos alios per quemcumque ecclesiarum pastorem mutari

Finally, they are out of the way which think that either one man, as the pope, or any certain calling of men, as the clergy, hath power to decree and appoint rites or ceremonies, though of themselves good, unto the whole church of God, dispersed over the universal world.

Proposition II.

The church may not ordain what rites and ceremonies she will.

The proof from God's word.

As it is a clear truth that the church may ordain ceremonies, so true is it also that the church hath no power to appoint what rites or ceremonies she will. For she must decree none which be

Either for their own nature impious, like the ordinances,
Jerem. x. 8. manners, and idols of our forefathers[a], teachers of vanity,
Heb. iii. 18. and of lies.

2 Kings xviii. 4. Or for use, superstitious; like the brazen serpent, which king Hezekiah brake in pieces.

Or for their weight, over-heavy, and grievous to be borne; like the Jewish constitutions[b].

Or for their worthiness, in the eyes of the ordainers, either of equal price, or of more account than the very ordinances of God; so as, for the performance of them, the laws of God

[a] Walk ye not in the ordinances of your fathers, neither observe their manner, nor defile yourselves with their idols. Ezek. xx. 18.

[b] Ye lade men with burdens grievous to be borne, Luke xi. 46. Why tempt ye God, to lay a yoke on the disciples' necks, which neither our fathers nor we were able to bear? Acts xv. 10. Why as though ye lived in the world, are ye burdened with traditions? Col. ii. 20.

---

posse; anathema sit.—Concil. Harduin. Paris. 1714. Tom. x. col. 52. Conc. Trid. Sess. VII. De Sacramentis in Genere. Can. 13.]

[[15] Furthermore, ye dearly beloved, behold and consider how that the Catholic Church of Rome hath obediently grounded itself on the foresaid services and ceremonies, which are the figures, or the prefiguration of the true Christianity and her services: and with diligence and fervency observed those same, to a good discipline, or ordinance of the congregations: and even so, in figures, borne the name of Christians.—H. N. Evang. Reg. Transl. out of Base-Almayne. p. 73. cap. XXXI. § 1.]

must be left undone; such were many of the Pharisaical rites and traditions[c].

Or against the liberty of Christians, and to the entangling of them again with the yoke of servile bondage[d].

Or last of all, any way contrary to the commandments, word, and will of God[e].

But the rites, ceremonies, and constitutions of the church they must make altogether, and tend both to the nourishing and increase of love, friendship, and quietness among Christians, and also to the retaining of God's people in the holy service, worship, and fear of God, according to the rule of the apostle aforementioned, "Let all things be done honestly, and by order." 1 Cor. xiv. 10.

All churches reformed[1] consent hereunto. Conf. Helv. II. cap. 5. Gall. Art. XXXIII. Belg. Art. XXXII. August. Art. VII. 15. Saxon. Art. XX. Wittemb. Art. XXXV. Suevica, cap. 14.

[c] Ye lay the commandment of God apart, and observe the tradition of men, as the washing of pots, and of cups, and many other such like things ye do, Mark vii. 8. Ye reject the commandments of God, that ye may observe your own traditions, &c.; making the word of God of none authority by your tradition, which you have ordained, Ibid. ix. 13.

[d] Stand in the liberty wherewith Christ hath made us free, and be not entangled again with the yoke of bondage, Gal. v. 1.

[e] Every plant which my Father hath not planted shall be rooted up, Matt. xv. 13.

[[1] Omnia autem decenter et ordine fiant in Ecclesia, omnia denique fiant ad ædificationem.—Harm. Conf. Sect. xv. Conf. Helv. Post. cap. XXII. In the place referred to, cap. v., there is a general condemnation of the worship of saints, relics, &c. Excludimus autem humana omnia commenta, et leges omnes, quæ cultus Dei prætextu, astringendis conscientiis invehuntur, et eas tantum admittimus, quæ fovendæ concordiæ et unicuique in obedientia debita retinendo subserviunt.—Ibid. sect. XVII. p. 216. Conf. Gall. Art. XXXIII. Nos itaque omnia humana inventa, omnesque leges rejicimus, quæ ad Dei cultum sunt introductæ ut iis conscientiæ ullo modo illaqueentur aut obstringantur. Easque solas suscipimus, quæ idoneæ sunt vel ad fovendam alendamque concordiam, vel ad nos in Dei obedientia retinendos.—Ibid. p. 217. Conf. Belg. Art. XXXII. Sed de hoc ipso genere (sc. rituum Eccles.) docent non esse onerandas conscientias superstitiosis opinionibus.... Rejiciuntur igitur traditiones quæ sine peccato non possunt observari, &c.—Ibid. pp. 217, 18. Conf. Aug. 1540. Art. xv. Sed de hac quæstione nostri sic docent, quod Episcopi non habet potestatem statuendi aliquid contra Evangelium, &c.—Ibid. p. 219. Conf. Aug. De Abus. Art. VII. In the edit. of 1531, ... tenenda est regula certissima quod nemini liceat condere leges pugnantes cum mandatis Dei.—Ibid. p. 221. Est igitur prima regula: Nulli creaturæ, non angelis non hominibus, non regibus non episcopis licet condere leges aut ritus pugnantes cum verbo Dei.—Ibid. p. 226. Conf. Saxon. Art. xx. Nec licet vel veteres ritus legis restaurare, vel novos comminisci ad adumbrandam veritatem Evangelio jam patefactam, &c.... Multo minus licet instituere ceremonias aut sacra quorum meritis expientur peccata, &c.—

Errors and adversaries unto this truth.

The premises being, as they are, most true, most false then is it which the papists do publish, *viz.* that

Conc. Trid. Sess. v. cap. 2. The church hath power to change the sacraments ordained even by Christ himself[1].

Test. Rhem. An. marg. 336. "Whatsoever the apostles and rulers of the church command, is to be kept and obeyed."

Conf. Patrocenien. cap. 15. The authority of the church is greater than of the sacred scripture[2].

Proposition III.

The church hath authority to judge and determine in controversies of faith.

The proof from God's word.

Authority is given to the church, and to every member of sound judgement in the same, to judge in controversies of faith; and so in their places to embrace the truth, and to avoid and improve[3] antichristianity and errors; and this is not the private opinion of our church, but both the straight commandment of God himself particularly unto all teachers[a] and hearers[b] of God's word, and generally unto the whole

[a] Cast away profane and old wives' fables, 1 Tim. iv. 7. O Timothy, keep that which is committed unto thee, 1 Tim. vi. 20. A bishop must, &c. hold fast the faithful word according to doctrine, that he also may be able to exhort with wholesome doctrine, and improve them that say against it, &c. Tit. i. 9, &c.

[b] Hear not the words of the prophets that prophesy unto you, and teach you vanities; they speak the vision of their own heart, and not of the mouth of the Lord, Jer. xxiii. 16. Beware of false prophets, Matt. vii. 15. Beware of dogs, beware of evil workers, Philip. iii. 2. The sheep know the shepherd's voice, and they will not follow a stranger; but they fly from him: for they know not the voice of strangers, John x. 4, 5. Be not carried about with divers and strange doctrines, Hebr. xiii. 9.

Ibid. pp. 229, 30. Conf. Virtemb. Art. xxxv. The reference to the Conf. Suev. is inferential.—Ibid. p. 230. Conf. Suev. cap. XIV.]

[[1] The reference should probably be, Conc. Trid. Sess. XXI. cap. 2. Præterea declarat hanc potestatem perpetuo in ecclesia fuisse, ut in sacramentorum dispensatione, salva illorum substantia, ea statueret, vel mutaret, quæ suscipientium utilitati, seu ipsorum sacramentorum venerationi, pro rerum, temporum et locorum varietate magis expedire judicaret.—Conc. Harduin. Tom. x. col. 120.]

[[2] Quin tamen prior sit authoritas Ecclesiæ quam Scripturæ negari non potest.—Conf. Cath. Fid. in Syn. Petricov. Vienn. 1560. cap. xv. p. 16. Where, however, *prior* seems to refer to time, not order.]

[[3] In the sense of the Latin *improbare*. The edition of 1675 has *reprove*.]

church[c]: and also the judgement of our godly brethren in foreign countries[4].

Confess. Wit-temb. Art. xxxii. Suevica, Art. xv.

The errors and adversaries unto this truth.

Unsound therefore in judgement are the Papists. For first they maintain,

That the pope of Rome hath the power[5] to judge all men and matters[6], but may be judged of no man; to decree (without controlment) against the epistles of St Paul[7]; to dispense even against the new Testament[8]; and to give the sense and meaning of the holy scripture: to which sense or interpretation of his all and every man, without contradiction, must yield and obey[9].

Dist. 40. c. Si Papa. Carol. Ruinus. Panor. Extra de Divortiis. Hervæus. de potestate Papæ.

Next they publish and hold, that the power to judge of religion and points of doctrine is either in bishops only, as

[c] Beware lest you be also plucked away with the error of the wicked, and fall from your own stedfastness, 2 Pet. iii. 17. If there come any unto you, and bring not this doctrine, receive him not to house; neither bid him God speed, 2 John 10. If any shall say unto you, Lo, here is Christ, or there, believe it not; for there shall arise false Christs, and false prophets, Matth. xxiv. 23, 24. I speak as unto them which have understanding; judge ye what I say, 1 Cor. x. 15. Try all things, and keep that which is good, 1 Thess. v. 21.

[[4] Quod hæc Ecclesia habeat jus judicandi de omnibus doctrinis, juxta illud, Probate spiritus, &c.—Harm. Conf. Sect. x. p. 27. Conf. Virtemb. Art. xxxii. Hanc porro Ecclesiam seu congregationem regit ipse Spiritus sanctus...Hæc etiam illa ipsa est, quam omnes audire jubentur et qui illi non auscultavit, habendus est ceu Ethnicus et Publicanus.—Ibid. p. 30. Conf. Suev. Art. xv.]

[[5] Hujus (sc. Papæ) culpas....redarguere præsumit mortalium nullus, quia cunctos ipse judicaturus a nemine est judicandus, &c.—Corpus Jur. Canon. Antv. 1648. Decret. Gratian. Pars i. Distinct. xl. cap. vi. p. 50. Si papa.]

[[6] Matter, 1607.]

[[7] Et idem tenet archiepiscopus Florentinus in 3 parte suæ summæ, sub titulo de potestate papæ...ac refert aliquos dicere, quod potest tollere singula, sed non omnia, quia hoc esset destruere utilem statum ecclesiæ, et præsertim sic potest fieri cum causa, quia et contra epistolas Pauli potest papa statuere cum causa, in his quæ non concernunt fidem.—Carol. Ruin. Concil. Venet. 1591. Vol. iii. p. 125. b. Tom. Quint. Cons. cix. Num. 1.]

[[8] He is speaking of the marriage of unbelievers, of which he says: Cessat inter eos ratio indissolubilitatis. Nec obstat quod dicitur, quos Deus conjunxit homo non separet; scilicet quia non est homo qui dissolvit in casu sed ecclesia autoritate divina: nam ecclesia interpretatur in hoc jus divinum.—Panormit. super Quart. Decretal. Lugd. 1534. Fol. 46. b. De Divort.]

[[9] Sed sentire quod (? non) omnis potestas et quod non omnes existentes in quacunque potestate in ecclesia Dei subsint correctioni ecclesiæ Romanæ est sentire

some of them do think[d]; or in their clergy only, as others deem[e], and in the church of Rome only, as all of them suppose[f].

[d] The mysteries of religion are committed to the trust of bishops, *plebi tantum sciendum est, quod ad mores formandos et vitam pertinet*, the common people are only to know that which pertaineth unto manners and good behaviour, saith Friar Laurence à Villavincence[1], De forman. concion. lib. I. cap. 10. *Nec gratia, nec* [*certe*] *interior aliqua virtus* [*occulta*] *requirenda est* [*vel*] *in membris, vel* [*in*] *ministris, in Ecclesia, præter publicam* [*et legitimam*] *professionem fidei.* It is sufficient for the members and ministers of the church to make open profession of the faith: more is not required of them, neither grace (to judge of doctrine), nor any other inward virtue, saith Petrus à Soto, Assert. Cath. [Antv. 1557.] de Eccl. [p. 148.]

[e] The common and faithful people may in a generality refuse, and forsake all new doctrine dissenting from that which they have learned and embraced. *Non autem, ut doctrinam in particulari ex causis et fundamentis suis examinent, ut sic proprio judicio discutiant quid verum, quid falsum sit.* But they have none authority to examine any doctrine in particular from the very causes and grounds, and thereby search out what is true, what false; *quod proprium est ecclesiarum magistris:* this they must leave to the masters of churches, to whom properly it belongeth; saith Stapleton, [Opp. Par. 1620, Tom. III. p. 24.] Antid. Evang. in Mat. 7. [15.]

[f] *Sacræ scripturæ sensus nativus et indubitatus ab ecclesia catholica est petendus* (saith the aforementioned Petrus à Soto.) The native and true sense of the sacred scripture is to be fetched from the catholic church (of Rome). Assert. Cath. de Eccl.[2] The whole church throughout the world knoweth that the holy church of Rome hath power to judge of all matters, *neque cuiquam licebit de ejus judicio judicare*, neither is it lawful for any man to give any sentence of her judgment. Gelasius IX. q. Cuncta[3].

---

oppositum ejus quod tenet ecclesia, &c....sentire oppositum ejus quod tenet ecclesia vel illius qui habet determinare ea quæ sunt fidei est sentire oppositum ejus quod tenet fides vel explicite vel implicite....Ergo ponere apostolicam potestatem in ecclesia non subesse potestati papæ est oppositum ejus quod tenet ecclesia.—Hervæ. de Potest. Pap. Paris. 1506. fol. 201.]

[[1] This reference the editor has been unable to verify.]

[[2] The reference should be to Lindanus, Panopl. Evang. Colon. Agrip. 1560. Lib. III. cap. 7. p. 180. ...proximum est ut commonstremus undenam certus indubitatusque illarum (sc. sacr. liter.) sensus sit tuto putendus....Quocirca de vero scripturarum sensu an eum ecclesia Christi catholica suis proponat filiolis necne dubitet Judæus, dubitet Paganus, &c.]

[[3] Cuncta per mundum novit ecclesia, quod sacrosancta Romana ecclesia fas de omnibus habeat judicandi: neque cuiquam de ejus liceat judicare judicio.—Corp. Jur. Canon. Antverp. 1648. Decret. Sec. Pars. Caus. IX. Quæst. 3. cap. 17. fol. 208.]

Proposition IV.

The church hath power to interpret and expound the word of God.

The proof from God's word.

To interpret the word of God is a peculiar blessing, given by God only to the church and company of the faithful, though not to all and every of them. For,

"No man knoweth the Son but the Father, neither knoweth any man the Father but the Son, and he to whom the Son will reveal him." Matt. xi. 27.

"It is given to you to know the secrets of heaven, (saith our Saviour unto his disciples), but to them it is not given." Matt. xiii. 11.

"The manifestation of the Spirit is given to every man to profit withal. For to one is given by the Spirit the word of wisdom, &c., and to another prophecy." 1 Cor. xii. 7, [8–10].

"If any thing be revealed to another that sitteth by, let the first hold his peace," saith St Paul unto the church at Corinth. 1 Cor. xiv. 30.

"Ye have an ointment from him that is holy, and ye have known all things, &c., ye need not that any man teach you;" saith the apostle John. 1 Joh. ii. 20, 21, 27.

Hereunto subscribe the churches in Helvetia, Wittemberg, Bohemia[4]. Confess. Helv. II. cap. 2. Confess. Wittemb. cap. 30. Confess. Bohem. cap. I.

The errors and adversaries unto this truth.

Many and sundry are the adversaries unto this truth; whereof some think, that to expound the word of God is so easy a matter, as any student endued with a good natural wit, by diligence and industry of his own, may do the same.

Some teach, how to interpret the scriptures is too hard a

[4 Scripturas sanctas dixit apostolus Petrus, non esse interpretationis privatæ. Proinde non probamus interpretationes quaslibet....Ergo non alium sustinemus in causa fidei judicem, quam ipsum Deum per scripturas sanctas pronuntiantem quid verum sit, quid falsum, &c....Ita judiciis non nisi spiritualium hominum ex verbo Dei petitis acquiescimus.—Harm. Conf. Sect. I. pp. 5, 6. Conf. Helv. Post. cap. II. Nam quod aiunt jus interpretandæ scripturæ esse penes summos pontifices, non est obscurum quod donum interpretandæ scripturæ non sit humanæ prudentiæ sed S. Spiritus. *Unicuique*, inquit Paulus, *datur manifestatio Spiritus ad utilitatem, &c.* Spiritus Sanctus autem est liberrimus, nec est ad certum genus hominum alligatus, sed distribuit dona hominibus pro suo ipsius beneplacito.—Ibid. p. 15. Conf. Virtemb. cap. XXX. Qui Spiritus et ipse sententiam quomodo intelligi debeat, et veritatem scripturæ hujus in ecclesia, eo modo quo ipsi placet aperit et patefacit: imprimis fideles ministros, qui sunt organa electa ipsius, excitando et donando.—Ibid. p. 8. Conf. Bohem. cap. I.]

thing for any mortal man to attain unto: so did Johannes de Wassalia[1], and do many Anabaptists.

Æneas Sylv.

Some, though they acknowledge that divers have the gift to open the sense of God's word, yet that some, say they, are not the known preachers and writers in the reformed and christian assemblies, whom the Family of Love, in scorn, do term the scripture-learned. For, saith the said Family[2], it is mere lies and untruth, &c., whatsoever the scripture-learned, through their knowledge out of the scriptures, institute, preach, and teach. They preach the letter, &c., but not the word of the living God[3]. But themselves only have that gift, neither every one of the Family, but the illuminate elders[4]. For to them it is given to know the truth, and they are the elders[5] of the godly-understanding, and of the manly-wisdom, the primates[6], or principals in the light.

H. N. Evang. chap. 33. § 11, 12, 13.

Idem 1 Exhort. chap. 16, § 18.

Idem. in his Prov. chap. 21. § 3. Spirit. Land, chap. 7. § 10. 1 Exhortat. chap. 14. § 1. See the proposition next immediately aforegoing.

Some do suppose, that to interpret the holy scriptures is not so much a special gift of God upon some chosen persons, as an ordinary power annexed to the state and calling of popes, bishops, and clergymen.

Others be so far from giving the people of God, not being of the clergy, power to expound, as they will not suffer them to read, nor so much as to have the scriptures by them in a vulgar tongue, except it be their own most corrupt and barbarous translation, which but of late years neither, and that in part too, is granted by the Papists; but in place thereof they thrust upon the laity their most idolatrous and blasphemous

[[1] The editor has been unable to verify the reference: but see Soames's Mosheim, Vol. III. p. 41. note 4.]

[[2] See above, p. 177, note 3. H. N. Evang. Reg. Translated out of Base-Almayne, cap. XXXIII. § 11, 12.]

[[3] They preach indeed the letter and the imagination of their knowledge, but not (Jer. 5. b. 6. 8. Ezech. 13. b. 34) the word of the living God.—Id. First Exhortation, translated, &c. cap. XVI. § 18.]

[[4] For at that same time of their elderdom it is given them to know the truth, and they are able to understand the mystery (Mat. 13. b. Luke 8. b.) of the kingdom of God, &c.—Id. Proverbs, cap. XXI. § 3.]

[[5] ...the travailer in the youngness of his godly understanding must in the beginning, when the wisdom groweth first in him, have his proceeding-forward according to the counsel of his elder in the Family of Love, who hath obediently performed the requiring of the gracious word and his service: and so is grown up therein unto the old age (Eph. 4. b.) of the godly understanding of the gracious word of the Lord...to the end that he may likewise....attain to the old age (Eccl. 6. 8. b. 1 Cor. 13. b.) of the manly wisdom, &c.—Id. Spiritual Land, &c. cap. VII. § 10.]

[[6] ...And so give ear, as single-minded children, to the primates or principal elders in the same light, &c.—Id. First Exhortation, cap. XIV. § 1.]

festivals, legends, rosaries, horaries, and psalteries of Our Lady, as falsely they called her.

Proposition V.

The analogy of faith must be respected in the exposition of the scripture.

The proof from God's word.

Forasmuch as no prophecy is of any private motion, and whatsoever interpretation man giveth, if it agree not to the analogy of faith, which St Paul gave in commandment to be observed, is a private interpretation; special heed is to be had that one place of scripture be so expounded as it agree with another; and all to the proportion of faith.

2 Pet. i. 20.
Rom. xi. 6.

The churches reformed approve this assertion by their subscriptions[7].

Conf. Helv. I. Art. II. and II. c. 2. Gal. Art. VII. Sax. Art. I. Wit. cap. 30, 31, 33. Suevica, Art. I.

Errors and adversaries to this truth.

Of another judgement are many. For

Some do think the scriptures may be expounded in what sense and to what purpose men list; as the Pharisees[8], the Severians[9], and Papists; among whom there be, which from this opinion do term the most holy word and scriptures of God, most reproachfully, a shipman's hose, a leaden rule, a nose of wax[10].

Iren. Lib. IV. cap. 25.
Euseb. Eccl. Hist. Lib. IV. c. 29.
Pighius, Controv. 3. de Eccl. & Hier. Lib. III. c. 3. Lindan Præf. Cens. Colon.

[7 Hujus (sc. scripturæ) interpretatio ex ipsa sola petenda est, ut ipsa interpres sit sui, charitatis fideique regula moderante.—Harm. Conf. Sect. I. p. 6. Conf. Helv. Prior. Art. II. ...sed illam duntaxat scripturarum interpretationem pro orthodoxa et genuina agnoscimus quæ ex ipsis est petita scripturis...cum regula fidei et charitatis congruit, &c.—Ibid. p. 5. Conf. Helv. Post. cap. II. ...vera sententia scripturæ quærenda est in ipsa scriptura, et apud eos qui divino Spiritu excitati, scripturam per scripturam interpretantur. Quare postquam prophetica et apostolica doctrina divinitus confirmata est, nullius vel hominum vel hominis cœtus sententia simpliciter pro oraculo Spiritus Sancti, sine judicio recipienda est: sed exigenda ad normam doctrinæ propheticæ et apostolicæ, ut quod cum hac convenit, agnoscatur: quod cum hac pugnat refutetur.—Ibid. pp. 16, 17. Conf. Virtemb. capp. XXX. XXXIII. There seems to be an error in the other references.]

[8 Non solum autem per prævaricationem frustrati sunt Legem Dei, miscentes vinum aqua; sed et suam legem e contrario statuerunt, quæ usque adhuc Pharisaica vocatur. In qua quædam quidem auferunt, quædam vero addunt, quædam autem, quemadmodum volunt, interpretantur.—Iren. Adv. Hær. Oxon. 1702. Lib. IV. cap. 25. p. 311.]

[9 Χρῶνται μὲν οὖν οὗτοι νόμῳ καὶ προφήταις καὶ εὐαγγελίοις, ἰδίως ἑρμηνεύοντες τῶν ἱερῶν τὰ νοήματα γραφῶν.—Euseb. Eccl. Hist. Cant. 1720. Lib. IV. cap. 29. p. 193.]

[10 Sunt enim scripturæ, velut cereus quidam nasus: qui sicut horsum illorsumque facile se trahi permittit....ita et illæ se flecti, duci, atque etiam in diversam sententiam trahi accommodarique ad quodvis patiuntur, &c.—Pighius, Explicat.

Some do mislike all interpretations, and written commentaries upon the scriptures, as unnecessary, and vain; such were Servetus, Valdesius, Coranus[1], with others of late years; and are the Libertines, Schwenkfeldians[2], and Family of Love[3].

Bez. epist. 59. Ibid. H. N. 1 Exhort. chap. 16. § 4.

Some depend wholly upon visions and revelations; as did the Enthusiasts[4], Nicholas Storch, Thomas Monetarius[5], the Anabaptists, and our late English reformer, Hacket[6].

Theod. Hæret. Fab. Lib. IV. D. Major. in Domin. 8. post Trinit. Homil. fol. 440. Arthing. Seduct. pag. 17.

Some dislike of the literal, and prefer the allegorical sense of the scriptures; and thereby devise what them list, most monstrously, from the word of God; as did the Origen-

Cathol. Paris. 1568. De Eccles. Controv. III. p. 90. Sunt enim illæ (sc. scripturæ), ut non minus vere quam festive dixit quidam, velut nasus cereus, qui se horsum, illorsum, et in quam volueris partem trahi, retrahi, fingique facile permittit, et tanquam plumbea quædam Lesbiæ ædificationis regula, quam non sit difficile accommodare ad quidvis volueris.—Id. Hierarch. Eccles. Colon. 1558. Lib. III. c. 3. fol. 103. D. Taceo, quod nulla scripturæ testimonia (quæ ut vulgo videre est ob facilem ipsius in varias sententiarum formas flexum recte naso fuit assimilata cereo) ad quæstiones nunc orbem prope universum perturbantes definiendas ita vix proferas aut perspicua aut efficacia, quibus non oppositionum aliquot plaustra adversarii opponant.—Lindanus Præf. in Panopl. Evang. Col. Agrip. 1560. There seems to be an error in the reference to the Censura Coloniensis.]

[[1] Quoting a letter which he had received from Coranus, Beza says, Tua hæc verba sunt, bona fide opinor Latine expressa....Inter cæteros velim habere libros D. Casparis et Valentini Crotoaldi, &c.... Nam certe me jam tædet Hebraismorum et Hellenismorum: et prolixi commentarii jam ad meum gustum et palatum nihil faciunt, &c....Ignatium dico et Servetum utrumque nec Hebraismis, nec Hellenismis, nec prolixis commentariis, sed suis vanissimis, inanissimis, Hispanissimis denique contemplationibus addictum....Sume Valdesii considerationes pro exemplo, id est, evanidas speculationes præ quibus mirum ni mulierculis et imperitis hominibus ipsum Dei verbum sordeat, &c.—Beza. Epist. Genev. 1575. Ep. lix. pp. 250, 253.]

[[2] The Caspar above mentioned was more commonly known by the name of Schvenfeldius. Quid ergo (inquies) tun' me Schvenfeldianum facis?—Ibid. p. 251.]

[[3] Certain other bring forth out of the freemindedness of their heart many-manner of witnessings and expositions according to the imagination of their knowledge, &c.—H. N. First Exhortation, cap. XVI. § 6.]

[[4] See above, p. 158, note 1. *Βρενθύονται δὲ καὶ τὸν Πατέρα βλέπειν, καὶ τὸν υἱὸν, καὶ τὸ πολυάγιον πνεῦμα τοῖς τοῦ σώματος ὀφθαλμοῖς, καὶ τῆς γινομένης τοῦ πνεύματος ἐπιφοιτήσεως τὴν αἴσθησιν δέχεσθαι.* And, lower down, speaking of the phrensies with which they were seized, he observes, *διὸ δὴ καὶ τῶν ἐνθουσιαστῶν ἐσχήκασιν ὄνομα.*—Theodoret. Opp. Paris. 1642-84. Tom. IV. Hær. Fab. Lib. IV. cap. 11.]

[[5] Et nos ipsi audivimus hujusmodi impostorem, Nicolaum Storch, seu Pelargum, autorem sectæ anabaptisticæ, falso gloriantem sibi apparuisse angelos visibili specie, qui vaticinati essent ipsum fore instauratorem et reformatorem ecclesiæ, &c.—Geo. Major. Opp. Witeberg. 1570. Tom. III. p. 440. In Dom. 8. post. Trin. Homil.]

[[6] ...M. Coppinger (after a solemn sort) began to declare what manner of men we were, viz.: That it was shewed him by vision from heaven, that himself was endued with the spirit of the Father, to be the greatest and last prophet of mercy, &c....as for Hacket, he was greater than either of us, &c.—Arthington's Seduction. Lond. (no date) p. 17.]

ists, and do the Libertines[7], and Family of Love[8], hence teaching one the other, that the spiritual understanding is the word of God, and that to embrace the literal sense is to commit idolatry. Calv. contra Anabapt. Allen's Conf.

Some of every place of scripture will have an exposition both analogical, allegorical, historical, and moral; as the curious Thomists and monks.

Some are addicted to an interpretation which they call mystical and prophetical; as Bocardus, Morelius, and others.

Some are of mind, that the gospel, or evangelical word, cannot be committed to letters and writings, saith Lindanus[9]. Lib. I. cap. 2.

Some do think (as afore also hath been shewn) how that is the old[10] and only true sense of the scriptures which is made and given by the church[a], and pope of Rome[b].

Some do maintain, that as the church in time doth alter, so the interpretation of the scripture also therewithal doth vary: whereby that which in the apostles' time was a truth,

[a] *Hæretici Scripturarum cognitionem, et intelligentiam extra ecclesiam ponunt: nos autem* (papistæ) *volumus ecclesiæ* (Romanæ) *esse annexam, nec ab ea separari patimur.* Stapl. [Opp. Par. 1620. Tom. III. p. 314.] Antid. Evang. in Joan. 19, 23, p. 418. *Sicut Christo Judæi: sic nos ecclesiæ (Romanæ) simpliciter credere debemus;* saith Stapleton, Antid. in Luc. 10, 16. [See above, p. 78. n. 6.] When the authority of the church leaveth the holy scriptures, then are they of no more account than Æsop's fables: Wolf. Herman[11].

[b] *Si papam, qui Christi vicarius est, et ejus omnimodam potestatem habet in terris, consulerent, non errarent (hæretici);* saith Stella in Lucæ 9. fol. 499.

[[7] Si quis locus ipsis objiceretur, respondebant, nos literæ minime obnoxios esse; sed spiritum, qui vivificat, sequi oportere...Semper hoc retinent principium, Scripturam in naturali sensu suo acceptam, literam mortuam esse atque occidere: ideoque missam esse faciendam, ut ad Spiritum vivificantem veniamus. In quo sibi duo proponunt. Primum ne simplici sensui Scripturæ acquiescamus, sed ludamus allegoricis interpretationibus. Deinde, ne adhæreamus iis quæ scripta sunt, ut assentiamur omnino: sed sublimius speculemur, et revelationes novas inquiramus.—Calv. Opp. Amstel. 1669-71. Tom. IX. p. 380. Instr. adv. Libertinos, cap. 9.]

[[8] This reference has not been found.]

[[9] Vides diserte a Propheta Dei voce prædictum verbum Dei Evangelium, quod Divo Paulo ad Hebræos commentatore est fœdus novum, non in tabula lapidea Mosaicæ legis modo, non in arido Bethulæ libello, non in vili papyro, sed in vivis hominum cordibus descriptum iri.—Lindan. Panopl. Evang. Lib. I. cap. X. p. 18.]

[[10] So 1607, in the text, but in the Corrigenda directed to be printed, 'odde,' which is the reading both of 1585 and 1633. The later editions as in the text.]

[[11] See Hosius Opp. Col. 1584. Tom. I. p. 530. De Autor. Sacr. Script. Lib. III. See also, Whitaker's Disputation on Scripture. Park. Soc. Edit. p. 276, note 3.]

Cusan. ad Bohemos, Epist. 2. in these days shall be a falsehood. In which error was Cardinal Cusanus[1].

Proposition VI.

The church is the witness and keeper of God's written word.

The proof from God's word.

Though the church hath authority to hear and determine in controversies of faith, yet hath the church power neither to judge the word of God, nor to judge otherwise than God's word doth judge. For it is said to the church and people of God,

Rom. xvi. 17. "I beseech you, brethren, mark them diligently which cause divisions and offences, contrary to the doctrine which you have learned, and avoid them."

Matt. xvii. 5. Acts x. 43. "Hear him." "To him give all the prophets witness."

John v. 39. 2 John 9. "Search the scriptures." "Whosoever transgresseth, and abideth not in the doctrine of Christ, hath not God."

Ephes. ii. 20. "Ye are, &c. built upon the foundation of the apostles and prophets."

And of the holy scriptures:

John xvii. 17. Luke xvi. 29. "Thy word is the truth." "They have Moses and the prophets, let them hear them," saith our Saviour Christ.

2 Pet. i. 19. "We have also a sure word of the prophets," saith St Peter.

2 Tim. iii. 16, 17. And St Paul, "The whole scripture is profitable to teach," &c.

1 Tim. vi. 3, 4. "If any man teach otherwise, and consenteth not to the wholesome words of our Lord Jesus Christ, he is puft up, and knowing nothing," &c.

Conf. Helv. II. cap 1. Bohem. cap. 1. Gal. Art. v. Belg. Art. VII. Wittem. Art. XXX. XXXI. XXXII. Saxon. Art. XI. And so with us do other churches[2] conceive both of the scriptures and church; yet all of us do grant, that the church, as a faithful witness, may, yea of necessity must, testify to the world what hath been the doctrine of God his people from time to time, and, as a trusty recorder, is to keep and make known what the word of God, which it hath received, is: which truly hath been performed afore the word

[[1] Quare nec mirum si praxis ecclesiæ uno tempore interpretatur scripturam uno modo et alio tempore alio modo. Nam intellectus currit cum praxi....Origenes enim et quidam alii textum, Si quis non renunciaverit omnibus quæ possidet non potest meus esse discipulus: secundum praxim primitivæ ecclesiæ intellexerunt præceptum esse. Intrante autem multitudine, non fuit possibile omnes resignare, &c....Ecclesia igitur sicut recipit scripturam ita et interpretatur. Sequuntur igitur scripturæ ecclesiam, quæ prior est, et propter quam scriptura, et non e converso.—Nic. de Cusa. Opp. Basil. 1565. p. 858. Epist. 7. De Amplect. Unit. Eccl. ad Bohem.]

[[2] See above, p. 195, note 7.]

was written, by the patriarchs, and after the same was committed to writing, before Christ his incarnation, by the Jews; in Christ his lifetime, in the primitive church, from the apostles' time, by the godly Christians throughout the world.

Luke iv. 17. Acts xiii. 27. Acts xv. 21. 2 Cor. iii. 15. 2 Cor. viii. 18.

Errors and adversaries unto this truth.

Be it far therefore from us to think, which the Papists do not stick to write and say; namely, that

The church is to judge the scriptures, and not the scriptures the church[3].

Jo. Maria Verractas. Pigh. in Controv. de Eccl.

The scripture is not of the essence of the church; because without it a church may be, though not very well[4]. So said cardinal Cusan.

Card. Cusan. Ep. 2. ad Boh.

The scripture, because (in their opinion) it is unperfect, cannot; obscure, may not; ambiguous, ought not to be the judge. So Lindan[5], Latomus[6], Petrus à Soto[7], Pighius[8], Coster[9], &c.

Lind. Lib. I. c. 1. [Latom.] Contr. Bucer. [Pet. à Soto] De S. Scrip. [Pigh.] Eccl. Hierar. Lib. I. cap. 4. [Coster] Enchirid. de S. Scrip. cap. 1.

[[3] Hac itaque fide, evidenti, inquam, divinæ veritatis contestatione, suam ab initio fidem, ab ipsis apostolis accepit ecclesia: et qua fide accepit, eadem et custodivit, et transmisit, &c....Illius siquidem ecclesiæ, magis tunc erat contestata ac manifesta veracitas, quam veritas scripturæ evangelicæ. Quippe quæ cognoscebatur sacra et vera, ab ea quæ tunc erat ecclesia.—Pighius, Explicat. Cathol. Paris. 1586. De Eccles. Controv. III. p. 91. Cf. Hierar. Eccl. Assert. p. 17. Determinatio igitur ecclesiæ evangelium appellatur, cui in omnibus est præstanda fides:—quoted as the words of J. M. Verratus in Norm. et Prax. Const. Relig. et Eccles. ad calc. Protest. Concion. August. Confess. adv. Convent. Trident. 1563. p. 118.]

[[4] Nam ecclesia sine litera fuit aliquando, ante Moysen, et etiam antequam apostolus Joannes evangelium vel Paulus epistolas scripserit. Et Christus ecclesiam ædificavit sine litera, quia nihil scripsit. Non est igitur litera, quæ per tyrannum penitus deleri posset, de essentia ecclesiæ, sed spiritus est qui vivificat.—Nic. de Cusa. Opp. Basil. 1565. Tom. II. fol. 857. Epist. 7. ad Bohem.]

[[5] Lindan. Panopl. Evang. Col. Agrip. 1560. Lib. cap. I. p. 1, sqq.]

[[6] Quis igitur judex erit in tanta controversia?....Scriptura, inquis, quæ falli non potest. Recte ais, et placet judex. Scriptura verax est...ad cujus veritatem tanquam ad certissimam regulam omnis doctrina de religione exigenda est....Sed illud abs te peto ut mihi respondeas, sicubi obscura aut ambigua scriptura est, id quod sæpe usu venit, et testatur Petrus de Paulini epistolis....quo utemur interprete?—Respons. Latom. ad Epist. Bucer. in Script. Duo Advers. Latom. et Bucer. Argentorat. 1544. p. 19.]

[[7] Potest quidem nonnunquam ex una scriptura altera explicari, verum id aut non semper, aut certe non ita, ut non possit etiam aliter præcipue a contentiosis intelligi. Ita ut nisi certum judicium sit, nunquam dubia terminari possint: quare nolle extra scripturam quidquam audire, est ipsam etiam scripturam negare, &c.—Petr. a Soto. Assert. Cathol. Fid. Antv. 1557. p. 104. b. Schol. Cathol. in Art. Conf. Virtemb. De Sacr. Script.]

[[8] ...Cum contra scripturæ plurimum frequenter obscuritatis habeant, et se trahi, accomodarique in diversam, et ad eam, quam quis secum ante præsumsit sententiam ....facile permittant.—Hierarch. Eccles. Assert. Colon. 1558. Lib. I. cap. IV. fol. 17.]

[[9] Dicendum enim omnia fidei mysteria ceteraque creditu et scitu necessaria, in

He is an heretic that cleaveth to the scriptures. So said Jacobus Hochstratus[1].

Again, the careful keeping of the holy scriptures by God's people from age to age, and time to time, declareth, first, how the mother-church of Rome is not the only keeper of the holy writ, and next, that cursedly they do offend, which either as greatly esteem the Ethicks of Aristotle as the commandments of God; the Odes of Pindar, as the Psalms of David[2]; the works and books of men, as the writings of God; which the council of Trent[3] doth: or before and above the scripture prefer unwritten traditions. Hence Petrus à Soto,

Ang. Polit.

Sess. iv.

Tradition (saith he) is both more ancient and more effectual than the holy scripture[4]. And Lindan[5]: the scriptures would be of no validity, neither had continued till this day, but for traditions.

Conf. Cath. de Eccles. Lind. Lib. I. cap. 4, 5.

corde ecclesiæ esse clarissime exarata, in membranis tam novi quam veteris testamenti multa desiderari....Eodem pertinent difficilium et dubiarum scripturarum interpretationes, quas in varios sensus hæretici trahunt.—Coster. Enchirid. Controv. Colon. Agrip. 1608. S. Scrip. cap. I. pp. 46, 47.]

[1 The editor has been unable to meet with any work of Hochstraten containing the statement imputed to him in the text. For some account of him, see Hagenbach, Vorlesungen über die Reformation, I. 163.]

[2 The editor has been unable to verify this reference.]

[3 See above, p. 29, note 6, and p. 31. n. 7.]

[4 Irenæus lib. tert. capit. quarto: Quid autem si neque apostoli quidem scripturam reliquissent nobis nonne oportebat ordinem sequi traditionis, &c....et mox efficacissima ratione confirmat quam sit traditio scriptura et antiquior, et efficacior, ita inquirens, &c.—Petr. à Soto, Assert. Cathol. Fid. Antv. 1557. p. 121. b. De Eccles. Cathol.]

[5 Illa ergo traditio quæ christianis indubitato persuadet hæc quatuor evangelia esse inter alia solum vera evangelia, epistolas vere esse Pauli, apocalypsin Joannis Theologi apostoli esse, an non harum evangelicarum scripturarum sunt fundamentum? Ea enim subtracta, nullus eis credat, aut fidem ullam ipsæ apud catholicos mereantur unquam.—Lindan. Panopl. Evang. Col. Agrip. 1560. Lib. I. cap. 4. p. 8. An non hæc traditio non scripta quæ nobis sacras tradit sine scripto literas esse suscipiendas ac credendas sit fidei fundamentum? De quo si quis ambigat, eum mihi citra traditionem indubiam ecclesiæ cogitet rogo, videat e vestigio, quam scripturæ sacræ autoritas evanescat penitus, ne in vanissimos plane fumos solvatur. —Ib. cap. 5.]

Proposition VII.

The church may not enforce anything to be believed, as necessary unto salvation, that is either contrary, or besides the word of God.

The proof from the word of God.

"Ye shall put nothing unto the word which I command you, neither shall ye take ought therefrom." Deut. iv. 2.

"Put nothing unto his words, lest he reprove thee, and thou be found a liar." Prov. xxx. 6.

"Though it be but a man's covenant, when it is confirmed, (yet) no man doth abrogate it, or addeth anything thereto." Gal. iii. 15.

"If any man shall add unto these things, God shall add unto him the plagues that are written in this book. And if any man shall diminish of the words of the book of this prophecy, God shall take away his part out of the book of life, and out of the holy city, and from those things which are written in this book." Rev. xxii. 18, 19.

And so witness with us the churches reformed[6].

Whatsoever also is grounded upon God's written word, though not by our common and vulgar terms to be read therein, we do reverently[7] embrace; which maketh us, for doctrine, to embrace the consubstantiality of our Saviour with the Father and the Holy Ghost, which the Arians would not; Conf. Helv. I. Art. IV. & II. cap. 2. Basil. Art. X. Bohem. cap. 1. Gal. Art. V. Belg. Art. VII. Saxon. Art. I. Witt. c. 30, 33. Suevica, Art. I.

[6 Ceterum de traditionibus hominum quantum vis speciosis et receptis, quæcunque nos abducunt vel impediunt ut de inutilibus et noxiis, sic illud Domini respondemus, frustra me colunt, docentes doctrinas hominum.—Harm. Conf. Sect. I. p. 6. Conf. Helv. Prior. Art. IV. Pariter repudiamus traditiones humanas, quæ tametsi insigniantur speciosis titulis, &c....compositæ tamen cum scripturis, ab his discrepant, &c.—Ibid. Conf. Helv. Post. cap. II. Confitemur quod quemadmodum nemo mandare potest ea quæ Christus non mandavit, &c.—Ibid. p. 7. Conf. Basil. Art. X. Scripta vero sanctorum doctorum, veterum præsertim, etiam ipsa pro veris et utilibus habenda...sed in iis tantum in quibus cum sacra scriptura consentiunt, &c.—Ibid. p. 9. Conf. Bohem. cap. I. Ex hoc autem efficitur neque antiquitatem neque consuetudines, neque multitudinem, &c....Scripturæ illi divinæ opponere licere, &c.—Ibid. p. 11. Conf. Gall. Art. V. ...cum hisce divinis scripturis, atque Dei nuda veritate, nulla alia hominum, quantavis sanctitate præditorum, scripta, nulla consuetudo, &c.....neque concilia ulla, nulla denique hominum decreta conferenda, comparandave sunt,.....Idcirco toto animo rejicimus, quæcunque cum certissima hac regula non conveniunt.—Ibid. p. 13. Conf. Belg. Art. VII. ...detestamur omnem doctrinam, cultum et religionem, pugnantem cum hac scriptura.—Ibid. p. 15. Conf. Virtemb. cap. XXX. Conf. Ibid. cap. XXXIII. Tanti vero sacra hæc scriptura ab omnibus sanctis pontificibus et doctoribus habita est, ut neque ullus pontifex suis statutis obediri, neque ullus doctor suis scriptis credi expetiverit, nisi ex iis ea comprobasset. The reference to the Conf. Saxon. is merely inferential.]

[7 Reverendly, 1607.]

a Trinity of persons in the Godhead, which the Sabellians would never do; the justification by faith only, which the Papists will not; the baptism of infants and young children, which the Anabaptists dare not: and for discipline, not to refuse, of church-officers, the names, archbishops, patriarchs, primates, metropolitans, suffragans, parsons, vicars, &c.; of ecclesiastical censures, the terms, suspension, excommunication; of ceremonies, none at all, which tend either unto order, comeliness, or edification.

But from the heart we abhor, in matters both of doctrine and discipline, whatsoever either agreeth not with the canon of the scripture, or is not grounded thereupon.

The errors and adversaries unto this truth.

Hence detest we both all the old heretics, and their fancies, with the new prophets of Basilides, the manifestation of Marcion, the mysteries of the Manichees, the Jobelæa of the Scythians, the Symbonia of the Archontics, the Cabala of the Jews, the Alcoran of the Turks, and also all new heretics and schismatics, with all their cursed opinions; as first, the Anabaptists, and namely the Libertines, the Davi-Georgians, and Family of Love, and all the co-deified elders thereof; as Henry Nicholas, Eliad, Fidelitas, Christopher Vitel, Theophilus the Exile, and the rest.

Next the Papists, whereof

Gratian. Dist. 19, *Sic.*

Some have commanded that all the pope's decrees should be taken, as confirmed by the mouth of God himself; so did pope Agatho the First[1].

Some write (as Busgradus) that if the pope believe there is no life to come (as some popes have done), we must believe it as an article of our faith.

Decr. Lib. III. Tit. 2. Crantz. Lib. VIII. cap. 36.

Some say, if the pope carry innumerable souls with him unto hell, yet he may not be judged: so did pope Boniface the Eighth[2].

[1 Sic omnes apostolicæ sedis sanctiones accipiendæ sunt, tamquam ipsius divini Petri voce firmatæ sint.—Corp. Jur. Canon. Antverp. 1648. Decr. Prim. Pars. Dist. XIX. cap. II. fol. 22.]

[2 Si papa suæ et fraternæ salutis negligens deprehenditur inutilis, et remissus in operibus suis...nihilominus innumerabiles populos catervatim secum ducit, primo mancipio gehennæ cum ipso plagis multis in æternum vapulaturus. Hujus culpas istic redarguere præsumit mortalium nullus: quia cunctos ipse judicaturus a nemine est judicandus,&c.—Corp. Jur. Canon. Antv. 1648. Grat. Decr. Prim. Pars. Dist. XL. cap. VI. fol. 50. This is 'ex dictis Bonifacii Martyris,' *not* Bonifac. VIII. There is an error in the reference to Crantzius.]

Some, as Bellarmine, conclude, that it is a point of faith to hold, that the bishop of Rome hath succeeded Peter in the universal regiment of the church[3]. Bellarm. de Pontif. Rom. Lib. II. cap. 12.

Others, as the Jesuits, persuade their catholics, that the king of Spain and their catholic faith are so linked together, as it is become a point of necessity in the catholic faith to put all Europe into the hands of the said king, otherwise the catholic religion will be utterly extinguished and perish[4]. Spar. Discov. of the English Jesuits, p. 7.

Others of them have published a new gospel, called *Evangelium Æternum, et Spiritus Sancti:* which they say doth so far excel the gospel of Christ as the kernel surpasseth the shell, the sun the moon, and light darkness. The author whereof was one Cyrillus, a Carmelite[5].

And lastly the Puritans, and all the speculations of Brown, Barrow, Green, Penry, Mar-Prelate, T. C., E. G., R. H., A. C., I. B., with the new Sabbatarians, and their fancies.

Article XXI.

Of the authority of General Councils.

General Councils (1) *may not be gathered together without the commandment, and will of princes. And* (2) *when they be gathered together, (forasmuch as they be an assembly of men, whereof all be not governed with the Spirit and word of God,) they may err, and* (3) *sometimes have erred, even in things pertaining unto God: wherefore* (4) *things ordained by them as necessary unto salvation have neither strength nor authority, unless it may be declared that they be taken out of Holy Scriptures.*

The propositions.

1. General councils may not be gathered together but by the commandment and will of princes.
2. General councils may err.

[[3] Demonstravimus hactenus Romanum pontificem Petro succedere in episcopatu Romano: nunc id ipsum demonstrare aggredimur de successione *in universæ ecclesiæ primatu.* Negant hoc hæretici, &c.—Bellarm. de Controv. Christ. Fid. Prag. 1721. Tom. I. fol. 350. De Summ. Pontif. Lib. II. cap. 12.]

[[4] A Sparing Discoverie of the English Jesuits, 1601. p. 7.]

[[5] The real author was one Frater Gerhardus, a Franciscan. The work first made its appearance at Paris in the year 1254. See Gieseler, Eccl. Hist. Third Period, Div. III. cap. 3. § 70. Vol. III. p. 257. Eng. Transl.]

3. General councils have erred, even in things pertaining unto God.

4. The things ordained by general councils are so far to be embraced and believed as they are consonant to God's holy word.

Proposition I.

General Councils may not be gathered together but by the commandment and will of princes.

The proof from God's word.

Great is the power and authority of kings and princes, by the word of God. For, as the defence of religion is committed unto them, so must they see that all men do their duties. That these things the better may be performed, they are, as just occasion is offered, not as men under the power of others, to summon, but as supreme governors within their own territories and dominions, to command all sorts of men to meet together; and that either to the implanting of the truth where it is not, or to the suppressing of sin, errors, idolatry, and superstition, where or in whomsoever it doth arise, or is rooted. Such councils were holden, both in the time of the Mosaical government, by the commandment of the most godly kings, David, Solomon, Asa, Hezekiah, and Josiah; and since the gospel hath been received into kingdoms and commonweals, by christian princes, kings, and emperors, who gathered councils both general, as the Nicene was by Constantine the Great[1], the council of Constantinople by Theodosius the elder[2], the council of Ephesus by Theodosius the younger[3], the council of Chalcedon by Marcian[4]; and national and provincial; so the council at Franckfort, Rhemes, Turon, Arelate, and Moguntia, by the will and commandment of Charles the Great[5]; at Matison, by Gunthranus[6];

1 Chron. i. 3; i. 2
1 Kings viii. 1.
2 Chron. xv. 9.
2 Chron. xxix. 4.
2 Chron. xxxiv. 29.
Ruff. Lib. x. c. 1.
Euseb. de vita. Const. l. iii. c. 6.
Theod. [Eccl. Hist.] Lib. v. cap. 6.
Evag. Lib. I. c 2.
Leo, Epist. 43, 53.
Aventin.
Carranza, Summa Conc.
Carion. Lib. III.
Turon. Lib. VIII. cap. 20.

[1 Histor. Eccles. Autores. Basil. 1535. Lib. x. c. 1. p. 218. Ruffin. Lib. I. cap. I. Euseb. de Vit. Const. Cant. 1720. Lib. III. c. 6. p. 179.]

[2 Theodoret. Opp. Par. 1642-84. Tom. III. Eccl. Hist. Lib. v. cap. 6. p. 711.]

[3 Evagr. Eccles. Histor. Cant. 1720. Lib. I. cap. 3. p. 252.]

[4 ...*πᾶσαι αἱ ἐκκλησίαι τῶν ὑμετέρων μερῶν, καὶ πάντες οἱ ἱερεῖς, τὴν ὑμετέραν ἡμερότητα μετὰ δακρύων ἱκετεύουσι...ὥστε κελεῦσαι ἰδικὴν σύνοδον ἐν τοῖς τῆς Ἰταλίας ἐπιτελεσθῆναι, κ.τ.λ.*—Leon. Mag. Opp. Venet. 1753-7. Tom. I. col. 905. Epist. 43. Simil. col. 957. Epist. 54. Both epistles are addressed to the emperor *Theodosius*.]

[5 Aventin. Annal. Boior. Lips. 1710. Lib. v. cap. XI. § 12. p. 524. Carranza, Summa Concil. Lovanii. 1681. pp. 321. 333. There seems to be an error in the reference to Carion.]

[6 Gregor. Turon. Opp. Lut. Par. 1699. Hist. Franc. Lib. VIII. cap. 20. col. 392.]

at Paris and Orleance, by the direction and appointment of Childebert[7], were kept and holden. Magdeburg. Eccles. Hist. Cent. 6. cap. 9.

And never yet hath there been a council, either general or national, or whatsoever, (I only except the councils held by the apostles and apostolical men in a troublesome state and time of the church, there being then no christian princes and emperors to countenance the truth,) either begun or ended to the glory of God, but it hath been, I say not *called* only, but *confirmed* also by some godly emperor, king or queen. This in effect is granted by all reformed churches[8]. Conf. Helv. I. Art. XXVI. and II. cap. 30. Bohem. cap. 16. Belg. Art. XXXVI. Saxon. Art. XXIII. Wittemb. cap. 35. Suevica, in Perorat.

The errors and adversaries unto this truth.

This assertion hath been oppugned, and that diversely, both by the Papists and Puritans. For the Papists, they say,

Emperors and kings be the pope his summoners, but, of themselves, are no absolute and powerful commanders, and callers of councils[9]. Hard. Confut. par. 5. c. VI. sect. 3.

There ought no council to be kept without the determinate consent of the bishop of Rome[10]. Harding.

No council ever yet had firm and lawful authority which was not confirmed by the bishop of Rome[11]. Duræus, contra Whitak. Lib. II. Cardil. in def. Concil. Trid. Disp. I.

[7 Magdeburg. Eccles. Hist. Basil. 1559, &c. Cent. VI. cap. IX. col. 544. De Synod. Aurel. Sec. Of the Synod at Paris it is only said that it was held *regnante Childeberto*. Conf. ibid. col. 585.]

[8 The passages referred to contain only a general acknowledgement of the office of the civil magistrate in respect to religion.—See Harm. Conf. Sect. XIX. p. 271, sqq.]

[9 Who hath authority to command the parts of the body but the head? And that the pope is head, where it is amply declared, ye heard even now. Where you ask, "Which ever said that the pope hath authority to call councils?" if you know not so much, &c.' Harding in Jewel's Defence of the Apol. Part v. Apol. chap. VI. Div. 3. Works, Vol. IV. p. 826. Park. Soc. Ed. But the passage meant is perhaps that in Vol. III. pp. 216, 17. But the latter new councils have made the same bishop of Rome head and prince over all primates and patriarchs throughout the world. And M. Harding saith, the said patriarchs were only the pope's deputies, that is to say, served him at commandment as his men.—Def. of Apol. Part I. Apol. chap. VIII. Div. 1. See also Vol. I. pp. 410, 11.]

[10 That the bishops of Rome by accustomed practise of the church had auctoritie to approve or disprove councilles I nede to say nothing for proufe of it, seing that the ecclesiasticall men (as we read in the Tripartite Storie) commaundeth that no councille be celebrated and kepte without the advise and auctoritie of the pope.—Harding's Answere to Juelle's Challenge, Antwerpe 1565. fol. 116. b. Art. IV.]

[11 Illud vero ferre non potes, quod tanquam absurdissimum subjicis: De conciliis papa judicare debet. Quasi vero ullum unquam concilium firmam in ecclesia auctoritatem habuerit, quod non à Romano pontifice fuerit confirmatum?—Jo. Duræus Scot. Confut. Respon. Gul. Whitak. Ingolst. 1585. p. 77. Est etiam

Test. Rhem. Annot. Matt. xvi. The popes of Rome (and not christian princes) have the authority and power of making laws ecclesiastical, and of calling councils[1].

And the Puritans do think that private persons, without the leave or privity of princes, may summon assemblies about church-causes at their pleasures, and consult about the public affairs of the church. Of this mind was Beza[a], and be the Disciplinarians both of [2]South[b] and North Britain[c].

Others (adversaries to both Puritans and Papists) are of mind, that were the pope a good man, (as he is nothing less) he might; and, he being wicked, other good bishops (though subject unto kings and emperors) may summon councils at Analect. p. 35. their discretions. An error of Selneccerus[3].

The Muscovites have a phantasy, that since the seventh general council that was, neither prince nor pope, nor any Surius, Comment. *an.* 1501, page 30. other men else, have power to call a general council[4].

[a] Perplacet autem mihi quod de conventu absque ulla principum, aut civitatum authoritate, privatim instituendo, scribis. Beza Epist. [Genev. 1575. Ep.] 68. pag. 292.

[b] Witness their classical assemblies at commencements, fairs, &c. See Discipline Grounds.

[c] The approbation or disallowance of a general assembly hath been, and should be a matter and cause spiritual, and always cognosced and judged by the church, as judges competent within this realm, say certain Scottish ministers in their letters unto the lords of the king's privy council in Scotland, which letter is printed in the said lords' declaration, &c. published *anno* 1606, and printed by *Robert Barker.*

---

pontifex instar omnium, quoniam nemo præter eundem jure concilium possit agere. Neque robur aut firmitatem habent quæ ille semel improbaverit.—Gasp. Cardill. Villalp. Apol. Indict. Conc. Trid. Ingolst. 1563. p. 19.]

[[1] Test. Rhem. Rhemes 1582. Annot. Matth. xvi. 19. p. 47.]

[[2] About two years since Master Snape did say...that there were three or four small classes of ministers in every shire, where there were any learned preachers, who did use (in their meetings) to debate of the discipline by pastors, doctors, elders, and deacons, and that the said several small classes did send their resolutions and opinions to the greater assemblies at Cambridge at Sturbridge Fair-time, and at London at Bartholomew Fair-time, which did meet together also for the same purpose.—Third Book of Disciplinary Grounds and Practices in Bancroft's Dangerous Positions, &c. Lond. 1640. cap. v. p. 85.]

[[3] Si Pontifex Rom. non esset persecutor evangelii, haberet potestatem convocandi concilium: qua in re si negligentior deprehenderetur, episcopi præstare illud deberent....Quod si nec episcopi officii sui rationem haberent, pii reges et principes facere illud possent, &c.—Selneccer. Analect. Francof. ad Mæn. 1571. Sect. 45. p. 95.]

[[4] Persuasum habent (Moscovitæ) post septimam synodum generalem, nulli

Proposition II.

General Councils may err.

The proof from God's word.

General councils, consisting

First of men, who may err, nothing more easily (for "all Gen. vi. 5.
the imaginations of man's heart are only evil continually, even Gen. viii. 21.
from his youth," but God only is true) and all men are, yea, Psal. cxvi. 11.
and "every man is a liar." Rom. iii. 4.

Next, of men differing in years, riches, learning, judgement, calling and authority: whereby distractions of opinions often do arise.

Thirdly, of many men, whereof the wicked be for number commonly the major part, and the better in outward countenance of the world.

Lastly, of men, not all, nor always either governed with God's Holy Spirit and word, or gathered together in the name of Christ.

None of sound judgement in religion do doubt but they may err.

If Paphnutius had been absent at Nice, that council had erred[5]. Sozom. Lib. I. cap. 23.

If Hierome had been away at Chalcedon, that council had erred[6]. Bishop Jewel's Defen. fol. 58.

At any time (if some be believed) be the pope of Rome not present at such meetings, either *per se*, or *per legatum*, by himself or his legate, no council but must err[7]. Roffensis contra Lutherum.

unquam neque licuisse neque licere concilium œcumenicum indicere, aut accedere sub pœna anathematis, quod etiam severissime observant.—Surius, Comment. Rer. Gest. Colon. 1574. p. 29.]

[5 'Η δὲ σύνοδος, ἐπανορθῶσαι τὸν βίον σπουδάζουσα τῶν περὶ τὰς ἐκκλησίας διατριβόντων, ἔθετο νόμους οὓς κανόνας ὀνομάζουσιν. ἐν δὲ τῷ περὶ τούτου βουλεύεσθαι, τοῖς μὲν ἄλλοις ἐδόκει νόμον ἐπεισάγειν, ἐπισκόπους καὶ πρεσβυτέρους, διακόνους τε καὶ ὑποδιακόνους, μὴ συγκαθεύδειν ταῖς γαμεταῖς ἃς πρὶν ἱερᾶσθαι ἠγάγοντο. ἀναστὰς δὲ Παφνούτιος ὁ ὁμολογητὴς ἀντεῖπε· τίμιόν τε τὸν γάμον ἀποκαλῶν, κ.τ.λ.....ἐπῄνεσε δὲ καὶ ἡ σύνοδος τὴν βουλήν.—Sozom. Eccl. Hist. Cant. 1720. p. 41. Lib. I. c. 23.]

[6 So St Hierome, being neither pope nor bishop, was received against this whole council of Chalcedon.—Jewel, Def. of the Apol. Lond. 1570. Part I. fol. 60. Works, Vol. III. p. 219. Park. Soc. Ed. See also Controv. with Harding. Vol. I. p. 423. Jerome died A.D. 420, and the council of Chalcedon was held A.D. 451.]

[7 Neque ego penitus cujuscunque concilii decreta probanda censeo, sed ejus quodcunque fuerit in Spiritu Sancto pontificis auctoritate cunctisque præmonitis quorum interest adesse convocatum.....Dilucidum esse potest multa concilia frequenter errasse: sed nos de plenariis loquimur quæ per pontifices convocata

Therefore councils may err.

That which one council doth establish another will disannul. They will not (we must think) revoke that which is well decreed. Therefore councils may err.

The adversaries unto this truth.

Therefore err do the Papists which say that the Holy Spirit is the director of all councils, and

Test. Rhem. An. Joh. xvi. 13. That councils cannot err[1].

Proposition III.

General Councils have erred even in things pertaining unto God.

The proof from God's word.

Confess Wittemb. cap. 33. Councils both general and particular have erred, and that in matters of faith[2].

For in the holy scriptures we find that it was ordained, if any man did confess that Jesus was the Christ he should be

Joh. ix. 22, and xii. 42. excommunicate: which could not be but by council.

John xi. 47. A council was gathered to suppress Christ and his doctrine.

Matt. xxvi. 3, 4. A council consulted how they might take Jesus by subtilty, and kill him.

Mark xiv. 53, 55. A council sought for false witness to put him to death.

Mark xv. 1. By a council Jesus was bound, led away, and delivered unto Pilate.

Matt. xxvii. 63. Luke xxii. 71. A council judged our S. Christ to be both a deceiver and a blasphemer.

Matt. xxviii. 12, 13. A council corrupted the soldiers, and willed them to tell a lie.

Acts iv. 5, 6, 18. A council withstood Peter and John, and commanded

fuerunt, &c....Nam semper mihi suspecta videntur, ubi vel a concilio pontifex dissideat vel concilium a pontifice, nisi manifestissima pontificis culpa factum id fuerit.—Fisher Episcop. Roff. Opp. Wirceb. 1597. Assert. Luther. Confut. Art. XXIX. col. 597, 8.]

[1 *The Spirit of Truth.* Ever note that the Holy Ghost, in that he is promised to the church, is called the Spirit of Truth. Which Holy Spirit for many other causes is given to divers private men, and to all good men, to sanctification: but to teach all truth and preserve in truth and from error, he is promised and performed only to the church and the chief governor, and general councils thereof.—Test. Rhem. Rhemes, 1582. Ann. Joh. xvi. 13. p. 266.]

[2 Testantur quoque exempla, non Pontifices tantum, sed etiam Concilia errasse.—Harm. Conf. Sect. I. p. 16. Conf. Virtemb. cap. XXXIII.]

them that in no wise they should speak or teach in the name of Jesus.

A council both caused the apostles to be beaten, and commanded them also that they should not preach in the name of Jesus. Acts v. 40.

In ancient writings of credit we may read, how (contrary to God's word) by councils Arianism hath been confirmed, as by the council at Ariminum[3]. D. Hieron. in vita Damasi Papæ.

By councils the traditions and books of foolish men have been made of equal authority with the word of God; as by the council of Trent[4]. Sess. IV. Decr. 1.

By councils hath been established both the adoration of images, as by the second council of Nice[5]; and the invocation of creatures, as by the Tridentine council[6]. Brevia. Rom. ex Decr. SS. Concil. Trid. Restitu. et Edit. à Pio V.

By councils the authority of princes hath been impaired, and the pope and clergy advanced above all earthly princes; as by the council of Lateran[7]. Council. Lateran. c. 5. apud Innocent.

The consideration of the premises, and the like, moved

[3 His itaque gestis Concilium (Ariminense) solvitur...Cœperunt postea Valens et Ursacius...palmas suas jactitare, dicentes se Filium non creaturam negasse, sed similem cæteris creaturis....Tunc usiæ nomen abolitum est; tunc Nicenæ fidei damnatio conclamata est....Concurrebant Episcopi, qui Ariminensibus dolis irretiti, sine conscientia hæretici proferebantur, contestantes Corpus Domini et quidquid in Ecclesia sanctum est, se nihil mali in sua fide suspicatos, &c.—Hieron. Opp. Par. 1693-1706. Tom. IV. Pars II. coll. 300, 1. Adv. Lucif. See also Concil. Coll. Reg. Par. 1644. Tom. III. p. 189, where it is said, Duo Concilia Ariminensis Synodi nomine insignita reperiuntur....Prius catholicum est,...Posterius vero Arianorum Conciliabulum fuit, meritoque a Bellarmino inter reprobata rejectum.]

[4 See above, p. 83, note 6.]

[5 Imagines porro Christi, Deiparæ Virginis, et aliorum Sanctorum in templis præsertim, habendas et retinendas, eisque debitum honorem et venerationem impertiendam, &c....Id quod conciliorum præsertim vero secundæ Nicænæ Synodi decretis contra imaginum oppugnatores est sancitum.—Concil. Harduin. Paris. 1714. Tom. x. col. 168. Conc. Trid. Sess. xxv.]

[6 The reference is probably to the Proprium Sanctorum and the Commune Sanctorum in the Breviarium Romanum ex Decret. SS. Conc. Trid. Pii V. jussu editum. But see also Concil. Harduin. Tom. x. col. 167, 8. Mandat Sancta Synodus omnibus episcopis, &c....ut...de Sanctorum intercessione, invocatione, &c....fideles diligenter instruant, docentes eos, sanctos una cum Christo regnantes orationes suas pro hominibus offerre: bonum atque utile esse suppliciter eos invocare, &c.—Conc. Trid. Sess. xxv.]

[7 Moneantur autem et inducantur, et si necesse fuerit, per censuram ecclesiasticam compellantur sæculares potestates, quibuscumque funguntur officiis; ut sicut reputari cupiunt et haberi fideles, ita pro defensione fidei præstent publice juramentum, &c.—Concil. Harduin. Tom. VII. col. 19. Concil. Lateran. IV. cap. 3.]

Hilar. Epist. ad Constant. Imperator.

S. Hilary[1] to call the synod of Mediolane, the Synagogue of the Malignant: and

D. August. contra Maxim. Lib. III.

St Augustine[2] to write unto Maximinus, "Neither ought I to object against thee the synod of Nice, nor thou against me the synod of Ariminum:" and

Nazianz. ad Procop. Ep. 42.

Nazianzene[3] openly to pronounce, that he "never saw any good end of a council:" and

Orat. Synod. Legat. Regis Franc. *anno* 1562.

The French king his embassador[4] to say unto the chapter of Trent, that "scarcely any good at all, or very little, came by councils unto the state of Christendom:" and

Bish. Jewel's Defen. part I. fol. 39.

Cornelius, bishop of Bitonto[5], to break out into these words in the face of the council at Trent: "I would that with one consent we had not altogether declined from religion unto superstition; from faith unto infidelity; from Christ unto Antichrist; from God unto Epicurus."

Adversaries unto this truth.

Test. Rhem. An. Joh. xvi. 13.

This notwithstanding, the papists do continue in the opinion, that councils cannot err[6].

Proposition IV.

The things ordained by general councils are so far to be embraced and believed as they are consonant to God's holy word.

The proof from God's word.

General councils we simply condemn not; yet do we not ground our faith upon any council, but only upon the written word of God.

[1 ...collecta jam illic (sc. Mediolani) malignantium synagoga.—Hilar. Opp. Paris. 1605. Ad Const. Aug. Lib. col. 305.]

[2 Sed nunc nec ego Nicænum, nec tu debes Ariminense tanquam præjudicaturus proferre concilium. Nec ego hujus auctoritate, nec tu illius detineris, &c.—August. Opp. Paris. 1836-8. Tom. VIII. col. 1082. B. Contr. Maxim. Lib. II. cap. 14. § 3.]

[3 *Ἔχω μὲν οὕτως, εἰ δεῖ τἀληθὲς γράφειν, ὥστε πάντα σύλλογον φεύγειν ἐπισκόπων, ὅτι μηδεμιᾶς συνόδου τέλος εἶδον χρηστὸν, μηδὲ λύσιν κακῶν μᾶλλον ἐσχηκυῖαν ἢ προσθήκην.*—Greg. Nazianz. Opp. Par. 1840. Tom. II. p. 110. c. Ad Procop. Epist. 130.]

[4 Nostra, patrumque nostrorum, et avorum memoria synodos indictas fuisse, episcopos convenisse, maximos in Germania atque in Italia conventus peractos esse scimus. Vix tamen ullus, aut perexiguus inde fructus Christianitati constitit.—Orat. Guid. Fab. Carol. Galliar. Reg. Legat. in App. ad Conc. Trid. Concil. Harduin. Paris. 1714. Tom. X. col. 266.]

[5 Jewell's Def. of the Apol. Lond. 1570. fol. 40.]

[6 See above, p. 208, note 1.]

Therefore in general councils, whatsoever is agreeable unto the written word of God we do reverently[7] embrace; but whatsoever is contrary unto, or besides the will of God revealed in the holy scriptures, we do carefully avoid.

And so we are commanded to do even by God himself.

"Whatsoever I command you, take heed you do it: thou shalt put nothing thereto, nor take ought therefrom." Deut. xii. 32.

"Walk ye not in the ordinances of your fathers, neither observe their manners, &c. I am the Lord your God: walk in my statutes, and keep my judgements, and do them." Ezek. xx. 18, 19.

"Though that we, or an angel from heaven, preach unto you otherwise than that which we have preached unto you, let him be accursed. As we said before, so say I now again, If any man preach unto you otherwise than that ye have received, let him be accursed." Gal. i. 8, 9.

And so think the churches reformed with us[8]. Conf. Helv. 2. cap. 18. Bohem. cap. 1. Gal. Art. v. Belg. Art. VII. Wittemb. c. 33.

The adversaries unto this truth.

Contrary hereunto are the opinions of the papists. For of them,

Some do think that the decrees of councils do bind all nations; as pope Hormisda[9] decreed they should.

Some, as pope Gregory the Great[10], supposed that some councils, and namely the council of Nice, of Constantinople, Ephesus, and Chalcedon; some, as Campian[11], thought that all Greg. I. Lib. I. Epist. 24 & Lib. II. Epist. 49. Campian. Rat.

[7 Reverendly, 1607.]

[8 Neque vero et œcumenica improbamus concilia, si ad exemplum celebrentur Apostolicum, ad Ecclesiæ salutem non perniciem.—Harm. Conf. Sect. XI. p. 42. Conf. Helv. Post. cap. XVIII. ...neque edicta, vel decreta ullà, neque concilia.... Scripturæ illi divinæ opponere licere.—Ibid. Sect. I. p. 11. Conf. Gall. Art. V.... The reference to the Conf. Bohem. is erroneous. For the Conf. Belg. and Conf. Virtemb. see above, p. 201, note 6.]

[9 Paternas igitur regulas et decreta sanctissimis definita conciliis ab omnibus servanda mandamus.—Epist. I. Hormisd. Pap. in Concil. Mansi. Tom. VIII. col. 383.]

[10 Præterea quia corde creditur ad justitiam, ore autem confessio fit ad salutem, sicut sancti Evangelii quatuor libros, sic quatuor Concilia suscipere et venerari me fateor. Nicænum scilicet.... Constantinopolitanum.... Ephesinum etiam primum...Chalcedonense.—Greg. Pap. I. Opp. Par. 1705. Tom. II. col. 515. E. Epist. Lib. I. 25. (al. 24.) Et sic quatuor synodos sanctæ universalis Ecclesiæ, sicut quatuor libros sancti Evangelii recipimus.—Ibid. col. 632. E. Epist. Lib. III. 10.]

[11 Secuta sunt ad extirpandam hæresim, quæ varia quibusque sæculis pullulavit, Œcumenica veterum Concilia quatuor, tantæ firmitudinis, ut iis, ante annos

councils were of equal authority with the word of God. Calv. Epist. Bulling. 231. Others, as the Guisian faction in France, be resolved in matters of religion to follow the footsteps of their ancestors, though (God's word and) a thousand councils decree to the contrary[1].

ARTICLE XXII.

Of Purgatory.

The Romish doctrine concerning (1) *purgatory,* (2) *pardons, worshipping and adoration, as well* (3) *of images as* (4) *of reliques, and* (5) *also invocation of saints, is a fond thing, vainly invented, and grounded upon no warranty of scripture, but rather repugnant to the word of God.*

The propositions.

The Romish doctrine concerning

1. Purgatory,
2. Pardons,
3. Worshipping, and adoration of images,
4. Reliques,
5. Invocation of saints,

is a fond thing, and not warranted by the holy scripture, nor consonant, but contrary unto the same.

Proposition I.

The Romish doctrine concerning purgatory is fond, and not warranted by the holy scripture, nor consonant, but contrary unto the same.

The proof from God's word.

It is granted as well by the Romish, or false, as by the true church, that none unclean thing can enter into the kingdom of God. And because all men either have been, or be still unclean, therefore they must be purged from sin.

But in the manner of purging them who are unpure they do greatly differ. For the true church, looking into the word of God, doth find that we are sanctified, or made clean

mille, singularis honos, tamquam divinis vocibus, haberetur.—Edm. Campian. Decem. Ration. Antv. 1631. Rat. IV. p. 44.]

[[1] Dux Guisianus...ausus est etiam dicere, quicquid decernerent mille concilia, sibi fixum esse majorum instituta sequi.—Calvin. Opp. Amstelod. 1671. Tom. VIII. Pars 2. p. 143. Inter Epistol. et Respon.]

in divers respects, diversely: as by baptism[a], by the word preached[b], by the blood of Christ[c], and by the Spirit of God[d], and that in this life, and not in the other world.

For in the sacred scripture there is mention but only of two ways, one leading unto destruction, the other bringing unto life: of two sorts of men, whereof some believe, and they are saved; some believe not, and they are damned: and of two states, one blessed, where Lazarus is; the other cursed, where Dives doth abide. A third way, or sort, or state, cannot be found in the word of God.

Matt. vii. 13, 14.
Matt. xvi. 16. John iii. 18.
Luke xvi.

And therefore the purgatory in another world, both denied hath always been by the Greek churches[2], and neither is, nor will be acknowledged by any of God's reformed churches in this world; as their confessions do testify[3].

Alphons. de Hæres. Lib. VIII. de Indulgentiis. Polydor. de Inventor. Lib. VIII. cap. 1. Conf. Helvet. 2. cap. 26. Gal. Art. XXIV. Saxon. Art. XI. August. Art. XI. Wittemb. cap. 25.

[a] Christ loved the church, and gave himself for it; that he might sanctify it, and cleanse it by the washing of water through the word, Eph. v. 25, 26.

[b] Now are ye clean through the word that I have spoken unto you, Joh. xv. 3.

[c] The blood of Jesus Christ his Son cleanseth us from all sin, 1 John i. 7.

[d] Ye are washed, ye are sanctified, ye are justified, in the name of the Lord Jesus, and by the Spirit of our God, 1 Cor. vi. 11.

[[2] Unus ex notissimis erroribus Græcorum et Armenorum est quo docent nullum esse purgatorium locum in quo animæ ab hac luce migrantes purgentur a sordibus quas in corpore contraxerant.—Alphons. à Castro Adv. Hær. Antv. 1556. Lib. XII. fol. 131. b. Nemo certe dubitat orthodoxus, an purgatorium sit, de quo tamen apud priscos nulla vel quam rarissima fiebat mentio: sed et Græcis ad hunc usque diem non est creditum esse.—Polydor. Vergil. De Inventor. Argent. 1606. Lib. VIII. cap. I. p. 456.]

[[3] Quod autem quidam tradunt de igne purgatorio, fidei Christianæ (credo remissionem peccatorum et vitam æternam) purgationique plenæ per Christum, et Christi Domini hisce sententiis adversatur, &c.—Harm. Conf. Sect. XVI. p. 177. Conf. Helv. Post. cap. XXVI. Denique Purgatorium arbitramur figmentum esse, ex eadem officina profectum, unde etiam manarunt vota monastica, &c.—Ibid. p. 181. Conf. Gall. Art. XXIV. Etsi dubitari non debet, quin suus sit sanctis in hac vita Purgatorius ignis, quem admodum testantur exempla Davidis, Ezechiæ, Jonæ et aliorum, tamen haud immerito dubitatur, num post hanc vitam tale sit Purgatorium, quale vulgus hominum putat, in quo animæ tantisper crucientur, dum vel supplicio satis pro peccatis faciant, vel indulgentiis redimantur. Si enim tale est Purgatorium, valde mirandum videtur, quod nec Prophetica, nec Apostolica scripta aliquid certi et perspicui de eo tradiderint, &c.—Ibid. p. 199. Conf. Virtemb. cap. XXV. Manifestum est autem, aliud genus doctrinæ dissentiens ab Evangelio, adversarios tradere et propugnare, qui docent....Satisfactiones Canonicas, compensationes esse pœnarum purgatorii.—Ibid. Sect. X. p. 22. Conf. Saxon. Art. XI. Rejiciuntur et isti qui canonicas satisfactiones docent necessarias esse ad redimendas pœnas æternas, aut pœnas purgatorii.—Ibid. Sect. VIII. p. 148. Conf. August. Art. XI.]

Adversaries unto this truth.

Erroneous therefore, and not warrantable by God's word, concerning purgatory, is the doctrine both of the old heretics, the Montanists, who thought there was a purging of souls after this life[1]; and of the new, and renewed heretics, the papists. For

Tertul. de Corona Militis, & de Anima, in fine.

They think it to be unsound doctrine, and not sufferable in any book, for Christians to deliver, that it is unpossible for godly and faithful men or women to be punished after they be dead. Therefore *Deleatur*[a], say they, Blot out such a doctrine[2].

Vaux Catec. cap. 3.

They teach by their catechisms, that to doubt whether there is a purgatory or no, is a breach of the first commandment[3].

Thus do they pray for the souls of the faithful (as they phantasy) boiling in torments of purgatory:

Horæ B. Virg. Mariæ secundum usum Sarum.

Avete, omnes animæ fideles, quarum corpora hic et ubique conquiescunt in pulvere: Dominus Jesus Christus, qui vos, et nos redemit suo pretiosissimo sanguine, dignetur vos à pœnis liberare, &c.[4] That is, "All hail, all faithful souls, whose bodies do here and everywhere rest in the dust: the Lord Jesus Christ, who hath redeemed both you and us with his most precious blood, vouchsafe to deliver you from pains," &c.

Conc. Trid. Dec. de Purg. Sess. 25, & Sess. 6, Can. 30.

They have ratified the doctrine of purging souls after this life in the council of Trent[5].

[a] Puniri pios post mortem, impossibile: deleatur. *Index Expurg.* p. 26.

[[1] Oblationes pro defunctis, pro natalitiis annua die facimus.—Tertull. Opp. Lutet. 1634. p. 121. D. De Corona Mil. 3. In summa, quum carcerem illum quem Evangelium demonstrat, inferos intelligamus, et novissimum quadrantem, modicum quodque delictum mora resurrectionis illic luendum interpretemur; nemo dubitabit animam aliquid pensare penes inferos, salva resurrectionis plenitudine, per carnem quoque.—Ibid. p. 357. c. De Anima, 58.]

[[2] Amongst the Delenda in Indice Chrysostomi Basiliæ a Frobenio excusi.—Index Expurgat. Lugd. 1586. p. 26.]

[[3] Vaux. Catech. Antv. 1574. chap. iii. p. 25. In reply to the question, Who be they that break the first Commandment by doubting in faith?]

[[4] Hor. B. Virg. Mariæ. ad Sarisbur. Eccl. Ritum. Paris. 1535. Fo. CXXIII. Orationes pro Defunctis. Where, *requiescunt*, and, *Dominus noster Jesus*, &c.]

[[5] Cum Catholica Ecclesia, Spiritu sancto edocta, ex sacris literis et antiqua patrum traditione in sacris conciliis, et novissime in hac œcumenica synodo, docuerit Purgatorium esse; animasque ibi detentas fidelium suffragiis, potissimum vero acceptabili altaris sacrificio, juvari; præcipit sancta synodus episcopis, ut sanam de

It is further to be noted, how the same papists, sliding back from the truth of God, have fallen into many noisome and divers opinions in the matter of purgatory: agreeing among themselves

Neither about the place where purgatory should be; some[6] placing the same in the bottom of the sea, some near unto the mount Hecla in Ireland[7], some, upon the mount Ætna[8] in Sicily, others[9], in the centre of the earth, others[10], in hell, whereof they make four rooms; the first of the damned, the second of infants dying unbaptized, the third purgatory, the fourth *Limbus Patrum*, whereinto Christ descended; and others[11] in a mind tossed and troubled betwixt hope and fear.

Eckius in Enchirid. Bernard. de Bustis, Rosar. par. 3. sect. 2. Spec. Pereg. Quæst. Dec. I. cap. 3. q. 5. See above, Art. XVII. Prop. 7. Position. Ing. de Purgat. Lorich. Instit. Cathol. de 12 Fidei articulis.

purgatorio doctrinam, a sanctis Patribus et sacris conciliis traditam, a Christi fidelibus credi, teneri, doceri, et ubique prædicari diligenter studeant.—Concil. Harduin. Paris. 1714. Tom. x. col. 167. Conc. Trid. Sess. xxv. Si quis post acceptam justificationis gratiam cuilibet peccatori pœnitenti culpam ita remitti, et reatum æternæ pœnæ deleri dixerit, ut nullus remaneat reatus pœnæ temporalis exsolvendæ, vel in hoc sæculo, vel in futuro in purgatorio, antequam ad regna cœlorum aditus patere possit; anathema sit.—Ibid. Sess. VI. De Justif. can. 30.]

[[6] The fifth chapter of the Apocalypse is cited among others in support of a Purgatory: Et omnem creaturam quæ in cœlo est, et super terram, et subtus terram, et mare et quæ in eo sunt, omnes audivi, &c.... Upon which the comment is, Triplicem hic ponit ordinem laudantium Deum, scilicet in cœlo beatorum, in terra justorum, sub terra purgandorum, quia damnati non laudant Deum, nec benedicunt sedentem in throno.—Eckii Enchir. Lugd. 1572. De Purgat. p. 225.]

[[7] So all the editions. See the Beehive of the Romish Church, Transl. out of Dutch, &c. Lond. 1580. Book II. cap. 8. p. 151, where the notion is thus referred to: St. Patrick's Purgatory in Ireland lies fast by the sea-side, near unto a mountain called Hecla, where our mother the holy Church of Rome doth believe that the silly souls are as ill punished in ice as in fire.]

[[8] There seems to be an error in the reference. See, however, Bellarmin. Disput. Prag. 1721. Tom. II. p. 366. De Purgat. Lib. II. cap. 6. § 10.]

[[9] Tertiam ideo catholicam et orthodoxam et veram de Purgatorio conclusionem aggrediamur, quæ est, quod in centro terræ vere et realiter locus purgatorii reperitur.—Bart. Sibylle. Spec. Peregr. Quæst. Lugd. 1516. Prim. Dec. cap. III. fol. 78. See also above, Art. XVII. Prop. 7.]

[[10] The work referred to, Position. Ingolst., has not been found: but see Bernard. de Bust. Rosar. Sermon. Predicab. Hagen. 1518. Pars Sec. Serm. II. fol. 5. G. Et sciendum est secundum Rich. (de Media Villa) in IV. dist. 45. art. i. q. 2. quod subter terram sunt quatuor loca. Unus super alterum, quæ omnia possunt appellari infernus, quasi inferius generaliter accipiendo. Sed particularia habent nomina. Nam ultimus dicitur infernus proprie. Secundus prope ipsum dicitur limbus. Tertius, purgatorium. Quartus, sinus Abrahæ. Luc. XVI. In quo nunc non est aliquis. Sed ibi steterunt sancti patres, ante Christi adventum, et aliquando etiam appellatur limbus. Qui ergo vadunt ad limbum sunt morientes sine baptismo, sine aliquo actuali peccato.]

[[11] This reference to Lorichius the editor has been unable to verify. But this seems at one time to have been the view of Luther according to Fisher (Assert. Luther. Confut. Art. XXXVII.) and Bellarmine, Disput. Tom. II. p. 327. De Purgat.

Albertus, & Roffensis.

Neither about the tormentors there; who are thought of some[1] to be holy angels, of others[2], to be very devils.

S. Th. More.

Neither about the torments. For some dream how they are tormented there with fire only, as Sir Thomas More[3]; some, with water and fire, as Roffensis[4]; and some, neither with fire nor water, but with troublesome affections of hope and fear, as Lorichius[5].

Instit. Cathol. ut supra. Greg. Dial. Lib. IV. cap. 39. Spec. Pereg. Quæst. Dec. I. c. 3. q. 4. Eckius, Posit. 6.

Neither about the causes of purgatory torments: because that some do think that only venial sins[6], others, that venial

Lib. I. cap. 2....Lutherus ipse varius fuit. Nam primo, Purgatorium plane Catholice admittebat...Deinde Purgatorium admisit quidem, sed multis admistis erroribus. *Primus* error fuit: Purgatorium non posse probari ex scripturis. *Secundus:* animas in Purgatorio non esse certas de salute consequenda....*Quartus*, animas in Purgatorio sine intermissione peccare, dum horrent pœnas, et requiem quærunt. He acknowledges however that, Ultimo, simpliciter sustulit Purgatorium.]

[1 Roffensis does not say that the holy angels are tormentors, but rather comforters of the souls in purgatory. Jam haud dubie consolantur (angeli) et admonentur (? admonent) quatenus bono sint animo, patienterque ferant illos cruciatus, nec est dubium quin salutis suæ certitudinem frequenter eis inculcent. Præter hæc bonus cujusque angelus, cui et custodiæ cura mandata fuit a Deo, quid jam non facit, quem non movet lapidem, quo nihil consolationis desit animæ jam inter Purgatorii cruciatus constitutæ?—Fisher, Opp. Wirceb. 1597. col. 730. Assert. Luther. Confut. Art. XXXVIII. Non enim videtur probabile quod dæmones illud ministerium (sc. bonos affligendi) exerceant, cum ibi purgetur peccati scoria, secundum quam ibi quodammodo anima similis erit diabolo: et diabolus suam similitudinem nolit delere, &c....Rursus non videtur hoc probabile, ut ministerio fiat angelorum bonorum, ut tam graviter affligant, et puniant concives suos....Ideo concedendum est, quod non fit ministerio dæmonum, nec etiam supernorum spirituum, nisi fortassis quantum ad directionem, &c.—Bonavent. Opp. Mogunt. 1609. Tom. V. fol. 270. In Libr. IV. Sentent. Dist. XX. Quæst. 5.]

[2 Youre kepers dooe you great ease, and put you in great cumfort: our kepers (sc. in purgatory) are such as God kepe you from, cruell damned spirites, &c.—Sir Thos. More's Works, Lond. 1557. The Supplicacion of Soules, p. 337. H.]

[3 Finally, if ye pittie anye man in payne, never knew ye payne comparable to ours, whose fyre as farre passeth in heate all the fyres that ever burned upon earth, as the hottest of al those passeth a feyned fyre paynted on a walle.—Ibid.]

[4 Cæterum quod per ignem et aquam purgandæ sint animæ quæ de prælio vitæ hujus exierint, priusquam cœlum ingrediantur, testatur Orig. Hom. 25. super Numeros, &c.—Fisher, Opp. col. 721. Assert. Luther. Confut. Art. XXXVII.]

[5 See p. 215, note 11.]

[6 Sed tamen de quibusdam levibus culpis esse ante judicium purgatorius ignis credendus est, pro eo quod veritas dicit, quia si quis in Sancto Spiritu blasphemiam dixerit, neque in hoc seculo remittetur ei, neque in futuro. In qua sententia datur intelligi, quasdam culpas in hoc seculo, quasdam vero in futuro posse laxari.—Greg. Magn. Opp. Par. 1705. Tom. II. col. 441. E. Dialog. Lib. IV. cap. 39. ...dicitur conclusionaliter cum Gregorio et Augustino...quod culpa venialis in eo qui cum gratia decedit post hanc vitam, dimittitur per ignem purgatorium: qui pœna illa aliqualiter voluntaria virtute gratiæ habebit vim expiandi culpam omnem, quæ simul cum gratia stare potest, &c.—Bart. Sibyll. Spec. Peregr. Quæst. Prim. Dec. cap. iii. quæst. 4. fol. 86.]

and mortal sins too (for which in this life men have done no penance) are there purged[7].

Nor about the time, which they that be tormented, shall abide in purgatory. For some have given out, how the poor souls there be continually in torments till the day of judgment, as Dionys. Carthusianus[8]; others, as Durandus[9], do think they have rest sometimes, as upon Sundays and holy days: others are of mind, that in time they shall be set free and at liberty, because their punishment is but temporary[10]; and others, that at any time they may be delivered, if either their friends will buy out their pains, or the priests will pray, or say any mass for them, or the pope will but say the word.

De 4. Hom. noviss. De officio mort. Lib. VII. Spec. Pereg. Quæst. ut supra, Quæst. 5.

Nor finally about the state of souls in purgatory. For

Our English papists at Rhemes do think the souls in purgatory to be in a more happy and blessed condition than any men that live in this world, and yet say the same Rhemists, that purgatory-fire passeth all the pains of this life.

Test. Rhem. Annot. Apocal. xiv. 13. Ibid. Annot. marg. pag. 431.

Thomas Aquinas[11] holdeth how the pains of hell-fire and of purgatory are all one, and in nothing differ, but that the

[7 Discussis tenebris et explosis erroribus Ludderanis, restat aperire lucem veritatis catholicæ, animas scilicet purgandas esse non propter imperfectam charitatem, vel reliquias veritatis, sed quia secum deferunt peccata mortalia contrita sine satisfactione debita: nam libro de remissione culpæ et pœnæ, deo adjutore, probabimus culpam remitti, &c.—Joh. Eck. Opp. Contr. Ludder. Ingolstad. 1530. Pars Sec. De Purgat. cap. XVI. fol. 71.]

[8 This is only said with regard to certain abominable crimes. In his tormentis (sc. loci purgat. tertii) inveni quendam mihi in seculo olim notum, decretorum doctorem famosum cui vehementer condolens, interrogavi eundem an speraret se aliquando misericordiam consecuturum. Qui respondit: Væ, væ, væ, scio quod ante diem judicii veniam non obtinebo. An autem tunc, incertum habeo.—Dionys. Carthus. De Quat. Hom. Noviss. Par. 1551. Art. XLVII. fol. 113. a.]

[9 Siquidem commemoratio omnium fidelium defunctorum instituta est fieri ab ecclesia tali die, ut generalibus beneficiis adjuventur, quia specialia habere non valent....Sicut enim Petrus Damianus ait: Sanctus Edibo comperiens quod apud Vulcanum Ceciliæ (*sic*) crebre voces et ululatus dæmonum audiebantur plangentium pro eo quod animæ defunctorum per eleemosynas et orationes de eorum manibus eripiebantur, ordinavit in suis monasteriis ut post festum omnium sanctorum fieret commemoratio defunctorum....Anniversarium autem si contigerit in die dominica vel in aliqua celebrari solemnitate, non debet mutari ad sequentem diem, prout fit in festis sanctorum, sed fiat in die præcedenti, ut citius occurratur pœnis defunctorum quas in purgatorio sustinent.—Durand. Rational. Divin. Offic. Lugd. 1512. Lib. VII. De Off. Mort. fol. 175, 6.]

[10 ....licet ignis purgatorii sit eternus quo ad substantiam sicut ignis inferni: tamen est temporalis quo ad effectum purgationis.—Spec. Peregr. Quæst. Prim. Dec. cap. iii. quæst. 4. fol. 89.]

[11 Ad primum ergo dicendum, quod ignis purgatorius est æternus quantum ad substantiam; sed temporalis quantum ad effectum purgationis.—Thom. Aquin. Summ. Theolog. Duaci. 1614. Suppl. ad Tert. Part. Quæst. 100. Art. 2. fol. 166.]

one is but temporal, and the other not so. And others, put in choice either to tarry in purgatory one day, or to endure the miseries of this world an 100 years, have chosen to suffer the troubles of this life an hundred years together, rather than to abide the pains of purgatory but one short winter's day[1].

Cap. Qui in aliud. Dist. 25.

Therefore in this contrariety of opinions, some of them, the papists themselves cannot deny must be, we say, all of them are fond, and contrary to the word of God.

Besides, they nourish most cursed and damnable errors; as, that all the souls of the faithful separated from their bodies are not at rest.

That all sins, in their own nature, be not mortal, or deadly, and that some deserve not everlasting torments. They are purged in purgatory.

That one sinful man may save, and satisfy the wrath of God for another, and that easily, by praying, saying, or doing something for them.

That, if friends in this world will do nothing for the poor soul in purgatory pains, yet may the said souls come at length unto happiness, by abiding their deserved torments until the last hour or day of judgement in purgatory.

Finally, that the pope is God, in that he can at his pleasure discharge guilty souls both from the guilt of sin, and from the punishments due for the same.

Proposition II.

The Romish doctrine concerning pardons is fond, and not warranted by the holy scripture, nor consonant, but contrary unto the same.

The proof from God's word.

Such hath been the exceeding mercy and love of God towards mankind, that as he hath purged us from all guiltiness of sin by the blood, so hath he pardoned us from the everlasting punishment due for sin, by the pains of Jesus Christ. For,

Acts iv. 12.

"There is salvation in none other: for among men there is given none other name under heaven whereby they must be saved."

[[1] Qui in aliud sæculum distulit fructum conversionis, prius purgabitur igne purgationis. Hic autem ignis etsi æternus non sit miro tamen modo gravis est. Excellit enim omnem pœnam quam unquam aliquis passus est in hac vita vel pati potest.—Corp. Jur. Canon. Antv. 1648. Decr. Prim. Pars. fol. 33. Dist. xxv. cap. 5.]

"Through his name all that believe shall receive remission of sins." Acts x. 43.

"He hath purchased the church by his own blood." Acts xx. 28.

"With his stripes we are healed." Isai. liii. 5.

"He that believeth in him shall neither be condemned," nor "ashamed." John iii. 18. Rom. x. 11.

Therefore, "Come unto me all ye that are weary and laden, and I will ease you, &c., and ye shall find rest for your souls," saith our Saviour Christ. Matt. xi. 28, 29.

"If thou shalt confess with thy mouth the Lord Jesus, and shalt believe with thine heart that God raised him from the dead, thou shalt be saved," saith St Paul. Rom. x. 9.

Errors and adversaries to this truth.

This being the doctrine even of God himself, we may evidently perceive, how not only vain, but besides, not only besides, but against the word of God[2], the Romish doctrine concerning pardons is: for that doth teach us, Whereof see more, Art. II. prop. 4. Art. XI. prop. 1. Art. XII. prop. 1.

1. To seek salvation not at God alone, but at the hands of sinful men. For would we have a pardon for the sins of 40 days? a bishop may give it: for the sins of 100 days? a cardinal may grant [it][3]: for all our sins committed, or to be committed? from the pope we may have it. Hence be his pardons; if you respect time, for 40, 50, 100, 1000, 10,000, 50,000, &c., years; if offences, homicide, parricide, perjury, sodomitery, treason, and what not[4], &c. Vide Taxam. pœnit.

2. That we may be our own saviours. So did that of purgatory.

3. How the precious blood of Christ was shed in vain. For corruptible gold and silver, with our own deeds and works, may, and will save us, if we will.

[[2] See above, pp. 55, 108, 17.] [[3] It, omitted in 1607.]

[[4] Absolutio pro eo qui virginem defloravit. g. vi.
Absolutio pro vicio sodomye pro layco. g. vi.
Idem pro presbytero. g. vii.
Idem pro monacho. g. viii.
Absolutio pro perjurio. g. vi.
Absolutio pro layco præsente qui abbatem aut alium presbyterum minorem episcopum monachum vel clericum interfecit. g. vii. viii. vel. ix.
Absolutio super homicidio laycali pro layco et potest committi suo rectori. g. v. —Taxe Sacre Penitent. Apostol. The Edition referred to (without place or date) is that numbered vii. in Mendham's Spiritual Venality of Rome, p. 24.]

See Art. xxv. Prop. 6.

4. That repentance is not of necessity unto the salvation of man. For without the same a popish pardon may save. But without either a pardon from the pope, or such like, or absolution of a priest, there is no salvation, by the doctrine of the church of Rome.

A further manifestation of the vanity and impieties of the Romish pardons, from a book of the papists, entitled, *Horæ beatissimæ Virginis Mariæ secundum usum Sarum.*

Quicunque, in statu Gratiæ existens, dixerit devote septem Orationes sequentes cum septem Pater noster, et totidem Ave Maria, ante imaginem pietatis, merebitur quinquaginta sex millia annorum indulgentiarum.

Joannes Papa xii. concessit omnibus dicentibus orationem sequentem, transeundo per cemiterium, tot annos indulgentiarum, quot fuerunt ibi corpora inhumata a constitutione ipsius cemiterii.

Oratio pro Defunctis.

Avete, omnes animæ fideles, quarum corpora hic, et ubique requiescunt in pulvere; Dominus [noster] Jesus Christus qui vos, et nos redemit suo pretiosissimo sanguine, dignetur vos a pœnis liberare, et inter choros suorum sanctorum angelorum collocare, ibique nostri memores suppliciter exorare, ut vobis associemur, et vobiscum in cœlis coronemur[1].

Innocentius Papa Secundus concessit cuilibet, qui hanc Orationem sequentem devote dixerit, quatuor millia annorum indulgentiarum, Ave, vulnus lateris nostri Salvatoris[2], *&c.*

Quicunque, devote dixerit istam Orationem, habebit tria millia dierum Indulgentiarum criminalium peccatorum, et duo millia dierum, venialium, a Domino Johanne Papa Vicesimo secundo concessarum, ut in Antidatorio Animæ habetur.

Quicunque Orationem sequentem devote dixerit, promerebitur undecim millia annorum indulgentiarum, &c. "*Ave Domina, sancta Maria, Mater Dei, Regina Cœli, Porta*

[[1] Hor. Beatiss. Virg. Mar. sec. Usum Sarisbur. Par. 1535. fol. cxxiii.]

[[2] Oure holy father pope Innocentius the ij. hath graunted to all them that say thys prayer devoutly in the worshyp of the wounde that our Lorde had in his blessyd syde when he was deed hangynge in the crosse iiij. thousande days of pardon. Pater noster. Ave Maria. Oratio. Ave vulnus, &c.—Ibid. fol. lxvi. b.]

Paradisi, Domina Mundi, Lux Sempiterna, Imperatrix Inferni, &c. Ora pro me Jesum Christum, dilectum Filium tuum, et libera me ab omnibus malis: ora pro peccatis meis. Amen."

Whosoever, being in the state of grace, shall devoutly say the seven prayers ensuing, with seven Our Fathers, and as many Hail Maries, afore the image of piety, shall thereby merit fifty-six thousand years of pardons.

Pope John the Twelfth hath granted to all persons, which, going through the churchyard, do say the prayer following, so many years of pardons as there have been bodies buried since it was a churchyard.

The Prayer for the Dead.

"Hail all faithful souls, whose bodies here and everywhere do rest in the dust. The Lord Jesus who hath redeemed you and us with his most precious blood, vouchsafe to deliver you from pains, and to place you in the company of his holy angels; and there, being mindful of us, meekly to pray, that we may both be joined unto you, and crowned with you in the heavens."

Pope Innocent the Second hath granted to every one, which devoutly shall say this prayer following, four thousand years of pardons; "Hail, wound of our Saviour's side," &c.

Whosoever devoutly shall say this prayer shall have three-thousand days' pardons of criminal sins, and twenty-thousand days of venial offences granted by the lord pope John the Two-and-twentieth; as it is to be read in the Antidotary of the Soul.

Whosoever devoutly will say the prayer following shall merit (thereby) eleven thousand years of pardons; "Hail, Lady, saint Mary, mother of God, queen of heaven, the gate of paradise, the lady of the world, the light eternal, the empress of hell, &c. Pray unto thy beloved Son Jesus Christ for me, and deliver me from all evils, pray for my sins. Amen."

Proposition III.

The Romish doctrine concerning images is fond, and not warranted by the holy scriptures, nor consonant, but contrary unto the same.

The proof from the word of God.

Images are such an abomination to the Lord, as to make

them among all men odious; he describeth the vanity of them by his prophets, as that they are the doctrine of vanity, the
Jer. x. 15. Hab. ii. 18. work of errors, the teachers of lies, silver and gold, the work
Psal. cxxxv. 15. of men's hands, vanity: they have a mouth, and speak not;
Isai. xli. 10, &c. eyes, and see not; ears, and hear not; hands, and touch not;
Psal. cxxxv. 16. feet, and walk not.

Psal. cxv. 17. Exod. xx. 5. 2. He giveth a strait commandment, Not to bow down
1 Cor. x. 7, 14. to them, nor worship them, nor to make them, to fly from
Exod. xx. 5. Deut. iv. 15, &c. them, yea, to destroy both the images themselves, the idola-
1 Cor. x. 14. 1 John v. 21. ters, and the enticers unto idolatry.

Deut. vii. 5, & xii. 2, 3. 3. He commendeth greatly and praiseth such men as
Deut. xvii. 2, 3. have destroyed images, and not bowed unto idols.

Deut. xiii. 5. 2 Kings xviii. 3, 4. 4. He finally curseth the images, the image-makers, and
2 Chron. xiv. 2, 3. the image-servers, or worshippers.

Deut. vii. 25, 26. Hereunto with us the protestant churches everywhere do
Jer. li. 1 Kings xix. 18. subscribe[1].

Dan. ii. *The adversaries unto this truth.*

Deut. xxvii. 15. Isai. xliv. The Romish church most fondly, and contrary to the word
Deut. xxvii. 26. of God, doth allow, and not only allow, but publicly erect,
Psal. xcvii. 7. and not only erect, but adore[a], and not only adore images[2],
Isai. xlii. 17. Confess. Helvet. 2. but doth accurse, and more than so, condemn to the fire, yea
cap. 3, 4. Basil. Art. x. 3. to hell-fire, as heretics, such persons as will not worship
Bohem. cap. 3, 16. Gal. Art. I. August. Art. I. Saxon. Art. XXII. Wittemb. cap. 1, 23. Suevica, Art. XXII. images, and the images too (which is most abominable)

[a] Dele statuas venerari, potiusquam statuarios, stolidum est. Index Expurg. pag. 31.

[[1] Quid autem convenit templo Dei cum simulacris. Et quando beati spiritus ac Divi cœlites dum hic viverent, omnem cultum sui averterunt, et statuas oppugnarunt, cui veri simile videatur divis cœlitibus et angelis suas placere imagines ad quas genua flectant homines, detegant capita, et quas aliis prosequantur honoribus?—Harm. Conf. Sect. II. p. 25. Conf. Helv. Post. cap. IV. Itaque cultum et invocationem demortuorum, sanctorum venerationem et extructionem idolorum, et id genus improbamus.—Ibid. p. 28. Conf. Basil. Art. x. § 3. [al. XI. Disput. 29 et 30.] Ita etiam instituitur ecclesia neminem debere sanctos homines nedum imagines eorum ita ut Deum colere, eove cultu hos, animique affectione, quæ soli et unico Deo tantum debetur, venerari: atque in summa nullo modo divino cultu eos afficere, aut hunc his tribuere.—Ibid. p. 32. Conf. Bohem. cap. XVII. Accedunt et alii furores. Alii apud alias statuas existimantur esse magis propicii. Hi furores, quum palam similes sunt ethnicorum, et haud dubie valde irritent iram Dei, et a docentibus taxandi sunt, et a piis magistratibus severe puniendi.—Ibid. p. 44. Conf. Saxon. Art. XXII. In the other places referred to there is no direct condemnation of image-worship.]

[[2] Inter Delenda in Censura in Christianos Poet. Georg. Fabric. in Indic. Expurgat. Trident. Lugd. 1578, p. 29.]

Of God himself, even of God the Father, and that in the likeness of an old man with a long white beard; of the Son, in the similitude of a man hanging on the cross; of the Holy Ghost, in the shape of a dove; of the wholly, holy, and incomprehensible Trinity, with three faces in one head[b].

Also of God his creatures; as of angels, always with wings, sometimes with a pair of balance, as St Michael; of men, as of Moses, (as it were) with horns; the apostles, with round orbs on their heads like trenchers; the blessed virgin, with frisled hair and costly garments.

And of other base things; as *Agnus Deis* of wax, wafer-cakes of flour, crosses of gold, silver, stone, wood, paper, copper[c], &c.[3]

Proposition IV.

The Romish doctrine concerning relics is fond, and not warranted by the holy scriptures, nor consonant, but contrary unto the same.

The proof from God's word.

Of all the erroneous opinions among the papists (which are infinite) none is more to the illusion of well-meaning Christians than their doctrine concerning worshipping and adoration of the reliques of saints: a doctrine which is so far from being found, as it is forbidden in the holy scripture[d]; and a doctrine in the purer times, and writers of the church, nowhere to be found, and in all the best churches at this day utterly condemned[4].

Confess. Helvet. 1. Art. XI. & II. cap. 5. Basil. Art. X. Bohem. cap. 17. Gal. Art. XXIV.

[b] In hoc plerisque Christianis ethnicus philosophus religiosior, qui etiam Trinitatis, quæ mente vix comprehendatur, figuras oculis corporis aspectabilis (Petri Rami verba in Scholiis [Meta]physicis) deleantur. Index Expurg. [ut supra] pag. 146. Atque hæc absurditas Patrem, Filium, et Sp. S. effigiantium Jacobitis à Nicephoro tribuitur. G. Cassand. Consul. pag. 164. [De Artic. Relig. &c. Lugd. 1508. p. 179.]

[c] Non inficiamur hac nos latriæ adoratione Christi præclarissimam crucem colere et venerari. Andrad. Orthod. Expo. Lib. IX. page 284.

[d] Thou shalt worship the Lord thy God, and him only shalt thou serve, Matt. iv. 20.

[3 Andradius. Orthodox. Explic. Colon. 1583. Lib. IX. pp. 705, 6.]

[4 Multo vero minus credimus reliquias divorum adorandas esse aut colendas.—Harm. Conf. Sect. II. p. 27. Conf. Helv. Post. cap. v. Nothing is said about *relics* in the other places referred to. But see above, p. 222, note 1.]

Adversaries unto this truth.

Such, notwithstanding, is the satanical boldness of the antichristian synagogue of Rome, that as they will delude men with the relics of saints which are not such, so likewise they teach the people (which is most offensive and execrable) to give divine adoration and honour unto them[a].

Vinc. Lir. Lib. XXIII. cap. 155.

Hence is it that some do pray unto St Bene't, whose relics they had stolen: "O Benedict, after God our only hope, leave us not orphans, who art come hither, not through our merits, but for the salvation of many souls[1]."

Rab. Lib. v. cap. 10. de Sec. propriet.

Others have published, that the bodies of saints, and specially the reliques of the blessed martyrs, are with all sincerity to be honoured, as the members of Christ[2], &c. If any deny this conclusion, he is to be thought not a Christian, but an Eunomian, and Vigilantian[3].

Concil. Trid. Sess. 25. decr. de Invocat. &c.

The council of Trent also hath decreed[4], that they are to be taken for damned which affirm, how worship and honour is not to be given unto the reliques of saints.

Missa de S. Cruce, et Officium de S. Cruce.

Of this preposterous devotion they have appointed a certain and common service for the holy cross[5] whereon Christ

[a] Prædicatio autem ecclesiastica hoc semper tenuit, sanctorum reliquias esse ex fide venerandos. Stapleton [Opp. Par. 1620. Tom. III. p. 27.] Antidot. Evang. in Matt. IX. 21, pag. 30. The catholic affirmeth worshipping of saints, prayer unto them, feasts of them, adoration of their relics, and images; the Protestant denieth all. Hills Quartron [Antwerp. 1600], 14. Reas. page 71.

[[1] There is evidently an error in the reference.]

[[2] Festivitates apostolorum sive in honorem martyrum solennitates, antiqui patres in venerationis mysterio celebrare sanxerunt, vel ad excitandam imitationem vel ut meritis eorum consociemur, atque orationibus adjuvemur, ita tamen ut nulli martyrum sed ipsi Deo martyrum, quamvis in memoriis martyrum constituamus altaria....Notandum vero quod Felix papa Romanus vigesimus septimus, post sanctum Petrum legitur constituisse supra memorias martyrum missas celebrari. Attamen beatus Greg. pap. sexagesimus sextus Romanæ urbis constituit supra corpus missas celebrari.—Rab. Mauri Opp. Col. Agripp. 1626. Tom. VI. fol. 26. De Institut. Cleric. Lib II. cap. 43. The editor has been unable to find any work of Rabanus bearing the title given by the author.]

[[3] See Surius, Comment. Brev. Rer. Gest. Colon. 1574. p. 392.]

[[4] Sanctorum quoque martyrum et aliorum cum Christo viventium sancta corpora....veneranda esse;....ita ut affirmantes sanctorum reliquiis venerationem atque honorem non deberi, vel eas, aliaque sacra monumenta a fidelibus inutiliter honorari....omnino damnandos esse, prout jampridem eos damnavit, et nunc etiam damnat ecclesia.—Concil. Harduin. Paris. 1714. Tom. x. col. 167. Conc. Trid. Sess. xxv. Decr. de Invoc. &c.]

[[5] See Missal. Roman. ex Decr. SS. Trid. Conc. Antv. 1573. Comm. Sanctor. &c. p. 50.]

was hanged, they have made a feast for the spear and nails Beehive, Lib. IV. cap. 3.
wherewith Christ was fastened to the cross[6], they have can- Gratian. Dist. 38. Nul.
onized for a saint the chains which bound St Peter[7]: to say volat.
nothing of the adoration they give unto the hair, milk, smock of the blessed Virgin; unto the head, hair, thumb, coat of St John Baptist; unto the breeches of Joseph, the sword and handkerchief of St Paul, the keys of St Peter; and unto many other things which of modesty I will not mention, but do over pass.

Proposition V.

Invocation of saints is a fond thing, not warranted by the holy scriptures, nor consonant, but contrary unto the same.

The proof from God's word.

The christian exercise of prayer is a duty, which may not be either securely omitted, or vainly abused. And though many things in prayer be necessarily to be observed, yet a special point is it, that in our supplications and prayers we do call only upon God. For so to do we are both commanded even
by God himself[b], and thereunto also allured by manifold as Psal. l. 15. Matth. vii.
well promises of large blessing, as by the examples of godly 11. Luke xi. 13.
men in all ages; patriarchs, Abraham, Isaac, Jacob; prophets, and xviii. 7, 8.
as Daniel, Elias, Jeremy; centurions, publicans; apostles, as John xvi. 23, 24.
Paul, Peter, &c.; yea, of all the elect of God in this world. Gen. xiii. 4. Gen. xxvi. 25, &c.

On the other side, to pray unto any creature that is out Gen. ix. 32. Dan. ix. 16,
of this world, besides Jesus Christ, there is in the scripture &c. 1 Kings xviii.
neither law to command, nor promise of blessing, nor any 36, 37, &c. Jer. xiv. 7,
example of godly men or women to provoke. &c. Acts x. 2.

Finally, as all God's people in the purer and former times Luke xviii. 23. Acts xvi. 25, and through his Epistles. Acts i. 24.

[b] Call upon me in the time of trouble, Psal. l. 15. After this
manner, pray, Our Father, which art in heaven, &c. Matt. vi. 6. Luke xviii. 7.
When ye pray, say, Our Father, which art in heaven, Luke xi. 2.

[[6] True it is that (most devoutly) she [i. e. the Romish Church] doth worship a heap of spears wherewith Christ his side was pierced, and two or three dozen of the very same nails which our Saviour was nailed with on the cross: yea, she hath also ordained a holy day in reverence of the same, and hath appointed a special mass for it, namely, *In Festo Lanceæ et Clavorum.*—The Beehive of the Romish Church. Translated out of Dutch into English by George Gilpin the Elder. London 1580. Book. IV. cap. 3. p. 247. b.]

[[7] There is an error in the reference.]

Conf. Helv. I. Art. XI. & II. cap. 5, 23. Basil. Art. X. Bohem. cap. 2, 17. Gal. Art. XIV. XXIV. Belg. Art. XXVI. August. Art. XXI. Wittemb. cap. 23. Suevica, Art. XI. XXI.

have, so in these days protestant churches[1] utterly condemn the invocating of, or praying unto, any creatures whatsoever.

The adversaries unto this truth.

Test. Rhem. p. 187. Orationem Dominicam fundimus sanctis. Censura Colon. fol. 208.

Therefore the Romish doctrine, that saints are to be prayed unto[2], and their daily praying, as occasion serveth, unto saint Agatha, that have sore breasts; unto St Benedict, that either be, or fear to be poisoned; unto St Clare, for them that have sore eyes; St Damian, that be sick, for health; St Erasmus, for help in the entrails; St Feriol, for geese; St Giles, for women that would have children: St Hubberts, for dogs: St Job, for them which have the pox: St Katherine, for knowledge; St Loys, for horses; St Margaret, for women in travail; St Nicholas, for little children; St Otilia, for the head-ache; St Petronil, for the ague; St Quintin for the cough; St Ruffin, for lunacy or madness; St Sebastian, for the plague; St Thomas Becket, for sinners; St Valentine, for the falling-sickness; St Winefrid[3], for virginity; St ✠ or Cross, for all

[1 ...hunc (sc. Christum) solum agnoscimus ac toto corde credimus conciliationem, redemptionem, satisfactionem, expiationem, sapientiam, protectionem, assertionem nostram solum, omne hic simpliciter vitæ salutisque medium præter hunc solum Christum rejicientes.—Harm. Conf. Sect. II. pp. 27, 8. Conf. Helv. Prior. Art. XI. Deum verum docemus solum adorare et colare. Hunc honorem communicamus nemini....Proinde sanctos cœlites sive divos nec adoramus neque colimus, nec invocamus, neque illos coram Patre in cœlis pro intercessoribus aut mediatoribus nostris agnoscimus.—Ibid. p. 26. Conf. Helv. Post. cap. V. ...et quicquid homines de mortuorum sanctorum intercessione commenti sunt (credimus) nihil aliud esse quam fraudes et fallacias Satanæ, ut homines a recta precandi forma abduceret.—Ibid. p. 34. Conf. Gall. Art. XXIV. Credimus etiam nos nullum accessum habere ad Deum, nisi per unicum illum mediatorem et advocatum Jesum Christum justum. ...Hujus tamen mediatoris...majestas et potentia minime nos eousque tenere debet, ut ideo nobis alium pro arbitrio quærendum putemus.—Ibid. pp. 38, 9. Conf. Belg. Art. XXVI. Invocatio est honos qui tantum Deo omnipotenti præstandum est.... Ideo totum morem invocandi sanctos homines, qui ex hac vita discesserunt, damnamus, &c.—Ibid. p. 41. Conf. August. 1540. Art. XXI. Sicut ex gemitu reliquarum creaturarum non est instituendus cultus invocandi eas, ita ex oratione sanctorum in cœlis, non est approbandus cultus invocandi sanctos, &c.—Ibid. p. 48. Conf. Virtemb. cap. XXIII. Adhæc abusus quoque ille taxatus et confutatus fuit quo nonnulli, ita jejuniis et precibus tum beatam virginem Mariam Deiparam, tum sanctos alios sibi conciliare et promereri posse putant, ut sperent se illorum intercessione et meritis ab omnibus tam animæ quam corporis adversitatibus liberari posse. —Ibid. p. 51. Conf. Suev. Art. XI. For the references to the other Confessions, see above, p. 222, note 1.]

[2 Saints do hear our prayers and have care of us.—Test. Rhem. Rhemes, 1582. Marg. Annot. p. 187. The reference to the Censura Colon. the editor has been unable to verify.]

[3 Winefield, 1607.]

things. It is vain, not warrantable by God's word, but altogether repugnant to the holy scriptures.

The vanity and idolatry of the popish invocation further demonstrated, from that book of theirs entitled, *Horæ Beatissimæ Virginis, &c.*

Oremus. Majestatem tuam, Domine, suppliciter exoramus, ut sicut Ecclesiæ tuæ beatus Andræas Apostolus tuus extitit prædicator et rector: ita apud te sit pro nobis perpetuus intercessor, per Dominum nostrum Jesum Christum[4].

Oremus. Deus, pro cujus Ecclesia gloriosus Martyr, et Pontifex, Thomas gladiis impiorum occubuit, præsta, quæsumus, ut omnes, qui ejus implorant auxilium, piæ petitionis ejus salutarem consequantur effectum, per Dominum nostrum[5].

Versus. *Ora pro nobis beata Katharina.* Resp. *Ut digni efficiamur promissionibus Christi*[6].

Versus. *Ora pro nobis beate Martyr, Sebastiane.* Resp. *Ut mereamur pestem epydimiæ illæsi [per] transire, et promissionem Christi obtinere*[7].

Virgo Christi egregia, pro nobis, Apollonia,
Funde preces ad Dominum, ut tollat omne noxium,
Ne, pro reatu criminum, morbo vexemur dentium[8].

"Let us pray. O Lord, we humbly beseech thy majesty, that as thy blessed apostle Andreas was a preacher, and ruler of thy church, so he may be a perpetual intercessor for us, through Jesus Christ our Lord."

"Let us pray. O God, for whose church's sake the glorious martyr and bishop, Thomas, was slain by the sword of the ungodly; grant, we beseech thee, that such as call unto him for help may obtain a good effect of his godly prayer, through our Lord."

"*The Vers.* O blessed Katherine, pray for us. *The Ans.* That we may be made worthy of the promises of Christ."

"*The Vers.* O blessed Martyr Sebastian, pray for us. *The Ans.* That we may deserve to escape the plague without hurt, and obtain the promises of Christ."

[[4] Hor. Beat. Virg. Mar. sec. Usum Sarisbur. Par. 1535. fol. xviii. b.]
[[5] Ibid. fol. xix. b. where *petitionis suæ*; and, *per Christum Dominum*, &c.]
[[6] Ibid. fol. xx. b.] [[7] Ibid. fol. xx.] [[8] Ibid. fol. lxxiii.]

"Christ his noble Virgin Apollonia, pray unto the Lord to remove whatsoever is hurtful, lest, for the guiltiness of our sins, we be vexed with the tooth-ache."

Whosoever saith this prayer following in the worship of God and St Roche (the very words in the said book[1]), shall not die of the pestilence, by the grace of God, &c.

Oremus. Omnipotens, sempiterne Deus, qui precibus, et meritis beatissimi Rochi Confessoris tui quandam pestem generalem revocasti, præsta supplicibus tuis, ut qui pro simili peste revocanda sub tua confidunt fiducia, ipsius gloriosi Confessoris tui precamine, ab ipsa peste epydimiæ, et ab omni perturbatione liberemur, per Christum Dominum nostrum[2].

Oratio ad tres Reges. Rex Jasper, Rex Melchior, Rex Balthasar, rogo vos per singula nomina, rogo vos per sanctam Trinitatem, rogo vos per Regem Regum, quem vagientem in cunis videre meruistis, ut compatiamini tribulationum mearum hodie, et intercedatis pro me ad Dominum, cujus desiderio exules facti estis[3].

Crux Christi, protege me; Crux Christi, salva me; Crux Christi, defende me ab omni malo[3].

"Let us pray. O Almighty and everlasting God, who by the prayers and merits of thy most blessed confessor, Roche, didst revoke a certain general plague; grant unto thy suppliants, who for the revocation of the like plague do trust in thy faithfulness, by the prayer of that thy glorious confessor we may be delivered from the plague, and from all adversity, through Christ our Lord."

"A prayer unto the three kings. O king Jasper, king Melchior, king Balthasar, I beseech you by every of your names, I beseech you by the Holy Trinity, I beseech you by the King of kings, whom ye deserved to see even in his swaddling-clothes, that you would take pity on my troubles this day, and make intercession for me unto the Lord, for whose desire ye make yourselves exiles."

[[1] The words are not found in the editions which the Editor has consulted.]

[[2] Ibid. fol. lxxvi. where, *meritis et precibus*; and, *ad ipsum sub tua confugiunt fiducia.*]

[[3] These prayers do not occur in the edition to which reference has been made.]

"O Christ's cross, protect me; O Christ's cross, save me; O Christ's cross, defend me from all evil."

Article XXIII.

Of Ministering in the Congregation.

(1) *It is not lawful for any man to take upon him the office of public preaching,* (2) *or ministering the Sacraments in the congregation,* (3) *before he be lawfully called, and sent to execute the same.* (4) *And those we ought to judge lawfully called, and sent, which be* (6) *chosen and called to this work* (5) *by men, who have public authority given unto them in the congregation, to call and send ministers into the Lord's vineyard.*

The propositions.

1. None publicly may preach but such as thereunto are authorized.
2. They must not be silent, who by office are bound to preach.
3. The sacraments may not be administered in the congregation, but by a lawful minister.
4. There is a lawful ministry in the church.
5. They are lawful ministers which be ordained by men lawfully appointed to the calling and sending forth of ministers.
6. Before ministers are to be ordained, they are to be chosen, and called.

Proposition I.

None publicly may preach but such as thereunto are authorized.

The proof from God's word.

This truth in the holy scripture is evident. For there we find how,

1. Godly men were both called by God, and commanded
to preach, before they would, or durst so do. So was Samuel, 1 Sam. iii. 3, 4, &c. 20.
Jeremy, John Baptist, Christ Jesus himself, who also to Jer. i. 4, 5. John i. 6. John xx. 21.
preach did send the twelve apostles and the seventy disciples. Matth. x. 5. Luke x. 1.

Jer. xiv. 14, xxiii. 21, xxvii. 15, xxix. 8, 9. 2. The wicked, and false prophets, for preaching afore their time, are blamed.

Matt. ix. 38. 3. A commandment is given us to pray the Lord of the harvest that he would send forth labourers into his harvest.

1 Cor. xii. 28. 4. Lastly, we do read that God hath ordained in the church some to be apostles, some prophets, some teachers,
Ephes. iv. 11. some to be workers of miracles. And Christ being ascended into heaven, gave some to be apostles, some prophets, some evangelists, and some pastors, and teachers.

Conf. Helv. 2, cap. 18. And all this is acknowledged by the reformed churches[1].
Bohem. cap. 9. Gal. Art. XXXI. Belg. Art. XXXI. August. Art. XIV. Wittemb. Art. XX. Suevic. Art. XIII.

The errors and adversaries to this truth.

And so are we against them

Answer to the Execut. of Just. ch. 3, p. 44. Ib. c. 9, p. 211. Ib. c. 5, p. 91. Ib. c. 3, p. 41. R. A. Confut. of Brow. p. 113. Which to their power do seek the abolishment of public preaching in the reformed churches; as do first the papists, who phrase the preachers to be uncircumcised Philistines, sacrilegious ministers, Hieroboam's priests, inordinate and unordered apostates[2]; and next the Barrowists, who say how the said preachers are sent of God in his anger to deceive the people with lies[3].

[[1] Nemo autem honorem ministerii ecclesiastici usurpare sibi, id est, ad se largitionibus, aut ullis artibus, aut arbitrio proprio rapere debet. Vocentur et eligantur electione ecclesiastica et legitima ministri ecclesiæ, &c.—Harm. Conf. Sect. XI. p. 37. Conf. Helv. Post. cap. XVIII. Non autem ministri sua sponte procurrere ad conditionem illam debent: sed secundum Domini et apostolorum exemplum legitime debent ordinari et constitui, &c.—Ibid. p. 47. Conf. Bohem. cap. IX. Credimus ministros, seniores et diaconos debere ad functiones illas suas vocari, et promoveri legitima ecclesiæ electione, adhibita ad eam seria Dei invocatione, atque eo ordine et modo qui nobis Dei verbo præscribitur.—Ibid. p. 56. Conf. Belg. Art. XXXI. De ordine ecclesiastico docent, quod nemo debeat in ecclesia publice docere aut sacramenta administrare, nisi rite vocatus, &c.—Ibid. p. 57. Conf. August. Art. XIV. Nec permittendum est cuivis, quamvis spirituali sacerdoti, ut sine legitima vocatione usurpet publicum ministerium in ecclesia.—Ibid. p. 62. Conf. Virtemb. Art. XX. ...manifestum est, Nihil aliud veros atque idoneos ecclesiæ ministros (veluti episcopos, presbyteros, unctos et consecratos) efficere, quam quod a Deo missi sint. Quomodo enim prædicabunt (inquit Paulus) nisi mittantur.—Ibid. p. 64. Conf. Suev. Art. XIII.]

[[2] As for the high praises and special testimonie of wisdome, learning and loialtie that it liked the maker of the libel to give...to certaine of the cheefe clergie... it is a condemnation to him and his fellowes that presumed to dispossesse so noble, wise, and learned prelates;...and much more to put into their places a number of incircumcised *Philistines*, taken of the raskalitie of the whole realme.—(Card. Alan's) Def. of Eng. Cath. An Answer, &c. chap. III. p. 44. In chap. IX. p. 211, sacrilegious ministeries.—In chap. V. p. 91. You see in what sort also Hieroboam king of Israel, had a special prophet sent to him...for creating of a wicked cleargie out of Aaron's order: I meane; new, hungrie, base, and inordered priestes (the paterne of heretical ministers), &c.—In chap. III. p. 41. Greedie wolves, unordered *Apostats.*]

[[3] Allison's Plaine Confutation, &c. Lond. 1590. p. 114.]

Who publish how the word is not taught by the sermons of ministers, but only by the revelation of the Spirit; so did Muncer the anabaptist[4], and so doth H. N.[5], and his Family of Love[6].

Sleidan. comment. Lib. v. Evang. cap. 13, sect. 6, & Spirit. Land, chap. 48, sect. 5. Letter to the Bish. of Roch.

Who run afore they be sent; as do many both anabaptists and puritans, as Penry, Greenwood, Barrow, &c.; or which hold, how they which are able to teach, and instruct the people, may, and must so do: and that not privately only, but publicly too, though they be not ordinarily sent and authorized thereunto; which was the doctrine of R. H.[7]

In Ps. cxxii.

Who teach that laymen may teach to get faith[8], and that every particular member of the church hath power, yea, and ought to examine the manner of administering the sacraments, &c., and to call the people to repentance: so teacheth Barrow[9].

R. A. Confut. of Brownism, p. 113.

Barrow's Discovery, p. 36.

[4 ...neque dubium esse quin...solicitatus (Deus) aliquo signo conspicuo sese declaret, animique sitim restinguat, et nobiscum agat, ut quondam cum patribus: hoc etiam docebat (Muncerus) patefacere Deum per somnia voluntatem suam, &c. —Sleidan. Commentt. Argentorat. 1555. Lib. v. fol. 65.]

[5 Where now then the law and the services do in such wise change by the believers of the anointed, to wit, out of the figures into the true being, and out of the letter and serviceable word, into the revealing of the holy Spirit of Christ, &c.—H. N. Evang. Reg. cap. XIII. § 6. Seeing then that the glorious Light of Life (2 Cor. 4. a.) as a day or clearness of Christ, is by God's grace given us to behold, therefore have we out of the same sight, or heavenly revelation, rehearsed likewise in thosame foresaid books and writings, many of the secret heavenly treasures (Rom. 16. c. Eph. 3. a. Col. 1. c.) or riches of God: which in times past, even hitherto, have not been made known unto the world, like as God doth now presently, through his love, reveal and make them known unto his saints.—Id. Spiritual Land of Peace, cap. XLVIII. § 5.]

[6 I could also with all my heart wish that man with man committed not filthiness, nor depended one upon another: but to stay them only on the Lord's truth, and not on flesh and blood, so were then all controversies at an end. It were well also to prove all things: but not as seemeth me by the crooked rule of man's own judgment, or fleshly mind and concerning, nor by his imagination (without the light of God's truth, or spirit of righteousness and love:) taken on in constructing and wresting of the right sense and mind of the scriptures, &c....Consider therefore every thing in his right degree (if you be endowed with ghostly understanding and possessed with the right spirit of judgment), and then out of your spiritualness judge all things, &c. —Letter of the Fam. to the Bp. of Rochester in Wilkinson's Confut. Lond. 1579. B. 1, 2.]

[7 This reference has not been found.]

[8 They teach that a layman may beget faith, and that we have no need of public administrations.—Allison's Confutation, &c. p. 114.]

[9 Barrow's Discovery, 1590. p. 35.]

Proposition II.

They must not be silent who by office are bound to preach.

The proof from God's word.

As publicly to preach, before men are sent, is a grievous fault: so not to preach being sent, is a great sin. Hereunto bear witness,

Luke iv. 43. 1. Our Saviour Christ, whose words are these; "Surely I must also preach the kingdom of God: for therefore am I sent."

Acts iv. 17, &c. 2. Peter and John, who being charged to speak no more in the name of Jesus, said, "We cannot but speak that which we have heard and seen."

1 Cor. ix. 16, 17. 3. St Paul, for he writeth, "Necessity is laid upon me, and woe is me if I preach not the gospel."

Acts i. 42. 4. The apostles of Christ. For though they were beaten for so doing; yet "they ceased not to teach and preach Jesus Christ."

Conf. Helv. 1, Art. xv. & II. cap. 18. Bohem. cap. 9. Gal. Art. xxv. Aug. Art. vii. Wittemb. Art. xx. Suevica, Art. xiii. 5. All the churches of God which be purged from superstition and errors[1].

Errors and adversaries unto this truth.

Then, as in glass, they may see their faults;

Bullin. cont. Anabap. c. 12. Who maintain how there ought to be no public preaching at all; as do the anabaptists[2].

[[1] Summum functionis hujus munus est pœnitentiam et peccatorum remissionem per Christum prædicare, &c.—Harm. Conf. Sect. xi. p. 43. Conf. Helv. Prior. Art. xix. ...minister ecclesiæ totus et in omnibus suis officiis, non suo arbitrio indulgere, sed illud duntaxat exequi jubetur quod in mandatis habet a suo domino. ...Proinde in hoc sunt vocati ministri ecclesiæ, ut evangelium Christi annuncient fidelibus et sacramenta administrent.—Ibid. pp. 38, 9. Conf. Helv. Post. cap. xviii. ...docetur, functione illius muneris, in quod legitime sint collocati, obligari ipsos ad hoc, ut pro animabus hominum, qui fidei ipsorum concrediti sunt...curam gerant, doctrinaque verbi divini et sacramentis ministrandis de Christi sententia et institutione, fideliter ipsis inserviant, &c.—Ibid. pp. 47, 8. Conf. Bohem. cap. ix. Credimus...requiri in ecclesia pastores, quibus onus docendi verbi et administrandorum sacramentorum incumbat, &c.—Ibid. p. 53. Conf. Gall. Art. xxv. Hæc potestas tantum exercetur docendo, seu prædicando evangelium, et porrigendo sacramenta, vel multis vel singulis, juxta vocationem.—Ibid. p. 58. Conf. August. De Abus. Art. vii. Nec est obscurum, quod Christus instituerit in ecclesia sua ministros, qui adnuntient euangelion suum, et dispensent sacramenta ejus.—Ibid. p. 62. Conf. Virtemb. Art. xx. Qui ergo hoc modo missi, uncti, consecrati, et ornati sunt, his solicitam curam gregis Christi gerunt, et fideliter in verbo atque doctrina laborant, ut illum majore fructu pascant.—Ibid. p. 64. Conf. Suev. Art. xiii.]

[[2] Dogma, quo scripturarum expositionem damnant, aliqua ex parte commune

Which deprave the office of preaching; as do the Libertines[3], saying, that preaching is none ordinary means to come unto the knowledge of the word: and especially the Family of Love, who term the public preachers, in derision, scripture-learned[4], licentious-scripture-learned[5], good-thinking-wise[6], ceremonial, and letter-doctors[7], teaching-masters[8]; and further say, "It is a great presumption, that any man, out of the learnedness of the letter, taketh upon him to be a teacher or preacher." Again, "It becometh not any man to busy himself about preaching of the word." So, and more too, the Family[9].

Wilkins. against the Family of Love, Art. xiv. p. 66. Theoph. against Wilk. Part. of the Pref. Temp. H. N. Proph. of the Spirit, cap. 2, sect. 7. Family Letter to the bishop of Rochester. H. N. Spirit. Land, chap. 25. Idem I. Exhortat. chap. 16, sect. 15, 16.

Which take upon them the office of public preaching, without performance of their duty, either through ignorance, that they cannot; worldly employments, that they may not; negligence, that they will not; or fear of troubles, that they dare not preach the word of God.

Yet think we not (which our Sabbatarians let not to publish) that

Every minister necessarily, and under pain of damnation, is to preach at least once every Sunday[10]; and,

D. B. Doct. of the Sabbath, 2 Book, p. 174.

Unless a minister preach every Sunday, he doth not hallow

Ibid. p. 277.

est anabaptistis cum illis hominibus quibus alioqui sacræ conciones molestæ sunt, easque quam brevissimas fieri cupiunt....Hi scripturarum interpretationem ægerrime ferunt, et multo ægrius cum ex illis corripiuntur. Itaque dicunt, se quidem verbum Dei non illibenter audire, sed interpretationem et adjecta ministrorum verba non posse agnoscere pro verbo Dei, aut libenter audire et recipere.—Bulling. Adv. Anabapt. (Simler. Vers. Lat.) Tiguri, 1560. p. 113. b. Lib. III. cap. 11.]

[3 Wilkinson's Confutation. Lond. 1579. Art. XIV. p. 66.]

[4 Ibid. Art. XII. p. 57.]

[5 The work referred to has not been met with.]

[6 H. N. Prophecy of the Spirit. An. 1574. cap. II. § 7.]

[7 In Wilkinson's Confutation. fol. A. 4. b.]

[8 H. N. Spiritual Land. cap. XXV. § 3.]

[9 I tell thee truly that it is a great presumption against God and his saints that the man becometh so free of heart that he out of the learnedness of the letter, or out of the imagination of the knowledge, taketh upon him to be a teacher or preacher, &c....For no man can rightly...deal in, or use the true God-services, nor the services of the holy Word (it becometh not likewise that any man should take-in-hand to busy himself thereabout) but only the illuminated (Mat. 13. f.) elders. &c.—H. N. First Exhortation, Translated, &c. cap. XVI. § 15, 16.]

[10 Let us confess as the truth is, that the Lord would have every sabbath to be sanctified by the minister and the people, and that in the church he ought to preach the word, and they to hear it every sabbath-day: and though we be not so grossly blinded to imagine that it is not necessary one whit upon that day, we must not also be deceived to think, that now and then is sufficient, once a month or twice a quarter, &c.—Nich. Bownde, Doct. of the Sabbath. Lond. 1595. Book II. p. 174.]

the Sabbath-day in the least measure of that which the Lord requireth of us[1].

Proposition III.

The Sacraments may not be administered in the congregation, but by a lawful minister.

The proof from God's word.

Matth. xxviii. 19. Luke xxii. 19. 1 Cor. xi. 24, 25. Acts ii. 38, 41, viii. 12, 13, x. 47, xvi. 32, 33. John i. 25. 1 Cor. i. 14, 16. Acts xx. 7. 1 Cor. x. 16.

In the holy scripture we read, that the public ministers of the word are to be the administers of the sacraments. For both our Saviour Christ commanded his disciples, as to preach, so to baptize, and celebrate the Supper of the Lord: and the apostles, and other ministers in the purest times (whom the godly ministers and preachers in these days do succeed), not only did preach, but also baptize, and minister the Lord's Supper.

Conf. Helv. 2, cap. 18. Bohem. cap. 9. Gal. Art. XXV. XXXI. August. Art. VII. Wittem. Art. XX. Suevic. Art. XIII. T. C. 1 Rep. p. 113.

And hereunto do the churches of God subscribe[2].

In saying, that none may administer the sacraments in the congregation afore he be lawfully called, and sent thereunto, we think not (as some do) that the very being of the sacraments dependeth upon this point, *viz.* whether the baptizer, or giver of the bread and wine, be a minister, or no[3]:

Neither is it the meaning of this Article, that privately in houses, either lawful ministers, upon just occasion, may not, or others not of the ministry, upon any occasion (in the peace of the church) may administer the sacraments.

The errors and adversaries unto this truth.

Hereby we declare ourselves not to favour the opinion, that publicly,

Some may minister the sacraments, which are not merely, and full ministers of the word and sacraments; and so think

Surius, Comment. p. 237.

both the Anabaptists[4], among whom their king (when it was)

[1 Therefore it ought to be provided that the preaching of the word be everywhere established: for in that especially the sanctifying of the Sabbath consisteth... and without the which the day cannot be hallowed in the least measure, &c.—Ibid. p. 277.]

[2 See above, p. 138, note 1.]

[3 ... the substance of the sacrament depended chiefly of the institution and word of God, which is the form, and as it were the life of the sacrament, of which institution this is one and of the chief parts, that it should be celebrated by a minister.—A Reply to an Answer made of M. Dr Whitgift against the Admonition to the Parliament, by T. C., 2nd Edit. p. 144.]

[4 There seems to be an error in the reference.]

after supper took bread, and reaching it among the communicants, did say, "Take, eat, and shew forth the Lord's death;" their queen also reaching the cup said, "Drink ye, and shew forth the Lord's death:" and the presbyterians at Geneva[5], where the elder (a layman) ministereth the cup ordinarily at the communion. Some ministers (and namely the puritan doctors) may not minister the sacraments. For (say the Disciplinarians[6]) the office of doctors is only to teach true doctrine; but in our church (of England) the doctor encroacheth upon the office of the pastor[7]. For both indifferently do teach, exhort, and minister the sacraments.

Survey of Disci. chap. 15, out of the Geneva Laws. Lear. Disc. pag. 17.

Fruct. Ser. on Rom. xii. p. 40.

None, though a lawful minister, may administer the sacraments, which either is no preacher[a], or when he ministereth them, doth not preach[b]; which be the errors of the Disciplinarians, or puritans[8].

Publicly, and privately too, the sacraments of baptism may be administered by any man, yea, by women, if necessity do urge. So hold the papists: for saith Javel, "In the time of necessity the minister of baptism is every man, both male and

Javel. Phil. Ch. par. 5. f. 555.

[a] The administration of the sacraments ought to be committed to none but such as are the preachers of the word. Lear. Disc. p. 60. It is sacrilege to separate the word (viz. preaching) from the sacraments. Ibid. The preaching of the word is the life of the sacraments. T. C. 1 Reply, p. 125.

[b] The unchangeable laws of God be (saith T. C.) that none minister the sacraments which do not preach. T. C. 1 Reply, p. 104, § 3. Where there is no preacher of the word, there ought to be no minister of the sacraments. Lear. Disc. p. 62.

[[5] Fourthly; at the time of the communion they (the elders) must....help and assist the pastor (at Geneva the elder ministereth the cup).—Bancroft, Survey of the Pretended Holy Discipline, Lond. 1593. cap. xv. p. 178.]

[[6] The work referred to has not been found, but see A Demonstrat. of Discipline. chap. XI. p. 53. For the further revealing of the trueth, God hath ordayned, that there shoulde be in the churche doctors, whose office is to be employed in teaching of doctrin, and is an office different from that of the pastour.]

[[7] See A Fruitful Sermon upon the 3, 4, &c. vss. of the 12th chap. to the Romans, Lond. 1589. p. 36, where is a slight verbal difference.]

[[8] ... the life of the sacraments dependeth of the preaching of the word of God.—A Reply to an Answer, &c. by T. C. p. 158. And S. Paul by the commandment that our Saviour Christ gave him to preach, undertook also to baptize, although there were no express words that licensed him thereunto: for he knew right well that it was the perpetual ordinance of God that the same should be the ministers of the word and sacraments.—Ibid. p. 140.]

female. A woman, be she young or old, sacred or wicked; every male, that hath his wits, and is neither dumb, nor so drunken but that he can utter the words, as well pagan, infidel, and heretic, the bad as the good, the schismatic as the catholic, may baptize[1]. And yet usually in the civil wars, both in France and in Netherland[2], the papists did rebaptize such children[3] as of the protestant, not lay-men, but ministers, had afore been baptized[a].

D. Aug. ad Quod-vult, c. 27. Epiph. Hæres. 42.

The private baptism by private persons was also taught long since both by the Marcionites and Pepuzians[4].

Proposition IV.

There is a lawful ministry in the church.

The proof from God's word.

God, for the gathering or erecting to himself a church out of mankind, and for the well-governing of the same, from time to time hath used, yea, and also doth, and to the end of

[a] So in the Netherland were children rebaptized when the duke of Alva there tyrannized. Trag. Hist. of Antwerp. The like rebaptization was used by the papists at Toulouse, Troys, and other cities in France, especially *anno* 1562. See the Chron. of France.

[[1] Quantum ad secundum (i. e. quis sit baptismi minister tempore necessitatis) adverte quod eveniente necessitate minister baptismi est omnis homo, et masculus, et fœmina....Ex quibus sequitur quod mulier, sive anus, sive sancta sive prava, omnis masculus habens usum rationis, et non mutus nec ebrius adeo quod non potest verba proferre, tam Christianus quam paganus, sive infidelis et hæreticus, tam bonus quam malus, tam schismaticus quam catholicus baptizare potest.—Chr. Javell. Opp. Lugd. 1580. Tom. II. p. 559. Philos. Christ. Quinta Pars, Tract. II. De Sacr. Bapt. cap. 6.]

[[2] And then were their children before baptized by other, againe rebaptized by them, and their wives before married by other againe remarried by them, as though the former baptisme were no baptisme, &c.—A Tragical Hist. of Antwerp's Trouble. Lond. 1586. fol. D. i.]

[[3] Illi, illi sane violatæ divinæ majestatis sunt rei...qui rem anabaptistis propriam faciunt, baptismum pueris ex Jesu Christi institutione baptizatis repetendo, &c.—Verba Condæi in Comment. de Statu Relig. et Reip. in Gall. 1577. Pars II. Lib. V. p. 76. b.]

[[4] *Δίδωσι καὶ ἐπιτροπὴν γυναιξὶ βάπτισμα διδόναι*, says Epiphanius of Marcion, not of the Pepuzians.—Epiphan. Opp. Paris. 1622. Tom. I. p. 305. Adv. Hær. Lib. I. Tom. III. Hær. 42. He tells us, however, that the Pepuzians allowed women to minister in the church: *Ἐπίσκοποί τε παρ' αὐτοῖς γυναῖκες, καὶ πρεσβύτεροι γυναῖκες, καὶ τὰ ἄλλα· ὡς μηδὲν διαφέρειν φησίν. ἐν γὰρ Χριστῷ Ἰησοῦ οὔτε ἄρσεν, οὔτε θῆλυ.*—Ibid. p. 418. Hær. 49.]

the world will, use the ministry of men lawfully called thereunto by men. A truth most evident in the holy scripture.

Jesus said unto his apostles, "Go, and teach all nations, baptizing them, &c. And, lo, I am with you alway, unto the end of the world." Matt. xxviii. 20.

Christ "gave some to be apostles, and some prophets, and some evangelists, and some pastors, and teachers; for the gathering together of the saints, for the work of the ministry, and for the edification of the body of Christ, till we all meet together (in the unity of faith, and knowledge of the Son of God) unto a perfect man." Ephes. iv. 11, 12, 13.

A truth also approved by the churches[5]. Conf. Helv. I. Art. XV. & II. c. 18. Bohem. cap. 8, 9, 14. Gal. Art. XXV. XXIX. XXX. XXXI. Belg. Art. XXX. XXXI. Aug. Art. VII. Saxon. Art. XI. Wittemb. Art. XX. Suevica, Art. XIII. XV.

Adversaries unto this truth.

Oppugners of this truth are,

First, The anabaptistical Swermers[6], who both term all ecclesiastical men the devil's ministers; and also, as very wicked, do utterly condemn the outward ministry of the word and sacraments. Althemar. Concil. Loc. pugnan. lo. 191.

And next the Brownists[7], who divulge that in these days no ministers have the calling, sending, or authority pertaining to a minister; and that it will hardly be found in all the world that any minister is or shall be lawfully called; such R. H. on Psal. cxxii.

[5 Ministros ecclesiæ cooperarios (quemadmodum et Paulus appellavit) esse Dei fatemur: per quos ille et cognitionem sui et peccatorum administret, homines ad se convertat, &c.—Harm. Conf. Sect. XI. p. 42. Conf. Helv. Prior. Art. XV. Nuncupant sane apostoli Christi omnes in Christum credentes sacerdotes, sed non ratione ministerii....Diversissima ergo inter se sunt sacerdotium et ministerium. Illud enim commune est christianis omnibus...hoc non item.—Ibid. p. 38. Conf. Helv. Post. cap. XVIII. Nulli igitur apud nos permittitur ministerii munere fungi, aut ullum sacrum Domini munus administrare, nisi hoc primæ ecclesiæ more, atque divinitus constituto ordine, ad eam functionem pervenerit, vocatusque sit et constitutus.—Ibid. p. 47. Conf. Bohem. cap. IX. Conf. Ibid. pp. 50, 1. cap. XIV. et Sect. X. p. 12. cap. VIII. Credimus veram ecclesiam gubernari debere ea politia, sive disciplina, quam Dominus noster Jesus Christus sancivit, ita videlicet, ut in ea sint pastores, presbyteri, et diaconi, ut doctrinæ puritas retineatur, &c.—Ibid. p. 53. Conf. Gall. Art. XXIX. For the other references to this and the other confessions, vid. ibid. and above, p. 230, note 1.]

[6 Hi Swermeri...ecclesiæ ministros diaboli clamant. Nostrum ministerium in verbo Dei et sacramentorum dispensatione damnant.—Althamer. Conciliat. Locor. Script. Noremberg. 1535. Loc. CXCI. p. 211.]

[7 Therefore except they can approve the lawfulnesse of their calling to the ministerie under some other title than y[t] which thei now have by y[e] clergie; it will fall out that there shal hardlie be found a minister duelie called in all the worlde, and also that there is small hope that ever there shalbe anie.—Treatise on 1st verse of Ps. 122. by R. H. fol. E. 1583.]

Barrow's Discov. p. 104. also be the Barrowists[1], which say there is no ministry of the gospel in all Europe.

Proposition V.

They are lawful ministers which be ordained by men lawfully appointed for the calling and sending forth of ministers.

The proof from God's word.

St Paul, in the beginning of his epistle unto the Galatians, giveth us to observe the divers sending forth of men into the holy ministry: whereof

John xx. 21. John i. 6. Some are sent immediately from God himself. So sent was by God the Father both Jesus Christ and John Baptist; by Matt. x. 15. God the Son, in his state mortal, the twelve apostles, in his Acts ix. 15. state immortal and glorious, St Paul.

This calling is special and extraordinary: and the men so called were adorned with the gift of miracles commonly, as were Jesus Christ and his apostles; but not always, for John Baptist wrought none.

Matt. xxviii. 20. Matt. xv. 14. And they were also enjoined, for the most part, as the apostles, to preach throughout the world, howbeit our Saviour was limited.

Some again were sent of men: as they be who are sent of men not authorized thereunto by the word of God, and that to the disturbance of the peace of the church: such in the apostles' time were the false apostles; in our days be the anabaptists, family-elders, and law-despising Brownists.

Acts xiv. 23. 1 Tim. iv. 14. And some, lastly, are by men sent: so in the primitive church by the apostles were pastors and elders ordained, who by the same authority ordained other pastors and teachers. Whence it is that the church as it hath been, so it shall till the end of the world be provided for. They, who are thus called, have power neither to work miracles, as the apostles had, nor to preach, and minister the sacraments where they will, as the apostles might, but they are tied every man to his charge, which they must faithfully attend upon, except urgent occasion do enforce the contrary.

The calling of these men is termed a general calling, and it is the ordinary, and in these days the lawful calling, allowed by the word of God.

[[1] Barrow's Discovery of the False Church, 1590. p. 104.]

So testify with us the true churches elsewhere in the world[2]. Conf. Helv. I. Art. XVII. & II. cap. 18. Bohem. c. 9. Gal. Art. XXXI. Belg. Art. XXXI. August. Art. XIV. Wittemb. Art. XXI. Suevica, Art. XIII.

Adversaries unto this truth.

This truth hath many ways been resisted. For there be which think how in these days there is no calling but the extraordinary, or immediate, calling from God, and not by men, as the Anabaptists, Familists, and Brownists: of whom afore.

The Papists[3], albeit they allow the assertion, yet take they all ministers to be wolves, hirelings, laymen, and intruders, who are not sacrificing priests, anointed by some antichristian bishop of the Romish synagogue. Concil. Trid. Sess. 7. Can. 7.

Either all, or the most part of the ministers of England, saith Howlet[4], be mere laymen, and no priests, and consequently have no authority in these things. It is evident, &c., because they are not ordained by such a bishop and priest as the catholic church hath put in authority. Howl. 7. reas.

Proposition VI.

Before ministers are to be ordained, they are to be chosen and called.

The proof from God's word.

Though it be in the power of them which have authority in the church to appoint ministers for God's people; yet may they admit neither whom they will, nor as they will themselves: they are both deliberately to choose, and orderly to call such as they have chosen.

[[2] Est enim functio hæc nulli quem non et legis divinæ peritia, et vitæ innocentia, et Christi nominis studio singulari esse compererint, et judicarint ministri et ii quibus id negotii per ecclesiam est commissum, concedenda. Quæ quum vere Dei electio sit, ecclesiæ suffragio, et manuum sacerdotis impositione, recte comprobatur.—Harm. Conf. Sect. XI. p. 43. Conf. Helv. Prior. Art. XVII. Vocentur et eligantur electione ecclesiastica et legitima ministri ecclesiæ...et qui electi sunt, ordinentur a senioribus cum orationibus publicis et impositione manuum.—Ibid. pp. 37, 8. Conf. Helv. Post. cap. XVIII. ...ut ad munerum sacrorum administrationem...vocentur qui sint firmi et potentes in fide, &c....itemque ut hi ante omnia, an tales sint, explorentur, atque examinentur, et postea a senioribus, precibus et jejuniis factis, manuum impositione confirmentur, seu approbentur.—Ibid. p. 47. Conf. Bohem. cap. IX. For the other references, see above, p. 230, note 1.]

[[3] The place meant is probably this: Si quis dixerit, Christianos omnes in verbo et omnibus sacramentis administrandis habere potestatem; anathema sit.—Concil. Harduin. Par. 1714. Tom. X. col. 53. Conc. Trid. Sess. VII. De Sacram. in Genere, Can. X. Conf. Ibid. col. 136. Sess. XXIII. cap. 4.]

[[4] Howlet, i. e. Robert Persons, the Jesuit. See A Brief Discourse containing certain Reasons why catholics refuse to go to church, &c.—Douay, 1580. Part I. Reas. VII. p. 41. Where, *in that authority*.]

1 Tim. v. 22.

This made the apostles and elders in the primitive church straitly to charge that suddenly hands should be laid on no man.

Acts i. 23.

To make a special choice of twain, whereof one was to be elected into the place of Judas.

Acts xiv. 23. 1 Tim. iv. 14.

By election to ordain elders in every church, and by prayer and fasting to commend them to the Lord, and by laying on of hands to consecrate them.

1 Tim. ii. 12. 1 Tim. iii. 2. 1 Pet. v. 3. Tit. i. 7. 2 Cor. vi. 3. 1 Tim. iii. 2. Tit. i. 9. 2 Tim. ii. 15. 1 Tim. v. 20. Tit. i. 9. Matt. ix. 38. 2 Tim. iv. 2. Acts xx. 28. Acts v. 41. 2 Tim. iv. 7, 8. 2 Cor. xi. 23.

To describe who were to be chosen and called. For they are to be men, not boys nor women. Men of good behaviour, not incontinent, nor given to wine, nor strikers, nor covetous, nor proud, nor froward, nor ireful, nor givers of offence; finally, men of special gifts, apt to teach, able to exhort, wise to divide the word of God aright, bold to reprove, willing to take pains, watchful to oversee, patient to suffer, and constant to endure all manner of afflictions.

And this do the churches protestant by their confessions approve[1].

Conf. Helv. I. Art. XV. & II. cap. 18. Bohem. c. 9. Gal. Art. XIII. Belg. Art. XXXI. Aug. Art. XIV. Witt. Art. XX. Suev. Art. XIII.

The errors and adversaries unto this truth.

In error they remain, who are of opinion that

The due election and calling of ministers according to the word of God is of no such necessity to the making of ministers; an erroneous fancy of the anabaptists and Family of Love.

Sigebert.

That women may be deacons, elders, and bishops: the former the Acephalians[2], the latter the Pepuzians did maintain.

A special care is not to be had both of the life and the learning of men; or that wicked men, of evil life; ignorant men, without learning; asses, of no gifts; loiterers, which do no good; or favourers of superstition and idolatry, which do great hurt, are to be admitted into the ministry.

They are causes, which indeed are none, to debar men from the ecclesiastical function; as if men have been twice married, (an error of the Russies[3]) be married, have had cer-

[[1] See above, p. 230, note 1, and p. 239, note 2.]

[[2] Acephalorum hæresis...qui dicunt Paulum apostolum in epistolis præcepisse feminas diaconas debere fieri, quia eas commemorat post diaconos.—Sigebert. Chron. Ann. 526. in Biblioth. Sanct. Patr. Par. 1589. Tom. VII. col. 1384.]

[[3] Quicunque sacerdos viduus ad secundas nuptias quod cuique liberum est, transierit, is nihil habet cum clero commune.—Sigism. Liber. Rex. Moscov. Comment. p. 21. Inter Rer. Moscov. Auctor. Francof. 1600.]

tain wives[4], have not received the sacrament of confirmation[5], have been baptized of hereticks[6], these may not be priests, say the Papists: or if either they have not been trained up in the Family, or be not elders in the said Family of [a]Love[7].

Test. Rhem. An. 1 Tim. iii. 2. Concil. Trid. Sess. 23. cap. 4. 1 Quæst. I. ventum.

ARTICLE XXIV.

Of speaking in the congregation in such a tongue as the people understand not.

It is a thing plainly repugnant to the word of God, and the custom of the primitive church, to have publick prayer in the church, or to minister the sacraments in a tongue not understood of the people.

The proposition.

Public prayer and the sacraments must be ministered in a tongue understood of the common people.

The proof from God's word.

This assertion needeth small proof. For whoso is persuaded (as all true Christians of understanding are) that what

[a] Such ought not to busy themselves about the word. H. N. Document. Sent. chap. III. § 1. Exhortat. chap. XVI. § 16.

[[4] Sanctissimus mos est Romanæ ecclesiæ, rationique et scripturis consentaneus, atque a majoribus acceptus; quo neminem ad sacros ordines admittit nisi cœlibem, aut qui de uxoris consensu castitatem suam Deo consecravit.—Coster. Enchirid. Controv. Colon. Agr. 1608. c. 15. De Cœl. Sacerd. p. 561.

The husband of one wife. The apostle, by this place we now treat of, neither commandeth, nor counselleth, nor wisheth, nor would have bishops or priests to marry, or such only to be received as have been married: but that such an one as hath been married (so it were but once, and that to a virgin) may be made bishop or priest. Which is no more than an inhibition that none having been twice married, or being *bigamus,* should be admitted to that holy order.—Test. Rhem. Rhemes, 1582. Ann. 1 Tim. iii. 2.]

[[5] Prima tonsura non initientur qui sacramentum confirmationis non susceperint. —Conc. Harduin. Par. 1714. Tom. x. col. 140. Conc. Trid. Sess. XXIII. cap. IV.]

[[6] Sed nostræ lex ecclesiæ est, venientibus ab hæreticis, qui tamen illic baptizati sunt, per manus impositionem laicam tantum tribuere communionem, nec ex his aliquem in clericatus honorem vel exiguum subrogare.—Corp. Jur. Canon. Antv. 1648. Decret. Gratian. Sec. Pars, Caus. I. Quæst. I. cap. 18. p. 122.]

[[7] Neither yet is there also any man that preacheth or teacheth the word or the doctrine of Christ, but such as have first been obedient disciples of the word and of the doctrine of Jesu Christ. And even so, under the obedience of the Love of Christ are taught, &c.—H. N. Dicta, or Documental Sentences. Translated, &c. p. 5. b. cap. III. § 1, and First Exhort. cap. XVI. § 16. See above, p. 138, note 9.]

1 Cor. xiv. 6, 9, 14. Ibid. 17, 26. Ibid. 9. Ibid. 14. Ibid. 7, 11. Ibid. 11, 16. Matt. xv. 8. 1 Cor. xiv. 23.

is done publicly in the church by a strange language, not understood of the people, profiteth not the congregation, edifieth not the weak, instructeth not the ignorant, inflameth not the zeal, offendeth the hearers, abuseth the people, displeaseth God, bringeth religion into contempt, easily will think, that where the prayers be said, or the sacraments administered in a tongue not understood of the vulgar sort, neither is the word of God regarded, nor the custom of the purer and primitive church observed.

Conf. Helv. II. c. 22. Witt. c. 27. August. de Missa, Art. III. Suevic. cap. 21.

This article no church doth doubt of, and very many by their extant confessions do allow[1].

Adversaries unto this truth.

But there is nothing either so true or apparent which hath by all men at any time been acknowledged. So contrary to this truth

Epiphan. Hæres. 19.

In old time the Ossenes[2] made their prayers unto God always in a strange language, which they learned of Elxeus

D. Iren. Lib. I. cap. 8.

their founder. And the Marcosians[3], at the ministration of baptism used certain Hebrew words, not to edify, but to terrify and astonish the minds of the weak and ignorant people.

An. Geufræus, Aulæ Tur. Lib. II.

In these days the Turks[4] perform all their superstitions

[1 Taceant ergo omnes peregrinæ linguæ in cœtibus sacris. Omnia proponantur lingua vulgari, et quæ eo in loco ab hominibus in cœtu intelligatur.—Harm. Conf. Sect. xv. Conf. Helv. Post. cap. XXII. Sicut enim conciones et precationes lingua ecclesiæ nota habendæ sunt, ita et sacramenta noto sermone dispensanda sunt...consensus catholicæ ecclesiæ hoc exigit, ut necessaria ministeria ecclesiæ fiant sermone vernaculo.—Ibid. p. 169. Conf. Virtemb. cap. XXVII. ...contra expressum Spiritus Sancti præceptum, in ea omnia dicuntur et canuntur lingua, quam non solum populus non intelligit, sed nonnunquam ne ipsi quidem, qui ex illis cantionibus et precibus vivunt.—Ibid. p. 170. Conf. Suev. cap. XXI. ...retinetur...missa apud nos ...servantur et usitatæ ceremoniæ fere omnes præterquam quod Latinis cantionibus admiscentur alicubi Germanicæ, quæ additæ sunt ad docendum populum....Et non modo Paulus præcipit uti lingua intellecta populo in ecclesia: sed etiam ita constitutum est humano jure.—Ibid. p. 132. Conf. August. Pars II. De Abus. Subl. Art. III. De Missa.]

[2 *Τίσι δὲ λόγοις καὶ κενοφωνίαις ὕστερον ἐν τῇ βίβλῳ ἀπατᾷ λέγων, μηδεὶς ζητήσῃ τὴν ἑρμηνείαν, ἀλλ' ἢ μόνον ἐν τῇ εὐχῇ τάδε λεγέτω. καὶ αὐτὰ δῆθεν ἀπὸ Ἑβραϊκῆς διαλέκτου μετενέγκας, ὡς ἀπὸ μέρους κατειλήφαμεν οὐδὲν ὄντα τὰ παρ' αὐτῷ φανταζόμενα.*—Epiphan. Opp. Paris. 1622. Tom. I. p. 42. Adv. Hær. Lib. I. Hær. 19.]

[3 *Ἄλλοι δὲ Ἑβραϊκά τινα ὀνόματα ἐπιλέγουσι πρὸς τὸ μᾶλλον καταπληξάσθαι τοὺς τελειουμένους.*—Iren. Adv. Hær. Oxon. 1702. Lib. I. cap. 18. p. 90.]

[4 Illi autem (sacerdotes) qui etiam interpretari secundum textum noverint,

in the Arabian language, thinking it not only unmeet, but also an unlawful thing, for the common sort of persons to understand their Mahometan mysteries.

The Jacobite priests[5] do use a tongue at their church ministrations and meetings which the vulgar people cannot comprehend.

Magdeburg. Eccles. Hist. Cent. 12. cap. 5.

The divine liturgy among the Russians[6] is compounded partly of the Greek, and partly of the Sclavonian language.

Alex. Guag. de Relig. Mosc. p. 230.

The papists will have all divine service, prayers, and sacraments, and that throughout the world, ministered only in the Latin tongue; but which few men of the common people do understand; some of them holding that it is not necessary that we understand our prayers; and that prayers[7] not understood of the people are acceptable to God; and all of them maintaining that he is accursed whosoever doth affirm how the mass ought to be celebrate only in the vulgar tongue[a].

Test. Rhem. [Marg.] Annot. p. 463.
Test. Rhem. An. Matt. xxi. 16

Article XXV.

Of the Sacraments.

Sacraments, ordained of Christ, (1) *be not only badges or tokens of Christian men's profession, but rather they be* (2) *certain sure witnesses, and effectual signs of grace, and God's good will towards us, by which he doth work invisibly in us,* (3) *and not only quicken, but also strengthen and con-*

[a] Si quis dixerit, Lingua tantum vulgari Missam celebrari debere, Anathema sit. Concil. Trid. Sess. 22. Can. 9. [Concil. Harduin. Tom. x. col. 129.]

---

peritissimi habentur: quoniam non vulgari lingua Turcica sed Arabica a Mehemmeto sunt tradita, quod nephas esse putant, si vulgari lingua interpretata describerentur.—Ant. Geufræus, Aul. Turc. (Latine reddita) Basil. 1577. Lib. II. p. 44.]

[[5] Sacerdotes lingua utuntur propria, quam laici non intelligunt.—Magdeburg. Eccl. Hist. Basil. 1560, &c. Cent. XII. cap. 5. fol. 855.]

[[6] Sacrum sive missa Sclavonica lingua apud illos peragitur intermixtis etiam aliquando cantionibus Græcis.—Guagn. de Relig. Moscov. Spiræ Nemet. 1582. p. 230.]

[[7] Young children's prayers proceeding from the instinct of God's Spirit be acceptable: and so the voices of the like, or of other simple folk now in the church, though themselves understand not particularly what they say, be marvellous grateful to Christ.—Test. Rhem. Rhemes, 1582. Ann. Matth. xxi. 16. p. 61.]

firm our faith in him. (4) *There be two sacraments ordained of Christ our Lord in the gospel, that is to say, Baptism, and the Supper of the Lord. Those five commonly called sacraments, that is to say,* (5) *Confirmation,* (6) *Penance,* (7) *Orders,* (8) *Matrimony, and* (9) *Extreme Unction, are not to be accounted*[1] *for sacraments of the gospel, being such as have grown partly of the corrupt following of the apostles, partly are states of life allowed in the scriptures; but yet have not like nature of sacraments with Baptism and the Lord's Supper, for that they have not any visible sign or ceremony ordained of God.*

(10) *The sacraments were not ordained of Christ to be gazed upon, or to be carried about, but that we should duly use them.* (11) *And in such only as worthily receive the same they have a wholesome effect or operation: but they that receive them unworthily, purchase to themselves damnation, as Saint Paul saith.*

The propositions.

1. The sacraments ordained of Christ be badges or tokens of our profession which be Christians.

2. The sacraments be certain sure witnesses, and effectual signs of grace, and God his good will towards us.

3. By the sacraments God doth quicken, strengthen, and confirm our faith in him.

4. Christ hath ordained but two sacraments in his holy gospel.

5. Confirmation,
6. Penance,
7. Orders,
8. Matrimony,
9. Extreme Unction,

} is no sacrament.

10. The sacraments are not to be abused, but rightly to be used of us all.

11. All which receive the sacraments[2] receive not therewithal the things signified by the sacraments.

[[1] Compted, 1607.] [[2] Sacrament, 1607.]

Proposition I.

The sacraments ordained of Christ be badges, or tokens of our profession, which be Christians.

The proof from God's word.

The sacraments are badges, or tokens, both of Christians, and of Christianity.

Of Christians. For by them are visibly discerned the faithful from pagans, and Christians from the Jews, Turks, and all profane atheists.

Of Christianity. For, as circumcision, in the old law, was a token how the corrupt and carnal affections of the mind should be subdued, and that the Lord requireth not so much an outward of the body, as an inward circumcision of the heart; so baptism telleth us, that being once dead unto sin, we are to live unto righteousness, that all we, which have been baptized into[3] Jesus Christ, have been baptized into his death, &c., and must walk in newness of life, &c., for we have put on Christ by baptism.

Deut. x. 16, & xxxix. 6. Jer. iv. 4. Acts vii. 51. Rom. ii. 28. Phil. iii. 3. Col. ii. 1. Rom. vi. 3, &c. Gal. iii. 27.

And as the Paschal Lamb was to the Jews a token that the flight of sin should always be fresh in memory, and that it should be celebrated, not with old leaven, neither in the leaven of maliciousness, but with the unleavened bread of sincerity and truth; so the participation of one loaf and of one cup in the Lord his supper doth commend unto our consideration a sweet concord, a brotherly unanimity, and a constant continuance in the true worship of God, without favouring of idolatry in any respct.

1 Cor. v. 8. 1 Cor. x. 7.

This do the godly in all their churches, and throughout the world, both teach and testify[4].

Conf. Helv. 2. cap. 9, & 1. Art. XX. August. Art. XIII. Saxon. Art. XII.

[[3] Unto, 1607.]

[[4] Et quantum quidem quod attinet ad illud quod in sacramentis est præcipuum, et res ipsa, paria sunt utriusque populi (sc. Judæorum et Christianorum) sacramenta ...Utrique populo data sunt illa ut signa, adeoque obsignationes gratiæ et promissionum Dei, quæ in memoriam reducant, reparentque maxima Dei beneficia, quibus item fideles ab omnibus aliis orbis religionibus sejungerentur, &c.—Harm. Conf. Sect. XII. p. 71. Conf. Helv. Post. cap. XIX. ...asserimus sacramenta non solum tesseras quasdam societatis humanæ: sed et gratiæ divinæ symbola esse, quibus ministri Domino (ad eum finem quem ipse promittit, offert, et efficit) cooperantur, &c.—Ibid. p. 74. Conf. Helv. Prior. Art. XX. De usu sacramentorum docent, sacramenta instituta esse, non modo ut sint notæ professionis inter homines, sed multo magis, ut sint signa et testimonia voluntatis Dei erga nos, proposita ad excitandam et confirmandam fidem in his qui utuntur eis.—Ibid. p. 83. Conf. August. Art. XIII. Discernunt ecclesiam a cæteris gentibus, et ritus quidam divi-

The adversaries unto this truth.

Magdeburg. Eccles. Histor. Cent. XII. c. 5. Bulling. cont. Anab. Lib. II. c. 4. Altham. Conc. Lo. pag. lo. 191. D. Saravia, Def. Tract. de divers. Ministr. gradibus, c. 14. Holinsh. Chr. fol. 1299.

Ungodly therefore, and in a cursed state are they, which equal other things with the sacraments, to discern Christians from pagans; so the Jacobites[1] imprint the sign of the cross on their arms, foreheads, &c. to be known from Christians.

Which contemn the sacraments, as of none account; so do the Anabaptists[2].

There be (saith D. Saravia[3]) which hold how the sacraments were to be administered only at the first planting of the church by the apostles and evangelists; but do not appertain unto us in these days. It was also one of Matthew Hamant's heresies, that the sacraments are not necessary in the church of God[4].

Theodor. Lib. IV. c. 11. Pattern of the pres. Tem. Ramsey's Confess.

Which think the sacraments are but only civil and ceremonial badges of an outward church: such generally be all atheists and hypocrites; particularly the Messalians[5] and Family of Love, who think that for obedience sake to magistrates the sacraments are to be received[6], but are to none effect to the perfect ones in the Family.

nitus instituti, qui nominantur usitate sacramenta, ut baptismus et cœna Domini: quæ tamen non sunt tantum signa professionis, sed multo magis (ut vetustus dixit) signa gratiæ, &c.—Ibid. p. 84. Conf. Saxon. Art. XII.]

[1 Cruces porro sibi inurunt, alii in brachiis, alii in genis, alii in fronte, ob reverentiam crucis utque a paganis sese discernant.—Magdeburg. Eccl. Hist. Basil. 1562, &c. Cent. XII. cap. 5. fol. 855.]

[2 Eodem modo sacramenta fidelibus supervacanea judicabant: aut saltem non necessaria esse, et exiguam utilitatem habere.—Bulling. Adv. Anabapt. (Simler. Vers. Lat.) Tiguri, 1560. p. 42. b. Lib. II. cap. 4. Horrendum dictu quantum suggillent pædobaptismum, Sathanæ traditionem, magno pietatis zelo, tradunt esse.... Dominicam cœnam evacuant, et diris modis corrumpunt....Præterquam quod pædobaptismum damnant, nihil omnino tribuunt baptismo nisi quod sit christianorum nota, qua discernuntur ab gentibus, more civili, &c.—Althamer. Concil. Loc. Noremberg. 1535. Loc. CXCI. pp. 211, 12.]

[3 Quid enim si quis...dicat sacramenta illis initiis fuisse tantum ab apostolis et evangelistis ministranda; nec quicquam ad nostra pertinere tempora? Non desunt qui hunc defendunt errorem.—Saravia, Def. Tract. de Divers. Ministr. Grad. Lond. 1594. cap. 14. p. 237.]

[4 Holinsh. Chron. Lond. 1587. Vol. III. fol. 1299.]

[5 *Μεσσαλίανοι δὲ...τὸ μὲν βάπτισμα φασὶ μηδὲν ὀνεῖν τοὺς προσίοντας.*—Theodoret. Opp. Par. 1642-84. Tom. IV. p. 242. D. Hær. Fab. Lib. IV. cap. 11. *ταύτης ἐγένοντο τῆς αἱρέσεως ἀρχηγοὶ Δαδόης τε καὶ Σάββας....οἱ τῆς μὲν ἐκκλησιαστικῆς οὐκ ἀπέστησαν κοινωνίας...οὐδὲν οὔτε ὀνίνασθαι, οὔτε λωβᾶσθαι φάσκοντες τὴν θείαν τροφὴν, περὶ ἧς ὁ δεσπότης ἔφη Χριστὸς, ὁ τρώγων μου τὴν σάρκα, κ.τ.λ.*—Id. Tom. III. p. 670. c. Eccl. Hist. Lib. IV.]

[6 These references the editor has been unable to verify.]

Proposition II.

The sacraments be certain sure witnesses, and effectual signs of grace, and God his good will towards us.

The proof from God's word.

Infinitely doth God declare his unspeakable and incomprehensible good will to manward, yet in these days by none outward things more notably and effectually than by the sacraments. For

Of baptism saith Christ, "He that believeth and is baptized shall be saved." (Mark xvi. 16.) And Peter, "Amend your lives, and be baptized every one, &c., for the remission of sins." (Acts ii. 38.) And Paul, "Husbands, love your wives, even as Christ loved the church, and gave himself for it, that he might sanctify it and cleanse it by the washing of water through the word," &c. (Ephes. v. 25, 26, &c.)

And of the Lord's supper saith our Saviour Christ, touching the bread, "This is my body, which is given, and broken for you:" (Luke xxii. 19. 1 Cor. xi. 24.) and of the cup, "This is my blood of the new Testament, that is shed for many, for the remission of sins." (Matt. xxvi. 28. Luke xxii. 20.)

This truth do the purer churches of these days everywhere acknowledge[7].

Conf. Helv. I. Art. XX. XXII. & II. cap. 19, 20, 21. Bohem. cap. 11, 12, 13. Gal. Art. XXXIV. XXVIII. Belg. Art. XXXIII. XXXV. August. Art. IX. XIII. Wittemb. Art. X. XIX. Suevica, Art. XVI. XVIII.

The adversaries unto this truth.

Contrary hereunto the Papists erroneously do hold, that

The sacraments of the new law do confer grace *ex opere operato*[8]. (Concil. Trid. Sess. 7. Can. 8.)

[[7] See above, p. 245, note 4, and add the following: Instituit (Deus sacramenta)....ut....propitiæ beneplacitæque voluntatis erga nos Dei, certa contestatio essent et confirmatio, et veritati quæ his significatur testimonium perhiberent.—Harm. Conf. Sect. XII. p. 78. Conf. Bohem. cap. XI. Credimus adjuncta esse verbo sacramenta amplioris confirmationis causa, nimirum ut sint gratiæ Dei pignora, et tesseræ quibus infirmæ et rudi fidei nostræ subveniatur.—Ibid. p. 81. Conf. Gall. Art. XXXIV. Credimus Deum...sacramenta nobis instituisse ut...essent divinæ erga nos benevolentia, donorumque ejus certissima nobis pignora, ad fidem nostram fovendam, et sustentandam comparata.—Ibid. p. 82. Conf. Belg. Art. XXXIII. ...docent sacramenta instituta esse, non modo ut sint notæ professionis inter homines, sed multo magis, ut sint signa et testimonia voluntatis Dei erga nos, proposita ad excitandam et confirmandam fidem in his qui utuntur eis.—Ibid. p. 83. Conf. August. Art. XIII. ...Baptisma et eucharistia quæ apud veteres sacramenti nomen non solum ideo credimus obtinuisse, quod sint invisibilis gratiæ visibilia signa...sed eo etiam quod per ea Christo nos consecramus, et veluti sacramento fidei obstringamus.—Ibid. p. 85. Conf. Suev. Art. XVI. For the remaining references, see in the Articles, Of Baptism, and Of the Supper of the Lord.]

[[8] Si quis dixerit per ipsa nova legis sacramenta ex opere operato non conferri gratiam...anathema sit.—Concil. Harduin. Tom. x. col. 52. Conc. Trid. Sess. VII. De Sacrament. can. 8.]

The sacraments of the old and new Testament in this do differ; for that the sacraments of the old Testament did only shadow forth salvation, but the sacraments of the new do confer, and work salvation[1], and do justify (not only signify God his good will toward us) by reason of the work done, which is the outward sacraments[2]. Concil. Flor. Bonavent. Lib. IV. Dist. I. q. 5. Gabr. Biel. Lib. IV. Dist. I. q. 3.

Proposition III.

By the sacraments God doth quicken, strengthen, and confirm our faith in him.

The proof from God's word.

Acts ii. 38. "Be baptized every one of you in the name of Jesus Christ for the remission of your sins, and ye shall receive the gift of the Holy Ghost," saith St Peter.

Eph. v. 25, 26. "Christ he gave himself for the church, that he might sanctify it, and cleanse it by the washing of water through the word."

1 Cor. x. 16. "The cup of blessing which we bless, is it not the communion of the blood of Christ? The bread which we break, is it not the communion of the body of Christ?" saith St Paul.

Conf. Helv. I. Art. XXI. & II. cap. 10, 20, 21. Basil. Art. VI. Boh. c. 11, 12. Gal. Art. XXXIV. Belg. Art. XXXIII. XXXIV. August. Art. XIII. Suevica, cap. 17. The same is affirmed by the reformed churches[3].

[1 Novæ legis septem sunt sacramenta...Quæ multum a sacramentis differunt antiquæ legis. Illa enim non causabant gratiam, sed eam solum per passionem Christi dandam esse figurabant: hæc vero nostra et continent gratiam et ipsam digne suscipientibus conferunt.—Decr. Eugen. Pap. in Concil. Florent. Concil. Harduin. Paris. 1714. Tom. IX. col. 437. D.]

[2 Sed certe multo probabilius est quod Magister Hugo posuit, quod cum in illo opere operato esset professio fidei facta, quod ratione fidei conjunctæ erat in illis primo et per illa (per accidens tamen) justificatio. Sed in hoc est differentia ipsorum (sc. sacramentorum veteris legis) ad nova, quod in sacramentis novæ legis quantum ad opera operata est justificatio, non tantum per accidens, sed etiam per se.—Bonavent. Opp. Mogunt. 1609. Tom. V. In Lib. Quart. Sent. Dist. I. Quæst. 5. fol. 12. Secundo notandum...quod signum aliquod conferre gratiam, dupliciter potest intelligi. Uno modo ex ipso signo seu sacramento; vel ut alii dicunt, ex opere operato: itaque eo ipso quod opus illud puta signum aut sacramentum exhibetur, nisi impediat obex peccati mortalis, gratia confertur: sicque præter exhibitionem signi foris exhibiti non requiritur bonus motus interior in suscipiente, quo de condigno vel de congruo gratiam mereatur, sed sufficit quod suscipiens non ponat obicem.—Gab. Biel. Comment. in Sent. Brixiæ, 1574. In Lib. Quart. Dist. I. Quæst. 3. p. 28.]

[3 See above, p. 150, note 1, and add the following: Baptisma quidem ex institutione Domini est lavacrum regenerationis quam Dominus electis suis visibili signo per ecclesiæ ministerium...exhibet.—Harm. Conf. Sect. XIII. p. 91. Conf. Helv. Prior. Art. XXI. Sunt autem sacramenta...sacræ actiones a Deo ipso institutæ...quibus...promissiones suas obsignat...adeoque fidem nostram Spiritu Dei in cordibus nostris operante, roborat et auget.—Ibid. Sect. XII. p. 70. Conf. Helv.

Howbeit this faith is not necessarily tied unto the visible signs and sacraments. For

Without the sacraments many have lived and died who pleased God, and are, no doubt, saved, either in respect of their own faith, (as we are to think of all the godly, both men who were born and died afore the institution of circumcision in the wilderness, and in the time of grace, &c., yet by some extremity could not receive the seal of the covenant, and women, who afore and under the law for many years were partakers of no sacrament, and never of one sacrament,) or that be heirs of the promise.

Some have faith, afore they receive any of the sacraments.

So had Abraham; the Jews, unto whom Peter preached; the Samaritans, the eunuch, Cornelius the centurion; and have the godly of discretion, wheresoever not yet baptized.

Rom. iv. 9, 10. Acts ii. 41. Acts viii. 12. Acts viii. 37. Acts x. 48.

Some neither afore, nor at the instant, nor yet afterward, though daily they receive the sacraments, will have faith; such are like unto Judas, Ananias and Sapphira, Simon Magus, the old Israelites, and the wicked Corinthians.

John xiii. 26. Acts v. Acts viii. 13. 1 Cor. x. 5. 1 Cor. xi. 27. Rom. x. 14.

In some the sacraments do effectually work in process of time, by the help of God's word read or preached, which engendereth faith: such is the state principally of infants, elected unto life and salvation, and increasing in years.

The adversaries unto this truth.

Therefore do they err which teach or hold that

They never go to heaven which die without the seals of the covenant: so think the Papists of infants which die unbaptized[4].

Javel. Phil. Chr. tract. 4. de felicit. Ch. c. 3. & Viguer. Instit. Theol. cap. 16. Sect. 4, &c. Spec. Pereg. Quæst. dec. I. cap. 3, q. 5.

Post. cap. XIX. Cf. Ibid. Sect. XIII. p. 89. cap. XX. et Sect. XIV. p. 109. cap. XXI. Credimus autem firmiter ipsummet Christum cibum esse credentium animarum ad vitam æternam, et nostras animas per veram fidem in crucifixum Christum carne et sanguine Christi cibari et potari.—Ibid. p. 116. Conf. Basil. Art. VI. Instituit autem et constituit ea (Deus sacramenta)...ut sicut prædicatione verbi, ita etiam per sacramentorum in oculos incurrentem administrationem et mysteria horum, fidei commodaretur atque inserviretur.—Ibid. Sect. XII. p. 78. Conf. Bohem. cap. XI. In the Conf. Saxon. and Conf. Suev. the statement of the Proposition is not directly corroborated. But see also the references under Arts. XXVII. VIII.]

[4 Ex prædictis apparet quod nullus per solam fidem interiorem fuit salvatus absque aliqua protestatione exteriori per aliqua signa, quæ dicuntur sacramenta, nec etiam parvuli nati.—Viguer. Inst. Theol. Col. Agrip. 1607. cap. xvi. De Sacram. v. 9. p. 401. ...Limbus puerorum et limbus sanctorum patrum differunt quantum ad quatuor. Primo quantum ad spem vitæ æternæ, quia pueris decedentibus cum peccato originali non adest spes beatæ vitæ....Secundo quantum ad crimen....Pueris

Concil. Triden. Sess. 7. can. 13. They are damned (though they receive the sacraments) that will not receive them after the received and approved manner of the church of Rome[1].

Lear. Disc. There is no way of salvation but by faith[2]; hereby excluding infinite souls from the kingdom of heaven which depart from this world before they do believe.

Test. Rhem. An. Gal. iii. 27. Lear. Disc. pag. 3. None believe but such as are baptized, say the Papists[3]; as hear the word of God preached, say the puritans.

Test. Rhem. An. mar. p. 357. Ibid. Annot. marg. pag. 391. The sacraments give grace *ex opere operato*, and bring faith *ex opere operato*[4].

Ibid. Annot. 1 Pet. iii. 21. The sacrament of baptism is cause of the salvation of infants[5].

Proposition IV.

Christ hath ordained but two sacraments in his gospel.

The proof from God's word.

A sacrament, according to the etymology of the word (as the schoolmen do write), is a sign of an holy thing. Which being true, then have there been and still are, by so many above either two or seven sacraments, as there be and have been above two or seven things, which are signs of sacred and holy things.

But according to the nature thereof, a sacrament is a covenant of God his favour to manward, confirmed by some outward sign or seal instituted by himself. Which also hath been sometimes special; either to some men, and that extra-

autem est impedimentum ex parte naturæ et personæ: et ideo eis debetur pena eternalis.—Spec. Peregr. Quæst. Prim. Dec. cap. III. Quæst. v. fol. 101. See above, p. 137, note 6. The reference to Javellus the editor has been unable to verify.]

[1 Si quis dixerit receptos et approbatos ecclesiæ catholicæ ritus in solemni sacramentorum administratione adhiberi consuetos aut sine peccato a ministris pro libito omitti, aut in novos alios per quemcumque ecclesiarum pastorem mutari posse; anathema sit.—Concil. Harduin. Tom. x. col. 53. Conc. Trid. Sess. VII. De Sacram. can. 13.]

[2 The work referred to here, and again below, has not been found.]

[3 Here we learn that by the sacrament of Baptism also we put on Christ, which is to put on faith, hope, charity and all christian justice....And the adversaries' evasion that it is faith which worketh in the sacrament, and not the sacrament itself, is plainly false: Baptism giving grace and faith itself to the infant that had none before.—Test. Rhem. Rhemes, 1582. Annot. Gal. iii. 27. p. 504.]

[4 Our sacraments of the new law give *ex opere operato* that grace and justice of faith which here is commended.—Ibid. Marg. Annot. p. 391.]

[5 ...infants, to whom the sacrament (of baptism) is cause of salvation.—Ibid. Annot. 1 Pet. iii. 21. p. 661.]

ordinarily by things natural sometimes, as the tree of life was to Adam, and the rainbow to Noah; and sometimes by things supernatural, as the smoking furnace was to Abraham, the fleece of wool to Gideon, and the dial to Hezekiah; or to some nation, as the sacrifices, circumcision, and the Paschal Lamb, was to the Jews.

Gen. iii. 3. Gen. ix. 9, 13. Gen. xv. 17, 18. Judges vi. 37. 1 Kings xx. 11. Isai. xxxviii. 8.

And sometimes general to the whole church militant, and ordinary, as in the time of the gospel. And then a sacrament is defined to be a ceremony ordained immediately by Christ himself, who by some earthly and outward element doth promise everlasting favour and felicity to such as with true faith and repentance do receive the same. And such sacraments in the New Testament we find only to be baptism and the Lord's supper.

Matt. xxviii. 19. Mark xvi. 16. John iii. 5. Acts ii. 38. Luke xxii. 19. John vi. 53. 1 Cor. xi. 24.

This is the judgment also of the churches protestant[6].

Confess. Helvet. I. Art. XX. & II. cap. 19. Basil. Art. V. sect. 2. Gal. Art. XXXV. Belg. Art. XXXIII. Saxon. Art. XII. Suevica, Art. XVI.

The errors and adversaries unto this truth.

In a contrary opinion are divers, and namely,

The Jews and Turks; for they deny all the sacraments of the church, as we do hold them.

The Euchites[7], who say, that prayer only, and not the sacraments, are to be used.

Theodoret.

The Schwenkfeldians, who contemn not only the word preached, but the sacraments also, as superfluous, depending wholly upon revelations.

The Banisterians[8], who think there will be a time, and that in this world, when we shall need no sacraments.

Unfold. of untruths.

[6 Signa, quæ in ecclesia Christi sacramenta vocantur, duo sunt, Baptismus et Eucharistia.—Harm. Conf. Sect. XII. p. 74. Conf. Helv. Prior. Art. XX. Novi populi sacramenta sunt, Baptismus et Cœna Dominica.—Ibid. p. 70. Conf. Helv. Post. cap. XIX. In ecclesia usurpantur eadem sacramenta videlicet Baptismus in introitu ad ecclesiam, et Cœna Domini suo tempore, &c.—Ibid. p. 77. Conf. Basil. Art. V. § 2. Agnoscimus duo tantum sacramenta, toti ecclesiæ communia, &c.—Ibid. p. 81. Conf. Gall. Art. XXXV. Sunt vero illa (sc. sacramenta) duo duntaxat, nimirum sacramentum Baptismi et Sacræ Cœnæ Domini nostri Jesu Christi.—Ibid. p. 82. Conf. Belg. Art. XXXIII. Cf. Ibid. p. 84. Conf. Saxon. Art. XII. et p. 85. Conf. Suev. Art. XVI.]

[7 The Messalian heretics were so called. See above, pp. 86, 149: ἑκάστῳ γὰρ φασὶν ἀνθρώπῳ τικτομένῳ παραυτίκα συνέπεσθαι δαίμονα, καὶ τοῦτον εἰς τὰς ἀτόπους πράξεις παραινεῖν. τοῦτον δὲ οὔτε τὸ βάπτισμα, οὔτε ἄλλο τι δύναται τῆς ψυχῆς ἐξελάσαι, ἀλλὰ μόνη τῆς προσευχῆς ἡ ἐνέργεια.—Theod. Opp. Tom. IV. p. 242. D. Hær. Fab. Lib. IV. cap. 11.]

[8 This reference the editor has been unable to verify.]

The Papists, who publish,

Howlet, Reas. 7. That we leave out no less than six of the seven sacraments[1].

Catec. Canis. Vaux. How there be seven sacraments of the new Testament[2].

Test. Rhem. An. Jam. v. 24. Concil. Trid. Sess. 7. Can. 1. That he is accursed that shall say there be either more or fewer than seven sacraments; or that any of them is not verily and properly a sacrament; or that they be not all seven instituted of Christ himself[3].

Stella Clericorum. That there are seven sacraments, whereof two are voluntary, and at the discretion of men to be taken or not, as matrimony and holy orders; and five are necessary, and must be taken; and of these five, three, to wit, baptism, confirmation, and orders, are but once to be taken, because they imprint an indelible character in the soul of the receivers; and four be reiterable, and may often be received, as the sacrament eucharistical, matrimony, penance, and extreme unction, because at their first ministration they leave in the soul no indelible character[4].

Proposition V.

Confirmation is no sacrament.

Touching confirmation, the sentence and judgment of the true church is, that rightly used, as it was in the primitive church, it is no sacrament; but a part of Christian discipline, profitable for the whole church of God. For the ancient confirmation was nothing else than an examination of such as in their infancy had received the sacrament of baptism, and were then, being of good discretion, able to yield an account of their belief, and to testify with their own mouths what their

[[1] The second thing, which the Protestants' service leaveth out, is no less than six of the seven sacraments which the Catholic service of God doth use.—Howlet, [i. e. Robert Persons] A Brief Discourse, &c. Douay, 1580. Reas. VII. p. 43. b.]

[[2] Quot sunt sacramenta? Septem, quæ a Christo per Apostolos accepta conservavit, ac fideliter dispensavit hucusque Christi sponsa et columna veritatis Ecclesia.—Canis. Op. Catech. Colon. 1606. Sacram. Quæst. 5. p. 206.

How many sacraments did Christ institute? Seven, which be expressed in the Scripture, &c.—Vaux, Catech. Antv. 1574. cap. IV. p. 60.]

[[3] Si quis dixerit sacramenta novæ legis non fuisse omnia a Jesu Christo Domino nostro instituta; aut esse plura vel pauciora quam septem: videlicet, Baptismum, Confirmationem, Eucharistiam, Pœnitentiam, Extremam Unctionem, Ordinem et Matrimonium: aut etiam aliquod horum septem non esse vere et proprie sacramentum; anathema sit.—Concil. Harduin. Tom. x. col. 52. Conc. Trid. Sess. VII. De Sacram. Can. 1.]

[[4] There is an error in the reference, but see Catech. Conc. Trident. Rom. 1566. pp. 92, 3.]

sureties in their names had promised at their baptism: which confession being made, and a promise of perseverance in the faith by them given, the bishop by sound doctrine, grave advice, and godly exhortations, confirmed them in that good profession; and laying his hands upon them, prayed for the increase of God his gifts and graces in their minds.

The popish confirmation all churches of God with us utterly do dislike, as no sacrament at all instituted by Christ[5].

Conf. Saxon. Art. XIX. Wittemb. c. 11. See the Proposition immediately precedent.

Errors and adversaries unto this truth.

Contrariwise the synagogue of Rome teacheth that confirmation is a sacrament, whereby the grace that was given in baptism is confirmed and made strong by the seven gifts of the Holy Ghost[6].

Of which their confirmation they give us four things principally to observe; viz.

I. The substance or matter, which is holy chrism confect (as they say), and made of oil-olive and balm, consecrated by a bishop[7].

See Canis. Catech. cap. 4.

II. The form and manner of ministering the same, consisting of the words of the bishop, which are, "I sign thee with the sign of the cross, and confirm thee with the chrism

[5 Notum est formulas consecrandi oleum, magicas et execrandas esse: ideo nec unctiones illæ, in quibus usus est olei, tolerandæ sunt. Et vetustas hos ritus longe aliter exercuit quam nunc exercentur....Sed ritus Confirmationis quem nunc Episcopi retinent, quid est nisi inanis Umbra?—Harm. Conf. Sect. XIII. p. 99. Conf. Saxon. Art. XIX. Non est nobis dubium quin Apostoli initio revelati et confirmati... contulerint impositione manuum admirandum donum Spiritus sancti....Sed ex personali et temporali facto Apostolorum, non est absque certo mandato Dei, generale et perpetuum sacramentum in Ecclesia statuendum. Et horribile auditu est, quod Sacramentum Confirmationis (quale episcopi suffraganei solent pueris impertire) excellat dignitate sua sacramentum Baptismi.—Ibid. p. 103. Conf. Virtemb. cap. XI. De Confirm.]

[6 In Baptismo regeneramur ad vitam: post Baptismum autem in hoc sacramento confirmamur ad pugnam...Nec dissentit ab eo quod Clemens testatur se ab Apostolis ipsis accepisse: cum regeneratus, inquiens, quis fuerit per aquam, postmodum septiformis Spiritus gratia ab Episcopo confirmetur.—Canis. Op. Catech. Colon. 1606. De Sacram. Confirm. Quæst. v. p. 242.]

[7 Quæ sunt necessaria ad conficiendum hoc Sacramentum (sc. Confirmationis)? A. Tria præcipue ad hoc requiruntur: sacramenti propria materia, certa verborum forma et Minister idoneus. B. Materia ex oleo et balsamo mixta est, quæ ab Episcopo consecrata, sacri Chrismatis nomen jam olim obtinuit, et in hoc Sacramento fronti solenni ritu illinitur. C. Forma verborum hæc præscripta est, Signo te signo Crucis, et confirmo te chrismate salutis, in nomine Patris et Filii et Spiritus Sancti. D. Minister Sacramenti hujus solus est Episcopus, ut Apostolorum exemplum forma et traditio retineantur.—Ibid. Quæst. III. pp. 237, 8.]

of salvation; in the name of the Father, &c.;" and of the actions both of a godfather or godmother already confirmed, holding up the child to the bishop; and of the bishop, first crossing him which is to be confirmed on the forehead with oil, and next striking the party confirmed on the ear[1].

III. The minister, who must be a bishop and none inferior [a]minister[2].

IV. The effect, or effects rather. For by confirmation they say, that

1. Sins are pardoned and remitted.
2. The grace of baptism is made perfect.
3. Such become men in Christ who afore were children.
4. Grace is given boldly to confess the name of Christ, and all things belonging to a Christian man.
5. The Holy Ghost is given to the full.
6. And perfect strength of the mind is attained[3].

But in so teaching dangerous and very damnable doctrine do they deliver. For

Catech. Trid. tit. de Confirm.

It is an error that confirmation is a sacrament, because it hath no institution from God, which is necessary to all and every sacrament; inasmuch as a sacrament cannot be ordained but by God only, even as the Papists themselves do confess[4].

[a] Nunquam erit Christianus, nisi in Confirmatione Episcopali fuerit confirmatus. *De consecrat.* Dist. 5. c. ut jejuni.

[[1] Consignat illis (Episcopus) Cruce frontem, quæ pudoris est sedes, ut constanter et intrepide nomen Domini confiteantur: impingit et alapam, ut Christianam militiam invicta patientia exercendam et ornandam esse sibi perpetua memoria retineant.—Ibid. Quæst. v. p. 242.]

[[2] Primum quidem illud proprie Confirmationi tribuitur, quod baptismi gratiam perficit. Qui enim per baptismum Christiani effecti sunt, quasi infantes modo geniti teneritatem adhuc et mollitiem quandam habent, ac deinde Chrismatis sacramento, adversus omnes carnis mundi et diaboli impetus robustiores fiunt, et eorum animus in fide omnino confirmatur ad confitendum et glorificandum nomen Domini nostri Jesu Christi, &c.—Catech. Conc. Trid. Rom. 1566. p. 128.]

[[3] Decr. Gratian. Tert. Pars, De Consecr. Dist. v. cap. 6. in Corp. Jur. Canon. Antv. 1648. p. 495; where, nisi confirmatione episcopali fuerit chrismatus.]

[[4] Deinceps videndum est, a quo hæc sacra et divina mysteria acceperimus... Sed ea quæstio difficilem explicationem habere non potest. Nam cum Deus sit, qui homines justos efficiat; ipsa vero sacramenta justitiæ adipiscendæ mirifica quædam instrumenta sint; patet unum eundemque Deum in Christo justificationis et sacramentorum auctorem agnoscendum esse. Præterea, sacramenta eam vim et efficientiam continent, quæ ad intimam animam penetrat. Cum vero unius Dei potentiæ proprium sit in corda et mentes hominum illabi; ex hoc etiam perspicitur, sacramenta a Deo ipso per Christum instituta esse.—Catech. Conc. Trid. Rom. 1566. p. 93.]

To say that popish confirmation is grounded upon God's word is to speak foul untruths. For in the scripture there is mention neither of the matter, that it must be chrism, and that made of oil-olive and balm, and the same consecrated of a bishop; nor of the form, that either a bishop must sign the party to be baptized with the sign of the cross, or that a godfather, &c. must be thereat; nor of the minister, that of necessity he must be a bishop that is to confirm; nor of the effects, that thereby sins are pardoned and released, and baptism consummated and made perfect.

It is an error to say there is any other ointment given to the strengthening of the church militant besides the Holy Ghost, 1 Joh. ii. 27.

It is an error to maintain that any bishop can give heavenly graces to any creature.

It is an error to ascribe salvation unto chrism, and not only unto Christ.

It savoureth of Donatism to measure the dignity of the sacraments by the worthiness of the ministers.

It is an error to say that men cannot be perfect Christians without popish confirmation.

It is an error that by confirmation the Holy Ghost is given to the full.

Proposition VI.

Penance is no sacrament.

Touching penance the Papists do publish four things to be noted, whereof none of them is truly grounded upon the word of God.

First, the matter, which they do say is partly the actions of the person penitent, which are sufficient contrition of his heart, perfect confession of all his sins, and that in particular with all the circumstances, as of time, place, &c., and satisfaction by deeds, which maketh an amends for all his offences; and partly the absolution of the priest.

Canis. Catech. cap. 4. Catech. Trid. de Pœnit

Secondly, the form, which in the priest is the words of absolution which he uttereth over the sinner: in the person penitent, it is his kneeling down at the priest's feet, his making the sign of the cross upon his breast, and his saying *Benedicite*, to his ghostly father. The priest (say they) beareth the person of God, and is the lawful judge over the penitent;

and may both absolve from the guilt of sin and inflict a punishment according to the offence[1].

Thirdly, the minister, who ordinarily is the curate of every parish, but extraordinarily and in the time of extreme necessity, or by licence, is any priest. And yet some sins are so grievous, as none may absolve but either the bishop or his penitentiary; as the crime of incest, breaking of vows, church-robbing, heresy, adultery: and some again none remit, or pardon, but the pope only or his legate; as burning of churches, violent striking a priest, counterfeiting of the pope's bulls, &c.

Fourthly, and last of all, the effect. Hereby, they say, the penitent sinner is purged, absolved, and made as clean from all sin as when he was newly baptized, and, besides, enriched with spiritual gifts and graces.

Conf. Helv. II. cap 14, 19. Bohem. cap. 5. August. Art. III. XI. XII. Sax. Art. XVI. XVII. Witt. Art. XIII. XV. Suevic. Art. XX.

The consideration hereof hath moved, besides the church of England, all other churches reformed, to shew their detestation of this new sacrament, as having no warrant from God's word[2].

[[1] Quando hoc sacramentum (sc. Pœnitentiæ) rite accipitur, et efficaciter operatur? *A.* Cum is qui remissionem peccatorum implorat, tres illas partes seu actiones adhibet, contritionem, confessionem et satisfactionem; quæ totam hominis ad Deum conversionem, pœnitentis officium, et renovationem complectuntur. De quibus ita Chrysostomus: Perfecta pœnitentia cogit peccatorem omnia libenter ferre: in corde ejus contritio, in ore confessio, in opere tota humilitas. Hanc esse frugiferam pœnitentiam Chrysostomus asserit, ut quibus modis Deum offendimus; offendimus autem corde, ore ac opere, iisdem reconciliemur Deo, corde quidem per contritionem, ore per confessionem, ac opere per satisfactionem.—Canis. Catech. Colon. 1606. p. 388. cap. IV. De Pœnit. Sacr. Quæst. IV. Jam, quoniam nihil fideli populo notius esse debet, quam hujus sacramenti materia; docendum est, in eo maxime hoc sacramentum ab aliis differre, quod aliorum sacramentorum materia est res aliqua naturalis, vel arte effecta; sacramenti vero pœnitentiæ quasi materia sunt actus pœnitentis, nempe contritio, confessio et satisfactio, ut a Tridentina Synodo declaratum est: qui quatenus in pœnitente, ad integritatem sacramenti, et plenam ac perfectam peccatorum remissionem ex Dei institutione requiruntur, hac ratione partes pœnitentiæ dicuntur....Sed formæ etiam explicatio pastoribus prætermittenda non est...est autem forma, Ego te absolvo....Diligenter vero ritus etiam qui ad hoc sacramentum adhibentur, fideles observabunt....nam quem peccatorum pœnitet, is se humili ac demisso animo ad pedes sacerdotis dejicit....In sacerdote autem qui in eum legitimus judex sedet, Christi Domini personam, et potestatem veneratur.—Catech. Conc. Trid. pp. 164, 5.]

[[2] Damnamus imprimis lucrosam papæ de pœnitentia doctrinam, &c.—Harm. Conf. Sect. VIII. p. 140. Conf. Helv. Post. cap. XIV. Sunt qui sacramenta novi populi septem numerent. Ex quibus nos pœnitentiam, ordinationem ministrorum non papisticam quidem illam sed apostolicam, et matrimonium agnoscimus instituta esse Dei utilia sed non sacramenta.—Ibid. Sect. XII. p. 70. Conf. Helv. Post. cap. XIX. Præterea ita instituuntur pœnitentes, ut curatores animarum suarum accedunt, et

The blasphemies are outrageous, and the errors many and monstrous, comprised in this doctrine of popish penance. For neither can the matter of this their sacrament, nor the form, nor the minister, nor the effect, be drawn from the word of God.

They say penance is a sacrament, and yet can they shew no element it hath to make it a sacrament.

Their contrition is against the truth: for no man is, or can be, sufficiently contrite for his sins.

To confess all sins, and that one after another with all circumstances, unto a priest, as it is impossible, so is it never enjoined by God, nor hath ever been practised by any of God's saints.

That any man in any measure can satisfy for his sins, it is blasphemy to say, and against the merits of Christ. And yet do the Papists teach it, as also that one man may satisfy for another[3]. Test. Rhem. in Col. i. 24.

An untruth is it, that any priest, bishop, or pope, hath power at his will to forgive sins; or can enjoin any punishment that can make an amends unto God for the least offence.

If penance purge men, and make them clean from all sin, then is there a time, and that very often in this life, when men in this life be perfect; which tendeth greatly to the error of the Catharans, Donatists, and Pelagians.

The doctrine of the Papists, that such persons as willingly depart out of this world without their shrift are damned, is damnable doctrine, and to be eschewed: and yet is it dispersed everywhere in their books[4]. Vaux, Catec. cap. 4. Catech. Trid. de Pœnit. Test. Rhem. Annotat. in Matt. xii. 31. Hill's Quartron. 13. Reas. p. 65. Petrus de Soto. Meth. Confess. par. 4. p. 156. A.

coram ipsis confiteantur Deo peccato sua; nemo tamen neque jubetur, neque urgetur enumerare peccata.—Ibid. Sect. VIII. p. 142. Conf. Bohem. cap. V. Damnant et illos qui...contendunt remissionem peccatorum contingere propter dignitatem contritionis, dilectionis, aut aliorum operum, &c.—Ibid. pp. 147, 8. Conf. Aug. Art. XI. De confessione peccatorum docent quod absolutio privata in ecclesiis retinenda sit, quanquam in confessione non sit necessaria delictorum enumeratio.—Ibid. Art. XII. Cf. Ibid. pp. 149, 50. De Abus. Art. III. Hic autem taxamus adversarios qui fingunt contritionem mereri remissionem peccatorum et oportere contritionem sufficientem esse.—Ibid. p. 153. Conf. Saxon. Art. XI. Cf. Ibid. p. 156. Art. XVII. Talem contritionem arbitramur quidem necessariam esse in vera pœnitentia, quam contritionem lex Dei in homine excitare solet: sed docere eam mereri remissionem peccatorum, et esse expiationem peccatorum coram Deo existimamus ab apostolica doctrina alienum esse.—Ibid. p. 158. Conf. Virtemb. Art. XIII. Cf. Ibid. p. 162. Art. XV. Nam innumeras animas illa de peccatis sacerdoti confitendis constitutio in gravem desperationem adegit, &c.—Ibid. Conf. Suev. Art. XX.]

[3 The works of one may satisfy for another.—Test. Rhem. Rhemes, 1582. Marg. Annot. on Coloss. i. 24. p. 538. See above, p. 58, note 7.]

[4 If any commit deadly sin after baptism, the only refuge is to the sacrament of

Proposition VII.

Orders is no sacrament.

The church of England, and of other places reformed, do acknowledge an order of making ministers in the church of God, where all things are to be done by order. But that order is a sacrament, none but disordered Papists will say: and yet they observe none order in speaking of the same; for among them

Canis. Catec. Some do make seven orders; whereof some they call inferior, and some superior: the inferior be the order, first, of porters, whose office is to keep the door, to expel the wicked, and to let in the faithful; next, exorcists, or conjurers, which have power to expel the devils; thirdly, lectors, or readers, who are to read lessons, and books in the church; and fourthly, acolytes, or candle-bearers, whose office is to bear cruets to the altar with wine and water, and to carry about candles and tapers[1].

penance: without which sacrament in act or in will, they that have committed mortal sin cannot be saved.—Vaux, Catech. Antv. 1574. ch. IV. p. 68.

Etenim sic statuant fideles, oportere eum, qui mortali scelere premitur, confessionis sacramento ad spiritualem vitam revocandum esse: quod quidem pulcherrima translatione a Domino aperte significatum videmus; cum hujus sacramenti administrandi potestatem clavem regni cœlorum appellavit. Ut enim locum aliquem ingredi nemo potest sine ejus opera cui claves commissæ sunt, sic intelligimus neminem in cœlum admitti, nisi fores a sacerdotibus quorum fidei claves Dominus tradidit, aperiantur.—Catech. Concil. Trident. Rom. 1566. p. 175.

Among all the sins against the Holy Ghost (which are commonly reckoned six) one only shall never be forgiven, that is dying without repentance wilfully, called final impenitence. Which sin he committeth that dieth with contempt of the Sacrament of Penance, obstinately refusing absolution by the church's ministry. —Test. Rhem. Ann. Matt. xii. 31. The catholic religion teacheth confession to a priest of all deadly sins which we can remember, under pain of damnation, &c.— Hill's Quartron of Reasons. Reason 13. p. 65.

The editor has been unable to find in the Methodus Confessionis any assertion corresponding to the statement made in the text.]

[1 Quot gradus in se continet hoc sacramentum (sc. ordinis)? *A.* Generatim quidem minores ordines, majoresque continet: minores scilicet quatuor, Ostiariorum, Lectorum, Exorcistarum, et Acolytorum: majores vero tres, nempe Subdiaconorum, Diaconorum ac Presbyterorum.—Canis. Catech. p. 388. cap. IV. De Ordinis Sacr. Quæst. iv. An account of the different orders, and their offices, is given in the "Testimonia" subjoined to this "Quæstio." The following are the passages which seem to be referred to in the text. *Ostiarii* sunt qui in veteri testamento janitores templi vocabantur, &c.—Hi denique inter sanctum et iniquum discernentes, eos tantum in ecclesia qui sunt fideles recipiunt.—Habent enim in potestate tam bonos recipiendi quam rejiciendi indignos (Isidor. Hispalen. de Off. Eccl. Lib. II. cap. 14). *Exorcistæ.* Invocant super catechumenos, vel super eos qui habent spiritum immundum, nomen Domini Jesu, adjurantes per eum ut egrediatur ab eis (Raban.

The superior is the order of sub-deacons, deacons, and of priests. The sub-deacons are to read the epistle at service-time, to prepare necessaries for ministration, and to assist the priest in ministration. The deacon's duty is to read the gospel, and also to assist the priest in ministration. The priest his part and office is, to minister sacraments, that is to say, baptism, penance, the Eucharist, and to sacrifice for the quick and the dead, anointing of the sick, and matrimony.

Others, numbering the seven sacraments, do quite overpass in silence the sacrament of order, and in place thereof mention the sacrament of priesthood, as Vaux[2]; of bishopdom, as Hugh the cardinal[3]; of archbishopdom, as W. Paris[3].

These seven orders, say some papists, as Lombard[4], are seven sacraments; which, added to the other six, make thirteen sacraments; and are from Christ and his apostles' time[5], yea, were instituted even by Christ himself[6].

Lib. IV. Dist. 24. cap. 1.

Test. Rhem. Annot. Marg. p. 572. Ibid. Annot. Luke xxii. 19.

Which their assertions are besides the word of God. For in the holy Scripture

Where can it be seen, that either orders, as some, can make one, or seven sacraments; or priesthood, as others think, is a sacrament? What element hath it? what form? what promise? what institution from Christ?

Where can any of those hideous titles of porter, exorcists, &c., be found ascribed to any minister of the New Testament? or the manner of their creation, or offices established?

Maur. de Inst. Cleric. Lib. I. c. 10). Sunt *Lectores* qui verbum Dei prædicant, quibus dicitur, Clama, ne cesses, &c. (Id. cap. 11). *Acolytus* quum ordinatur.... accipiat ceroferarium cum cereo, ut sciat se ad accendenda ecclesiæ luminaria mancipari. Accipiat et urceolum vacuum, ad suggerendum vinum in eucharistiam sanguinis Christi.]

[[2] This seems to be an error. Vaux says: The Sacraments be these: Baptism, Confirmation, Penance, the Sacrament of the Altar, Extreme Unction, Order, and Marriage.—Catech. Antv. 1574. p. 60.]

[[3] These statements the editor has been unable to verify.]

[[4] Si autem quæritur, quid sit quod hic vocatur ordo: sane dici potest signaculum esse, id est sacrum quoddam, &c....et dicuntur hi ordines sacramenta, quia in eorum perceptione res sacra, id est gratia confertur, quam figurant ea, quæ ibi geruntur.—Lombard. Sentent. Col. Agrip. 1576. Lib. IV. Dist. 24. p. 395.]

[[5] All the seven orders ancient, even from Christ and the apostles' time.—Test. Rhem. Rhemes, 1582. Marg. Annot. p. 572.]

[[6] *Do this.* In these words the holy sacrament of Order is instituted, because power and commission to do the principal work of priesthood is given to the apostles: that is to do that which Christ then did concerning his body: which was to make and offer his body as a sacrifice for us, and for all that have need of sacrifice, and to give it to be eaten as Christ's body sacrificed to all faithful.—Ibid. p. 104. Annot. Luk. xxii. 19.]

Majoran. Clyp. Milit. Eccles. Lib. I. cap. 9.

Lomb. Lib. IV. Dist. 24.

Some Papists themselves do write[1] that all inferior orders are not grounded upon Scripture, but some of them come by tradition. And Peter Lombard[2] saith plainly, that five of the seven orders neither can be read in the word of God, nor yet were heard of in the primitive church.

Where is it appointed to the ministers of the New Testament only to minister sacraments? or to minister more than two, *viz.* baptism, and the Lord's supper?

By what one place of Scripture have priests authority to offer sacrifice, and that for the quick and the dead also?

Where, without extreme blasphemy, can they shew that our Saviour[3] Christ was a porter, an exorcist, an acolyte, &c., and not always in his church a king, a prophet, and a priest?

Proposition VIII.

Matrimony is no sacrament.

Heb. xiii. 4.

Concil. Trid. Sess. 7. Can. 1.
Test. Rhem. Annot. Eph. v. 32.
Catech. Vaux, & Canis.

Matrimony is a state of life holy and honourable among all men. Howbeit to say that the same is a sacrament instituted, and that by Christ, as the Papists[4] do, we cannot be induced, and that for divers reasons.

For marriage, or the wedded state, was never commanded by God to be taken for a sacrament.

Again, it hath neither outward element, nor prescribed form, nor promise of salvation, as a sacrament should, and baptism and the Lord's supper have.

[1 Minores ordines ex apostolica traditione fuisse testes sunt Ignatius, Dionysius, Clemens, et Anacletus.—Majoran. Scutum Fid. Antverp. 1589. Lib. I. cap. 9. p. 13.]

[2 Ecce de septem ecclesiæ gradibus breviter elocuti, quid ad quenquam pertinent insinuavimus, cumque omnes spirituales sint et sacri, excellenter tamen canones duos tantum sacros ordines appellari censent. Diaconatus scilicet et presbyteratus, quia hos solos primitiva ecclesia legitur habuisse, et de his solis præceptum apostoli habemus.—Lombard. Sent. Col. Agrip. 1576. Lib. IV. Dist. 24. p. 395.]

[3 Saviour, omitted in 1607.]

[4 *This is a great Sacrament.* Marriage a great sacrament of Christ and his church prefigured in the first parents, &c.—Test. Rhem. Ann. Ephes. v. 32. Matrimony, which is a sign of the conjunction of Christ and the church his spouse is a sacrament, &c.—Vaux, Catech. ch. IV. Of the Seven Sacraments, p. 85.

Qua ratione matrimonium est sacramentum? *A.* Quatenus ea conjunctio, quæ inter virum et uxorem arctissima intercedit, congruum et sacrum est signum divinitus institutum, quo Christi sponsi et ecclesiæ sponsæ conjunctio sanctissima firmissimaque designatur.—Canis. Catech. p. 413. cap. IV. De Matrim. Sacr. Quæst. II.

For the reference to Concil. Trid. see above, p. 252, note 3.]

Besides, matrimony may be entered into or not, at our discretion. But it is not at our choice to be partakers, or not to participate of the sacraments, if we may come by them.

Moreover, matrimony was ordained even by God himself in the time of man's innocency; but the sacraments of the New Testament were instituted by Christ.

Gen. ii. 24. Matt. xix. 4, 5, 6.

Finally, it was no sacrament to the fathers afore, and in the time of the law; and therefore is no sacrament to us.

Hereunto subscribe the churches of God elsewhere[5]; all of us opposing ourselves against the manifold adversaries of this truth: whereof

Some have too highly conceived of the wedded state; such are the papists, when they will have it to be a sacrament, as hath been said; and such were the Vigilantian bishops[6], who would take no men into the clergy except they would be married first.

Others again too basely and badly think of matrimony, defending (some of them) how it is not meet

That any man or woman should marry at all; such were the Gnostics[7], the Marcionites[8], the Tatians[9], the Montanists[10], the Manichees[11], the Hieracites[12], and the Apostolics[13].

Conf. Helv. I. Art. XX. XXXVII. & II. c. 19, 29. Basil. Art. V. Bohem. cap. 9. Gal. Art. XXIV. XXXV. Belg. Art. XXXIII. August. Art. II. V. VI. Saxon. Art. XII. XVIII. Wittemb. cap. 21, 26. Suevica, cap. 12, 15. D. Hieron. adv. Vigil. c. 1. Epiphan. Tertul. cont. Marcion. Lib. IV. Epiphan. Euseb. D. August. de Hæres. August. Ibid. Epiphan.

[5 There is no direct condemnation of the Romish view of matrimony considered as a *sacrament* in the places referred to.—See Harm. Conf. Sect. XII. p. 70, sqq. and Sect. XVIII. p. 236, sqq.]

[6 Proh nefas, episcopos sui sceleris dicitur habere consortes; si tamen episcopi nominandi sunt, qui non ordinant diaconos, nisi prius uxores duxerint.—Hieron. Opp. Par. 1693-1706. Tom. IV. Pars II. col. 281. Adv. Vigilant.]

[7 ...πρῶτον μὲν κοινὰς τὰς ἑαυτῶν γυναῖκας ἔχουσι.—Epiphan. Opp. Paris. 1622. p. 85. Adv. Hær. Lib. I. Tom. II.]

[8 Teneo meum Christum, etiam in nomine sponsi, de quo Psalmus, Ipse tanquam sponsus egrediens de thalamo suo, &c.... Qui etiam per Esaiam gaudens ad patrem, Exultet, inquit, anima mea in Domino, induit enim me...tunicam jucunditatis velut sponso...Nega te nunc dementissimum, Marcion. Ecce legem tui quoque Dei impugnas: Nuptias non conjungit, conjunctas non admittit, neminem tinguit nisi cœlibem aut spadonem, morti aut repudio baptisma servat.—Tertull. Opp. Lutet. 1634, p. 516. A. adv. Marcion. Lib. IV. cap. 11. Cf. etiam, p. 528. A.]

[9 Ἐγκράτειαν δὲ οὗτος (sc. Τατίανος) κηρύττει, τὸν δὲ γάμον πορνείαν καὶ φθορὰν ἡγεῖται· φάσκων μηδὲν διαλλάττειν πορνείας τὸν γάμον, ἀλλὰ τὸ αὐτὸ εἶναι.—Epiphan. Opp. Tom. I. p. 391. Adv. Hær. Lib. I. Tom. III. Hær. 46.]

[10 The editor has been unable to verify this reference.]

[11 Unde nuptias sine dubitatione condemnant, et quantum in ipsis est, prohibent.—August. Opp. Par. 1836-8. Tom. VIII. col. 52. B. Lib. de Hær. ad Quod vult deum. cap. 46.]

[12 Monachos tantum et monachas, et conjugia non habentes in communionem recipiunt.—Ibid. col. 53. D. cap. 47.]

[13 Τὰ ὅμοια δὲ τοῖς ἀνωτάτω λεγομένοις (i.e. the Encratites, Tatians and Ca-

D. August. de Hæres. In Hom. xix. Tertul. libro de Monog.

That any man or woman should twice marry, the husband or wife being dead; of this mind were the Catharans[1], Origen[2], and Tertullian[3].

Test. Rhem. Annot. 1 Tim. iii. 2. See more afterward, Art. XXXII.

That some kind of persons should ever marry; as namely those which have taken holy orders[4], or be of spiritual [a]kindred[5]; these errors the Papists do hold.

Lastly, that any person should be married but by popish priests; thinking all those men and women not lawfully married, which are coupled together by protestant ministers: and therefore have new-married such persons. So did the Papists both in the Low Countries[6], and in France[7].

Supplication of the Pr. of Orange unto K. Philip. Calvin. Epist. fol. 266, and Chronicle of France.

[a] Petrus Lombard, Lib. IV. Dist. 42. By spiritual kindred, which is between the party that is baptized, or confirmed, and his godfathers and godmothers, and also between the godfather or godmother, and the parents of the child so baptized, or confirmed, matrimony may not be either contracted, or continued.—Canis. Catech. cap. 4.

---

tharans) φρονοῦσι περί τε τοῦ γάμου καὶ τῶν ἄλλων πραγμάτων.—Epiphan. Tom. I. p. 506. Adv. Hær. Lib. II. Tom. I.]

[[1] ...secundas nuptias non admittunt.—August. Opp. Paris. 1836-8. Tom. VIII. col. 45. D. cap. 38.]

[[2] Nunc vero et secundæ, et tertiæ, et quartæ nuptiæ, ut de pluribus taceam, reperiuntur, et non ignoramus quod tale conjugium ejiciet nos de regno Dei. Sicut enim ab ecclesiasticis dignitatibus non solum fornicatio, sed et nuptiæ repellunt,... sic forsitan et de cœtu primitivorum immaculatorumque ecclesiæ, quæ non habet maculam, neque rugam: ejicietur digamus, &c.—Orig. Opp. Par. 1740. Tom. III. p. 953. In Lucam, Hom. XVII.]

[[3] Hæretici nuptias auferunt, Psychici ingerunt. Illi nec semel, isti non semel nubunt...Unum matrimonium novimus, sicut unum Deum.—Tertull. Opp. Lutet. 1634. p. 673. De Monogam. cap. 1.]

[[4] The apostle then by this place we now treat of neither commandeth, nor counselleth, nor wisheth; nor would have bishops or priests to marry, or such only to be received as have been married: but that such an one as hath been married (so it were but once, and that to a virgin) may be made bishop or priest.—Test. Rhem. Rhemes, 1582. Ann. 1 Tim. iii. 2. p. 570.]

[[5] Jam de spirituali cognatione addamus, quæ etiam personas impedit, ut non sint legitimæ ad inuendas nuptias...Spiritualis proximitas est inter compatrem et commatrem: et inter eos quorum unus alterum de sacro fonte levavit vel in catechizatione aut confirmatione tenuit. Est etiam inter filios ejusdem hominis carnales et spirituales.—Lombard. Sent. Col. Agrip. 1576. Lib. IV. Dist. 42. p. 43. There seems to be an error in the reference to Canisius.]

[[6] The reference has not been found.]

[[7] ...nostrarum ecclesiarum matrimonia irrita habeantur, et ex iis prognati mares vel fœminæ inter spurios numerentur. Quid amplius? ut quos baptizavimus, alieni ab ecclesia censeantur.—Calvin. Opp. Amstelod. 1669-71. Tom. VIII. Pars 2. p. 166. Epist. Bezæ Calvino. See also above, p. 236, note 2.]

Proposition IX.

Extreme unction is no sacrament.

The Papists do take anoiling of the sick (which they call extreme unction) for a sacrament[8]: whereof (as they write)

The matter is oil hallowed by a bishop, wherewith the sick person is anoiled upon the eyes, ears, mouth, nose, hands, and feet[9].

The form is the words which the priest speaketh, when he doth anoint the sick person in the foresaid places, saying, "By this oil God forgive thee thy sins which thou hast committed by thine eyes, nose, ears, and mouth, by thine hands, and by thy feet: all the angels, archangels, patriarchs, prophets, apostles, evangelists, martyrs, confessors, virgins, widows, infants, heal thee[10]."

The minister thereof usually is a priest, but may be any other Christian[11].

[8 Quod autem extremæ unctioni propria sacramenti ratio conveniat, in primis explanandum est. Id vero perspicuum fiet, si verba quibus sanctus Jacobus apostolus hujus sacramenti legem promulgavit, attendamus. Infirmatur quis in vobis? inquit: Inducat presbyteros ecclesiæ, et orent super eum, ungentes eum oleo in nomine Domini, et oratio fidei salvabit infirmum, et alleviabit eum Dominus: et si in peccatis sit, remittentur ei. Nam quod peccata condonari Apostolus affirmat, in eo declarat sacramenti vim et naturam.—Catech. Conc. Trid. Rom. 1566. p. 189. De Extremæ Unctionis Sacramento.]

[9 Ejus igitur elementum sive materia, quemadmodum concilia, ac præcipue Tridentinum decrevit, est oleum ab episcopo consecratum, liquor scilicet non ex quavis pingui et crassa natura, sed ex olearum baccis tantummodo expressus.—Ibid. p. 190. Non sunt autem omnes corporis partes ungendæ, sed eæ tantum, quas veluti sensuum instrumenta natura homini attribuit, oculi propter visionem, aures propter auditum, nares propter odoratum, os propter gustum vel sermonem, manus propter tactum....Ac quoniam in corporis morbis, quamvis universum corpus male affectum sit, tamen illi tantum parti curatio adhibetur, a qua, tanquam a fonte et origine, morbus manat; iccirco non totum corpus, sed ea membra, in quibus potissimum sentiendi vis eminet, renes etiam, veluti voluptatis et libidinis sedes unguntur; tum pedes qui nobis ingressus, et ad locum movendi principium sunt.—Ibid. pp. 192, 3.]

[10 Forma vero sacramenti est verbum, et solemnis illa precatio, quam sacerdos ad singulas unctiones adhibet, cum inquit: Per istam sanctam unctionem indulgeat tibi Deus, quidquid oculorum, sive narium, sive tactus vitio deliquisti.—Ibid. p. 190.]

[11 The author seems here to be mistaken. The Catechism allows none but priests to administer the rite. Jam vero, quis extremæ unctionis minister sit, ab eodem apostolo, qui Domini legem promulgavit, didicimus: inquit enim: Inducat presbyteros, quo nomine non eos significat, qui ætate provectiores sunt, quemadmodum sapienter Tridentina Synodus exposuit, aut qui in populo principem locum obtinent, sed sacerdotes, qui ab ipsis episcopis per manuum impositionem rite ordinati sunt. Sacerdoti igitur hujus sacramenti administratio commissa est.—Catech. Conc. Trid. p. 193.]

The effect of anoiling is to purge and put away venial sins, committed by misspending of our senses; as also sins forgotten[1].

In this antichristian doctrine many errors be contained. For,

In respect of the matter, the Papists make of greasy matter a spiritual ointment; whereas there is none ointment spiritual but the Holy Ghost.

In respect of the form, the only propitiator and mediator between God and man, Christ Jesus, is blasphemed, and the merit and power of his death ascribed unto greasy oil. Besides, Christ is not acknowledged for the only Saviour of mankind, and physician of our souls; but other physicians be called upon besides him.

In respect of the minister, they hold how any man hath power to forgive sins; which belongeth unto God alone: also, that other men, yea women (and not the ministers of the word only) may be ministers of the sacraments.

In respect of the effect, they teach us (which is utterly untrue) that neither all sins be mortal, nor that Christ hath cleansed such as be his from all their sins by his precious blood.

Proposition X.

The sacraments are not to be abused, but rightly to be used of us all.

The proof from God's word.

In the word of God the right use of the sacraments, and the ends of their institution, are evidently set down. For,

Matt. xxviii. 19. Mark xvi. 16. Concerning baptism, Christ he saith, "Teach all nations, baptizing them," &c. He that shall believe, and be baptized, shall be saved.

Touching the Lord his supper, saith our Saviour, of the bread, "Take, eat," &c., and of the cup, "Drink ye all of it;" and Saint Paul, "The cup of blessing which we bless, is it not the communion of the blood of Christ? The bread which we break, is it not the communion of the body of Christ?" Matt. xxvi. 26, 27. 1 Cor. x. 16.

[1 Docebunt igitur pastores hoc sacramento gratiam tribui, quæ peccata, et in primis quidem leviora, et ut communi nomine appellantur, venialia, remittit.—Ibid. p. 194.]

This truth do the churches reformed by their confession subscribe unto[2].

Conf. Helv. I. Art. XXII. & II. cap. 20, 21. Bohem. cap. 11, 13. Gal. Art. XXXV. XXXVIII. Belg. Art. XXXIV. XXXV. August. Art. II. IX. Saxon. Art. XIII. XV. Wittemb. cap. 10, 19. Suevica, cap. 13, 18.

The errors and adversaries unto this truth.

Then greatly do they sin, who either do not use the sacraments at all, as do the Schwenkfeldians[3]; or minister them but unto whom they list; so is baptism of the Servetians[4] and Anabaptists[5] ministered only unto elder persons, and denied unto infants; and so is the same sacrament of the Marcionites[6] ministered unto single persons, but denied unto married folks.

See in this Art. Prop. I.

Calv. Epist. p. 118.

Sleidan. comment. Lib. VI.

Tertul. contra Marcion. Lib. I. & IV.

[2 Itaque immerito nostro maximo fit quod quidam parum nos tribuere sacris symbolis putant. Sunt enim hæ res sanctæ venerandæque, &c.—Harm. Conf. Sect. XIV. p. 113. Conf. Helv. Prior. Art. XXII. Credimus perfectissimam esse baptisandi formam qua Christus ipse baptisatus est, et qua baptisarunt apostoli.—Ibid. Sect. XIII. p. 90. Conf. Helv. Post. cap. XX. Ritum, modum, vel formam cœnæ illam existimamus esse simplicissimam et præstantissimam quæ proxime accedit ad primam Domini institutionem, &c.—Ibid. Sect. XIV. p. 112. Conf. Helv. Post. cap. XXI. Qui igitur hæc (sacramenta) contemnunt, et contumaciter apud se nihil ponderis habere sinunt, parvique facientes pro rebus levibus habent, aut alioqui contra institutionem, voluntatem et mandatum Christi abutuntur, hi universi adversus auctorem horum qui ea instituit, peccant, &c.—Ibid. Sect. XII. p. 78. Conf. Bohem. cap. XI. Cf. Ibid. Sect. XIV. p. 119. cap. XIII. Itaque fanaticos illos omnes rejicimus, qui hæc signa et symbola repudiant, quum Christus Dominus noster pronuntiarit, Hoc est corpus meum; et hoc poculum est sanguis meus.—Ibid. Sect. XIV. p. 122. Conf. Gall. Art. XXXVIII. Itaque nos hic quidem merito omnes hominum ludificationes, et damnanda commenta (quæ illi sacramentis addiderunt, et admiscuerunt) tanquam veram profanationem rejicimus, &c.—Ibid. p. 126. Conf. Belg. Art. XXXV. Admonentur etiam homines de dignitate et usu sacramenti, quantam consolationem proponat iis qui agunt pœnitentiam: ut discant homines et timere Deum et credere, &c.—Ibid. p. 127. Conf. August. De Abus. Art. I. Ut igitur reverentia major sit in hujus sacramenti usu, veræ causæ institutionis cogitentur, quæ ad publicam congregationem et ad singulorum consolationem pertinent.—Ibid. p. 138. Conf. Saxon. Art. XV. Nec damnandæ sunt piæ lectiones et precationes, quæ consecrationem ut vocant et dispensationem eucharistiæ præcedere et sequi solent, sed interea non licet nobis errores, qui ad hoc sacrum imperitia magis privatorum hominum quam legitimo consensu veræ catholicæ ecclesiæ, accesserunt, dissimulare, et approbare.—Ibid. p. 145. Conf. Virtemb. cap. XIX. ...factum est, ut divina sacramenta...quam religiosissime reverentiaque singulari apud nos et administrentur et sumantur.—Ibid. p. 149. Conf. Suev. cap. XVIII.]

[3 See above, p. 246, note 3.]

[4 ...Et ne a fanaticis nostrorum temporum sectis abhorrere videatur (Servetus) baptismum infantium horrendis modis flagellat, et abominabilem reddere conatur.—Calvin. Opp. Amstelod. 1669-71. Tom. VIII. Pars 2. p. 73.]

[5 In hoc tempore vigebat novum doctrinæ genus eorum qui dicuntur Anabaptistæ. Parvulorum hi damnant baptismum et rebaptisantur ipsi, et bonorum docent communionem.—Sleidan. Comment. Argentorat. 1555. Lib. VI. fol. 87.]

[6 Non tinguitur apud illum (sc. Marcionem) caro, nisi virgo, nisi vidua, nisi

Or do abuse them. So abused is baptism by them who baptize things without reason, yea sometimes without life, or sense: so have the Papists baptized both bells and babels; as the great bell of St John de Lateran, at Rome, by pope John the Fourteenth, who named it John, after his own name[1], and the great bell of Christchurch, in Oxford, which Dr Tresham, the vice-chancellor, named Mary[2]; babels, as the duke of Alva's chief standard, which he used in the Low Countries, was baptized by Pius Quintus, an. 1568, and called Margaret by the said pope[3]: and so the Cataphrygians baptized the dead bodies of men[4].

Cypr. Valera, of the Pope, &c. p. 55.

D. Humfred. in vita Juelii, p. 81.
D. Morison, de Deprav. Re Orig. p. 24.

Philastrius.

Again, baptism was abused by the Marcionites, when they baptized the living for the dead[5], also by the Novatians[6]; and Papists, when they rebaptized infants afore baptized, as they termed them, by heretics[7].

Tertul. contra Marcion. Lib. IV.
D. Cyprian. ad Jubaian.
See Art. XXIII. prop. 3.

And so abused was the Lord's Supper by certain heretics, condemned in a council at Carthage[8], whose manner was to

Conc. Carthag. 3. Can. 6.

cœlebs, nisi divortio baptisma mercata.—Tertull. Opp. Lutet. 1634. p. 451. D. Adv. Marcion. Lib. I. 29. Si omnino negas permitti divortium a Christo, quomodo tu nuptias dirimis? nec conjungens marem et feminam, nec alibi conjunctos ad sacramentum baptismatis et eucharistiæ admittens, &c.—Ibid. p. 538. B. Adv. Marc. Lib. IV. 32. Cf. supra, p. 160.]

[1 He (John XIV.) it was that baptized the great bell of St John de Lateran, and gave it his name.—Cyp. Valera, Two Treatises, &c. Transl. Lond. 1600. Of the Lives of the Popes, p. 55.]

[2 Dum vero hoc scriptum legit D. Treshamo procancellario, animus illius ut delectari videbatur cum recitantem attendit, ita vagari cœpit cum magnam nolam ædis Christi sonantem audivit, quam ille ut ad missam clare vocaret, ante paucos dies reparatam novo nomine donavit, et Mariam baptizavit.—Humfred. Vita Juell. Lond. 1573. pp. 80, 1.]

[3 ...et anno 1568 Papa baptizat vexillum Italorum et Hispanorum, qui regi Hispaniarum militabant in Flandria, vocavitque Margaretam, quæ postea ut fertur vicit in acie diabolum collatis signis, &c.—Moresin. Papatus, seu Deprav. Relig. Orig. Edinburg. 1594. pp. 23, 4.]

[4 Hi (Cataphryges) mortuos baptizant.—Philastr. Lib. de Hær. in Biblioth. Patr. Paris. 1624. Tom. IV. col. 13.]

[5 It does not appear that Tertullian speaks of baptism for the dead as a practice adopted by the Marcionites. He twice alludes to the passage in the first Epistle to the Corinthians, where baptism for the dead is mentioned. In the tract De Resurrect. Carnis, he treats it as a custom of certain heretics in the time of the apostle: but in his work against Marcion, he employs it in argument against Marcion's denial of the resurrection of the flesh.—Tertull. Opp. Lutet. 1634. p. 594. Adv. Marc. Lib. V. cap. 10.]

[6 Nec nos movet, frater carissime, quod in literis tuis complexus es; Novatianenses rebaptizare eos, quos a nobis sollicitant.—Cypr. Opp. Oxon. 1682. Epist. 73. p. 198.]

[7 See above, p. 236, notes 2, 3.]

[8 Item placuit ut corporibus defunctorum eucharistia non detur.—Concil. Harduin. Paris. 1715. Tom. I. col. 961. Conc. Carthag. III. cap. 6.]

thrust the sacrament into the mouths of dead men; and is by the Papists, whose guise is to use it magically, as a salve against bodily sickness and adversity; also to carry the same about pompously and superstitiously in the open streets, to be adored of the beholders.

Articles of the peace between Spain and England, *anno* 1604. Article II. concerning a Moderation. See more in the Article of Baptism, the Lord's Supper; also Article XXVIII. prop. 5.

Proposition XI.

All which receive the sacraments receive not therewithal the things signified by the sacraments.

The proof from God's word.

We read in the holy Scripture, that

Some persons do receive the sacraments, and the things signified by the sacraments, which are the remission of sins, and other spiritual graces from God: and so received was the sacrament of baptism of Cornelius; and the Lord's supper, of the good disciples, and the godly Corinthians.

Acts x. 47. Matt. xxvi. 26, &c. 1 Cor. xi. 22.

Some again receive the sacraments, but not the things by them signified: so received was baptism of Simon Magus, and the Lord's Supper of Judas; and so receive the atheists, libertines, and impenitent persons.

Acts viii. 13. John xiii. 26. 1 Cor. xi. 27, &c.

And some receive not the sacraments at all, and yet are partakers of the things by the sacraments signified: such a communicant was the thief upon the cross.

Luke xxiii. 43, 44.

This maketh us to conceive well both of those men and women, which would, and yet cannot, communicate in the public and christian assemblies, and of the children of christian parents, which depart this world unbaptized.

Furthermore, it is apparent how

Salvation is promised to such as are baptized; yet not simply in respect of their baptism, but if they do believe.

Mark xvi. 16.

Again, St Paul saith, "Whosoever shall eat the bread, or drink the cup of the Lord unworthily, shall be guilty of the body and blood of Christ."

1 Cor. xi. 27.

And this the purer churches everywhere do acknowledge[9].

Conf. Helv. I. Art. XX. & II. cap. 19, 21. Basil. Art. V. VI. Bohem. cap. 11, 13. Gal. Art. XXXIV. XXXVI. XXXVII. Belg. Art. XXXIII. XXXV. August. Art. III. XIII. Saxon. Art. XIII. XIV. Wittemb. cap. 10. Suevica, cap. 17.

[[9] In baptismo enim aqua signum est, ac res ipsa regeneratio, adoptioque in populum Dei. In eucharistia panis et vinum signa sunt. Res autem, communicatio corporis Christi, parta salus, et peccatorum remissio. Quæ quidem percipiuntur fide, quemadmodum signa ore corporeo. Et in ipsa re totus fructus sacramentorum est.—Harm. Conf. Sect. XII. p. 74. Conf. Helv. Prior. Art. XX. Neque vero approbamus istorum quoque doctrinam, qui docent gratiam et res

The adversaries unto this truth.

The Papists therefore be in a wrong opinion, which deliver that

Test. Rhem. An. 1 Pet. iii. 21. The sacraments are not only seals, but also causes of grace[1]; and

Ibid. Annot. Marg. p. 357. The sacraments do give grace, even because they be delivered, and received, *ex opere operato*[2].

ARTICLE XXVI.

Of the unworthiness of the ministers, which hinders not the effect of the sacraments.

Although in the visible Church the evil be ever mingled with the good, and sometimes the evil have chief authority in the ministration of the Word and Sacraments: yet forasmuch as they do not the same in their own name, but in Christ's, and do minister by his commission and authority, (1) *we may use their ministry, both in hearing the Word of God, and in the receiving the Sacraments. Neither is the effect of Christ's ordinance taken away by their wickedness, nor the grace of God's gifts diminished from such, as by faith, and rightly, do receive the sacraments ministered unto them; which are effectual, because of Christ's institution and promise, although they be ministred by evil men.*

significatas signis ita alligari et includi ut quicunque signis exterius participent, etiam internis gratiæ rebusque significatis participent, quales quales illi sint.—Ibid. p. 73. Conf. Helv. Post. cap. XIX. Docetur et hoc, sacramenta a se vel ex sese, ex opere operato, seu externa actione sola, id est, nuda communicatione atque perceptione aut usu sui, nemini qui antea non sit intus a Spiritu Sancto vivificatus, &c....neque gratiam neque justificantem aut vivificantem fidem conferre.—Ibid. p. 79. Conf. Bohem. cap. XI. Sunt enim sacramenta signa ac symbola visibilia rerum internarum et invisibilium, per quæ, ceu per media Deus ipse virtute Spiritus Sancti in nobis agit.—Ibid. p. 82. Conf. Belg. Art. XXXIII. Damnant igitur Pharisaicam opinionem, quæ obruit doctrinam de fide, nec docet fidem in usu sacramentorum requiri, quæ credat propter Christum nobis gratiam dari, sed fingit homines justos esse propter usum sacramentorum ex opere operato, et quidem sine bono motu utentium.—Ibid. p. 83. Conf. Aug. Art. XIII. For the other references, see below, Art. XXVII. Prop. 2. and Art. XXVIII. Propp. 2, 4.]

[1 The water bearing up the ark from sinking, and the persons in it from drowning, was a figure of baptism, that likewise saveth the worthy receivers from everlasting perishing, &c.—Test. Rhem. Rhemes, 1582. Ann. 1 Pet. iii. 21. p. 661.]

[2 ...the sacraments give grace *ex opere operato*, that is, by the force and virtue of the work and word done and said in the sacrament.—Ibid. Marg. Annot. p. 357.]

Nevertheless, it appertaineth to the discipline of the Church, that (2) enquiry be made of evil ministers, and that they be accused by those that have knowledge of their offences; and finally being found guilty, by just judgment be deposed.

The propositions.

1. The effect of the word and sacraments is not hindered by the badness of ministers.
2. Evil ministers are to be searched out, convicted, and deposed; but orderly, and by the discipline of the church.

Proposition I.

The effect of the word and sacraments is not hindered by the badness of ministers.

The proof from God's word.

Of the ministers ecclesiastical the church is to conceive neither too sinisterly, as though their unworthiness could make the word and sacraments the less effectual to such as worthily do hear, and receive them: nor, on the other side, too highly, as if the dignity of their calling were cause good enough, that what they do, or say, *ex opere operato*, take happy effects.

These things from the Scriptures are manifest; which teach us, that wicked ministers, even the scribes and Pharisees sit- Matt. xxiii. 2, 3.
ting in Moses' chair, and preaching Christ, though through Phil. i. 15.
envy, strife, and contention, are to be heard; and many administer the sacraments, as did the ordinary priests among the Jews, whereof very many, both afore and after that our 1 Cor. iv. 1. 1 Cor. iii. 9.
Saviour came into the world, were most wicked men: and the best are but the ministers of God, and God's labourers.

Also the purer churches[3] bear witness hereunto. Conf. Helv. I. Art. xv. xx. xxii. Helv. II. c. 18, 21. Bohem. cap. 11, 12. Gal. Art. xxxiii. xxxv. August. Art. viii. Saxon. Art. xi. xiii. Wittemb. Art. xxxi. Suevica, Art. xiii.

[3 ...ita tamen ut virtutem et efficaciam in his omnem Domino, ministerium ministris tantum ascribamus....Nihil enim est qui rigat, neque qui plantat, &c.—Harm. Conf. Sect. xi. pp. 42, 3. Conf. Helv. Prior. Art. xv. Cf. Ibid. p. 74. Art. xx. Scimus sacramenta ex institutione et per verbum Christi sanctificari, et efficacia esse piis, tametsi offerantur ab indignis ministris.—Ibid. p. 42. Conf. Helv. Post. cap. xviii. Postremo sciendum et hoc quod sacramenta nunquam destituat virtus ipsorum...sed in institutione Christi semper exercent virtutem atque efficacitatem suam in contestando, obsignando, confirmando, dignis quidem gratiam et salutem præsentem, indignis autem culpam et condemnationem, sive a bono honestoque sacerdote administrentur et distribuantur, sive ab occulto peccatore.—Ibid. Sect. xii. p. 80. Conf. Bohem. cap. xi. Quum autem in hac vita admixti sint ecclesiæ multi

1 Cor. iii. 7. Neither is he (whosoever) that planteth any thing, neither he that watereth; but God that giveth the increase, saith St Paul. And a sign of a good spirit is it to regard not so much who speaketh or ministereth, as what is uttered and offered from God.

Errors and adversaries to this truth.

The due consideration of the premises will both settle us the more firmly in the truth, and make us the more carefully to abhor all adversaries thereof; as in old time were the Donatists and the Petilians, who taught that the sacraments are holy when they be administered by holy men, but not else[1]: also the Apostolics, or Henricians, who had a fancy that he was no bishop which was a wicked man[2].

D. August. in Psal. x. & xxxii. Idem contra Petil. Lib. I. c. 4. Magd. Eccles. Hist. Cent. 12. cap. 5, fol. 844. D. Cyprian. Epist. Lib. I. Lib. ad Mag. Ep. 6. Ibid. Epist. 4.

Among the fathers also, Cyprian and Origen were not sound in this point. For Cyprian published, that no minister could rightly baptize who was not himself endued with the Holy Ghost[3]; he further delivered, that whosoever do communicate with a wicked minister do sin[4].

Origen. in Matt. Tract. I. Origen held, that in vain did any minister either bind or loose who was himself bound with the chains of sin and wickedness[5].

mali et hypocritæ, qui tamen societatem habent externorum signorum cum ecclesia, licet uti sacramentis, quæ per malos administrantur, &c.—Ibid. p. 83. Conf. August. Art. VIII. Donatistas improbamus, qui finxerunt ministerium eorum qui non sunt sancti, non esse efficax.—Ibid. Sect. x. p. 24. Conf. Saxon. Art. XI. Neque tamen eousque cujusquam (ministri) vita culpanda est, ut propterea qui Christianus est recuset audire, si quis fortasse e cathedra Mosis aut Christi (hoc est vel ex Dei lege, vel ex sacro evangelio) aliquid quod ad ædificationem inservire possit, proferat.—Ibid. Sect. XI. p. 64. Conf. Suev. Art. XIII. The other references are either erroneous, or merely inferential.]

[[1] Non enim confidunt in Domino qui tunc esse dicant sancta sacramenta si per sanctos homines dantur.—August. Opp. Paris. 1836-8. Tom. IV. col. 87. B. Enarr. in Psalm. x. § 5. Id enim agunt isti, ut origo, radix et caput baptizati non nisi ille sit a quo baptizatur, &c.—Ibid. Tom. IX. col. 344. B. Cont. Litt. Petil. Lib. I. cap. 4.]

[[2] Episcopum esse non posse, qui peccator sit.—Magdeburg. Eccl. Hist. Basil. 1560, &c. Cent. XII. c. 5. fol. 844.]

[[3] In hoc ipso a nobis tenentur, ut ostendamus nec baptizare omnino eos posse, qui non habeant Spiritum Sanctum.—Cyp. Opp. Oxon. 1682. Epist. 69. p. 185. It must be remembered that Cyprian is speaking here not of individual ministers *in the church*, but of those, who as having separated themselves from the church, were in his opinion neither endowed with spiritual gifts, nor capable of exercising a spiritual authority.]

[[4] Nec sibi plebs blandiatur quasi immunis esse a contagio delicti possit, cum sacerdote peccatore communicans.—Ibid. Epist. 67. p. 172.]

[[5] Εἰ δὲ σειραῖς τῶν ἁμαρτημάτων αὐτοῦ ἔσφικται, μάτην καὶ δεσμεῖ καὶ λύει.—Orig. Opp. Paris. 1740. Tom. III. p. 531. C. Comment. in Matt. xvi. 19.]

Such adversaries in our time be the Anabaptists, the Family of Love, the Disciplinaries (usually termed Puritans), the Sabbatarians, the Brownists, and the Papists. For

The Anábaptists[6] will not have the people to use the ministry of evil ministers; and think the service of wicked ministers unprofitable, and not effectual; affirming, that no man, who is himself faulty, can preach the truth to others. Wilkinson against the Fam. Art. XIV. p. 66.

The Family of Love do say[7], that no man can minister the upright service or ceremonies of Christ but the regenerate: also[8], that wicked men cannot teach the truth. H. N. Evang. c. 23. § 2. Fam. I. Epist. to M. Rogers.

The disciplinarian Puritans do bring all ministers which cannot preach, and their services, into detestation. For their doctrine is, that

Where there is no preacher there ought to be no minister of the sacraments[9]. Lear. Disc. p. 62.

None must minister the sacraments which do not preach[10]. T. C. 1 cap. p. 104.

The sacrament is not a sacrament if it be not joined to the word of God preached[11]. Ber. de Loque, Reas. of the Church, c. 10.

It is sacrilege to separate the ministration of the word preached from the sacraments[12]. Lear. Disc. p. 60.

Of these men's opinions be the Sabbatarians among us. For their doctrine is to the common people, that, unless they leave their unpreaching ministers every sabbath-day, and go to some place where the word is preached, they do profane the sabbath, and subject themselves unto the curse of God[13]. D. B. doct. of the Sabbath, 2 Book, p. 173.

[[6] Secondly (they affirm), that no man which is faulty himself can preach the truth to others.—Wilkinson's Confutation. Lond. 1579. Art. XIV. p. 66.]

[[7] Therefore no man knoweth Christ, nor the Father, (Matth. 11. c.), nor yet the upright services or ceremonies of Christ, for to minister those-same according to the truth, but such as are evenso, (Joh. 3. a. Rom. 8. 12. a. Eph. 4. c.) renewed, or born-again through Christ (as we have declared) in their spirit and mind.—H. N. Evang. Reg. p. 52. b. cap. XXIII. § 2.]

[[8] The scripture affirmeth that Christ (the only truth) hath said: My kingdom is not of this world; and how can the truth be taught where the kingdom is not? And again, I pray you tell me, what ministration (that ever was true) came from other than God's own mouth.—First Epistle of the Fam. to J. R. in the Displaying of the Fam. Lond. 1579. I. 6. 8.]

[[9] The work referred to has not been found.]

[[10] See above, p. 235, notes a, b. Art. XXIII. Prop. 3.]

[[11] Bertrand de Loque, Treatise of the Church. Translated out of French into English by T. W. Lond. 1581. cap. 10. p. 175.]

[[12] See note 9.]

[[13] ... Wheresoever the preaching of the word is not, or where men have it and come not to it, there can they not sanctify the day in that manner that they should, because they want the principal part of God's service, &c.—Nich. Bownde, Doct. of the Sabbath. Lond. 1595. p. 172.]

R. H. on Psal. cxxii. So the Brownists: No man is to communicate (say they) where there is a blind or dumb ministry[1].

The Papists do cross this truth, but after another sort. For

Bish. Jewel on Ag. i. Ser. • Pope Hildebrand decreed, and commanded, that no man should hear mass from the mouth of a priest which hath a wife[2].

The Rhemists do publish how,

Test. Rhem. Ann. Tit. iii. 10. The sermons of heretics (and so term they all protestant ministers) must not be heard, though they preach the truth[3].

Ibid. Annot. Mark iii. 13. Their prayers and sacraments are not acceptable to God, but are the howling of wolves[4].

Proposition II.

Evil ministers are to be searched out, convicted, and deposed; but orderly, and by the discipline of the church.

Matt. xxv. 26. Matt. xviii. 9. Matt. v. 13. The wicked and evil ministers must not always be endured in the church of God. For they are the evil and unprofitable servants; the eyes which do offend; the unsavoury salt; which are carefully to be seen unto, and, if admonitions will not serve, deposed; yet orderly, and by the discipline of the church. For that God, which appointed a government for the civil state, hath also given authority unto his church to punish offenders according to the quality of their transgressions. And so may we read in the word of God.

Matt. xviii. 17. "Tell the church," saith our Saviour.

1 Cor. v. 4, 5. "Let such a one, by the power of our Lord Jesus Christ, be delivered unto Satan, for the destruction of the flesh, that the spirit may be saved in the day of our Lord Jesus," saith St Paul.

[1 See above, p. 185, note 5.]

[2 Jewel, Sermon on Haggai i. 2—4. Works, Vol. II. p. 989. Park. Soc. Ed.]

[3 Let our protestants behold themselves in this glass, and withal let them mark all other properties that old heretics ever had, and they shall find all definitions and marks of an heretic to fall upon themselves. And therefore they must not marvel if we warn all catholic men by the words of the apostle in this place, to take heed of them, and to shun their preachings, books, conventicles, and companies.—Test. Rhem. Rhemes, 1582. Ann. Tit. iii. 10.]

[4 The confession of the truth is not grateful to God proceeding from every person. The devil acknowledging our Saviour to be the Son of God, was bidden hold his peace: Peter's confession of the same was highly allowed and rewarded. *Aug. tract.* 10. *in Ep. Joann. Ser.* 30. 31. *de verb. Apostoli.* Therefore neither heretics' sermons must be heard, no, not though they preach the truth. So is it of their prayer and service, which being never so good in itself, is not acceptable to God out of their mouths, yea, it is no better than the howling of wolves. *Hiero. in* 7. *Osee.*—Ibid. Ann. Mark iii. 13.]

So the neighbour churches[4]. Helv. 2. c. 18. Bohem. cap. 9. Saxon. Art. XI. Suevic. Art. XIII.

Adversaries unto this truth.

Then deceived, and out of the way, are the Brownists and Barrowists; which are of mind, that

Private persons in themselves have authority to depose unmeet ministers, and to punish malefactors[5]. R. H. in Psal. cxxii. p. 117.

Every particular member of a church in himself hath power to examine the manner of administering the sacraments, &c., to call men unto repentance[6], &c., to reprove the faults of the church, and to forsake that church, which will not reform her faults upon any private admonition[7]. Barr. Discov. p. 36. Giff. Repl. unto Bar. & Gr. in the end.

For want of the due execution of discipline against persons offending, and malefactors, both women may leave their husbands (as some have done), and husbands their wives, and go where it is in force[8]. See more in Art. XXXIII. Prop. I. Brown, Tract. of the Life and Mann. Bredw. Detect. p. 122.

[[4] Atqui debet interim justa esse inter ministros disciplina. Inquirendum enim diligenter in doctrinam et vitam ministrorum in synodis: corripiendi sunt peccantes a senioribus, et in viam reducendi, si sunt sanabiles, aut deponendi, et velut lupi abigendi, per veros pastores a grege Dominico, si sunt incurabiles.—Harm. Conf. Sect. XI. p. 42. Conf. Helvet. Post. cap. XVIII. Quod si vero ex præsidibus his aliquis in peccatum aut errores labatur, aut in munere suo curando negligentior sit, is per ordinariam et legitimam ecclesiæ disciplinam in viam reduci, castigarique debet. Sin vero resipiscere nolit...tum primum a muneris sui curatione...removeri, et postea e communitate ecclesiæ, &c.—Ibid. p. 50. Conf. Bohem. cap. IX. Ceterum quod quorundam concionatorum doctrinam aut ferre amplius non potuerimus, sed pro nostra necessitate alios in eorum locum substituerimus, &c....non alia de causa id factum est, quam quod hi vocem Domini nostri Jesu Christi clare et fideliter, illi vero alii humanis figmentis permixtam proferrent.—Ibid. p. 65. Conf. Suev. Art. XIII. There seems to be an error in the reference to the Conf. Saxon.]

[[5] By the vertue of which libertie and authoritie, the church of God have to trie and examine the giftes and conversation of those which should leade them, and finding them meet, to chuse them, and perceiving them afterwarde to fall to anie evill heresie in doctrine, or to looseness of life, and will not be reclaymed by dewe admonition, to depose them. Also...the church of God have to use their dewe admonitions, and rebukinges of offendours....And such offendours as will not hear the church and bee reformed, must feele the sworde of excommunication by the woorde of God to bee cutte of, &c.—A Treatise on Ps. 122. by R. H. 1583. fol. H. 3.]

[[6] ...Who can deny, but every particular member hath power, yea, and ought to examine the manner of administering the sacraments, as also the estate, disorder, or transgressions of the whole church, yea, and not to join in any known transgression with them, but rather to call them all to repentance.—Barrowe, Discov. of the False Church. 1590. p. 35.]

[[7] Ye hold it a due convincing, not only of particular persons, but also of whole churches, and such as doth cast them forth as heathen, so soon as any private man doth reprove the least error, and they forthwith do not reform the same.—Gyfford's Reply unto Barrow and Greenwood.—London, 1591, p. 97.]

[[8] As for the covenant here between husband and wife, we understand not the covenant which is in the communion of marriage, but that which is in the communion of government. And this covenant is broken if either do seek the destruction

Article XXVII.

Of Baptism.

(1) *Baptism is not only a sign of profession, and mark of difference, whereby christian men are discerned from other that be not christened, but* (2) *it is also a sign of Regeneration, or New-birth, whereby, as by an instrument, they that receive baptism rightly, are graffed into the church, the promises of the forgiveness of sin, and of our adoption to be the sons of God by the Holy Ghost, are visibly signed and sealed; faith is confirmed, and grace increased by virtue of prayer unto God.*

(3) *The Baptism of young children is in any wise to be retained in the Church, as most agreeable with the institution of Christ.*

The propositions.

1. Baptism is a sign of profession, and mark of difference, whereby Christians are discerned from other men that be no Christians.

2. Baptism is a sign or seal of the regeneration, or new birth of Christians.

3. Infants and young children, by the word of God, are to be baptized.

Proposition I.

Baptism is a sign of profession, and mark of difference, whereby Christians are discerned from other men that be no Christians.

The proof from God's word.

How the sacraments are tokens; and therefore that baptism is a sign of the true church, which be Christians, it is apparent from God's word in the fifth proposition of the nineteenth article aforegoing; and the same do the churches of God acknowledge[1].

Conf. Helv. I. Art. xx. & II. cap. 19, 20. Basil. Art. v. sect. 2. Gal. Art. xxxv. Belg. Art. xxxiv. August. Art. xiii. Saxon. Art. xii.

of other, or do persecute religion or goodness: likewise also it is broken, if by keeping together the one cannot hold the true religion through the untowardness of the other in a wicked and false religion. And therefore in such cases a brother or a sister is not in bondage, but that the husband may depart from the wife, or the wife from the husband. 1 Cor. 7. Yet this departing is not a breach of the communion of marriage, but of that communion in government, through leaving one another for a good conscience.—A Book which sheweth the Life and Manner of all true Christians, &c. by Robert Browne. Middelburgh. 1582. § 120, note.

He accounted discipline the groundwork of the church....so far he proceedeth in reducing, that he saith, the wife ought to go away from her husband (if he will not go with her), in the case of want of this discipline.—Bredwell's Detect. Lond. 1568, p. 122.]

[[1] Separat item nos Deus baptismi symbolo ab omnibus alienis religionibus et

Errors and adversaries unto this truth.

This declareth us to be sound Christians, and

Not Nazarenes, who were with the Jews circumcised, and baptized with Christians, and so (as Hierom[2] writeth of them) were neither Jews nor Christians. D. Hieron. in Epist. ad Aug. de Hæres.

Not Manicheans[3], which baptize not any. D. August.

Not false Christians, or Marcionites[4], which did baptize the living for the dead. Which Marcionites also denied baptism unto all married persons, and baptized none but persons single, virgins, widows, and women divorced from their husbands[5]. 1 Cor. xv. Tertul. contra Marc. Lib. IV. Tertul. Ibid.

Not Origenists[6], who maintain a baptism by fire; as also that after the resurrection of our bodies we shall have need of baptism. Origen. in Luc. Hom. 14.

Not of Matthew Hamant's opinion (that Norfolk heretic), which stood in it to the death, that baptism is not necessary in the church. Holinsh. Chr. fol. 1299.

Not Anabaptists[7], which number baptism among things indifferent, and so to be used, or refused, at our discretion. Bulling. contra Anabapt. Lib. II. cap. 4.

Not Familists[8], which say there is no true baptism but only among themselves. H. N. I. Exhort. cap. 7.

populis, et sibi consecrat ceu peculium.—Harm. Conf. Sect. XIII. p. 90. Conf. Helv. Post. cap. XX. ...Baptismum...quo in Dei ecclesiam recipimur, et a cunctis aliis gentibus, ac peregrinis omnibus religionibus segregamur.—Ibid. p. 96. Conf. Belg. Art. XXXIV. For the other references, see above, Art. XXV. Prop. 1.]

[2 ...inter Judæos hæresis est...quos vulgo Nazaræos nuncupant, qui credunt in Christum, filium Dei...in quem et nos credimus: sed dum volunt et Judæi esse et Christiani, nec Judæi sunt, nec Christiani.—Hieron. Opp. Paris. 1693-1706. Tom. IV. Pars II. col. 623. Epist. ad August. 74.]

[3 Quid eis prodest, Baptismum omnibus ætatibus necessarium confiteri; quod Manichæi dicunt in omni ætate superfluum: cum isti dicant esse in parvulis falsum, quantum ad remissionem attinet peccatorum?—August. Opp. Paris. 1836-8. Tom. X. col. 876. D. contr. Duas Epist. Pelagian. Lib. IV. cap. 4.]

[4 See above, p. 266, note 5.] [5 See above, p. 261, note 8, and p. 265, note 6.]

[6 Ego puto, quod et post resurrectionem ex mortuis indigeamus sacramento eluente nos atque purgante: nemo enim absque sordibus resurgere poterit: nec ullam posse animam reperiri quæ universis statim vitiis careat.—Origen. Opp. Paris. 1740. Tom. III. p. 948. A. In Lucam Hom. 14.]

[7 Statuebant pædobaptismum, magistratum, jusjurandum, esse res liberas et medias, quibus fideles suo arbitrio uti, aut non uti possint.—Bulling. adv. Anabapt. Tiguri. 1560. p. 42. Lib. II. cap. 4.]

[8 We confess that they all, which become not grounded in this same upright faith of Jesu Christ, nor become evenso baptized...in the name of the Father, under the obedience of the love of the Father and his law;...in the name of the Son, &c.... and in the name of the Holy Ghost, &c....are no true Christians: and that they also all that boast themselves to be Christians, without this same upright faith and baptism, are doubtless false Christians, Mat. 34. a. Luk. 21. a.—H. N. First Exhortation. Translated out of Base-Almayne, cap. VII. § 32.]

Not Papists, who both baptize bells and babels, as afore hath been shewed, Art. xxv. Prop. x., and also make the vow and profession of the monachal, or life of a monk, as good a token of Christians as baptism[1].

T. Aquinas, 2, 21. De Ingr. Relig. p. 119.

Proposition II.

Baptism is a sign, or seal of the regeneration, or new birth, of Christians.

The proof from God's word.

Titus iii. 5.

Baptism of St Paul is called the washing of the new birth, of others the sacrament of the new birth, to signify how they which rightly (as all do not) receive the same[2], are ingrafted into the body of Christ, as by a seal be assured from God that their sins be pardoned, and forgiven, and themselves adopted for the children of God, confirmed in the faith, and do increase in grace, by virtue of prayer unto God.

See afore, Art. xxv. Prop. 11. 1 Cor. xii. 13. Acts ii. 38. Titus iii. 5. Mark xvi. 16. Acts ii. 41, 42.

And this is the constant doctrine of all churches protestant and reformed[3].

Conf. Helv. I. Art. xxi. & II. cap. 20. Bohem. cap. 12. Gal. Art. xxxv. Belg. Art. xxxiv. Augustana, Art. ix. Saxon. Art. xiii. Wittemb. cap. 10. Suevica, cap. 19.

[1 The passage intended is probably this:....Hoc etiam ex multorum laudabili consuetudine approbatur: qui ab infidelitate quacunque ad fidem Christi conversi, statim habitum religionis assumunt. Quis autem erit tam improbus disputator, qui audeat eis consulere, ut potius in seculo remaneant, quam in religione perceptam baptismi gratiam studeant conservare? Quis sanæ mentis ab hoc proposito eum impediat ne Christum quem per sacramentum baptismi jam induit, perfecta imitatione induere mereatur?—Tho. Aquin. Antv. 1612. fol. 106. b. Cont. Retrahen. ab Ingress. Relig. cap. 4.]

[2 See above, p. 267.]

[3 Baptisma quidem ex institutione Domini est lavacrum regenerationis quam Dominus electis suis visibili signo per ecclesiæ ministerium...exhibet.—Harm. Conf. Sect. xiii. p. 91. Conf. Helv. Prior. Art. xxi. Etenim baptisari in nomine Christi est inscribi, initiari, et recipi in fœdus atque familiam, adeoque in hæreditatem filiorum Dei, imo jam nunc nuncupari nomine Dei, id est, appellari filium Dei, purgari item a sordibus peccatorum, et donari varia Dei gratia ad vitam novam et innocentem.—Ibid. p. 89. Conf. Helv. Post. cap. xx. ...quod (sc. sacramentum baptismi) consistit in externa ablutione quæ fit aqua cum invocatione nominis sanctæ Trinitatis...fitque ea ablutio et ad significandam et contestandam spiritualem ablutionem, et internam mundationem Sancti Spiritus, ab hereditarii peccati morbo, cæterisque peccatis, quorum reatus hic remittitur et tollitur, et ad consequendum novum ortum nascendi seu regenerationem, unde sacramentum nominatur novi ortus, id est regenerationis, &c.—Ibid. pp. 92, 3. Conf. Bohem. cap. xii. ...Baptismus nobis testificandæ nostræ adoptioni datus, quoniam in eo inserimur Christi corpori, ut ejus sanguine abluti, simul etiam ipsius Spiritu ad vitæ sanctimoniam renovemur.—Ibid. pp. 94, 5. Conf. Gall. Art. xxxv. Suos igitur omnes jussit Dominus in nomine Patris et Filii et Spiritus Sancti pura aqua baptisari, ut significaret sanguinem Christi per Spiritum Sanctum idem præstare et efficere interne in anima quod aqua externe operatur in corporibus. Sicuti enim aqua....sordes corporis abluit, sic et sanguis Christi animam abluens, a peccatis illam emundat;

The errors and adversaries unto this truth.

But no part of the true church thinketh, as did many old heretics, *viz.* that

The baptized of the orthodoxal ministers are to be rebaptized, as said the Novatians[4]. Cyp. ad Jub.

Original sin is not pardoned in infants, as said the Pelagians, because they have no such sin in them at all[5]. D. August. de pec. mer. Lib. c. 20.

Only sins past, and not sins future, or not yet committed, are by baptism cleansed; as the Messalians held[6]. Theod. Dimider. cap. de Bap.

Being once baptized, we can no more be tempted; as thought the Jovinians: which was the error also of the Pelagians[7]. Magd. Eccles. Hist. Cent. IV. cap. 5, fol. 381.

The baptism of water is now ceased, and the baptism of voluntary blood by whipping is come in place thereof, without which none can be saved; as the Flagelliferans published[8]. Gerson, Tract. contra Flagel.

nosque filios iræ in filios Dei regenerat.—Ibid. p. 96. Conf. Belg. Art. XXXIV. De baptismo docent, quod necessarius sit ad salutem tanquam ceremonia a Christo instituta. Et quod per baptismum offeratur gratia Dei...et quod infantes per baptismum Deo commendati recipiantur in gratiam Dei, et fiant filii Dei.—Ibid. p. 97. Conf. August. Art. IX. Ego baptiso te: id est, ego testificor hac mersione te ablui peccatis, et recipi jam a vero Deo qui est Pater Domini nostri Jesu Christi, qui te per Filium Jesum Christum redemit, et sanctificat te Spiritu Sancto.—Ibid. p. 98. Conf. Saxon. Art. XIII. ...docemus eum qui baptisatur in nomine Patris, &c.... tingi spirituali chrismate, hoc est fieri membrum Christi per fidem, et donari Spiritu Sancto ut ad percipienda cœlestia, aures mentis ejus aperiantur, et oculi cordis illuminentur.—Ibid. p. 101. Conf. Virtemb. cap. X. De baptismate itaque confitemur, id quod passim scriptura de illo prædicat, eo sepeliri nos in mortem Christi, coagmentari in unum corpus, Christum induere: esse lavacrum regenerationis, peccata abluere, nos salvare.—Ibid. p. 104. Conf. Suev. cap. XVIII.]

[[4] Id enim agit illa disputatio contra cujus novitatem antiqua veritate nitendum est, ut infantes omnino superfluo baptizari videantur.—Cypr. Opp. Oxon. 1682. Epist. 73. p. 198. See above, p. 266, note 6.]

[[5] Terrentur autem isti sententia Domini dicentis, *Nisi quis natus fuerit denuo, non videbit regnum Dei.* Quod cum exponeret, ait, *Nisi quis renatus fuerit ex aqua et Spiritu, non intrabit in regnum cœlorum.* Et propterea conantur parvulis non baptizatis innocentiæ merito salutem ac vitam æternam tribuere; sed quia baptizati non sunt, eos a regno cœlorum facere alienos, &c.—August. Opp. Par. 1836-8. Tom. X. col. 207. De Peccat. Mer. et Remiss. Lib. I. cap. 20. § 26.]

[[6] Ξύρου γὰρ δίκην ἀφαιρεῖται (sc. τὸ βάπτισμα) τῶν ἁμαρτημάτων τὰ πρότερα, τὴν δὲ ῥίζαν οὐκ ἐκκόπτει τῆς ἁμαρτίας.—Theodoret. Opp. Lut. Par. 1642-84. Tom. IV. p. 242. D. Hær. Fab. Lib. IV. cap. 11.]

[[7] Non posse peccare hominem, aut a diabolo subverti, lavacro regenerationis plena fide accepto. Idem autem ascribitur Pelagio.—Magdeburg. Eccl. Hist. Basil. 1562, &c. Cent. IV. cap. 5. fol. 381.]

[[8] Constat autem per experientiam in multis, quod taliter se flagellantes non curant de sacramento confessionis, vel pœnitentiæ sacramentalis, dicentes, quod hæc flagellatio potior est ad delendum peccata, quam quæcunque confessio: immo eam æquiparant nonnulli vel præponunt martyrio, &c.—Gerson. Opp. Antv. 1706. Tom. II. col. 660. D. Tract. contr. Sect. Flagell.]

We also condemn the opinion

Russia Com. weal, chap. 23, p. 98, B. Of the Russes, that there is such necessity of baptism, as that all that die without the same are damned[1].

Bannister's Errors, printed by T. Man. Also of the Bannisterians[2], which say, that the water at baptism is not holy in respect that it is applied to an holy use; and that the ordinary and common washings among the Turks and Jews, is the same to them that baptism is to us.

H. N. Evang. c. 19. sect. 5, 6. Likewise of the Family of Love[3], which conceive basely of this sacrament, calling it in derision, "elementish water," and of no better validity, or virtue, than common water.

Althamer. Concil. loc. Pugnan. loc. 131. Also the Anabaptists[4], who ascribe no more unto baptism than unto any other thing civilly discerning one man from another: and say, that the sacraments of the New Testament are no instruments to raise or confirm faith.

And lastly, of the Papists who maintain, that

D. Thom. de sacr. Altaris. Baptism serveth to the putting away of original sin only[5].

Test. Rhem. Ann. Gal. iii. 27. Baptism bringeth grace, even *ex opere operato*[6].

Proposition III.

Infants and young children, by the word of God, are to be baptized.

The proof from God's word.

Although by express terms we be not commanded to baptize young children, yet we believe they are to be baptized, and that for these, among other reasons:

1. The grace of God is universal, and pertaineth unto

[[1] Russe Commonweal. Lond. 1591. chap. xxiii. p. 98. b.]

[[2] This reference the editor has been unable to verify.]

[[3] H. N. Evang. Reg. p. 46. cap. XIX. § 5. See above, page 177, note 10.]

[[4] Nihil omnino tribuunt baptismo, nisi quod sit christianorum nota qua discernantur ab gentibus, more civili, sicut toga Romanos ab aliis gentibus discernebat: ac civilia militariaque signa inter cives militesque discernunt: aut velut cucullus monachos ab reliquo hominum genere separat, et discriminis symbolum est....Negant sacramenta novi testamenti instrumenta esse per quæ fides excitetur, erigatur et confirmetur.—Althamer. Concil. Loc. Norimb. 1535. Loc. cxci. p. 211.]

[[5] There is apparently an error in the reference, but see Thom. Aquin. Script. Sec. in Quat. Lib. Sentent. Antv. 1612. In Lib. IV. Dist. IV. Art. 4. fol. 115. Sicut pœnitentia data est in remedium actualis, ita baptismus in remedium originalis: sed non potest aliquis salvari ab actuali mortali nisi per pœnitentiam; ergo nec ab originali nisi per baptismum.]

[[6] See above, p. 250, note 4.]

all; therefore the sign or seal of grace is universal, and belongeth unto all, so well young as old.

2. Baptism is unto us as circumcision was unto the Jews: but the infants of the Jews were circumcised; therefore the children of Christians are to be baptized.

3. Children belong unto the kingdom of heaven, and are in the covenant; therefore the sign of the covenant is not to be denied them. Matt. xiii. 14.

4. Christ gave in commandment that all should be baptized; therefore young children are not to be exempted. Matt. xxviii. 19.

5. Christ hath shed his blood as well for the washing away the sins of children, as of the elder sort; therefore it is very necessary that they should be partakers of the sacrament thereof.

All christian churches allow of the baptism of infants[7]. Conf. Helv. I. Art. XXI. & II. cap. 20. Bohem. cap. 12. Gall. Art. XXXV. Belg. Art. XXXIV. August. Art. IX. Saxon. Art. XIII. Wittemb. cap. 10. Suevica, cap. 17.

Adversaries unto this truth.

The premises declare, that

They slander us which say, that all Protestants deny the baptism of children to be necessary; and this is runagate Hill's[8] report. Hill's Quart. Reas. 14.

[7 Damnamus Anabaptistas qui negant baptisandos esse infantulos recens natos a fidelibus. Nam juxta doctrinam evangelicam horum est regnum Dei, et sunt in fœdere Dei, &c.—Harm. Conf. Sect. XIII. p. 90. Conf. Helv. Post. cap. XX. ...quo quidem sacro lavacro infantes nostros iccirco tingimus quoniam e nobis (qui populus Dei sumus) genitos, e populi Dei consortio rejicere nefas est, tantum non divina voce designatos: præsertim quum de eorum electione pie est præsumendum. —Ibid. p. 91. Conf. Helv. Prior. Art. XXI. Etsi autem sacer baptismus in prima ecclesia maxima ex parte adultis...collatus fuit: docetur tamen hoc, etiam infantibus, qui et ipsi in numero populi Dei referuntur, hoc ministerio ad salutem similiter inserviri debere.—Ibid. p. 93. Conf. Bohem. cap. XII. ...quum una cum parentibus posteritatem etiam illorum in ecclesia Deus recenseat, affirmamus infantes sanctis parentibus natos, esse ex Christi auctoritate baptisandos.—Ibid. p. 95. Conf. Gall. Art. XXXV. Nos vero eos (sc. infantes) eadem ratione baptisandos et signo fœderis obsignandos esse credimus, qua olim in Israele parvuli circumcidebantur, nimirum propter easdem promissiones infantibus nostris factas.—Ibid. p. 97. Conf. Belg. Art. XXXIV. ...docent...quod infantes sint baptisandi.—Ibid. Conf. August. Art. IX. Retinemus et infantium baptismum, quia certissimum est, promissionem gratiæ etiam ad infantes pertinere, et ad eos tantum qui ecclesiæ inseruntur.—Ibid. p. 99. Conf. Saxon. Art. XIII. Agnoscimus baptismum tam infantibus quam adultis in ecclesia, &c.—Ibid. p. 100. Conf. Virtemb. cap. X. Quum autem baptisma sit sacramentum fœderis quod Deus cum suis icit, pollicitus se illorum et seminis eorum Deum ac vindicem futurum...infantibus quoque illud conferendum nostri docent, &c.—Ibid. p. 104. Conf. Suev. cap. XVII.]

[8 The Catholic affirmeth baptism of children to be necessary, the Protestant denieth it.—Hill's Quartron Reason, 14. p. 70.]

They err which oppugn this truth; as do many persons, but not after one and the same sort. For

D. August. de Verb. Apost. de Bap. parv. Magdeburg. Eccles. Histor. Cent. 12, c. 5. Bulling. contra Anab. Lib. I. Ib. Lib. II. c. 13. Althamer. Conciliat. Locorum, Pug. loc. 191. Epist. Minist. Bern. in Calv. Epist. fol. 118. Displ. H. 7. A.

Some utterly deny that infants, or young children, are to be baptized; so did the Pelagians[1], the Heracleans, and the Henricians[2], and so do the Anabaptists, whereof said some[3], how baptism is the invention of pope Nicholas, and therefore naught: others, that baptism is of the devil; so thought Melchior Hoffman[4], so also do the Swermerians[5], (a sect among the said Anabaptists,) the Servetians[6], and the Family of Love[7], which doth hold that none should be baptized until he be thirty years old.

Bar. Disc. p. 9. Gifford's Reply. [Lond. 1591. p. 97.]

Others refuse to baptize not all, but some infants. So denied is baptism by the Barrowists[8] unto the seed of whores and witches; by the Brownists, unto the children of open sinners; by the Disciplinarians, unto their children which subject not themselves (as Dudly Fenner saith) unto the discipline of the church, or obey not the presbyterial decrees[a].

Others allow the baptism of infants, yet think those infants not lawfully baptized which are baptized either by the now

[a] Sacramentorum autem primum pro natura sua administrari debet vel infantibus, vel adultis. Infantibus autem iis, qui sunt liberi eorum, qui sunt intra. Intra autem, qui ecclesiæ εὐταξίᾳ se subjiciunt.—D. Fenner, Lib. v. Theol. cap. ult.[9]

[[1] Id enim agit illa disputatio, contra cujus novitatem antiqua veritate nitendum est, ut infantes omnino superfluo baptizari videantur. Sed aperte hoc non dicitur ne tam firmata salubriter ecclesiæ consuetudo violatores suos ferre non possit.—August. Opp. Paris. 1836-8. Tom. x. col. 302. A. De Peccat. Mer. &c. Lib. III. cap. 13.]

[[2] Infantes non baptisandos.—Magdeburg. Eccl. Hist. Basil. 1562, &c. Cent. XII, c. 5. fol. 844.]

[[3] Accusant autem nos, quod infantes nuper in lucem editos, qui ratione et intellectu carent, baptizemus, cum tamen baptismus parvulorum pontificem et diabolum authores habeat.—Bulling. Adv. Anabapt. (Simler. Vers. Lat.) Tiguri. 1560. p. 202. b. Lib. VI. cap. 1.]

[[4] Parvulorum baptismum ex diabolo esse, neque ulli Christiano ferendum.—Ibid. p. 65. Lib. II. cap. 13.]

[[5] See above, p. 246, note 2.]

[[6] ...(Servetus) baptismum infantium horrendis modis flagellat, et abominabilius reddere conatur.—Calv. Opp. Amstelod. 1669-71. Tom. VIII. Pars II. p. 73. Inter Epist. et Respons. Epist. Ministr. Eccles. Bern.]

[[7] Displaying of the Family. Lond. 1579. fol. H. 7. a.]

[[8] All without exception or respect of person are received into, and nourished in the bosom of this church (the church of England) with the word and sacraments, ...not denying baptism to the seed even of whores and witches.—Barrowe, Discov. of the False Church. 1590. p. 9.]

[[9] There seems to be an error in the reference.]

ministers of the church of England; as the Brownists[10] do think; or by Protestant ministers, as the Papists are of mind, witness their rebaptizing of infants in France, and in Netherland[11]; or by unpreaching ministers, as the Disciplinarian Puritans do hold[12].

R. A. Confut. of Brow. p. 113. See afore, Art. XXIII. Prop. 3. See Art. XXVI. Prop. 1.

And others are of opinion, that none are to be baptized which believe not first.

Hence the Anabaptists: Infants believe not; therefore be not to be baptized. Hence the Lutherans[b]: Infants do believe; therefore to be baptized[13].

ARTICLE XXVIII.

Of the Supper of the Lord.

The Supper of the Lord is not only (1) *a sign of the love that Christians ought to have among themselves, one to another; but rather* (2) *it is a sacrament of our redemption by Christ's death: insomuch that to such, as worthily and with faith receive the same, the bread which we break is a partaking of the body of Christ; and likewise the cup of blessing is a partaking of the blood of Christ.* (3) *Transubstantiation (or the change of the substance of bread and wine) in the Supper of the Lord, cannot be proved by holy writ; but it is repugnant to the plain words of scripture, overthroweth the nature of a sacrament, and hath given occasion to many superstitions.* (4) *The body of Christ is given, taken, and eaten in the Supper, only after an heavenly*

[b] Declarent ubinam legerint, tam necessario esse copulandam cœlestis verbi prædicationem cum administratione sacramenti, ut nisi concio habeatur, renascentium lavacro infans adspergi non possit?—Querim. Eccl. [Lond. 1592.] p. 80. Heshus. de 600. Fr. Pontif. lo. 16.

[[10] They hold it not lawful to baptize children among us.—Allison's Plaine Confut. &c. Lond. 1590. p. 114.]

[[11] The Netherlands, 1675. See above, p. 236, note 2.]

[[12] See above, p. 271.]

[[13] Heshusius enumerates the following among the 'Errores Pontificiorum:' Docent infantes fide propria carere, et tantum in fide parentum vel ecclesiæ baptizari.—Heshusius, Sexcenti Errores, &c. Francof. ad Mœnum, 1585. XVI. Locus de Baptismo. p. 112.]

and spiritual manner. And the mean whereby the body of Christ is received and eaten in the Supper is faith. (5) *The sacrament of the Lord's Supper was not by Christ's ordinance reserved, carried about, lifted up, or worshipped.*

The propositions.

1. The supper of the Lord is a sign of the love that Christians ought to have among themselves.

2. The Lord's supper is a sacrament of our redemption by Christ's death, and to them, which receive the same worthily by faith, a partaking of the body and blood of Christ.

3. The bread and wine in the Lord's supper be not changed into another substance.

4. The body of Christ is given, taken, and eaten after an heavenly and spiritual, not after a carnal sort.

5. To reserve, carry about, lift up, or worship the sacrament of the Lord's supper, is contrary to the ordinance of Christ.

Proposition I.

The supper of the Lord is a sign of the love that Christians ought to have among themselves.

The proof from God's word.

The supper of the Lord is a token of the love that Christians ought to have among themselves. For which cause
1 Cor. x. 21. 1 Cor. xi. 20. it is called the Lord's Table, the Lord's Supper, a Communion of the body of Christ; and they that partake thereof, though
1 Cor. x. 16, 17. they be many, yet are but one bread, and one body.
Conf. Helv. II. cap. 21. Basil. Art. VI. Bohem. cap. 13. Belg. Art. XXXV. Saxon. Art. XIV. Suevica, cap. 18. This is the doctrine of all christian churches[1].

[[1] Admonemur præterea celebratione cœnæ Dominicæ ut memores simus corporis cujus membra facti sumus, et idcirco concordes simus cum omnibus fratribus, &c.—Harm. Conf. Sect. XIV. p. 111. Conf. Helv. Post. cap. XXI. Confitemur Dominum Jesum sanctam suam cœnam instituisse ad memorandam sanctam suam passionem cum gratiarum actione ad annunciandam mortem suam, atque ad testificandam Christianam charitatem et unitatem cum vera fide.—Ibid. p. 116. Conf. Basil. Art. VI. Hoc enim modo (sc. spirituali perceptione) Christo inserimur... atque...fit vera illa unio et communicatio Christi cum sua ecclesia: et vicissim ecclesiæ sanctæ quæ est spirituale corpus quoddam inter se et secum communio, de quo scribit apostolus, Unus panis est, &c.—Ibid. p. 119. Conf. Bohem. cap. XIII. Usu porro hujus sacramenti accenditur in nobis flagrantissimus amor tum in Deum ipsum, tum in proximum.—Ibid. p. 126. Conf. Belg. Art. XXXV. ...Cœnam Domini simul etiam voluit Dominus nervum esse publicæ congregationis, &c.....Vult (Deus) et ipsis ecclesiæ membris inter sese vinculum esse mutuæ benevolentiæ.—Ibid. pp. 137, 8. Conf. Saxon. Art. XIV. ....a Christo servatore nostro spectatum

The errors and adversaries unto this truth.

So think not those men, who either with heretic Hamant deny the use of the Lord's supper to be necessary, or with the Rhemists rail on it and the Protestants that use the same, calling it, "a profane and detestable table," "the cup of devils[2]."

Holin. Chron. fol. 1299.

Test. Rhem. Annot. 1 Cor. x. 21.

Proposition II.

The Lord's supper is a sacrament of our redemption by Christ's death, and to them which receive the same worthily by faith, a partaking of the body and blood of Christ.

The proof from God's word.

The sacrament of the Lord's supper is to all Christians a sacrament of our redemption by Jesus Christ. For "This is my blood of the new Testament, which is shed for many for the remission of sins;" "This is my body, which is given for you," &c. "This cup is the new Testament in my blood, which is shed for you," saith our Saviour.

Matt. xxvi. 28. Luke xxii. 19, 20. Mark xiv. 24. 1 Cor. xi. 24.

And to such as receive the same worthily, and by faith, it is the partaking of the body and blood of Christ.

1 Cor. xi. 28, &c. 2 Cor. xiii. 5. John vi. 35. 1 Cor. x. 16, 17.

This is a truth openly both maintained and testified by the neighbour churches[3].

Confess. Helvet. 1. Art. XXII. & II. cap. 21. Basil. Art. VI. Bohem. cap. 13. Gal. Art. XXXVII. Belg. Art. XXXV. August. touching the Mass, Art. I. III. Saxon. Art. XIV. Wittemb. cap. 19. Suevica, cap. 19.

est...ut ipso pasti, in ipso et per ipsum vivamus...simusque inter nos omnes unus panis, unum corpus, qui de uno pane in sacra cœna participamus.—Ibid. p. 149. Conf. Suev. cap. XVIII.]

[2 ...God...acknowledgeth none to be his that is not partaker of his one only table and sacrifice in his church: and acquitteth himself of all such as join in fellowship with...heretics and schismatics at their profane and detestable table. Which ...is indeed a very sacrifice, or (as the apostle here speaketh) a table and cup of devils, &c.—Test. Rhem. Rhemes, 1582. Ann. 1 Cor. x. 21. pp. 447, 8.]

[3 Cœnam vero mysticam esse in qua Dominus corpus et sanguinem suum (id est seipsum) suis vere ad hoc offerat, ut magis magisque vivat in illis et illi in ipso. —Harm. Conf. Sect. XIV. p. 112. Conf. Helv. Prior. Art. XXII. Obsignatur item hac cœna sacra, quod revera corpus Domini pro nobis traditum, et sanguis ejus in remissionem peccatorum nostrorum effusus est, ne quid fides nostra vacillet....Ergo accipiunt fideles quod datur a ministro Domini, et edunt panem Domini ac bibunt de poculo Domini: intus interim opera Christi per Spiritum sanctum percipiunt etiam carnem et sanguinem Domini, et pascuntur his in æternam vitam.—Ibid. p. 109. Conf. Helv. Post. cap. XXI. Credimus autem firmiter ipsummet Christum cibum esse credentium animarum ad vitam æternam et nostras animas per veram fidem in crucifixum Christum, carne et sanguine Christi cibari et potari.—Ibid. p. 116. Conf. Basil. Art. VI. See also above, p. 282, note 1. ...corde credimus et ore confitemur hunc cœnæ Dominicæ panem esse corpus Domini Jesu Christi, pro nobis traditum: et calicem seu vinum in hoc, similiter esse sanguinem ipsius pro nobis profusum ad remissionem peccatorum, &c.—Ibid. p. 118. Conf. Bohem. cap. XIII. ...affirmamus eos qui ad sacram mensam Domini puram fidem tanquam vas quoddam afferunt, vere recipere quod ibi signa testificantur, nempe corpus et

Errors and adversaries to this truth.

Diversely hath this proposition been oppugned. For

Some either denying, or not acknowledging, the benefit of so heavenly a sacrament, do say, how

Leon. Rams. Conf. an. 1580.

It is to be received only for obedience sake to the prince's commandment, but is of none effect to the perfect ones. An opinion of the Family's[1].

Theodoret. Eccles. Hist.

It doth neither good nor hurt to the receivers. The Messalians' error[2].

It doth much hurt and no good, to participate the Lord's supper among Protestants, say the Papists[a].

It is no sign assuring us that all our sins through Christ

[a] What can the Protestant churches afford you? &c. the Communion? O poisoned cup! better it were for you to eat so much ratsbane than that polluted bread, and to drink so much dragon's gall, or viper's blood, than that sacrilegious wine.—Garnish of the Soul, &c. Printed at Antwerp, *an.* 1596, by Joach. Tro. [In the Pref. to the Catholique-lyke Protestantes.]

---

sanguinem Jesu Christi non minus esse cibum ac potum animæ quam panis et vinum sunt corporis cibus.—Ibid. p. 121. Conf. Gall. Art. XXXVII. Ut autem panem hunc spiritualem et cœlestem Christus nobis figuraret...instituit panem et vinum, terrenum et visibilem, in corporis et sanguinis sui sacramentum. Iis vero testificatur nos quam vere accipimus et tenemus manibus nostris sacramentum, illudque ore comedimus...tam vere etiam nos fide....recipere verum corpus et verum sanguinem Christi, &c.—Ibid. p. 125. Conf. Belg. Art. XXXV. ....docentur...quod sacramentum....sit pignus quo Christus testetur se nobis præstare promissa, et quod promissiones ad nos pertineant, quod Christus exhibeat nobis corpus suum, ut testetur se in nobis efficacem esse tanquam in membris suis: exhibeat sanguinem, ut testetur nos ablui sanguine suo.—Ibid. p. 131. Conf. August. De Abus. Art. I. Docentur etiam homines...in hac communione vere et substantialiter adesse Christum, et vere exhiberi sumentibus corpus et sanguinem Christi: Christum testari quod sit in eis, et faciat eos sibi membra, et quod abluerit eos sanguine suo, &c.—Ibid. p. 139. Conf. Saxon. Art. XIV. Etsi eucharistia juxta institutionem Christi ita celebratur ut in ea annuntietur mors Christi et dispensetur ecclesiæ sacramentum corporis et sanguinis Christi, recte vocatur applicatio meriti passionis Christi, his videlicet, qui sacramentum sumunt.—Ibid. p. 145. Conf. Virtemb. cap. XIX. ...non minus hodie quam in novissima illa cœna omnibus qui inter illius discipulos ex animo nomen dederunt, quum hanc cœnam, ut ipse instituit, repetunt, verum suum corpus, verumque suum sanguinem vere edendum et bibendum in cibum potumque animarum, quo illæ in æternam vitam alantur, dare per sacramenta dignatur.—Ibid. p. 149. Conf. Suev. cap. XVIII.]

[[1] This reference the editor has been unable to verify.]

[[2] *...οὐδὲν οὔτε ὀνίνασθαι, οὔτε λωβᾶσθαι φάσκοντες τὴν θείαν τροφὴν, περὶ ἧς ὁ δεσπότης ἔφη Χριστὸς, ὁ τρώγων μου τὴν σάρκα κ.τ.λ.*—Theodoret. Opp. Lut. Par. 1642-84. Tom. III. p. 670. D. Eccl. Hist. Lib. IV. cap. 10.]

are pardoned. For only venial and mortal sins are thereby remitted[3], and we must always doubt of the forgiveness of our sins[4], say the same Papists. Catec. Trid. Concil. Trid. Sess. 6, cap. 9.

Others do teach, that

It can profit such as have no faith, as babes and infants[5]; in which errors be the Russians; yea, the dead bodies of men[6]. Alex. Guag. de Relig. Mosc. p. 268. Concil. Carthag. 3. Can. 6.

It can benefit such as receive it not at all, if on their behalf it be administered; as persons absent upon the seas, in the wars, yea, and dead; and present too, when yet they participate not, but the priest for them. These errors the Papists defend.

Proposition III.

The bread and wine in the Lord's supper be not changed into another substance.

The proof from God's word.

Transubstantiation, or the change of the substance of bread and wine in the supper of the Lord, we do utterly deny; and the reasons moving us thereunto are, for that it is repugnant to the plain words of the scripture. For

"I will not drink henceforth of this fruit of the vine," saith our Saviour Christ. Which fruit had it really been either the blood, or, by way of concomitance, the very body and blood of Jesus Christ, then our Lord had eaten himself; which is not only blasphemous to be spoken, but also impossible to be done, and directly against the word of God, where commandment is often given, that the blood with flesh (not of beast, much less of man) must not be eaten. Matt. xxvi. 29. Mark xiv. 25. Gen. ix. 4. Lev. xvii 14.

"The heaven must contain Jesus Christ until the time that all things be restored," saith St Peter. If Christ there- Acts iii. 21.

[[3] Remitti vero eucharistia, et condonari leviora peccata, quæ venalia dici solent, non est quod dubitari debeat.—Catech. Conc. Trid. Rom. 1566. p. 149.]

[[4] Nemini tamen fiduciam et certitudinem remissionis peccatorum suorum jactanti, et in ea sola quiescenti, peccata dimitti vel dimissa esse dicendum est, &c.—Concil. Harduin. Paris. 1714. Tom. x. col. 36. Conc. Trid. Sess. VI. cap. 9.]

[[5] Pueros qui septem annos transigerunt ad sacramentum admittunt.—Guag. Rel. Moscov. Spiræ Nemet. 1582. p. 268. But perhaps the reference should rather be to Faber. Rel. Mosc. p. 183, of the same volume. Unicum est quod a nobis sane probari non potest...quod pueris vixdum tres annos natis, eucharistiæ sacramentum præbent.]

[[6] See above, p. 266, note 8.]

fore corporally, according to his humanity, be in heaven, then is he not in the sacrament.

1 Cor. xi. 20. "As often as ye shall eat this bread (not Christ his real body) and drink this cup (not the real blood of Christ) you shew the Lord's death till he come;" saith St Paul. Therefore he is not come; which he must be, being under the forms of bread and wine.

Transubstantiation besides overthroweth the nature of the sacrament. For where there is no element there can be no sacrament. Because God's word coming unto the element maketh a sacrament.

Finally, it hath been the occasion of much superstition and idolatry. For from hence proceeded the reservation of the transubstantiated bread for sundry superstitious purposes: hence the adoration of the bread, even as God himself, and that both of priest and people: hence the carrying about, in pompous procession, of the wafer-god; and hence the popish feast called Corpus Christi day.

Conf. Helv. I. Art. XXII. & II. cap. 21. Basil. Art. VI. Bohem. c. 13. Wittemb. c. 19. The right consideration hereof hath moved all the churches reformed to shew their detestation hereof, both by their sermons and writings[1].

The adversaries unto this truth.

Abominable therefore be the popish errors, *viz.* that

Concil. Trid. Sess. 13, Can. 2. In the Eucharist there is not the substance of bread and wine, but only the mere accidents and qualities[2].

[[1] Non quod pani et vino corpus et sanguis Domini vel naturaliter uniantur, vel hic localiter includantur, vel ulla hac carnali præsentia statuantur, &c.—Harm. Conf. Sect. XIV. p. 112. Conf. Helv. Prior. Art. XXII. Ergo corpus Domini et sanguinem ejus cum pane et vino non ita conjungimus, ut panem ipsum dicamus esse corpus Christi, nisi ratione sacramentali, aut sub pane corporaliter latitare corpus Christi, ut etiam sub speciebus panis adorari debeat, aut quicunque signum percipiat, idem et rem percipiat ipsam.—Ibid. p. 111. Conf. Helv. Post. cap. XXI. ...in cœna Domini (in qua nobis cum pane et vino Domini, verum corpus et verus sanguis Christi per ministrum ecclesiæ præfiguratur et offertur) panis et vinum manet.—Ibid. p. 116. Conf. Basil. Art. VI. ...docetur amplius, etiamsi panis sit corpus Christi de institutione ipsius et vinum sanguis hujus sit, neutrum tamen horum naturam suam exuere, aut substantiam mutare aut amittere; sed panem verum panem, et vinum verum vinum esse et manere.—Ibid. p. 118. Conf. Bohem. cap. XIII. ...quum de pane dicitur, Hoc est corpus meum, non est necesse ut substantia panis mutetur in substantiam corporis Christi, sed ad veritatem sacramenti sufficit quod corpus Christi vere sit cum pane præsens, atque adeo necessitas ipsa veritatis sacramenti exigere videtur, ut cum vera præsentia corporis Christi verus panis maneat.—Ibid. p. 144. Conf. Virtemb. cap. XIX.]

[[2] Si quis dixerit in sacrosancto eucharistiæ sacramento remanere substantiam panis et vini, una cum corpore et sanguine Domini nostri Jesus Christi, negaveritque

Substantially and really the body and blood, together with the soul and divinity of our Lord Jesus Christ, and therefore whole Christ, is contained in the Sacrament Eucharistical[3]. Test. Rhem. An. Matt. xxvi. 26.

Under each kind, and under every part of each kind severally, whole Christ is comprised[4]. Concil. Trid. Sess. 13, can. 3. Vaux Cat. c. 4.

After the consecration in the wonderful sacrament of the Eucharist the body and blood of our Lord Jesus Christ is; and that not only in the use, while it is taken, but afore also, and after in the hosts, or consecrated pieces, reserved or remaining after the communion[5]. Conc. Trid. Sess. 13, can. 6.

In the holy sacrament, Christ, the only-begotten Son of God, is to be adored with the very worship of Latria[6]. Concil. Trid. Sess. 13, can. 6.

Marcus also, that detestable heretic, held, that the wine of the Lord's supper was converted into blood[7]. Epiphan. Hæres. 34.

mirabilem illam et singularem conversionem totius substantiæ panis in corpus, et totius substantiæ vini in sanguinem, manentibus duntaxat speciebus panis et vini; quam quidem conversionem catholica ecclesia aptissime transubstantiationem appellat; anathema sit.—Concil. Harduin. Tom. x. col. 83. Conc. Trid. Sess. XIII. De Euch. Sacram. can. 2.]

[3 ...though now not only in heaven, but also in the sacrament he (Christ) be indeed *per concomitantiam* (as the church calleth it, that is by sequel of all his parts to each other) whole, alive, and immortal, &c.—Test. Rhem. Rhemes, 1582. Ann. Matt. xxvi. 26. p. 79.]

[4 Si quis negaverit in venerabili sacramento eucharistiæ sub unaquaque specie, et sub singulis cujusque speciei partibus, separatione facta, totum Christum contineri; anathema sit.—Conc. Trid. Sess. XIII. can. 3.

Vaux, Catechism. Antv. 1574. chap. iv. p. 75. See below, p. 289, note b.]

[5 Si quis dixerit, peracta consecratione, in admirabili eucharistiæ sacramento non esse corpus et sanguinem Domini nostri Jesu Christi; sed tantum in usu dum sumitur, non autem ante vel post: et in hostiis, seu particulis consecratis, quæ post communionem reservantur vel supersunt, non remanere verum corpus Domini; anathema sit.—Conc. Trid. Sess. XIII. can. 4.]

[6 Si quis dixerit in sancto eucharistiæ sacramento Christum unigenitum Dei filium non esse cultu latriæ, etiam externo, adorandum......anathema sit.—Ibid. can. 6.]

[7 *Φασὶ γὰρ τρία ποτήρια λευκῆς ὑάλου παρ' αὐτοῖς ἑτοιμάζεσθαι, κεκραμένα λευκῷ οἴνῳ. καὶ ἐν τῇ ἐπιτελουμένῃ παρ' αὐτοῦ ἐπῳδῇ τῇ νομιζομένῃ εὐχαριστίᾳ μεταβάλλεσθαι εὐθὺς, τὸ μὲν ἐρυθρὸν ὡς αἷμα, τὸ δὲ πορφύρεον, τὸ δὲ κυάνεον.*—Epiphan. Opp. Paris. 1622. Tom. I. p. 233. Adv. Hær. Lib. I. Tom. III. Hær. 34.]

Proposition IV.

The Body of Christ is given, taken, and eaten, after an heavenly and spiritual, not after a carnal sort.

The proof from God's word.

The regenerate have in them a double life, one carnal, the other spiritual.

1 Pet. i. 23. The life carnal and temporary they brought with them into this world: the spiritual was given unto them afterward in their second birth through the word.

The life carnal and corporal is common to all men, good and bad, and is maintained and preserved by earthly and corruptible bread, common also to all and every man. The life spiritual is peculiar only to God's elect, and is cherished by the bread of life which came down from heaven, which is Jesus Christ, who nourisheth and sustaineth the spiritual life of Christians, being received of them by faith. (John vi. 51. John vi. 35.)

Which spiritual bread, that he might the better represent, he hath instituted earthly and visible bread and wine, for a sacrament of his body and blood. Whereby he doth testify, that as verily as we receive the bread with the hands, and chew the same with the teeth and tongue, to the nourishing of this life temporal, even so by faith (which is in place of hands and mouth to the soul) we verily receive the true body, and the true blood of Christ, our only Saviour, to the cherishing of the spiritual life in our souls.

Conf. Helv. I. Art. XXII. & II. c. 21. Basil. Art. VI. Bohem. c. 13. Gal. Art. XXXVI. Belg. Art. XXXV.

And herein there is a goodly consent with the most of the reformed churches and us [1].

[[1] ...sed quod panis et vinum ex institutione Domini symbola sint, quibus ab ipso Domino per ecclesiæ ministerium vera corporis et sanguinis ejus communicatio non in periturum ventris cibum, sed in æternæ vitæ alimoniam exhibeatur.—Harm. Conf. Sect. XIV. p. 113. Conf. Helv. Prior. Art. XXII. Est et spiritualis manducatio corporis Christi, non ea quidem, qua existimemus cibum ipsum mutari in Spiritum, sed qua, manente in sua essentia et proprietate corpore et sanguine Domini ea nobis communicantur spiritualiter, utique non corporali modo, sed spirituali, per Spiritum Sanctum, &c.—Ibid. p. 109. Conf. Helv. Post. cap. XXI. ...in cœna Domini (in qua nobis cum pane et vino Domini, verum corpus et verus sanguis Christi, per ministrum ecclesiæ præfiguratur et offertur) panis et vinum manet. Credimus autem firmiter ipsummet Christum cibum esse credentium animarum, &c.—Ibid. p. 116. Conf. Basil. Art. VI. Et quanquam utrique (sc. boni et mali) verum sacramentum et hanc veritatem ejus sacramentaliter, et externo modo accipiunt, credentes tamen soli spiritualiter, atque ita cum salute sua accipiunt; absque qua spirituali perceptione, nulla in usu sacramentali digna fit perceptio.—Ibid. p. 119. Conf. Bohem. cap. XIII. Quamvis enim nunc sit (Christus) in cœlis...credimus tamen eum arcana et incomprehensibili Spiritus sui virtute nos

The adversaries unto this truth.

Jointly we withstand the adversaries thereof whosoever; as the Capernaites, which thought the flesh of our Lord might be eaten with corporal mouths.

The Synusiasts, or Ubiquitaries[a], which think the body of Christ so is present in the supper, as his said body, with bread and wine, by one and the same mouth, at one and the same time, of all and every communicant, is eaten corporally and received into the belly.

The Metusiasts and Papists[b], which believe the substance of bread and wine is so changed into the substance of Christ his body, as nothing remaineth but the real body of Christ, besides the accidents of bread and wine.

The Symbolists, Figurists, and Significatists, who are of opinion that the faithful at the Lord's supper do receive nothing but naked and bare signs.

[a] Aliqui μετουσίασιν fugimus, sed in cognatum delabimur συνουσίασιν, pani et vino substantiam equidem relinquendo, sed corporale Christi corpus ita coaduniendo, ut substantia substantiam vel localiter, vel definitive, vel repletive, vel omnibus istis modis simul contineat: quod ipsum profecto nil est aliud, quam Transubstantiationis quoddam quasi involucrum, &c.—Jezler De Diutur. bell. Euchar. [Tigur. 1584] p. 18. a.

[b] After consecration there is neither bread nor wine left in this sacrament, saith Vaux in his Catech. By virtue of the words of consecration the substance of bread is turned and changed into the very body of Christ; and the substance of wine is turned into the blood of Christ, the Holy Ghost working by a divine power, so that Christ is wholly under the form of bread, and in every part of the Host, being broken, Christ is wholly: also under the form of wine and every part thereof, being separated, Christ is wholly.—Canis. Catech. c. 4[2]. Romanenses introduxerunt μετουσίασιν, vos (Lutherani) συνουσίασιν, ejus sororem, et plurimorum errorum matrem, πανταχότητα.—Jezler. De Diutur. bell. Euchar. [ut supra] p. 31. b.

---

nutrire et vivificare sui corporis et sanguinis substantia per fidem apprehensa. Dicimus autem hoc spiritualiter fieri, &c.—Ibid. p. 121. Conf. Gall. Art. XXXVI. Ceterum nequaquam erraverimus dicentes, id quod comeditur esse ipsissimum Christi corpus naturale et id quod bibitur, verum ipsius sanguinem. At instrumentum, seu medium quo hæc comedimus et bibimus, non est os corporeum, sed spiritus ipse noster, idque per fidem. Christus itaque semper ad dexteram Patris in cœlis residet, nec ideo minus se nobis per fidem communicat. Porro hæc cœna mensa est spiritualis, &c.—Ibid. p. 126. Conf. Belg. Art. XXXV.]

[[2] This should be Vaux, Catech. Antv. 1574. ch. iv. p. 75, where the words are found.]

Proposition V.

To reserve, carry about, lift up, or worship the Sacrament of the Lord's Supper, is contrary to the ordinance of Christ.

The proof from God's word.

Matt. xxvi. 26. Mark xiv. 22. Luke xxii. 19. 1 Cor. x. 16, & xi. 2. Matt. xxvi. 27. Mark xiv. 23. Luke xxii. 17. 1 Cor. xi. 25. Luke xxii. 19.

The true and lawful use of this sacrament hath been afore set down; and therefore it may suffice us to be remembered, how the Lord's supper was ordained that the bread should only[1] be broken, and eaten, the cup should only be given, and drunken; and all this done in remembrance of Christ.

And so also testify the churches reformed[2].

1 Cor. xi. 24, 25. Conf. Helv. II. cap. 21. Basil. Art. VI. Bohem. cap. 13. August. de Missa, Art. I. Saxon. Art. XIV. Wittemb. cap. 19.

Adversaries unto this truth.

Concil. Trid. Sess. 13. cap. 6.

But, contrary to the institution of Christ, the Papists abuse the holy sacrament. For

Ibid. Can. 6.

They reserve the same; and not only so, but take it to be a catholic, a pious, and a necessary custom, so to reserve it[3]. And besides, they think every piece and particle of the sacrament so reserved is the very body of Christ[4].

[1 Not only, 1607.]

[2 Corpus Christi in cœlis est, ad dexteram Patris. Sursum ergo elevanda sunt corda, et non defigenda in panem, nec adorandus Dominus in pane.—Harm. Conf. Sect. XIV. p. 111. Conf. Helv. Post. cap. XXI. Non includimus autem naturale, verum et substantiale corpus Christi...in Domini panem et potum. Itaque nec adoramus Christum in signis panis et vini...sed in cœlis, &c.—Ibid. p. 117. Conf. Basil. Art. VI. Ita igitur...corpus et sanguis Domini nostri Jesu Christi distribui tantum, et a fidelibus...percipi debet, non autem sacrificari, aut proponi aut venerationis causa attolli, monstrarique et asservari aut circumferri debet.—Ibid. p. 119. Conf. Bohem. cap. XIII. Hic honos sacrificii Christi non debet transferri in opus Sacerdotis.....Institutione cœnæ Domini, non mandat Christus ut offerant sacerdotes pro aliis vivis ac mortuis. Qua igitur auctoritate hic cultus tanquam oblatio pro peccatis sine mandato Dei in ecclesia institutus est?—Ibid. p. 129. Conf. August. Pars II. De Abus. Art. I. Quum autem hæc omnia manifeste sint impia, facere oblationem, ut loquuntur, ut mereatur vivis et mortuis...horribiliter peccant qui hæc scelera retinent et defendunt....Est et manifesta profanatio, partem Cœnæ Domini circumgestare et adorare, &c.—Ibid. p. 141. Conf. Saxon. Art. XIV. ...Alius error est quod Eucharistia sit tale sacrificium, quod debeat jugiter in Ecclesia, ad expianda peccata vivorum et mortuorum, &c....offerri...Alius error est, quod una pars Eucharistiæ soleat in singularem cultum Dei circumgestari, et reponi.—Ibid. pp. 146, 8, Conf. Virtemb. cap. XIX.]

[3 Consuetudo asservandi in sacrario sanctam Eucharistiam adeo antiqua est, ut eam seculum etiam Nicæni concilii agnoverit. Porro deferri ipsam sacram Eucharistiam ad infirmos, et in hunc usum diligenter in ecclesiis conservari, præterquam quod cum summa æquitate et ratione conjunctum est, tum multis in conciliis præceptum invenitur, et vetustissimo Catholicæ Ecclesiæ more est observatum.—Concil. Harduin. Tom. x. col. 81. Conc. Trid. Sess. XIII. cap. 6.]

[4 See above, p. 287, note 5.]

They carry it about, both unto sick folks; hence saith the Festival, "As often as any man seeth that body at mass, or borne about to the sick, he shall kneel down devoutly, and say his *Pater noster*, or some other good prayer in worship of his sovereign Lord[5]."

Festival, 4 Sermons, fol. 170. B.

And also through cities and towns. For whensoever the pope goeth any journey, the sacramental bread is carried before him on an ambling jennet; as the Persian kings have before them carried their Orsmada, or holy [a]fire[6].

In Spain, even at this day, in the time of the peace between the two mighty kings of Great Britain and Spain, those Englishmen, as meeting the sacrament in the streets will neither do reverence thereunto, nor go aside, nor turn into some house, do fall into the danger of the not holy, but bloody inquisition[7].

Act of the Peace, &c. *anno* 1604, Art. II. in the end touching a moderation, &c.

They worship it, and for the same have ordained a certain set and solemn feast, called Corpus Christi day, on which the sacrament is borne about, lifted up, and most idolatrously adored[8].

Concil. Trid. Sess. 13. cap. 5.

[a] See Cerem. Pontif. Lib. I. When the pope goeth from one people to another, he sendeth before him, yea, and sometime a day or two days' journey, his sacrament upon an horse, carrying at his neck a little bell, accompanied with the scum and baggage of the Roman court. Thither go the dishes and spits, old shoes, cauldrons and kettles, and all the scullery of the court, whores, and jesters. Thus the sacrament arriveth, with this honourable train, to the place whither the pope is to come: it there awaiteth his coming, and when the master is known to approach near the people, it goeth forth to receive him. So Cypr. Valera, a Spaniard, in his treatise Of the Pope and his Authority, p. 17.

[5 The Festyvall. Ed. Faques. Quat. Serm. Fol. 170, b.]

[6 Et post eos ducitur per familiarem sacristæ...equus albus, mansuetus, ornatus...portans sacramentum, habens ad collum tintinnabulum bene sonantem.—Sacr. Ceremon. Rom. 1560. Lib. I. Tit. ii. fol. 16. b. See also Cyp. Valera, Two Treatises, Of the Lives of the Popes, &c. Transl. into Eng. Lond. 1600, where *scullery of the court of Rome*, and *at the place*. Of the Orismada he says: The popes in this carrying of the Sacrament before them do imitate the kings of Persia, before whom went a horse carrying a little altar upon him: whereupon among a few ashes shone a small flame of holy fire: which they call Orismada.—Ibid.]

[7 The editor has been unable to verify the reference.]

[8 Declarat præterea sancta Synodus pie et religiose admodum in Dei Ecclesia inductum fuisse hunc morem, ut singulis annis peculiari quodam et festo die præcelsum hoc et venerabile Sacramentum singulari veneratione ac solemnitate celebrare-

ARTICLE XXIX.

Of the Wicked which do not eat the body and blood of Christ in the use of the Lord's Supper.

The wicked, and such as be void of a lively faith, although they do carnally and visibly press with their teeth (as St Augustine saith) the Sacrament of the Body and Blood of Christ, yet in no wise are they partakers of Christ, but rather, to their condemnation, do eat and drink the sign or sacrament of so great a thing.

The proposition.

The wicked, and such as be void of a lively faith, do not eat the body, nor drink the blood of Jesus Christ, in the use of the Lord's supper.

The proof from God's word.

1 Cor. xi. 28. Ibid. 29. 1 Cor. x. 21. St Paul doth shew how the supper of the Lord is received of some worthily, which do examine and judge themselves, and discern the Lord's body, as also do abstain from the table of devils. How these do participate of the body and blood of Christ, it hath already been shewn in the last-mentioned Article, Proposit. IV.

1 Cor. xi. 27, 29. Ibid. 28, 31. Ibid. 29. 1 Cor. x. 21. Again, of others the same is unworthily received; that is to say, which themselves do not examine, nor judge, neither discern the Lord's body, and do communicate at the table of the Lord and at the table of devils. These may receive the sacrament, but not the true body of Christ. The reasons be, for that

Matt. xxii. 11, 12. They lack the wedding-garment, which is faith, and the righteousness of Christ.

Eph. iv. 15, &c. They are no members of the true church, the head whereof is Jesus Christ.

John vi. 35. They have no promise of heavenly refreshing, because they are without a lively faith.

1 Cor. xi. 27. Therefore they procure unto themselves most heavy punishments; as diseases, death, guiltiness of the body and blood of Christ, and therewith damnation.

tur: utque in processionibus reverenter et honorifice illud per vias et loca publica circumferretur.—Conc. Trid. Sess. XIII. cap. 5.]

Of this judgement be other churches, Christian and reformed besides[1].

Conf. Helv. in the declaration of the Lord's supper.

Helv. II. cap. 21. Basil. Art. VI. Bohem. cap. 13. Gal. Art. XXXVII. Belg. Art. XXXV.

Errors and adversaries unto this truth.

The adversaries of this doctrine are

The Ubiquitaries, both Lutheran and popish; they saying the very body of Christ, at the Lord's supper, is eaten as well of the wicked as of the godly[2]; these affirming, that all communicants, bad and good, do eat the very and natural body of Christ Jesus[3]; they saying that the true and real body of Christ, in, with, under the bread and wine, may be eaten, chewed, and digested, even of Turks, which never were of the church[4]; and these maintaining, that under the form of bread the same true and real body of Christ may be devoured of dogs, hogs, cats, and rats[5].

Sturmius, Anti-Pap. 4, par. 1, p. 58.

Test. Rhem. Annot. 1 Cor. xi. 27.

So reporteth Sturmius in his Anti-Pap. 4, par. 2, p. 106.

Alex. Hales, par. 4, q. 45, & D. Thom. par. 3, q. 8, Art. III.

[1 Qui autem indigne, id est, sine fide (per quam solam Domini et salutis efficimur participes) de pane hoc ederit et de poculo biberit, [fatemur] sibi judicium manducare et bibere.—Harm. Conf. Sect. XIV. p. 115. Conf. Helv. Prior. Declarat. de Sacr. Dom. Cœn. Ceterum qui nulla cum fide ad hanc sacram Domini mensam accedit, sacramento duntaxat communicat, et rem sacramenti, unde est vita et salus, non percipit: et tales indigne edunt de mensa Domini, &c.—Ibid. p. 111. Conf. Helv. Post. cap. XXI. Utuntur autem hoc (sacramento) utrique, boni et mali, et tamen vere credentes ad vitam, non credentes autem ad judicium, et condemnationem.—Ibid. p. 119. Conf. Bohem. cap. XIII. ...affirmamus eos, qui ad sacram mensam Domini, puram fidem, tanquam vas quoddam afferunt, vere recipere quod ibi signa testificantur, &c.—Ibid. p. 121. Conf. Gall. Art. XXXVII. Præterea quamvis sacramenta sint conjuncta rei ipsi significatæ, ambæ tamen res istæ non ab omnibus recipiuntur. Malus enim recipit quidem sacramentum in suam condemnationem, at rem seu veritatem sacramenti non recipit.—Ibid. p. 126. Conf. Belg. Art. XXXV.]

[2 There is an error in the reference, but see below, note 4.]

[3 *Guilty of the body.* First hereupon mark well, that ill men receive the body and blood of Christ, be they infidels or ill livers.—Test. Rhem. Rhemes, 1582. Ann. 1 Cor. xi. 27. p. 453.]

[4 Aiunt pontificii, verum corpus natum ex Maria virgine, ut natum est, ut vixit, ut cruci suspensum fuit, illud inquam in cruce cruentatum, esse ita corporaliter cum pane, ut panis specie sit, revera non sit panis, corpus autem totum sit, et ore comedi illud et manducari ab indignis et malis et improbis Christianis sive fidelibus. Lutherani qui nunc sunt et dici volunt, excepta transubstantiatione idem dicunt: et amplius videntur addere, etiam ab impiis et Turcis manducari et ore masticari.—Sturmius, Quart. Antipapp. Neap. Palat. 1580. Pars Sec. Antiproœm. p. 106.]

[5 Prima autem opinio quæ dicit, quod corpus Christi defertur quocunque species deferuntur, et in ventrem canis vel suis, vel in alia loca immunda, videtur vera: salvo enim vero esse specierum, adhuc non desinit esse sacramentum, nec Christus sub specie.—Alex. Alens. Summ. Theolog. Col. 1622. Pars IV. Quæst. XI. Art. 4. § 3. p. 407. Ad tertium dicendum quod etiam si mus vel canis hostiam consecratam manducet substantia corporis Christi non desinit esse sub speciebus quamdiu species illæ manent &c.—Thom. Aquin. Summ. Theolog. Duac. 1614. Pars III. Quæst. LXXX. Art. 3. fol. 181.]

ARTICLE XXX.

Of both kinds.

The cup of the Lord is not to be denied to the lay-people; for both the parts of the Lord's Sacrament, by Christ's ordinance and commandment, ought to be ministered to all Christian men.

The proposition.

The people must be partakers, not only of the bread, but also of the wine, when they approach unto the Lord's table.

The proof from God's word.

Our Lord and Saviour Christ hath so instituted his supper, as he will have not only the bread, but also the cup, to be delivered unto all communicants. So find we in the word of God, namely,

Matt. xxvi. 26. Mark xiv. 22. Luke xxii. 19. 1 Cor. x. 16, & xi. 23, 24, 25. Matt. xxvi. 27. Mark xxv. 23. Luke xxii. 20. 1 Cor. x. 16, & xi. 25. Conf. Helv. I. Art. XXII. & II. cap. 21. Bohem. cap. 13. Gal. Art. XXXVI. XXXVIII. Belg. Art. XXXV. August. de Missa, Art. I. II. Saxon. Art. XV. Wittemb. cap. 19. Suevica, cap. 18.

That the bread must be given to all, and eaten of all.

The cup is to be given to all, and to be drunken of all.

Hereunto subscribe the churches[1].

The adversaries unto this truth.

Gal. iii. 15. "Though it be a man's covenant, yet when it is confirmed, no man doth abrogate, or addeth anything thereunto." What impudency then, yea, what impiety, do they shew which alter this ordinance of God!

[[1] Improbamus itaque illos qui alteram speciem, poculum inquam Domini, fidelibus subtraxerunt. Graviter enim peccant contra institutionem domini dicentis, Bibite ex hoc omnes, &c.—Harm. Conf. Sect. XIV. p. 112. Conf. Helv. Post. cap. XXI. ...et distinctis elementis hæc ambo accipi debent: peculiariter et separatim corpus, et separatim sanguis ejus sanctus, sicut singula separatim a Domino instituta, porrecta, et universis communiter tradita fuerunt.—Ibid. p. 119. Conf. Bohem. cap. XIII. Itemque panem illum, et vinum illud quod nobis in Cœna datur, &c.—Ibid. p. 122. Conf. Gall. Art. XXXVIII. Et quoniam communis missa apud nos celebratur, ut intelligat populus se quoque sanctificari sanguine Christi et discat verum usum ceremoniæ, datur laicis utraque pars sacramenti in Cœna Domini, &c.—Ibid. p. 135. Conf. August. De Abus. Art. II. Norunt omnes Cœnam Domini ita institutam esse, ut detur populo integrum sacramentum, sicut scriptum est, Bibite ex hoc omnes...fatendum est prohibitionem unius partis injustam esse.—Ibid. p. 143. Conf. Saxon. Art. XV. Quod autem ad Eucharistiæ usum attinet, primum etsi non negamus quin totus Christus tam pane quam vino Eucharistiæ dispensetur, tamen docemus usum utriusque partis debere universæ Ecclesiæ communem esse.—Ibid. p. 145. Conf. Virtemb. cap. XIX. The other references are inferential. See above, p. 288, note 1.]

Some, by adding thereto: so added was unto the bread cheese by the Artotarites[2]; blood by the Cataphrygians[3]; the seed of man by the Manichees[4]; unto the wine warm water by the Moscovites[5].

Epiphan. Philastrius. Aug. de Hær. J. Faber. de Relig. Moscov.

Some, by taking therefrom: so the Encratites[6], the Tatians[7], the Severians[8], use no wine at all; the Manichees do minister only the bread[9]: the Papists, though they use both kinds, yet they always deny the cup unto the people, and unto priests also when they say not mass[10]; affirming that

Epiphan. Theodoret. Epiphan. Leo, Ser. 4. Quadrages. Concil. Trid. Sess. 5, cap. 1, & sess. 21, c. 1, 2, 3.

The people, participating of the cup, thereby perceive no fruit of spiritual comfort, but receive to themselves damnation[11].

Censura Colon. p. 289.

[2 *'Αρτοτυρίτας δὲ αὐτοὺς καλοῦσιν ἀπὸ τοῦ ἐν τοῖς αὐτῶν μυστηρίοις ἐπιτιθέντας ἄρτον καὶ τυρὸν, καὶ οὕτως ποιεῖν τὰ αὐτῶν μυστήρια.*—Epiphan. Opp. Paris. 1622. Tom. I. p. 418. Adv. Hær. Lib. II. Tom. I. Hær. 49.]

[3 Dicunt enim eos de infantis sanguine in Pascha miscere in suum sacrificium.—Philastr. Lib. de Hær. in Biblioth. Patr. Paris. 1624. Tom. IV. col. 13.]

[4 ...coguntur electi eorum velut eucharistiam conspersam cum semine humano sumere.—August. Opp. Paris, 1836-8. Tom. VIII. col. 50. De Hær. Lib. Hær. xlvi.]

[5 Calici item tantum aquæ quantum vini rubei miscent: quam aquam et calidam esse volunt, quod ex latere Domini, &c.—Faber. Relig. Moscov. Spiræ Nemet. 1582. p. 175.]

[6 *...τὰ παρ' αὐτοῖς μυστήρια δι' ὕδατος μόνου γίνεται, καὶ οὔτε μυστήρια ὄντα, ἀλλὰ κατὰ μίμησιν τῶν ἀληθινῶν, τὰ ψεύδη γινόμενα.*—Epiphan. Opp. Tom. I. p. 401. Adv. Hær. Lib. II. Tom. I. Hær. 47.]

[7 *ἠρανίσατο δὲ* (Τατίανος)*...τὴν τοῦ οἴνου μετάληψιν. τοῦτον* (i. e. Tatian) *ἔχουσιν ἀρχηγὸν οἱ λεγόμενοι 'Υδροπαραστάται καὶ 'Εγκρατιταί. 'Υδροπαραστάται δὲ ὀνομάζονται, ὡς ὕδωρ ἀντὶ οἴνου προσφέροντες, κ.τ.λ.*—Theodoret. Opp. Tom. IV. p. 208. a. Hær. Fab. Lib. I. cap. 20.]

[8 *...ἀπέχονται οἴνου πολυτελῶς οἱ τοιοῦτοι.*—Epiphan. Opp. Tom. I. p. 388. Adv. Hær. Lib. I. Tom. III. Hær. 45.]

[9 Cumque ad tegendam infidelitatem suam nostris audeant interesse conventibus, ita in sacramentorum communione se temperant, ut interdum ne penitus latere non possint, ore indigno Christi Corpus accipiant, sanguinem autem redemptionis nostræ haurire omnino declinent.—Leon. Magn. Opp. Venet. 1753-7. Tom. I. col. 161. Serm. xlii. De Quadrages. iv.]

[10 Itaque sancta ipsa synodus...declarat ac docet, nullo divino præcepto laicos et clericos non conficientes obligari ad Eucharistiæ sacramentum sub utraque specie sumendum: neque ullo pacto salva fide dubitari posse, quin illis alterius speciei communio ad salutem sufficiat. Licet ab initio Christianæ religionis non infrequens utriusque speciei usus fuisset, tamen progressa temporis, latissime jam mutate illa consuetudine, gravibus et justis causis adducta [Ecclesia] hanc consuetudinem sub altera specie communicandi approbavit....Insuper declarat quamvis Redemptor noster...in suprema illa cœna hoc sacramentum in duabus speciebus instituerit, et Apostolis tradiderit; tamen fatendum esse, etiam sub altera tantum specie, totum atque integrum Christum, verumque sacramentum sumi. Ac propterea, quod ad fructum attinet nulla gratia necessaria ad salutem eos defraudari, qui unam speciem solam accipiunt.—Concil. Harduin. Tom. x. col. 119, 120. Concil. Trid. Sess. XXI. capp. 1, 2, 3.]

[11 This reference the editor has been unable to verify.]

Ibid. p. 283.

It is not by God's, but man's law, that lay-persons communicate, either in both kinds, or in one[1].

Conc. Constan. Sess. 13.

Notwithstanding that Christ instituted the sacrament to be received under both kinds, and the primitive church accordingly did so administer the same: *Hoc tamen non obstante*, yet, this notwithstanding, it is to be taken of the laity but under one kind[2].

Surius, Comment. an. 1501, p. 31. Catec. Trid.

Some, by confounding the elements. So the Muscovites do mingle bread and wine together[3]; and the Papists make a mixture of wine and water, maintaining that water must be

Ibid.

mixed with wine at the consecration of the blood[4], and that the mixture of water with wine without sin cannot be omitted[5].

Theodoret.

Some, by changing the elements. So the Aquarians, and the Hydroparastatites, for wine, administered and gave water unto the people[6].

ARTICLE XXXI.

Of the one Oblation of Christ finished upon the Cross.

The offering of Christ once made (1) *is that perfect redemption, propitiation, and satisfaction for all the sins*

[1 See last note.]

[2 ...licet Christus post cœnam instituerit et suis discipulis administraverit sub utraque specie panis et vini hoc venerabile sacramentum; tamen hoc non obstante, sacrorum Canonum auctoritas laudabilis et approbata consuetudo ecclesiæ servavit et servat, quod hujusmodi sacramentum non debet confici post cœnam, &c.... Et sicut hæc consuetudo ad evitandum aliqua pericula et scandala est rationabiliter introducta, quod licet in primitiva Ecclesia hujusmodi sacramentum reciperetur a fidelibus sub utraque specie, tamen postea a conficientibus sub utraque, et a laicis tantummodo sub specie panis suscipiatur, cum firmissime credendum sit, et nullatenus dubitandum, integrum Christi corpus et sanguinem tam sub specie panis quam sub specie vini contineri...hujusmodi consuetudo...habenda est pro lege quam non licet reprobare, &c.—Concil. Harduin. Paris. 1714. Tom. VIII. col. 381. Concil. Constant. Sess. XIII.]

[3 Communicant sub utraque specie, sed ita ut corpus sanguini misceant in calice, unde sacerdos cum cochleari portiunculam accipit, et porrigit communicanti.—Surius, Comment. Brev. Rer. Gest. &c. Colon. 1574. p. 29.]

[4 Superest ut de altera hujus sacramenti materia, et elemento dicatur. Est autem vinum ex vitis fructu expressum, cui modicum aquæ permixtum sit...Aquam vero Dei Ecclesia vino semper admiscuit.—Catech. Conc. Trid. Rom. 1566. p. 134.]

[5 Sed quamvis aquæ admiscendæ ita graves rationes sint, ut eam sine mortali peccato prætermittere non liceat, &c.—Ibid.]

[6 See above, p. 295, note 7.]

of the whole world, both original and actual; and there is none other satisfaction for sin but that alone. Wherefore (2) *the sacrifice of masses, in the which it was commonly said that the priests did offer Christ for the quick and the dead to have remission of pain and guilt, were blasphemous fables, and dangerous deceits.*

The propositions.

1. The blood of Jesus Christ once shed for mankind upon the cross is a perfect redemption, propitiation, and satisfaction for all the sins of the whole world.

2. Sacrifices of the mass are most blasphemous fables and dangerous deceits.

Proposition I.

The blood of Jesus Christ once shed for mankind upon the cross is a perfect redemption, propitiation, and satisfaction for all the sins of the whole world.

The proof from God's word.

Of the benefits redounding unto mankind by Christ his offering up of himself upon the cross, we have in sundry places afore spoken, and by the word of God proved him to be the perfect redemption, propitiation, and satisfaction for all the sins of the whole world, both original and actual.

See Art. II. prop. 4. Art. XXII. prop. 2. Art. XXVIII. prop. 2. Acts xx. 28. Rom. v. 6, &c. Gal. iii. 13. 1 Cor. vi. 28. 1 Pet. i. 18, 19. Acts x. 43. Rom. iii. 25. Heb. ix. 12, &c. 28. 1 John ii. 2. 1 John iv. 10. John i. 29. 1 Pet. iii. 18. 1 John i. 7.

Hereunto the churches of God bear witness[7].

Conf. Helv. I. Art. XI. & II. cap. 11, 15. Basil. Art. IV. Bohem. c. 6. Gal. Art. XIII. XVI. XVII. Belg. Art. XX. XXII. August. Art. XXXIV. Saxon. Art. III. Wittemb. c. 2, 5. Suevic. c. 2, 3.

The errors and adversaries unto this truth.

Hereby it is evident to the eyes of all godly persons, that most accursed be the errors of them which do affirm that

From the beginning of the world until the fifteenth year of the Emperor Tiberius none at all were saved. The error of Manes the heretic[8]. Epiphan.

Man's body is not capable of happiness, but the soul only; and yet no souls shall be saved but their own, said the Marcionites[9]. D. Iren. Lib. I. cap. 29.

All men and women that sin after baptism are undoubtedly

[7 See above, pp. 56, 219, 283.]

[8 See above, p. 137, note 5.]

[9 Salutem autem solum animarum esse futuram, earum quæ ejus doctrinam didicissent; corpus autem, videlicet quoniam a terra sit sumptum, impossibile esse participare salutem.—Iren. Adv. Hær. Oxon. 1702. Lib. I. cap. 29. p. 104.]

D. Hieron. ad Marcel. Lib. II. D. Cyp. Lib. IV. Epist. 2. Bullinger contra Anab. Lib. II. cap. 13. Holinsh. Chr. fol. 1299.

damned. In this error were the Montanists[1] and the Novatians[2].

"Our salvation is of ourselves;" so said Melchior Hoffman, an arch-heretic[3].

Man is restored to grace of God's mere mercy, without the means of Christ's blood, death, and passion; one of Matthew Hamant's blasphemous assertions.

Dial. of Div. & Paup. 6, com. Jesuits' Cat. 1. b. c. 10. p. 28, b. Conf. S. Fran.

The Saviour of men is Jesus Christ, a man, and came into the world to save no women, but men, say some[4] Papists, and redeemed the superior world only, which is man, said Postellus[5] the Jesuit: and yet not all men neither; for St Francis hath redeemed so many as are saved since his days, say the Franciscan friars[6].

P. Mornæus, Tract. de Eccl. c. 9. Jesuits' Cat. 1, b. c. 10.

The Saviour of women, from her time till the end of the world, is St Clare, affirm[7] one: and other Papists, as Postellus[8], saith it is one Mother Jane.

Dialogue of Dives and Paup. 6. com. c. 10. Dionys. Car. de 4. Hom. Novis. Art. 50.

The Saviour of men and women is St Mary, through her virginity, say[9] some; is St Christina, by her passion, say other[10] Papists.

There is no sufficient sacrifice yet offered for the sins of the world; one of F. Ket's errors.

Christ hath satisfied, and was offered only for original sin; an error of Thomas Aquinas.

[1 See above, p. 141, note 2.] [2 See above, p. 135, note 6.]

[3 Salutem in nostris viribus positam esse arbitrabatur [Hofmannus].—Bulling. adv. Anabapt. (Simler. Vers. Lat.) Tiguri. 1560. p. 65. b. Lib. II. cap. 13.]

[4 Cryste becam not woman but man to save mankynde. That as mankynde was loste by man, soo mankynde sholde be saved by man. And therefore in manhede he wolde dye for mankynde, for manhede had lost mankynde. And also he becam man and not woman to save the ordre of kynde....Only of woman's kyn he made medycyine to the synne of Adam and to hele mankynde of ye harde sekeness of Adam's synne.—Dives and Pauper. Printed by Wyken de Worde. Westmónstre. 1496. Com. VI. c. 10.]

[5 See above, Art. II. Prop. 4. page 58, note 3.]

[6 This reference the editor has been unable to verify; but see Mornæus, Tract. de Eccles. 1599. cap. ix. p. 400. Nimirum Franciscum tanquam alterum Christum nobis peperit (Papatus) de quo hujusmodi portenta...evulgata sunt: Hunc videlicet suis meritis a morte æterna salvare posse quotquot a suis temporibus ad finem usque mundi victuri essent.]

[7 Porro Claram iisdem temporibus quibus Franciscum in mundum prodiisse ut eas omnes servaret, quæ eam ad finem usque mundi invocaturæ essent.—Mornæus, Ibid.]

[8 See note 5.]

[9 By our lady blessed mote she be, the fendes power is destroyed.—Dives and Pauper. Com. VI. c. 10.]

[10 Dionys. Carthus. De Quat. Hom. Noviss. Paris. 1551. Art. 50. fol. 119.]

Sins actual and venial are taken away by sacred ceremonies[11], by a bishop's blessing[12], by a priest's absolution[13].

Test. Rhem. Annot. marg. pag. 258. Ibid. Annot. Matt. x. 12. Vaux, Cat. cap. 4. See Art. XXII. prop. 2.

Sins actual and mortal be remissed by a pardon from some bishop, or from the pope of Rome[14].

Proposition II.

The sacrifices of the mass are most blasphemous fables, and dangerous deceits.

The Papists deliver how the mass is a sacrifice[15], a sacrifice propitiatory[16], a sacrifice propitiatory for the quick and the dead[17], the same propitiatory sacrifice that was offered by Christ himself upon the cross[18].

Test. Rhem Annotat. Matt. xxiv. 15. Concil. Trid. Sess. 22. Can. 3. Catech. Trid. de S. Eucharist. Concil. Trid. Ibid. Catech. Trid. Ibid. Concil. Trid. Sess. 3, Can. 4. Concil. Trid. Sess. 22. cap. 2. Howl. 7. Reas.

A sacrifice in which, by virtue of a few, even five words, (mumbled by a priest) Christ, even that Christ which hung upon the cross, is contained[19].

A sacrifice, serving for all persons, quick and dead[20], to purge them from their sins, to ease them of their pains, to satisfy for their punishment, and for all necessities corporal and spiritual[21].

[[11] See above, p. 110, note 4.]

[[12] Among other spiritual benefits it (a bishop's blessing) taketh away venial sins.—Test. Rhem. Rhemes, 1582. Annot. Matt. x. 12. p. 27.]

[[13] The form of the sacrament of penance is the words of absolution that the priest speaketh over the sinner; by virtue of the which the Holy Ghost worketh remission and forgiveness of sin, so that the sinner being penitent is purged and made clean from sin, as he was in baptism.—Vaux, Catech. Antv. 1574. cap. IV. p. 68.]

[[14] See above, p. 219.]

[[15] This abomination of desolation foretold...shall be fulfilled by antichrist and his precursors, when they shall abolish the holy mass, which is the sacrifice of Christ's body and blood.—Test. Rhem. Rhemes, 1582. Annot. Matt. xxiv. 15. p. 71.]

[[16] Si quis dixerit missæ sacrificium tantum esse laudis et gratiarum actionis, aut nudam commemorationem sacrificii in cruce peracti, non autem propitiatorium... neque pro vivis et defunctis...offerri debere; anathema sit.—Concil. Trid. Sess. XXII. De Sacrif. Miss. can. 3. Sine ulla dubitatione docendum est, id quod etiam sancta synodus explicavit, sacrosanctum missæ sacrificium esse non solum laudis et gratiarum actionis, aut nudam commemorationem sacrificii quod in cruce factum est: sed vere etiam propitiatorium sacrificium, quo Deus nobis placatus et propitius redditur.—Catech. Conc. Trid. Rom. 1566. p. 158.]

[[17] See last note.]

[[18] Unum itaque et idem sacrificium esse fatemur, et haberi debet, quod in missa peragitur, et quod in cruce oblatum est: quemadmodum una est et eadem hostia Christus, &c.—Catech. Conc. Trid. p. 158.]

[[19] See above, p. 286, note 2, and p. 287, notes 4,5.]

[[20] Si quis dixerit Missæ sacrificium...soli prodesse sumenti; neque pro vivis et defunctis, pro peccatis, pœnis satisfactionibus, et aliis necessitatibus offerri debere; anathema sit.—Concil. Trid. Sess. XXII. De Sacrif. Miss. can. 3.]

[[21] See below, p. 300, note 3.]

Concil. Trid. Sess. 22, cap. 3. Sess. 22, can. 5.

A sacrifice propitiatory[1] of Jesus Christ really offered to God the Father, and that often, in the honour of dead saints.

Ibid. Sess. 13. cap. 5.

A sacrifice[2], wherein Christ is so gloriously, as it is to be adored, even with divine worship, both of priest and people.

Albert. Mag. de Sacr. Euch. Howl. 7. Reas.

A sacrifice meritorious[3] to all them for whom it is offered, although they be not living, but dead; not present, but absent; not endued either with zeal or knowledge, but quite destitute of faith; and that *ex opere operato*.

Hereby are we to note, first, blasphemous fables. For

It is a fable that the mass is a sacrifice, and that propitiatory; a fable, that a few words of a priest can change bread into a living body, yea, many bodies with their souls, and that of Jesus Christ, God and man; a fable, that one and the same sacrifice is offered in the mass which was offered on the cross; a fable, that the said mass is any whit profitable for the quick, much less for the dead.

Next, dangerous deceits. For hereby men are to believe that

Creatures may be adored; contrary to God's word[a].

Christ is often offered; contrary to the scripture[b].

[a] Thou shalt not bow to them, nor serve them, Exod. xx. 5.

[b] By his own blood entered he in once unto the holy place, &c. Heb. ix. 12, &c. He was once offered, Ibid. 28.

[[1] Et quoniam in divino hoc sacrificio, quod in missa peragitur, idem ille Christus continetur, et incruente immolatur, qui in ara crucis semel seipsum cruente obtulit, docet sancta synodus sacrificium istud vere propitiatorium esse, &c. Et quamvis in honorem et memoriam sanctorum nonnullas interdum missas ecclesia celebrare consueverit, non tamen illis sacrificium offerri docet, sed Deo soli qui illos coronavit.—Concil. Trid. Sess. XXII. cap. 2, 3. Si quis dixerit imposturam esse missas celebrare in honorem sanctorum, et pro illorum intercessione apud Deum obtinenda; anathema sit.—Ibid. can. 5.]

[[2] Nullus itaque dubitandi locus relinquitur, quin omnes Christi fideles, pro more in catholica ecclesia semper recepto, latriæ cultum qui vero Deo debetur huic sanctissimo sacramento in veneratione exhibeant.—Ibid. Sess. XIII. cap. 5.]

[[3] Offertur Christus in humana natura corporis et sanguinis. Offertur autem pro omnibus. Sapientia autem divina oblatum univit offerenti...univit offerentem cum eo cui fit oblatio....Univit oblatum cum his pro quibus offertur, &c....Propter hæc et similia non utimur aliquo sacrificio nisi isto unico: quia sicut dicit Gregor. Hoc magis vivis proficit ad gratiam inveniendam, retinendam et recuperandam: hoc magis desiderant mortui purgandi ad impetrandum veniam.—Albert. Mag. Opp. Lugd. 1651. Tom. XXI. De Sacram. Euchar. Dist. v. cap. 3. foll. 90, 1.

...the blessed sacrifice of Christ his body and blood, appointed by Christ to be offered up every day for thanksgiving to God, for obtaining of grace, and avoiding of all evil, and for the remission of sins both of quick and dead.—A Brief Discours contayning certayne Reasons, &c. Douay, 1580. Reas. VII. p. 43. See note, p. 239, note 4.]

The priest offereth up Christ; contrary to the scripture[c].

Sins be forgiven without blood; contrary to the scripture[d].

Christ died not once, but dieth daily; contrary to the scripture[e].

Faith is not necessary in communicants; contrary to the scripture[f].

We are to adore Christ as always present; contrary to the scripture, where we are taught to remember him absent. Luke xxii. 19. 1 Cor. xi. 25.

The favour of God by money may be purchased from a priest; contrary to the scripture. 1 Pet. i. 18, 19.

All which their fables and deceits do tend to the utter abolishing of true religion. Therefore justly have we and our godly brethren[4] abandoned the mass. Conf. Helv. I. Art. XXII. & II. cap. 19, 21. Basil. Art. VI. Bohem. c. 13. Belg. Art. XXXV. August. de Missa, Art. I. Saxon. Art. XIV. Wittemb. cap. 19. Suevic. c. 19.

Accursed then stand those Papists before God which take the mass to be the sacrifice of Christ his body and blood[5], and "the only sovereign worship due to God in his church[6]." Concil. Trid. Sess. 6. Can. 2, & Catech. Trid. de Sacr. Euchar. Test. Rhem. Annot. Matt. xxiv. 15.

[c] He offered up himself, Heb. vii. 27.

[d] Without shedding of blood is no remission, Heb. ix. 22.

[e] It is appointed unto men that they shall once die, Heb. ix. 27.

[f] Without faith it is impossible to please God, Heb. xi. 6.

[[4] ...hoc autem libere dicimus, missam, quæ hodie in usu est per universam Romanam ecclesiam, plurimas et justissimas quidem ob causas, in ecclesiis nostris esse abrogatam....Certe approbare non potuimus, quod...in ea sacerdos dicitur conficere ipsum Domini corpus, et hoc offerre realiter, &c.—Harm. Conf. Sect. XIV. p. 112. Conf. Helv. Post. cap. XXI. Non includimus autem naturale verum et substantiale corpus Christi ex pura virgine Maria natum, pro nobis passum, et quod in cœlos ascendit, in Domini panem et potum, &c.—Ibid. p. 117. Conf. Basil. Art. VI. Sic interpretantur sacrificium quum Missam vocant sacrificium, opus videlicet quod applicatum pro aliis meretur eis remissionem culpæ et pœnarum, &c. ....Qua igitur auctoritate hic cultus, tanquam oblatio pro peccatis, sine mandato Dei, in ecclesia institutus est?—Ibid. pp. 128, 9. Conf. August. De Abus. Art. I. De Missa. Et Filius Dei ipse sese obtulit, ingrediens in sanctum sanctorum....Quid igitur nunc intelligunt sacrificuli, qui dicunt sese offerre Christum.—Ibid. p. 142. Conf. Saxon. Art. XIV. Alius error est, quod eucharistia sit tale sacrificium quod debeat jugiter in ecclesia, ad expianda peccata vivorum et mortuorum...offerri.—Ibid. p. 146. Conf. Virtemb. cap. xix. ...et contra qui missas celebrant, præsumunt Christum Patri offerre pro vivis et defunctis, missamque tale opus faciunt, quo solo fere favor et salus comparetur, &c.—Ibid. p. 150. Conf. Suev. cap. XIX. See also above, p. 286, note 1.]

[[5] The reference to the Concil. Trid. should be, Sess. xiii. Can. 4. See above, p. 286, note 2, and p. 287, notes 4, 5.]

[[6] Test. Rhem. Rhemes, 1582. Annot. Matt. xxiv. 15. p. 71.]

ARTICLE XXXII.

Of the Marriage of Priests.

Bishops, priests, and deacons (1) *are not commanded by God's law either to vow the estate of single life, or to abstain from marriage; therefore it is lawful also for them,* (2) *as for all other Christian men, to marry at their own discretion, as they shall judge the same to serve better to godliness.*

The propositions.

1. By the word of God it is lawful for bishops, and all other ecclesiastical ministers, to marry at their own discretion.

2. It is lawful by the word of God for all Christian men and women to marry at their own discretion in the fear of God.

Proposition I.

By the word of God it is lawful for bishops, and all other ecclesiastical ministers, to marry at their own discretion.

The proof from God's word.

Neither the single nor the wedded life is enjoined on any man, much less any calling of men, by the word of God. And that ecclesiastical ministers in particular may marry it is evident both from the Old and the New Testament.

Lev. xxi. 7. Lev. xxii. 1. 1 Sam. iii. 13. Luke i. 5.

From the Old Testament, both by the commandments given unto the priests for the choice of their wives, and by the examples also of the religious priests, as Aaron, Eli, Zacharias, &c., and prophets, which were all married, as it is thought, except Jeremy.

1 Tim. iii. 2, 4. Tit. i. 5, 6. 1 Tim. ii. 11, 12. Matt. viii. 14. Phil. iv. 2. 1 Cor. vi. 5.

From the New Testament, by the words of St Paul, who saith, "A bishop must be the husband of one wife; one that hath children under obedience." "An elder must be unreprovable, the husband of one wife, having faithful children." "Deacons must be the husbands of one wife; and have wives that be honest, not evil-speakers, &c.;" and by the example of Peter, Paul, yea, of the apostles, who were all married men, John the evangelist only except, as some think.

Conf. Helv. I. Art. XXXVII. & II. cap. 29. Basil. Art. I. sect. 1, 2. Bohem. c. 9, 1. Gal. Art. XXIV. August. de Abusu. Saxon. Art. XVIII. XXI. Wittemb. c. 21, 26. Suevica, c.12.

All sincere churches and professors subscribe hereunto[1].

[[1] Conjugium omnibus hominibus aptis, et alio non vocatis, divinitus institutum

Adversaries unto this truth.

And none of God's churches or people be of the mind

Either of the Vigilantians, that all and every one of the clergy is necessarily to marry, or not to be admitted for a minister[2];

D. Hieron. advers. Vigil.

Or of the Jovinians, whose elect or priests might not marry[3].

D. August. epist. 74.

nullius ordinis sanctimoniæ repugnare censemus.—Harm. Conf. Sect. XVIII. p. 238. Conf. Helv. Prior. Art. XXVII. Qui cœlitus donum habent cœlibatus...serviant in ea vocatione Domino, donec senserint se divino munere præditos, et ne præferant se cæteris....Aptiores autem hi sunt curandis rebus divinis, quam qui privatis familiæ negotiis distrahuntur. Quod si adempto rursus dono, ustionem senserint durabilem, meminerint verbi apostolici, melius est nubere quam uri.—Ibid. p. 236. Conf. Helv. Post. cap. XXIX. ...nostri ad ministerium ecclesiasticum expeditiores magisque idoneos esse ducunt cœlibes: eos tamen cœlibes, qui hoc peculiare donum a Deo concessum habent, &c....non tamen pro peccato habetur neque quisquam hoc aversatur, si sacerdotes justis seu legitimis de causis conjuges sunt aut fiunt.—Ibid. pp. 238, 9. Conf. Bohem. cap. IX. ...a nostris tamen sicut salus Christiana, ita etiam ministerii ecclesiastici dignitas, sanctitas, et virtus, neutro ex his vitæ generibus, neque cœlibe, neque conjugii conditione fundatur.—Ibid. p. 239. cap. XIX. Nam hæc nova lex, quæ nunc defenditur ab adversariis, quæ et prohibet sacerdotibus conjugia et contracta distrahit, pugnat cum jure naturali, divino, cum evangelio, cum veterum synodorum constitutionibus, cum exemplis veteris ecclesiæ.—Ibid. p. 244. Conf. August. De Abus. Art. V. Damnamus et legem pontificiam, quæ prohibet sacerdotibus conjugia, et causam præbet exitii magnæ multitudini hominum, et ob eandem causam vota monastica cœlibatus improbamus.—Ibid. p. 258. Conf. Saxon. Art. XVIII. Cf. Ibid. p. 260. Art. XXI. Præterea non dubitamus, quin qui sunt vere honestatis amantes sentiant conjugium non tantum laicis ut vocant, verum etiam ministris ecclesiæ liberum esse....Et Paulus probat conjugium in episcopo et adfirmat prohibitionem conjugii esse spiritum erroris et doctrinam demoniorum.—Ibid. p. 263. Conf. Virtemb. cap. XXI. Nam manifestum est, quod cœlibatus non sit verbo Dei præceptus.—Ibid. p. 264. Art. XXVI. Proinde nemini obsistere potuimus qui vitam monasticam, indubitatam, jam Satanæ servitutem, cum Christiana mutare voluisset. Sicut nec aliis ex ordine ecclesiastico qui ductis uxoribus, &c. Denique nec eos qui apud nos in verbi Dei ministerio perseverarunt arcere a jure conjugii...nobis permisimus.—Ibid. p. 268. Conf. Suev. cap. XII. In the Gall. Conf. Art. XXIV. *interdicta matrimonii* are condemned. For the reference to Conf. Basil. see Coll. Conf. Lips. 1840. p. 102. Conf. Basil. Art. XI. Disp. 28. Sicut contra, ministrorum matrimonium non prohibitum scimus.]

[[2] Proh nefas, episcopos sui sceleris dicitur habere consortes; si tamen episcopi nominandi sunt, qui non ordinant diaconos, nisi prius uxores duxerint:—et nisi prægnantes uxores viderint clericorum, infantesque de ulnis matrum vagientes, Christi sacramenta non tribuunt.—Hieron. Opp. Paris. 1693-1706. Tom. IV. Pars II. col. 281. Adv. Vigilant.]

[[3] The assertion made applies to the *Manichees*. Auditorem sane Manichæorum, non electum se esse confessus est. Auditores autem qui appellantur apud eos, et carnibus vescuntur, et agros colunt, et si voluerint, uxores habent: quorum nihil faciunt, qui vocantur electi. Sed ipsi auditores ante electos genua figunt, ut eis manus supplicibus imponantur, non a solis presbyteris, vel episcopis aut diaconibus eorum sed a quibus libet electis.—August. Opp. Paris. 1836-8. Tom. II. col. 1289. B. Epist. 236. (al. 74.)]

Or of the Papists, who teach that

Major. Clyp. milit. Eccles. From the apostles' time it was never lawful for priests to marry[1].

Test. Rhem. Annot. marg. p. 571. The three orders of deacons, sub-deacons, and priests, are bound not to marry[2].

Ibid. Annot. 1 Tim. iii. 2. Ibid. Annot. 1 Tim. v. 15. After orders, to marry it is not lawful[3]; it is to turn back unto Satan, and apostasy[4].

Ibid. Annot. 1 Tim. iii. 2. None may be a priest, though he will vow a single life, if he have been a married man[5].

Sleid. Com. 1 Tim. v. 9. i. 4. For a priest to play the whore-master it is less offence than to take a wife. This was the speech of cardinal Campeius[6]. And most infamous is the Romish clergy for their unclean and incontinent life. Hence written is it

Of pope Paul the Second,

> Anxia testiculos Pauli ne Roma requiras:
> Filia huic nata est; hæc docet esse marem.

Of pope Innocent the Eighth,

> Bis quatuor nocens genuit puellulos,
> Totidem sed et nocens genuit puellulas;
> O Roma! possis hunc merito dicere patrem.

Of pope Alexander the Sixth,

[[1] There seems to be an error in the reference.]

[[2] Under the name of deacons are here contained sub-deacons, as before under the name of bishop, priests also were comprehended; for to these four pertaineth the apostle's precept and order touching one wife, and touching continency and chastity, &c.—Test. Rhem. Rhemes, 1582. Annot. 1 Tim. iii. 8. p. 571. The marginal annotation is, The three holy orders only bound to chastity.]

[[3] ...it was never lawful in God's church to marry after orders.—Test. Rhem. Rhemes, 1582. Annot. 1 Tim. iii. 2. p. 570.]

[[4] We may here learn, that for those to marry which are professed, is to turn back after Satan.—Ibid. Ann. 1 Tim. v. 15. p. 581.]

[[5] The author is mistaken here. The annotation to which he refers is as follows: The apostle then by this place we now treat of neither commandeth, nor counselleth, nor wisheth, nor would have bishops or priests to marry, or such only to be received as have been married: but that such an one as hath been married (so it were but once, and that to a virgin) may be made bishop or priest. Which is no more than an inhibition that none having been twice married, or being *bigamus*, should be admitted to that holy order.—Test. Rhem. Rhemes, 1582. Ann. 1 Tim. iii. 2. And the marginal annotation on the same page (p. 570) is, "They that were made priests of married men, abstained from their wives."]

[[6] Quod autem alii scortentur et inhoneste vivant, non ideo scelus istorum expurgari: non recte facere qui sic vivant...sed tamen idcirco non istis licere matrimonium contrahere: et quod sacerdotes fiant mariti multo esse gravius peccatum, quam si plurimas domi meretrices alant: nam illos habere persuasum, quasi recte faciant, hos autem scire et peccatum agnoscere.—Sleidan. Comment. Argentorat. 1555. Lib. IV. fol. 58.]

Non spado Alexander fuerat, Lucretia nempe
Illius conjux, nata, nurusque fuit.

Of the priests,

Multi vos sanctos, multi vos dicere patres,
Gaudent, et vobis nomina tanta placent:
Ast ego vos sanctos non possum dicere; patres
Possum, cum natos vos genuisse sciam.

Of the Jesuits,

"With women ye lie not, but with males rather,
Speak, Jesuit, how canst thou be a father, &c.[7]?" Jesuits' Cat. 2. B. cap. 5, p. 114, b.

Proposition II.

It is lawful by the word of God for all Christian men and women to marry at their own discretion, in the fear of God.

The proof from God's word.

The Spirit of God saith unto men and women in all ages, "Bring forth fruit, and multiply, and fill the earth." Gen. i. 27, 28.

"Marriage is honourable among all men, and the bed undefiled." Heb. xiii. 4.

"To avoid fornication, let every man have his wife, and every woman have her husband." 1 Cor. vii. 2.

"If they cannot abstain, let them marry." Ibid. 9.

Notwithstanding, in saying that Christians may marry at their discretion, the meaning is not that any may marry, if they think good, either within the degrees of kindred and affinity prohibited by wholesome laws; or without the consent of parents, or of others in the room of parents, if they be under tuition; or to other ends than God hath prefixed.

So testify with us the reformed churches[8]. Conf. Helv. I. Art. XXVII. & II. c. 29. Bohem. c. 19. Gal. Art. XXIV. August. de Abus. Art IV. V. Saxon. Art. XVIII. Wittemb. cap. 21, 26. Suevica, cap. 2.

[7 Jesuits' Catechisme, 1602. Bk. II. cap. 5. p. 114. b.]

[8 See above, p. 302, note 1, and add the following: Docemus contrahenda esse conjugia legitime in timore Domini, et non contra leges prohibentes aliquot in conjugio gradus, ne incestæ fiant nuptiæ. Contrahantur cum consensu parentum, aut qui sunt loco parentum, ac in illum maxime finem, ad quem Dominus conjugia instituit, &c.—Harm. Conf. Sect. XVIII. p. 236. Conf. Helv. Post. cap. XXIX. De conditione vitæ cœlibis, virginitate et viduitate, docetur in uniuscujusque arbitrio esse positum, deligere eam sibi aut repudiare.—Ibid. p. 239. Conf. Bohem. cap. XIX. Natura homines ita conditi sunt, ut sint fœcundi. Quare jurisconsulti dicunt, conjunctionem maris et fœminæ esse juris naturæ...Deinde quum Paulus inquit: Unusquisque habeat uxorem ad vitandam fornicationem, certe præcipit omnibus, qui non sunt idonei ad cœlibatum, ut contrahant conjugia.—Ibid. p. 245. Conf. August. De Abus. Art. V. Conjugium est legitima et indissolubilis conjunctio, tantum unius maris et unius fœminæ, observanda propter mandatum Dei,...Ne concedatur commixtio personarum, quibus jure divino non est concessa commixtio.

Errors and adversaries unto this truth.

Greatly hath this truth been crossed and contradicted. For

Heyden, de Descript. urbis Hierosol. Lib. III.

Some leave it not to men and women's discretions, but compel them, whether they will or no, to marry: so did the Ossenes[1].

D. Irenæus. D. August. de Hæres. Leo, Epist. 93, cap. 7. Euseb. Epiphan. Philastr. Epiphan.

Some utterly condemn marriage; as did the Gnostics[2], the Hieracites[3], the Priscillianists[4], the Montanists[5], the Saturnians[6], the Arians[7], the Apostolics[8].

Some allow of the wedded life, yet not in all sorts of persons. For

1 Test. Rhem. An. 1 Tim. v. 9. See above, Art. xxv. Prop. 8.

The Papists forbid all clergymen to marry[9]: as also all godfathers, godmothers, and whosoever be of spiritual kindred[10].

Servantur et regulæ juris canonici de aliis propioribus gradibus, &c. Scimus autem voluntatem Dei esse ne prohibeatur conjugium ullis personis, quæ sunt idoneæ ad conjugium.—Ibid. p. 258. Conf. Saxon. Art. XVIII. ...docemus quod liceat conjugium inire in his gradibus consanguinitatis et affinitatis quos politicæ leges, quæ sunt divinæ ordinationes, permittunt. Docemus etiam quod juvenes non debeant temere sine parentum suorum autoritate conjugium inire.—Ibid. p. 262. Conf. Virtemb. cap. XXI. Nam stat edictum illud Dei per Paulum promulgatum, quod nulla hominum vota possunt reddere irritum: propter stupra vitanda, quisque (neminem excipit) suam uxorem habeat, et unaquæque suum maritum.—Ibid. p. 267. Conf. Suev. cap. XII.]

[1 Osseni adversabantur virginitati odio habentes continentiam, et ad nuptias cogentes.—Reisner. Descript. Urb. Ierusalem, Lat. Vers. per Joann. Heyden. Francof. 1563. Lib. III. cap. 3. p. 110.]

[2 Ἀπὸ Σατορνίνου καὶ Μαρκίωνος οἱ καλούμενοι ἐγκρατεῖς ἀγαμίαν ἐκήρυξαν, ἀθετοῦντες τὴν ἀρχαίαν πλάσιν τοῦ Θεοῦ.—Iren. Adv. Hær. Oxon. 1702. Lib. I. cap. 30. p. 105.]

[3 Monachos tantum et monachas et conjugia non habentes in communionem recipiunt (Hieracitæ).—August. Opp. Paris. 1836-8. Tom. VIII. coll. 53, 4. Lib. De Hær. ad Quodvultdeum.]

[4 Septimo loco sequitur, quod nuptias damnant, et procreationem nascentium perhorrescunt.—Leon. Mag. Opp. Venet. 1753. Tom. I. col. 701. Epist. XIV. cap. 7.]

[5 See above, p. 261, note 10.]

[6 Τὸ γαμεῖν δὲ καὶ τὸ γεννᾶν ὁ αὐτὸς ἀγύρτης ἐκ τοῦ Σατανᾶ ὑπάρχειν λέγει.—Epiphan. Opp. Paris. 1622. Tom. I. p. 63. Adv. Hær. Lib. I. Tom. II. Hær. 23.]

[7 Damnant etiam [Aerii] de lege nuptias, non a Deo institutas adserentes.—Philastr. Lib. de Hær. in Biblioth. Patr. Paris. 1624. Tom. IV. col. 18.]

[8 Epiphan. Opp. Tom. I. pp. 506-12. Adv. Hær. Lib. II. Tom. I. Hær. 60.]

[9 This is a conclusion drawn from the rule which the apostle lays down with regard to those who should be received into the number of widows, that they should not have been married more than once. From which the Annotators argue, "that the apostle...must needs much more mean that...as none were admitted to be widows of the church that ever intended to marry again, so none should ever be received to minister the sacraments (which is a thing infinitely more, and requireth more purity and continency than the office or state of the said widows) that intended to marry again."—Test. Rhem. Ann. 1 Tim. v. 9. pp. 579, 80.]

[10 See above, p. 262, n. a.]

Some will have none to marry but virgins, and single persons; as the Henricians[11]. Magd. Eccl. Hist. Cent. 12, cap. 25.

Some condemn all iteration of marriage, or twice marrying, the husband or wife being dead; such heretics were the Catharans[12], &c. D. August. de Hæres.

Some would have women, though married, to be all common, as the Nicolaitans[13], and Davi-Georgians[14]. D. Irenæus. Hist. David. Georgii.

Some will not marry according to God's ordinance, but think that one man, at one and the same time, may have many wives. In which error were the Hermogenians[15], and are the Ochinites[16]. Test. advers. Hermogen. Beza, epist. 1, p. 11.

Article XXXIII.

Of excommunicate Persons, how they are to be avoided.

That person, (1) *which by open denunciation of the Church, is right cut off from the unity of the Church, and excommunicate, ought to be taken of the whole multitude of the faithful as an heathen and publican,* (2) *until he be openly reconciled by penance, and received into the Church by a judge that hath authority thereto.*

The propositions.

1. The person that is rightly by the church excommunicate, is of all the faithful to be taken for an heathen and publican.

[11 Virgines tantum matrimonio copulandas; quia Deus virgines crearit marem et feminam.—Magdeburg. Eccl. Hist. Basil. 1562. &c. Cent. XII. cap. 5. fol. 844.]

[12 Cathari...secundas nuptias non admittunt.—August. Opp. Tom. VIII. col. 45. Lib. de Hær. ad Quodvultd. &c.]

[13 Plenissime autem per Joannis Apocalypsin manifestantur qui sint (Nicolaitæ) nullam differentiam esse docentes in mœchando, et idolothyton edere.—Iren. Adv. Hær. Oxon. 1702. Lib. I. cap. 27. p. 103.]

[14 Qui autem in jugi pœnitentia et assiduo contra hos carnis stimulos motus et assultus certamine eo progressi sunt ut, &c....eos deinde ulterius eluctari oportere ut libenter videant atque etiam flagitent ut ejusdem religionis spiritualis frater eorum uxores in possessionem sumat, cumque ea congrediatur, &c.—Hist. David. Georg. à Nicol. Blesdik. Daventr. 1642. Art. XIV. p. 29.]

[15 Præterea pingit illicite (Hermogenes), nubit assidue. Legem Dei in libidinem defendit...totus adulter et prædicationis et carnis, &c.—Tertull. Opp. Lutet. 1634. p. 265. c. Adv. Hermog. cap. 1.]

[16 Speaking of Ochinus, Beza applies to him amongst other epithets that of Polygamiæ defensor.—Bez. Epist. Genev. 1575. Ep. i. p. 11.]

2. An excommunicate person, truly repenting, is to be received into the church again.

Proposition I.

The person that is rightly by the church excommunicate is of all the faithful to be taken for an heathen and publican.

The proof from God's word.

The most severe and uttermost punishment that the visible church can inflict upon the wicked and ungodly of this world is excommunication, which is a part of discipline to be exercised, and that upon urgent occasions; and it is commended unto the church even by God himself, who in his word hath prescribed,

Matt. xviii. 17. 1 Cor. v. 4, 5. 2 Cor. iii. 13, 14. 1 Tim. iii. 6.

1. Who are to excommunicate; namely, such as have authority in the church.

2. Who are to be excommunicate; even two sorts of men, whereof the one pervert the sound doctrine of the truth, as
1 Tim. i. 20. did Hymenæus and Alexander; the other be defiled with noto-
1 Cor. v. 1. rious wickedness, as that incestuous person at Corinth was.

Tit. iii. 10. Matt. xviii. 15. Gal. vi. 1. 2 Thess. iii. 15. 1 Tim. v. 20. 1 Cor. v. 13. Ibid. Matt. xviii. 17.

The manner of proceeding in excommunication; namely, first by gentle admonition, and that once or twice given, with the "spirit of meekness," even as to a brother, if the fault be not notoriously known; and next by "open reprehension," afterward by the public sentence of the church, to put him from the company of the faithful, "to deliver him unto Satan," and to denounce him an heathen and a publican, if none admonitions will serve, and the crime and persons be very offensive.

Rom. xvi. 17. 1 Cor. v. 11. Ibid. 9. 2 John 10.

A man so cut off from the congregation, and excommunicated, is of every godly professor to be avoided, and not to be eaten withal, not to be companied withal, nor to be received into house.

Conf. Helv. I. Art. xix. & II. c. 18. Bohem. c. 9, 14. Gal. Art. xxix. xxxiii. Belg. Art. xxx. Saxon. Art. xi. xvii. August. de Abusu, Art. vii. Wittemb. Art. xi. Suevic. Art. xiii.

This censure is had in great reverence and estimation among the faithful servants of God[1].

[[1] Summum functionis hujus (sc. ministrorum) munus est...Christi cives sanos quidem tueri, vitiosos autem monere, reprehendere, coercere; et grassantes longius conspiratione pia eorum qui ex ministris magistratuque delecti sunt disciplina excludere, vel alia ratione commoda mulctare tantisper dum resipiscant, ac salvi fiant.—Harm. Conf. Sect. xi. pp. 43, 4. Conf. Helv. Prior. Art. xix. Quumque omnino oporteat esse in ecclesia disciplinam et apud veteres quondam usitata fuerit excommunicatio, fuerintque judicia ecclesiastica in populo Dei....ministrorum quoque fuerit ad ædificationem disciplinam moderari hanc, &c.—Ibid. p. 41. Conf.

Errors and adversaries unto this truth.

1. Adversaries unto this doctrine be they

Who utterly condemn all censures ecclesiastical, and so excommunication, saying how the wicked are not excommunicable; so did the Paulicians[2]. Paulus Diaconus.

Heretics, holding other points of religion soundly, for their private and singular opinions, are not to be excommunicate; so the Pelagians[3]. Prosper de ingratis.

Christians cleaving unto the foundation, which is Christ, are not by excommunication to be thrust out of the church, for any other errors or misdemeanors whatsoever. Of which opinions be sundry divines of good regard[4]. Wolf. Musc. Carm. p. 63. Jezler, Lib. de Diutur. Bel Euchar. p. 73, b.

Helv. Post. cap. XVIII. Ab altera parte, clavium Christi munus et opus proprium est claudere et ligare...atque ita verbo Christi pro ratione ejus quod admissum est, peccatum arguere, a Christi salvatoris nostri communitate et sacramentorum fructu perceptioneque separare, et ex ecclesia Christiana ejicere, atque in summa regnum cœlorum eis claudere, tandem et Satanæ eos tradere.—Ibid. p. 51. Conf. Bohem. cap. XIV. Credimus veram ecclesiam gubernari debere ea politia seu disciplina... ut doctrinæ puritas retineatur, vitia cohibeantur, &c.—Ibid. p. 53. Conf. Gall. Art. XXIX. ...sequendum nobis putamus quod Dominus noster Jesus Christus de excommunicatione statuit, quam quidem approbamus, et una cum suis appendicibus necessariam esse arbitramur.—Ibid. Sect. XVII. p. 216. Conf. Gall. Art. XXXIII. Credimus veram hanc ecclesiam debere regi ac gubernari spirituali illa politia quam nos Deus ipse verbo suo edocuit, ita ut...homines vitiis dediti spiritualiter corripi et emendari ac veluti fræno quodam disciplinæ cohiberi (possint).—Ibid. Sect. XI. p. 56. Conf. Belg. Art. XXX. Et ad ministerium hæc pertinent...exercere judicia ecclesiæ legitimo modo de iis qui manifestorum criminum in moribus aut doctrina rei sunt, et contra contumaces sententiam excommunicationis ferre, &c.—Ibid. Sect. X. p. 24. Conf. Saxon. Art. XI. ...fatemur reos manifestorum scelerum legitimo judicio et ordine excommunicandos esse, nec est inane fulmen justa excommunicatio.—Ibid. Sect. VIII. p. 157. Conf. Saxon. Art. XVII. Item, (competit episcopis) cognoscere doctrinam...et impios quorum nota est impietas, excludere a communione ecclesiæ, sine vi humana sed verbo.—Ibid. Sect. XI. p. 59. Conf. August. De Abus. Subl. Art. VII. Ministerium enim remittendi aut retinendi peccata, quod alias vocatur clavis regni cœlorum non est liberæ potestati personæ hominum traditum sed est in ipsum evangelii verbum ita inclusum, &c.—Ibid. Sect. X. p. 25. Conf. Virtemb. Art. XXXI. Hi sunt enim qui claves regni cœlestis, et potestatem ligandi ac solvendi peccataque aut remittendi aut retinendi obtinent.—Ibid. Sect. XI. p. 63. Conf. Suev. Art. XIII.]

[2 This reference the editor has been unable to verify.]

[3 Non segnior inde Orientis
Rectorum cura emicuit: captumque nefandi
Dogmatis auctorem constrinxit lege benigna
Commentum damnare suum: nisi corpore Christi
Abjungi et sancto mallet grege dissociari.

Prosper. Opp. Venet. 1782. Tom. I. p. 72. De Ingratis, Carm. l. 46.]

[4 Indubitatum sit igitur atque fixum, neminem in fundamento persistentem, quod Christus est, ex ecclesia Christi esse exterminandum, &c.—Jezler. De Diutur. Bell. Euchar. Tiguri. 1584. p. 73. b. The reference to Wolf. Musculus has not been found.]

2. Which allow the censure of excommunication, so it be done,

Sold. of Bar. Demon. of dis. c. 12.

Not (as with us it is) by commissaries, chancellors[1], or [a]bishops[2], but in every parish[3], and that either

Hunt of the Fox, E. 1. T. C. 1 Rep. p. 146. Answ. to Mr Cartw. Letter, p. 30. Bar. discov. p. 27. Petition of the 1000.

By the whole congregation[4], or by the eldership and the whole church[5]; or by every minister[6], yea, every member of the church[7]; or finally, if not by, yet not without, the consent of his pastor who is to be excommunicate[8].

[a] Assert. Polit. *an.* 1604. Bishops are to be obeyed neither when they cite, nor when they inhibit, nor when they excommunicate, saith the Mar-prelate, Thes. 46, 82, 83.

[[1] *The Commissarie his courte.* 1. This robbeth the church of hir government used both in the olde and newe Testament. 2. This is contrarie to Christes commaundement, *Dic Ecclesiæ*, and to the example and doctrine of Paule, to excommunicate alone.—A pleasaunt Dialogue betweene a souldier of Barwicke and an English Chaplaine, 1581. fol. M.]

[[2] That none ever defended this hierarchie of bishops to be lawfull but papists, or such as were infected with popish errors.—Theses Martin. 46. That according to the doctrine of our churche, the citations, processes, excommunications, &c. of the prelates, are neyther to be obeyed nor regarded.—Ibid. 82. That, according unto the doctrine of the church of England, men ought not to appeare in their courtes, seeing their proceedings are so directly against the trueth, &c.—Ibid. 83.]

[[3] Every congregation ought to have elders to see into the manners of the people, and to be assistaunt unto the ministers in the government ecclesiasticall.—A Demonstration of Discipline, chap. XII. p. 54. It (excommunication) may not be done by any one man, but by the eldership, the whole church consenting thereunto.—Ibid. chap. XIX. p. 95.]

[[4] But if these church-robbers (for so I call them that bye that thing which they know is stolen from Christes church, and will not deliver it up unto the church againe that which they have bought and received of that robber the pope) will not restore them againe, let them be compelled thereto by an acte of parliament, or if yee be to weake in the parliament house to compell them, then let all the reste of the churche excommunicate them, &c.—The Hunting of the Fox and the Wolfe, &c. fol. E. 1.]

[[5] It is certain that St Paul did both understand and observe the rule of our Saviour Christ. But he communicateth this power of excommunication with the church [referring to the case of the incestuous person], and therefore it must needs be the meaning of our Saviour Christ, that the excommunication should be by many and not by one, and by the church, and not by the minister of the church.—T. C. First Reply, p. 184.]

[[6] It is manifest that the synagogues of the Jews in Antiochia and Ephesus were the churches of God: yet when Christ was preached unto them, and they withstood Paul and Barnabas, did Paul or Barnabas stay for the consent of the most part to cast them off?...Then belike it is true that one man, or a few persons, may cast off whole churches for some greater sins and offences.—An Answere to M. Cartwright, his Letter, &c. London, p. 30.]

[[7] But now if it be not possible...to keep any holy communion or Christian order without the diligent watch of every member, but chiefly of the rulers and elders...to censure all errors and transgressions, to excommunicate the obstinate impenitent, &c.—Barrow's Discovery, 1590, p. 27.]

[[8] See, The Humble Petition of the Ministers of the Church of England desiring

3. Which rightly use not, but abuse the censure of excommunication; drawing the same forth

Against what they list, even against dead bodies, dumb fishes, flies, and vermin, when they have annoyed them. For this the Papists are famous, or infamous rather. The dead Act. & Mon. bodies of Wickliff, Bucer, P. Fagius, were excommunicated after they were dead and buried[9].

The bishop of Canaglion, anno Domini 1593, very catho- Merc. Gallo, Lib. VI. p. 592. licly accursed the mute fishes[10].

St Bernard denounced the sentence of excommunication Pet. de Natal. in vita Bernar. against flies[11].

And against whom they please: so the Apostolics excom- Epiphan. municated all that were married, only for that they were married[12]. Diotrephes thrust the brethren out of the church. 3 John 10. The Brownists excommunicate whole cities and churches[13]; Answ. to Mr Cart. Let. p. 30. the Papists excommunicate even kings and emperors. Queen Elizabeth of blessed memory was excommunicate by three popes, Pius Quintus, Gregory the Thirteenth, and Sixtus Quintus. The Puritans mislike, and find great fault, that ex- T. C. Rep. 2. communication is not exercised against kings and princes[14]. Barrow saith that a prince contemning the censures of the Bar. Discov. p. 14. church is to be disfranchised out of the church, and delivered over unto Satan[15].

Also for what things they list[16], even for May-games and Surv. of Dis. c. 25, p. 284.

Reformation, &c. prefixed to the Answer of the Vice-Chancellor, Doctors, &c. in the University of Oxford to the same. Oxford, 1604.]

[9 Foxe, Acts and Monum. Lond. 1844. Vol. III. p. 418, and VIII. 268, 9.]

[10 Memorabile est quod scribunt nonnulli sub id tempus in mari Massiliensi tantam delphinorum visam esse copiam, quanta vix in toto mari Mediterraneo fuisse putabatur....Episcopus Canaglioneus qui tunc in urbe erat, a pontifice missus ad controversiam quandam componendam, in littus exiens, piscibus solitis ecclesiæ ceremoniis interdixit.—Janson. Mercurius, Gallo-Belgicus, Colon. Agrip. 1594. Lib. VI. p. 592.]

[11 Monasterium quoddam multitudo infinita muscarum occupaverat, quæ monachos graviter infestabat. Quas vir Dei excommunicavit, et mane omnes musce mortue sunt reperte.—Pet. de Natal. Catalog. Sanctor. Lugd. Lib. VII. cap. 84. De S. Bernard. fol. 187.]

[12 Καὶ εἰ μόνον τυγχάνει ἡ ἁγία τοῦ Θεοῦ Ἐκκλησία τῶν τῷ γάμῳ ἀποταξαμένων, κ.τ.λ.—Epiphan. Opp. Paris. 1622. Tom. I. p. 506. Adv. Hær. Lib. II. Tom. I. Hær. 60.]

[13 ...yet Christ for all disobedience in refusing any message of God doth give commandment even to all and every one of his messengers to cast off whole cities and churches, as being in a worse case than Sodom and Gomorrha.—An Answere to Master Cartwright his Letter, &c. p. 30.]

[14 The Rest of the second Replie of Thomas Cartwright, 1577. pp. 92. &c.]

[15 Barrow's Discovery of the False Church, 1594, p. 14.]

[16 ...for some disorders committed in Edinburgh about a Robin-hood, which the

Robin-Hood matters, as sometimes it was denounced in Scotland by the new presbytery; and for all crimes which by God's law deserve death; and for all things that to God's people be scandalous; yea, not only for all matters criminal, but also for the very suspicion of avarice, pride, &c.[1]

Knox, Order of Excom. in Scotland, p. 2.

4. Lastly, which favour the right and true excommunication, but exercise it not, being bound thereunto.

Proposition II.

An excommunicate person, truly repenting, is to be received into the church again.

The proof from God's word.

Sundry be the reasons and ends why excommunication is used: as,

That a wicked liver, to the reproach of the gospel, be not suffered among the godly and Christian professors of true religion.

That many good men be not evil spoken of for a few bad.

1 Cor. v. 6. That good and virtuous persons may not be infected through the continual or much familiarity of the wicked. For, as St Paul saith, "a little leaven leaveneth the whole lump."

1 Tim. i. 20. And that he which hath fallen, through shame of the world, may at length "learn to blaspheme no more," and
1 Cor. v. 5. through "repentance be saved."

2 Cor. ii. 7, &c. Among all other causes therefore of excommunication one is, and not the least, that the person excommunicate may not be condemned utterly, but return unto the Lord by repentance, and so be received again into the visible church, as St Paul willed the incestuous man should be.

The adversaries unto this truth.

D. Hieron. adv. Marc. Lib. II. D. Cyprian. Lib. IV. Epist. 2.

Contrariwise, the Montanists[2] and the Novatians[2] are of opinion, that so many as after baptism do fall into sin be utterly damned of God, and therefore be not to find favour at the church's hands.

provost and bailiffs would have stayed, the whole multitude were holden excommunicate.—Bancroft, Survey of Discipline. Lond. 1593. cap. xxv. p. 284.]

[1 This reference the editor has been unable to verify.]

[2 For these references, see above, p. 141, note 2, and p. 135, note 6.]

Article XXXIV.

Of the Traditions of the Church.

(1) *It is not necessary that Traditions and Ceremonies be in all places one, or utterly like; for at all times they have been diverse, and changed, according to the diversity of countries, times, and men's manners, so that nothing be ordained against God's Word.* (2) *Whosoever through his private judgement willingly and purposely doth openly break the traditions and ceremonies of the Church,* (3) *which be not repugnant to the Word of God, and be ordained and approved by common authority, ought to be rebuked openly, (that other may fear to do the like) as he that offendeth against the common order of the Church, and woundeth the consciences of the weak brethren.* (4) *Every particular or national church hath authority to ordain, change, and abolish ceremonies or rites of the Church, ordained only by man's authority, so that all things be done to edifying.*

The propositions.

1. Traditions or ceremonies are not necessary to be like and the same in all places.

2. No private man, of a self-will and purposely, may in public violate the traditions and ceremonies of the church, which by common authority be allowed, and are not repugnant to the Word of God.

3. Ceremonies and traditions ordained by authority of man, if they be repugnant to God's word, are not to be kept and observed of any man.

4. Every particular or national church may ordain, change, and abolish ceremonies or rites, ordained only by man's authority, so that all things be done to edifying.

Proposition I.

Traditions and ceremonies are not necessarily to be like, or the same in all places.

The proof from God's word.

If a necessity were laid upon the church of God to observe the same traditions and ceremonies at all times, and in all places, assuredly neither had the ceremonies of the old law been, as they are now, abolished; neither would the apostles ever have given such precedents of altering them, upon special reasons, as they have done.

Acts vi. 14, x. 15, & xv. 1, &c.

Gal. ii. 3, &c. Eph. ii. 14. Col. ii. 16.

Acts ii. 46, v. 21. Acts xiii. 14, xvii. 2, xviii. 4. Acts ii. 46. iii. 1, v. 24. Acts ix. 20, xiv. 1, xvii. 10, xviii. 4. Acts xix. 9. Acts v. 42. Acts i. 13, 20, viii. 28, 30, 31.

For the said apostles changed the times and places of their assembling together; the people of God meeting, and the apostles preaching, sometimes on the week, sometimes on the Sabbath-days; sometimes publicly in the temple, in the synagogue, and in the schools; sometimes "privately in house after house," and in chambers; sometimes in the day-time, sometimes in the night.

Acts ii. 46, iii. 1. Acts xx. 7.

Neither kept they the same course in the ministration of the sacraments.

Acts ii. 46. Acts x. 33, x. 27, 28. Acts xviii. 12, x. 27, 28. Acts viii. 36. Acts ii. 46. Acts xx. 11. 1 Cor. xi. 17. Acts xx. 7, ii. 46.

For, as occasion was offered, they both baptized in public assemblies, and in private houses, before many, and when none of the faithful, but the minister only and the party to be baptized, were present; and ministered likewise the supper of the Lord in the daytime, and at midnight, in the open churches, and in private houses.

So nothing therefore be done against the word of God, traditions and ceremonies, according to the diversity of countries and men's manners, may be changed, and divers.

Of this judgement with us be all reformed churches[1].

Conf. Helv. II. c. 17, 27. Bohem. c. 15. Gal. Art. XXII. Belg. Art. XXXII. August. Art. XV. & Art. VII. touching abuses. Saxon. Art. XX. Wittemb. Ar XXXV. Suevica, c. 14.

The errors and adversaries unto this truth.

They are greatly deceived therefore which think, that

Acts xv.

The Jewish ceremonies, prescribed by God himself for a time unto the Jews, are to be observed of us Christians. Such were the old heretics, the false apostles, the Cerdonites[2], the Cerinthians[3], and the Nazarites[4], and are the Familists[5].

Tertul. contra Mar. Lib. IV. Philaster. D. Hieron. in Epist. ad Aug. H. N. Evang. c. 13, § 8.

[1 ...legimus apud veteres rituum fuisse diversitatem variam, sed eam liberam qua nemo unquam existimavit dissolvi unitatem ecclesiasticam.—Harm. Conf. Sect. X. p. 8. Conf. Helv. Post. cap. XVII. Quod in ecclesiis dispares inveniuntur ritus, nemo ecclesias existimet ex eo esse dissidentes.—Ibid. Sect. XVII. p. 210. Conf. Helv. Post. cap. XXVII. For the other references, see above, p. 184, note 1.]

[2 Tertullian says of Cerdon, Hic Prophetias et Legem repudiat.—Opp. Lutet. 1634, p. 253. De Præscript. Hæret. cap. 51. The place meant may perhaps be this: Est præterea his omnibus etiam Blastus accedens, qui latenter Judaismum vult introducere. Pascha enim dicit non aliter custodiendum esse, nisi secundum legem Moysi XIV. mensis.—Ibid. p. 254. cap. 53.]

[3 See above, p. 89, note 4.]

[4 Usque hodie per totas Orientis synagogas inter Judæos hæresis est, quæ dicitur Mineorum, et a Pharisæis nunc usque damnatur, quos vulgo Nazaræos nuncupant, qui credunt in Christum, filium Dei natum de virgine Maria, et eum dicunt esse qui sub Pontio Pilato passus est, et resurrexit: in quem et nos credimus: sed dum volunt et Judæi esse et Christiani; nec Judæi sunt nec Christiani.—Hieron. Opp. Paris. 1693-1706. Tom. IV. Pars II. col. 623. Epist. 74. ad Augustin.]

[5 Oh alas! how grossly have then certain wise of the world and scripture-

The traditions, and namely the tradition and ceremony of the seventh day for the Sabbath, and the manner of sanctifying thereof, must necessarily be one and the same always, and in all places. Hence the demi-Jews, our English Sabbatarians, affirm, first touching the sanctification of the seventh day, how

It is not lawful for us to use the seventh day to any other end, but to the holy and sanctified end for which God in the beginning created it. D. B. Sab. Doct. I. p. 4.

So soon as the 7. day was, so soon was it sanctified, that we might know, that as it came in with the first man, so must it not go out but with the last. Ibid. p. 6.

The Sabbath (or seventh day of rest) which hath that commendation of antiquity, ought to stand still in force[6]. Ibid. p. 9.

All the Judaical days and feasts being taken away, only the Sabbath remaineth[7]. Ibid. p. 128.

And next, concerning the form and manner of keeping the day, they deliver, that

We are bound unto the same rest with the Jews on the Sabbath-day. Ibid. p. 125.

As the first seventh day was sanctified, so must the last be. Ibid. p. 6.

We be restrained upon the Sabbath from work, both hand and foot, as the Jews were[8]. Ibid. p. 127.

Every ecclesiastical minister in his charge necessarily must preach, and make a sermon every Sabbath-day; every man or woman, under pain of utter condemnation, must hear a sermon every Sabbath-day[9]. Ibid. p. 174. Ibid. p. 175.

Every pastor in his charge must execute the discipline and (presbyterial) government in his parish every Sabbath-day[10]. Ibid. p. 165.

Last of all, deceived be the Roman Catholics, which are Conc. Trid. Sess. 7, can. 13.

learned overreached them herein, which have, without diversity, forsaken the law and the service of the elder's testament, and of the priest's office after the ordinance of Aaron.—H. N. Evang. cap. XIII. § 8.]

[6 Nich. Bownde, Doct. of the Sabbath. Lond. 1595. Book I. pp. 4, 6, 9.]

[7 Ibid. p. 128. Where, only the Sabbath *is reserved for us.*]

[8 Ibid. p. 125, p. 6, p. 127.]

[9 See above, p. 233, note 10.]

[10 Therefore whereas the Lord is served in the ministry of his word, sacraments, prayer, and all other parts of his holy discipline and government, which he hath appointed for his church, these are the very things in which the day is to be consumed.—Ibid. Book II. p. 165.]

of opinion, how the ceremonies of their church are universally, and under the pain of the great curse, necessarily to be used in all places and countries[1].

Proposition II.

No private man, of a self-will, and purposely, may in public violate the traditions and ceremonies of the church, which by common authority be allowed, and are not repugnant to the word of God.

The proof from God's word.

Great is the privilege, great also the liberty and freedom of God's church and people.

For they are delivered

Gal. iii. 13. From the curse of the law.

Rom. viii. 2. From the law of sin and of death.

Acts xv. 24. From all Jewish rites and ceremonies.

Col. ii. 8. And from all human ordinances and traditions whatsoever, when they are imposed upon the consciences of men, to be observed under pain of eternal condemnation.

Notwithstanding, the church, and every member thereof, in his place is bound to the observation of all traditions and
1 Cor. iv. 16, 20. ceremonies, which are allowed by lawful authority, and are not repugnant to the word of God. For he that violateth them, contemneth not man, but God, who hath given power
1 Cor. xiv. 40. to his church to establish whatsoever things shall make unto comeliness, order, and edification.

Conf. Helv. I. Art. xxv. & II. c. 24. Bohem. c. 15, 18. August. Art. IV. XV. Saxon. Art. XX. Suevica, c. 14. This of our godly brethren, in their published writings, is approved[2].

[[1] See above, p. 187, note 14.]

[[2] Quæ media vocantur, et sunt proprie, iis uti vir pius, quanquam libere ubique et semper potest: tamen scienter, et ex charitate, nempe ad gloriam Deo et ad ecclesiæ proximorumque ædificationem omnibus utetur solum.—Harm. Conf. Sect. XVII. p. 211. Conf. Helv. Prior. Art. XXV. Non licet autem cuivis pro suo arbitrio ecclesiæ ordinationem hanc convellere.—Ibid. Sect. XVI. p. 174. Conf. Helv. Post. cap. XXIV. ...ne quis speciem Christianæ libertatis prætexendo, piis et bono usui servientibus constitutionibus se subtrahat.—Ibid. pp. 212, 213. Conf. Bohem. cap. XV. Sunt quidem Christiani hac in parte legibus soluti; ita tamen ne imbecillioribus sint scandalo.—Ibid. p. 181. Conf. Bohem. cap. XVIII. Omnes moderati homines libentius parent traditionibus, postquam intelligunt, privatim conscientias periculo liberatas esse, et eatenus parendum esse, ne perturbetur communis tranquillitas, neve imbecilles lædantur.—Ibid. p. 186. Conf. August. De Abus. Art. IV. Sed sentiendum est, quod sint (ritus ecclesiastici) res adiaphoræ quæ extra casum scandali omitti possint. Sed illi peccant, qui cum scandalo eas violant, ut qui suarum ecclesiarum tranquillitatem temere perturbant, &c.—Ibid. p. 218. Conf. August. Art. XV. ...postea ritus aliquos honestos, boni ordinis causa factos,

The adversaries unto this truth.

Notwithstanding, say the Anabaptists[3], the people of God are free from all laws, and owe obedience to no man; are not to be bound with the bands of any jurisdiction of this world, say the Brownists[4]; are freed from the observation of all rites and ecclesiastical ceremonies, say certain ministers of the precise faction both in Scotland and England[5].

Bulling. contra Anabap. Lib. II. c. 2.
R. H. on Psal. cxxii.
D. Barlow, Conference at Hampton Court, p. 70, 71.

Again, there be of the clergy, who, rather than they will use, or observe any rites, ceremonies, or orders, though lawfully ratified, which please them not, will disquiet the whole church, forsake their charges, leave their vocations, raise stirs, and cause divisions in the church; as did many, when it was in Germany about the Rhine, Frankland, and Sueavland, whereby most lamentable effects did ensue[6]; and do the refractory ministers in the church of England at this day[a]; the more is the pity.

Phil. Melanct. ep. ad Pastores, & in Comitat. Mansfield.

[a] Burges in his Letter unto King James, *anno* 1604, saith, the number of those ministers so refusing conformity were 600, or 700, viz. (as it is in the Lincolnshire ministers' Apology) in Oxfordshire, 9; Staffordshire, 14; Dorsetshire, 17; Hertfordshire, 17; Nottinghamshire, 20; Surrey, 21; Norfolk, 28; Wiltshire, 31; Buckinghamshire, 33; Sussex, 47; Leicestershire, 57; Essex, 57; Cheshire, 12; Bedfordshire, 16; Somersetshire, 17; Derbyshire, 20; Lancashire, 21; Kent, 23; London, 30; Lincolnshire, 33; Warwickshire, 44; Devonshire and Cornwall, 51; Northamptonshire, 57; Suffolk, 71.

---

et servamus et servandos esse docemus; ut sine ordine homines vivere non possunt. —Ibid. p. 228. Conf. Saxon. Art. xx. ...multas (traditiones) sane ecclesia hodie jure observat...quas qui rejecerit, is non hominum sed Dei, cujus traditio est quæcunque utilis est, auctoritatem contemnit.—Ibid. p. 231. Conf. Suev. cap. XIV.]

[3 Nam eo quod a Christo liberati essent, ab omnibus legibus liberi et immunes esse volebant. Ideoque existimabant se jure neque annuos reditus, neque decumas, neque etiam ulla servitia debere.—Bulling. adv. Anabapt. (Simleri Vers. Lat.) Tiguri, 1560. p. 37. Lib. II. cap. 2.]

[4 See above, p. 185, note 5.]

[5 ...but for matters of ceremony they were to be left in christian liberty unto every man, as he received more and more light from the illumination of God's Spirit.—Barlow, Summe of the Conference, &c. at Hampton Court. Lond. 1604, p. 71.]

[6 In aliis rebus adiaphoris servitutem quamlibet duram tolerabimus; nec propter eves causas occasionem præbendam censemus iis qui pellere pastores conantur: qua de re cum a multis interrogati simus, scripsi quid mihi videretur. Quamquam autem scio quibusdam horridiores sententias magis probari, tamen hæc magna causa est cur servitutem toleremus ne fiat in ecclesia solitudo qualis jam in multis locis est ad Rhenum et in Suevia.—Phil. Melancthon. Epist. Lond. 1642. Lib. I. Ep. 81. col. 104, 5.]

The principal author of all these tragical furies about ceremonial matters was Flacius Illyricus, whose preachings were, that rather than ministers should yield unto the servitude of ceremonies, they should abandon their calling, and give over the ministry, to the end, that princes and magistrates, even for fear of uproars and popular tumults, might be forced at the length to set their ministers free from the observation of all ceremonies, more than they were willing to use [a]themselves[1].

Proposition III.

Ceremonies and traditions, ordained by the authority of man, if they be repugnant to God's word, are not to be kept and observed of any man.

The proof from God's word.

Of ceremonies and traditions, repugnant to the word of God, there be two sorts: whereof some are of things merely
Exod. xxxii. 4, &c. Dan. iii. 1, &c. See afore, Art. XXII. Prop. 3, 4, 5. impious and wicked; such was the Israelites' calf, and Nebuchadnezzar's idol, and be the papistical images, relics, Agnus-Deis, and crosses, to which they do give divine adoration[2]. These, and such like, be all flatly forbidden[b]. Others are of things by God in his word neither commanded nor forbidden; as of eating or not eating flesh; of wearing or not wearing some apparel; of keeping or not keeping some days holy by abstinence from bodily labour, &c.; the which are not to be observed of any Christian, when for sound doctrine it is delivered that such works either do merit remission of sins, or be the acceptable service of God; or do more please than the observation of the laws prescribed by God himself; or be necessarily to be done, insomuch as they are damned who do them not.

[a] Fateor me suasisse, et Francis, et aliis, ne desererent ecclesias propter servitutem, quæ sine impietate sustineri posset. Nam quod Illyricus vociferatur, potius vastitatem fuisse faciendam in templis, et metu seditionum terrendos principes, ego ne nunc quidem tam tristis sententiæ autor esse velim; inquit Phil. Melancthon. Epist. ad Pium Lectorem inter Epist. Theolog. suas. p. 455. [Epist. Lond. 1642. Lib. I. Ep. 107. col. 134.]

[b] Thou shalt make thee no graven image, neither any similitude of things, &c. Thou shalt not bow down to them, neither serve them, &c. Exod. xx. 4, 5.

[[1] See above, p. 186, note 1.] [[2] See above, pp. 222, 3.]

We must therefore have always in mind that we are "bought with a price," and therefore may not be the "servants of men:" and that none human constitution in the church doth bind any man to break the least commandment of God.

1 Cor. vii. 23. Acts iv. 19.

The consideration hereof hath caused other churches also, with a sweet consent, to condemn such wicked ceremonies and traditions of men[3].

Conf. Helv. I. Art. IV. & II. cap. 14, 27. Basil. Art. x. sect. 3. Bohem. c. 15. Gal. Art. XXIV. XXXIII. Belg. Art. VII. XXIX. XXXII. August. Art. XV. Wittemb. Art. XXVIII. XXIX. XXXII. XXXIII. Suevica, c. 8, 14, 15.

Errors and adversaries to this truth.

Such ungodly traditions and ceremonies are all the ceremonies and traditions in a manner of the anti-christian synagogue of Rome.

Such also be the Sabbatarian traditions and ceremonies, lately broached, because they be imposed upon the church, necessarily, and perpetually to be observed of all and every Christian under pain of damnation both of soul and body. For, say they, (speaking yet of their private and classical injunctions about the Sabbath-day) "The Lord hath commanded so precise a rest unto all sorts of men, that it may not by any fraud, deceit, or circumvention whatsoever, be broken, but that he will most severely require it at our hands, under the pain of his everlasting displeasure."

D. B. Sab. Doct. I. Book, p. 98.

This (viz. the manner of keeping the Sabbath prescribed by themselves) the Lord requireth of all, and every one continually from the beginning to the end of our lives, without any interruption, under the pain of everlasting condemnation[4].

Ibid. p. 146.

[[3] See above, p. 189, note 1, and p. 201, note 6, and add the following: Quanto magis accedit cumulo rituum in ecclesiæ, tanto magis detrahitur non tantum libertati Christianæ, sed et Christo et ejus fidei; dum vulgus ea quærit in ritibus, quæ quæreret in solo Dei Filio Jesu Christo per fidem. Sufficiunt itaque piis, pauci, moderati, simplices, nec alieni a verbo Dei ritus.—Harm. Conf. Sect. XVII. p. 210. Conf. Helv. Post. cap. XXVII. Secundum hæc igitur non tantum non servandæ, sed fugiendæ sunt omnes traditiones humanæ, ritusque ejusmodi qui gloriam, honorem, cultum et gratiam Domini nostri Jesu Christi obscurant aut tollunt, populumque a vera et sincera fide abducunt.—Ibid. p. 213. Conf. Bohem. cap. XV. His igitur notis vera ecclesia a falsa discernetur...si denique (ut uno verbo cuncta complectamur) ad normam verbi Dei omnia exigat, et quæcunque huic adversantur, repudiet.—Ibid. Sect. x. p. 18. Conf. Belg. Art. XXIX. The other references are either inferential, or concern only special cases of rites and traditions, such as the use of fasting, holy water, &c.]

[[4] Nich. Bownde, Doct. of the Sabbath. Lond. 1595. Book I. pp. 98, 146.]

Pattern of the pres. Temp. Another sort of people there is amongst us, which will observe, and use all ceremonies whatsoever[1], as the temporizing Familists, who at Rome, and such like places of superstition, will go unto idolatrous services, and do adoration
Ibid. unto idols; and nowhere will they strive, or vary with any one about religion, but keep all external orders, albeit in their hearts they scorn all professions and services but their own;
H. N. Spirit. land. chap. 5, § 1. Ibid. terming all temples and churches in derision, common-houses; and all God's services or religions besides their own, foolishness[2].

To the Christian Reader.

Christian and beloved reader, let me request thee to observe well the first section of the proof of this present proposition; and therein how I speak of ceremonies and traditions apparently impious, among which I do reckon papistical crosses, whereunto the Romanists do attribute divine adoration, as elsewhere in this book, and subscription of mine, I have declared, and could more copiously; but the reliques of a libel of theirs, left in the parish-church of Euborn in Berkshire, anno 1604, sufficiently shall express the thoughts of Papists, touching their cross and crossing; whose words be these:

Now Mr Parson, for your welcome home,
Read these few lines you know not from whom.
You hold cross for an outward token and sign,
And remembrance only in religion thine.
And of the profession the people do make,
For more than this comes to, thou doest it not take.
Vide Coster. Jesu. Enchirid. controvers. c. 21, de S. Cruc. p. 358, &c. Yet holy church tells us of holy cross much more[3],
Of power and virtue to heal sick and sore;
Of holiness to bless us, and keep us from evil,
From foul fiend to fend us, and save us from devil;

[[1] The work referred to has not been found.]
[[2] See above, p. 186, note 2.]
[[3] Utilitates ejus (sc. crucis) sunt varia. Est enim sancta et efficax oratio fidelium, qua sese signantes, implorant divinum auxilium, &c....Est deinde oblatio qua nos nostraque omnia hoc signo crucis Deo offerimus, &c....Tertio hoc signum crucis est conjuratio quædam ad depellendum dæmonem, ejusque vires frangendas, &c....Quarto excitatur spes nostra signo hoc crucis, et fiducia remissionis peccatorum assequendæ....Quinto: Hoc signo excitatur in nobis charitas, dum per id renovatur memoria passionis Dominicæ....Sexto: Hoc signo crucis excitamur ad imitationem crucifixi, &c.—Coster. Enchirid. Controv. Col. Agrip. 1608. c. XXI. De Sanct. Cruce, pp. 619-621.]

And of many miracles which holy cross hath wrought,
All which by tradition to light church hath brought.
Wherefore holy worship holy church doth it give;
And surely so will we, so long as we live.
Though thou sayest idolatry, and vile superstition,
Yet we know it is holy church's tradition.
Holy cross then disgrace not, but bring it in renown,
For up shall the cross go, and you shall go down.

Of this cross I spake, and meant, and of none other, when I number it among things merely impious and unlawful: and therefore have I not a little wondered at those my brethren, which draw these words of mine in this section unto the cross used in our church at baptism[5] which I never thought, nor take to be either papistical or impious, because none adoration, not so much as civil, much less divine, is given thereunto, either by our church in general, or of any minister, or member thereof in particular. If they have no other patrons for their not using, or refusing the ceremony of the cross, than myself, they are in an ill case. For both in my judgement and practice I do allow thereof. This their perverting of my words contrary to their sense, and my meaning, telleth me that other men's words and names are but too much abused by them in that book, to the backing of schism and faction in the church and state, which from our souls we do abhor.

Abridgment of the Lincoln ministers' Apology unto King James, *anno* 1605, p. 30.

Proposition IV.

Every particular, or national church, may ordain, change, and abolish ceremonies, or rites, ordained only by man's authority, so that all things be done to edifying.

It hath pleased our most merciful Lord and Saviour Christ, for the maintenance of his church militant, that two sorts of rites and ceremonies should be used, whereof

Some, God his most excellent Majesty hath himself ordained, as the ceremony of baptism and the Lord's supper: which are till the end of the world, without all addition, diminution, and alteration, with all zeal and religion to be observed.

[[5] The sign of the Cross also is notoriously known to be abused to superstition and idolatry by the Papists....This hath caused many of our chief divines to condemn the use of it even in Baptism, as Hellopeus, Beza, &c....Thomas Rogers, and others.—An Abridgement of that Booke which the Ministers of Lincoln Diocese delivered to his Majestie, &c. 1605. Argum. I. Except. 2. pp. 29, 30.]

Others be ordained by the authority of each provincial, or national church, and that partly for comeliness, that is to say, that by these helps the people of God the better may be inflamed with a godly zeal; and that soberness and gravity may appear in the well-handling of ecclesiastical matters: and partly for order sake, even that governors may have rules and directions how to govern by; auditors and inferiors may know how to prepare, and behave themselves in sacred assem-
In this Art., Prop. 1. blies; and a joyful peace may be continued, by the well-ordering of church-affairs.

Confess. Helv. II. c. 27. Bohem. c. 15. Gal. Art. XII. Belg. Art. XXXII. August. de Abusu. Art. VII. Wittemb. Art. XXXV. Suevica, c. 14.

We have already proved that these latter sort of ceremonies may be made, and changed, augmented, or diminished, as fit opportunity and occasions shall be ministered, and that by particular or national churches; which thing is also affirmed by our neighbours[1].

Adversaries unto this truth.

See Art. XXV. Prop. 10. Concil. Trid. Sess. 7. can. 13.

This manifesteth to the world the intolerable arrogancy of the Romish church, which dare take upon her to alter, and apply to wrong uses, the very sacraments instituted even by Christ himself[2], and to prescribe ceremonies and rites, not to some particular, but to all churches, in all times and places[3].

T. C. 1 Rep. p. 120. D. B. Doct. of Sab. I. B. p. 31.

It sheweth also the boldness of our home adversaries, the Puritan Dominicans, which say, that the church nor no man can take away the liberty (of working six days in the week) from men, and drive them to a necessary rest of the body (upon any day saving the seventh[4]).

Ibid. p. 47.

Again, say these men, the church hath none authority, ordinarily and perpetually, to sanctify any day but the seventh day, which the Lord hath sanctified; nor to set up any day like to the Sabbath-day[5].

The latter sort, what in them is, quench the people's devotion, and hinder them from frequenting of churches upon all holy-days falling on the week-days, and ordained by the lawful authority of the church.

[[1] See above, p. 184, note 1; p. 189, note 1; and p. 201, note 6.]
[[2] See above, p. 266, notes 1, 2, 3.]
[[3] See above, p. 187, note 14.]
[[4] See above, p. 187, note 11.]
[[5] Nich. Bownde, Doct. of the Sabbath. Lond. 1595. Book I. pp. 31, 47.]

Article XXXV.

Of Homilies.

The second Book of Homilies, the several titles whereof we have joined under this Article, doth contain a godly and wholesome doctrine, and necessary for these times, as doth the former Book of Homilies, which were set forth in the time of Edward the Sixth: and therefore we judge them to be read in churches by the ministers diligently and distinctly, that they may be understood of the people.

Of the Names of the Homilies.

1. *Of the right use of the Church.*
2. *Against Peril of Idolatry.*
3. *Of repairing and keeping clean of Churches.*
4. *Of good Works; first of Fasting.*
5. *Against Gluttony and Drunkenness.*
6. *Against excess of Apparel.*
7. *Of Prayer.*
8. *Of the Place and Time of Prayer.*
9. *That Common Prayers and Sacraments ought to be ministered in a known Tongue.*
10. *Of the reverend Estimation of God's Word.*
11. *Of Alms-doing.*
12. *Of the Nativity of Christ.*
13. *Of the Passion of Christ.*
14. *Of the Resurrection of Christ.*
15. *Of the worthy receiving of the Sacrament of the Body and Blood of Christ.*
16. *Of the Gifts of the Holy Ghost.*
17. *For the Rogation-Days.*
18. *Of the Estate of Matrimony.*
19. *Of Repentance.*
20. *Against Idleness.*
21. *Against Rebellion.*

Touching this article, the greatest matter is not, whether these homilies meant and mentioned do contain doctrine both godly, wholesome, and necessary; but whether homilies, or any apocrypha writings at all, may be read in the open church, and before the congregation; which I think they may, and prove thus.

Great is the excellency, great also the utility, of God's word preached. Therefore saith St Paul, "None can believe without a preacher;" and, "Woe is me if I preach not the gospel." Howbeit the manner of preaching is not always one and the same. For the apostles were to teach as well by the pen as by the lively voice[6].

Rom. x. 14. 1 Cor. ix. 16. D. Whitak. cont. Bel. Con. I. q. 6, p. 385.

[[6] Itaque summam religionis nostræ scriptam esse affirmamus, quæ quidem

D. Fulk against the Rhem. Annot. Rom. i. 15.

Paul did preach the gospel by writing[1]: we owe in a manner more to the bonds of Paul (for his books) than to his liberty for [a]preaching[2].

The ministers of Geneva's epistle before Calvin, on Deuteronomy. Soiter de Vinda de bello Pa. Lib. II.

Calvin's writings will edify all men continually in the time to come[3]. Protestant books are witnesses of sound doctrine and sincere Christianity[4].

For my part, I cannot but magnify the goodness of God for all good means to bring us unto faith, and so unto salvation, but especially for the written labours of holy and learned men, whose doings in all ages not only have been approved, but also used and read many of them in the most sacred assemblies. So

D. Chrysost. & Muscul. in Ad Col. iv. Eus. Lib. IV. c. 23.

In the primitive church was publicly read the epistle of the Laodiceans[5] in the church of the Colossians, the epistle of Clemens unto the Corinthians[6].

[a] Pauli vinculis plura pene quam libertati debemus.—Beza, Epist. Dedicat. Olevian. Com. in epist. ad Galat.

---

eadem est cum eorum etiam apostolorum doctrina, qui nihil scripserunt. Idem enim docuerunt evangelium qui non scripserunt, quod illi qui scripserunt.—Whitaker, Disput. de Sacra Script. Cantab. 1588. Controv. I. Quæst. VI. cap. 6. p. 385.]

[[1] St Paul did preach the gospel also by writing, and the people did hear by reading.—Fulke's Rhemish New Test. Lond. 1617. p. 438. Annot. Rom. i. 7.]

[[2] Sic fiet ut...Paulum ipsum imitatus videare, cujus etiam vinculis plura pene quam libertati debemus.—Bez. Epist. Dedicat. in Olevian. Comm. in Epist. ad Galat. Genev. 1578. prope fin.]

[[3] The editor has been unable to discover any such epistle. But see Beza's Epistle Dedicatory to the Comment. on Job. (Calvin. Opp. Amstelod. 1667-71. Tom. II.) Calvinus...magis ac magis inter vere pios et eruditos in posterum eminebit.]

[[4] Curiam ingressi et habito senatu in primis novi dogmatis de religione rem ordiri cœpere, et ipse imperator Augustus....monere jussit: Dogma illud novum, &c....At hi in eadem perseverantia...perstitere....Composuisse namque suos jampridem antea quos evulgaverint in lucemque ediderint libellos multos, sanæ doctrinæ atque purioris Christianismi testes et indices synceros, &c.—Melch. Soiter. a Vinda, Bell. Pannon. Lib. II. pp. 516, 17, subjoined to Laon. Chalcond. de Orig. Turc. Basil. 1556.]

[[5] Καὶ τὴν ἐκ Λαοδικείας ἵνα καὶ ὑμεῖς ἀναγνῶτε. Τινὲς λέγουσιν ὅτι οὐχὶ τὴν Παύλου πρὸς αὐτοὺς ἀπεσταλμένην, ἀλλὰ τὴν παρ' αὐτῶν Παύλῳ.—Chrysost. Opp. Paris. 1839. Tom. XI. p. 478. D. In Epist. ad Colos. cap. IV. Hom. 12. Non satis observant verba apostoli, qui putant illum loqui de quadam epistola quam scripserit ad Laodicenses, quæ interciderit. Non dicit, Et eam quam scripsi ad Laodicenses: sed, Et eam quæ est ex Laodicea vos quoque legatis.—Wolf. Musc. in Pauli Epist. Basil. 1578. In Ep. ad Coloss. cap. IV. p. 201.]

[[6] Ἐν αὐτῇ δὲ ταύτῃ καὶ τῆς Κλήμεντος πρὸς Κορινθίους μέμνηται ἐπιστολῆς, δηλῶν ἀνέκαθεν ἐξ ἀρχαίου ἔθους ἐπὶ τῆς ἐκκλησίας τὴν ἀνάγνωσιν αὐτῆς ποιεῖσθαι.—Euseb. Eccl. Hist. Cant. 1720. Lib. IV. cap. 23. p. 187.]

Hermes his Pastor[7], and the homilies of the fathers[8].

In the reformed churches in Flanders[9] and France[b] read are M. Calvin's sermons upon Job: and in the Italian, French, Dutch and Scottish churches, the said Calvin his catechism is both read and expounded publicly, and that before the whole congregation[10].

Idem, Lib. III. c. 3.
T. C. 2 Rep. p. 110.
D. Sutclif, Answer to the Petit. c. 1, p. 23.
Smeton. contra Hamilton, p. 106.

The errors and adversaries unto this truth.

Deceived then, and out of the way of truth, are they, which of preaching by the mouth conceive either too basely, or too highly: too basely, as do the Anabaptists and Family of Love, they affirming there ought to be no preaching at all[11], and that preachers are not sent of God, neither do preach God's word, but the dead letter of the scripture[12]; these, with the said Anabaptists, terming them letter-doctors[13], preaching the letter, and imagination of their own knowledge, but not the word of the living God[14].

Wilkinson against the Fam. of Love, p. 75.
Bullinger. contra Anab.
H. N. lamen. Complaint.
Idem, I. Exhort. 16, 18.

[b] Editæ sunt igitur jampridem Gallicæ istæ conciones (Calvini in Jobum) &c. Neque id vero temere factum fuisse res ipsa mox ostendit, maximo cum remotissimarum etiam Gallicarum ecclesiarum fructu, quibus usque adeo privatim et publice placuerunt, ut plurimis in locis, quibus quotidiani pastores deerant, [conciones istæ in communi cœtu ex pulpito recitatæ] pastorum vice fuerint.—Beza, Præf. Concionum, J. Calv. in Jobum. [Opp. Tom. II.]

[7 Ἐπεὶ δὲ ὁ αὐτὸς ἀπόστολος, ἐν ταῖς ἐπὶ τέλει προσρήσεσι τῆς πρὸς Ῥωμαίους, μνήμην πεποίηται μετὰ τῶν ἄλλων καὶ Ἑρμᾶ, οὗ φασὶν ὑπάρχειν τὸ τοῦ ποιμνίου βιβλίον· ἰστέον ὡς καὶ τοῦτο πρὸς μὲν τινῶν ἀντιλέλεκται, δι' οὓς οὐκ ἂν ἐν ὁμολογουμένοις τεθείη· ὑφ' ἑτέρων δὲ ἀναγκαιότατον οἷς μάλιστα δεῖ στοιχειώσεως εἰσαγωγικῆς κέκριται. ὅθεν ἤδη καὶ ἐν ἐκκλησίαις ἴσμεν αὐτὸ δεδημοσιευμένον, κ.τ.λ.—Ibid. Lib. III. cap. 3. p. 90.]

[8 Another council decreed that in the minister's sickness one deacon should read the homilies of the fathers, &c.—The rest of the Second Replie of Thomas Cartwright, 1577. p. 110.]

[9 There seems to be an error in the reference.]

[10 Summam Christianæ fidei brevi libello complexus est Genevæ Joan. Calvinus; quam Itali, Galli, Belgæ, Scoti, &c. publice in ecclesiis suis interpretantur.—Smeton. contr. Hamilton. Edinburg. 1579. p. 106.]

[11 They said there ought to be no more any preaching because the door was shut. Apoc. I.—Wilkinson's Confut. Lond. 1579. p. 75. (from Bullinger against the Anabaptists.)]

[12 Hi scripturarum interpretationem ægerrime ferunt, et multo ægrius cum ex illis corripiuntur. Itaque dicunt, se quidem verbum Dei non illibenter audire, sed interpretationem et adjecta ministrorum verba non posse agnoscere pro verbo Dei, aut libenter audire et recipere.—Bulling. adv. Anabapt. (Simler. Vers.) Tigur. 1560. cap. XI. p. 114.]

[13 See Wilkinson's Confut. p. 57.]

[14 H. N. First Exhortation, Translated, &c. cap. XVI. § 18.]

T. C. 1 Rep. p. 173. Too highly, as do the Puritans of all sorts. For say they, Except God work miraculously and extraordinarily, (which is not to be looked for of us) the bare reading (yea not) of the scriptures, without preaching, cannot deliver so much as one poor soul from destruction[1]: reading (of whatsoever in the church) without preaching, is not feeding, but as ill as playing upon a stage, and worse too[2]. 1 Admon. to the Parliam.

D. B. Sab. Doct. 2 B. p. 277. Without preaching of the word (viz. by the lively voice of a minister, and without the book) the Sabbath cannot be hallowed either of a minister or people, in the least measure which the Lord requireth of us[3].

Next, err do they, which set their wits and learning, either against all books in general, except the sacred Bible, or against the public reading of any learned men's writings, be they never so divine and godly, in the open and sacred assemblies.

Sleidan. Com. Lib. x. Of the former sort are the Anabaptists; who, as Sleidan[4] recordeth, did burn the books, writings, and monuments of learned men, reserving and preserving only the holy scriptures from the fire.

Of the latter be the Brownists, Disciplinarians, and Sabbatarians.

Gifford against the Brown. 15. Fruct. Ser. on Rom. xii. p. 60. Def. of the god. Min. p. 116. The Brownists do say, that no Apocrypha must be brought into the christian assemblies[5]: so the Disciplinarians; ministers ought not to read openly in the congregation any writings, but only the canonical scriptures[6]: they complain that human writings are brought into the church[7]: they cry out,

[1 And indeed unless the Lord work miraculously and extraordinarily (which is not to be looked for of us) the bare reading of the scriptures without the preaching cannot deliver so much as one poor sheep from destruction.—A Reply to an Answer, &c. by T. C. p. 173.]

[2 For bare reading of the word, and single service saying is bare feeding, yea, it is as evil as playing upon a stage, and worse too.—An Admonition to the Parliament, fol. B.]

[3 Nich. Bownde, Doct. of the Sabbath, Lond. 1595. Bk. II. p. 277.]

[4 Post hæc idem propheta (Joannes Mathæus) mandabat, ne quis ullum deinceps librum haberet, aut sibi servaret, præter sacra Biblia: reliquos omnes in publicum deferri jussit et aboleri: hoc se mandatum divinitus accepisse dicebat: itaque magno numero libri comportati flamma fuerunt omnes absumpti.—Sleidan. Comment. Argentorat. 1555. Lib. x. fol. 151.]

[5 See, A Plaine Declaration that our Brownists be full Donatists, &c. by George Gyffard. London, 1590. p. 83.]

[6 ...so ought not the ministers of God to expound or read openly, &c.—A Fruitful Sermon on the 3, 4, &c. verses of the 12th chap. of the Epistle to the Romans. London, 1589. p. 53.]

[7 From this we come unto the Homilies, which are allowed by one of the

Remove homilies[8]; and they supplicate unto K. James, that the canonical scriptures only may be read in the church[9].

1 Admon. to the Parliament.
The Petit. of the thousand.

And so, but much more bitterly and erroneously, the Sabbatarians. We damn ourselves (say they) if we go not from those ministers and churches where the scriptures and homilies only be read, and seek not unto the prophets, when (and so often as) we have them not at home[10].

D. B. Sabbat. Doct. 2 Book, pag. 173.

Article XXXVI.

Of Consecration of Bishops and Ministers.

The Book of Consecration (1) *of Archbishops and Bishops, and Ordering of Priests and Deacons, set forth in the time of Edward the Sixth, and confirmed at the same time by authority of Parliament, doth contain all things necessary to such Consecration and Ordering: neither hath it anything that of itself is superstitious or ungodly. And therefore* (2) *whosoever are consecrated or ordered according to the Rites of that Book, since the second year of the aforenamed K. Edward unto this time, or hereafter shall be consecrated or ordered according to the same Rites; we decree all such to be rightly and orderly and lawfully consecrated and ordered.*

The propositions.

1. It is agreeable to the word of God, and practice of the primitive church, that there should be archbishops,

Articles, where beside the contrariety they have in the order itself, that the human writings of men are brought to be read in the church, and that to underpropt (*sic*), a yet more foul abuse, even the inability of ministers to teach, &c.—A Defense of the Godly Ministers against the Slaunders of D. Bridges. 1587. p. 116.]

[8 Remove Homilies, Articles, Injunctions, and that prescript order of service made out of the mass-book.—An Admonition, &c. fol. A. 4.]

[9 See the Humble Petition of the Ministers of the Church of England, desiring Reformation, &c. prefixed to the Answer of the Vice-Chancellor, Doctors, &c. in the University of Oxford to the same. Oxford, 1604. Art. I.]

[10 What cause have we to be sorry for ourselves and others? which have so many times broken this law by wilful absenting ourselves from the church without any just cause, or by not seeking to the prophets to teach us when we had not them at home, &c.—Nich. Bownde, Doct. of the Sabbath. Book II. p. 173.]

bishops, and such like differences and inequalities of ecclesiastical ministers.

2. Whosoever be, or shall be consecrated or ordered according to the rites of the Book of Consecration of Archbishops, Bishops, and Ordering of Priests and Deacons, they be rightly, orderly, and lawfully consecrated and ordered.

Proposition I.

It is agreeable to the word of God, and practice of the primitive church, that there should be archbishops, bishops, and such like differences and inequalities of ecclesiastical ministers.

The proof from God's word.

Albeit the terms and titles of archbishops we find not, yet the superiority which they enjoy, and authority which the bishops and the archbishops do exercise, in ordering and consecrating of bishops, and ecclesiastical ministers, is grounded upon the word of God. For we find that

Beza in Act. Apost. i. 2.

In the apostles' days how themselves both were in dignity above the evangelists, and the seventy disciples, and for authority both in and over the church, as twelve patriarchs, saith Beza[1], and also established an ecclesiastical hierarchy.

D. Chrysost. in Act. Hom. 33. D. Hieron. in Galat. Euseb. D. Hieron. ad Evagr. D. Hieron. in 2 Tim. iv. D. Chrysost. in 1 Tim. v.

Hence came it that bishop was of Jerusalem, James[2];

Of Antioch, Peter[3]; of the Asian churches, John[4]; of Alexandria, Mark[5]; of Ephesus[6], yea, and all Asia, Timothy[7];

[1 ...illos omnino oportuit, novæ ecclesiæ quasi duodecim patriarchas futuros, peculiari quadam forma divinitus consecrari. Sicut etiam ipsis peculiariter promissus fuerat Spiritus Sanctus, &c.—Bez. Annot. in Nov. Test. Genev. 1598. Pars I. p. 455. In Act. ii. 1.]

[2 *'Επίσκοπος ἦν τῆς ἐν 'Ιεροσολύμοις ἐκκλησίας οὗτος ('Ιάκωβος)· διὸ καὶ ὕστερος λέγει.*—Chrysost. Opp. Par. 1839. Tom. IX. p. 279. In Act. Apost. xv. 13.]

[3 Denique primum episcopum Antiochenæ ecclesiæ Petrum fuisse accepimus, &c.—Hieron. Opp. Paris. 1693-1706. Tom. IV. Pars I. col. 244. In Epist. ad Galat. cap. 2.]

[4 *'Επὶ τούτοις κατὰ τὴν 'Ασίαν ἔτι τῷ βίῳ περιλειπόμενος αὐτὸς ἐκεῖνος, ὃν ἠγάπα ὁ 'Ιησοῦς, ἀπόστολος ὁμοῦ καὶ εὐαγγελιστὴς 'Ιωάννης, τὰς αὐτόθι διεῖπεν ἐκκλησίας, κ.τ.λ.*—Euseb. Eccl. Hist. Cantab. 1720. Lib. III. cap. 23, p. 112.]

[5 Nam et Alexandriæ a Marco evangelista usque ad Heraclam et Dionysium episcopos, presbyteri semper unum ex se electum, in excelsiori gradu collocatum, episcopum nominabant.—Hieron. Opp. Tom. IV. Pars 2. col. 803. Epist. 101. ad Evang.]

[6 *Ministerium tuum imple*...episcopatus scilicet.—Id. Opp. Tom. V. col. 1100. In Ep. 2. ad Tim. cap. 4.]

[7 This does not seem to be directly stated: it may be inferred perhaps from Chrysost. Hom. XIII. in 1 Tim. cap. IV. 11—14. Opp. Tom. XI. p. 671, b.]

of all Crete, Titus[8]; of Philippos, Epaphroditus[9]; of Corinth and Achaia, Apollos; of Athens, Dionysius; of France, Crescens[10]; of Britain, Aristobulus[11].

Theod. arg. in Epist. ad Tit.
Theod. in Ep. ad Philip.
Euseb. Lib. II.
Doroth. in Apost. Synop.

In the purer times, succeeding the apostles, so approved was the administration of the church-affairs by these kind of men, as

They ordained patriarchs and chor-episcopi[12].

They ratified the decrees of ecclesiastical super-eminency, at the first and most famous council at Nice[13].

Heming. Syntag. tit. de Guber. Eccles.
Beza, Epist. 1.

They gloried much, and greatly, that they had received the apostles' doctrine by a succession of bishops[14], that they were the successors in the apostles' doctrine of the godly bishops[15], and that bishops succeeded in the room of apostles[16].

D. Iren. 13, c. 3.
Sadeel. de Leg. Voc. p. 20.
D. August. in Psal. xliv.

Their godly monuments, and worthy labours and books yet extant, do shew, that bishop was of Lyons, Irenæus; of Antioch, Ignatius; of Carthage, Cyprian; of Hierusalem, Cyril; of Alexandria, Athanasius; Basil, of Cæsarea; of all Thracia, Asia, and Pontus, Chrysostom; Hilary of Poictiers;

[8 Theod. Opp. Paris. 1642-84. Tom. III. p. 507. c.] [9 Id. p. 322. c.]

[10 It is only said: *Κρίσκης μὲν ἐπὶ τὰς Γαλλίας στειλάμενος ὑπ' αὐτοῦ* (sc. *τοῦ Παύλου*) *μαρτυρεῖται.*—Euseb. Eccles. Histor. Lib. III. cap. 4. pp. 91, 2.]

[11 Aristobulus et ipse ab apostolo ad Roman. commemoratus episcopus Brittaniæ factus est.—Doroth. Synopsis, Wolf. Musc. Interpret. in Euseb. Eccles. Hist. Basil. 1570. p. 664.]

[12 Hinc ecclesia secuta tempora apostolorum, alios patriarchas, alios episcopos, alios chorepiscopos quos Justinus Martyr *προεστῶτας* vocat, nos præpositos, &c. instituit.—Nic. Hemming. Opusc. Theolog. 1636. p. 799. Syntagm. Inst. Christ. cap. XXIII. Art. 15.]

[13 Beza is arguing against the pretensions of the church of Rome. The passage is as follows: Primates et archiepiscopos esse politiæ Romanæ umbram et imaginem quæ paulatim emerserit, omnes vel mediocriter historiarum periti norunt. Confirmavit illam graduum distinctionem Nicena Synodus.—Bez. Epist. Genev. 1575. Ep. I. pp. 17, 18.]

[14 Traditionem itaque apostolorum in toto mundo manifestatam, in omni ecclesia adest perspicere omnibus qui vera velint videre, et habemus annumerare eos qui ab apostolis instituti sunt episcopi in ecclesiis, et successores eorum usque ad nos, qui nihil tale docuerunt neque cognoverunt quale ab his [sc. hæreticis] deliratur.—Iren. Opp. Oxon. 1702. Adv. Hær. Lib. III. cap. 3.]

[15 Ergo sic apud Tertullianum exclamans ecclesia nobis objiciebatur, "sum," inquit, "hæres apostolorum, sicut caverunt testimonio, sicut fidei commiserunt, sicut adjuraverunt, ita teneo." Quibus verbis apertissime significat se de successione doctrinæ gloriari.—Sadeel. De Legitim. Vocat. Pastor. Eccl. Reform. Morgiis. 1580. p. 20.]

[16 Quid est, *Pro patribus tuis nati sunt tibi filii?* Patres missi sunt apostoli, pro apostolis filii nati sunt tibi constituti sunt episcopi. Hodie enim episcopi qui sunt per totum mundum, unde nati sunt? Ipsa ecclesia patres illos appellat, ipsa illos genuit, et ipsa illos constituit in sedibus Patrum.—August. Opp. Paris. 1836-8. Tom. IV. col. 564. c. Enarr. in Psalm. xliv. v. 17. cap. 32.]

Augustine of Hippo; Ambrose of Millain: all of these most notable instruments for the advancement of God's honour and glory in their days.

Finally, from the apostles' days hitherto there never wanted a succession of bishops, neither in the east nor western churches, albeit there have been from time to time both mar-prelates, and mock-prelates, to supplant their states, and ill-prelates abusing their functions and places, to the discredit of their calling and profession. So provident hath the Almighty been for the augmentation of his glory, and people, by this kind and calling of men.

The errors and adversaries unto this truth.

This manifesteth the erroneous and evil minds,

Sleidan. Com. Lib. v. 1. Of the Anabaptists[1], who condemn all superiority among men, saying, That every man should be equal for calling; and that there should be no difference of persons among Christians.

Niceph. Lib. XVIII. c. 49. 2. Of the old heretics, viz. the Contobaptites[2], which allowed of no bishops.

Magd. Eccles. Hist. Cent. 7, c. 5. & Niceph. The Acephalians[3], who would not be at the command, or yield obedience unto bishops.

August. de Hæres. cap. 53. The Aerians[4], that equalled bishops and priests, making them all one.

D. Bernard. in Can. Ser. 66. The Apostolicks[5], which condemned prelacy.

3. Of the late schismatics, namely,

[1 Bonorum quoque communionem et humanitati cum primis esse consentaneum, ut et dignitate sint omnes æquales, docebat (Muncerus) et conditione liberi, et promiscue bonis omnibus utantur.—Sleidan. Comment. Argentorat. 1555. Lib. v. fol. 65.]

[2 ....οὓς (sc. ἐπισκόπους) οἱ Κοντοβαβδῖται μόνοι οὐ δέχονται.—Niceph. Eccl. Hist. Lut. Par. 1630. Lib. XVIII. cap. 49. p. 876. D.]

[3 Pertinet et hæc secta ad Severitas, dicta Acephalorum, ut inquit Nicephorus; quia sub episcopis non fuerunt.—Magdeburg. Eccl. Hist. Basil. 1562, &c. Cent. VII. c. 5. fol. 124.

Οἱ δὲ καὶ Ἀκέφαλοι ὠνομάζοντο· οἳ τὸ ἑνωτικὸν τοῦ βασιλέως Ζηνώνος οὐ προσίεντο, οἷς μὴ τῷ ἀναθέματι καὶ τὴν ἁγίαν τετάρτην καθυπέβαλε σύνοδον. διὰ δὲ τὸ ὑπὸ ἐπισκόποις μὴ ἄγεσθαι, Ἀκέφαλοι ὠνομάσθησαν.—Niceph. Eccl. Hist. Lib. XVIII. cap. 45. p. 869. See also Evagrius, Hist. Eccl. Lib. III. cap. 14.]

[4 ...cum esset presbyter (Aerius), doluisse fertur quod episcopus non potuit ordinari....Dicebat etiam presbyterum ab episcopo nulla differentia debere discerni. —August. Opp. Paris. 1836. Tom. VIII. col. 55. A. Liber de Hæres. cap. 53. See also Epiphan. Opp. Paris. 1622. Tom. I. Hæres. lxxv. p. 904.]

[5 The Apostolici, or Henricians, a sect in the time of S. Bernard. After

The Jesuits, who cannot brook episcopal pre-eminence[6]; and in their high court of reformation have made a law for the utter abrogation of all episcopal jurisdiction[7]. Declar. motuum, &c. c. 20. Quodlibets, p. 142.

The Disciplinarians or Puritans among ourselves. For

They abhor, and altogether do loath the callings of archbishops, bishops, &c., as the author of the Fruitful Sermon doth[8], and say, that by the prelatical discipline the liberty of the church is taken away[9], and that, instead of archbishops and bishops, an equality must be made of ministers[10]. Fruct. Ser. on Rom. xii. p. 37. Assert. Polit. p. 29. Admon. to the Parliam.

They term the differences of ministers, A proud ambitious superiority of one minister above another[11]; and archbishops and bishops they call the supposed governors of the church of England[12]. Discov. of D. Ban. ser. p. 37. Demon. of Dis. Epist. ded.

Some of them will not have bishops to be obeyed either when they cite, or when they inhibit, or when they excommunicate[13]. Mar. thes. 46, 82, 83.

Some of them have not only archbishops and bishops, but also parsons and vicars in detestation. For

Miles Monopodios numbereth parsons and vicars among the hundred points of popery yet remaining in our church[14]. Sold. of Bar. in the end.

charging them with denying infant baptism, purgatory, &c., he proceeds: Jam vero qui ecclesiam non agnoscunt, non est mirum si ordinibus ecclesiæ detrahunt,... Peccatores, inquiunt, sunt apostolici, archiepiscopi, episcopi, presbyteri, ac per hoc nec dandis nec accipiendis idonei sacramentis.—Bernard. Opp. Paris. 1667. Tom. III. col. 111. In Cantic. Serm. LXVI. § 11.]

[6 This reference the editor has been unable to verify.]

[7 I told you before, if you remember, that they (the Jesuits) have made a Puritanian division of the ecclesiastical state in their high Council of Reformation for England: wherein, amongst other things, a statute is made for abrogation of all episcopal dignity.—A Decacordon of Quodlibetical Questions, 1602. p. 142.]

[8 Even so is it with the church and spouse of Christ in England. For as she is grieved for the lack of those parts which are wanting: so she abhorreth and loatheth such as are abounding: as, namely, the callings, Arch-Bp., Deans, Archdeacons, Deacons, Chancelers, Comissaries, officials, and all such as be rather members and parts of the whore and strumpet of Rome than of the pure virgin and spouse of the immaculate Lamb.—Fruitful Sermon upon the 3, 4, &c. verses of Rom. xii. Lond. 1589. pp. 33, 4.]

[9 This reference has not been found.]

[10 Instead of an Archbishop or Lord-bishop you must make equality (2 Cor. 10. 7. Coloss. 1. 1. Philip. 1. 1. 1 Thess. 1. 1.) of ministers.—An Admon. to the Parliament. fol. A. 5.]

[11 A Brief Discovery of the Untruths and Slanders against Reformation, &c. contained in D. Bancroft's Sermon, p. 37.]

[12 See, A Demonstration of Discipline. The Dedication is, "To the Supposed Governours of the Church of England, the Archbyshops, lord Byshops, Archdeacons, and the rest of that order."]

[13 See above, p. 310, note 2.]

[14 "The Parson" and "the Vicar" are mentioned among "An hundred pointes

1 Admon. to the Parliam.

Others say, That birds of the same feather, *viz.* with archbishops and bishops, and parsons and vicars[1].

Bar. discov. p. 54.

Barrow publisheth, that parsonages and vicarages be in name, office and function, as popish and antichristian as any of the other[2].

Burges' Letter to king James before his Apology.

It is therefore an egregious untruth, that Puritans (or which is equivalent, the good men, the faithful and innocent ministers, for so do they style themselves) affect not any popularity or parity in the church of God, as some of them would make his majesty believe[3].

Proposition II.

Whosoever be or shall be confirmed or ordered according to the rites of the Book of Consecration of archbishops and bishops and Ordering of priests and deacons, they be rightly, orderly and lawfully consecrated and ordered.

D. Fulk against the Rhem. fol. 39.

Archbishops, bishops, and ministers, which according to the Book of Consecration be, or shall be consecrated or ordered, they are consecrated and ordained rightly, orderly and lawfully, because afore their consecration and ordination they be rightly tried or examined; by imposition of hands, needful and seasonable prayers, they be consecrated and ordained: and all this is performed by those persons, that is, by bishops, to whom the ordination and consecration of bishops and ministers was always principally committed[4]; and also after the same form and fashion (corruptions being afore taken away and removed) as bishops and priests afore the reign of King Edward the sixth formerly were.

of poperie which deforme the Englishe reformation."—A pleasaunt Dialogue between a Souldier of Barwicke and an English Chaplaine. 1581. fol. L. 5.]

[1 And birds of the same feather are covetous patrons of benefices, parsons, vicars, readers, parish priests, &c.—that under the authority of their masters (i.e. the bishops, archbishops) spoil their flocks of the food of their souls.—An Admon. to the Parliament. fol. B. 5.]

[2 Barrow's Discovery of the False Church, 1590. p. 54.]

[3 This reference has not been found.]

[4 The passage intended is probably this: ...for order and seemly government, there was always one principal to whom, by long use of the church, the name of Bishop or Superintendent hath been applied....Therefore although in scripture a Bishop and an Elder is of one order and authority in preaching, &c.....yet in government, by ancient use of speech, he is only called a Bishop....to whom the ordination or consecration by imposition of hands was always principally committed.—Fulke's New Test. Lond. 1617. Note on Tit. i. 5. fol. 718, 19.]

The adversaries unto this truth.

Well therefore may they disgorge their stomachs, but trouble our consciences they shall never, which condemn or deprave our callings, as do

1. The Family of Love[5], which dislike, and labour to make contemptible, the outward admission of ministers. H. N. Evang. c. 31, § 2.

2. The Papists, who say their pleasure of the bishops and ministers of the church of England, and of other reformed churches.

None is to be admitted for a bishop, (say they) which is not ordained by imposition of three or four (Romish) catholic bishops at the least, of which none are to be found among the Protestants[6]. Howlet's 7 reas.

Whosoever taketh upon him to preach, to minister sacraments, and is not ordered of a true catholic (that is, a popish) bishop, to be a curate of souls, parson, bishop, &c., he is a thief and a murderer[7]. Test. Rhem. An. John x. 1.

Our bishops and ministers, they are not come in by the door (saith Stapleton); they have stolen in like thieves[8]; they be unordered apostates, pretended, and sacrilegious ministers, intruders[9], mere laymen, and not priests, because, first, they have received none under[10] orders; and next, they are not ordained by such a bishop, and priest, as the catholic (Roman) church hath put in authority[11]. Stapl. Fort. 2 part. 3. 8, p. 141. Answer to the Exec. c. 3, p. 41. Ibid. chap 7, p. 148. Ibid. cap. 9, p. 211. Ibid c. 8, p. 171. Howl. 7 reas.

3. The Puritans. For they write, that

The bishops of our church have none ordinary calling of

[5 *Christians* signify unto us, Those that are anointed. For the Holy ones of *Christ* were in times past so named, which were anointed (Act. 2. a.) with the holy Spirit of *Christ* to priests or elders of the holy understanding.—H. N. Evang. Reg. c. XXXI. § 2, p. 73.]

[6 ...(The Catholic church) admitteth no man for bishop which is not ordained by imposition of three or two catholic bishops' hands at the least. Of all which things none are to be found amongst the Protestants.—A Brief Discours, &c. Douay, 1581. Reas. VII. p. 41. b. See above, p. 239, note 4.]

[7 Test. Rhem. Rhemes, 1582. Annot. Joh. x. 1. p. 250, where, *to preach without lawful sending*, and *is not canonically ordered.*]

[8 Stapleton, Fortresse of the Faith, Antwerpe, 1565. Part II. cap. 8. p. 141, with a slight verbal difference.]

[9 (Card. Alan's) Sincere and Modest Defence, &c. against the Exec. of Justice, &c., where in chap. 7, p. 148, *pretended ministry:* chap. 9, p. 211, sacrilegious ministries: chap. 8, p. 171, First and foremost for the clergy...it is wholly destained and destroyed...as these other good fellows their intruders have lived in joy and felicity.]

[10 Other, the later editions.]

[11 See above, p. 239, note 4.]

T. C. def. 21, sect. 1. Dial. of the Strife, præf. God, and function in the scriptures, for to exercise[1]. They are not sent of God; they be not the ministers of Jesus Christ, by whom he will advance his gospel[2].

1 Admon. to the Parliament. Inferior ministers, they are not (say they) according to God's word either proved, elected, called or ordained[3]. Hence the church of England wanteth (say they) her pastors and teachers[4], and hence they urge divers afore ordained to seek at their classis a new approbation[5], which they term the Lord's Ordinance, and to take new callings from classical ministers, renouncing their calling from bishops[6].

Fruct. Ser. on Rom. xii. p. 36. Eng. Scotiz. 3 B. c. 14, p. 113. Ibid.

Article XXXVII.

Of the Civil Magistrate.

(1) *The King's Majesty hath the chief power in this realm of England, and other his dominions,* (2) *unto whom the chief government of all estates of this realm, whether they be Ecclesiastical or Civil, in all causes doth appertain, and is not, nor ought to be subject to any foreign jurisdiction. Where we attribute to the King's Majesty the chief government, by which titles we understand the minds of some slanderous folks to be offended;* (3) *we give not to our prince the ministering either of God's word, or of the Sacraments; the which thing the injunctions also, sometime set forth by Elizabeth our (late) Queen, do most plainly testify;*

[1 A Replie to an Answere, &c. by T. C. p. 21.]

[2 A Dialogue Concerning the Strife of our Churche. Lond. 1584. Pref. p. 4.]

[3 An Admon. to the Parliam. fol. A. 2.]

[4 The Church of God in England (dear Christians)...wanteth her Pastors, Teachers, Elders, Deacons, and her attenders upon the poor, &c.—Fruitful Sermon on 3, 4, &c. verses of Rom. xii. Lond. 1589. pp. 32, 3.]

[5 The first degree they have entered into is this, that, teaching all ministers which are called according to the order of the church of England to be unlawful, they do urge such as they dare trust (and who are ministers already) to seek at their classis a new approbation which they term the Lord's Ordinance.—English Scottizing, for Discipline by Practise, the Third Book of Disciplinary Grounds and Practises, cap. XIV. p. 113. The Title of the work is, Dangerous Positions and Proceedings, &c. for the Presbyterial Discipline, by Richard Bancroft, &c. Lond. 1640.]

[6 They renounce the calling they have had of the bishops: and do take it again from the approbation of the classis.—Ibid.]

but that only prerogative, which we see to have been given always to all godly princes in holy Scriptures by God himself, that they should rule all estates and degrees committed to their charge by God, whether they be ecclesiastical or temporal, (4) *and restrain with the civil sword the stubborn and evil-doers.* (5) *The bishop of Rome hath no jurisdiction in this realm of England.* (6) *The laws of the realm may punish Christian men with death, for heinous and grievous offences.* (7) *It is lawful for Christian men, at the commandment of the magistrate, to wear weapons, and serve in the wars.*

The propositions.

1. The king's majesty hath the chief power in this realm of England and other his dominions.
2. The king's majesty hath the chief government of all estates ecclesiastical and civil, in all causes within his dominions.
3. His highness may not execute the ecclesiastical duties of preaching and ministering the sacraments, and yet is to prescribe laws and directions unto all estates, both ecclesiastical and temporal.
4. The king by his authority is to restrain with the material sword, and to punish malefactors.
5. The bishop of Rome hath no jurisdiction in this realm of England (nor other of the king's dominions).
6. By the laws of this realm Christian men, for heinous and grievous offences, may be put to death.
7. It is lawful for Christian men, at the commandment of the magistrate, to wear weapons, and serve in the wars.

Proposition I.

The king's majesty hath the chief power in this realm of England, and other his dominions.

The proof from God's word.

Divers and sundry be the forms of commonweals and magistracy. For some, where many, and they of the inferior people, bear the sway, as in a democracy; some, where a few, and that of choice, and the best men do govern, as in an aristocracy; and some, where one man or woman hath the pre-eminence, as in a monarchy: such is the government of this kingdom.

Notwithstanding whatsoever the government is, either democratical, aristocratical, or monarchical, God's word doth teach us, that

Rom. xiii. 1, 2 "There is no power but of God; the powers that be are ordained of God; and that whosoever resisteth the power, resisteth the ordinance of God."

Tit. iii. 1. "We must be subject to the principalities and powers, and obedient and ready to every good work."

1 Pet. ii. 13. "We must submit ourselves unto all manner of ordinance of man, for the Lord's sake."

1 Tim. ii. 1, 2. "We must pray for kings, and for all that be in authority."

Rom. xiii. 7. Finally, "we must give to all men their duty; tribute to whom tribute; custom to whom custom; fear to whom fear; and honour to whom honour is due."

But of the monarchical government, special mention is made in the writings of the prophets and apostles.

Isai. xlix. 23. "Kings shall be thy[1] nursing-fathers, and queens shall be thy nurses," saith Isai.

1 Pet. ii. 13. The apostle Peter calleth the king the superior (or him that hath the chief power), as our King James hath in his dominions.

Conf. Helv. I. Art. XXVI. & II. cap. 30. Basil. Art. VII. Bohem. c. 16, & in the Concil. Belg. Art. XXXVI. August. Art. XVI. XVII. Saxon. Art. XXIII. Suevic. in Petor. All churches protestant and reformed subscribe unto this doctrine, as both apostolical and orthodoxal[2].

[[1] Their, 1607.]

[[2] Magistratus omnis a Deo quum sit....Huic nos etiamsi liberi simus, et corpore et facultatibus omnibus nostris, et animi studio, vera cum fide sancte subjiciendos esse, fidelitatem ac sacramentum præstare, quantisper hujus imperia cum eo, propter quem hunc reveremus, palam non pugnant, scimus.—Harm. Conf. Sect. XIX. p. 273. Conf. Helv. Prior. Art. XXVI. Magistratus omnis generis ab ipso Deo est institutus....Damnamus itaque omnes magistratus contemptores, rebelles, Reip. hostes, et seditiosos nebulones, denique omnes quotquot officia debita præstare, vel palam vel arte renuunt.—Ibid. pp. 271, 2. Conf. Helv. Post. cap. XXX. Præterea, Deus magistratui, suo ministro, gladium et summam externam potestatem, bonis ad defensionem, malis ad vindictam et pœnam delegavit.—Ibid. p. 274. Conf. Basil. Art. VII. Amplius ex sacris literis docetur, politicum magistratum esse ordinationem Divinam, et a Deo constitutam....Ad hæc docetur etiam populus de suo officio, et re ipsa verbo Dei eo adigitur, ut universi et singuli in omnibus quæ Deo tantum non sunt contraria, eminenti potestati subjectionem præstent; primum Regiæ Majestati vestræ, postea omnibus magistratibus, &c.—Ibid. pp. 275, 7. Conf. Bohem. cap. XVI. Credimus Deum optimum maximum...reges, principes et magistratus constituisse, velleque ut mundus hic legibus ac certa politia gubernetur, &c.—Ibid. p. 281. Conf. Belg. Art. XXXVI. De rebus civilibus docent, quod

The errors and adversaries unto this truth.

These churches with us, and we with them, utterly condemn the opinions

Of the dreamers whereof the apostle speaketh, which despise government, and speak evil of them which are in authority. Jude, ver. 8.

Of the Manichees[3], Fratricellians[4], Flagelliferies[5], Anabaptists[6], and Family of [a]Love[7]; all which rail upon and condemn magistracy. D. August. contra Faust. Lib. XXII. c. 74. W. Thomas's Description of Italy, p. 59. Prateol. Hæres. de Flagel. Alth. Conc. lo. pug. lo. 191.

Of them who allow not of the government by women, but utterly detest the same: such were they in Italy, which said, *Interitus mundi est a muliere regi*[8]; again, speaking unto women, *Abunde magna civitas vobis sit domus, publicum neque noscatis, neque vos noscat*[9]: such in France, who think how the laws of God and nature is violated where a woman is suffered to reign and [b]govern[10]: such in Scotland, or Scottish men rather from Geneva, which wrote that W. Thomas's Descr. of Italy, p. 129, a. Lud. Vives, de Instit. fœm. Chr. Lib.

[a] H. N. calleth a king "the scum of ignorance," Spirit. Land, cap. 6, sect. 5.

[b] Neque solum naturæ jura convelluntur; sed etiam omnium

---

legitimæ ordinationes civiles sint bona opera et ordinationes Dei, sicut Paulus testatur....Scimus enim cum pii debeant obedire præsentibus magistratibus, non eripere eis imperia, &c.—Ibid. pp. 281, 3. Conf. August. Artt. XVI. XVII. Vult Deus regi et coerceri politica gubernatione omnes homines, etiam non renovatos.—Ibid. p. 285. Conf. Saxon. Art. XXIII. In superioribus exposuimus nostros ecclesiasticos obedientiæ quæ exhibetur magistratibus inter primi ordinis bona opera locum dedisse, et docere hoc unumquemque studiosius sese accommodare publicis legibus, quo syncerior fuerit Christianus, &c.—Ibid. pp. 292, 3. Conf. Suev. cap. XXIII.]

[[3] ...Sed quia Manichæi Joannem (Baptistam) aperte blasphemare consueverunt, ipsum Dominum Jesum Christum audiant hoc stipendium jubentem reddi Cæsari, quod Joannes dicit debere sufficere militi, &c.—August. Opp. Paris. 1836-8. Tom. VIII. col. 625. D. Contr. Faust. Manich. Lib. XXII. cap. 74.]

[[4] He [Clement the fifth] oppressed the sect called Fratricelli: that were then newly risen in Lombardy, who would have had all things in common without magistrates or rulers.—W. Thomas, Hist. of Italy. Lond. 1549. p. 59.]

[[5] Cujus alioqui erroris fucus ut nihil differebat ab Anabaptistarum opinione religiosa, ita secta non minus perniciosa fuit illis temporibus.—Gabr. Prateol. Marcos. de Vit. &c. Hæret. Colon. 1569. Lib. VI. § 8. col. 180.]

[[6] Legitimos magistratus conviciis proscindunt [Swermeri], ac tollere studuerunt.—Altham. Concil. Loc. Norimberg. 1535. Loc. CXCI. p. 211.]

[[7] This reference has not been found.]

[[8] W. Thomas, Hist. of Italy, p. 129.]

[[9] Lud. Viv. Opp. Basil. 1555. Tom. II. De Christ. Fœm. Lib. II. p 726.]

[[10] Bodin. Method. ad Facil. Histor. Cognit. Lugd. 1583. cap. VI. p. 258.]

Against the Regim. of Women, Blast præf. A woman's government is a monstriferous empire, most detestable and damnable[1].

Again, I am assured that God hath revealed to some in this age, that it is more than a monster in nature that a woman shall reign, and have empire above man[2], &c. (Ibid.)

Martin Mar-prelate, Epist. of Dr Bridges. And little differing from these men are they in England, which termed "The Harborough for Faithful Subjects," a carnal and unlearned book, smelling altogether of earth, without rhyme and without reason, for defending the regiment of women over men (when it falleth unto them by inheritance to govern) to be lawful and good[3]. He which so censureth the said "Harborough" was the Mar-prelate; and this his censure declareth that he was the Mar-prince, as well as the Mar-prelate.

Proposition II.

The king's majesty hath the chief government of all estates ecclesiastical and civil, in all causes within his dominions.

The proof from God's word.

We ascribe that unto our king by this assertion, which is given to every king or queen in their own dominion by the word of God. For

Luke xxii. 25. Rom. xiii. 3. Ibid. 4. Isai. xlix. 23. Psal. lxxxii. 1. 1 Pet. ii. 13. 1 Tim. ii. 1, 2.

They are, for titles, "gracious lords," "princes," "the ministers of God," "the nurses of the church," "gods:" for authority, the "chief." Which moveth St Paul to exhort, that supplications be made for all men, but first for kings as the chief.

Rom. xiii. 1. Again, every soul is commanded to be subject to the higher powers, &c.

Finally, the examples are manifold, and pregnant, shewing the principality of kings over all persons and causes. For

Exod. xxxii. 22. 1 Sam. xxii. 12. Aaron the high priest called Moses the chief prince, his lord: so did Abimelech term Saul his lord.

gentium, quæ nunquam fœminas regnare permiserunt, &c.—Bodin, Meth. Hist. c. 6, p. 257.

[[1] And therefore I say that of necessity it is that this monstriferous empire of women (which amongst all enormities that this day do abound upon the face of the whole earth is most detestable and damnable) be openly revealed, &c.—The First Blast of the Trumpet against the Monstrous Regiment of Women (by John Knox) Pref. p. 5. Genev. 1558.]

[[2] Ibid. pp. 3, 4.] [[3] This reference has not been found.]

K. Jehoshaphat, as chief in Judah, appointed judges, Levites, and priests. 2 Chron. xix. 5, 6, 7, 8.

K. Hezekias also, as chief, sent unto all Israel and Judah, that they should come to the house of the Lord at Jerusalem, to keep the passover: also he appointed the courses of the priests[4] and Levites by their turns: and commanded all the priests to offer sacrifice, &c.; and they obeyed him: and enjoined all the congregation to bring offerings; and they brought them. 2 Chron. xxx. 1. 2 Chron. xxxi. 2. Ibid. xxix. 21, 22. 2 Chron. xxix. 31.

Which we do unto ours, the very same do the churches of God ascribe unto christian magistrates in their principalities[5]. Confess. Helv. I. Art. XXVI. & II. cap. 30. Basil. Art. VII. Bohem. c. 16. Belg. Art. XXXVI. August. Art. XVI. XVII. Saxon. Art. XXIII. Suevic. Peror.

Errors and adversaries unto this truth.

Which being true, then false is it which the Papists deliver; *viz.* that

The king's excellency of power is in respect of the nobility and lay-magistrates under him, and not of popes, bishops, or priests, as they have cure of souls[6]. Kings and princes, be they never so great, must be subject unto some bishop, priest, or prelate[7]. Test. Rhem. Annotat. 1 Pet. ii. 13. Ibid. Annot. Heb. xiii. 17.

The whole clergy ought to be free from paying tribute[8]. Ibid. Annot. Matt. xvii. 26.

Sacerdotes etiam principibus jure divino subditi, deleatur, say the Expurgators: "Priests are not by God's law subject unto princes[9]." Index Expurg. p. 26.

"No man is to be subject unto his temporal prince and superior, in matters of religion, or regiment of his soul, Test. Rhem. An. Rom. xiii. 1.

[4 Course of priests, 1607.]

[5 See above, last Proposition, p. 336, note 1.]

[6 It is evident that he calleth the king the precellent or more excellent, in respect of his vicegerents which he calleth dukes or governors that be at his appointments: and not in respect of popes, bishops, or priests, as they have the rule of men's souls.—Test. Rhem. Rhemes, 1582. Ann. 1 Pet. ii. 13. p. 659.]

[7 *Obey your Prelates.* There is nothing more inculcated in the holy Scriptures, than obedience of the lay people to the priests and prelates of God's church in matters of soul conscience and religion....From this obedience there is no exception nor exemption of kings nor princes, be they never so great.—If they have souls, and be christian men, they must be subject to some bishop, priest, or other prelate.—Ibid. Ann. Heb. xiii. 17. p. 639.]

[8 Though Christ to avoid scandal paid tribute, yet indeed he sheweth that both himself ought to be free from such payments...and also his Apostles...and in them their successors the whole clergy, &c.—Ibid. Ann. Matt. xvii. 26. p. 50.]

[9 Inter Delenda in Indice Chrysostomi Basileæ a Frobenio excusi.—Index Expurgat. Lugd. 1586. p. 26.]

but in such things only as concern the public peace and policy[1]."

False also is it which the puritans do hold; namely, that
T. C. Rep. p. 144. Princes must be servants unto the church, be subject unto the church, submit their sceptres unto the church, and throw down their crowns before the church[2].

Eccl. Disp. p. 185. Magistrates, as well as other men, must submit themselves and be obedient to the just and lawful authority of the church[3], that is, of the [a]presbytery[4].

Beza, de Presb. p. 124. *Quis tandem reges et principes*, who can exempt even kings and princes from this *non humana, sed divina dominatione*, not human, but divine domination? (meaning of the presbytery) saith Beza[5]: which presbytery they would have to be in every [b]parish.

[a] That which our Saviour calleth presbyterian, and so doth Luke.—Lear. Dis. p. 89.

[b] There ought to be in every church a consistory, or seigniory of elders or governors.—Lear. Dis. p. 84.

Every congregation ought to have elders and an eldership.—Demon[stration]. of Dis[cipline]. chap. 12, p. 55, chap. 14, p. 69.

Instead of chancellors, archdeacons, officials, commissaries, proctors, summoners, churchwardens, and such like, you (parliament men) have to plant in every congregation a lawful and godly seigniory.—1 Admon. to the Parliament. [fol. A. 6.]

I would that every little parish should have seven such (elders) at

---

[[1] ...S. Paul here...expressly chargeth every man to be subject to his temporal prince and superior: not every man to all that be in office or superiority, but every one to him whom God hath put in authority over him, by that he is his Master, Lord, King or such like: neither to them in matters of religion or regiment of their souls (for most part were pagans, whom the apostle could not will men to obey in matters of faith) but to them in such things only as concern the public peace and policy, &c.—Ibid. Ann. Rom. xiii. 1. p. 415.]

[[2] But it must be remembered that civil magistrates...as they are nurses so they be servants unto the church, and as they rule in the church, so they must remember to subject themselves unto the church, to submit their sceptres, to throw down their crowns before the church, yea as the prophet speaketh to lick the dust of the feet of the church.—A Reply to an Answer made of M. Doctor Whitgifte, &c. by T. C. p. 144.]

[[3] A Full and Plain Declaration of Ecclesiastical Discipline, &c. 1574. Where, '*also as well as the rest*;' and, '*authority of the officers of the church*.']

[[4] The work referred to has not been met with.]

[[5] ...quis tandem reges et principes ab ista dominatione non humana sed divina exemerit, quin læsæ divinæ Christi majestatis reus constituatur.—Beza, Tract. de Vera Excomm. et Christ. Presbyt. Genev. 1590. pp. 124, 5.]

Quotquot ecclesiæ Christi, as many as be members of Christ, and of the church, they must subject themselves to the consistorian discipline. *Non hic excipitur episcopus, aut imperator:* "Neither bishop or emperor is excepted here." *Nulla hic acceptio, aut exceptio [est] personarum:* "Here is no acception, or exception, of persons[6]." Snecan. de Discipl. Ecles. p. 456.

Proposition III.

His highness may not execute the ecclesiastical duties of preaching and ministering the Sacraments, and yet is to prescribe laws and directions unto all estates both ecclesiastical and temporal.

The proof from God's word.

K. Hezekiah said unto the priests and Levites of his time, "My sons, be not deceived: for the Lord hath chosen you to stand before him, and to serve him, and to be his ministers, and to burn incense." 2 Chron. xxix. 11.

So do we say, The Lord hath appointed a company, and calling of men, to teach the people, to expound the scriptures, to celebrate the sacraments, to handle the keys of the celestial kingdom: insomuch as he whosoever that shall presume to do these things, not called thereunto, and that lawfully, though he be a king or prince, he may fear that punishment which fell upon Uzziah. See afore, Ar. 2 Chron. xxvi. 19.

Notwithstanding, all kings, queens, and princes in their places, may, yea, and must, as occasion serveth, with K. Solomon "build an house for the Lord," and set the courses of priests to their office; with K. Hezekiah break the images, cut down the groves, take away the high places, appoint the courses of the priests and Levites, and enjoin all the people to minister sustenance unto the priests[c]; with K. Josiah put down and burn the horses of the sun, break down the houses of the Sodomites, purge Judah and Jerusalem from the 2 Chron. ii. 1. 2 Chron. viii. 14. 2 Chron. xxxi. 1. 2 Kings xxiii. 11. Ibid. 7. 2 Chron. iii. 34.

the least, and every mean church thirteen, and every great church twenty-three.—Hunt of the Fox, &c. E. 2. a.

[c] Thus did Hezekiah throughout all Judah, and did well, and uprightly, and truly, before the Lord his God. 2 Chron. xxxi. 20.

[[6] Gall. Snecan. Frisius. Method. Descrip. Lugd. Bat. 1584. p. 456. De Discip. Eccl. where, Detur hic quoque locus dicendi, ut quotquot Christi aut Ecclesiæ homines censeri volunt, disciplinæ sese subjiciant, &c.]

Ibid. iii. 5, 2. Ib. c. xxxiii. xxxiv. Jonas iii. 7.

high places, groves, carved and molten images, appoint the priests to their charges, and compel all that are found in Israel to serve the Lord their God; and with the king of Nineveh proclaim a fast, and command every man to turn from his evil way, &c.

Conf. Helv. I. Art. XXVI. & II. c. 30. Basil. Art. VII. Bohem. c. 16. Gal. Art. XXXIX. Belg. Art. XXXVI. Saxon. Art. XXIII. Wittemb. c. 35.

Of the same judgement be other churches[1].

The errors and adversaries unto this truth.

Much therefore out of the way are, and offend greatly do, first, the papists, who publish that

Index Expurg. p. 145.

The care of religion pertaineth not unto kings: *Religionis curam semper pertinuisse ad reges, dele,* say the Expurgators; "Blot it out[2]."

Test. Rhem. Annotat. 1 Cor. xiv. 33.

Queens may not have or give voice, either deliberative or definitive in councils and public assemblies, concerning

[1 ...officium ejus (sc. magistratus)...præcipuum est; religionem ab omni blasphemia defendere et procurare...Qua quidem in parte locum primum pura atque libera divini verbi prædicatio, juventutis civium et scholarum recta et sedula institutio, disciplina justa, liberalis ministrorum ecclesiæ pauperumque solicita cura, habet:...Deinde secundum leges æquas divinasque, judicare populum, judicium et justitiam colere, &c.—Harm. Conf. Sect. XIX. p. 273. Conf. Helv. Prior. Art. XXVI. Ejus (sc. magistratus) officium præcipuum est, pacem et tranquillitatem publicam procurare et conservare...docemus religionis curam imprimis pertinere ad magistratum sanctum.—Ibid. p. 271. Conf. Helv. Post. cap. XXX. Præterea Deus magistratui, suo ministro, gladium et summam externam potestatem, bonis ad defensionem: malis, ad vindictam et pœnam, delegavit. Quilibet igitur christianus magistratus...omnes vires eo dirigit ut apud suæ fidei commissos, nomen Dei sanctificetur, regnum ipsius propagetur, &c.—Ibid. p. 274. Conf. Basil. Art. VII. Quum autem magistratus non tantum sit potestas Dei eo modo, quo scriptura ethnico etiam magistratui hoc tribuit...sed christianus magistratus consors etiam quasique minister...docetur...ut hoc munere suo veritatem sancti evangelii ornet, portas veritati ubicunque potest, aperiat, ministrorum et populi Christi defensor sit, idololatriam ac tyrannidem Antichristi ne approbet, &c.—Ibid. p. 276. Conf. Bohem. cap. XVI. Ideo etiam gladium in magistratuum manus tradidit (Deus), reprimandis nimirum delictis, non modo contra secundam tabulam, sed etiam contra primam commissis.—Ibid. p. 280. Conf. Gall. Art. XXXIX. Horum (sc. magistratuum) porro est non modo de civili politia conservanda esse solicitos, verum etiam dare operam ut sacrum ministerium conservetur, omnis idololatria et adulterinus Dei cultus e medio tollatur, regnum Antichristi diruatur, Christi vero regnum propagetur.—Ibid. p. 281. Conf. Belg. Art. XXXVI. Primum vult Deus sine ulla dubitatione magistratus sonare vocem legis moralis in genere humano quod ad disciplinam attinet...Sint membra ecclesiæ ipsi quoque reges et principes et doctrinam recte intelligant, non adjuvent eos qui falsam doctrinam stabiliunt, et injustam sævitiam exercent, sed sint memores hujus dicti: Glorificantes me glorificabo.—Ibid. pp. 286, 7. Conf. Saxon. Art. XXIII. Nota sunt diræ et maledictiones quibus divina lex violatores verbi Dei devovet. Et Josias rex Judæ in instauranda ecclesia plane heroico animo præditus, &c.—Ibid. p. 291. Conf. Virtemb. cap. XXXV.]

[2 Index Expurgat. Lugd. 1586. p. 145.]

matters of religion; nor make ecclesiastical laws concerning religion; nor give any man right to rule, preach, or execute any spiritual function, as under them, and by their authority[3].

In matters of religion, and of their spiritual charge, neither heathen nor christian kings ought to direct clergymen, but rather to take direction from them[4]. Answ. to the Execut. of Just. d. 3. p. 56.

The emperor of the whole world, if he take upon him to prescribe laws of religion to the bishops and priests, &c., he shall be damned assuredly, except he repent[5]. Test. Rhem. Annot. Heb. xiii. 17.

Next, the Anabaptists, who being private men, and no princes, will take upon them the ordering, and reformation of the church; as did Monetarius[6], and Muncer[7], in Germany. Carranz. Sum. Conc. p. 365. Bullinger. contra Anab.

And thirdly, the Disciplinarian Puritans, whose doctrine is, that

1. The making of ecclesiastical constitutions and ceremonies belongeth unto the ministers of the church and ecclesiastical governors[8], unto the elders who are to consult, admonish, correct, and order all things pertaining to the congregation[9]. T. C. 1 Repl. p. 163. 1 Admon. to the Parliam.

2. Civil magistrates have no power to ordain ceremonies

[[3] There is an error in the reference.]

[[4] ...though in matters of religion and of their spiritual charge neither heathen nor christian kings be their superiors (sc. of catholic bishops and prelates of the church) or ought to direct them, but rather to take direction from them.—Alan's Sincere and Modest Defence, an Answer, &c. cap. iii. p. 56.]

[[5] And whatsoever he be (though Emperor of all the world), if he take upon him to prescribe and give laws of religion to the bishops and priests, whom he ought to obey and be subject unto in religion, he shall be damned undoubtedly, except he repent.—Test. Rhem. Ann. Heb. xiii. 17. p. 639.]

[[6] ... ibidem anno 1525 concionator ecclesiasticus, Thomas Monetarius dictus, palam docuit, restauraturum collapsum ecclesiæ statum.—Carranza, Summ. Concil. Lovan. 1681. p. 417. col. a.]

[[7] Divinitus etiam sibi revelatum dicebat [Muncerus], omnes magnates et principes dejiciendos esse, datum sibi esse gladium Gedeonis contra omnes tyrannos, ad asserendam veram libertatem, et ad instituendum novum regnum Christi in his terris, etc.—Bulling. Adv. Anabapt. Tiguri. 1560. p. 3. Lib. I. cap. 1.]

[[8] As for the making of the orders and ceremonies of the church, they do (where there is a constituted and ordered church) pertain unto the ministers of the church and to the ecclesiastical governors, and that as they meddle not with the making of civil laws, and laws for the commonwealth, so the civil magistrate hath not to ordain ceremonies pertaining to the church.—A Reply to an answer made of M. Doctor Whitgifte, &c. by T. C. p. 154.]

[[9] Their office was to govern (Act. 15. 4. 1 Cor. 12. 28) the church, with the rest of the ministers, to consult, to admonish, to correct and to order all things appertaining to the state of the congregation.—An Admonition to the Parliament. fol. A. 5.]

T. C. 1 Repl. p. 153. Idem, 2 Rep. 2 par. p. 4. pertaining unto the church[1]; but are to ordain civil discipline only[2]: as being no church-officers, at all.

Lear. Dis. p. 10. Fruct. Serm. on Rom. xii. p. 35, 71. 3. The ecclesiastical officers be doctors, pastors, elders, and deacons, the only officers instituted of God[3], or, at the most, pastors, doctors, elders, deacons, and widows. These are all, no more, no fewer; and are only sufficient; and we are to content ourselves with these, and rest in them, saith the preacher[4]. In which number unless the king be included, he cannot possibly have anything to do in church-affairs, in these men's opinions.

Barrow's Refut. p. 169. Conspiracy for pretended Reform. p 34. Without the prince, the people may reform the church, and must not tarry for the magistrate: so thought Barrow[5], Greenwood, and Wiggington[6]. Hence Hacket's, Coppinger's, and Arthington's insurrection at London, an. 1591.

Without the prince also the lords and burgesses of the parliament have power of themselves to reform the abuses, and take away the corruptions of the church. Hence their manifold petitions, supplications, politic assertions, exhibited unto the parliament from time to time. In one of which their supplications, saith one (speaking unto the parliament),

"You must enjoin every one, according to his place, to have a hand in this work."

[[1] See above, p. 343, note 8.]

[[2] And if it be true that he saith after, *the pastor must use such discipline as seemeth good to the magistrate*, when the magistrate ordereth civil discipline only, &c.—The Rest of the Second Replie of Thomas Cartwright, &c. 1577. p. 4.]

[[3] This reference the editor has been unable to verify.]

[[4] Now if you ask me how many members there be in the body, what they be, and how they be named and called, and what be their duties and callings, the apostle himself will answer plainly...saying: These members are either doctors to teach, pastors to exhort, elders to rule, deacons to distribute, attenders upon the poor strangers and the sick, or else the people and saints which are taught, exhorted, ruled, and receive alms and relive (? relief). These are all: no more, no fewer.—A Fruitful Sermon on the 3, 4, &c. vss. of Rom. xii., &c. Lond. 1589. pp. 31, 2.]

[[5] Againe, our question is not whether it is the office and dutie of the Prince to see abuses reformed both in the Church and Common-wealth (which we think no man to be so ignorant or barbarous to deny, except the Anabaptistes). But whether the Church ought not now amongst themselves freely to practice Christes Testament either in erecting her officers and ordinances, or in reforming or correcting any fault or abuse that ariseth amongst them without staying for the Prince's licence: yea though the Prince should upon the paynes of death forbid. This we affirme to be the dutie of everie particular congregation, &c.—Barrowe's Plaine Refutation of M. Giffard's Booke, &c. 1591. p. 200.]

[[6] Hacket further declared...he heard Wigginton say, that if the magistrates do not govern well, the people might draw themselves together and to see a reformation.—Conspir. for Pretended Reform. London. 1592. p. 33.]

"You must encourage and countenance the gentlemen and people that shall be found forward," &c.

"And you (of the parliament) must not suffer an uncircumcised mouth to bring a slander upon that land," &c. *scil.* upon their discipline. This hath Penry[7]. Penry, Supp. p. 60.

Proposition IV.

The king by his authority is to restrain with the material sword, and to punish malefactors whosoever they be.

The proof from God's word.

The office of the civil magistrate is to restrain, and if need be, to punish according to the quality of their offences, the disturbers of the quiet and peace of the commonweal; and that as occasion shall require, sometimes by force of arms, if the enemies of his state be either foreign or domestical, and they gathered together be many and mighty. To this end kings and princes have both men, munition, subsidies, and tributes. So against the enemies of God and good men went of Israel and Judah the valiant judges and the noble and puissant princes.

And sometimes they execute their wholesome and penal statutes upon the goods, cattle, lands, and bodies of their disorderly and rebellious subjects.

For the king is the minister of God, to take vengeance on him that doth evil. Therefore princes are to be feared, not of them which do well, but of such as do wickedly. Rom. xiii. 3, 4.

And this do the people of God acknowledge to be true[8]. Conf. Helv. I. Art. XXIV. XXVI. & II. cap. 30. Basil. Art. VII. Bohem. c. 19. Gal. Art. XXXIII. Belg. Art. XXXVI. August. Art. XVI. Saxon. Art. XXIII.

Adversaries unto this truth.

Contrarily hereunto,

The Cresconians were of opinion, that magistrates were to punish no malefactors[9]. D. August. contra Cresc. Gra. Lib. III. c. 15.

[7 A viewe of some part of such publike wants and disorders as are in the service of God within her Maiesties countrie of VVales, togither vvith an humble Petition, vnto this high Court of Parliament for their speedy redresse. (By John Penri) 1588. pp. 60, 61; where *according unto his place,* and *encourage the gentlemen and people that shall be found forward by gracing and countenancing them,* and *upon that good land.*]

[8 See above, p. 342, note 1.]

[9 Frustra dicis, "Relinquar libero arbitrio." Cur enim non in homicidiis, et in stupris et in quibusque aliis facinoribus et flagitiis libero te arbitrio dimittendum esse

Magd. Eccl. Hist. Cent. 9, c. 4, fol. 216.

One Rabanus maintained that magistrates were not of God's ordinance for the good, but an human institution for the hurt of men[1].

Many have a fancy, that before the general resurrection there shall be no magistrates at all, because, as they dream, all the wicked shall be rooted out. Of this mind are the Anabaptists[2] and Family of Love[3].

Conf. Aug. I. Art. XVII. H. N. 1 Exh. c. 12, § 39, 40. Ramsey's Conf.

Proposition V.

The bishop of Rome hath no jurisdiction in this realm of England, (nor other of the king's dominions).

The proof from God's word.

1 Tim. v. 17.

The bishop of Rome, did he, according to the will of God, preach the gospel, labour in the Lord's harvest, divide the word of God aright, minister the sacraments instituted by Christ, and that sincerely, and shew by his life and conversation the good fruits of a godly bishop; doubtless he were worthy of double, yea, of triple honour.

Yet will not the word of God, were he never so holy and religious, warrant him any jurisdiction out of his diocese, especially not within this realm; much less when he doth perform no part of a Christian, but every part of an antichristian bishop, in corrupting the doctrine of the truth with errors and cursed opinions; in polluting the sacraments of Christ by superstitious ceremonies; in persecuting the church and saints with fire and sword; in making merchandise of the souls of men through covetousness; in playing the lord over God's heritage; in sitting in the temple of God, as God,

2 Pet. ii. 3. 1 Pet. v. 3. 2 Thess. ii. 4.

proclamas? Quæ tamen omnia justis legibus comprimi utilissimum ac saluberrimum est. Dedit quidem Deus homini liberam voluntatem, sed nec bonam infructuosam, nec malam esse voluit impunitam.—August. Opp. Paris. 1836-8. Tom. IX. col. 716. A. Contr. Crescon. Gramm. Donat. Lib. III. cap. 51.]

[[1] Rabanus inquit: Magistratum politicum ab hominibus esse, cum ab ipso Deo habeat originem. Sic enim inquit: Duæ dignitates atque potestates inter homines constitutæ reperiuntur. una ex humana inventione reperta, hoc est imperialis atque regalis. altera vero ex divina autoritate instituta, hoc est sacerdotalis. quarum una hominum corpora parat ad mortem, altera animas nutrit ad vitam.—Magdeburg. Eccl. Hist. Basil. 1562, &c. Cent. IX. c. 4. fol. 216.]

[[2] Damnamus Anabaptistas qui nunc Judaicas opiniones spargunt, fingunt ante resurrectionem pios regna mundi occupaturos esse, ubique deletis aut oppressis impiis. Scimus enim quod pii debeant obedire præsentibus magistratibus, &c.—Syll. Conf. Oxon. 1827. pp. 175, 6. Conf. August. 1540. Art. XVII.]

[[3] The references have not been found.]

shewing himself that he is God; and in exalting himself against all that is called God, or that is worshipped. 2 Thess. ii. 4.

In respect of which fruits of impieties the said bishop of Rome in the holy scripture is described to be very antichrist, that wicked man, the man of sin, the son of perdition, and the adversary of God. Ibid.

He was openly proclaimed antichrist by a council in France, in the reign of Hugh Capet. He is termed by the truly and godly-learned, the basilisk of the church[4]; neither the head nor the tail of the church[5]. Luther. præf. Epist. L. Huss. Hemming. in 5, c. Jac. Epist.

His jurisdiction hath been, and is justly renounced and banished out of England, by many kings and parliaments; as by K. Edward the First, Third and Sixth, by K. Richard the Second, by K. Henry the Fourth, Sixth and Eighth, by queen Elizabeth, and by our most noble K. James.

His pride and intolerable supremacy over all christian people is renounced and condemned, as well by the mouths as writings of all the purer churches[6]; and that deservedly. Conf. Helv. I. Art. XVIII. & II. cap. 17, 18. Bohem. c. 8, 9. Belg. Art. XXVIII. XXXII. Wittemb. Art. XXXI. Aug. de Abus. Art. VII.

The errors and adversaries unto this truth.

But with the Papists, the bishop of Rome, he is forsooth, for supremacy, Abel; for governing the ark, Noah; for patriarchship, Abraham; for order, Melchisedech; for dignity, Aaron; for authority, Moses; for justice, Samuel; for zeal, Elias; for humility, David; for power, Peter; for his unction, Christ[7]; the general pastor, the common father of all Christians, the high pastor of God's universal church, the prince Majoran. Clyp. Milit. Eccl. Lib. III. c. 35. Answer to the Execut. of Just.

[4 The passage has not been found.]

[5 Voco autem ecclesiasticam prohibitionem non Papæ, quem nec caput nec caudam Ecclesiæ agnoscimus, sed, &c.—Hemming. Comment. in Epist. Lips. 1572. p. 958. In Epist. Jac. cap. v.]

[6 ...caputque Romanum minime agnoscimus.—Harm. Conf. Sect. XI. p. 43. Conf. Helvet. Prior. Art. XVIII. Servat quidem caput Romanum tyrannidem suam et corruptelam inductam in ecclesiam: sed impedit interim, oppugnat, et quantis potest viribus, exscindit justam ecclesiæ reformationem.—Ibid. p. 5. Conf. Helv. Post. cap. XVII. Cf. Ibid. p. 39. cap. XVIII. Simul cum his docetur, quod Antichristus ille sceleratus et nequam in templo Dei in ecclesia sedeat, de quo Prophetæ, Christus Dominus et Apostoli ipsius prædixerint, &c.—Ibid. p. 13. Conf. Bohem. cap. VIII. Sunt qui tribuunt Romano Pontifici quod sit caput universali Ecclesiæ et habeat potestatem non in terris tantum, &c.—Ibid. p. 25. Conf. Virtemb. Art. XXXI. The other references seem to be inferential.]

[7 Inveniet quod Romanus pontifex est....primatu Abel, gubernatu Noë, patriarchatu Abraham, ordine Melchisedec, dignitate Aaron, authoritate Moyses, judicatu Samuel, potestate Petrus, unctione Christus.—Majoran. Scutum Fidei, &c. Antverp. 1589. Lib. III. cap. 35. p. 137.]

Panorm. de Transl. Præl. cap. quarto. Cere. Lib. I. c. 2. Distinct. xl. c. 5, Papa. Extravag. de Transl. Episc. cap. quarto. Test. Rhem. Annot. marg. p. 280. Bonif. VIII. de Major. et Obed. in Extravag. Bristow, Motive 40.

of God's people[1]; for title, God, even the Lord God the Pope[2]; for power, God; For

By him kings reign[3]; he may judge all men, but must of none be judged[4]; he can do what him list, as well as God, except sin[5].

His jurisdiction is universal, even over the whole world[6].

Him, upon pain of eternal damnation, all Christians are to obey[7].

And by his sovereign authority both all Papists in England were discharged from their obedience and subjection unto queen Elizabeth, and the same queen disabled to govern her own people and dominions[8].

Proposition VI.

By the laws of this realm Christian men for heinous and grievous offences may be put to death.

The proof from God's word.

As the natures of men be divers, and some sins in some countries more abound than in others; so are the punishments to be imposed upon malefactors, according to the quantity and quality of their offences; and any country and kingdom may punish offenders even with death, if the laws thereof, and their offence, do require it. For

Matt. xxvi. 52.

"All that take the sword shall perish with the sword."

[[1] The Apostolique Bishop is...a spiritual and most loving parent and common Father of al Christians, and speciallie of Princes.—(Card. Alan's) Sincere and Modest Defence, &c. An Answer, &c. x. cap. VI. p. 121. ...our holie and highe Pastor.—Ibid. p. 130. ...the cheefe Bishops of Christes Church, our supreme Pastors in earth, &c.—Ibid. cap. VII. p. 144.]

[[2] See above, p. 38, note 2.]

[[3] Sacr. Ceremon. Lib. Rom. 1500. Lib. I. foll. 24, 5.]

[[4] See above, Art. xx. Prop. 3. p. 191, note 5.]

[[5] See above, p. 38, note 4.]

[[6] The title of universal Bishop refused, but universal jurisdiction always acknowledged and practised.—Test. Rhem. Rhemes, 1582. Marg. Annot. p. 280.]

[[7] See above, page 172, note 1.]

[[8] And if at any time it happen, after long toleration, humble beseeching and often admonition, of very wicked and notorious apostates or heretics, no other hope of amendment appearing, but the filthy more and more daily defiling himself and others to the huge great heap of their own damnation, that after all this the sovereign authority of our common pastor in religion, for the saving of souls, do duly discharge us from subjection, and the prince offender from his dominion, &c.—Motives to the Catholic Faith by Richard Bristow. Antwerp, 1599. cap. xl. p. 153. b.]

"Governors be sent of the king for the punishment of evil-doers." 1 Pet. ii. 14.

"A wise king scattereth the wicked, and causeth the wheel to turn over them." Prov. xx. 26.

"The magistrate beareth not the sword for nought, and is the minister of God to take vengeance on them that do evil." Rom. xiii. 4.

Which punishments testify to the world, that

God is just, which will have some sins more severely punished than others, and the magistrates to cut off dangerous and ungodly members:

God is merciful, and hath care both of his servants and of human society:

God is all wise and holy, in that he will have it known who are just, who wicked, who holy, and who profane, by cherishing and preserving of the one, and by punishing and rooting out of the other.

Our godly and christian brethren in other countries approve this doctrine[9]. Conf. Helv. I. Art. XXIV. XXVI. & II. c. 30. Basil. Art. VII. Bohem. c. 16. Gal. Art. XXXIX. Belg. Art. XXXVI. August. Art. XVI. Saxon. Art. XXIII.

The adversaries unto this truth.

The adversaries of this doctrine be divers. For

Some are of opinion, that no man for any offence should be put to death. Such in old time were the Manichees and the Donatists[10], and such in our days be the Anabaptists[11]. D. August. in Johan. xi. Conf. Helv. II. cap. 30.

And some do think, that howsoever for other[12] offences

[9 ...officium ejus (sc. magistratus)...est...sortes pro delicti ratione mulctare, opibus, corpore, vita.—Harm. Conf. Sect. XIX. p. 273. Conf. Helv. Prior. Art. XXVI. Stringat ergo Dei gladium in omnes maleficos, seditiosos, latrones, vel homicidas, oppressores, blasphemos, perjuros, et in omnes eos quos Deus punire ac etiam cædere jussit.—Ibid. p. 272. Conf. Helv. Post. cap. XXX. Idcirco magistratus ipsos gladio armavit (Deus) ut malos quidem plectant pœnis, &c.—Ibid. p. 281. Conf. Belg. Art. XXXVI. ...quod Christianis liceat magistratus gerere....supplicia jure constituere, &c.—Ibid. p. 282. Conf. August. Art. XVI. For the other references, see above, page 342, note 1.]

[10 Isti etiam audent dicere quia persecutionem solent pati a catholicis regibus.—August. Opp. Paris. 1836-8. Tom. III. col. 1812. c. In Joann. Tract. XI. § 13. Nam videte qualia faciunt et qualia patiuntur. Occidunt animas, affliguntur in corpore: sempiternas mortes faciunt, et temporales se perpeti conqueruntur.—Ibid. col. 1814. B. § 15. See also Ibid. Tom. IX. col. 75. Contr. Epist. Parmen. Lib. I. cap. 10.]

[11 Damnamus Anabaptistas, qui ut Christianum negant fungi posse officio magistratus, ita etiam negant quenquam a magistratu juste occidi.—Collect. Confess. Lips. 1840. Conf. Helv. Post. cap. XXX. p. 535.]

[12 Their, the later editions.]

against the second table malefactors may be put to death; yet for heretical and erroneous opinions in points of religion none are so to suffer. Of this mind are the Familists. For

Display I. a. They hold that no man should be put to death for his opinion.

Ibid. They blame M. Cranmer and Ridley for burning Joan of Kent for an heretic[1].

Fam. 2, Letter unto M. Ro. Ibid. It is not Christian-like that one man should persecute another for any cause touching conscience[2]. Is not that punishment sufficient (say they) which God hath ordained, but that one Christian must vex, torment, bely and persecute another[3]?

Proposition VII.

It is lawful for Christian men, at the commandment of the magistrate, to wear weapons, and serve in wars.

The proof from God's word.

Eccles. iii. 8. There is (saith K. Solomon) a time of war, and a time of peace: and princes are, by war and weapons, to repress the power of enemies, whether foreign or intestine. For they are in authority placed for the defence of quiet and harmless subjects, as also to remove the violence of oppressors, and

Prov. ii. 31. enemies, whatsoever they be. For these causes have they

Rom. xiii. 6, 7. horses prepared for the battle; tributes paid them as well of Christians as others; and subjects to serve them in their wars, of what nature soever.

Acts x. Cornelius, being a Christian, was not forbidden to play

Luke iii. 14. the centurion, or bidden to forsake his profession; nor the soldiers that came unto John's baptism willed to leave the wars, but to offer no violence unto any man.

Conf. Helvet. II. cap. 30. Bohem. c. 16. Saxon. Art. XXIII. This truth is granted by the churches[4].

[1 Displaying of the Family of Love. Lond. 1579. fol. I. a.]

[2 Second Letter of the Family to M. Rogers in the Displaying, L. 4. b. where, *envy belie and persecute.*]

[3 Ibid. fol. L. 5. b.]

[4 Et si salus publica patriæve et justitia requirat, et magistratus ex necessitate bellum suscipiat, deponant (subditi) etiam vitam, et fundant sanguinem pro salute publica.—Harm. Conf. Sect. XIX. p. 272. Conf. Helv. Post. cap. XXX. ...ad hæc eos (sc. magistratus) peculiariter obligari...ut...subjectos pacificos suos, jura, facultates, vitam,...defendant: adversus eos qui hæc violant, in hæc grassantur, et damnis malisve hæc afficiunt, itemque contra Turcarum injustam vim, una cum aliis qui hoc agunt, defensionem eis præstent.—Ibid. pp. 275, 6. Conf. Bohem.

The adversaries unto this truth.

Many are against this assertion: whereof some doubt of the truth thereof; as [a]Ludovicus Vives[5].

Others deny it altogether as untrue. So did in ancient time the Manichees, whose doctrine was, that no man might go to war[6]. D. Aug. contr. Man. Lib. XXII. c. 74.

Lactantius thought it altogether unlawful for a good man or a Christian either to go to war, or to bring any man to a violent death, though by law he were adjudged to die[7]. Lact. de Vero Cultu, cap. 20.

In these days the Anabaptists think it to be a thing most execrable for Christians to take weapons or to go to war[8]. Conf. Helv. II. cap. 30.

The Family of Love also do so condemn all wars, as the time was when they would not bear or wear a weapon[9]: and they write first of themselves, how all their nature is love and peace[10], and that they are a people peaceable, concordable, amiable, loving, and living peaceably[11]; but all other men in the world besides they do wage war, kill, and destroy; for which ends they have divers sorts of swords, halberds, spears, bows and arrows, guns, pellets and gunpowder, armour, Display, H. 5, b. H. N. Spirit. Land, c. 37, sect. 2. Ibid. Præf. sect. 31. Ibid. chap. 5, § 9.

[a] Arma Christianum virum tractare nescio an fas fit.—Lud. Vives, Institut. Fœm. Chr. Lib. I.

---

cap. XVI. Sunt igitur res suo genere bonæ...gerere bella legitima, et esse militem in bellis legitimis, &c. Et potest his rebus uti homo Christianus, &c.—Ibid. p. 285. Conf. Saxon. Art. XXIII.]

[[5] The passage has not been found.]

[[6] Quid enim culpatur in bello? An quia moriuntur quandoque morituri, ut domentur in pace victuri? Hoc reprehendere timidorum est non religiosorum. Nocendi cupiditas, ulciscendi crudelitas...culpantur: quæ plerumque at etiam jure puniantur...gerenda ipsa bella suscipiuntur a bonis....Alioquin Joannes cum ad eum baptizandi milites venirent, dicentes, *Et nos quid facimus?* responderet iis, Arma abjicite, militiam ipsam deserite, neminem percutite, vulnerate, prosternite....Sed quia Manichæi Joannem aperte blasphemare consueverunt, &c.—August. Opp. Paris. 1836-8. Tom. VIII. col. 625. Contr. Faust. Manich. Lib. XXII. cap. 74.]

[[7] Ita neque militare justo licebit, cujus militia est in ipsa justitia; neque vero accusare quenquam crimine capitali.—Lact. Opp. Div. Inst. Lib. VI. cap. 20. p. 618.]

[[8] Damnamus Anabaptistas, qui...negant...magistratum bellum gerere posse.—Collect. Confess. Lips. 1840. Conf. Helv. Post. cap. XXX. p. 535.]

[[9] They did prohibit bearing of weapons, but at the length, perceiving themselves to be noted and marked for the same, they have allowed the bearing of staves.—Displaying of the Fam. Lond. 1579. fol. H. 5. b.]

[[10] All their nature and mind is nothing else but love, peace, (Gal. 5. c.) and righteousness.—H. N. Spirit. Land of Peace, cap. XXXVII. § 2.]

[[11] ...so have we...found a lovely land (Esa. 26. 60. b. Zach. 8. a. b.) or a peaceable city, whose people (and none other) is a peaceable, concordable, and lovely people, agreeably-minded, living peaceably, &c.—Ibid. Pref. § 31.]

harness, and gorgets[1]; none of which the Familists do use or allow of.

ARTICLE XXXVIII.

Of Christian men's Goods, which are not common.

The riches and goods of Christians (1) *are not common, as touching the right, title, and possession of the same, as certain Anabaptists do falsely boast. Notwithstanding* (2) *every man ought, of such things as he possesseth, liberally to give alms to the poor, according to his ability.*

The propositions.

1. The riches and goods of Christians, as touching the right, title, and possession of the same, are not common.
2. Every man is to give liberal alms to the poor of that which he possesseth, according to his ability.

Proposition I.

The riches and goods of Christians, as touching the right, title, and possession of the same, are not common.

The proof from God's word.

Against community of goods and riches be all those places (which are infinite) of holy scripture, that either condemn the unlawful getting, keeping, or desiring of riches, which, by covetousness[a], thievery[b], extortion[c], and the like wicked means, many do attain; or do commend liberality[d], frugality[e],

[a] If any one that is called a brother be a fornicator, or covetous, &c. with such an one eat not, 1 Cor. v. 11. Covetousness, let it not be once named among you, as it becometh saints, Ephes. v. 3.

[b] Let none of you suffer as a thief, &c. 1 Pet. iv. 15.

[c] With a brother that is an extortioner, eat not, 1 Cor. v. 11. Neither thieves, nor covetous (persons), nor extortioners, shall inherit the kingdom of God, 1 Cor. vi. 10.

[d] It is a blessed thing to give rather than to receive, Acts xx. 35. Yea, and that thing ye do unto all the brethren throughout all Macedonia, 1 Thess. iv. 10. If a brother or a sister be naked, and destitute

---

[[1] Ibid. cap. v. § 9, where, ordinance or guns,...armour or harness.]

free and friendly lending[f], honest labour[g], and lawful vocations to live and thrive by[h]. All which do shew that Christians are to have goods of their own, and that riches ought not to be common.

Of this judgement be the reformed churches[2]. Conf. Helvet. II. c. 29.

Gal. Art. XL. Belg. Art XXXVI. August. Art. XVI. Wittemb. c. 21.

The adversaries unto this truth.

Of another mind were the Esseis[3], the Manichees[4], the Pelagians[5], the Apostolicks[6], and Fratricellians[7], and are the Anabaptists[8], and Family of Love[9]. Heyden, Des. urbis Hierosolym. Lib. III. c. 3. D. August. De mor. Eccles. Cath. Lib. I. Magdeburg.' Eccles. Hist. cent. 5, fol. 586. D. Humfred. De Romanæ Curiæ praxi. pag. 39, ex Epiph. W. Thomas's Description of Italy, pag. 59. Sleidan. Comment. Lib. VI. Display, H. 3. b.

of daily food, &c. notwithstanding ye give them not these things, which are needful to the body, what helpeth it? James ii. 15, 16.

[e] If there be any that provideth not for his own, and namely for them of his household, he denieth the faith, and is worse than an infidel, 1 Tim. v. 8.

[f] From him that would borrow of thee turn not away, Matth. v. 42. And lend, looking for nothing again, Luke vi. 35.

[g] Let him that stole, steal no more, but rather let him labour, &c. that he may have to give unto him that needeth, Ephes. iv. 28. We warned you that if there were any which would not work that he should not eat, 2 Thess. iii. 8.

[h] Ye know that these hands have ministered unto my necessities, and to them that were with me, Acts xx. 34. We laboured day and night, because we would not be chargeable unto any of you, 1 Thess. ii. 9. We took not bread of any man for nought, 2 Thess. iii. 8.

[[2] Divitias et divites, si pii sint et recte utantur divitiis, non reprobamus. Reprobamus autem sectam Apostolicorum, &c.—Harm. Conf. Sect. XVIII. p. 237. Conf. Helv. Post. cap. XXIX. ...detestamur omnes eos qui dominationes repudiant, communitatem et confusionem bonorum invehunt, omnem denique juris rationem evertere moliuntur.—Ibid. Sect. XIX. p. 280. Conf. Gall. Art. XL. ...Anabaptistas et turbulentos omnes detestamur, qui...bona omnia communia faciunt, &c.—Ibid. p. 281. Conf. Belg. Art. XXXVI. De rebus civilibus docent, quod....liceat....lege contrahere, tenere proprium, &c.—Ibid. pp. 281, 2. Conf. August. Art. XVI. Facultates tuas autem sic deserere, ut eas in commune conferas, non est paupertatem sectari, sed de certiore et copiosiore victu tibi prospicere.—Ibid. p. 265. Conf. Virtemb. Art. XXVI.]

[[3] Esseni seu Essæi...facultates in commune possidebant.—Reisner. Descript. Urb. Ierosol. (Lat. per Joann. Heyden.) Francof. 1563. Lib. III. cap. 3. p. 109.]

[[4] Quid calumniamini, quod fideles jam baptismate renovati, procreare filios, et agros ac domos pecuniamque ullam possidere non debeant? Permittit hoc Paulus, &c.—August. Opp. Paris. 1836-8. Tom. I. col. 1154. c. De Mor. Eccl. et Manich. Lib. I. cap. 35.]

H. N. Spirit. land, chap. 35, § 4.

Among the Familists (saith H. N.) none claimeth anything proper to himself for to possess the same to any owedness[1] or privateness. For no man, &c. can desire to appropriate or challenge anything to himself, either yet to make any private use to himself from the restward: but what is there is free, and is also left free in his upright form[2].

Proposition II.

Every man is to give liberal alms to the poor of that which he possesseth, according to his ability.

The proof from God's word.

Unto liberality towards the poor, according to our ability, we are in the holy scriptures provoked,

Deut. xv. 11. Prov. v. 15, 16. Eccles. xi. 1, 2. Matt. v. 42, &c. vi. 2, 3, &c. Luke vi. 30, &c. Rom. xii. 13. 1 Cor. xvi. 2.

1. By the commandments from God, by his servants the prophets, by his Son our Saviour, and by his apostles.

2. By sweet promises of ample blessings[a].

3. By threatenings of punishments to the covetous and stony-hearted[b].

[a] Eccles. xi. 1. The liberal person shall have plenty: and he that watereth shall also have rain, Prov. xi. 24.

[b] He that stoppeth his ear at the crying of the poor, he shall cry and not be heard, Prov. xxi. 13. He that giveth unto the poor shall

---

[5 Divites baptizatos, Pelagius docet, nisi omnibus abrenuncient, regnum Dei ingredi non posse.—Magdeburg. Eccl. Hist. Basil. 1562. Cent. v. c. 5. fol. 586.]

[6 ...ἄλλοι ἑαυτοὺς Ἀποστολικοὺς ὠνόμασαν...φυλάττεται δὲ παρ' αὐτοῖς τὸ μηδὲν κεκτῆσθαι....Καὶ ἔχει...ἡ ἐκκλησία...ἀκτημοσύνην, ἀλλὰ οὐκ ἐπαίρεται τῶν ἐν κτήσει δικαιοσύνης ὑπαρχόντων.—Epiphan. Opp. Paris. 1622. Tom. I. p. 506. Adv. Hær. Lib. II. Tom. I. Hær. 61.]

[7 See above, p. 337, note 4.]

[8 ...Anabaptistæ....bonorum docent communionem.—Sleidan. Comment. Argentorat. 1555. Lib. VI. fol. 87. See also above, Art. 36. Prop. 1.]

[9 When any person shall be received into their congregation, they cause all their brethren to assemble, and the bishop or elder doth declare unto the new elected brother, that if he will be content, that all his goods shall be in common amongst the rest of all his brethren, he shall be received, &c.—Displaying of the Fam. Lond. 1579. fol. H. 3. b.]

[1 Owness, the later editions.]

[2 Moreover, there is no man that claimeth anything to be his own, as to possess the same to his own private use. For no man (and that out of every one's good disposition) can desire anything to be his own, or yet to make anything proper (Act. 4. d.) to himself from another. But all whatsoever is there is free, and is there left free in his upright form.—H. N. Spiritual Land of Peace, p. 54. cap. xxxv.]

4. By the examples of the best men, viz. the apostles and primitive church.

So the churches[3].

Acts xi. 29, 30. Rom. xv. 25. 2 Cor. viii. 1, 2, 3, &c. 2 Cor. ix. 2, &c. Confess. Helv. II. c. 23, 28, 29. Saxon. Art. XXI. Wittemb. c. 18.

The adversaries unto this truth.

Of strange minds, therefore, and impious are,

First, the Anabaptists, which would have no man either to give or receive. For all things, in their opinion, should be common; (as afore also hath been said) and none among them be either poor to receive, or wealthy to minister any alms[4].

Bale, Myst. of Iniquit. p. 53.

Secondly, the hypocritical sectaries, who are bountiful only to those who side with them. Such were, first, the publicans in our Saviour his days; and after them the Manichees, who would minister neither bread nor water unto any hungry and pining beggar, unless he were a [c]Manichean[5].

Matt. v. 46, 47.

And such are the Family of Love, who say they are not bound to give alms but to their own sect; and if they do, they give the same to the devil[6].

Displ. H. 7. b.

not lack; but he that hideth his eyes shall have many curses, Prov. xxviii. 27.

[c] Homini mendico esurienti, nisi Manichæus sit, panem, aut aquam non porrigunt Manichæi.—D. Aug. de Mor. Manich. Lib. II.

[[3] Ac verus usus opum ecclesiæ quondam fuit, et nunc est...in primis pauperibus juvandis atque alendis.—Harm. Conf. Sect. XV. p. 159. Conf. Helv. Post. cap. XXVIII. In multis locis desunt pastores ecclesiis, aut deest victus pastoribus. His primum opitulandum erat ex reditibus monasteriorum locupletium. Postea pauperum quoque studia inde juvanda sunt, &c....Hospitalia etiam inde juvanda sunt, in quibus pauperes, qui diuturnis morbis laborant, ali necesse est.—Ibid. p. 165. Conf. Saxon. Art. XXI. Eleemosynam diligenter commendamus: et hortamur ecclesiam, ut proximum quisque suum quoquo officio potest, adjuvet ac charitatem suam testificetur.—Ibid. p. 167. Conf. Virtemb. cap. XVIII.]

[[4] They would have all men's goods in common.—Bale, Myst. of Iniquity, Genev. 1545. p. 53.]

[[5] Hinc est quod mendicanti homini, qui Manichæus non sit, panem vel aliquid frugum, vel aquam ipsam, quæ omnibus vilis est dari prohibetis; ne membrum Dei quod his rebus admixtum est, suis peccatis sordidatum a reditu impediat.—August. Opp. Paris. 1836-8. Tom. I. col. 1177. D. De Mor. Eccl. et Manich. Lib. II. cap. 15.]

[[6] Displaying of the Fam. of Love. Lond. 1579. fol. H. 7. b.]

ARTICLE XXXIX.

Of a Christian Man's Oath.

As we confess that (1) *vain and rash swearing is forbidden christian men by our Lord Jesus Christ, and James his apostle, so we judge that* (2) *christian religion doth not prohibit, but that a man may swear when the magistrate requireth, in a cause of faith and charity; so it be done according to the prophet's teaching, in justice, judgement, and truth.*

The propositions.

1. We may not swear vainly and rashly.
2. A lawful oath may be given and taken, according to the word of God, in justice, judgement, and truth.

Proposition I.

We may not swear vainly and rashly.

The proof from God's word.

The better to avoid vain and rash oaths and swearing, it is good to have in remembrance that which is said by our Saviour Christ and his apostle James.

Matt. v. 34. Our Saviour saith, "Swear not at all; neither by heaven; for it is the throne of God: nor by the earth; for it is his footstool: nor by Jerusalem; for it is the city of the great King: nor by thine head, because thou canst not make one hair white or black. But let your communication be Yea, yea; Nay, nay."

James v. 12. So the apostle St James: "Before all things, my brethren," (saith he) "swear not, either by the heaven, or by the earth, or by any other oath: but let your yea be yea, and your nay, nay, lest ye fall into condemnation."

Conf. Helv. II. cap. 5. Basil. Art. XI. All churches do, and some in their public writings, condemn vain, rash, and idle oaths[1].

[[1] Illi ipsi veteres non jurarunt nisi per nomen solius Jehovah sicuti lege divina est præceptum: quia sicut vetitum est jurare per nomina alienorum Deorum, sic nos juramenta per divos requisita non præstamus.—Harm. Conf. Sect. II. p. 27. Conf. Helv. Post. cap. v. Clare protestamur nos peregrinas et erroneas doctrinas... damnare, ut quum dicunt, In nullo casu jurandum esse, etsi gloria Dei, et charitas proximi id requirant. *Et in Annot. Margin.* Suo tempore juramento uti licet. Deus enim jussit hoc in veteri testamento et in novo Christus non prohibuit. Imo Christus et Apostoli ipsi jurarunt.—Ibid. p. 28. Conf. Basil. Art. XI. (Disput. 33.)]

The adversaries unto this truth.

This declareth many sorts of men to be very impious, as,

The wantons, which, for their pleasure, and the covetous worldlings, who, for gain and profit, blush not to take the name of God in vain by idle, rash, and usual oaths.

Next, the Basilidians[2], Helchisaites[3], Priscillianites[4], and Family of Love, who for ease, and to avoid troubles and persecution, dread not to swear and forswear themselves. Philastrius. Euseb. ex Orig. Lib. VI. c. 38. Bulling. contra Anab. Lib. II. cap. 4.

Thirdly, the Papists, whose common guise is to swear either by saints or idols, or by God and creatures together[5]. Rams. Conf. Pet. de Soto, Meth. Conf. p. 40, a.

Fourthly, the Puritans, who used to swear, though not by God, &c., yet as wickedly, using horrible imprecations, as "I renounce God," "God damn me;" or, as Hacket's manner was, "God confound me[6]." Conspiracy for pretended Reform, p. 5.

Lastly, the Bannisterians, who deem it hypocrisy for one Christian to reprove another for common and rash swearing, which are but trifles in their opinions[7]. Unfold. of Bannist.

Proposition II.

A lawful oath may be given and taken, according to the word of God, in justice, judgement, and truth.

The proof from God's word.

The truth of this doctrine appeareth plentifully in the holy scriptures. For in the same there be both command-

[2 See above, p. 119, note 10.]

[3 Φησὶ δὲ (ἡ γνώμη Ἑλκεσαϊτῶν) ὅτι τὸ ἀρνήσασθαι ἀδιάφορόν ἐστι. Καὶ ὁ μὲν νοήσας, τῷ στόματι ἐν ἀνάγκαις ἀρνήσεται, τῇ δὲ καρδίᾳ οὐχί.—Orig. apud Euseb. Eccl. Hist. Cant. 1720. Lib. VI. cap. 38.]

[4 Statuebant etiam liberum esse fidem confiteri necne, pro temporum ratione. Si enim gravia pericula urgeant, tum posse fideles dissimulare ac tacere. Satis enim esse coram Deo si quis veritatem in corde retineat etiamsi externis coram hominibus contrarium faciat. Neque enim homines debere seipsos fidei causa tormentis et morti exponere.—Bulling. adv. Anabapt. (Simler. Vers. Lat.) Tiguri. 1560. p. 43. Lib. II. cap. 4.]

[5 Vetatur etiam omne jusjurandum sine causa legitima sive fiat per Deum, per sanctos, per crucem, per sanctum evangelium, per fidem, per animam, per caput, sive per alias creaturas, ut scilicet in illis Deus et est et invocatur. Nam in omnibus his non juratur nisi per Deum, qui sanctos sanctificavit, pro nobis in cruce pependit, evangelium et fidem dedit; obligasque animam et caput tuum pœnæ a Deo infligendæ.—Petr. à Soto, Method. Confess. Antv. 1577. Decalog. Expos. p. 39. b.]

[6 Conspiracy for Pretended Reformation. Lond. 1592. p. 5.]

[7 The reference has not been found.]

ments that we must, and may, and forms prescribed how we shall swear.

Deut. vi. 12, 13. For the first, "Thou shalt fear the Lord thy God, and serve him; and shalt swear by his name," saith Moses. Again, Ibid. x. 20. "Thou shalt swear, The Lord liveth, and thou shalt cleave unto him, and shalt swear by his name."

Jer. xii. 16. Josh. xxiii. 7. Zeph. i. 5. Matt. v. 34. And, touching the other, swear may we not, either by Baal, or by strange gods, or by the Lord, and by Malcham, (that is by idols), or by any creatures.

Deut. vi. 13. Jer. xii. 16. Jer. iv. 2. Exod. xxii. 8. 1 Kings viii. 31. But our oaths must be made in the name of the Lord, as, "The Lord liveth;" and all is to be done in truth, judgement, and righteousness, and when the magistrate calleth us thereunto.

Conf. Helv. I. Art. XXVI. & II. cap. 30, Gal. Art. XL. Basil. Art. XI. sect. 1. August. Art. XVI. All churches join with us in this assertion, and some testify the same in their public writings[1].

The errors and adversaries unto this truth.

Many be the adversaries, one way or other, crossing this truth. For

Fardl. of Fashions, 2 part. Conf. Basil. Art. XI. sect. 1. 1. Some condemn all swearing, as did the Esseis, who deem all swearing as bad as forswearing[2], and do the Anabaptists, which will not swear, albeit thereby both the glory of God may be much promoted, and the church of Christ, or commonweal, furthered[3].

2. Others condemn some kind of oaths, and will not swear, though urged by the magistrate, but when themselves Test. Rhem. An. Act. xxiii. 12. think good; so the Papists. No man, say they, ought to take an oath to accuse a Catholic (a Papist) for his religion[4],

[[1] Huic (magistratui) nos...sancte subjiciendos esse, fidelitatem ac sacramentum præstare, &c.—Harm. Conf. Sect. XIX. p. 273. Conf. Helv. Prior. Art. XXVI. Damnamus Anabaptistas qui...negant...juramenta magistratui præstanda esse.—Ibid. p. 272. Conf. Helv. Post. cap. XXX. In the other places referred to only a general obedience to magistrates and laws is required.]

[[2] The Esseis ware in all poinctes verie like unto our cloisterers....Swearing thei compted forswearyng.—(W. Waterman's) Fardle of Facions, Lond. 1555. Part II. chap. iv. fol. I. 6.]

[[3] See above, p. 356, note 1.]

[[4] If thou be put to an oath to accuse catholics for serving God as they ought to do, or to utter any innocent man to God's enemies and his, thou oughtest first to refuse such unlawful oaths, but if thou have not courage and constancy so to do, yet know thou that such oaths bind not at all in conscience and law of God, but

and such as by oaths accuse Catholics (that is, Papists) are damned. Ibid.

So the Puritans oftentimes either will take no oath at all when it is ministered unto them by authority, if it may turn to the molestation of their brethren[5], or if they swear (finding their testimony will be hurtful to their cause) they will not deliver their minds after they be sworn[6]. Hook. of Eccles. Pol. præf. D. Sutcliff's answer to Job Throc. p. 46, b.

3. Others, having taken the oath, do foully abuse the same, as the Knights of the Post, like the Turkish Seiti and Chagi[7], who for a ducat will take a thousand false oaths afore the magistrate; as also the Jesuits, who, in swearing, (which is little better than forswearing) do *uti scientia,* that is, cunning and equivocations[8]; as also do they who conscionably and religiously keep not their faith; such are the Policy of the Turkish Emp. c. 24, p. 74. Quodlibet, p. 34, 68, Garner's Araign.

may and must be broken under pain of damnation.—Test. Rhem. Rhemes, 1582. Ann. Act. xxiii. 12. p. 361.]

[5 And lest examination of principal parties therein should bring those things to light which might hinder and let your proceedings; behold, for a bar against that impediment, one opinion ye have newly added unto the rest even upon this occasion, an opinion to exempt you from taking oaths which may turn to the molestation of your brethren in that cause.—Hooker, Eccles. Pol. Pref. chap. viii. § 13. Works, Oxford, 1845. Vol. I. pp. 140, 1.]

[6 Afterward when ye insolencie of this faction grew intollerable, some of ye principal leaders were called for. But so far were they from submission that some of them refused to take their oathes before her majesties commissioners and the judges, and others being sworn refused to answere: and that so obstinatly, that neither the perswasions of friendes, nor resolutions of judges, could worke anything with them, for which divers of them were committed.—M. Sutcliffe's Answere to Job Throkmorton, Lond. 1595. p. 46. b.]

[7 See above, p. 120, note 1.]

[8 ...just like to the Jesuits' absurd equivocating or counterfeited perjuries, sacriledges and cousinage in abusing the words of S. Paul, with, *factus sum omnia omnibus ut omnes lucrifaciam:* as much to say in a Jesuiticall sense, as to be a seminarie priest among seminaries, a secular priest among seculars, a religious man amongst religious, a seditious person amongst seditious, &c.—A Decacordon of Quodlibet. Quæst. 1602. p. 33. Out of this directing and doing of all things in order *ad Deum,* and for obedience sake, they frame a new devise, how to make themselves not only above seculars in authority, but also more mundane than any temporal worldling in practice. And this devise is grounded upon a principle amongst them called *uti scientia,* that is, a rule prescribed unto them (if you please to know it) in plain English, how to learn to shift and live by their wits.—Ibid. p. 68. Their dissimulation appeareth out of their doctrine of equivocation...concerning the treatise of equivocation seen and allowed by Garnet and by Blackwell the archpriest, wherein under the pretext of the lawfulness of a mixt proposition to express one part of a man's mind and retain another, people are indeed taught not only simple lying, but fearful and damnable blasphemy.—A True Relation of the Proceedings against Garnet, &c. Lond. 1606. fol. T. 2.]

Test. Rhem. an. Act. xx. 12. Concil. Constan. forenamed Papists. For (say they) "An oath taken for the furtherance of false religion" (as they take the profession of all Protestants to be[1]) "bindeth [a] not." Again, "Faith is not to be kept with heretics[2]." Which assertion little differeth from the opinion of some Puritans, who teach that promise (or faith) is not to be kept, when (as perhaps by the not erecting of presbyteries in every parish) God's honour and preaching of his word is [b] hindered[3].

Merc. Gallo-Belg. Lib. II. p. 89. Subjects be discharged from their oath of allegiance, and may gather forces against their liege sovereign, if he enterprize anything to the hurt of his realm, or of (the Romish) religion, was a determination of the Sorbonists in a certain conventicle of theirs at Paris[4]. Buchan. Rerum Scotic. Lib. XVII. p. 202, b. And that magistrates, by their subjects, may be brought under the obedience of laws, was a conclusion of certain Scottish ministers in a private conventicle of Edinburgh[5].

Euseb. Philadelph. Dial. 2, p. 57. *Seditiosi non sunt, qui resistunt principibus politicum aut ecclesiasticum statum perturbantibus. Nam qui resistit*

[a] Juramentum propter falsam religionem præstitum non obligat.—Bap. Fickler. de Jure Magist. [Ingolstad. 1578] p. 11. [in Marg.]

[b] Geneva, Annot. Matt. ii. 12. [See, The Bible transl. according to the Ebrew and Greeke, &c. with most profitable Annotations. Lond. 1578. Marg. Annot. on Matt. ii. 12.] One of them hath delivered, that if the prince do hinder the building of the church, the people may by force of arms resist him.—Answer to the Abstract, p. 194.

[[1] See above, p. 358, note 4.] [[2] See above, p. 119, note 15.]

[[3] Divers of the French reformers are also too violentlie affected that waie. One of them hath delivered, that *If the prince doo hinder the building of the church, or doo affect the seat of God:* that is (in their sense and meaning) deale in ecclesiasticall causes and hinder the presbyterie: the people may by force of arms resist him.—An Answer to an Abstract of certeine Acts of Parliament, &c. Lond. 1584. Append. to the First Treatise, p. 194.]

[[4] Congregatum est...collegium Sorbonicum...conclusum itaque est, populum sacramento esse solutum, et licere ei contra regem suum pecunias colligere, confederationes inire, arma ferre, pugnare.—D. M. Janson. Mercur. Gallo-Belg. Col. Agripp. 1594. Lib. II. p. 87.]

[[5] ...controversia in domo privata inter paucos est agitata: possentne idololatriam jamjam in omnium perniciem grassaturam compescere, et summum magistratum, quando ipse nullum sibi modum statuat, intra legum præscripta per vim reducere.—Georg. Buchanan. Rer. Scoticar. Hist. Edinburg. 1582. Lib. XVII. fol. 202. b.]

principi seditioso seditiosus non est, sed seditionem tollit, saith a Frenchman[6]. Yea (saith an Englishman) whose works by T. C. are highly approved and commended, *Hunc tollant vel pacifice, vel cum bello, qui ea potestate donati sunt, ut regni ephori, vel omnium ordinum conventus publicus*[7]. Subjects may not respect their oaths made unto such princes which trouble the state of the church or commonweal.

Dud. Fen. S. Theol. Lib. v. cap. 13

Finally, whatsoever princes be (good or bad), if they be women (say some), oaths of allegiance unto them are not to be kept. Their words be these,

"First, (as well the states of the kingdom as the common people) they ought to remove from honour and authority that monster in nature, (so call I woman in the habit of man, yea, a woman against nature reigning above man). Secondarily, if any presume to defend that impiety they ought not to fear, first to pronounce, and then after to execute against them (that is to say, against women governors) the sentence of death. If any man be afraid to violate the oath of obedience which they have made to such monsters, let them be most assuredly persuaded, that, as the beginning of their oaths proceeding from ignorance was sin, so is the obstinate purpose to keep the same nothing but plain rebellion against God[8]."

Against the Regim. of Women, 1 Blas. p. 53, b.

Last of all, whereas every minister of the word and sacraments at his ordination doth swear to obey his diocesan in all lawful matters, certain gentlemen of the Puritan faction writ thus unto the bishops of the Church of England, and printed the same, viz. "The canon law is utterly void within the realm; and therefore your oath of canonical obedience is of no force, and all your canonical admonitions not worth a rush[9]."

The gentlemen's demands unto the bishops (printed *anno* 1605) p. 46.

[[6] The editor has been unable to verify the reference.]

[[7] *Exercitio tyrannus* est qui consulto pacta reip. omnia vel præcipua pessundant. Hunc tollant, &c.—Dud. Fenner. Sacr. Theolog. apud Eust. Vignon. 1589. Lib. v. cap. 13. p. 80. b.]

[[8] The First Blast, &c. against the Regiment of Women, p. 53. b. Genev. 1558. where, *a woman clad in the habit, &c.*]

[[9] Certaine Demandes with their grounds, &c. propounded &c. by some religious Gentl. unto the reverend father, Richard, Archbp. of Cant. &c. 1605. p. 49.]

D. Hilar. *Contra Constantium August.*

Non recipit mendacium veritas; nec patitur religio impietatem[1]*:* "The truth admits no lie; neither can religion abide impiety."

1 Tim. i. v. 17.

"Unto the king everlasting, immortal, invisible, unto
God only wise (be) honour (and) glory for
ever and ever. Amen."

[[1] Hilar. Opp. Paris. 1605. Contr. Const. August. col. 298. A.]

FINIS.

INDEX.

A.

B.

F.

G.

K.

L.

M.

www.ingramcontent.com/pod-product-compliance
Lightning Source LLC
LaVergne TN
LVHW020523100826
845148LV00010B/1320

* 9 7 8 1 5 9 7 5 2 2 0 4 5 *